Chapter 1

Overview of Financial Reporting, Financial Statement Analysis, and Valuation

Learning Objectives

1. Understand the six-step analytical framework that is the logical structure for financial statement analysis and valuation, and establishes the foundation for this book. This framework enables the analyst to link the economic characteristics and strategies of a firm, its financial statements and notes, assessments of its current and forecasted profitability and risk, and its market value.

2. Apply three tools for assessing the economic characteristics and dynamics that drive competition in an industry: (a) value chain analysis, (b) Porter's five forces framework, and (c) an economic attributes framework.

3. Review the purpose, underlying concepts, and format of the balance sheet, income statement, and statement of cash flows.

4. Become familiar with PepsiCo, the firm analyzed throughout the book, obtaining an overview of its economics, strategy, and financial statements.

5. Examine the provisions of the Sarbanes-Oxley Act of 2002 that relate to financial statement information.

6. Obtain an introduction to the tools used to analyze a firm's profitability and risk, including financial ratios, common-size financial statements, and percentage change financial statements.

7. Obtain an overview of how to use financial statement information to forecast the future business activities of a firm and to value a firm.

8. Examine the role of financial statement analysis in an efficient capital market.

9. Review sources of financial information available for publicly held firms.

10. Obtain guidance and direction for conducting a financial statement analysis project (Appendix 1.1).

The principal activity of security analysts is to value firms. Security analysts collect and analyze a wide array of information from financial statements and other sources to evaluate a firm's current and past performance and to predict its future performance. Then they use the expected future performance to measure the value of the firm's shares. Comparisons of the analysts' estimates of the firm's share value with the market price for the shares provide the basis for making good investment decisions.

This book has three principal purposes, each designed to help you gain important knowledge and skills necessary for financial statement analysis and valuation:

1. To demonstrate how you can link the economics of an industry, a firm's strategy, and its financial statements, gaining important insights about the firm's profitability and its risk. Chapters 1–5 discuss the principal financial statements and tools for analyzing profitability and risk.

2. To enhance your understanding of the accounting principles and methods under U.S. GAAP (Generally Accepted Accounting Principles) and IFRS (International Financial Reporting Standards) that firms use to measure and report their financing, investing, and operating activities in a set of financial statements and the adjustments the analyst may make to reported amounts to increase their relevance and reliability. Chapters 6–9 explore accounting principles in depth.

3. To demonstrate how you can use financial statement data to build forecasts of future financial statements and then use the expected future amounts of earnings, cash flows, and dividends in the valuation of firms. Chapters 10–14 focus on forecasting and valuation.

Financial analysis is an exciting and rewarding activity, particularly when the objective is to assess whether the market is pricing a firm's shares fairly. Studying the intrinsic characteristics of a firm (for example, its business model; product and service market share; and operating, investing, and financing decisions) and using this information to make informed judgments can be a very satisfying endeavor. Financial statements play a central role in the study and analysis of a firm.

Besides being used to measure firm value, the tools of effective financial statement analysis can be applied in many different decision-making settings, including the following:

- Assigning credit ratings or extending credit for a short-term period (for example, a bank loan used to finance accounts receivable or inventories) or a long-term period (for example, a bank loan or public bond issue used to finance the acquisition of property, plant, or equipment)
- Assessing the operating performance and financial health of a supplier, customer, competitor, or potential employer
- Managing a firm and communicating results to investors, creditors, employees, and other stakeholders
- Consulting with a firm and offering helpful strategic advice
- Evaluating firms for potential acquisitions or mergers or divestitures
- Valuing a firm in the initial public offering of its stock
- Forming a judgment about damages sustained in a lawsuit
- Assessing the extent of auditing needed to form an opinion about a client's financial statements

OVERVIEW OF FINANCIAL STATEMENT ANALYSIS

We view effective financial statement analysis as a three-legged stool, as Exhibit 1.1 depicts. The three legs of the stool in the figure represent effective analysis based on the following:

1. Identifying the economic characteristics of the industries in which a firm participates and the relation of those economic characteristics to various financial statement ratios

2. Describing the strategies that a firm pursues to differentiate itself from competitors as a basis for evaluating a firm's competitive advantages, the sustainability of a firm's earnings, and its risks

Integrated Issues in Accounting ACTG 495

James M. Wahlen | Stephen P. Baginski | Mark T. Bradshaw

CENGAGE
Learning·

Australia • Brazil • Japan • Korea • Mexico • Singapore • Spain • United Kingdom • United States

Integrated Issues in Accounting ACTG 495

Financial Reporting, Financial Statement Analysis, and Valuation: A Strategic Perspective, Seventh Edition
James M. Wahlen | Stephen P. Baginski | Mark T. Bradshaw

ExamView® is a registered trademark of eInstruction Corp. Windows is a registered trademark of the Microsoft Corporation used herein under license. Macintosh and Power Macintosh are registered trademarks of Apple Computer, Inc. used herein under license.

Library of Congress Control Number: 2010930107

Senior Project Development Manager:
Linda deStefano

Market Development Manager:
Heather Kramer

Senior Production/Manufacturing Manager:
Donna M. Brown

Production Editorial Manager:
Kim Fry

Sr. Rights Acquisition Account Manager:
Todd Osborne

For product information and technology assistance, contact us at
Cengage Learning Customer & Sales Support, 1-800-354-9706

For permission to use material from this text or product,
submit all requests online at **cengage.com/permissions**
Further permissions questions can be emailed to
permissionrequest@cengage.com

This book contains select works from existing Cengage Learning resources and was produced by Cengage Learning Custom Solutions for collegiate use. As such, those adopting and/or contributing to this work are responsible for editorial content accuracy, continuity and completeness.

Compilation © 2013 Cengage Learning
ISBN-13: 978-1-285-55679-6

ISBN-10: 1-285-55679-8
Cengage Learning
5191 Natorp Boulevard
Mason, Ohio 45040
USA

Cengage Learning is a leading provider of customized learning solutions with office locations around the globe, including Singapore, the United Kingdom, Australia, Mexico, Brazil, and Japan. Locate your local office at:
international.cengage.com/region.
Cengage Learning products are represented in Canada by Nelson Education, Ltd.
For your lifelong learning solutions, visit **www.cengage.com/custom.**
Visit our corporate website at **www.cengage.com.**

Printed in the United States of America

David Layzell

Brief Contents

Chapter 1   Overview of Financial Reporting, Financial Statement Analysis, and Valuation   **1**

Chapter 4   Profitability Analysis   **246**

Chapter 5   Risk Analysis   **345**

Chapter 6   Financing Activities   **439**

Chapter 7   Investing Activities   **522**

Chapter 9   Accounting Quality   **729**

Chapter 10   Forecasting Financial Statements   **783**

Chapter 11   Risk-Adjusted Expected Rates of Return and the Dividends Valuation Approach   **884**

Chapter 12   Valuation: Cash-Flow-Based Approaches   **928**

Appendix A: Financial Statements and Notes for PepsiCo, Inc. and Subsidiaries   **1097**

Appendix B: Management's Discussion and Analysis for PepsiCo, Inc. and Subsidiaries   **1129**

Appendix C: Financial Statement Analysis Package (FSAP)   **1159**

Appendix D: Financial Statement Ratios: Descriptive Statistics by Industry and by Year   **1197**

Index   **1247**

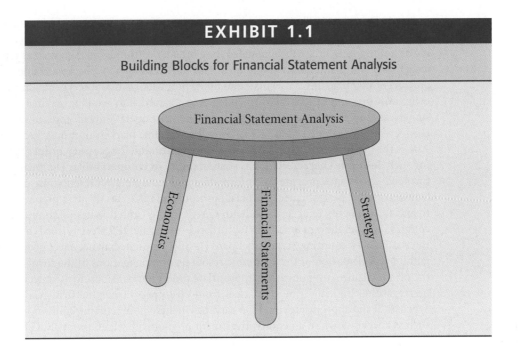

EXHIBIT 1.1

Building Blocks for Financial Statement Analysis

3. Evaluating the financial statements, including the accounting concepts and methods that underlie them and the quality of the information they provide

Our approach to effective analysis of financial statements for valuation and many other decisions involves six interrelated sequential steps, depicted in Exhibit 1.2.

1. **Identify the economic characteristics and competitive dynamics of the industry in which a particular firm participates.** What dynamic forces drive competition in the industry? For example, does the industry include a large number of firms selling similar products, such as grocery stores, or only a small number of competitors selling unique products, such as pharmaceutical companies? Does technological change play an important role in maintaining a competitive advantage, as in computer software? Are industry sales growing rapidly or slowly?

2. **Identify the strategies the firm pursues to gain and sustain a competitive advantage.** What business model is the firm executing to be different and successful in its

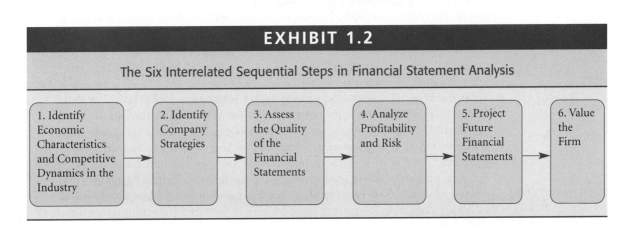

EXHIBIT 1.2

The Six Interrelated Sequential Steps in Financial Statement Analysis

industry? Does the firm have competitive advantages? If so, how sustainable are they? Are its products designed to meet the needs of specific market segments, such as ethnic or health foods, or are they intended for a broader consumer market, such as typical grocery stores and family restaurants? Has the firm integrated backward into the growing or manufacture of raw materials for its products, such as a steel company that owns iron ore mines? Has the firm integrated forward into retailing to final consumers, such as an athletic footwear manufacturer that operates retail stores to sell its products? Is the firm diversified across several geographic markets or industries?

3. **Assess the quality of the firm's financial statements and, if necessary, adjust them for such desirable characteristics as sustainability or comparability.** Do the firm's financial statements provide an informative and complete representation of the firm's economic performance, financial position, and risk? Has the firm prepared its financial statements in accordance with GAAP in the United States or some other country, or are they prepared in accordance with the IFRS established by the International Accounting Standards Board (IASB)? Does the balance sheet provide a faithful representation of the economic resources and obligations of the firm? Does the firm recognize revenues at the appropriate time, after considering the uncertainties regarding the collectibility of cash from customers? Does the firm recognize expenses at the appropriate time? Do earnings include nonrecurring gains or losses, such as a write-down of an equity investment or goodwill, which the analyst should evaluate differently from recurring components of earnings? Has the firm structured transactions or commercial arrangements or has it selected accounting principles to appear more profitable or less risky than economic conditions otherwise suggest?

4. **Analyze the current profitability and risk of the firm using information in the financial statements.** Most financial analysts assess the profitability of a firm relative to the risks involved. What rate of return is the firm generating from the use of its assets? How much return is the firm generating for the equity capital invested? Is the firm's profit margin increasing or decreasing over time? Are returns and profit margins higher or lower than those of its key competitors? How much leverage does the firm have in its capital structure? How much of the leverage consists of debt financing that will come due in the short-term versus the long-term? Ratios that reflect relations among particular items in the financial statements are the tools used to analyze profitability and risk.

5. **Prepare forecasted financial statements.** What will be the firm's future resources, obligations, investments, cash flows, revenues, and expenses? What will be the likely future profitability and risk and, in turn, the likely future returns from investing in the company? Forecasts of a firm's ability to manage risks, particularly those elements of risk with measurable financial consequences, permit the analyst to estimate the likelihood that the firm will experience financial difficulties in the future. Forecasted financial statements that rely on the analyst's projections of the firm's future operating, investing, and financing activities provide the basis for projecting future profitability and risk.

6. **Value the firm.** What is the firm worth? What is the value of the firm's common shares? Financial analysts use their estimates of share value to make recommendations to buy, sell, or hold the equity securities of various firms whose market price they think is too low, too high, or about right. Investment banking firms that underwrite the initial public offering of a firm's common stock must set the initial offering price. Financial analysts in corporations considering whether to acquire a company (or to divest a subsidiary or division) must assess a reasonable range of values to bid in order to acquire a target (or to expect to receive from a divestiture). Translating information

from the financial statements into reliable estimates of firm value (and therefore into intelligent investment decisions) is the principal activity of financial analysts.

These six interrelated steps represent the subject matter of this book. We use these six steps as the analytical framework for analysts to follow in their efforts to analyze and value a company. This chapter briefly explores each step. Subsequent chapters develop the important concepts and tools in considerably more depth.

Throughout this book, we use financial statements, notes, and other information provided by PepsiCo, Inc. and Subsidiaries (PepsiCo) to illustrate the various topics discussed. Appendix A at the end of the book includes the fiscal year 2008 financial statements and notes for PepsiCo, as well as statements by management and the opinion of the independent accountant regarding these financial statements. Appendix B includes excerpts from a financial review provided by management that discusses the business strategy of PepsiCo; it also offers explanations for changes in PepsiCo's profitability and risk over time. Appendix C presents the output of the FSAP (Financial Statements Analysis Package), which is the financial statement analysis software that accompanies this book. The FSAP model is an Excel add-in that enables analysts to enter financial statement data, after which the model computes a wide array of profitability and risk ratios and creates templates for forecasting future financial statements and estimating a variety of valuation models. Appendix C presents the use of FSAP for PepsiCo for recent years, including PepsiCo's profitability and risk ratios, projected future financial statements, and valuation. FSAP is available at www.cengage.com/accounting/wahlen. You can use FSAP for many of the problems and cases in this book to aid in your analysis (FSAP applications are highlighted with the FSAP icon in the margin of the text). FSAP contains a user manual with guides to assist you. Appendix D presents tables of descriptive statistics on a wide array of financial ratios across 48 industries.

STEP 1: IDENTIFY THE INDUSTRY ECONOMIC CHARACTERISTICS

The economic characteristics and competitive dynamics of an industry play a key role in influencing the strategies firms in the industry will employ and therefore the types of financial statement relationships the analyst should expect to observe when analyzing a set of financial statements. Consider, for example, the financial statement data for firms in four different industries shown in Exhibit 1.3. This exhibit expresses all items on the balance sheets and income statements as percentages of revenue. Consider how the economic characteristics of these industries affect their financial statements.

Grocery Store Chain

The products of a particular grocery store chain are difficult to differentiate from similar products of other grocery store chains, a trait that characterizes such products as *commodities*. In addition, low barriers to entry exist in the grocery store industry; an entrant needs primarily retail space and access to food products distributors. Thus, extensive competition and nondifferentiated products result in a relatively low net income to sales, or profit margin, percentage (3.5 percent in this case). Grocery stores, however, need relatively few assets to generate sales (34.2 cents in assets for each dollar of sales in this case). The assets are described as turning over 2.9 times (= 100.0%/34.2%) per year. (Each dollar invested in assets generated, on average, $2.90 of revenues.) Each time the assets of this grocery store chain turn over, or generate one dollar of revenue, it generates a profit of 3.5 cents. Thus, during a one-year period, the grocery store earns 10.15 cents (= 3.5% × 2.9) for each dollar invested in assets.

EXHIBIT 1.3

Common-Size Financial Statement Data for Four Firms

	Grocery Store Chain	Pharmaceutical Company	Electric Utility	Commercial Bank
BALANCE SHEET				
Cash and marketable securities	0.7%	11.0%	1.5%	261.9%
Accounts and notes receivable	0.7	18.0	7.8	733.5
Inventories	8.7	17.0	4.5	—
Property, plant, and equipment, net	22.2	28.7	159.0	18.1
Other assets	1.9	72.8	29.2	122.6
Total Assets	34.2%	147.5%	202.0%	1,136.1%
Current liabilities	7.7%	30.8%	14.9%	936.9%
Long-term debt	7.6	12.7	130.8	71.5
Other noncurrent liabilities	2.6	24.6	1.8	27.2
Shareholders' equity	16.3	79.4	54.5	100.5
Total Liabilities and Shareholders' Equity	34.2%	147.5%	202.0%	1,136.1%
INCOME STATEMENT				
Revenue	100.0%	100.0%	100.0%	100.0%
Cost of goods sold	(74.1)	(31.6)	(79.7)	—
Operating expenses	(19.7)	(37.1)	—	(41.8)
Research and development	—	(10.1)	—	—
Interest	(0.5)	(3.1)	(4.6)	(36.6)
Income taxes	(2.2)	(6.0)	(5.2)	(8.6)
Net Income	3.5%	12.1%	10.5%	13.0%

Pharmaceutical Company

The barriers to entry in the pharmaceutical industry are much higher than for grocery stores. Pharmaceutical firms must invest considerable amounts in research and development to create new drugs. The research and development process is lengthy with highly uncertain outcomes. Very few projects result in successful development of new drugs. Once new drugs have been developed, they must undergo a lengthy government testing and approval process. If the drugs are approved, firms receive patents that give them exclusive rights to manufacture and sell the drugs for an extended period. These high entry barriers (research and development expenditures, government approval process, patent protection) permit pharmaceutical firms to realize much higher profit margins on approved patent-protected products compared to the profit margins of grocery stores. Exhibit 1.3 indicates that the pharmaceutical firm generated a profit margin of 12.1 percent, more than three times that reported by the grocery store chain. Pharmaceutical firms, however, face product liability risks as well as the risk that competitors will develop superior drugs that make a particular firm's drug offerings obsolete. Because of these business risks, pharmaceutical firms tend to take on relatively small amounts of debt financing as compared to firms in industries such as electric utilities and commercial banks.

Electric Utility

The principal assets of an electric utility are its capital-intensive generating plants. Thus, property, plant, and equipment dominate the balance sheet. Because of the large investments required in such assets, in the past, electric utility firms generally demanded a monopoly position in a particular locale. Government regulators permitted this monopoly position but set the rates that utilities charged customers for electric services. Thus, electric utilities have traditionally realized relatively high profit margins (10.5 percent in this case) to offset their relatively low total asset turnovers (.495 = 100.0%/202.0% in this case). The monopoly position and regulatory protection reduced the risk of financial failure and permitted electric utilities to invest large amounts of capital in long-lived assets and take on relatively high proportions of debt in their capital structures. The economic characteristics of electric utilities have changed dramatically in recent years. The gradual elimination of monopoly positions and the introduction of competition that affects rates are reducing profit margins considerably.

Commercial Bank

Through their borrowing and lending activities, commercial banks serve as intermediaries in the supply and demand for financial capital. The principal assets of commercial banks are investments in financial securities and loans to businesses and consumers. The principal financing for commercial banks comes from customers' deposits and short-term borrowings. Because customers can generally withdraw deposits at any time, commercial banks invest in securities that they can quickly convert into cash if necessary. Money is a commodity: money borrowed from one bank is similar to money borrowed from another bank. Thus, one would expect a commercial bank to realize a small profit margin on the revenue it earns from lending (interest revenue) over the price it pays for its borrowed funds (interest expense). The profit margins on lending are indeed relatively small. The 13.0 percent margin for the commercial bank shown in Exhibit 1.3 reflects the much higher profit margins it generates from offering fee-based financial services such as structuring financing packages for businesses, guaranteeing financial commitments of business customers, and arranging mergers and acquisitions. Note that the assets of this commercial bank turn over just .09 (= 100.0%/1,136.1%) times per year, reflecting the net effect of interest revenues from investments and loans of 6–8 percent per year, which requires a large investment in financial assets, and fee-based revenues, which require relatively few assets.

TOOLS FOR STUDYING INDUSTRY ECONOMICS

Three tools for studying the economic characteristics of an industry are (1) value chain analysis, (2) Porter's five forces classification framework, and (3) an economic attributes framework. The microeconomics literature suggests other analytical frameworks as well.

Value Chain Analysis

The value chain for an industry sets forth the sequence or chain of activities involved in the creation, manufacture, and distribution of its products and services. Exhibit 1.4 portrays a value chain for the pharmaceutical industry. Pharmaceutical companies invest in research and development to discover and develop new drugs. When promising drugs emerge, a lengthy drug approval process begins. Estimates suggest that it takes seven to ten years and almost $1 billion to discover and obtain approval of new drugs. To expedite the approval process, reduce costs, and permit their scientists to devote energies to the more creative

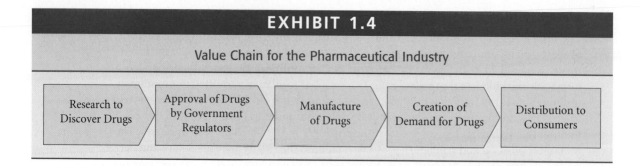

EXHIBIT 1.4

Value Chain for the Pharmaceutical Industry

Research to Discover Drugs → Approval of Drugs by Government Regulators → Manufacture of Drugs → Creation of Demand for Drugs → Distribution to Consumers

drug discovery phase, pharmaceutical companies often contract with clinical research firms to conduct the testing and shepherding of new drugs through the approval process.

The manufacture of drugs involves combining various chemicals and other elements. For quality control and product purity reasons, pharmaceutical companies use highly automated manufacturing processes. Pharmaceutical companies employ sales forces to market drugs to doctors, hospitals, and health maintenance organizations. In an effort to create demand, these companies have increasingly advertised new products through multiple advertising media, suggesting that consumers ask their doctors about the drug. Drug distribution typically channels through pharmacies, although bulk mail-order and Internet purchases are increasingly common (and encouraged by health insurers).

To the extent prices are available for products or services at each stage in the value chain, the analyst can study where value is added within an industry. For example, the analyst can look at the prices paid to acquire firms with promising or newly discovered drugs to ascertain the value of the drug discovery phase. The prices that clinical research firms charge to test and obtain approval of new drugs signal the value added by this activity. The higher the value added from any activity, the higher the profitability should be from engaging in that phase.

The analyst also can use the value chain to identify the strategic positioning of a particular firm within the industry. Traditionally, pharmaceutical firms have maintained a presence in the discovery through demand creation phases, leaving distribution to pharmacies and increasingly contracting out the drug testing and approval phase.

Refer to Note 1, "Basis of Presentation and Our Divisions," to the financial statements of PepsiCo (Appendix A) for an organizational chart of PepsiCo's divisions and segments. PepsiCo operates three business units: PepsiCo Americas Foods (PAF), PepsiCo Americas Beverages (PAB), and PepsiCo International (PI). PepsiCo Americas Foods is organized into three divisions: Frito-Lay North America (FLNA; branded snacks, chips, and other food products), Quaker Foods North America (QFNA; cereal and related products), and Latin America Foods (LAF; branded snacks, chips, and other food products). PepsiCo Americas Beverages operates as a single-segment division, and it manufactures and distributes soft drinks and other beverages throughout North America. PepsiCo International operates in markets outside North America and manufactures and sells branded snack foods, breakfast foods, soft drinks, and other beverages. The PepsiCo International unit is organized into two geographic divisions: the United Kingdom and Europe (UKEU) and the Middle East, Africa & Asia (MEAA). Exhibit 1.5 shows the amounts taken from Note 1 to PepsiCo's financial statements in Appendix A, the proportions of revenues and operating profit that PepsiCo derived from each division, and the operating profit margin (operating profit divided by revenues) of each division for 2008.

Exhibit 1.6 illustrates a value chain for one of PepsiCo's principal businesses, the soft drink/beverage industry. Note that this is PepsiCo's legacy business, so for completeness an

EXHIBIT 1.5

Division Revenues and Operating Profits for PepsiCo for 2008
(Dollar amounts in millions)

	Revenues		Operating Profits		Operating Profit Margin
PepsiCo Americas Foods					
Frito-Lay North America	$12,507	28.9%	$2,959	37.3%	23.7%
Quaker Foods North America	1,902	4.4%	582	7.3%	30.6%
Latin America Foods	5,895	13.6%	897	11.3%	15.2%
PepsiCo Americas Beverages	10,937	25.3%	2,026	25.5%	18.5%
PepsiCo International					
United Kingdom & Europe	6,435	14.9%	811	10.2%	12.6%
Middle East, Africa & Asia	5,575	12.9%	667	8.4%	12.0%
Total	$43,251	100.0%	$7,942	100.0%	18.4%

analyst should also evaluate PepsiCo's other principal businesses, particularly in the snack food and breakfast food industries.

Although the classic PepsiCo soft drinks (for example, Pepsi, Diet Pepsi, Mountain Dew®, and Slice™) have not changed for many years, the company continually engages in new product development. Once a product appears to have commercial feasibility, PepsiCo combines raw materials into a concentrate or syrup base. The ingredients and their mixes are highly confidential. PepsiCo ships the concentrate to its franchise bottlers (or, in the case of syrup, to its national fountain accounts), which combine it with water and sweeteners to produce the finished soft drink.

PepsiCo relies on noncontrolled affiliates to bottle and distribute a large percentage of its beverages. That is, PepsiCo contracts out the bottling operation. (We discuss the rationale for this arrangement in the strategy section later in this chapter.) The bottlers transport the bottled beverages and syrups to independent distributors and retail establishments.

Because the analyst can obtain separate financial statements for PepsiCo and its bottlers, one can observe where value is added along the value chain. We examine the profitability and risk of PepsiCo and its bottlers in greater depth in Chapters 4, 5, 8, and 9.

EXHIBIT 1.6

Value Chain for the Soft Drink/Beverage Industry

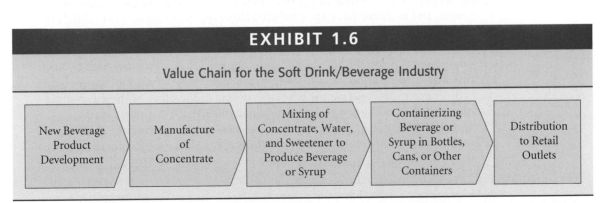

Porter's Five Forces Classification Framework

Porter suggests that five forces influence the level of competition and the profitability of firms in an industry.[1] Three of the forces—rivalry among existing firms, potential entry, and substitutes—represent horizontal competition among current or potential future firms in the industry and closely related products and services. The other two forces—buyer power and supplier power—depict vertical competition in the value chain, from the suppliers through the existing rivals to the buyers. We discuss each of these forces next and illustrate them within the soft drink/beverage industry. Exhibit 1.7 depicts Porter's five forces in the soft drink/beverage industry.

1. **Rivalry among Existing Firms.** Direct rivalry among existing firms is often the first order of competition in an industry. Some industries can be characterized by concentrated rivalry (such as a monopoly, a duopoly, or an oligopoly), whereas others have diffuse rivalry across many firms. Economists often assess the level of competition with industry concentration ratios, such as a four-firm concentration index that measures the proportion of industry sales controlled by the four largest competitors. Economics teaches that in general, the greater the industry concentration, the lower the competition between existing rivals and thus the more profitable the firms will be.

    PepsiCo and Coca-Cola dominate the soft drink/beverage industry in the United States. Because some consumers view the two companies' products as being similar, intense competition based on price could develop. Also, the soft drink market in the United States is mature (that is, not growing rapidly), so price cutting could become a strategy to gain market share. Although intense rivalries have a tendency to reduce profitability, in this case, PepsiCo and Coca-Cola appear to tacitly avoid competing based on price and compete instead on brand image, access to key distribution channels (for example, fast-food chains and grocery store shelf space), and other attributes. Growth opportunities do exist in other countries, which these companies pursue aggressively. Thus, we characterize industry rivalry as moderate.

2. **Threat of New Entrants.** How easily can new firms enter a market? Are there entry barriers such as large capital investment, technological expertise, patents, or regulations that inhibit new entrants? Do the existing rivals have distinct competitive advantages (such as brand names) that will make it difficult for other firms to enter and compete successfully? If so, firms in the industry will likely generate higher profits than if new entrants can enter the market easily and compete away the excess profits.

    The soft drink/beverage industry has no barriers to entry. This is evident by the numerous small juice, sports drink, water, and soft drink companies that exist; the frequency with which new firms enter the industry; and the availability of generic and no-name beverage products. However, the existing major players in the soft drink/beverage industry have competitive advantages that reduce the threat of new entrants. Brand recognition by PepsiCo and Coca-Cola serves as a very powerful deterrent to potential new competitors. Another deterrent is these two firms' domination of distribution channels. Most restaurant chains sign exclusive contracts to serve the beverages of one or the other of these two firms. Also, PepsiCo and Coca-Cola often dominate shelf space in grocery stores.

3. **Threat of Substitutes.** How easily can customers switch to substitute products or services? How likely are they to switch? When there are close substitutes in a market,

[1]Michael E. Porter, *Competitive Strategy: Techniques for Analyzing Industries and Competitors* (New York: Free Press), 1998.

EXHIBIT 1.7

Porter's Five Forces in the Soft Drink/Beverage Industry

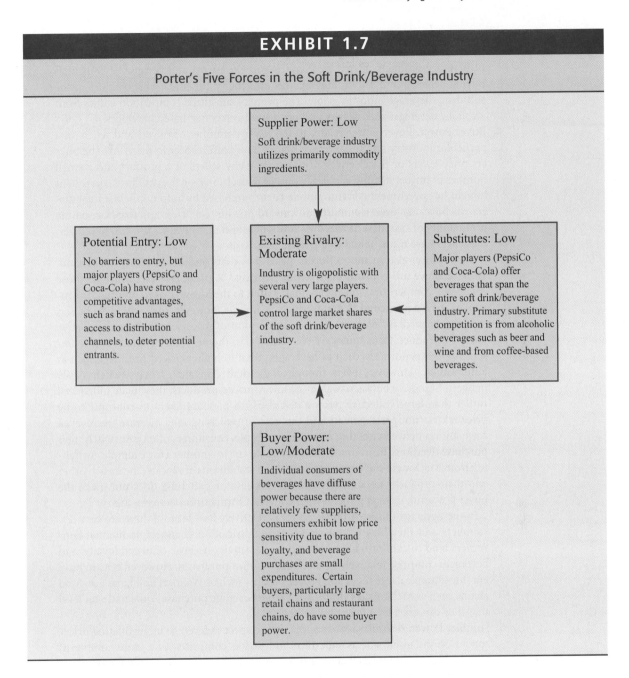

Supplier Power: Low

Soft drink/beverage industry utilizes primarily commodity ingredients.

Potential Entry: Low

No barriers to entry, but major players (PepsiCo and Coca-Cola) have strong competitive advantages, such as brand names and access to distribution channels, to deter potential entrants.

Existing Rivalry: Moderate

Industry is oligopolistic with several very large players. PepsiCo and Coca-Cola control large market shares of the soft drink/beverage industry.

Substitutes: Low

Major players (PepsiCo and Coca-Cola) offer beverages that span the entire soft drink/beverage industry. Primary substitute competition is from alcoholic beverages such as beer and wine and from coffee-based beverages.

Buyer Power: Low/Moderate

Individual consumers of beverages have diffuse power because there are relatively few suppliers, consumers exhibit low price sensitivity due to brand loyalty, and beverage purchases are small expenditures. Certain buyers, particularly large retail chains and restaurant chains, do have some buyer power.

competition increases and profitability diminishes (for example, between restaurants and grocery stores for certain types of prepared foods and between airlines, automobiles, and other means of transportation for traveling short distances). Unique products with few substitutes, such as certain prescription medications, enhance profitability.

The carbonated soft drink industry faces substitute competition from an array of other beverages that consumers can substitute to quench their thirst. Fruit juices, bottled waters, sports drinks, teas, coffees, milk, beers, and wines serve a similar thirst-quenching function to that of soft drinks. Over the years, Coca-Cola and PepsiCo have expanded their beverage portfolios to encompass virtually all nonalcoholic beverages except coffee. For example, PepsiCo purchased Tropicana and Gatorade to enhance its product offerings in juices, sports drinks, and bottled water. Because of the wide range of beverage products offered by PepsiCo and Coca-Cola and because of consumer buying habits, brand loyalty, and channel availability, the threat of substitutes in the soft drink/beverage industry is low. The primary substitute competition comes from alcoholic beverages such as beer and wine and from coffee-based beverages.

4. **Buyer Power.** Buyer power relates to the relative number of buyers and sellers in a particular industry and the leverage buyers have with respect to price. Are the buyers price takers or price setters? If there are many sellers of a product and a small number of buyers making very large purchase decisions, such as military equipment bought by governments or automobile parts purchased by automobile manufacturers, the buyer can exert significant downward pressure on prices and therefore on the profitability of suppliers. If there are few sellers and many buyers, as with beverages, the sellers have more bargaining power.

Buyer power also relates to buyers' price sensitivity and the elasticity of demand. How sensitive are consumers to product prices? If products are similar to those offered by competitors, consumers may switch to the lowest-priced offering. If consumers view a particular firm's products as unique, however, they will likely be less sensitive to price differences. Another dimension of price sensitivity is the relative cost of a product. Consumers are less sensitive to the prices of products that represent small expenditures, such as beverages, than to higher-priced products, such as automobiles. However, even though individual consumers may switch easily between brands or between higher- or lower-priced products, they make individual rather than large collective buying decisions; so they are likely to continue to be price takers (not price setters) and the ease of switching may increase the level of competition between existing rivals. For example, consumers often can switch their purchase decisions from one fast-food restaurant to another (for example, switching from McDonald's to Subway) because the restaurants are located near each other and their products are similarly priced. But ease of switching does not make the buyer powerful; instead it increases the level of competition between the rivals.

In the beverage industry, buyer power is relatively low because there are very few suppliers and they have access to essential distribution channels. Individual consumers tend to exhibit relatively low price sensitivity because of brand loyalty, and beverages comprise relatively small dollar amount purchases. However, certain buyers (for example, large retail and grocery chains such as Walmart and large fast-food chains such as McDonald's) make such large beverage purchases on a national level that they can exert significant buyer power.

5. **Supplier Power.** A similar set of factors with respect to leverage in negotiating prices applies on the input side as well. If an industry is comprised of a large number of potential buyers of inputs that are produced by relatively few suppliers, the suppliers will have greater power in setting prices and generating profits. For example, many firms assemble and sell personal computers and laptops, but these firms face significant supplier power because Microsoft is a dominant supplier of operating systems and application software and Intel is a dominant supplier of microprocessors.

Beverage companies produce their concentrates and syrups with raw materials that are commodities. Although PepsiCo does not disclose every ingredient, PepsiCo is not likely to be dependent on one supplier (or even a few suppliers) for its raw materials. It also is unlikely that any of these ingredients are sufficiently unique that the suppliers could exert much power over PepsiCo. Given PepsiCo's size, the power more likely resides with PepsiCo than with its suppliers.

In sum, competition in the soft drink/beverage industry rates low on supplier power, threat of new entrants, and threat of substitutes; the industry rates low on buyer power of consumers but moderate on buyer power of fast-food chains and large retail and grocery chains; and the industry rates moderate on rivalry within the industry. Unless PepsiCo or Coca-Cola decides to compete on the basis of low price, the analyst might expect these firms to continue to generate relatively high profitability.

Economic Attributes Framework

We find the following framework useful in studying the economic attributes of a business, in part because it ties in with items reported in the financial statements.

1. **Demand**
   - Are customers highly price-sensitive, as in the case of automobiles, or are they relatively insensitive, as in the case of soft drinks?
   - Is demand growing rapidly, as in the case of long-term health care, or is the industry relatively mature, as in the case of grocery stores?
   - Does demand move with the economic cycle, as in the case of construction of new homes and offices, or is demand insensitive to business cycles, as in the case of food products and medical care?
   - Does demand vary with the seasons, as in the case of summer clothing and ski equipment, or is demand relatively stable throughout the year, as in the case of most grocery store products?

2. **Supply**
   - Are many suppliers offering similar products, or are few suppliers offering unique products?
   - Are there high barriers to entry, or can new entrants gain easy access?
   - Are there high barriers to exit, as in the case of firms that face substantial environment cleanup costs?

3. **Manufacturing**
   - Is the manufacturing process capital-intensive, as in the case of electric power generation; labor-intensive, as in the case of advertising, investment banking, auditing, and other professional services; or a combination of the two, as in the case of automobile manufacturing and airline transportation?
   - Is the manufacturing process complex with low tolerance for error, as in the case of heart pacemakers and microchips, or relatively simple with ranges of products that are of acceptable quality, as in the case of apparel and nonmechanized toys?

4. **Marketing**
   - Is the product promoted to other businesses, in which case a sales staff plays a key role, or is it marketed to consumers, so that advertising, location, and coupons serve as principal promotion mechanisms?
   - Does steady demand pull products through distribution channels, or must firms continually create demand?

5. **Investing and Financing**
   - Are the assets of firms in the industry relatively short-term, as in the case of commercial banks, which require short-term sources of funds to finance them? Or are assets relatively long-term, as in the case of electric utilities, which require primarily long-term financing?

- Is there relatively little risk in the assets of firms in the industry, such as from technological obsolescence, so that firms can carry high proportions of debt financing? Alternatively, are there high risks resulting from short product life cycles or product liability concerns that dictate low debt and high shareholders' equity financing?
- Is the industry relatively profitable and mature, generating more cash flow from operations than is needed for acquisitions of property, plant, and equipment? Alternatively, is the industry growing rapidly and in need of external financing?

Exhibit 1.8 summarizes the economic attributes of the soft drink/beverage industry.

EXHIBIT 1.8

Economic Attributes of the Soft Drink/Beverage Industry

Demand

- Demand is relatively insensitive to price.
- There is low growth in the United States, but more rapid growth opportunities are available in other countries.
- Demand is not cyclical.
- Demand is higher during warmer weather.

Supply

- Two principal suppliers (PepsiCo and Coca-Cola) sell branded products.
- Branded products and domination of distribution channels by two principal suppliers create significant competitive advantages.

Manufacturing

- Manufacturing process for concentrate and syrup is not capital-intensive.
- Bottling and distribution of final product is capital-intensive.
- Manufacturing process is simple (essentially a mixing operation) with some tolerance for quality variation.

Marketing

- Brand recognition and established demand pull products through distribution channels, but advertising can stimulate demand to some extent.

Investing and Financing

- Bottling operations and transportation of products to retailers require long-term financing.
- Profitability is relatively high and growth is slow in the United States, leading to excess cash flow generation. Growth markets in other countries require financing from internal domestic cash flow or from external sources.

STEP 2: IDENTIFY THE COMPANY STRATEGIES

Firms establish business strategies to differentiate themselves from competitors, but an industry's economic characteristics affect the flexibility that firms have in designing these strategies. In some cases, firms can create sustainable competitive advantages. PepsiCo's size, brand name, and access to distribution channels give it sustainable competitive advantages over smaller, less well-known beverage companies. Coca-Cola enjoys similar advantages. The reputation for quality family entertainment provides Disney with a sustainable advantage. A reputation for low prices generates advantages in high customer traffic and high sales volume for Walmart.

In many industries, however, products and ideas quickly get copied. Consider, for example, computer hardware; chicken, pizza, and hamburger restaurant chains; and financial services. In these cases, firms may achieve competitive advantage by being the first with new concepts or ideas (referred to as *first mover advantage*) or by continually investing in product development to remain on the leading edge of change in an industry. Such competitive advantages are difficult (but not impossible) to sustain for long periods of time.

Framework for Strategy Analysis

The set of strategic choices confronting a particular firm varies across industries. The following framework dealing with product and firm characteristics helps the analyst identify and structure the set of trade-offs and choices a firm must face.

1. **Nature of Product or Service.** Is a firm attempting to create unique products or services for particular market niches, thereby achieving relatively high profit margins (referred to as a *product differentiation strategy*)? Or is it offering nondifferentiated products at low prices, accepting a lower profit margin in return for a higher sales volume and market share (referred to as a *low-cost leadership strategy*)? Is a firm attempting to achieve both objectives by differentiating (perhaps by creating brand loyalty or technological innovation) and being price competitive by maintaining tight control over costs?

2. **Degree of Integration in Value Chain.** Is the firm pursuing a vertical integration strategy, participating in all phases of the value chain, or selecting just certain phases in the chain? With respect to manufacturing, is the firm conducting all manufacturing operations itself (as usually occurs in steel manufacturing), outsourcing all manufacturing (common in athletic shoes), or outsourcing the manufacturing of components but conducting the assembly operation in-house (common in automobile and computer hardware manufacturing)?

   With respect to distribution, is the firm maintaining control over the distribution function or outsourcing it? Some restaurant chains, for example, own all of their restaurants, while other chains operate through independently owned franchises. Computer hardware firms have recently shifted from selling through their own sales staffs to using various indirect sellers, such as value-added resellers and systems integrators—in effect shifting from in-house sourcing to outsourcing of the distribution function.

3. **Degree of Geographical Diversification.** Is the firm targeting its products to its domestic market or integrating horizontally across many countries? Operating in other countries creates opportunities for growth but exposes firms to risks from changes in exchange rates, political uncertainties, and additional competitors.

4. **Degree of Industry Diversification.** Is the firm operating in a single industry or diversifying across multiple industries? Operating in multiple industries permits

firms to diversify product, cyclical, regulatory, and other risks encountered when operating in a single industry but raises questions about management's ability to understand and manage multiple and different businesses effectively.

Application of Strategy Framework to PepsiCo's Beverage Division

To apply this strategy framework to PepsiCo's beverage division, we rely on the description provided by PepsiCo's management (Appendix B). Most U.S. firms include this type of management discussion and analysis in their Form 10-K filing with the Securities and Exchange Commission (SEC).

1. **Nature of Product or Service.** PepsiCo's beverage division competes broadly in the beverage industry, with offerings in soft drinks, fruit juices, bottled waters, sports drinks, teas, and coffees. However, its principal beverage products are soft drinks. Although one might debate whether its products differ from similar products offered by Coca-Cola and other competitors (a debate that invariably involves taste), brand recognition and domination of distribution channels permit PepsiCo to sell a somewhat differentiated product.

2. **Degree of Integration in Value Chain.** PepsiCo engages in new product development, manufactures concentrates and syrups, and promotes its products while it allows its bottlers to manufacture and distribute soft drink products. This arrangement exists because PepsiCo realizes that the principal value added comprises the secret formulas that make up the concentrates and syrups as well as the product and brand promotion that maintain its brand name and brand loyalty. Maintaining product quality and efficient and effective distribution channels are critical to PepsiCo's success, so PepsiCo emphasizes the important role that bottlers play and the oversight role PepsiCo plays to ensure its financial strength and efficient operation. Thus, a close operational relationship exists between PepsiCo and its bottlers. However, bottling operations are relatively simple, yet capital-intensive; require long-term financing, typically debt; and are not particularly value-enhancing. By not owning a majority interest in the bottling and distribution operations, PepsiCo reports greater profitability. The company also appears less risky because it does not include the debt of the bottling operations on its balance sheet.

    Because of its heavy influence (supplier power) over its bottlers, PepsiCo is able to price its concentrate sales to these bottlers to garner a significant portion of the profit margin for itself. The bottlers are willing to accept a lower margin because of the control PepsiCo gives them in a particular locale and the strong demand for the PepsiCo products they produce. (Subsequent chapters consider PepsiCo's strategy with respect to its bottlers when assessing the company's profitability, quality of financial information, and risk.)

    Interestingly, PepsiCo's main competitor in the soft drink industry, Coca-Cola, structures its operations similar to PepsiCo's. As with PepsiCo, Coca-Cola's principal products are the concentrates it sells to bottlers, which are responsible for bottling and distributing the final Coca-Cola soft drinks.

3. **Degree of Geographical Diversification.** Note 1, "Basis of Presentation and Our Divisions," to PepsiCo's financial statements (Appendix A) and Exhibit 1.5 indicate that the PepsiCo Americas Beverages division generated 25.3 percent of the firm's revenues during 2008 from beverage sales in North America, South America, and Central America. PepsiCo derived 27.8 percent of its revenues during 2008 from the

PepsiCo International division, but PepsiCo does not disclose the proportion of international revenues it derived from beverages alone. Overall, PepsiCo derived about two-thirds of its revenues from the Americas and one-third from other parts of the world.

4. **Degree of Industry Diversification.** To focus and streamline the presentation of industry analysis and strategic analysis techniques, our discussion thus far has focused on PepsiCo's beverages business. However, PepsiCo generates greater revenues and higher operating profit margins from the snack food and breakfast foods divisions than from the beverage division. Exhibit 1.5 indicates that during 2008, PepsiCo generated 28.9 percent of its revenues from the Frito-Lay North America snack food division, 13.6 percent from the Latin America Foods division, and 4.4 percent from the Quaker Foods North America division selling breakfast foods and cereal products. Because PepsiCo does not disclose the proportions of PepsiCo International revenues that derive from sales of snack foods, soft drinks and beverages, and cereal and related products, we cannot measure PepsiCo's worldwide mix of product sales.

Although PepsiCo is more industry-diverse than Coca-Cola, many economic characteristics of the beverage, snack food, and cereal industries are similar in nature, involving the selling of branded consumer products. These industries can be characterized as having low barriers to entry but a small number of powerful rivals with brand recognition and access to key distribution channels. These industries rely on commodity raw materials for inputs, facing low supplier power, and relatively price-insensitive buyers because of brand loyalty and distribution channels. As a result, PepsiCo's strategies are similar between the beverage and foods divisions, focusing on product development and promotion to leverage the brand recognition and maintaining access to important distribution channels.

STEP 3: ASSESS THE QUALITY OF THE FINANCIAL STATEMENTS

Business firms prepare three principal financial statements to report the results of their activities: (1) balance sheet, (2) income statement, and (3) statement of cash flows. Many firms prepare a fourth statement, the statement of shareholders' equity, which provides further detail of the shareholders' equity section of the balance sheet. Firms also include a set of notes that elaborate on items included in these statements. Together, the financial statements and notes provide an extensive set of information about the firm's financial position, performance, and cash flows. The statements provide insights to an analyst about the firm's profitability, risk, and growth.

Using the financial statements and notes for PepsiCo in Appendix A as examples, this section presents a brief overview of the purpose and content of each of these three financial statements. Understanding accounting concepts and methods and evaluating the quality of a firm's financial statements is a central element of effective financial statement analysis and therefore one of the three central purposes of this book. Chapters 2 and 3 describe the fundamental accounting concepts and methods for measuring and reporting:

- Assets, liabilities, and shareholders' equity
- Revenues, expenses, and income
- Cash flows associated with operating, investing, and financing activities

Chapters 6–9 describe specific accounting principles and methods in depth. The sequencing of these chapters is powerful and intuitive because it follows the natural sequencing of firms' economic activities. Chapter 6 begins the sequence by describing accounting for financing activities because firms initiate business activities by raising capital. Chapter 7 then describes accounting for investing activities, which occur after the firm has raised capital. Once capital has been raised and invested in productive resources, the firm commences operating activities by producing products and services for customers and incurring costs of conducting those operations, which are discussed in Chapter 8. Chapter 9 concludes the sequence by demonstrating how to evaluate the quality of a firm's accounting and discussing the faithfulness with which the financial statements represent the firm's economic resources, obligations, and performance.

Accounting Principles

Firms produce financial statements and notes based on accounting standards and principles established by the accounting profession. For U.S. firms, GAAP determines the valuation and measurement methods used in preparing financial statements. Official rule-making bodies set these principles. The SEC (Securities and Exchange Commission), an agency of the federal government, has the legal authority to specify acceptable accounting principles in the United States (http://www.sec.gov). The SEC has, for the most part, delegated the responsibility for setting GAAP to the FASB (Financial Accounting Standards Board), a private-sector body within the accounting profession (http://www.fasb.org). The FASB is an independent board comprising five members and a full-time professional staff. The FASB specifies acceptable accounting principles only after receiving extensive comments on proposed accounting standards from various preparers, auditors, and users of financial statements.

The IASB is an independent entity comprising 15 members (to be expanded to 16 members in 2012) and a full-time professional staff (http://www.iasb.org). The IASB specifies acceptable accounting principles known as IFRS. Many countries have dropped their own country-specific accounting rules, formally accepting IFRS as the applicable accounting standards. Beginning in 2005, the financial statements of firms in the European Community were required to conform to the pronouncements of the IASB.

The SEC accepts financial statement filings prepared under IFRS from non-U.S. registrants, although it has not yet accepted IFRS-based financial statement filings from U.S. firms. In 2008, the SEC pronounced a road map for convergence, providing a timetable under which it would be willing to accept filings from U.S. companies using IFRS instead of U.S. GAAP. The road map projected acceptance of such filings beginning as early as 2011 for large firms and as late as 2014 for small firms. Since publicizing the road map, the SEC has had to deal with some major crises in the U.S. capital markets, including the subprime crisis, the credit crunch, the failure and bailout of many large banks and insurers, and several major frauds. As a result, in February of 2010 the SEC issued a Work Plan for the SEC staff to determine by the end of 2011 whether, and if so, when and how to incorporate IFRS into the U.S. financial reporting system. The SEC's Work Plan indicates that, if IFRS-based filings are approved, the soonest U.S. companies would report financial statements under IFRS would be no earlier than 2015.

The FASB and IASB are working together closely to harmonize financial reporting worldwide. Although substantial differences must be resolved between the two sets of standards (we will highlight existing differences throughout this book), the two Boards have managed to find common ground on most major principles. Now when the two Boards propose a new principle or a revision of an existing principle, they typically work jointly to develop the proposed principle and to collect and evaluate comments from various constituencies. They then agree on the final principle, which becomes part of U.S. GAAP and IFRS. Working together, the IASB and FASB are reducing diversity in accounting principles across countries to encourage greater standardization. Global harmonization in accounting standards will simplify financial statements analysis, enabling analysts to evaluate and compare financial statements from firms across many countries, prepared under similar accounting principles. This should make allocation of capital more efficient worldwide.

Balance Sheet—Measuring Financial Position

The balance sheet, or statement of financial position, presents a snapshot of the resources of a firm (assets) and the claims on those resources (liabilities and shareholders' equity) as of a specific date. The balance sheet derives its name from the fact that it reports the following balance, or equality:

$$\text{Assets} = \text{Liabilities} + \text{Shareholders' Equity}$$

That is, a firm's assets are in balance with, or equal to, the claims on those assets by creditors (liabilities) and owners (shareholders' equity). The balance sheet views resources from two perspectives: a list of the specific resources the firm holds (for example, cash, inventory, and equipment) and a list of the persons or entities that provided the funds to finance the business and therefore have claims on the assets (for example, suppliers, employees, governments, financial institutions, and shareholders).

The assets portion of the balance sheet reports the effects of a firm's operating decisions (principally those involving assets used in day-to-day activities to produce and deliver products and services to customers) and investing decisions (principally those involving financial assets to generate interest income, dividends, and other returns on investment). Refer to the balance sheets for PepsiCo as of fiscal year-end 2004 through 2008 in Exhibit 1.9. PepsiCo's principal operating assets are cash and cash equivalents; accounts and notes receivable; inventories; prepaid expenses; property, plant, and equipment; and goodwill and intangible assets. PepsiCo's principal financial assets from investing activities include short-term investment securities and investments in the equity securities of noncontrolled affiliates.

The liabilities and shareholders' equity portion of the balance sheet reports obligations that arise from a firm's operating decisions (involving obligations to pay employees and suppliers of goods and services) and financing decisions (raising debt capital from banks and other lenders as well as raising equity capital from investors in common stock). PepsiCo obtains financing from suppliers of goods and services (reported as accounts payable, other current liabilities, and other long-term liabilities), banks and other lenders (reported as both short- and long-term obligations), preferred equity investors (reported as preferred stock, offset by repurchased preferred stock), and common equity investors (reported as common shareholders' equity).

For sake of comparison, also refer to the balance sheets for The Coca-Cola Company as of fiscal year-end 2004 through 2008 in Exhibit 1.10. Notice that Coca-Cola's principal assets, liabilities, and financing from banks, lenders, and common equity investors are similar to those of PepsiCo.

Under U.S. GAAP, firms are required to report assets and liabilities in descending order of liquidity; so the assets that are closest to cash are listed first while the assets that are hardest to convert to cash are reported last. Similarly, the liabilities that are likely to be settled soonest are listed first while the liabilities likely to be settled furthest in the future are shown last.

Formats of balance sheets in some countries can differ from the format used in the United States. Under IFRS, for example, firms can choose to report the balance sheet with assets and liabilities listed in descending order of liquidity or they can report the balance

EXHIBIT 1.9

PepsiCo, Inc. and Subsidiaries
Consolidated Balance Sheets (in millions)

As of Fiscal Year-End:	2008	2007	2006	2005	2004
ASSETS					
Cash and cash equivalents	$ 2,064	$ 910	$ 1,651	$ 1,716	$ 1,280
Short-term investments	213	1,571	1,171	3,166	2,165
Accounts and notes receivable, net	4,683	4,389	3,725	3,261	2,999
Inventories	2,522	2,290	1,926	1,693	1,541
Prepaid expenses and other current assets	1,324	991	657	618	654
Total Current Assets	$10,806	$10,151	$ 9,130	$10,454	$ 8,639
Property, plant, and equipment, net	11,663	11,228	9,687	8,681	8,149
Amortizable intangible assets, net	732	796	637	530	598
Goodwill	5,124	5,169	4,594	4,088	3,909
Other nonamortizable intangible assets	1,128	1,248	1,212	1,086	933
Investments in noncontrolled affiliates	3,883	4,354	3,690	3,485	3,284
Other assets	2,658	1,682	980	3,403	2,475
Total Assets	$35,994	$34,628	$29,930	$31,727	$27,987
LIABILITIES AND SHAREHOLDERS' EQUITY					
Short-term obligations	$ 369	$ —	$ 274	$ 2,889	$ 1,054
Accounts payable and other current liabilities	8,273	7,602	6,496	5,971	5,599
Income taxes payable	145	151	90	546	99
Total Current Liabilities	$ 8,787	$ 7,753	$ 6,860	$ 9,406	$ 6,752
Long-term debt obligations	7,858	4,203	2,550	2,313	2,397
Other liabilities	7,017	4,792	4,624	4,323	4,099
Deferred income taxes	226	646	528	1,434	1,216
Total Liabilities	$23,888	$17,394	$14,562	$17,476	$14,464
Preferred stock, no par value	$ 41	$ 41	$ 41	$ 41	$ 41
Repurchased preferred stock	(138)	(132)	(120)	(110)	(90)
Common stock, par value	30	30	30	30	30
Capital in excess of par value	351	450	584	614	618
Retained earnings	30,638	28,184	24,837	21,116	18,730
Accumulated other comprehensive loss	(4,694)	(952)	(2,246)	(1,053)	(886)
Treasury stock	(14,122)	(10,387)	(7,758)	(6,387)	(4,920)
Total Common Shareholders' Equity	$12,203	$17,325	$15,447	$14,320	$13,572
Total Liabilities and Shareholders' Equity	$35,994	$34,628	$29,930	$31,727	$27,987

EXHIBIT 1.10

The Coca-Cola Company
Consolidated Balance Sheets (in millions)

As of Fiscal Year-End:	2008	2007	2006	2005	2004
ASSETS					
Cash and cash equivalents	$ 4,701	$ 4,093	$ 2,440	$ 4,701	$ 6,707
Short-term investments	278	215	150	66	61
Accounts and notes receivable, net	3,090	3,317	2,587	2,281	2,244
Inventories	2,187	2,220	1,641	1,424	1,420
Prepaid expenses and other current assets	1,920	2,260	1,623	1,778	1,849
Total Current Assets	$12,176	$12,105	$ 8,441	$10,250	$12,281
Property, plant, and equipment, net	8,326	8,493	6,903	5,786	6,091
Amortizable intangible assets, net	2,417	5,153	2,045	1,946	2,037
Goodwill	4,029	4,256	1,403	1,047	1,097
Other nonamortizable intangible assets	6,059	2,810	1,687	828	702
Investments in noncontrolled affiliates	5,779	7,777	6,783	6,922	6,252
Other assets	1,733	2,675	2,701	2,648	2,981
Total Assets	$40,519	$43,269	$29,963	$29,427	$31,441
LIABILITIES AND SHAREHOLDERS' EQUITY					
Short-term obligations	$ 6,066	$ 6,915	$ 3,235	$ 4,518	$ 4,531
Accounts payable and other current liabilities	6,205	5,919	5,055	4,493	4,403
Current maturies of long-term debt	465	133	33	28	1,490
Income taxes payable	252	258	567	797	709
Total Current Liabilities	$12,988	$13,225	$ 8,890	$ 9,836	$11,133
Long-term debt obligations	2,781	3,277	1,314	1,154	1,157
Other liabilities	3,401	3,133	2,231	1,730	2,814
Deferred income taxes	877	1,890	608	352	402
Total Liabilities	$20,047	$21,525	$13,043	$13,072	$15,506
Common stock, par value	$ 880	$ 880	$ 878	$ 877	$ 875
Capital in excess of par value	7,966	7,378	5,983	5,492	4,928
Retained earnings	38,513	36,235	33,468	31,299	29,105
Accumulated other comprehensive loss	(2,674)	626	(1,291)	(1,669)	(1,348)
Treasury stock	(24,213)	(23,375)	(22,118)	(19,644)	(17,625)
Total Shareholders' Equity	$20,472	$21,744	$16,920	$16,355	$15,935
Total Liabilities and Shareholders' Equity	$40,519	$43,269	$29,963	$29,427	$31,441

sheet with long-term assets such as property, plant, and equipment and other noncurrent assets appearing first, followed by current assets. On the financing side, balance sheets prepared under IFRS may list shareholders' equity first, followed by noncurrent liabilities and current liabilities. Both formats under IFRS maintain the balance sheet equality but present accounts in a different sequence.

In the United Kingdom, for example, the balance sheet equation commonly takes the following form:

$$\text{Noncurrent Assets} + [\text{Current Assets} - \text{Current Liabilities}] - \text{Noncurrent Liabilities} = \text{Shareholders' Equity}$$

This format takes the perspective of shareholders by reporting the net assets available for shareholders after subtracting claims by creditors. Financial analysts can rearrange the components of published balance sheets to the format they consider most informative, although ambiguity may exist for some balance sheet categories.

Assets—Recognition, Valuation, and Classification

Which of its resources should a firm recognize as assets? At what amount should the firm report these assets? How should it classify them in the assets portion of the balance sheet? U.S. GAAP and IFRS establish the principles that firms must use to determine responses to those questions.

Defining what resources firms should recognize as assets is one of the most important definitions among all of the principles established by U.S. GAAP and IFRS:[2]

Assets are probable future economic benefits obtained or controlled by a particular entity as a result of past transactions or events.

Assets are resources that have the potential to provide a firm with future economic benefits: the ability to generate future cash inflows (as with accounts receivable, inventories, and investment securities) or to reduce future cash outflows (as with prepayments) or to provide future service potential for operating activities (as with property and equipment and intangibles). Therefore, asset recognition depends on managers' expectations for future economic benefits. A firm can recognize as assets only those resources (1) for which it has the rights to future economic benefits as a result of a past transaction or event and (2) for which the firm can predict and measure, or quantify, the future benefits with a reasonable degree of precision and reliability. If an expenditure does not meet both criteria, it cannot be capitalized and must be expensed. A firm should derecognize assets (that is, write off assets from the balance sheet) that it determines no longer represent future economic benefits (such as writing off not uncollectible receivables or unsalable inventory). Resources that firms do not normally recognize as assets because they fail to meet one or both of the criteria include purchase orders received from customers; employment contracts with corporate officers and employees; and a quality reputation with employees, customers, or citizens of the community.

Most assets on the balance sheet are either *monetary* or *nonmonetary*. (We will define these categories more specifically in the discussion of foreign currency translation in Chapter 7.) Monetary assets include cash and claims to future payments of cash (such as receivables). PepsiCo's monetary assets include cash, accounts and notes receivable, and investments in debt and equity securities of other firms. Under U.S. GAAP and IFRS,

---

[2]Financial Accounting Standards Board, *Statement of Financial Accounting Concepts No. 6*, "Elements of Financial Statements" (1985), par. 25.

balance sheets report monetary assets using a variety of measurement attributes intended to enhance the relevance and reliability of reported asset values. Some monetary assets such as cash are reported at current value. Others, such as accounts receivable, are reported at net realizable value (the amounts the firm expects to collect). For other assets, such as notes receivable and loans with cash receipts that extend beyond one year, the firm reports the monetary asset at the present value of the future cash flows using a discount rate that reflects the underlying uncertainty of collecting the cash as assessed at the time the claim initially arose. Still other assets, such as debt and equity investment securities, are typically reported at fair value, which represents those cash amounts the firm could expect to realize if it sold the securities. Chapter 2 provides more discussion on the various measurement attributes that accounting principles employ to achieve relevant and reliable asset valuations.

Nonmonetary assets include assets that are *tangible,* such as inventories, buildings, and equipment, and assets that are *intangible,* including brand names, patents, trademarks, licenses, and goodwill. In contrast to monetary assets, nonmonetary assets do not represent claims to fixed amounts of cash. The amount of cash firms receive from using or selling nonmonetary assets depends on market conditions at the time of their use or sale. Under U.S. GAAP and IFRS, firms might report nonmonetary assets at the amounts initially paid to acquire them (acquisition, or historical, cost), at the original acquisition cost adjusted for the use of the asset over time (acquisition cost net of accumulated depreciation or amortization), at the amounts currently required to replace them (replacement cost), at the amounts for which firms could currently sell the asset (net realizable value), or at the present values of the amounts firms expect to receive in the future from selling or using the assets (present value of future cash flows). The valuation attribute used typically depends on the nature of the asset. U.S. GAAP and IFRS generally require the reporting of most nonmonetary assets on the balance sheet at their acquisition cost amounts (adjusted for accumulated depreciation or amortization if long-lived) because cost-based valuation is usually more objective and verifiable than other valuation bases. IFRS also permits periodic revaluation of certain types of nonmonetary assets to current values (such as real estate held for investment purposes rather than for operating use). Chapter 2 discusses alternative valuation methods and their implications for measuring earnings.

Perhaps PepsiCo's most valuable resources are its brand names (for example, Pepsi, Frito-Lay®, and Quaker® Oats). PepsiCo and its subsidiaries created and developed these brand names through past expenditures on advertising, event sponsorships, product development, and quality control. Yet ascertaining the portion of these expenditures that creates reliably predictable future economic benefits and the portion that simply stimulates sales during the current period is too uncertain to justify recognizing an asset. The amounts that PepsiCo does report for amortizable intangible assets, goodwill, and other nonamortizable intangible assets (see Note 4, "Property, Plant, and Equipment and Intangible Assets," to PepsiCo's financial statements in Appendix A) result from PepsiCo's purchases of other companies, transaction-based events that provide market evidence of the value of acquired intangibles. PepsiCo's balance sheet reports $732 million of amortizable intangible assets and $1,128 million of nonamortizable intangibles, principally brand names. The remaining $5,124 million of intangible assets is goodwill, which represents the portion of the purchase price of other businesses that PepsiCo could not allocate to identifiable assets and liabilities. Every year PepsiCo tests the value of all of its intangible assets for impairment, and if the evaluation indicates impairment, the intangible asset is written down to its estimated fair value. Chapter 7 discusses the accounting for goodwill and intangibles.

The classification of assets in the balance sheet varies widely in published annual reports. The principal asset categories are as follows:

Current Assets. Current assets include cash and other assets that a firm expects to collect, sell, or consume during the normal operating cycle of a business, usually one year. Cash; short-term investments; accounts and notes receivable; inventories; and prepayments for rent, insurance, and advertising appear as current assets for PepsiCo.

Investments. This category includes short-term and long-term investments in the debt and equity securities of other entities. If a firm makes such investments for short-term purposes, it classifies them under current assets. A principal asset for PepsiCo is the investments in noncontrolled affiliates, which are primarily its bottlers (Pepsi Bottling Group, PepsiAmericas, and other bottlers). Note 8, "Noncontrolled Bottling Affiliates," to PepsiCo's financial statements (Appendix A) indicates that it owns very substantial proportions but less than 50 percent of the common stock of these bottlers. Therefore, PepsiCo does not prepare consolidated financial statements with these bottlers; instead, it reports the investments on the balance sheet using the equity method (discussed in Chapter 7).

Property, Plant, and Equipment. This category includes the tangible, long-lived assets that a firm uses in operations over a period of years. Note 4, "Property, Plant, and Equipment and Intangible Assets," to PepsiCo's financial statements (Appendix A) indicates that property, plant, and equipment includes land and improvements, buildings and improvements, machinery and equipment, and construction in progress. It reports property, plant, and equipment at acquisition cost and then subtracts the accumulated depreciation recognized on these assets since acquisition.

Intangibles. Intangibles include the rights established by law or contract to the future use of property. Patents, trademarks, licenses, and franchises are intangible assets. The most troublesome asset recognition questions revolve around which rights satisfy the criteria for an asset. As Chapter 7 discusses in more depth, firms generally recognize as assets intangibles acquired in external market transactions with other entities (as is the case for brand names and goodwill included in PepsiCo's balance sheet under the categories of amortizable and nonamortizable intangible assets, which it details in Note 4, "Property, Plant, and Equipment and Intangible Assets," in Appendix A), but do not recognize as assets intangibles developed internally by the firm (the Pepsi and Frito-Lay® brand names, for example). The rationale for the different accounting treatment is that the value of intangibles acquired in external market transactions is more reliable than the value of internally developed intangibles.

Liabilities—Recognition, Valuation, and Classification

Under U.S. GAAP and IFRS, firms must report obligations as liabilities if they meet the **definition** of a liability:[3]

> **Liabilities are probable future sacrifices of economic benefits arising from present obligations of a particular entity to transfer assets or provide services to other entities in the future as a result of past transactions or events.**

Therefore, liabilities represent a firm's existing obligations to make payments of cash, goods, or services in a reasonably predictable amount at a reasonably predictable future time as a result of a past transaction or event. Liabilities reflect managers' expectations of future sacrifices of resources to satisfy existing obligations. Liabilities for PepsiCo include obligations to suppliers of goods and services (accounts payable and other current liabilities), governments (income taxes payable), and banks and other lenders (short-term and long-term debt obligations).

---

[3]*Ibid.,* par. 35.

Most troublesome questions regarding liability recognition relate to *executory contracts* and *contingent obligations.* Under U.S. GAAP and IFRS, firms do not recognize executory contracts for labor, purchase order commitments, and some lease agreements as liabilities because the firm has not yet received the benefits from these items and is not yet obligated to pay for them. For example, a firm should not recognize a liability when it places an order to purchase inventory, which is a contingent obligation; the obligation arises only when the firm receives the inventory. Likewise, the firms should not recognize a liability for future wages to employees; instead, it should recognize the liability once the employees have earned the wages. Notes to the financial statements disclose material executory contracts and other contingent claims. For example, refer to PepsiCo's long-term contractual commitments in Note 9, "Debt Obligations and Commitments" (Appendix A). PepsiCo lists noncancelable operating leases, purchasing commitments, and marketing commitments among its executory contracts. The note also describes $2.3 billion of guarantees it has issued for long-term debt of Bottling Group, LLC. Chapters 6 and 8 discuss these claims more fully.

Most liabilities are monetary, requiring future payments of cash. U.S. GAAP and IFRS report those due within one year at the amount of cash the firm expects to pay to discharge the obligation. If the payment dates extend beyond one year, U.S. GAAP and IFRS state the liability at the present value of the required future cash flows (discounted at an interest rate that reflects the underlying uncertainty of paying the cash as assessed at the time the obligation initially arose). Some liabilities, such as warranties, require delivery of goods or services instead of payment of cash, and the balance sheet states those liabilities at the expected future cost of providing these goods and services. Other liabilities also involve obligations to deliver goods or services when customers prepay, giving rise to deferred revenue liabilities. For example, such obligations can arise from the sale of gift cards redeemable for products or services, insurance premia, airfares, subscriptions, and memberships. The balance sheet reports these liabilities at the amount of revenues that have been received from customers and not yet earned.

Published balance sheets classify liabilities in various ways. Virtually all firms (except banks) use a current liabilities category, which includes obligations a firm expects to settle within one year. Balance sheets report the remaining liabilities in a section labeled "noncurrent liabilities" or "long-term debt." PepsiCo uses three noncurrent liability categories: long-term debt obligations, other liabilities, and deferred income taxes. Chapters 2 and 8 discuss deferred income taxes.

Shareholders' Equity Valuation and Disclosure

The shareholders' equity in a firm is a residual interest or claim. That is, the owners have a claim on all assets not required to meet the claims of creditors. Therefore, the valuation of assets and liabilities in the balance sheet determines the valuation of total shareholders' equity.[4]

Balance sheets separate total shareholders' equity into (1) amounts initially contributed by shareholders for an interest in a firm (PepsiCo uses the accounts common stock and capital in excess of par value), (2) cumulative net income in excess of dividends declared (PepsiCo's account is retained earnings), (3) shareholders' equity effects of the recognition or valuation of certain assets or liabilities (PepsiCo includes items related to available-for-sale investment securities, foreign currency translation, derivatives, and pensions in accumulated other comprehensive loss), and (4) treasury stock (PepsiCo

---

[4]The issuance of bonds with equity characteristics (such as convertible bonds), the issuance of equity claims with debt characteristics (such as redeemable preferred or common stock), and the issuance of obligations to be settled with the issuance of equity shares (such as stock options) cloud the distinction between liabilities and shareholders' equity.

shares repurchased by PepsiCo). PepsiCo also reports a small amount of contributed capital as preferred stock (which had been issued by Quaker prior to PepsiCo's acquisition of Quaker) less the amount of repurchased preferred stock.

Changes in Balance Sheet Accounts

The total assets of a firm and the claims on assets change over time because of investing and financing activities. For example, a firm may issue common stock for cash, acquire a building by mortgaging a portion of the purchase price, or issue common stock in exchange for convertible bonds. These investing and financing activities affect the amount and structure of a firm's assets, liabilities, and shareholders' equity.

The total assets of a firm and the claims on assets also change every day because of operating activities. The firm engages in daily business operations to generate revenues and create assets, but to do so, the firm must consume resources and incur obligations. Ideally, the firm sells goods or services to customers for an amount larger than the firm's cost to acquire or produce the goods and services. Creditors and owners provide capital to a firm with the expectation that the firm will use the capital to conduct profitable business operations and provide an adequate return to the suppliers of capital for the level of risk involved. The balance sheet is the summary of the firm's financial position at the end of each period; therefore, it summarizes the results of the operating, investing, and financing activities.

Assessing the Quality of the Balance Sheet as a Complete Representation of Economic Position

Analysts frequently examine the relation between items in the balance sheet when assessing a firm's financial position and credit risk. For example, an excess of current assets over current liabilities suggests that a firm has sufficient liquid resources to pay short-term creditors. A relatively low percentage of long-term debt to shareholders' equity suggests that a firm likely has sufficient long-term assets to repay the long-term debt at maturity, or at least an ability to take on new debt financing using the long-term assets as collateral to repay debt coming due.

However, when using the balance sheet for these purposes, the analyst must recognize the following:

1. Certain valuable resources of a firm that generate future cash flows, such as a patent for a pharmaceutical firm or a brand name for a consumer products firm such as PepsiCo, appear as assets only if they were acquired from another firm and therefore have a measurable acquisition cost.
2. Nonmonetary assets are reported at acquisition cost, net of accumulated depreciation or amortization, even though some of these assets may have current market values that exceed their recorded amounts. An example is the market value versus recorded value of land on the balance sheets of railroads and many urban department stores.
3. Certain rights to use resources and commitments to make future payments may not appear as assets and liabilities. On the balance sheet of airlines, you generally do not see, for example, leased aircraft or commitments to make future lease payments on those aircraft. Also, on the balance sheets of steel, tire, and automobile companies, you do not see the rights to receive labor services or the commitments to make future payments for labor services under labor union contracts.
4. Noncurrent liabilities appear at the present value of expected cash flows discounted at an interest rate determined at the time the liability initially arose instead of at a current market interest rate.

For certain firms under these circumstances, the balance sheet reporting may provide incomplete measures of the economic position of the firms. When using the balance sheet, the analyst should consider making adjustments for items that impact balance sheet quality. Chapters 6–9 discuss these issues more fully.

Income Statement—Measuring Operating Performance

The second principal financial statement, the income statement, provides information about the profitability of a firm for a period of time. As is common among analysts and investors, we use the terms *net income, earnings,* and *profit* interchangeably when referring to the bottom-line amount in the income statement. Exhibit 1.11 presents the income statements for PepsiCo for the five years 2004 through 2008.

Net income equals revenues and gains minus expenses and losses. Revenues measure the inflows of assets and the settlements of obligations from selling goods and providing services

---

EXHIBIT 1.11

PepsiCo, Inc. and Subsidiaries
Consolidated Statements of Income (in millions except per share amounts)

For Fiscal Year:	2008	2007	2006	2005	2004
Net revenue	$43,251	$39,474	$35,137	$32,562	$29,261
Cost of sales	20,351	18,038	15,762	14,176	12,674
Gross Profit	$22,900	$21,436	$19,375	$18,386	$16,587
Selling, general, and administrative expenses	15,901	14,208	12,711	12,314	11,031
Other operating charges	64	58	162	150	147
Restructuring charges	0	0	0	0	150
Operating Profit	$ 6,935	$ 7,170	$ 6,502	$ 5,922	$ 5,259
Bottling equity income	374	560	553	557	380
Interest expense	(329)	(224)	(239)	(256)	(167)
Interest income	41	125	173	159	74
Income before Income Taxes	$ 7,021	$ 7,631	$ 6,989	$ 6,382	$ 5,546
Provision for income taxes	1,879	1,973	1,347	2,304	1,372
Income from Continuing Operations	$ 5,142	$ 5,658	$ 5,642	$ 4,078	$ 4,174
Tax benefit from discontinued operations	0	0	0	0	38
Net Income	$ 5,142	$ 5,658	$ 5,642	$ 4,078	$ 4,212
Net income per common share:					
Basic	$ 3.26	$ 3.48	$ 3.42	$ 2.43	$ 2.45
Diluted	$ 3.21	$ 3.41	$ 3.34	$ 2.39	$ 2.41

to customers. Expenses measure the outflows of assets that a firm consumes and the incurrence of obligations in the process of operating the business to generate revenues. As a measure of performance, revenues report the resources generated by a firm and expenses report the resources consumed. Gains and losses result from selling assets or settling liabilities for more or less than their book values in transactions that are only peripherally related to a firm's central operations. For example, the sale of a building by PepsiCo for more than its book value would appear as a gain on the income statement. Chapter 2 describes income measurement in detail, and Chapter 3 contrasts income measurement with cash flows. Chapter 8 describes accounting for operating activities, particularly recognizing revenues and expenses.

PepsiCo generates revenues from selling goods in three principal product categories: snack foods; various soft drink concentrates, syrups, and bottled beverages; and cereals and related items. Revenues also include interest income from investments in debt instruments and equity method income from investments in affiliated but noncontrolled bottlers.

Costs of sales include the cost of manufacturing snack foods; the cost of producing concentrates, syrups, and bottled beverages; and the cost of manufacturing cereals and related items. Expenses also include selling, general, and administrative expenses (including advertising and other promotion costs) and interest expense on short- and long-term borrowing. PepsiCo reports amortization of intangible assets as a separate expense.

Compare PepsiCo's income statements to those of its closest rival, Coca-Cola. Exhibit 1.12 presents the income statements for Coca-Cola for the five years 2004 through 2008. Although PepsiCo is larger than Coca-Cola in terms of annual revenues, Coca-Cola is generally more

EXHIBIT 1.12

The Coca-Cola Company
Consolidated Statements of Income (in millions except per share amounts)

For Fiscal Year:	2008	2007	2006	2005	2004
Net revenue	$31,944	$28,857	$24,088	$23,104	$21,742
Cost of sales	11,374	10,406	8,164	8,195	7,674
Gross Profit	$20,570	$18,451	$15,924	$14,909	$14,068
Selling, general, and administrative expenses	11,774	10,945	9,431	8,739	7,890
Other operating charges	350	254	185	85	480
Operating Profit	$ 8,446	$ 7,252	$ 6,308	$ 6,085	$ 5,698
Bottling equity income	(874)	668	102	680	621
Interest expense	(438)	(456)	(220)	(240)	(196)
Interest income	333	236	193	235	157
Other income (loss) net	(28)	173	195	(70)	(58)
Income before Income Taxes	$ 7,439	$ 7,873	$ 6,578	$ 6,690	$ 6,222
Provision for income taxes	1,632	1,892	1,498	1,818	1,375
Net Income	$ 5,807	$ 5,981	$ 5,080	$ 4,872	$ 4,847
Net income per common share:					
Basic	$ 2.51	$ 2.59	$ 2.16	$ 2.04	$ 2.00
Diluted	$ 2.49	$ 2.57	$ 2.16	$ 2.04	$ 2.00

profitable in terms of annual net income. For example, in 2008, PepsiCo generated total revenues of $43,251 million and net income of $5,142 million; during the same year, Coca-Cola generated total revenues of $31,944 and net income of $5,807.

When using the income statement to assess a firm's profitability, the analyst is interested not only in its current and past profitability, but also in the likely level of sustainable earnings in the future (Step 5 in our six-step framework). When forecasting future earnings, the analyst must project whether past levels of revenues and expenses will likely continue and grow. Chapters 4 and 9 discuss some of the factors the analyst should consider before making these judgments. Chapter 10 provides an extensive discussion of building forecasts of future financial statements.

Accrual Basis of Accounting

Exhibit 1.13 depicts the operating, or earnings, cycle for a manufacturing firm. Net income from this series of activities equals the amount of cash received from customers minus the amount of cash paid for raw materials, labor, and the services of production facilities. If the entire operating cycle occurred in one accounting period, few difficulties would arise in measuring operating performance. Net income would equal cash inflows minus cash outflows related to these operating activities. However, firms acquire raw materials in one accounting period and use them in several future accounting periods. They acquire buildings and equipment in one accounting period and use them during many future accounting periods. Firms commonly sell goods or services in an earlier period than the one in which customers pay. Firms often consume resources or incur obligations in one accounting period and pay for those resources or settle those obligations in subsequent periods.

Under a cash basis of accounting, a firm recognizes revenue when it receives cash from customers and recognizes expenses when it pays cash to suppliers, employees, and other providers of goods and services. Because a firm's operating cycle usually extends over several accounting periods, the cash basis of accounting provides a poor measure of economic performance for specific periods of time because it provides a poor matching of resources earned (revenues) with resources used (expenses). To overcome this deficiency of the cash basis, both U.S. GAAP and IFRS require that firms use the accrual basis of accounting in measuring performance.

Under the accrual basis of accounting, a firm recognizes revenue when it meets the following two criteria:

- **It has completed all (or substantially all) of the revenue-generating process by delivering products or services to customers.**
- **It is reasonably certain it has satisfied a liability or generated an asset that it can measure reliably.**

Most firms recognize revenue during the period in which they sell goods or render services. Consider the accrual basis of accounting applied to a manufacturing firm. The cost

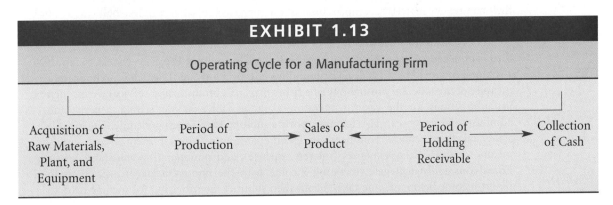

EXHIBIT 1.13

Operating Cycle for a Manufacturing Firm

Acquisition of Raw Materials, Plant, and Equipment ← Period of Production → Sales of Product ← Period of Holding Receivable → Collection of Cash

of manufacturing a product remains on the balance sheet as an asset (inventory) until the time of sale. At the time of sale, the firm recognizes revenue in the amount of cash it expects to collect. It recognizes the cost of manufacturing the product as a cost of the goods sold. Most costs cannot be matched to particular revenues because they are costs of operating the business for a particular period of time (for example, the salary of the chief executive officer and rent on corporate offices.). Therefore, the firm recognizes such costs as expenses on the income statement in the period in which it consumes those resources (that is, matching expenses to a period rather than to specific revenues).

Note that under accrual accounting a firm should not delay revenue recognition until it receives cash from customers as long as the firm can estimate with reasonable precision the amount of cash it will ultimately receive. The amount will appear in accounts receivable prior to the receipt of cash. The accrual basis provides a better measure of operating performance than the cash basis because it matches inputs with outputs more accurately.

Classification and Format in the Income Statement

Investors commonly assess a firm's value based on the firm's expected future sustainable earnings stream. As Chapter 10 discusses more fully, analysts predict the future earnings, or net income, of a firm by projecting future business activities that will drive future revenues, expenses, and profits. To inform analysts and other financial statement users about sustainable earnings, firms often report income from recurring business activities separately from income effects from unusual or nonrecurring activities (such as asset impairments, restructuring, discontinued business segments, and extraordinary events). To provide more useful information for prediction, U.S. GAAP requires that the income statement include some or all of the following sections or categories depending on the nature of the firm's income for a period:

- Income from continuing operations
- Income, gains, and losses from discontinued operations
- Extraordinary gains and losses

Income from Continuing Operations. The first section, Income from Continuing Operations, reports the revenues and expenses of activities in which a firm anticipates an ongoing involvement. When a firm does not have items in the second and third categories of income in a particular year, all of its income items are related to continuing operations; so it does not need to use the continuing operations label.

Firms report their expenses in various ways. Most firms in the United States report expenses by their function: cost of goods sold for manufacturing, selling expenses for marketing, administrative expenses for administrative management, and interest expense for financing. Other firms, particularly those in the European Community, tend to report expenses by their nature: raw materials, compensation, advertising, and research and development.

Many variations in income statement format appear in corporate annual reports. Most commonly, firms list various sources of revenues from selling their goods and services and then list the cost of goods sold. Some firms (Coca-Cola but not PepsiCo) choose to report a subtotal of gross profit (sales revenues minus cost of goods sold), which is an important measure of the inherent profitability of a firm's principal products and services. Firms then list subtractions for the various operating expenses (for example, selling, general, and administrative expenses). This format reports a subtotal for operating income. The income statement then reports nonoperating income amounts (interest income and equity income), nonoperating expenses (interest expense), and nonoperating gains and losses. Firms commonly aggregate operating income with the nonoperating income items to report income before income taxes. Firms then subtract the provision for income taxes to compute and report the bottom-line net income. As shown in Exhibit 1.11 and Appendix A, PepsiCo uses this multistep format to report its income statement.

Income from Discontinued Operations. A firm that intends to remain in a line of business but decides to sell or close down some portion of that line (such as closing a single plant or dropping a line of products) generally will report any income, gain, or loss from such an action under continuing operations. On the other hand, if a firm decides to terminate its involvement in a line of business (such as selling or shuttering an entire division or subsidiary), it will report the income, gain, or loss in the second section of the income statement, labeled "Income, Gains, and Losses from Discontinued Operations."

For example, on August 14, 1997, PepsiCo announced that it would spin off its restaurant businesses (which included Pizza Hut, Taco Bell, and KFC), forming a new restaurant company named Tricon Global Restaurants, Inc. (now known as Yum! Brands, Inc.). For 1997, PepsiCo reported income from continuing operations separately from discontinued operations. In that year, PepsiCo reported a total of $1,491 million of income (net of tax) from continuing operations and $651 million of income (net of tax) associated with the discontinued restaurants segment.

Extraordinary Gains and Losses. Extraordinary gains and losses arise from events that are (1) unusual given the nature of a firm's activities, (2) nonrecurring, and (3) material in amount. Corporate annual reports rarely disclose such items.

Many firms, including PepsiCo, have reported restructuring charges and impairment losses in their income statements in recent years. Such items often reflect the write-down of assets or the recognition of liabilities arising from changes in economic conditions and corporate strategies. Because restructuring charges and impairment losses do not usually satisfy the criteria for discontinued operations or extraordinary items, firms report them in the continuing operations section of the income statement. If the amounts are material, they appear on a separate line to distinguish them from recurring income items. Chapters 4 and 9 discuss the benefits and possible pitfalls of segregating such amounts when analyzing profitability.

Income, gains, and losses from discontinued operations and extraordinary gains and losses appear in the income statement net of any income tax effects. The majority of published income statements include only the first section because discontinued operations and extraordinary gains and losses occur infrequently.

Comprehensive Income

The FASB and IASB have determined that the balance sheet is the cornerstone of accounting and that income should be measured by changes in the values of assets and liabilities. To provide relevant and reliable measures of assets and liabilities, U.S. GAAP and IFRS use a variety of measurement attributes, some of which require firms to adjust asset or liability values to reflect changes in net realizable values, fair values, or present values. Valuation adjustments to assets and liabilities usually give rise to revenues (or gains) or to expenses (or losses). For example, if a firm determines that it will not collect some of its accounts receivable or will not be able to sell some items of inventory, it should adjust receivables and inventory to their net realizable values and recognize those adjustments as expenses or losses in net income.

The FASB and IASB have determined that four particular types of valuation adjustments represent unrealized gains or losses that should be classified as "other comprehensive income" items. Other comprehensive income items are accumulated over time in a special account in shareholders' equity titled Accumulated Other Comprehensive Income or Loss (similar to how net income is accumulated over time in the shareholders' equity account titled Retained Earnings). These other comprehensive income items are not recognized in net income until they are realized in an economic transaction, such as when the related assets are sold or the liabilities are settled.

Review the Consolidated Statement of Common Shareholders' Equity for PepsiCo in Appendix A. It details the four types of unrealized gain/loss items that are triggered by the valuation of assets and liabilities and are recognized as other comprehensive income items. It also reports the components of Accumulated Other Comprehensive Loss: (1) currency translation adjustments; (2) cash flow hedges, net of tax; (3) certain changes in pension and retiree medical plan obligations, net of tax; and (4) unrealized losses/gains on securities, net of tax. Later chapters discuss the accounting for each of these items.

The FASB and IASB are aware that unrealized gains and losses of this nature affect the market value of firms, but users of financial statements might overlook them because they do not yet appear in net income. Therefore, firms must report an amount in one of their financial statements that the FASB refers to as *Comprehensive Income*.[5] Comprehensive income equals *all* revenues, expenses, gains, and losses for a period. Comprehensive income includes net income plus or minus the other comprehensive income items. Refer again to PepsiCo's consolidated statement of common shareholders' equity in Appendix A. The bottom portion of the statement shows the computation of PepsiCo's comprehensive income each year. Comprehensive income for PepsiCo for 2008 is as follows (in millions):

Net income	$5,142
Currency translation adjustment	(2,484)
Cash flow hedges, net of tax	21
Pension and retiree medical plan liability adjustments, net of tax	(1,303)
Unrealized losses on securities, net of tax	(21)
Other	(6)
Comprehensive income	$1,349

Firms have considerable flexibility as to where they report comprehensive income in the financial statements. It may appear in the income statement, in a separate statement of comprehensive income, or as part of the analysis of changes in shareholders' equity accounts. PepsiCo uses this last method of disclosure.

Firms also have flexibility as to how they label disclosures related to comprehensive income. That is, firms need not use the term *comprehensive income*, but instead may label the amount as, for example, net income plus or minus changes in other non-owner equity accounts. The balance sheet disclosure might use the term *accumulated other comprehensive income/loss* for the portions of comprehensive income not related to reported earnings or use a term such as *accumulated non-owner equity account changes*.

Appendix A indicates that PepsiCo uses the term *Accumulated Other Comprehensive Loss* in its Consolidated Balance Sheet. In addition, PepsiCo reports the accumulated balances for each component of its other comprehensive income in Note 13, "Accumulated Other Comprehensive Loss," to the financial statements.

Assessing the Quality of Earnings as a Complete Representation of Economic Performance

Common stock prices in the capital markets usually react quickly when firms announce new earnings information, indicating that earnings play an important role in the valuation

---

[5]Financial Accounting Standards Board, *Statement of Financial Accounting Standards Statement No. 130*, "Reporting Comprehensive Income" (1997).

of firms. We provide some striking empirical evidence of the association between earnings and stock returns later in this chapter. In using earnings information for valuation, however, the analyst needs to be alert to the possibility that reported earnings for a particular period represent an incomplete measure of current period profitability or are a poor predictor of ongoing sustainable profitability. For example, reported net income may include amounts that are not likely to recur in the future, such as restructuring or impairment charges; income, gains, and losses from discontinued operations; or extraordinary gains or losses. The analyst may want to eliminate the effects of nonrecurring items when assessing operating performance for purposes of forecasting future earnings. (Chapters 9 and 10 discuss these ideas more fully.)

In some circumstances managers use subtle means to manage earnings. For example, a firm might accelerate recognition of revenues, understate its estimate of bad debt expense or warranty expense, cut back on advertising or research and development expenditures, or delay maintenance expenditures as a means of increasing earnings in a particular period. Chapter 9 discusses the quality of accounting information and illustrates adjustments the analyst might make to improve the quality of earnings.

Statement of Cash Flows

The third principal financial statement is the statement of cash flows. This statement reports for a period of time the net cash flows (inflows minus outflows) from three principal business activities: operating, investing, and financing. The purpose of the statement of cash flows is important but simple: to inform analysts about the sources and uses of cash. The statement provides useful information to complement the income statement, demonstrating how cash flows differ from accrual-based income. Because the cash flows statement reveals how a firm is generating and using cash, it also is a useful tool for gauging how the firm is executing its strategy.

Rationale for the Statement of Cash Flows

The statement of cash flows provides information on the sources and uses of cash. Even profitable firms—especially those growing rapidly—sometimes find themselves strapped for cash and unable to pay suppliers, employees, and other creditors. This can occur for two principal reasons:

- The timing of cash receipts from customers does not necessarily coincide with the recognition of revenue, and the timing of cash expenditures does not necessarily coincide with the recognition of expenses under the accrual basis of accounting. In the usual case, cash expenditures precede the recognition of expenses and cash receipts follow the recognition of revenue. Thus, a firm might have positive net income for a period but a negative net cash flow from operations.
- The firm may need to acquire new property, plant, and equipment; retire outstanding debt; or reacquire shares of its common stock when sufficient cash is not available.

In many cases, a profitable firm finding itself short of cash can obtain the needed funds from short- or long-term creditors or from equity investors. The firm must repay with interest the funds borrowed from creditors. Owners may require that the firm pay periodic dividends as an inducement to invest in the firm. Eventually, the firm must generate sufficient cash from operations if it is to survive.

Sometimes firms are flush with cash. In such cases, the analyst should determine why the firm has excess cash, which can occur for two principal reasons:

- Firm operations may be profitable, with cash flows from operations equal to or greater than profits. This can occur, for example, when the firm is mature, stable, and profitable and does not need to invest excess cash flows in capital or growth opportunities (sometimes referred to as cash-cow firms).

- The firm may have engaged in cash-raising transactions by selling assets or divesting subsidiaries, issuing short-term or long-term debt, or issuing equity shares.

The analyst will find it useful to know which of the two reasons explain the firm's excess cash because they have different implications for the firm's strategy and are likely to influence how the analyst values the firm.

Classification of Cash Flows

Cash flows are the connecting link between operating, investing, and financing activities. They permit each of these three principal business activities to continue functioning smoothly and effectively. The statement of cash flows also can be helpful in assessing a firm's past ability to generate free cash flows and for predicting future free cash flows. The concept of free cash flows is first introduced in Chapter 3. As discussed in Chapter 12, free cash flows are central to cash-flow-based valuation models.

The statement of cash flows classifies cash flows as relating to operating, investing, or financing activities.

Operating. Selling goods and providing services are among the most important ways a financially healthy company generates cash. Assessing cash flow from operations over several years indicates the extent to which operating activities have provided the necessary cash to maintain operating capabilities (and the extent to which firms have had to rely on other sources of cash).

Investing. The acquisition of long-lived productive assets, particularly property, plant, and equipment, usually represents major ongoing uses of cash. Firms must replace such assets as they wear out. If firms are to grow, they must acquire additional long-lived productive assets. Firms obtain a portion of the cash needed to acquire long-lived productive assets from sales of existing assets. However, such cash inflows are seldom sufficient to cover the cost of new acquisitions.

Financing. A firm obtains cash from short- and long-term borrowing and from issuing preferred and common stock. It uses cash to repay short- and long-term borrowing, to pay dividends, and to reacquire shares of outstanding preferred and common stock.

Exhibit 1.14 presents the statement of cash flows for PepsiCo for 2004 through 2008. The statement reveals that cash flow from operating activities exceeded the net cash outflow for investing activities in each of the three years. In 2006, PepsiCo used a portion of the excess cash flow for financing activities, reducing short-term and long-term debt. But PepsiCo shifted its financing strategy in 2007 and 2008, generating large amounts of net cash inflows from proceeds of short-term and long-term borrowings. In all three years, PepsiCo used large amounts of cash to pay dividends to shareholders and to repurchase shares of its common stock. For comparative purposes, Exhibit 1.15 (see page 37) presents the statement of cash flows for Coca-Cola for 2004 through 2008.

Firms sometimes engage in investing and financing transactions that do not directly involve cash. For example, a firm might acquire a building by assuming a mortgage obligation. It might issue common stock upon conversion of long-term debt. Firms disclose these transactions in a supplementary schedule or note to the statement of cash flows in a way that clearly indicates that the transactions are investing and financing activities that do not affect cash. In Note 14, "Supplemental Financial Information," (Appendix A), PepsiCo reports the portion of its acquisitions in recent years that did not directly involve the use of cash.

EXHIBIT 1.14

PepsiCo, Inc. and Subsidiaries
Consolidated Statements of Cash Flows (in millions)

For Fiscal Year:	2008	2007	2006	2005	2004
OPERATING ACTIVITIES					
Net income	$ 5,142	$ 5,658	$ 5,642	$ 4,078	$ 4,212
Adjustments to reconcile net income to net cash provided by operating activities					
Depreciation and amortization	1,543	1,426	1,406	1,308	1,264
Stock-based compensation expense	238	260	270	311	368
Restructuring and impairment charges	543	102	67	—	150
Excess tax benefits from share-based payment arrangements	(107)	(208)	(134)	—	—
Cash payments for restructuring charges	(180)	(22)	(56)	(22)	(92)
Pension and retiree medical plan contributions	(219)	(310)	(131)	(877)	(534)
Pension and retiree medical plan expenses	459	535	544	464	395
Bottling equity income, net of dividends	(202)	(441)	(442)	(411)	(297)
Deferred income taxes and other tax charges and credits	573	118	(510)	585	(75)
Change in accounts and notes receivable	(549)	(405)	(330)	(272)	(130)
Change in inventories	(345)	(204)	(186)	(132)	(100)
Change in prepaid expenses and other current assets	(68)	(16)	(37)	(56)	(31)
Change in accounts payable and other current liabilities	718	522	279	188	216
Change in income taxes payable	(180)	128	(295)	609	(268)
Other, net	(367)	(209)	(3)	79	(24)
Net Cash Provided by Operating Activities	$ 6,999	$ 6,934	$ 6,084	$ 5,852	$ 5,054
INVESTING ACTIVITIES					
Capital spending	$(2,446)	$(2,430)	$(2,068)	$(1,736)	$(1,387)
Sales of property, plant, and equipment	98	47	49	88	38
Acquisitions and investments in noncontrolled affiliates	(1,925)	(1,293)	(547)	(1,095)	(64)
Cash restricted for pending acquisitions	(40)	—	—	—	—
Cash proceeds from sale of PBG and PAS stock	358	315	318	214	—
Divestitures	6	—	37	3	52
Short-term investments, by original maturity					
More than three months—purchases	(156)	(83)	(29)	(83)	(44)
More than three months—maturities	62	113	25	84	38
Three months or less, net	1,376	(413)	2,021	(992)	(963)
Net Cash Used for Investing Activities	$(2,667)	$(3,744)	$ (194)	$(3,517)	$(2,330)

(Continued)

EXHIBIT 1.14 (Continued)

For Fiscal Year:	2008	2007	2006	2005	2004
FINANCING ACTIVITIES					
Proceeds from issuances of long-term debt	$ 3,719	$ 2,168	$ 51	$ 25	$ 504
Payments of long-term debt	(649)	(579)	(157)	(177)	(512)
Short-term borrowings, by original maturity					
More than three months—proceeds	89	83	185	332	153
More than three months—payments	(269)	(133)	(358)	(85)	(160)
Three months or less, net	625	(345)	(2,168)	1,601	1,119
Cash dividends paid	(2,541)	(2,204)	(1,854)	(1,642)	(1,329)
Share repurchases—common	(4,720)	(4,300)	(3,000)	(3,012)	(3,028)
Share repurchases—preferred	(6)	(12)	(10)	(19)	(27)
Proceeds from exercises of stock options	620	1,108	1,194	1,099	965
Excess tax benefits from share-based payment arrangements	107	208	134	—	—
Net Cash Used for Financing Activities	$(3,025)	$(4,006)	$(5,983)	$(1,878)	$(2,315)
Effect of exchange rate changes on cash and cash equivalents	$ (153)	$ 75	$ 28	$ (21)	$ 51
Net Increase (Decrease) in Cash and Cash Equivalents	$ 1,154	$ (741)	$ (65)	$ 436	$ 460
Cash and Cash Equivalents, Beginning of Year	910	1,651	1,716	1,280	820
Cash and Cash Equivalents, End of Year	$ 2,064	$ 910	$ 1,651	$ 1,716	$ 1,280

The statement of cash flows is required under both U.S. GAAP and IFRS, but it is not a required financial statement in some countries. Increasingly, however, most large international firms are providing the statement on a voluntary basis. Chapter 3 describes and illustrates analytical procedures for preparing a statement of cash flows in situations where firms provide only a balance sheet and income statement. Chapter 10 demonstrates techniques for projecting future statements of cash flows from projected balance sheets and income statements.

Important Information with the Financial Statements

A firm's accounting system records the results of transactions, events, and commercial arrangements and generates the financial statements, but the financial statements do not stand alone. To provide more relevant and reliable information for financial statement users, firms typically provide a substantial amount of important additional information with the financial statements. This section briefly introduces three important additional elements of information: (a) Notes, (b) Management Discussion and Analysis, and (c) Managers' and Independent Auditors' Attestations.

Notes

The financial statements report the accounts and amounts that comprise the balance sheet, income statement, and statement of cash flows, but they do not explain how those accounts

EXHIBIT 1.15

The Coca-Cola Company
Consolidated Statements of Cash Flows
(in millions)

For Fiscal Year:	2008	2007	2006	2005	2004
OPERATING ACTIVITIES					
Net income	$ 5,807	$ 5,981	$ 5,080	$ 4,872	$ 4,847
Adjustments to reconcile net income to net cash provided by operating activities					
Depreciation and amortization	1,228	1,163	938	932	893
Stock-based compensation expense	266	313	324	324	345
Deferred income taxes	(360)	109	(35)	(88)	162
Bottling equity income, net of dividends	1,128	(452)	124	(446)	(476)
Foreign currency adjustments	(42)	9	52	47	(59)
Gains on sales of assets	(130)	(244)	(303)	(32)	(44)
Other operating charges	209	166	159	85	480
Other items	153	99	233	299	437
Net change in operating assets and liabilities	(688)	6	(615)	430	(617)
Net Cash Provided by Operating Activities	$ 7,571	$ 7,150	$ 5,957	$ 6,423	$ 5,968
INVESTING ACTIVITIES					
Acquisitions and investments	$ (759)	$(5,653)	$ (901)	$ (637)	$ (267)
Purchases of other investments	(240)	(99)	(82)	(53)	(46)
Proceeds from disposals of acquisition and investments	479	448	640	33	161
Purchases of property, plant, and equipment	(1,968)	(1,648)	(1,407)	(899)	(755)
Proceeds from disposals of property, plant, and equipment	129	239	112	88	341
Other investing activities	(4)	(6)	(62)	(28)	63
Net Cash Used for Investing Activities	$(2,363)	$(6,719)	$(1,700)	$(1,496)	$ (503)
FINANCING ACTIVITIES					
Issuances of debt	$ 4,337	$ 9,979	$ 617	$ 178	$ 3,030
Payments of debt	(4,308)	(5,638)	(2,021)	(2,460)	(1,316)
Issuances of stock	586	1,619	148	230	193
Purchases of stock for treasury	(1,079)	(1,838)	(2,416)	(2,055)	(1,739)
Dividends	(3,521)	(3,149)	(2,911)	(2,678)	(2,429)
Net Cash Used for Financing Activities	$(3,985)	$ 973	$(6,583)	$(6,785)	$(2,261)
Effect of exchange rate changes on cash and cash equivalents	$ (615)	$ 249	$ 65	$ (148)	$ 141
Net Increase (Decrease) in Cash and Cash Equivalents	$ 608	$ 1,653	$(2,261)	$(2,006)	$ 3,345
Cash and Cash Equivalents, Beginning of Year	4,093	2,440	4,701	6,707	3,362
Cash and Cash Equivalents, End of Year	$ 4,701	$ 4,093	$ 2,440	$ 4,701	$ 6,707

and amounts have been determined. The notes to financial statements provide important details about the accounting methods and principles the firm has used to measure assets, liabilities, revenues, expenses, gains, and losses. The first note typically provides a summary of the key accounting principles the firm has used. Because each account in the financial statements requires application of judgments, estimates, and accounting principles, the notes typically describe and explain how each account has been determined (except accounts that are deemed not to be material). For example, the notes explain how the firm is accounting for inventory and what cost methods the firm used to value inventory on hand as well as cost of goods sold. The notes explain how property, plant, and equipment are valued; how they are being depreciated; how much depreciation has been accumulated to date; and what the expected useful lives of the underlying assets are. Notes also provide important details about key financial statement estimates, such as fair values of investment securities, pension and postemployment benefit liabilities, income taxes, and intangible assets.

In the 2008 Annual Report (Appendix A), PepsiCo provides a total of 14 notes to explain the accounting principles, methods, and estimates used to prepare the financial statements. Immediately following the financial statements, the notes comprise an additional 21 pages of the annual report. You should read the notes carefully because they provide important information that is useful for understanding the firm's accounting and assessing its accounting quality.

Management Discussion and Analysis

Many firms accompany the financial statements and notes with extensive narrative and quantitative discussion and analysis from the managers. The MD&A (Management Discussion and Analysis) section of the financial statements provides insights into managers' strategies and their assessments and evaluation of the firm's performance. In some cases, MD&A disclosures provide glimpses into managers' expectations about the future of the company.

In the 2008 Annual Report, PepsiCo provides a total of 24 pages of MD&A (Appendix B). In the MD&A, PepsiCo describes the business as a whole, as well as the operations of the business in each of the six divisions. In addition to qualitative descriptions, the MD&A section provides valuable details about the financial performance of each division, with managers' analysis comparing results of 2008 to 2007 and 2007 to 2006. In addition, PepsiCo's MD&A section provides important insights into the firm's business risks and the way PepsiCo is managing them, critical accounting policies PepsiCo has applied, and PepsiCo's liquidity and capital resource situation. The MD&A section also provides valuable glimpses into a few of PepsiCo's plans for the future, such as its intention in 2009 to repurchase up to $2.5 billion in common shares. Because the MD&A section provides insight into the company from the managers' point of view, you should read it carefully to obtain all of the information available. But you also should read it with a bit of skepticism because managers tend to be optimistic when evaluating the strategies and performance of their firms.

Managers' and Independent Auditors' Attestations

The design and operation of the accounting system are the responsibility of a firm's managers. However, the SEC and most stock exchanges require firms with publicly traded common stock to have their accounting records and financial statements audited by independent auditors. The independent auditor's attestation as to the fairness and reliability of a firm's financial statements relative to U.S. GAAP or IFRS is an essential element in the efficiency of the capital markets. Investors and other users of the financial statements can rely on financial statements for essential information about a firm only if they are confident that the independent auditor has examined the accounting records and has concluded that the financial statements are fair and reliable according to U.S. GAAP or IFRS.

In response to some managers' misrepresenting their financial statements and audit breakdowns in now infamous cases involving Enron, Global Crossing, Qwest Communications, and other firms, Congress passed the Sarbanes-Oxley Act of 2002. This act more clearly defines the explicit responsibility of managers for financial statements, the relation between the independent auditor and the firm audited, and the kinds of services permitted and not permitted. Exhibit 1.16 summarizes some of the more important provisions of the Sarbanes-Oxley Act as they relate to financial statements.

For many years, firms have included with their financial statements a report by management that states its responsibility for the financial statements. The Sarbanes-Oxley Act of 2002 now requires that the management report include an attestation that managers assume responsibility for establishing and maintaining adequate internal control structure and procedures (referred to as the *Management Assessment*). This new requirement now makes explicit management's responsibility not only for the financial statements, but also

---

EXHIBIT 1.16

Summary of the Principal Provisions of the Sarbanes-Oxley Act of 2002

1. Violation of the provisions of the Sarbanes-Oxley Act of 2002 is a violation of the Securities Exchange Act of 1934. The Securities Exchange Act of 1934 governs the public trading of securities.

2. The Sarbanes-Oxley Act of 2002 created the Public Company Accounting Oversight Board (PCAOB), which has responsibility for setting generally accepted auditing standards, ethics standards, and quality-control standards for audits.

3. The SEC has oversight and enforcement authority over the PCAOB.

4. The act precludes a registered public accounting firm from performing non-audit services contemporaneously with the audit. Certain services, such as tax work, are allowed if they are preapproved by the firm's audit committee or constitute less than 5 percent of the billing price for audit and other services.

5. The lead audit or coordinating partner and the reviewing partner of the public accounting firm must rotate, or change, every five years.

6. Members of the audit committee of a firm's board of directors will have primary responsibility for appointment, oversight, and compensation of the registered public accounting firm.

7. At least one member of the audit committee of the board of directors must be a "financial expert."

8. The firm's chief executive officer and the chief financial officer must issue a statement along with the audit report stating that the financial statements and notes fairly present the operations and financial position of the firm.

9. Each annual report must contain an "internal control report" that states management's responsibility for establishing and maintaining an adequate internal control structure and procedures (Management Assessment Report). The annual report must also contain an assessment of the effectiveness of the internal control structure and procedures by the firm's auditor (Assurance Opinion). The assurance opinion can be unqualified, qualified, adverse, or a disclaimer, the same as the independent accountant's opinion on the financial statements and notes.

for the underlying accounting and control system that generates the financial statements. The chief executive officer and the chief financial officer must sign this management report. PepsiCo's management report appears in Appendix A.

The independent auditor also assesses a firm's internal control system, designs its audit tests in light of the quality of these internal controls, and then forms an opinion about the fairness of the amounts reported in the financial statements based on its audit tests. The independent auditor must now include opinions on the effectiveness of the internal control system (referred to as the *Assurance Opinion*) and the fairness of the amounts reported in the financial statements. This dual opinion makes explicit the independent auditor's responsibility for testing the effectiveness of the internal control system and judging the fairness of the amounts reported. The report of PepsiCo's independent auditor (KPMG, LLP) appears in Appendix A after Note 14, "Supplemental Financial Information." Note that the last paragraph includes opinions on both the internal control system and the financial statements and reads as follows:

> In our opinion, the consolidated financial statements referred to above present fairly, in all material respects, the financial position of PepsiCo, Inc. as of December 27, 2008 and December 29, 2007, and the results of their operations and their cash flows for each of the fiscal years in the three-year period ended December 27, 2008, in conformity with U.S. generally accepted accounting principles. Also, in our opinion, PepsiCo, Inc. maintained, in all material respects, effective internal control over financial reporting as of December 27, 2008, based on criteria established in *Internal Control-Integrated Framework* issued by COSO.

Summary of Financial Statements, Notes, MD&A, and Managers' and Auditors' Attestations

The three principal financial statements, the notes, the MD&A section, and managers' and auditors' attestations provide analysts with an immense amount of useful information for understanding various aspects of a firm's operating, investing, and financing activities.

- The balance sheet reports the results of firms' decisions to acquire assets and the financing of those assets. Most assets result from decisions about operating activities (for example, credit policies for customers, production and control systems for inventories, and plant and productive capacity), yet other assets result from investing decisions (for example, holding investment securities and investing in noncontrolled affiliates). Many liabilities of firms also result from decisions about operating activities (such as policies for paying suppliers of good and services and compensation and benefits plans for employees) or from claims from government tax authorities. Financing decisions also determine many liabilities, including the firm's decisions about the use of short-term and long-term borrowings and common stock to finance assets.

- The income statement primarily reflects the results of operating decisions (for example, product mix and pricing, sourcing of production and marketing, and use of plant and equipment). The income statement also reports amounts related to investing decisions (for example, interest and dividend income) and financing decisions (for example, interest expense). The other comprehensive income items, which are reported as part of comprehensive income in the statement of shareholders' equity, reflect gains and losses from changes in values of certain assets and liabilities that are not reported in net income until such gains and losses are realized.

- The statement of cash flows reflects the sources of uses of cash during a period. The statement of cash flows classifies cash changes during a period into operating, investing, and financing categories.
- The notes to the financial statements explain and describe the accounting methods, assumptions, estimates, and judgments used to prepare the statements.
- The MD&A section provides managers' insights and evaluation of the firm's performance and risks.
- The managers' attestation and the independent auditor's attestation provide statements about (and take responsibility for) the quality and effectiveness of the firm's internal control system and the fairness of its financial statements and notes in reporting a firm's financial position, performance, and cash flows. The independent audit adds credibility and reliability to the financial statements and notes prepared by management.

STEP 4: ANALYZE PROFITABILITY AND RISK

The first three steps of the six-step analytical framework establish three key building blocks:

- An understanding of the economics of the industry in which a firm competes
- An understanding of the particular strategies that the firm has chosen to compete in its industry
- An understanding of the information contained in the financial statements and notes that report the results of a firm's operating, investing, and financing activities and an assessment of the quality of the financial statements

The analyst is now ready to conduct a financial statement analysis.

Most financial statement analysis aims to evaluate a firm's profitability and risk. This twofold focus stems from the emphasis of investment decisions on returns and risk. Investors acquire shares of common stock in a company because of the return they expect from such investments. This return includes any dividends received plus the change in the market price of the shares of stock while the investor holds them. A rational investor will not be indifferent between two investments that are expected to yield, for example, a 20 percent return if there are differences in the uncertainty, or risk, of earning that 20 percent return. The investor will demand a higher expected return from higher-risk investments to compensate for the additional risk assumed.

The income statement reports a firm's net income during the current year and prior years. Assessing the profitability of the firm during these periods, after adjusting as appropriate for nonrecurring or unsustainable items, permits the analyst to evaluate the firm's current and past profitability and to begin forecasting its likely future profitability. Empirical research has shown an association between earnings and market rates of return on common stock, a point discussed in the next section in this chapter and in greater depth in Chapters 13 and 14.

Financial statements also are useful for assessing the risk of a firm. Empirical research has shown that volatility in reported earnings over time is correlated with stock market-based measures of firm risk, such as market equity beta. In addition, firms that cannot generate sufficient cash flow from operations will likely encounter financial difficulties and perhaps even bankruptcy. Firms that have high proportions of debt in their capital structures will experience financial difficulties if they are unable to repay the debt at maturity or replace maturing debt with new debt. Assessing the financial risk of a firm assists the investor in identifying the level of risk incurred when investing in the firm's common stock.

Tools of Profitability and Risk Analysis

Most of this book describes and illustrates tools for analyzing financial statements. The purpose here is simply to introduce several of these tools as a broad overview.

Common-Size Financial Statements

One simple but powerful analytical tool is common-size financial statements, a tool that is helpful in highlighting relations in a financial statement. Common-size income statements and balance sheets express all items in the statement as a percentage of a common base. Common-size balance sheets often use total assets as the base. Sales revenue is a common base in a common-size income statement.

The first five columns of Exhibit 1.17 present common-size balance sheets for PepsiCo for 2004 through 2008. Note that various common-size percentages for PepsiCo remain quite stable while others change over this period. For example, PepsiCo experienced a significant increase in the proportion of assets comprising cash, but a sharp drop in the short-term investments during 2008. To better understand the reasons for the increased proportion of cash and marketable securities, refer to PepsiCo's statement of cash flows in Exhibit 1.14. It shows that significant amounts of short-term investments matured or were sold, explaining the drop in short-term investments. In addition, Exhibit 1.14 shows that the cash flow from operations was more than sufficient to finance expenditures on property, plant, and equipment. In addition, PepsiCo raised more cash by issuing a significant amount of long-term debt. PepsiCo used a large amount of cash to pay dividends and repurchase shares of its own stock. PepsiCo invested the remaining excess cash in cash and cash equivalents, leading to the increased common-size percentage.

The common-size balance sheets also show that the proportion of financing from liabilities rose from 51.7 percent in 2004 to 66.4 percent in 2008. In particular, the long-term debt obligations grew from 8.6 percent of assets in 2004 to 21.8 percent in 2008. This is consistent with the prior observation from the statement of cash flows that PepsiCo increased its long-term borrowing. The common-size balance sheet also reveals that large increase in treasury stock. Again, PepsiCo's statement of cash flows in Exhibit 1.14 reports repurchases of common shares totaled $4,720 million in 2008. The common-size balance sheets for Coca-Cola for 2004 through 2008, presented in the first five columns of Exhibit 1.19 (see pages 46–47), do not reveal the same trends: Coca-Cola's proportions of liabilities and common shareholders' equity remained relatively constant over the same period.

The first five columns of Exhibit 1.18 (see page 45) present common-size income statements for PepsiCo for 2004 through 2008. Note that net income as a percentage of sales (also known as the *profit margin*) decreased from 16.1 percent in 2006 to 11.9 percent in 2008. The common-size income statements show that most expenses as a percentage of sales revenue increased during this period. The decreasing profit margin results primarily from cost of sales increasing by 2.2 percent of sales and selling general and administrative expenses increasing by 0.6 percent of sales from 2006 through 2008. Management's discussion and analysis of operations presented in Appendix B explains some of these changes. The task of the financial analyst is to delve into the reasons for such changes, taking into consideration industry economics, company strategies, management's explanations, and the operating results for competitors. Chapter 4 explores the reasons for PepsiCo's decreased profit margin.

The common-size income statements for Coca-Cola for 2004 through 2008, presented in the first five columns of Exhibit 1.20 (see page 48), reveal a decline in profit margin over the same period of time. Coca-Cola's profit margin was 22.3 percent of revenues in 2004 and dropped to 18.2 percent of revenues in 2008.

EXHIBIT 1.17

Common-Size and Percentage Change Balance Sheets for PepsiCo (allow for rounding)

	Common-Size Balance Sheets:					Percentage Change Balance Sheets:			
	2008	2007	2006	2005	2004	2008	2007	2006	2005
ASSETS									
Cash and cash equivalents	5.7%	2.6%	5.5%	5.4%	4.6%	126.8%	(44.9%)	(3.8%)	34.1%
Short-term investments	0.6%	4.5%	3.9%	10.0%	7.7%	(86.4%)	34.2%	(63.0%)	46.2%
Accounts and notes receivable, net	13.0%	12.7%	12.4%	10.3%	10.7%	6.7%	17.8%	14.2%	8.7%
Inventories	7.0%	6.6%	6.4%	5.3%	5.5%	10.1%	18.9%	13.8%	9.9%
Prepaid expenses and other current assets	3.7%	2.9%	2.2%	1.9%	2.3%	33.6%	50.8%	6.3%	(5.5%)
Total Current Assets	30.0%	29.3%	30.5%	32.9%	30.9%	6.5%	11.2%	(12.7%)	21.0%
Property, plant, and equipment, net	32.4%	32.4%	32.4%	27.4%	29.1%	3.9%	15.9%	11.6%	6.5%
Amortizable intangible assets, net	2.0%	2.3%	2.1%	1.7%	2.1%	(8.0%)	25.0%	20.2%	(11.4%)
Goodwill	14.2%	14.9%	15.3%	12.9%	14.0%	(0.9%)	12.5%	12.4%	4.6%
Other nonamortizable intangible assets	3.1%	3.6%	4.0%	3.4%	3.3%	(9.6%)	3.0%	11.6%	16.4%
Investments in noncontrolled affiliates	10.8%	12.6%	12.3%	11.0%	11.7%	(10.8%)	18.0%	5.9%	6.1%
Other assets	7.4%	4.9%	3.3%	10.7%	8.8%	58.0%	71.6%	(71.2%)	37.5%
Total Assets	100.0%	100.0%	100.0%	100.0%	100.0%	3.9%	15.7%	(5.7%)	13.4%
LIABILITIES AND SHAREHOLDERS' EQUITY									
Short-term obligations	1.0%	0.0%	0.9%	9.1%	3.8%	n.m.	(100.0%)	(90.5%)	174.1%
Accounts payable and other current liabilities	23.0%	22.0%	21.7%	18.8%	20.0%	8.8%	17.0%	8.8%	6.6%
Income taxes payable	0.4%	0.4%	0.3%	1.7%	0.4%	(4.0%)	67.8%	(83.5%)	451.5%
Total Current Liabilities	24.4%	22.4%	22.9%	29.6%	24.1%	13.3%	13.0%	(27.1%)	39.3%
Long-term debt obligations	21.8%	12.1%	8.5%	7.3%	8.6%	87.0%	64.8%	10.2%	(3.5%)
Other liabilities	19.5%	13.8%	15.4%	13.6%	14.6%	46.4%	3.6%	7.0%	5.5%
Deferred income taxes	0.6%	1.9%	1.8%	4.5%	4.3%	(65.0%)	22.3%	(63.2%)	17.9%
Total Liabilities	66.4%	50.2%	48.7%	55.1%	51.7%	37.3%	19.4%	(16.7%)	20.8%

(Continued)

EXHIBIT 1.17 (Continued)

	Common-Size Balance Sheets:					Percentage Change Balance Sheets:			
	2008	2007	2006	2005	2004	2008	2007	2006	2005
Preferred stock, no par value	0.1%	0.1%	0.1%	0.1%	0.1%	0.0%	0.0%	0.0%	0.0%
Repurchased preferred stock	(0.4%)	(0.4%)	(0.4%)	(0.3%)	(0.3%)	4.5%	10.0%	9.1%	22.2%
Common stock, par value	0.1%	0.1%	0.1%	0.1%	0.1%	0.0%	0.0%	0.0%	0.0%
Capital in excess of par value	1.0%	1.3%	2.0%	1.9%	2.2%	(22.0%)	(22.9%)	(4.9%)	(0.6%)
Retained earnings	85.1%	81.4%	83.0%	66.6%	66.9%	8.7%	13.5%	17.6%	12.7%
Accumulated other comprehensive loss	(13.0%)	(2.7%)	(7.5%)	(3.3%)	(3.2%)	393.1%	(57.6%)	113.3%	18.8%
Treasury stock	(39.2%)	(30.0%)	(25.9%)	(20.1%)	(17.6%)	36.0%	33.9%	21.5%	29.8%
Total Common Shareholders' Equity	33.9%	50.0%	51.6%	45.1%	48.5%	(29.6%)	12.2%	7.9%	5.5%
Total Liabilities and Shareholders' Equity	100.0%	100.0%	100.0%	100.0%	100.0%	3.9%	15.7%	(5.7%)	13.4%

EXHIBIT 1.18

Common-Size and Percentage Change Income Statements for PepsiCo (allow for rounding)

	Common-Size Income Statements					Percentage Change Income Statements			
	2008	2007	2006	2005	2004	2008	2007	2006	2005
Net revenue	100.0%	100.0%	100.0%	100.0%	100.0%	9.6%	12.3%	7.9%	11.3%
Cost of sales	47.1%	45.7%	44.9%	43.5%	43.3%	12.8%	14.4%	11.2%	11.9%
Gross Profit	52.9%	54.3%	55.1%	56.5%	56.7%	6.8%	10.6%	5.4%	10.8%
Selling, general, and administrative expenses	36.8%	36.0%	36.2%	37.8%	37.7%	11.9%	11.8%	3.2%	11.6%
Other operating charges	0.1%	0.1%	0.5%	0.5%	0.5%	10.3%	(64.2%)	8.0%	2.0%
Restructuring charges	0.0%	0.0%	0.0%	0.0%	0.5%	n.m.	n.m.	n.m.	n.m.
Operating Profit	16.0%	18.2%	18.5%	18.2%	18.0%	(3.3%)	10.3%	9.8%	12.6%
Bottling equity income	0.9%	1.4%	1.6%	1.7%	1.3%	(33.2%)	1.3%	(0.7%)	46.6%
Interest expense	(0.8%)	(0.6%)	(0.7%)	(0.8%)	(0.6%)	46.9%	(6.3%)	(6.6%)	53.3%
Interest income	0.1%	0.3%	0.5%	0.5%	0.3%	(67.2%)	(27.7%)	8.8%	114.9%
Income before Income Taxes	16.2%	19.3%	19.9%	19.6%	19.0%	(8.0%)	9.2%	9.5%	15.1%
Provision for income taxes	4.3%	5.0%	3.8%	7.1%	4.7%	(4.8%)	46.5%	(41.5%)	67.9%
Income from Continuing Operations	11.9%	14.3%	16.1%	12.5%	14.3%	(9.1%)	0.3%	38.4%	(2.3%)
Tax benefit from discontinued operations	0.0%	0.0%	0.0%	0.0%	0.1%	n.m.	n.m.	n.m.	n.m.
Net Income	11.9%	14.3%	16.1%	12.5%	14.4%	(9.1%)	0.3%	38.4%	(3.2%)

EXHIBIT 1.19

Common-Size and Percentage Change Balance Sheets for Coca-Cola (allow for rounding)

	Common-Size Balance Sheets:					Percentage Change Balance Sheets:			
	2008	2007	2006	2005	2004	2008	2007	2006	2005
ASSETS									
Cash and cash equivalents	11.6%	9.5%	8.1%	16.0%	21.3%	14.9%	67.7%	(48.1%)	(29.9%)
Short-term investments	0.7%	0.5%	0.5%	0.2%	0.2%	29.3%	43.3%	127.3%	8.2%
Accounts and notes receivable, net	7.6%	7.7%	8.6%	7.8%	7.1%	(6.8%)	28.2%	13.4%	1.6%
Inventories	5.4%	5.1%	5.5%	4.8%	4.5%	(1.5%)	35.3%	15.2%	0.3%
Prepaid expenses and other current assets	4.7%	5.2%	5.4%	6.0%	5.9%	(15.0%)	39.2%	(8.7%)	(3.8%)
Total Current Assets	30.1%	28.0%	28.2%	34.8%	39.1%	0.6%	43.4%	(17.6%)	(16.5%)
Property, plant, and equipment, net	20.5%	19.6%	23.0%	19.7%	19.4%	(2.0%)	23.0%	19.3%	(5.0%)
Amortizable intangible assets, net	6.0%	11.9%	6.8%	6.6%	6.5%	(53.1%)	152.0%	5.1%	(4.5%)
Goodwill	9.9%	9.8%	4.7%	3.6%	3.5%	(5.3%)	203.3%	34.0%	(4.6%)
Other nonamortizable intangible assets	15.0%	6.5%	5.6%	2.8%	2.2%	115.6%	66.6%	103.7%	17.9%
Investments in noncontrolled affiliates	14.3%	18.0%	22.6%	23.5%	19.9%	(25.7%)	14.7%	(2.0%)	10.7%
Other assets	4.3%	6.2%	9.0%	9.0%	9.5%	(35.2%)	(1.0%)	2.0%	(11.2%)
Total Assets	100.0%	100.0%	100.0%	100.0%	100.0%	(6.4%)	44.4%	1.8%	(6.4%)
LIABILITIES AND SHAREHOLDERS' EQUITY									
Short-term obligations	15.0%	16.0%	10.8%	15.4%	14.4%	(12.3%)	113.8%	(28.4%)	(0.3%)
Accounts payable and other current liabilities	15.3%	13.7%	16.9%	15.3%	14.0%	4.8%	17.1%	12.5%	2.0%
Current maturities of long-term debt	1.1%	0.3%	0.1%	0.1%	4.7%	249.6%	303.0%	17.9%	(98.1%)
Income taxes payable	0.6%	0.6%	1.9%	2.7%	2.3%	(2.3%)	(54.5%)	(28.9%)	12.4%
Total Current Liabilities	32.1%	30.6%	29.7%	33.4%	35.4%	(1.8%)	48.8%	(9.6%)	(11.7%)
Long-term debt obligations	6.9%	7.6%	4.4%	3.9%	3.7%	(15.1%)	149.4%	13.9%	(0.3%)
Other liabilities	8.4%	7.2%	7.4%	5.9%	9.0%	8.6%	40.4%	29.0%	(38.5%)
Deferred income taxes	2.2%	4.4%	2.0%	1.2%	1.3%	(53.6%)	210.9%	72.7%	(12.4%)
Total Liabilities	49.5%	49.7%	43.5%	44.4%	49.3%	(6.9%)	65.0%	(0.2%)	(15.7%)

Common stock, par value	2.2%	2.0%	2.9%	3.0%	2.8%	0.0%	0.2%	0.1%	0.2%
Capital in excess of par value	19.7%	17.1%	20.0%	18.7%	15.7%	8.0%	23.3%	8.9%	11.4%
Retained earnings	95.0%	83.7%	111.7%	106.4%	92.6%	6.3%	8.3%	6.9%	7.5%
Accumulated other comprehensive loss	(6.6%)	1.4%	(4.3%)	(5.7%)	(4.3%)	(527.2%)	(148.5%)	(22.6%)	23.8%
Treasury stock	(59.8%)	(54.0%)	(73.8%)	(66.8%)	(56.1%)	3.6%	5.7%	12.6%	11.5%
Total Common Shareholders' Equity	50.5%	50.3%	56.5%	55.6%	50.7%	(5.8%)	28.5%	3.5%	2.6%
Total Liabilities and Shareholders' Equity	100.0%	100.0%	100.0%	100.0%	100.0%	(6.4%)	44.4%	1.8%	(6.4%)

EXHIBIT 1.20

Common-Size and Percentage Change Income Statements for Coca-Cola (allow for rounding)

	Common-Size Income Statements					Percentage Change Income Statements			
	2008	2007	2006	2005	2004	2008	2007	2006	2005
Net revenue	100.0%	100.0%	100.0%	100.0%	100.0%	10.7%	19.8%	4.3%	6.3%
Cost of sales	35.6%	36.1%	33.9%	35.5%	35.3%	9.3%	27.5%	(0.4%)	6.8%
Gross Profit	64.4%	63.9%	66.1%	64.5%	64.7%	11.5%	15.9%	6.8%	6.0%
Selling, general, and administrative expenses	36.9%	37.9%	39.2%	37.8%	36.3%	7.6%	16.1%	7.9%	10.8%
Other operating charges	1.1%	0.9%	0.8%	0.4%	2.2%	37.8%	37.3%	117.6%	(82.3%)
Operating Profit	26.4%	25.1%	26.2%	26.3%	26.2%	16.5%	15.0%	3.7%	6.8%
Bottling equity income	(2.7%)	2.3%	0.4%	2.9%	2.9%	(230.8%)	554.9%	(85.0%)	9.5%
Interest expense	(1.4%)	(1.6%)	(0.9%)	(1.0%)	(0.9%)	(3.9%)	107.3%	(8.3%)	22.4%
Interest income	1.0%	0.8%	0.8%	1.0%	0.7%	41.1%	22.3%	(17.9%)	49.7%
Other income (loss), net	(0.1%)	0.6%	0.8%	(0.3%)	(0.3%)	(116.2%)	(11.3%)	(378.6%)	20.7%
Income before Income Taxes	23.3%	27.3%	27.3%	29.0%	28.6%	(5.5%)	19.7%	(1.7%)	7.5%
Provision for income taxes	5.1%	6.6%	6.2%	7.9%	6.3%	(13.7%)	26.3%	(17.6%)	32.2%
Net Income	18.2%	20.7%	21.1%	21.1%	22.3%	(2.9%)	17.7%	4.3%	0.5%

The analyst must interpret common-size financial statements carefully. The amount for any one item in these statements is not independent of all other items. The dollar amount for an item might increase between two periods, but its relative percentage in the common-size statement would decrease (or remain the same) if the dollar amount increased at a slower (or the same) rate as total assets. For example, PepsiCo's dollar amounts for property, plant, and equipment increased between 2007 and 2008, but the common-size percentages remained the same because they increased at the same rate as total assets. Common-size percentages provide a general overview of financial position and operating performance, but the analyst must supplement them with other analytical tools.

Percentage Change Financial Statements

Another powerful analytical tool is percentage change financial statements, a tool that is helpful in highlighting the relative rates of growth in financial statement amounts from year to year and over longer periods of time. These statements present the percentage change in the amount of an item relative to its amount in the previous period or the compounded average percentage change over several prior periods.

The four rightmost columns of Exhibit 1.17 present percentage changes in balance sheet items during 2005 through 2008 for PepsiCo. Note that the increase in cash and the decrease in short-term investment securities are the largest percentage changes in assets between 2007 and 2008, consistent with the preceding observations with respect to changes in the common-size balance sheet. Another large percentage change between 2007 and 2008 occurred for long-term obligations, consistent with the prior observation from the statement of cash flows that PepsiCo issued a large amount of long-term debt in 2008. Also note that the huge percentage increase in accumulated other comprehensive loss for 2008 was 393 percent. This change reflects an increase in the accumulated loss from a negative $952 million in 2007 to a negative $4,694 million in 2008. This is an example in which a large percentage change in an account corresponds with a large dollar amount of change. For comparison, the four rightmost columns of Exhibit 1.19 present the percentage changes in balance sheet items for Coca-Cola during 2005 through 2008.

The analyst must exert particular caution when interpreting percentage change balance sheets for a particular year. If the amount for the preceding year that serves as the base is relatively small, even a small change in dollar amount can result in a large percentage change. This is the case, for example, with PepsiCo's deferred tax liability. The liability declined by 65.0 percent in 2008, but it amounted to only a drop from $646 million in 2007 to $226 million in 2008. However, note that the deferred tax liability comprises only 0.6 percent of total assets at the end of 2008. A large percentage change in an account that makes up a smaller portion of total financing is not as meaningful as a smaller percentage change in an account that makes up a larger portion of total assets or total financing.

The four rightmost columns of Exhibit 1.18 present percentage change income statement amounts for PepsiCo. Note that during 2008, 2007, and 2005, net income growth did not keep pace with revenue growth. An analyst might direct particular concern to the rapid growth rates in cost of sales, which have exceeded the growth rates in sales each of the four years. This implies a lower degree of cost control, a loss of pricing power, or a shift in product mix to lower margin products, leading to shrinking gross profit margins. The analyst should carefully investigate the reasons for this deterioration in PepsiCo's profitability. By comparison, the four rightmost columns of Exhibit 1.20 present the percentage change income statement amounts for Coca-Cola during the same span of years, and they reveal that (with the exception of 2007) Coca-Cola exhibited stronger control over cost of sales as a percentage of revenues.

Financial Statement Ratios

Perhaps the most useful analytical tools for assessing profitability and risk are financial statement ratios. Financial statement ratios express relations among various items from the three financial statements. Researchers and analysts have found that such ratios are effective indicators of various dimensions of profitability and risk and serve as useful signals of future profitability and risk. Chapters 4 and 5 discuss these financial ratios in depth. The discussion here merely introduces several of them. Appendix D presents descriptive statistics for many of the most commonly used financial ratios across 48 industries over the past eleven years.

Profitability Ratios. Perhaps the most commonly encountered financial ratio is EPS (earnings per share). Basic EPS equals net income available to the common shareholders (that is, net income minus dividends on preferred stock) divided by the weighted average number of common shares outstanding. For 2008, basic EPS for PepsiCo (see Exhibit 1.11 and Note 11, "Net Income per Common Share," in Appendix A) is $3.26 [(= $5,142 − $8)/1,573 shares]. Firms typically report both basic and diluted EPS in their income statements, with per share amounts for continuing operations, discontinued operations, and extraordinary gains and losses shown separately. Chapter 4 discusses the computation of EPS. Furthermore, as Chapter 14 makes clear, financial analysts often use a multiple of EPS to derive what they consider an appropriate price for a firm's common stock.

Another profitability ratio is the ROCE (rate of return on common shareholders' equity). ROCE equals net income available to the common shareholders divided by average common shareholders' equity for the year. ROCE for PepsiCo for 2008 is 34.8 percent [= ($5,142 − $8)/(0.5{$12,203 + $17,325})]. This ROCE is large relative to those of many firms. However, we should expect PepsiCo to generate a high rate of return for its shareholders because it has developed an effective and sustainable strategy as one of only two major players in the soft drink industry and one of the global leaders in the snack food industry, which we assessed to have relatively favorable competitive conditions. This example illustrates that it is difficult to interpret ROCE and other financial ratios without a frame of reference, which the analyst builds by conducting the industry analysis, the strategic analysis, and the accounting quality analysis. Analysts compare ratios to corresponding ratios of earlier periods (time-series analysis), to corresponding ratios of other firms in the same industry (cross-sectional analysis), and to industry averages in order to interpret the ratios. Chapter 4 provides an in-depth analysis of PepsiCo's ROCE and other profitability ratios.

Risk Ratios. To assess the volatility in a firm's earnings over time and to gauge the uncertainty inherent in the firm's future earnings, analysts can calculate the standard deviation in ROCE over time.

To assess the ability of firms to repay short-term obligations, analysts frequently calculate various short-term liquidity ratios such as the current ratio, which equals current assets divided by current liabilities. The current ratio for PepsiCo at the end of 2008 is 1.23 (= $10,806/$8,787). As with profitability ratios, this ratio is meaningful only when the analyst performs a time-series and cross-sectional analysis. Like most firms, PepsiCo's current ratio has exceeded 1.0 in each of the past five years; so PepsiCo appears to have minimal short-term liquidity risk.

To assess the ability of firms to continue operating for a longer term (that is, to avoid bankruptcy), the analyst looks at various long-term solvency ratios, such the relative amount of long-term debt in the capital structure. The ratio of long-term debt to common shareholders' equity for PepsiCo at the end of 2008 is 0.644 (= $7,858/$12,203). This ratio for PepsiCo jumped significantly in 2008, from 0.244 in 2007, because PepsiCo issued large amounts of long-term debt and paid large amounts of cash to common shareholders through common stock dividends and repurchases. Clearly, PepsiCo is increasing its leverage, but given PepsiCo's level of profitability, strong cash flows, and solid short-term liquidity position, bankruptcy risk is low. Chapter 5 provides an in-depth analysis of PepsiCo's debt-to-equity ratio and other risk ratios.

STEP 5: PREPARE FORECASTED FINANCIAL STATEMENTS

Each of the steps in our six-step analysis and valuation framework is important, but the crucial (and most difficult) step is forecasting future financial statements. Such forecasts are the inputs into valuation models or other financial decisions, and the quality of the decisions rests on the reliability of the forecasts. Thus, the analyst uses a thorough understanding of the firm's industry, strategy, accounting quality, and financial statement ratios, including common-size and percentage change statements and other analytical tools, to evaluate the profitability and risk of the firm in the current and recent past and to provide useful information to begin forecasting future financial statements. Forecasted financial statements rely on assumptions the analyst makes about the future: Will the firm's strategy remain the same or change? At what rate will the firm generate revenue growth? Will the firm likely gain or lose market share relative to competitors? Will revenues grow because of increases in sales volume, prices, or both? How will its costs change? How much will the firm need to increase operating assets (inventory, plant, and equipment) to achieve its growth strategies? How much capital will the firm need to raise to finance growth in assets? Will it change the mix of debt versus equity financing? How will a change in the debt-equity mix change the risk of the firm? Responses to these and other questions provide the basis for preparing forecasted income statements, balance sheets, and statements of cash flows. The analyst can compare financial ratios of forecasted financial statement items with the corresponding ratios from the reported financial statements to judge the reasonableness of the assumptions made. Amounts from the forecasted financial statements serve as the basis for the valuation models in Step 6, discussed next. Chapter 10 describes and illustrates the techniques to project future financial statements and applies the techniques to build financial statement projections for PepsiCo for the next five years.

STEP 6: VALUE THE FIRM

Capital market participants most commonly use financial statement analysis to value firms, which is the culmination of the previous five steps of the framework incorporated into a valuation model. Financial statements—specifically, key metrics from the statements such as earnings, dividends, and cash flows—play a central role in firm valuation. Thus, the emphasis of this book is to arm the analyst with the knowledge necessary to apply sophisticated and comprehensive valuation models.

To develop reliable estimates of firm value, and therefore to make intelligent investment decisions, the analyst must rely on well-reasoned and objective forecasts of the firm's future profitability and risk. Forecasts of future dividends, earnings, and cash flows form the basis for the most frequently used valuation models.

In some cases, analysts prefer to assess firm value using the classical dividends-based approach, which takes the perspective of valuing the firm from the standpoint of the cash that investors can expect to receive through dividends (or the sale of their shares). It also is common for analysts to assess firm value using measures of the firm's expected future free cash flows—cash flows that are available to be paid as dividends after necessary payments are made to reinvest in productive assets and meet required debt payments. An equivalent approach to valuation involves computing firm value based on the book value of equity and the earnings of the firm the analyst expects to exceed the firm's cost of capital (similar in logic to "economic value-added" computations). In many circumstances, analysts find it necessary or desirable to estimate firm value quickly using valuation heuristics such as price-earnings ratios and market-to-book value ratios. Chapters 11–14 describe the theory and demonstrate the practical applications of each of these approaches to valuation using PepsiCo.

ROLE OF FINANCIAL STATEMENT ANALYSIS IN AN EFFICIENT CAPITAL MARKET

Market efficiency describes the degree to which the market impounds information into security prices. The larger the set of information that is priced and the greater the speed with which security prices reflect new information, the higher the degree of market efficiency. A highly efficient capital market would impound all publicly available value-relevant information (such as an announcement of surprisingly good or poor earnings in a particular period) quickly and completely and without bias into share prices. In a less efficient market, share prices would react more slowly to value-relevant information. In the U.S. capital markets, for example, share prices of the largest market capital firms, which tend to have a wide following by buy-side and sell-side analysts, many institutional investors, and frequent coverage in the financial press tend to be more efficient than share prices for small market capital stocks, which have no analyst following, no institutional investors, and rare press coverage.

There are differing views as to the benefits of analyzing a set of financial statements in the context of market efficiency. One view is that stock market prices react with a high degree of efficiency to published information about a firm. That is, market participants react intelligently and quickly to information they receive so that market prices continually reflect underlying economic values. One implication of a highly efficient capital market is that analysts and investors have more difficulty finding "undervalued" or "overvalued" securities by analyzing financial statements because the capital market quickly impounds new financial statement information into security prices.

Opposing views include the following:

- For markets to be efficient, analysts and investors must do the analysis to bring about the appropriate prices. With their expertise and access to information about firms, financial analysts do the analysis quickly and engage in the trading necessary to achieve efficient pricing. They are agents of market efficiency.
- Research on capital market efficiency aggregates financial data for individual firms and studies the average reaction of the market to earnings and other financial statement information. A finding that the market is efficient on average does not preclude temporary mispricing of individual firms' shares. A principal task of the financial analyst is to identify and buy/sell mispriced securities of particular firms.
- Research has shown that equity markets are not perfectly efficient. Anomalies include the tendency for market prices to adjust with a lag to new earnings information, systematic underreaction to the information contained in earnings announcements, and the ability to use a combination of financial ratios to detect under- and overpriced securities.[6]

---

[6] For a summary of the issues and related research, see Ray Ball, "The Theory of Stock Market Efficiency: Accomplishments and Limitations," *Journal of Applied Corporate Finance* (Spring 1995), pp. 4–17.

- Management has incentives related to job security and compensation to report as favorable a picture as possible in the financial statements within the constraints of GAAP. Therefore, these reports may represent biased indicators of the economic performance and financial position of firms. Analysts must analyze and adjust these financial statements to remove such biases if market prices are to reflect underlying economic values.

Financial statement analysis is valuable in numerous settings outside equity capital markets, including credit analysis by a bank to support corporate lending, competitor analysis to identify competitive advantages, and merger and acquisition analysis to identify buyout candidates.

THE ASSOCIATION BETWEEN EARNINGS AND SHARE PRICES

As discussed earlier in this chapter, performing financial analysis that relies on analysis, forecasting, and valuation of key accounting measures (such as earnings) from a firm's financial statements can be very rewarding. To illustrate the striking relation between accounting earnings and stock returns and to foreshadow the potential to generate positive excess returns through analysis and forecasting, consider the results from empirical research by D. Craig Nichols and James Wahlen.[7] They studied the average cumulative market-adjusted returns generated by firms during the 12 months leading up to and including the month in which each firm announced annual earnings numbers. For a sample of 31,923 firm-years between 1988 and 2001, they found that the average firm that announced an increase in earnings (over the prior year's earnings) experienced stock returns that exceeded market average returns by roughly 19.2 percent. On the other hand, the average firm that announced a decrease in earnings experienced stock returns that were roughly 16.4 percent lower than the market average. Their results suggest that merely the sign of the change in earnings was associated with a 35.6 percent stock return differential in one year, on average, over their sample period. Exhibit 1.21 presents a graph of their results.

To an analyst, the results of the Nichols and Wahlen study indicate how informative accounting earnings are to the capital markets and emphasize the importance of forecasting the changes in earnings one year ahead. Analysts should view the Nichols and Wahlen results as encouraging and intriguing because they imply that if analysts can forecast earnings changes correctly more often than not, they should be able to earn some portion of the excess returns documented in this study. To be sure, analysts will not be able to beat the market consistently by 35 percent per year—Nichols and Wahlen's research had the advantage of perfect foresight, which analysts do not have. Using historical earnings data, Nichols and Wahlen knew with certainty which firms would announce earnings increases or decreases one year ahead. Analysts must forecast earnings changes and take positions in stocks on the basis of their earnings expectations.

Note in the graph of the Nichols and Wahlen results in Exhibit 1.21 that their study also examined the relation between changes in cash flows from operations and cumulative market-adjusted stock returns. Using the same firm-years and study period, Nichols and Wahlen documented that firms experiencing positive changes in cash from operations

---

[7] D. Craig Nichols and James Wahlen, "How Do Earnings Numbers Relate to Stock Returns? A Review of Classic Accounting Research with Updated Evidence," *Accounting Horizons* (December 2004), pp. 263–286. The portion of the Nichols and Wahlen study described here is a replication of path-breaking research in accounting by Ray Ball and Philip Brown, "An Evaluation of Accounting Income Numbers," *Journal of Accounting Research* (Autumn 1968), pp. 159–178.

EXHIBIT 1.21

The Association between Changes in Annual Earnings and Cumulative Abnormal Returns

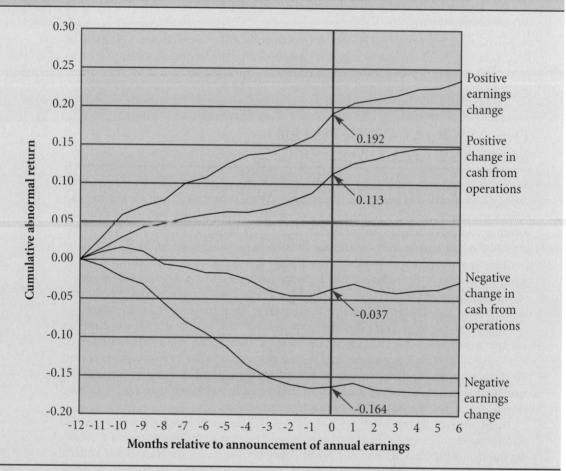

Source: D. Craig Nichols and James Wahlen, "How Do Earnings Numbers Relate to Stock Returns? A Review of Classic Accounting Research with Updated Evidence," *Accounting Horizons* (December 2004), pp. 263–286. Reprinted with permission from American Accounting Association.

experienced stock returns that beat the market by an average of 11.3 percent, whereas firms experiencing decreases in cash from operations experienced stock returns that were lower than the market by an average of 3.7 percent. These results suggest that the sign of the change in cash from operations was associated with a 15.0 percent stock return differential in one year, on average, during the study period. This implies that changes in cash flows also are strongly related to stock returns, but they are not as informative for the capital markets as are changes in earnings. This should not be surprising because changes in cash flow are less indicative of a firm's performance in one period than are changes in earnings. For example, a firm experiencing a negative change in cash from operations could be attributable to cash flow distress (bad news) or a large investment of cash in growth opportunities (good news). A negative change in earnings, on the other hand, is almost always bad news. This explains, in part, why analysts, firm managers, the financial press, boards of directors, auditors, and therefore financial statement analysis textbook writers focus so much attention on analyzing and forecasting earnings numbers.

Empirical research in accounting has deepened our understanding of the many dimensions of the role of accounting numbers in the capital market by documenting that share prices react strongly to the magnitude of the change in earnings and the persistence of the change in earnings for future periods and that financial statement ratios are useful for predicting future earnings changes. We will refer to important research results such as these throughout this book.

SOURCES OF FINANCIAL STATEMENT INFORMATION

Firms whose bonds or common shares trade in public capital markets in the United States typically make the following information available:

- **Annual Report to Shareholders.** The glossy annual report includes balance sheets for the most recent two years and income statements and statements of cash flows for the most recent three years, along with various notes and supporting schedules. The annual report also includes a letter from the chairperson of the board of directors and from the chief executive officer summarizing the activities of the most recent year. The report typically includes management's discussion and analysis of the firm's operating performance, financial position, and liquidity. Firms vary with respect to the information provided in this Management Discussion and Analysis of operations. Some firms, such as PepsiCo, give helpful information about the firm's strategy and reasons for the changes in profitability, financial position, and risk. (See Appendix B.) Other firms merely repeat amounts presented in the financial statements without providing helpful explanations for operating results.
- **Form 10-K Annual Report.** The Form 10-K annual report filed with the SEC includes the same financial statements and notes as the corporate annual report in addition to supporting schedules required by the SEC. For example, compared to the corporate annual report, Form 10-K often includes more detailed information on changes in the allowance for uncollectible accounts and other valuation accounts. Firms are required by the SEC to report several key items in the Form 10-K that are necessary reading for the analyst. These include a description of the business (Item 1); risk factors (Item 1A); a description of company properties (Item 2); the management discussion and analysis (Item 7); and, of course, the financial statements, notes, and supplemental schedules (Item 8). Large firms must file their annual reports with the SEC within 60 days after the end of their annual accounting period.
- **Form 10-Q Quarterly Report.** The Form 10-Q quarterly report filed with the SEC includes condensed balance sheet and income statement information for the most recent three months, as well as comparative data for earlier quarters. Unlike the annual filing of Form 10-K, the financial statements included in Forms 10-Q are not audited.
- **Prospectus or Registration Statement.** Firms intending to issue new bonds or capital stock file a prospectus with the SEC that describes the offering (amount and intended uses of proceeds). The prospectus includes much of the financial information found in the Form 10-K annual report.

A large number of firms include all or a portion of their annual reports and SEC filings on their corporate websites. For example, PepsiCo provides all of the financial data and analysis provided in Appendices A and B on its website (http://www.pepsico.com). In addition, many firms provide additional financial data on their sites that is not published in the annual reports. For example, Gap Inc., consisting of Gap, Banana Republic, and Old

Navy clothing store chains, provides monthly sales data for each chain and information on the opening and closing of stores. Firms also provide other useful information in the investor relations section of their corporate websites, such as (1) presentations made to analysts; (2) press releases pertaining to new products, customer acquisitions, and earnings announcements; and (3) transcripts or archived webcasts of conference calls with analysts.

Firms are required to file reports electronically with the SEC, and filings for recent years are available at the SEC website (http://www.sec.gov). Numerous commercial online and CD-ROM services also provide financial statement information (for example, Thomson One Analytics, Bloomberg, Standard & Poor's, and Moody's).

Appendix 1.1 discusses sources of financial information more fully.

SUMMARY

The purpose of this chapter is to provide a broad overview of the six-step analysis and valuation framework that is the focus of this book and is a logical process for analyzing and valuing companies:

1. Identify the economic characteristics of the industry in which a firm participates.
2. Identify the corporate strategy that a firm pursues to compete in its industry.
3. Read the information in a set of financial statements and notes carefully and assess the quality of a firm's financial statements, adjusting them, if necessary, for items lacking sustainability or comparability.
4. Analyze and interpret the profitability and risk of a firm, assessing the firm's performance and the strength of its financial position.
5. Prepare forecasted financial statements.
6. Value the firm.

You should not expect to fully understand these six steps at this stage of your studies. The remaining chapters discuss each step in greater depth. Chapter 2 discusses the important links between the valuation of assets and liabilities on the balance sheet and revenues and expenses on the income statement. Chapter 3 details the preparation and interpretation of the statement of cash flows for firms in different industries at various stages of growth. Chapter 4 describes common financial statement ratios used to assess profitability and illustrates their calculation and interpretation for PepsiCo. Chapter 5 parallels the preceding chapter by describing common financial statement ratios used to assess risk. Chapters 6–9 examine U.S. GAAP and IFRS for financing, investing, and operating activities and address concerns that affect the quality of earnings and financial position. Chapters 10–14 shift the focus to valuation. Chapter 10 demonstrates the preparation of forecasted financial statements. Chapters 11–14 examine various valuation models based on dividends, cash flows, earnings, and amounts for comparable firms. With firm valuation being the most frequent objective of financial statement analysis, these chapters represent a fitting culmination to the book.

Appendix **1.1**

Preparing a Term Project

Our reading of the course syllabi by various users of previous editions of this book indicates that many instructors require their students to apply the concepts and tools of analysis in this book to the financial statements of one or more companies. This appendix provides helpful hints for you in conducting such a project. Our students find it useful to complete each part of the project as the topic is covered in class. For example, soon after completing Chapter 1, you should select the companies you intend to study and complete the industry economics and company strategy portion of the project. Obtaining financial statement data and performing a first pass on profitability and risk ratios follows coverage of Chapters 4 and 5. Assessments of the quality of the financial statements should coincide with coverage of Chapters 6–9. Forecasts of future financial statement amounts follow coverage of Chapter 10. Applying various valuation models must await coverage of Chapters 11–14. Based on our experience, we can assure you that by following this approach, your learning experience will be much richer and more rewarding than if you wait until the last few weeks of the course to do the major work on the project. For this reason, we ask our students to submit progress reports throughout the term. These progress reports help students stay on schedule and permit us to provide suggestions to assist them going forward.

SELECTING COMPANIES FOR THE TERM PROJECT

Some instructors ask students to analyze a single company over time (a time-series analysis), while other instructors ask students to compare two or more companies over time (a cross-sectional analysis). We have found that comparing companies in the same industry over time provides the most interesting insights.

When selecting companies to analyze, select an industry and firms in which you have an interest. You will likely spend considerable time on the project. Selecting firms of interest enhances motivation. Some students select firms for which they hope or expect to work. The in-depth analysis of the firm often enhances the job interview and early work experience once the student is hired. Our students find that selecting firms with somewhat different strategies usually provides better insights than selecting firms with similar strategies. Some students' richest term projects have involved analyzing firms in the same industry but headquartered in different countries. However, such projects involve additional work to learn U.S. GAAP as well as IFRS and institutional and cultural differences in each country that might affect interpretation of the financial analyses.

Various online databases list firms in the United States and worldwide in various industries. Your library may or may not subscribe to all of the databases discussed in this appendix. Packaged with this book is access to the Gale Business & Company Resource Center. This site provides information about particular industries and companies. Information includes company overviews and histories, newspaper and magazine articles, financial data, and investment reports. A similar online information service is OneSource, published by Global Business Browser (http://www.onesource.com).

UNDERSTANDING INDUSTRY ECONOMICS AND COMPANY STRATEGIES

The Form 10-K report the firm filed with the SEC (http://www.sec.gov) may be the best place to begin learning about the economics of an industry and the particular strategy a firm has selected for competing in the industry. The first section of Form 10-K is a descriptive narrative entitled "Item 1. Business." This section usually describes the firm's principal businesses and provides information about suppliers, competitors, regulation, and other items. Reading this section of Form 10-K for the other firms selected for study usually provides sufficient information so that you can summarize the economics of the industry using a value chain, Porter's five forces framework, or the economics attributes framework discussed in the chapter. These sources will not likely set forth precise economics to fit any of the industry economics frameworks, so some interpretation and synthesis on your part will be necessary.

Reading the Business description section of the Form 10-K report should provide you with information on the strategy of each firm studied. We find it useful to search the notes to the financial statements to find the segment data by products or services and by geographical location. We convert the reported numbers to mix percentages, as we did for PepsiCo in Exhibit 1.5, to obtain an overview of the firm's principal involvements.

Another source for industry information is Standard & Poor's Industry Surveys. These surveys describe the most important factors affecting the industry, key firms in the industry, and key financial ratios for each firm. The Gale Business & Company Resource Center and OneSource resources, described previously, also provide helpful information about the industry.

ASSESSING THE QUALITY OF THE FINANCIAL STATEMENTS

Two steps are necessary: (1) reading the financial statements carefully and thoroughly and creating a data file with the amounts from the financial statements and (2) adjusting the reported financial statement amounts to improve the quality of the financial statement data.

Reading the Financial Statements and Creating a Data File

Our experience, and that of our students, is that careful and thorough reading of the financial statements yields a great deal of information about the firm. The financial statements, the notes, and management's discussion and analysis provide valuable insights into the business strategies, profitability, and risk of the firm. Many firms explicitly disclose elements of the business that are performing well or poorly, also providing explanations about the performance. Many firms explicitly disclose (or one can infer) projections of future business activities, such as expected future sales growth rates or capital expenditures, which is helpful information for projecting future financial statements. Analysts who do not carefully read the financial statements stand to miss this valuable information.

After careful reading, the analyst should enter the financial statement data into a data file. One initial choice in creating a data file is whether to use the accounts and amounts that the firm provides in its Form 10-K or annual report to shareholders or to download and use amounts from various online sources or databases that format the amounts into a standardized template. One advantage of following the first approach is that you rely on the primary source of the financial statements, not on a secondary source about which you may not know all of the reclassifications and adjustments made to conform the reported amounts to the standardized template. Another advantage of following the first approach is that the financial statement data will be classified into accounts consistent with the notes to the financial statements, the main source of information for assessing the quality of the reported amounts, a topic discussed shortly. The principal advantages of using amounts in a standardized template are that use of the template can save time and the financial statement amounts are reasonably comparable across firms.

The next decision to be made is whether to input the financial statement data into FSAP, a financial statement analysis package that accompanies this text, or to create a new spreadsheet file. The principal advantages of FSAP are that it provides spreadsheets that have embedded formulas for the various profitability and risk ratios, it provides a template for preparing forecasted financial statements using the previously reported actual amounts as a base, and it inputs the forecasted amounts into several valuation models to arrive at equity values. (Appendix C illustrates the use of FSAP to analyze and value PepsiCo. FSAP contains a user manual that explains how to create a data file.) The disadvantage of using FSAP from a learning perspective is that much of the work is done for you. The advantage of creating a new spreadsheet file is that you must program the spreadsheets to compute the financial ratios, prepare forecasted financial statements, and apply the various valuation models. To enhance learning, many instructors prefer that students program the spreadsheet themselves.

Downloading financial statement data from online sources means that the data are already in a standard format. You can program the spreadsheet for this format and use it for all firms analyzed. Downloading financial statement data from a firm's Form 10-K requires that, at least initially, the spreadsheet use the firm's specific categories and grouping of accounts. The other firms analyzed are not likely to use precisely the same accounts. Thus, you must transform the reported amounts to a standard format or program each firm's spreadsheet to conform to its specific accounts and categories.

It is a good idea to program various mathematical checks into the spreadsheet. For example, check whether the sum of the individual assets equals the sum of the individual liability and shareholders' equity accounts. The net of individual revenues and expenses must equal net income. The cash flow from operating, investing, and financing activities must equal the change in cash. The latter should agree with the change in cash on the balance sheet from the beginning to the end of the year.

One issue you must face is how many years of financial statement data to obtain. We recommend using at least three years of income statements and statements of cash flows and four years of balance sheets (although this many years of data may not be available for very young firms or for initial public offering firms). We recommend using an extra year of balance sheet data because computing certain ratios requires average amounts for certain accounts on the balance sheet. FSAP permits the inputting of six years of balance sheet, income statement, and cash flow data. The longer historical time frame is useful when deciding on appropriate growth rates for forecasting financial statements, particularly when the recent past was unusual (for example, because of a recession).

Another issue you must face is whether to use the originally reported amounts for each year or to use amounts as retroactively restated for discontinued operations, acquisitions, divestitures, or for other factors. The advantage of using restated numbers is that the financial statements amounts may be more consistent with amounts that might be expected going forward. The disadvantage is that firms seldom provide restated data beyond the three income statements and statements of cash flows and the two balance sheets commonly found in annual reports. Thus, using restated data is not likely to yield financial statements that are fully consistent over time. Chapter 9 discusses this issue more fully.

Assessing the Quality of the Reported Amounts

One of the most important steps in financial statement analysis is to assess the quality of the reported amounts and make appropriate adjustments before proceeding to the analysis of profitability and risk. The saying "garbage in, garbage out" applies with particular importance to financial statements. To assess quality, you must read the financial statements and notes. Chapters 6–9 describe the most important factors to look for in this quality assessment. Material nonrecurring or unusual income items are candidates for adjustment. Significant off-balance-sheet assets or liabilities also are candidates. Some adjustments may be needed to increase the comparability of the financial statement amounts for each of the firms analyzed in the term project. You might consider keeping a log of adjustments made to refer to later when interpreting profitability and risk ratios and forecasting future financial statements.

ANALYZING PROFITABILITY AND RISK

If you use FSAP to create data files, FSAP will automatically calculate the profitability and risk ratios discussed in Chapters 4 and 5. If you create your own spreadsheet file for the financial statement data, you should include a separate worksheet within that file to compute the financial statement ratios. This worksheet should contain the formulas for the financial ratios, referring back to the worksheets with the financial statement data to obtain the amounts for the numerator and denominator of each ratio. If you change any of the amounts in the financial statements portion of the worksheet later in the project (for example, making adjustments to improve the quality of the data), the financial ratios will automatically update.

When analyzing profitability and risk using the financial statement ratios, you may find it helpful to do a time-series analysis for each firm and then do cross-sectional comparisons across firms. As a first pass, look for financial ratios that have changed significantly over time or that differ significantly across firms. Then relate the changes and differences to the economics of the industry and strategies of the firms. You will find it helpful to read the MD&A section of the annual report to shareholders or the Form 10-K (Item 7) to find explanations for the time-series changes. A useful sequence is as follows:

- Time-series analysis of profitability for each firm using (1) common-size and percentage change financial statements, (2) rate of return on assets and its components, and (3) ROCE and its components
- Cross-sectional profitability analysis of profitability for all firms using (1) common-size and percentage change financial statements, (2) rate of return on assets and its components, and (3) ROCE and its components
- Time-series and cross-sectional comparisons of short-term liquidity risk
- Time-series and cross-sectional comparisons of long-term liquidity risk

PREPARING FORECASTED FINANCIAL STATEMENTS

Having analyzed the profitability and risk of each firm in the recent past, you are ready to project the financial statement amounts into the future. As Chapter 10 discusses, you should identify any important factors that are likely to change, such as a major divestiture or acquisition, changes in the economic or regulatory environment, or a change in business strategy.

Spreadsheets are particularly powerful tools for preparing forecasted financial statements. It is desirable to link the forecasted financial statements with the financial statement data and related ratios from the recent past. FSAP does this automatically. If you program your own spreadsheet file with the financial statement data, you can program additional worksheets in this file for the forecasted amounts. We suggest that you build the same kind of mathematical data checks into the forecasted amounts that you included for the reported amounts. We also find it useful to include a spreadsheet that computes the same financial ratios for the forecasted amounts as it does for the reported amounts. Then you can study the financial ratios to see if the assumptions underlying the forecasted amounts make sense relative to the past and to expected changes going forward.

VALUE THE FIRMS

You should program the spreadsheet to use the projected financial statements to compute the amounts used in valuation models. Chapters 11–14 describe and illustrate various models to value firms, including the following:

- Present value of projected dividends (Chapter 11)
- Present value of expected free cash flows (Chapter 12)
- Residual income valuation (Chapter 13)
- Market-based comparables (Chapter 14)

All of these valuation models rely on data from the forecasted financial statements. Your instructor may ask you to follow one or more than one of these approaches in your valuations. We have programmed FSAP to compute all of these valuation approaches and to conduct analysis to determine the sensitivity of the value estimate to different assumptions about the discount rate and the long-run growth rate.

Good luck and enjoy!

QUESTIONS, EXERCISES, PROBLEMS, AND CASES

Questions and Exercises

1.1 VALUE CHAIN ANALYSIS APPLIED TO THE TIMBER AND TIMBER PRODUCTS INDUSTRY. Create a value chain for the timber and timber products industry, beginning with the growing of timber and ending with the retailing of timber and paper products. Briefly describe each link in the value chain and list the name of one U.S. company involved in each link. (Hint: Access Gale's Business & Company Resource Center, Global Business Browser, or Standard & Poor's Industry Surveys to obtain the needed information.)

1.2 PORTER'S FIVE FORCES APPLIED TO THE AIR COURIER INDUSTRY. Apply Porter's five forces to the air courier industry. Industry participants include such firms as FedEx, UPS, and DHL. (Hint: Access Gale's Business & Company Resource Center, Global Business Browser, or Standard & Poor's Industry Surveys to obtain the needed information.)

1.3 ECONOMIC ATTRIBUTES FRAMEWORK APPLIED TO THE SPECIALTY RETAILING APPAREL INDUSTRY. Apply the economic attributes framework discussed in the chapter to the specialty retailing apparel industry, which includes such firms as Gap, Limited Brands, and Abercrombie & Fitch. (Hint: Access Gale's Business & Company Resource Center, Global Business Browser, or Standard & Poor's Industry Surveys to obtain the needed information.)

1.4 IDENTIFICATION OF COMMODITY BUSINESSES. A recent article in *Fortune* magazine listed the following firms among the top ten most admired companies in the United States: Dell, Southwest Airlines, Microsoft, and Johnson & Johnson. Access the websites of these four companies or read the Business section of their Form 10-K reports (http://www.sec.gov). Describe whether you would view their products or services as commodities. Explain your reasoning.

1.5 IDENTIFICATION OF COMPANY STRATEGIES. Refer to the websites and the Form 10-K reports of Home Depot (http://www.homedepot.com) and Lowe's (http://www.lowes.com). Compare and contrast their business strategies.

1.6 RESEARCHING THE FASB WEBSITE. Go to the website of the Financial Accounting Standards Board (http://www.fasb.org). Identify the most recently issued financial reporting standard and summarize briefly (in one paragraph) its principal provisions. Also search under Project Activities to identify the reporting issue with the most recent update. Describe the issue briefly and the nature of the action taken by the FASB.

1.7 RESEARCHING THE IASB WEBSITE. Go to the website of the International Accounting Standards Board (http://www.iasb.org). Search for the International Financial Reporting Standards (IFRS) summaries. Identify the most recently issued international financial reporting standard and summarize briefly (in one paragraph) its principal provisions.

1.8 EFFECT OF INDUSTRY ECONOMICS ON BALANCE SHEET. Access the investor relations or corporate information section of the websites of American Airlines (http://www.aa.com), Intel (http://www.intel.com), and Disney (http://disney.go.com). Study the business strategies of each firm. Examine the financial ratios below and indicate which firm is likely to be American Airlines, Intel, and Disney. Explain your reasoning.

	Firm A	Firm B	Firm C
Property, Plant, and Equipment/Assets	27.9%	34.6%	62.5%
Long-Term Debt/Assets	18.2%	3.7%	35.7%

1.9 EFFECT OF BUSINESS STRATEGY ON COMMON-SIZE INCOME STATEMENT. Access the investor relations or corporate information section of the websites of Apple Computer (http://www.apple.com) and Dell (http://www.dell.com). Study the strategies of each firm. Examine the following common-size income statements and indicate which firm is likely to be Apple Computer and which is likely to be Dell. Explain your reasoning. Indicate any percentages that seem inconsistent with their strategies.

	Firm A	Firm B
Sales	100.0%	100.0%
Cost of Goods Sold	(82.1)	(59.9)
Selling and Administrative	(11.6)	(9.7)
Research and Development	(1.1)	(3.1)
Income Taxes	(1.4)	(8.9)
All Other Items	0.2	0.8
Net Income	4.1%	19.2%

1.10 EFFECT OF BUSINESS STRATEGY ON COMMON-SIZE INCOME STATEMENT. Access the investor relations or corporate information section of the websites of Dollar General (http://www.dollargeneral.com) and Macy's Inc. (http://www.macysinc.com). Study the strategies of each firm. Examine the following common-size income statements and indicate which firm is likely to be Dollar General and which is likely to be Macy's. Explain your reasoning. Indicate any percentages that seem inconsistent with their strategies.

Firm A	Firm A	Firm B
Sales	100.0%	100.0%
Cost of Goods Sold	(70.7)	(60.3)
Selling and Administrative	(23.4)	(34.1)
Income Taxes	(0.8)	(0.5)
All Other Items	(4.0)	(0.1)
Net Income	1.0%	5.2%

Problems and Cases

1.11 EFFECT OF INDUSTRY CHARACTERISTICS ON FINANCIAL STATEMENT RELATIONSHIPS.

Effective financial statement analysis requires an understanding of a firm's economic characteristics. The relations between various financial statement items provide evidence of many of these economic characteristics. Exhibit 1.22 (see pages 66–67) presents common-size condensed balance sheets and income statements for 12 firms in different industries. These common-size balance sheets and income statements express various items as a percentage of operating revenues. (That is, the statement divides all amounts by operating revenues for the year.) Exhibit 1.22 also shows the ratio of cash flow from operations to capital expenditures. A dash for a particular financial statement item does not necessarily mean the amount is zero. It merely indicates that the amount is not sufficiently large for the firm to disclose it. Amounts that are not meaningful are shown as *n.m.* A list of the 12 companies and a brief description of their activities follow.

A. Amazon.com: Operates websites to sell a wide variety of products online. The firm operated at a net loss in all years prior to that reported in Exhibit 1.22.

B. Carnival Corporation: Owns and operates cruise ships.

C. Cisco Systems: Manufactures and sells computer networking and communications products.

D. Citigroup: Offers a wide range of financial services in the commercial banking, insurance, and securities business. Operating expenses represent the compensation of employees.

E. eBay: Operates an online trading platform for buyers to purchase and sellers to sell a variety of goods. The firm has grown in part by acquiring other companies to enhance or support its online trading platform.

F. Goldman Sachs: Offers brokerage and investment banking services. Operating expenses represent the compensation of employees.

G. Johnson & Johnson: Develops, manufactures, and sells pharmaceutical products, medical equipment, and branded over-the-counter consumer personal care products.

H. Kellogg's: Manufactures and distributes cereal and other food products. The firm acquired other branded food companies in recent years.

I. MGM Mirage: Owns and operates hotels, casinos, and golf courses.

J. Molson Coors: Manufactures and distributes beer. Molson Coors has made minority ownership investments in other beer manufacturers in recent years.

K. Verizon: Maintains a telecommunications network and offers telecommunications services. Operating expenses represent the compensation of employees. Verizon has made minority investments in other cellular and wireless providers.

L. Yum! Brands: Operates chains of name-brand restaurants, including Taco Bell, KFC, and Pizza Hut.

Required

Use the ratios to match the companies in Exhibit 1.22 with the firms listed above.

1.12 EFFECT OF INDUSTRY CHARACTERISTICS ON FINANCIAL STATEMENT RELATIONSHIPS.

Effective financial statement analysis requires an understanding of a firm's economic characteristics. The relations between various financial statement items provide evidence of many of these economic characteristics. Exhibit 1.23 (see pages 68–69) presents common-size condensed balance sheets and income statements for 12 firms in different industries. These common-size balance sheets and income statements express various items as a percentage of operating revenues. (That is, the statement divides all amounts by operating revenues for the year.) Exhibit 1.23 also shows the ratio of cash flow from operations to capital expenditures. A dash for a particular financial statement item does not necessarily mean the amount is zero. It merely indicates that the amount is not sufficiently large for the firm to disclose it. A list of the 12 companies and a brief description of their activities follow.

- **A.** Abercrombie & Fitch: Sells retail apparel primarily through stores to the fashion-conscious young adult and has established itself as a trendy, popular player in the specialty retailing apparel industry.
- **B.** Allstate Insurance: Sells property and casualty insurance, primarily on buildings and automobiles. Operating revenues include insurance premiums from customers and revenues earned from investments made with cash received from customers before Allstate pays customers' claims. Operating expenses include amounts actually paid or expected to be paid in the future on insurance coverage outstanding during the year.
- **C.** Best Buy: Operates a chain of retail stores selling consumer electronic and entertainment equipment at competitively low prices.
- **D.** E. I. du Pont de Nemours: Manufactures chemical and electronics products.
- **E.** Hewlett-Packard: Develops, manufactures, and sells computer hardware. The firm outsources manufacturing of many of its computer components.
- **F.** HSBC Finance: Lends money to consumers for periods ranging from several months to several years. Operating expenses include provisions for estimated uncollectible loans (bad debts expense).
- **G.** Kelly Services: Provides temporary office services to businesses and other firms. Operating revenues represent amounts billed to customers for temporary help services, and operating expenses include amounts paid to the temporary help employees of Kelly.
- **H.** McDonald's: Operates fast-food restaurants worldwide. A large percentage of McDonald's restaurants are owned and operated by franchisees. McDonald's frequently owns the restaurant buildings of franchisees and leases them to franchisees under long-term leases.
- **I.** Merck: A leading research-driven pharmaceutical products and services company. Merck discovers, develops, manufactures, and markets a broad range of products to improve human and animal health directly and through its joint ventures.
- **J.** Omnicom Group: Creates advertising copy for clients and is the largest marketing services firm in the world. Omnicom purchases advertising time and space from various media and sells it to clients. Operating revenues represent commissions and fees earned by creating advertising copy and selling media time and space. Operating expenses includes employee compensation.
- **K.** Pacific Gas & Electric: Generates and sells power to customers in the western United States.
- **L.** Procter & Gamble: Manufactures and markets a broad line of branded consumer products.

EXHIBIT 1.22

Common-Size Financial Statement Data for Firms in 12 Industries
(Problem 1.11)

	1	2	3
BALANCE SHEET			
Cash and marketable securities	2,256.1%	4.1%	20.1%
Receivables	352.8%	2.8%	15.2%
Inventories	0.0%	2.4%	7.9%
Property, plant, and equipment, at cost	0.0%	286.8%	43.0%
Accumulated depreciation	(0.0%)	(59.8%)	(20.4%)
Property, plant, and equipment, net	0.0%	227.0%	22.5%
Intangibles	0.0%	36.5%	43.4%
Other assets	57.3%	7.2%	24.0%
Total Assets	2,666.2%	280.0%	133.2%
Current liabilities	2,080.8%	37.8%	32.7%
Long-term debt	390.9%	69.1%	12.7%
Other long-term liabilities	92.6%	5.6%	21.1%
Shareholders' equity	101.9%	167.5%	66.7%
Total Liabilities and Shareholders' Equity	2,666.2%	280.0%	133.2%
INCOME STATEMENT			
Operating revenues	100.0%	100.0%	100.0%
Cost of sales (excluding depreciation) or operating expenses[a]	(54.6%)	(61.6%)	(29.0%)
Depreciation and amortization	(2.0%)	(9.9%)	(4.4%)
Selling and administrative	(1.4%)	(12.1%)	(29.3%)
Research and development	(1.6%)	0.0%	(12.2%)
Interest (expense)/income	9.5%	(2.8%)	(0.1%)
Income taxes	(14.3%)	(0.1%)	(6.2%)
All other items, net	(8.0%)	0.1%	1.6%
Net Income	27.6%	13.6%	20.3%
Cash flow from operations/capital expenditures	n.m.	1.0	4.9

[a] See the problem narrative for items included in operating expenses.

EXHIBIT 1.22 (Continued)

4	5	6	7	8	9	10	11	12
2.0%	10.6%	96.9%	4.1%	2,198.0%	26.0%	4.5%	1.9%	39.3%
8.9%	12.0%	8.8%	4.2%	1,384.8%	4.0%	13.3%	2.0%	5.1%
7.0%	2.1%	3.0%	1.5%	0.0%	8.9%	4.0%	1.3%	0.0%
55.4%	221.5%	33.8%	278.8%	0.0%	7.8%	41.4%	61.1%	32.9%
(32.5%)	(132.6%)	(22.6%)	(52.8%)	(0.0%)	(2.6%)	(14.1%)	(28.3%)	(18.9%)
22.9%	88.9%	11.2%	226.0%	0.0%	5.3%	27.3%	32.9%	14.0%
39.8%	75.2%	40.5%	6.0%	101.9%	5.0%	109.4%	8.3%	90.9%
4.8%	19.0%	28.3%	81.0%	208.5%	7.2%	59.7%	11.4%	33.3%
85.4%	207.9%	188.6%	322.9%	3,893.3%	56.4%	218.2%	57.9%	182.6%
27.7%	26.6%	37.8%	41.7%	2,878.4%	30.0%	20.7%	15.3%	43.4%
31.7%	48.2%	28.5%	172.2%	596.1%	0.4%	38.4%	31.6%	0.0%
14.6%	90.2%	15.3%	53.8%	171.3%	4.4%	33.9%	12.0%	9.4%
11.3%	42.8%	107.0%	55.1%	247.5%	21.4%	125.3%	(1.0%)	129.8%
85.4%	207.9%	188.6%	322.9%	3,893.3%	56.4%	218.2%	57.9%	182.6%
100.0%	100.0%	100.0%	100.0%	100.0%	100.0%	100.0%	100.0%	100.0%
(58.1%)	(40.1%)	(36.1%)	(56.0%)	(73.4%)	(85.8%)	(59.5%)	(75.1%)	(26.1%)
(2.9%)	(15.0%)	(1.5%)	(10.8%)	(5.0%)	(1.5%)	(5.7%)	(4.9%)	(2.8%)
(23.7%)	(27.6%)	(27.6%)	(19.3%)	(5.1%)	(2.6%)	(27.9%)	(7.6%)	(33.7%)
0.0%	0.0%	(14.6%)	0.0%	(7.7%)	(5.1%)	0.0%	0.0%	(8.5%)
(2.5%)	(1.9%)	1.0%	(8.5%)	78.4%	0.0%	(1.8%)	(2.0%)	1.3%
(3.8%)	(3.4%)	(4.3%)	(2.6%)	(16.0%)	(1.0%)	(2.2%)	(2.8%)	(4.7%)
0.0%	(5.5%)	0.0%	2.3%	(28.8%)	(0.3%)	5.2%	0.4%	0.0%
9.0%	6.6%	17.0%	5.3%	42.3%	3.7%	8.0%	8.0%	25.5%
2.7	1.5	9.8	1.0	n.m.	8.8	1.8	1.6	5.1

Required

Use the ratios to match the companies in Exhibit 1.23 with the firms listed above.

1.13 EFFECT OF INDUSTRY CHARACTERISTICS ON FINANCIAL STATEMENT RELATIONSHIPS: A GLOBAL PERSPECTIVE. Effective financial statement analysis requires an understanding of a firm's economic characteristics. The relations between various financial statement items provide evidence of many of these economic characteristics. Exhibit 1.24 (see pages 70–71) presents common-size condensed balance sheets and income statements for 12 firms in different industries. These common-size balance sheets and income statements express various items as a percentage of operating revenues. (That is, the statement divides all amounts by operating revenues for the year.) A dash for a particular

EXHIBIT 1.23

Common-Size Financial Statement Data for Firms in 12 Industries
(Problem 1.12)

	1	2	3
BALANCE SHEET			
Cash and marketable securities	11.6%	23.0%	9.2%
Receivables	18.2%	48.4%	25.0%
Inventories	17.8%	9.6%	2.9%
Property, plant, and equipment, at cost	87.8%	101.2%	272.3%
Accumulated depreciation	(52.8%)	(50.9%)	(92.8%)
Property, plant, and equipment, net	35.0%	50.3%	179.5%
Intangibles	15.2%	8.2%	0.0%
Other assets	15.8%	58.4%	60.5%
Total Assets	113.7%	197.9%	277.1%
Current liabilities	30.5%	60.0%	51.2%
Long-term debt	24.0%	16.5%	70.1%
Other long-term liabilities	36.9%	42.7%	88.9%
Shareholders' equity	22.4%	78.7%	66.9%
Total Liabilities and Shareholders' Equity	113.7%	197.9%	277.1%
INCOME STATEMENT			
Operating revenues	100.0%	100.0%	100.0%
Cost of sales (excluding depreciation) or operating expenses[a]	(75.6%)	(23.4%)	(60.7%)
Depreciation and amortization	(4.5%)	(6.8%)	(12.6%)
Selling and administrative	(6.8%)	(24.1%)	0.0%
Research and development	(4.4%)	(20.1%)	0.0%
Interest (expense)/income	(1.2%)	(1.1%)	(4.8%)
Income taxes	(1.2%)	(8.4%)	(3.3%)
All other items, net	0.0%	16.7%	(10.6%)
Net Income	6.3%	32.7%	8.1%
Cash flow from operations/capital expenditures	1.6	5.1	0.8

[a] See the problem narrative for items included in operating expenses.

financial statement item does not necessarily mean the amount is zero. It merely indicates that the amount is not sufficiently large for the firm to disclose it. A list of the 12 companies, the country of their headquarters, and a brief description of their activities follow.

A. Accor (France): World's largest hotel group, operating hotels under the names of Sofitel, Novotel, Motel 6, and others. Accor has grown in recent years by acquiring established hotel chains.

B. Carrefour (France): Operates grocery supermarkets and hypermarkets in Europe, Latin America, and Asia.

C. Deutsche Telekom (Germany): Europe's largest provider of wired and wireless telecommunication services. The telecommunications industry has experienced increased deregulation in recent years.

EXHIBIT 1.23 (Continued)

4	5	6	7	8	9	10	11	12
362.6%	6.0%	1.1%	1.6%	14.7%	8.3%	27.3%	8.8%	11.6%
47.7%	8.9%	4.1%	15.7%	2.7%	43.2%	697.5%	4.0%	16.8%
0.0%	8.7%	10.6%	0.0%	10.5%	5.0%	0.0%	0.5%	5.3%
10.3%	46.4%	15.4%	6.9%	66.1%	13.1%	3.2%	132.4%	18.3%
(6.7%)	(21.8%)	(6.1%)	(3.7%)	(26.6%)	(7.7%)	(1.3%)	(46.3%)	(8.5%)
3.6%	24.6%	9.3%	3.1%	39.5%	5.4%	1.9%	86.1%	9.8%
2.8%	112.8%	6.0%	2.6%	0.0%	55.7%	40.9%	9.5%	34.7%
120.7%	9.5%	4.1%	4.7%	12.9%	12.0%	26.7%	12.2%	22.0%
537.5%	170.6%	35.2%	27.8%	80.5%	129.6%	794.3%	121.0%	100.2%
391.7%	39.1%	18.7%	10.3%	12.7%	73.0%	122.1%	10.8%	37.5%
19.4%	26.1%	2.5%	0.9%	2.8%	22.9%	565.5%	43.3%	12.2%
51.3%	25.5%	3.6%	2.7%	12.8%	7.4%	20.2%	10.0%	15.1%
75.1%	79.8%	10.3%	13.9%	52.1%	26.4%	86.5%	56.9%	35.4%
537.5%	170.6%	35.2%	27.8%	80.5%	129.6%	794.3%	121.0%	100.2%
100.0%	100.0%	100.0%	100.0%	100.0%	100.0%	100.0%	100.0%	100.0%
(91.6%)	(49.2%)	(75.6%)	(82.5%)	(33.3%)	(87.4%)	(29.1%)	(63.3%)	(76.4%)
(0.9%)	(3.9%)	(1.8%)	(0.8%)	(5.1%)	(1.8%)	(1.7%)	(5.1%)	(4.2%)
(10.7%)	(23.9%)	(18.2%)	(15.3%)	(49.4%)	0.0%	(25.0%)	(4.9%)	(6.0%)
0.0%	(2.6%)	0.0%	0.0%	0.0%	0.0%	0.0%	0.0%	(2.5%)
21.0%	(1.7%)	(0.2%)	0.0%	0.3%	(0.6%)	(32.7%)	(2.2%)	(0.6%)
(6.9%)	(5.1%)	(1.5%)	(0.5%)	(5.0%)	(4.1%)	(3.7%)	(7.8%)	(1.5%)
4.2%	0.7%	(0.5%)	(0.1%)	0.0%	1.2%	(3.3%)	1.7%	(2.1%)
15.2%	14.3%	2.2%	0.8%	7.4%	7.5%	4.5%	18.3%	6.7%
18.7	4.6	1.4	1.6	1.3	6.6	100.9	2.8	3.6

D. E.ON AG (Germany): One of the major public utility companies in Europe and the world's largest privately owned energy service provider.

E. Fortis (Netherlands): Offers insurance and banking services. Operating revenues include insurance premiums received, investment income, and interest revenue on loans. Operating expenses include amounts actually paid or amounts it expects to pay in the future on insurance coverage outstanding during the year.

F. Interpublic Group (U.S.): Creates advertising copy for clients. Interpublic purchases advertising time and space from various media and sells it to clients. Operating revenues represent the commissions or fees earned for creating advertising copy and selling media time and space. Operating expenses include employee compensation.

EXHIBIT 1.24

Common-Size Financial Statement Data for Firms in 12 Industries
(Problem 1.13)

	1	2	3
BALANCE SHEET			
Cash and marketable securities	313.7%	2.2%	21.8%
Receivables	412.9%	8.4%	48.8%
Inventories	0.0%	27.7%	6.9%
Property, plant, and equipment, at cost	6.6%	186.9%	66.2%
Accumulated depreciation	(2.8%)	(125.4%)	(36.5%)
Property, plant, and equipment, net	3.8%	61.4%	29.7%
Intangibles	2.4%	0.0%	0.0%
Other assets	66.2%	33.2%	16.2%
Total Assets	829.8%	133.0%	123.5%
Current liabilities	120.3%	18.3%	45.4%
Long-term debt	630.8%	40.9%	22.8%
Other long-term liabilities	55.6%	24.7%	10.1%
Shareholders' equity	23.1%	49.0%	45.1%
Total Liabilities and Shareholders' Equity	829.8%	133.0%	123.5%
INCOME STATEMENT			
Operating revenues	100.0%	100.0%	100.0%
Cost of sales (excluding depreciation) or operating expenses[a]	(18.7%)	(80.3%)	(76.2%)
Depreciation and amortization	(0.6%)	(6.0%)	(5.7%)
Selling and administrative	(4.8%)	(1.4%)	(5.9%)
Research and development	0.0%	0.0%	(3.6%)
Interest (expense)/income	(69.7%)	(0.3%)	0.5%
Income taxes	(1.1%)	(5.1%)	(3.5%)
All other items, net	(0.4%)	0.0%	0.9%
Net Income	4.7%	6.8%	6.5%
Cash flow from operations/capital expenditures	(5.5)	1.1	2.1

[a] See the problem narrative for items included in operating expenses.

G. Marks & Spencer (U.K.): Operates department stores in England and other retail stores in Europe and the United States. Offers its own credit card for customers' purchases.

H. Nestlé (Switzerland): World's largest food processor, offering prepared foods, coffees, milk-based products, and mineral waters.

I. Roche Holding (Switzerland): Creates, manufactures, and distributes a wide variety of prescription drugs.

J. Sumitomo Metal (Japan): Manufacturer and seller of steel sheets and plates and other construction materials.

K. Sun Microsystems (U.S.): Designs, manufactures, and sells workstations and servers used to maintain integrated computer networks. Sun outsources the manufacture of many of its computer components.

EXHIBIT 1.24 (Continued)

4	5	6	7	8	9	10	11	12
4.9%	16.2%	32.7%	19.5%	17.9%	43.4%	4.7%	6.0%	6.5%
12.0%	17.0%	69.6%	21.8%	38.8%	20.4%	6.9%	6.6%	12.2%
2.1%	1.3%	0.0%	4.9%	5.8%	12.2%	5.9%	7.8%	8.5%
195.3%	92.8%	23.2%	35.2%	134.7%	62.9%	82.6%	34.5%	42.0%
(127.9%)	(36.9%)	(15.2%)	(23.6%)	(76.0%)	(24.9%)	(29.3%)	(17.7%)	(22.8%)
67.4%	55.9%	8.1%	11.6%	58.7%	38.0%	53.3%	16.8%	19.2%
87.5%	31.6%	46.3%	27.2%	26.5%	32.3%	4.4%	14.1%	34.1%
25.9%	25.5%	17.5%	18.4%	28.5%	12.7%	4.9%	7.7%	16.1%
199.7%	147.5%	174.1%	103.3%	176.2%	158.8%	80.1%	59.0%	96.6%
40.3%	70.2%	98.8%	40.8%	40.6%	25.3%	25.5%	32.2%	30.2%
8.8%	24.9%	25.7%	9.1%	21.3%	6.2%	23.4%	10.8%	5.8%
80.7%	6.3%	14.2%	13.1%	43.5%	15.0%	8.1%	3.6%	10.7%
69.9%	46.0%	35.6%	40.3%	70.8%	112.4%	23.2%	12.4%	50.0%
199.7%	147.5%	174.1%	103.3%	176.2%	158.8%	80.1%	59.0%	96.6%
100.0%	100.0%	100.0%	100.0%	100.0%	100.0%	100.0%	100.0%	100.0%
(56.1%)	(70.4%)	(62.4%)	(53.5%)	(64.5%)	(28.5%)	(62.8%)	(77.9%)	(51.3%)
(17.8%)	(5.8%)	(2.5%)	(3.4%)	(5.1%)	(3.5%)	(4.5%)	(2.1%)	(2.4%)
(15.9%)	0.0%	(26.4%)	(25.1%)	(22.7%)	(20.5%)	(24.7%)	(16.3%)	(30.2%)
0.0%	0.0%	0.0%	(13.4%)	0.0%	(18.5%)	0.0%	0.0%	(1.8%)
(4.0%)	(1.1%)	(1.7%)	1.2%	(1.4%)	0.5%	(1.8%)	(0.6%)	(1.0%)
(2.3%)	(3.5%)	(2.2%)	(1.5%)	(0.1%)	(6.9%)	(2.2%)	(0.8%)	(3.4%)
(0.1%)	(11.3%)	(0.5%)	0.2%	1.1%	0.1%	1.6%	0.1%	7.6%
3.8%	7.9%	4.2%	4.5%	7.3%	22.6%	5.6%	2.3%	17.3%
2.3	2.0	6.3	3.0	1.7	4.0	2.7	1.8	2.2

L. Toyota Motor (Japan): Manufactures automobiles and offers financing services to its customers.

Required

Use the ratios to match the companies in Exhibit 1.24 with the firms listed above.

1.14 VALUE CHAIN ANALYSIS AND FINANCIAL STATEMENT RELA-TIONSHIPS. Exhibit 1.25 (see page 74) presents common-size income statements and balance sheets for seven firms that operate at various stages in the value chain for the pharmaceutical industry. These common-size statements express all amounts as a percentage of sales revenue. Exhibit 1.25 also shows the cash flow from operations to capital expenditures ratios for each firm. A dash for a particular financial statement item does not necessarily mean the amount is zero. It merely indicates that the amount is not sufficiently large for the firm to disclose it. A list of the seven companies and a brief description of their activities follow.

A. Wyeth: Engages in the development, manufacture, and sale of ethical drugs (that is, drugs requiring a prescription). Wyeth's drugs represent primarily mixtures of chemical compounds. Ethical-drug companies must obtain approval of new drugs from the U.S. Food and Drug Administration (FDA). Patents protect such drugs from competition until other drug companies develop more effective substitutes or the patent expires.

B. Amgen: Engages in the development, manufacture, and sale of drugs based on biotechnology research. Biotechnology drugs must obtain approval from the FDA and enjoy patent protection similar to that for chemical-based drugs. The biotechnology segment is less mature than the ethical-drug industry, with relatively few products having received FDA approval.

C. Mylan Laboratories: Engages in the development, manufacture, and sale of generic drugs. Generic drugs have the same chemical compositions as drugs that had previously benefited from patent protection but for which the patent has expired. Generic-drug companies have benefited in recent years from the patent expiration of several major ethical drugs. However, the major ethical-drug companies have increasingly offered generic versions of their ethical drugs to compete against the generic-drug companies.

D. Johnson & Johnson: Engages in the development, manufacture, and sale of over-the-counter health care products. Such products do not require a prescription and often benefit from brand recognition.

E. Covance: Offers product development and laboratory testing services for biotechnology and pharmaceutical drugs. It also offers commercialization services and market access services. Cost of goods sold for this company represents the salaries of personnel conducting the laboratory testing and drug approval services.

F. Cardinal Health: Distributes drugs as a wholesaler to drugstores, hospitals, and mass merchandisers. Also offers pharmaceutical benefit management services in which it provides customized databases designed to help customers order more efficiently, contain costs, and monitor their purchases. Cost of goods sold for Cardinal Health includes the cost of drugs sold plus the salaries of personnel providing pharmaceutical benefit management services.

G. Walgreens: Operates a chain of drugstores nationwide. The data in Exhibit 1.25 for Walgreens include the recognition of operating lease commitments for retail space.

Required

Use the ratios to match the companies in Exhibit 1.25 with the firms listed above.

INTEGRATIVE CASE 1.1

STARBUCKS

The first case at the end of this chapter and each of the remaining chapters is a series of integrative cases involving Starbucks. The series of cases applies the concepts and analytical tools discussed in each chapter to Starbucks' financial statements and notes. The preparation of responses to the questions in these cases results in an integrated illustration of the six sequential steps in financial statement analysis discussed in this chapter and throughout the book.

Introduction

"They don't just sell coffee; they sell the *Starbucks Experience*," remarked Deb Mills while sitting down to enjoy a cup of Starbucks cappuccino with her friend Kim Shannon. Kim, an investment fund manager for a large insurance firm, reflected on that observation and what it might mean for Starbucks as a potential investment opportunity. Glancing around the store, Kim saw a number of people sitting alone or in groups, lingering over their drinks while chatting, reading, or checking e-mail and surfing the Internet through the store's Wi-Fi network. Kim noted that in addition to the wide selection of hot coffees, French and Italian style espressos, teas, and cold coffee-blended drinks, Starbucks also offered food items and baked goods, packages of roasted coffee beans, coffee-related accessories and equipment, and even its own line of CDs. Intrigued, Kim made a mental note to do a full-blown valuation analysis of Starbucks to evaluate whether its business model and common equity shares were as good as their coffee.

Growth Strategy

Kim's research quickly confirmed her friend's observation that Starbucks is about the *experience* of enjoying a good cup of coffee. The Starbucks 2008 Form 10-K (page 2) boldly asserts that

> "The Company's retail goal is to become the leading retailer and brand of coffee in each of its target markets by selling the finest quality coffee and related products, and by providing each customer a unique *Starbucks Experience*. The *Starbucks Experience*, or third place beyond home and work, is built upon superior service as well as clean and well-maintained Company-operated retail stores that reflect the personalities of the communities in which they operate, thereby building a high degree of customer loyalty."

The *Starbucks Experience* strives to create a "third place"—somewhere besides home and work where a customer can feel comfortable and welcome—through friendly and skilled customer service in clean and personable retail store environments. This approach enabled Starbucks to grow rapidly from just a single coffee shop near Pike's Place Market in Seattle to a global company with 16,680 locations worldwide at the end of fiscal 2008. Of that total, Starbucks owns and operates 9,217 stores (7,238 U.S. stores and 1,979 international stores), while licensees own and operate 7,463 stores (4,329 U.S. stores and 3,134 international stores).

Most of Starbucks' stores at the end of fiscal 2008 were located in the United States (11,567 stores), amounting to one Starbucks retail location for every 27,000 U.S. residents. However, Starbucks was clearly not a company content to focus simply on the U.S. market, as it was extending the reach of its stores globally, with 5,113 stores outside the United States. At the end of fiscal 2008, Starbucks owned and operated stores in a number of countries around the world, including 731 stores in Canada, 664 stores in the United Kingdom, and 178 stores in China. In addition, by the end of 2008, Starbucks' licensees operated 1,933 stores in the Asia-Pacific region; 685 stores in Europe, the Middle East, and Africa; and 472 stores in Canada and Mexico.

Starbucks' success can be attributed in part to its successful development and expansion of a European idea—enjoying a fine coffee-based beverage and sharing that experience with others in a comfortable, friendly environment with pleasant, competent service. Starbucks imported the idea of the French and Italian café into the busy North American lifestyle. Ironically, Starbucks successfully extended its brand and style of café into the European continent. On January 16, 2004, Starbucks opened its first coffeehouse in

EXHIBIT 1.25

Common-Size Financial Statement Data for Seven Firms in the Pharmaceutical Industry (Problem 1.14)

	1	2	3	4	5	6	7
BALANCE SHEET							
Cash and marketable securities	12.5%	1.9%	63.7%	63.7%	12.1%	4.1%	20.1%
Receivables	22.7%	5.7%	13.8%	16.0%	18.7%	3.9%	15.2%
Inventories	20.7%	7.2%	13.8%	13.1%	3.7%	10.7%	7.9%
Property, plant, and equipment, at cost	34.2%	3.9%	66.6%	73.9%	74.2%	22.6%	43.0%
Accumulated depreciation	(13.5%)	(2.0%)	(27.4%)	(24.9%)	(27.1%)	(5.5%)	(20.4%)
Property, plant, and equipment, net	20.7%	1.9%	39.2%	49.0%	47.1%	17.1%	22.5%
Intangibles	109.3%	6.1%	95.5%	20.5%	5.8%	2.3%	43.4%
Other assets	16.8%	2.5%	16.9%	30.5%	8.5%	1.6%	24.0%
Total Assets	202.6%	25.2%	242.9%	192.8%	96.0%	39.7%	133.2%
Current liabilities	30.1%	11.5%	32.6%	30.0%	25.2%	10.7%	32.7%
Long-term debt	100.5%	3.3%	61.2%	47.4%	0.0%	3.7%	12.7%
Other long-term liabilities	19.4%	1.7%	13.3%	31.5%	5.4%	2.6%	21.1%
Shareholders' equity	52.6%	8.8%	135.9%	84.0%	65.4%	22.7%	66.7%
Total Liabilities and Shareholders' Equity	202.6%	25.2%	242.9%	192.8%	96.0%	39.7%	133.2%
INCOME STATEMENT							
Operating revenues	100.0%	100.0%	100.0%	100.0%	100.0%	100.0%	100.0%
Cost of sales (excluding depreciation) or operating expenses	(59.7%)	(94.4%)	(15.3%)	(27.4%)	(62.5%)	(72.2%)	(29.0%)
Depreciation and amortization	(8.3%)	(0.4%)	(7.2%)	(4.1%)	(3.9%)	(1.5%)	(4.4%)
Selling and administrative	(12.2%)	(3.1%)	(20.1%)	(25.9%)	(13.7%)	(21.1%)	(29.3%)
Research and development	(6.2%)	0.0%	(20.2%)	(14.8%)	0.0%	0.0%	(12.2%)
Interest (expense)/income	(6.9%)	(0.2%)	0.2%	(0.1%)	0.4%	(0.1%)	(0.1%)
Income taxes	(2.7%)	(0.5%)	(7.0%)	(8.4%)	(4.3%)	(1.8%)	(6.2%)
All other items, net	0.1%	0.0%	(2.5%)	(0.1%)	(5.3%)	0.0%	1.6%
Net Income	4.1%	1.3%	28.0%	19.3%	10.5%	3.2%	20.3%
Cash flow from operations/ capital expenditures	2.3	3.0	8.9	4.4	4.0	2.2	4.9

France—in the heart of Paris at 26 Avenue de l'Opera—and had a total of 46 stores in France by the end of 2008. The success of Starbucks' retail coffeehouse concept is illustrated by the fact that by the end of 2008, Starbucks had opened over 1,000 company-operated and licensed locations in Europe, with the majority of them in the United Kingdom.

Not long ago Starbucks' CEO Howard Schultz stated that his vision and ultimate goal for Starbucks was to have 20,000 Starbucks retail locations in the United States, to have another 20,000 retail locations in international markets worldwide, and to have Starbucks recognized among the world's leading brands. Kim Shannon wondered whether Starbucks could ultimately achieve that level of global penetration because she could name only a few such worldwide companies. Among those that came to mind were McDonald's, with 31,677 retail locations in 119 countries; Subway, with 32,191 locations in 90 countries (of which, 21,995 were in the United States); and Yum! Brands, with 36,000 restaurants in 110 countries under brand names such as KFC, Pizza Hut, and Taco Bell.

Until 2009, growth in the number of retail stores had been one of the primary drivers of Starbucks' growth in revenues. The most significant area of expansion of the Starbucks model in recent years has been the rapid growth in the number of licensed retail stores. At the end of fiscal 1999, Starbucks had only 363 licensed stores, but by the end of fiscal 2008, the number of licensed stores had mushroomed to 7,463.

Recent Performance

Starbucks' performance in 2008 caused Kim to question whether Starbucks had already reached (or perhaps exceeded) its full potential. She wondered whether it could generate the impressive growth in new stores and revenues it had created in the past.

In fiscal year 2008, Starbucks opened 1,669 net new retail locations (681 net new company-owned stores and 988 new licensed stores), but this number was well below the initial target (2,500 new stores) and well below the 2,571 new stores opened in 2007. Late in 2008, Starbucks announced a plan to close approximately 600 underperforming stores in the United States as well as 64 underperforming stores in Australia. Early in fiscal 2009, it increased the restructuring plan to close a total of approximately 800 U.S. stores (an increase of 200) and announced a plan to close 100 additional stores in various international markets during 2009. During fiscal 2008, Starbucks managed to close 205 U.S. stores and the 64 underperforming stores in Australia. The restructuring plans called for closing 595 stores in the United States and 100 international stores during fiscal 2009. The store closings triggered restructuring charges that reduced Starbucks' operating income by $267 million in 2008. Similar charges would likely reduce 2009 operating income by $360 million. Overall in fiscal 2009, for the first time in company history, Starbucks' projected that net store growth in the United States would be negative, with company-operated store closings outnumbering new store openings. Growth in U.S.-licensed stores also was expected to be slow, with less than 100 new stores planned. Internationally, Starbucks' plans for store opening for 2009 were conservative, owing in part to the difficult economic conditions in its primary markets. Starbucks planned to open 100 new company-operated international stores in 2009 and 300 new licensed stores.

In fiscal 2008, total revenues grew to $10.383 billion from $9.411 billion in fiscal 2007, a growth rate of 10.3 percent. Prior to 2008, Starbucks had generated impressive revenue growth rates of 20.9 percent in fiscal 2007 and 22.2 percent in fiscal 2006.

Starbucks' revenue growth was driven not only by the opening of new stores, but also by sales growth among existing stores. Through 2007, Starbucks could boast of a streak of 16 consecutive years in which it achieved comparable store sales growth rates equal to or greater than 5 percent, but that string was broken with –3 percent comparable store sales growth in 2008. Unfortunately, given the economic conditions in Starbucks' primary markets, it was not clear whether same store sales growth rates would improve in 2009.

In January 2008, Howard Schultz returned from retirement and resumed his role as president and CEO of Starbucks to restructure the business and its potential for growth. Focal points of his transformation plan included overseeing the restructuring efforts, taking a more disciplined approach to opening new stores, reinvigorating the *Starbucks Experience*, and developing and implementing even better service and quality while cutting operating and overhead costs. In addition, the transformation plans included introducing new beverage and food offerings, including baked goods, breakfast items, and chilled foods. A key to Starbucks profit growth lies in increasing same store sales growth via new products. Starbucks regularly introduces new specialty coffee-based drinks and coffee flavors as well as iced coffee-based drinks, such as the successful line of Frappuccino® and Iced Shaken Refreshment drinks.

Starbucks also planned to continue to expand the scope of its business model through new channel development in order to "reach customers where they work, travel, shop, and dine." To further expand the business model, Starbucks entered into a licensing agreement with Kraft Foods to market and distribute Starbucks whole bean and ground coffee to grocery stores and warehouse club stores. By the end of fiscal 2008, Starbucks whole bean and ground coffees were available throughout the United States in approximately 39,000 grocery and warehouse club stores. In addition, Starbucks sells whole bean and ground coffee through institutional foodservice companies that service business, education, office, hotel, restaurant, airline, and other foodservice accounts. For example, in 2008, Starbucks (and its subsidiary Seattle's Best Coffee) was the only superpremium national brand of coffee promoted by Sysco Corporation to such foodservice accounts. Finally, Starbucks had formed partnerships to produce and distribute bottled Frappuccino® and Doubleshot® drinks with PepsiCo and premium ice creams with Dreyer's Grand Ice Cream, Inc.

Despite Starbucks' difficulties with store closings, restructuring charges, and negative comparable store sales growth rates, Kim could see positive aspects of Starbucks' financial performance and condition. She noted that Starbucks had been profitable in 2008 despite the restructuring charges and falling revenues. The restructuring plan was expected to help Starbucks reduce costs, even during these difficult times. Further, she noted that Starbucks' operating cash flows had remained fairly strong throughout this period, amounting to $1,259 million in fiscal 2008. Starbucks had a cash balance of nearly $270 million. Perhaps Starbucks could weather the economic recession and its restructuring and look to better days ahead.

Product Supply

Starbucks purchases green coffee beans from coffee-producing regions around the world and custom roasts and blends them to its exacting standards. Although coffee beans trade in commodity markets and experience volatile prices, Starbucks purchases higher-quality coffee beans that sell at a premium to commodity coffees. Starbucks purchases its coffee beans under fixed-price purchase contracts with various suppliers, with purchase prices reset annually. Starbucks also purchases significant amounts of dairy products from suppliers located near its retail stores. Starbucks purchases paper and plastic products from several suppliers, the prices of which vary with changes in the prices of commodity paper and plastic resin.

Competition in the Specialty Coffee Industry

After some reflection, Kim realized that Starbucks faced intense direct competition. Kim could think of a wide array of convenient retail locations where a person can purchase a cup of coffee. Kim reasoned that Starbucks competes with a broad scope of coffee beverage retailers, including fast-food chains (for example, McDonald's), doughnut chains (for example, Krispy Kreme, Dunkin' Donuts, and Tim Hortons), and convenience stores associated with many gas stations, but that these types of outlets offer an experience that is very different from what Starbucks offers. In particular, Kim was aware that McDonald's had started to expand development of its McCafé shops, which sold premium coffee drinks (lattes, cappuccinos, and mochas) in McDonald's restaurants. It appeared to Kim that the McCafé initiative was intended to be a direct competitive challenge to Starbucks' business.

Kim also identified a number of companies that were growing chains of retail coffee shops that could be compared to Starbucks, including firms such as Panera Bread Company; Diedrich Coffee; New World Restaurant Group, Inc.; and Caribou Coffee Company, Inc. (a privately-held firm). However, these firms were much smaller than Starbucks, with the largest among them being the Panera Bread Company, with 1,325 bakery-cafés systemwide (763 franchised and 562 company-owned) as of the end of fiscal 2008. On the other end of the spectrum, Kim was aware that Starbucks faced competition from local mom-and-pop coffee shops and cafés.

Kim recognized that despite facing extensive competition, Starbucks had some distinct competitive advantages. Very few companies were implementing a business strategy comparable to that of Starbucks, with emphasis on the quality of the experience, the products, and the service. In addition, only the fast-food chains and the doughnut chains operated on the same scale as Starbucks. Finally, Starbucks had developed a global brand that was synonymous with the quality of the *Starbucks Experience.* Recently, Interbrand ranked the Starbucks brand as one of the world's top 100 most valuable brand names, estimating it to be worth in excess of $3 billion.

Financial Statements

Exhibit 1.26 presents comparative balance sheets, Exhibit 1.27 presents comparative income statements, and Exhibit 1.28 (see page 80) presents comparative statements of cash flows for Starbucks for the four fiscal years ending September 28, 2008.

Required

Respond to the following questions relating to Starbucks.

Industry and Strategy Analysis

    a. Apply Porter's five forces framework to the specialty coffee retail industry.

    b. How would you characterize the strategy of Starbucks? How does Starbucks create value for its customers? What critical risk and success factors must Starbucks manage?

Balance Sheet

    c. Describe how Cash differs from Cash Equivalents.

    d. Why do investments appear on the balance sheet under both current and noncurrent assets?

    e. Accounts receivable are reported net of allowance for uncollectible accounts. Why? Identify the events or transactions that cause accounts receivable to increases and

EXHIBIT 1.26

Starbucks Corporation Comparative Balance Sheets
(amounts in millions)
(Integrative Case 1.1)

As of Fiscal Year End September:	2005	2006	2007	2008
ASSETS				
Current Assets				
Cash and equivalents	$ 173.8	$ 312.6	$ 281.3	$ 269.8
Short-term investments	133.2	141.0	157.4	52.5
Receivables	190.8	224.3	287.9	329.5
Inventories	546.3	636.2	691.7	692.8
Prepaid expenses and other assets	94.4	126.9	148.8	169.2
Deferred income taxes, net	70.8	88.8	129.5	234.2
Total Current Assets	$1,209.3	$1,529.8	$1,696.5	$1,748.0
Long-term investments	60.5	5.8	21.0	71.4
Equity and other investments	201.1	219.1	258.8	302.6
Property and equipment, gross	$3,467.6	$4,257.7	$5,306.6	$5,717.3
Accumulated depreciation	(1,625.6)	(1,969.8)	(2,416.1)	(2,760.9)
Property and equipment, net	$1,842.0	$2,287.9	$2,890.4	$2,956.4
Other assets	72.9	186.9	219.4	261.1
Other intangible assets	35.4	38.0	42.0	66.6
Goodwill	92.5	161.5	215.6	266.5
Total Assets	$3,513.7	$4,428.9	$5,343.9	$5,672.6
LIABILITIES AND STOCKHOLDERS' EQUITY				
Current Liabilities				
Accounts payable	$ 221.0	$ 340.9	$ 390.8	$ 324.9
Short-term borrowings	277.0	700.0	710.2	713.0
Accrued compensation and related costs	232.4	289.0	292.4	253.6
Accrued occupancy costs	44.5	54.9	74.6	136.1
Accrued taxes	78.3	94.0	92.5	76.1
Insurance reserves	–	–	137.0	152.5
Other accrued expenses	198.1	224.2	160.3	164.4
Deferred revenue	175.0	231.9	296.9	368.4
Current portion of long-term debt	0.7	0.8	0.8	0.7
Total Current Liabilities	$1,227.0	$1,935.6	$2,155.6	$2,189.7
Long-term debt	2.9	2.0	550.1	549.6
Other long-term liabilities	193.6	262.9	354.1	442.4
Total Liabilities	$1,423.4	$2,200.4	$3,059.8	$3,181.7
Shareholders' Equity				
Common stock	91.0	0.8	0.7	0.7
Paid-in capital	39.4	39.4	39.4	39.4
Retained earnings	1,939.0	2,151.1	2,189.4	2,402.4
Accum. other comprehensive income	20.9	37.3	54.6	48.4
Total Shareholders' Equity	$2,090.3	$2,228.5	$2,284.1	$2,490.9
Total Liabilities and Shareholders' Equity	$3,513.7	$4,428.9	$5,343.9	$5,672.6

EXHIBIT 1.27

**Starbucks Corporation Comparative Income Statements
(amounts in millions except per share figures)
(Integrative Case 1.1)**

Fiscal Years Ended September:	2005	2006	2007	2008
Company-operated retail stores	$5,391.9	$6,583.1	$7,998.3	$ 8,771.9
Specialty:				
Licensing	673.0	860.7	1,026.3	1,171.6
Foodservice and other	304.4	343.2	386.9	439.5
Total Specialty	977.4	1,203.9	1,413.2	1,611.1
Net Revenues	**$6,369.3**	**$7,787.0**	**$9,411.5**	**$10,383.0**
Cost of sales including occupancy costs	(2,605.2)	(3,178.8)	(3,999.1)	(4,645.3)
Gross Profit	**$3,764.1**	**$4,608.2**	**$5,412.4**	**$ 5,737.7**
Store operating expenses	(2,165.9)	(2,687.8)	(3,215.9)	(3,745.1)
Other operating expenses	(192.5)	(253.7)	(294.1)	(330.1)
Depreciation and amortization	340.2	387.2	467.2	549.3
General and administrative expenses	(361.6)	(479.4)	(489.2)	(456.0)
Restructuring charges	—	—	—	266.9
Income from equity investees	(76.6)	(93.9)	(108.0)	(113.6)
Operating Income	**$ 780.5**	**$ 894.0**	**$1,054.0**	**$ 503.9**
Interest and other income	17.1	20.7	40.6	9.0
Interest expense	(1.3)	(8.4)	(38.2)	(53.4)
Income Before Income Taxes	**$ 796.3**	**$ 906.3**	**$1,056.4**	**$ 459.5**
Provision for income taxes	(302.0)	(324.8)	(383.7)	(144.0)
Cumulative effect of an accounting change	—	(17.2)	—	—
Net Income	**$ 494.3**	**$ 564.3**	**$ 672.7**	**$ 315.5**
Net Income Per Share				
Basic	$ 0.63	$ 0.76	$ 0.90	$ 0.43
Diluted	$ 0.61	$ 0.73	$ 0.87	$ 0.43

decrease. Also identify the events or transactions that cause the allowance account to increase and decrease.

f. How does the account Accumulated Depreciation on the balance sheet differ from Depreciation Expense on the income statement?

g. Deferred income taxes appear as a current asset on the balance sheet. Under what circumstances will deferred income taxes give rise to an asset?

h. Accumulated Other Comprehensive Income includes unrealized gains and losses from marketable securities and investments in securities as well as unrealized gains and losses from translating the financial statements of foreign subsidiaries into U.S. dollars. Why are these gains and losses not included in net income on the income statement? When, if ever, will these gains and losses appear in net income?

EXHIBIT 1.28

Starbucks Corporation Comparative Statements of Cash Flows
(amounts in millions)
(Integrative Case 1.1)

Fiscal Years Ended September:	2005	2006	2007	2008
OPERATING ACTIVITIES:				
Net income	$ 494.5	$ 564.3	$ 672.6	$ 315.5
Depreciation and amortization	367.2	412.6	491.2	604.5
Provisions for impairments and disposals	20.2	19.6	26.0	325.0
Deferred income taxes, net	(31.3)	(84.3)	(37.3)	(117.1)
Equity in income of investees	(49.6)	(60.6)	(65.7)	(61.3)
Distributions of income from equity investees	30.9	49.2	65.9	52.6
Stock-based compensation	110.0	105.7	103.9	75.0
Other non-cash items in net income	10.1	(96.9)	(84.7)	(11.0)
Changes in operating assets and liabilities:				
Inventories	(121.6)	(85.5)	(48.6)	(0.6)
Accounts payable	9.7	105.0	36.1	(63.9)
Accrued expenses and taxes	22.7	132.7	86.4	7.3
Deferred revenues	53.3	56.6	63.2	72.4
Other operating assets and liabilities	7.6	13.2	22.2	60.3
Cash Flow from Operating Activities	**$ 923.7**	**$1,131.6**	**$ 1,331.2**	**$ 1,258.7**
INVESTING ACTIVITIES:				
Purchases, sales, maturities of investment securities	$ 452.2	$ 61.1	$ (11.7)	$ 24.1
Net additions to property, plant, and equipment	(644.0)	(771.2)	(1,080.3)	(984.5)
Acquisitions and other investments	(29.5)	(130.9)	(109.9)	(126.2)
Cash Flow Used in Investing Activities	**$(221.3)**	**$ (841.0)**	**$(1,201.9)**	**$(1,086.6)**
FINANCING ACTIVITIES:				
Net (payments on) proceeds from short-term borrowings	$ 277.0	$ 423.0	$ 10.2	$ 2.2
Net (payments on) proceeds from long-term debt	(0.7)	(0.9)	548.2	(0.6)
Net (repurchases of) issues of common equity shares	(950.1)	(694.8)	(819.9)	(199.1)
Excess tax benefit from exercise of stock options	—	117.4	89.6	13.0
Cash Flow Used in Financing Activities	**$(673.8)**	**$ (155.3)**	**$ (171.9)**	**$ (184.5)**
Effects of exchange rate changes on cash	$ 0.1	$ 3.5	$ 11.3	$ 0.9
Net Change in Cash and Cash Equivalents	**$ 28.7**	**$ 138.8**	**$ (31.3)**	**$ (11.5)**
Beginning Cash and Cash Equivalents	145.1	173.8	312.6	281.3
Ending Cash and Cash Equivalents	**$ 173.8**	**$ 312.6**	**$ 281.3**	**$ 269.8**

Income Statement

i. Starbucks reports three principal sources of revenues: company-operated stores, licensing, and foodservice and other consumer products. Using the narrative information provided in this case, describe the nature of each of these three sources of revenue.

j. What types of expenses does Starbucks likely include in (1) Cost of Sales, (2) Occupancy Costs, and (3) Store Operating Expenses?

k. Starbucks reports Income from Equity Investees in its income statement. Using the narrative information provided in this case, describe the nature of this type of income.

Statement of Cash Flows

l. Why does net income differ from the amount of cash flow from operating activities?

m. Why does Starbucks add the amount of depreciation and amortization expense to net income when computing cash flow from operating activities?

n. Why does Starbucks show an increase in inventory as a subtraction when computing cash flow from operations?

o. Why does Starbucks show a decrease in accounts payable as a subtraction when computing cash flow from operations?

p. Starbucks includes short-term investments in current assets on the balance sheet, yet it reports purchases and sales of investment securities as investing activities on the statement of cash flows. Explain why changes in investment securities are investing activities while changes in most other current assets (such as accounts receivable and inventories) are operating activities.

q. Starbucks includes changes in Short-Term Borrowings as a financing activity on the statement of cash flows. Explain why changes in Short-Term Borrowings are a financing activity when most other changes in current liabilities (such as accounts payable and other current liabilities) are operating activities.

Relations between Financial Statements

r. Prepare an analysis that explains the change in Retained Earnings from $2,189.4 at the end of fiscal 2007 to $2,402.4 at the end of fiscal 2008.

s. Prepare an analysis that explains the changes in Property, Plant, and Equipment from $5,306.5 at the end of fiscal 2007 to $5,717.3 at the end of fiscal 2008 and Accumulated Depreciation from $2,416.1 at the end of fiscal 2007 to $2,760.9 at the end of fiscal 2008. You may need to deduce certain amounts that Starbucks does not disclose. For simplicity, assume that all of the depreciation and amortization expense is depreciation.

Interpreting Financial Statement Relations

Exhibit 1.29 presents common-size and percentage change balance sheets and Exhibit 1.30 (see page 84) presents common-size and percentage change income statements for Starbucks for 2005–2008. The percentage change statements report the annual percentage change in each account as well as the compound annual growth rate from 2005 through 2008. Respond to the following questions.

t. The dollar amount shown for property and equipment net of accumulated depreciation (see Exhibit 1.26) increased between the end of fiscal 2007 and the end of fiscal 2008, yet the percentage of total assets comprising these assets declined (see Exhibit 1.29). Explain.

EXHIBIT 1.29

Starbucks Corporation Common-Size and Percentage Change Balance Sheets (allow for rounding)
(Integrative Case 1.1)

| As of Fiscal Year-End September: | Common-Size Balance Sheets | | | | | Percentage Change Balance Sheets | | | |
	2005	2006	2007	2008		2006	2007	2008	Compound Growth
ASSETS									
Current Assets									
Cash and equivalents	4.9%	7.1%	5.3%	4.8%		79.9%	(10.0%)	(4.1%)	15.8%
Short-term investments	3.8%	3.2%	2.9%	0.9%		5.9%	11.6%	(66.7%)	(26.7%)
Receivables	5.4%	5.0%	5.4%	5.8%		17.6%	28.4%	14.4%	20.0%
Inventories	15.6%	14.4%	12.9%	12.2%		16.5%	8.7%	0.2%	8.2%
Prepaid expenses and other assets	2.7%	2.8%	2.8%	3.0%		34.4%	17.2%	13.7%	21.5%
Deferred income taxes, net	2.0%	2.0%	2.4%	4.1%		25.4%	45.8%	80.9%	49.0%
Total Current Assets	**34.4%**	**34.5%**	**31.7%**	**30.8%**		**26.5%**	**10.9%**	**3.0%**	**13.1%**
Long-term investments	1.7%	0.1%	0.4%	1.3%		(90.4%)	261.8%	239.6%	5.7%
Equity and other investments	5.7%	4.9%	4.9%	5.3%		9.0%	18.1%	16.9%	14.6%
Property and equipment, gross	98.7%	96.1%	99.3%	100.8%		22.8%	24.6%	7.7%	18.1%
Accumulated depreciation	(46.3%)	(44.5%)	(45.2%)	(48.7%)		21.2%	22.7%	14.3%	19.3%
Property and equipment, net	52.4%	51.7%	54.1%	52.1%		24.2%	26.3%	2.3%	17.1%
Other assets	2.1%	4.2%	4.1%	4.6%		156.4%	17.4%	19.0%	53.0%
Other intangible assets	1.0%	0.9%	0.8%	1.2%		7.2%	10.8%	58.4%	23.4%
Goodwill	2.7%	3.7%	4.0%	4.7%		74.6%	33.5%	23.6%	42.3%
Total Assets	**100.0%**	**100.0%**	**100.0%**	**100.0%**		**26.0%**	**20.7%**	**6.2%**	**17.3%**

LIABILITIES AND STOCKHOLDERS' EQUITY

Current Liabilities

Accounts payable	6.3%	7.7%	7.3%	5.7%	54.3%	14.6%	(16.9%)	13.7%
Short-term borrowings	7.9%	15.8%	13.3%	12.6%	152.7%	1.5%	0.4%	37.0%
Accrued compensation and related costs	6.6%	6.5%	5.5%	4.5%	24.4%	1.2%	(13.3%)	3.0%
Accrued occupancy costs	1.3%	1.3%	1.4%	2.4%	23.3%	35.9%	82.5%	45.2%
Accrued taxes	2.2%	2.1%	1.7%	1.3%	20.1%	(1.6%)	(17.7%)	(0.9%)
Insurance reserves	0.0%	0.0%	2.6%	2.7%	n.m.	n.m.	11.3%	n.m.
Other accrued expenses	5.6%	5.1%	3.0%	2.9%	13.2%	(28.5%)	2.6%	(6.0%)
Deferred revenue	5.0%	5.2%	5.6%	6.5%	32.5%	28.0%	24.1%	28.2%
Current portion of long-term debt	0.0%	0.0%	0.0%	0.0%	1.9%	1.7%	(9.7%)	(2.2%)
Total Current Liabilities	**34.9%**	**43.7%**	**40.4%**	**38.6%**	**57.8%**	**11.4%**	**1.6%**	**21.3%**
Long-term debt	0.1%	0.1%	10.3%	9.7%	(31.8%)	27,996.1%	(0.1%)	476.4%
Other long-term liabilities	5.5%	5.9%	6.6%	7.8%	35.8%	34.7%	24.9%	31.7%
Total Liabilities	**40.5%**	**49.7%**	**57.3%**	**56.1%**	**54.6%**	**39.1%**	**4.0%**	**30.7%**
Shareholders' Equity								
Common stock	2.6%	0.0%	0.0%	0.0%	(99.2%)	(2.4%)	0.0%	(79.9%)
Paid-in capital	1.1%	0.9%	0.7%	0.7%	0.0%	0.0%	0.0%	0.0%
Retained earnings	55.2%	48.6%	41.0%	42.4%	10.9%	1.8%	9.7%	7.4%
Accumulated other comprehensive income	0.6%	0.8%	1.0%	0.9%	78.2%	46.5%	(11.4%)	32.3%
Total Shareholders' Equity	**59.5%**	**50.3%**	**42.7%**	**43.9%**	**6.6%**	**2.5%**	**9.1%**	**6.0%**
Total Liabilities and Shareholders' Equity	**100.0%**	**100.0%**	**100.0%**	**100.0%**	**26.0%**	**20.7%**	**6.2%**	**17.3%**

EXHIBIT 1.30

Starbucks Corporation Common-Size and Percentage Change Income Statements (allow for rounding)
(Integrative Case 1.1)

Fiscal Year End September:	Common-Size Income Statements				Percentage Change Income Statements			
	2005	2006	2007	2008	2006	2007	2008	Compound Growth
Company-operated retail stores	84.7%	84.5%	85.0%	84.5%	22.1%	21.5%	9.7%	17.6%
Specialty:								
Licensing	10.5%	11.1%	10.9%	11.3%	27.9%	19.2%	14.2%	20.3%
Foodservice and other	4.8%	4.4%	4.1%	4.2%	12.8%	12.7%	13.6%	13.0%
Total specialty	15.3%	15.5%	15.0%	15.5%	23.2%	17.4%	14.0%	18.1%
Net Revenues	**100.0%**	**100.0%**	**100.0%**	**100.0%**	**22.3%**	**20.9%**	**10.3%**	**17.7%**
Cost of sales including occupancy costs	(40.9)	(40.8)	(42.5)	(44.7)	22.0%	25.8%	16.2%	21.3%
Gross Profit	**59.1%**	**59.2%**	**57.5%**	**55.3%**	**22.4%**	**17.5%**	**6.0%**	**15.1%**
Store operating expenses	34.0%	34.5%	34.2%	36.1%	24.1%	19.6%	16.5%	20.0%
Other operating expenses	3.0%	3.3%	3.1%	3.2%	31.8%	15.9%	12.2%	19.7%
Depreciation and amortization	5.3%	5.0%	5.0%	5.3%	13.8%	20.6%	17.6%	17.3%
General and administrative expenses	5.7%	6.2%	5.2%	4.4%	32.6%	2.1%	(6.8%)	8.0%
Restructuring charges	0.0%	0.0%	0.0%	2.6%	n.m.	n.m.	n.m.	n.m.
Income from equity investees	1.2%	1.2%	1.2%	1.1%	22.6%	15.0%	5.2%	14.0%
Operating Income	**12.3%**	**11.4%**	**11.2%**	**4.8%**	**14.5%**	**17.9%**	**(52.2%)**	**(13.6%)**
Interest and other income	0.2%	0.3%	0.4%	0.1%	20.8%	96.3%	(77.8%)	(19.3%)
Interest expense	0.0%	(0.1%)	(0.4%)	(0.5%)	546.2%	354.8%	39.8%	245.0%
Income before income taxes	12.5%	11.6%	11.2%	4.4%	13.8%	16.6%	(56.5%)	(16.7%)
Provision for income taxes	4.7%	4.2%	4.1%	1.4%	7.5%	18.2%	(62.5%)	(21.9%)
Net Income	**7.8%**	**7.2%**	**7.1%**	**3.0%**	**14.1%**	**19.2%**	**(53.1%)**	**(13.9%)**

u. From 2005 through 2008, the proportion of total liabilities increased while the proportion of shareholders' equity declined. What are the likely explanations for these changes?

v. How has the revenue mix of Starbucks changed from 2005 to 2008? Relate these changes to Starbucks' business strategy.

w. Net income as a percentage of total revenues increased from 7.8 percent in fiscal 2005 to 3.0 percent in fiscal 2008. Identify the most important reasons for this change.

CASE 1.2

NIKE: SOMEWHERE BETWEEN A SWOOSH AND A SLAM DUNK

Nike's principal business activity involves the design, development, and worldwide marketing of high-quality footwear, apparel, equipment, and accessory products for serious and recreational athletes. Almost 25,000 employees work for the firm. Nike boasts the largest worldwide market share in the athletic-footwear industry and a leading market share in sports and athletic apparel.

This case uses Nike's financial statements and excerpts from its notes to review important concepts underlying the three principal financial statements (balance sheet, income statement, and statement of cash flows) and relationships among them. The case also introduces tools for analyzing financial statements.

Industry Economics

Product Lines

Industry analysts debate whether the athletic footwear and apparel industry is a performance-driven industry or a fashion-driven industry. Proponents of the performance view point to Nike's dominant market position, which results in part from continual innovation in product development. Proponents of the fashion view point to the difficulty of protecting technological improvements from competitor imitation, the large portion of total expenses comprising advertising, the role of sports and other personalities in promoting athletic shoes, and the fact that a high percentage of athletic footwear and apparel consumers use the products for casual wear rather than the intended athletic purposes (such as playing basketball or running).

Growth

There are only modest growth opportunities for footwear and apparel in the United States. Concern exists with respect to volume increases (how many pairs of athletic shoes will consumers tolerate in their closets) and price increases (will consumers continue to pay prices for innovative athletic footwear that is often twice as costly as other footwear).

Athletic footwear companies have diversified their revenue sources in two directions in recent years. One direction involves increased emphasis on international sales. With dress codes becoming more casual in Europe and East Asia and interest in American sports such as basketball becoming more widespread, industry analysts view international markets as the major growth markets during the next several years. Increased emphasis on soccer (European football) in the United States aids companies such as Adidas that have reputations for quality soccer footwear.

The second direction for diversification is sports and athletic apparel. The three leading athletic footwear companies capitalize on their brand name recognition and distribution channels to create a line of sportswear that coordinates with their footwear. Team uniforms and matching apparel for coaching staffs and fans have become a major growth avenue recently. For example, to complement Nike's footwear sales, Nike recently acquired Umbro, a major brand-name line of jerseys, shorts, jackets, and other apparel in the soccer market.

Production

Essentially all athletic footwear and most apparel are produced in factories in Asia, primarily China (40 percent), Indonesia (31 percent), Vietnam, South Korea, Taiwan, and Thailand. The footwear companies do not own any of these manufacturing facilities. They typically hire manufacturing representatives to source and oversee the manufacturing process, helping to ensure quality control and serving as a link between the design and the manufacture of products. The manufacturing process is labor-intensive, with sewing machines used as the primary equipment. Footwear companies typically price their purchases from these factories in U.S. dollars.

Marketing

Athletic footwear and sportswear companies sell their products to consumers through various independent department, specialty, and discount stores. Their sales forces educate retailers on new product innovations, store display design, and similar activities. The market shares of Nike and the other major brand-name producers dominate retailers' shelf space, and slower growth in sales makes it increasingly difficult for the remaining athletic footwear companies to gain market share. The slower growth also has led the major companies to increase significantly their advertising and payments for celebrity endorsements. Many footwear companies, including Nike, have opened their own retail stores, as well as factory outlet stores for discounted sales of excess inventory.

Athletic footwear and sportswear companies have typically used independent distributors to market their products in other countries. With increasing brand recognition and anticipated growth in international sales, these companies have recently acquired an increasing number of their distributors to capture more of the profits generated in other countries and maintain better control of international marketing.

Finance

Compared to other apparel firms, the athletic footwear firms generate higher profit margins and rates of return. These firms use cash flow generated from this superior profitability to finance needed working capital investments (receivables and inventories). Long-term debt tends to be relatively low, reflecting the absence of significant investments in manufacturing facilities.

Nike

Nike targets the serious athlete with performance-driven footwear and athletic wear, as well as the recreational athlete. The firm has steadily expanded the scope of its product portfolio from its primary products of high-quality athletic footwear for running, training, basketball, soccer, and casual wear to encompass related product lines such as sports apparel, bags, equipment, balls, eyewear, timepieces, and other athletic accessories. In addition, Nike has expanded its scope of sports, now offering products for swimming, baseball, cheerleading, football, golf, lacrosse, tennis, volleyball, skateboarding, and other leisure activities. In recent years, the firm has emphasized growth outside the United States. Nike also has grown by acquiring other apparel companies, including Cole Haan (dress and casual footwear),

Converse (athletic and casual footwear and apparel), Hurley (apparel for action sports such as surfing, skateboarding, and snowboarding), and Umbro (footwear, apparel, and equipment for soccer). The firm sums up the company's philosophy and driving force behind its success as follows: "Nike designs, develops, and markets high quality footwear, apparel, equipment and accessory products worldwide. We are the largest seller of athletic footwear and apparel in the world. Our strategy is to achieve long-term revenue growth by creating innovative, 'must-have' products; building deep, personal consumer connections with our brands; and delivering compelling retail presentation and experiences."

To maintain its technological edge, Nike engages in extensive research at its research facilities in Beaverton, Oregon. It continually alters its product line to introduce new footwear, apparel, equipment, and evolutionary improvements in existing products.

Nike maintains a reputation for timely delivery of footwear products to its customers, primarily as a result of its "Futures" ordering program. Under this program, retailers book orders five to six months in advance. Nike guarantees delivery of the order within a set time period at the agreed price at the time of ordering. Approximately 89 percent of the U.S. footwear orders received by Nike during 2009 came though its Futures program. This program allows the company to improve production scheduling, thereby reducing inventory risk. However, the program locks in selling prices and increases Nike's risk of increased raw materials and labor costs.

Independent contractors manufacture virtually all of Nike's products. Nike sources all of its footwear and approximately 95 percent of its apparel from other countries.

The following exhibits present information for Nike:

Exhibit 1.31: Consolidated balance sheets for 2007, 2008, and 2009
Exhibit 1.32: Consolidated income statements for 2007, 2008, and 2009
Exhibit 1.33: Consolidated statements of cash flows 2007, 2008, and 2009
Exhibit 1.34: Excerpts from the notes to Nike's financial statements
Exhibit 1.35: Common-size and percentage change income statements
Exhibit 1.36: Common-size and percentage change balance sheets

Required

Study the financial statements and notes for Nike and respond to the following questions.

Income Statement

    a. Identify the time at which Nike recognizes revenues. Does this timing of revenue recognition seem appropriate? Explain.

    b. Identify the cost-flow assumption(s) that Nike uses to measure cost of goods sold. Does Nike's choice of cost-flow assumption(s) seem appropriate? Explain.

    c. Nike reports property, plant, and equipment on its balance sheet and discloses the amount of depreciation for each year in its statement of cash flows. Why doesn't depreciation expense appear among its expenses on the income statement?

    d. Identify the portion of Nike's income tax expense of $469.8 million for 2009 that is currently payable to governmental entities and the portion that is deferred to future years. Why is the amount currently payable to governmental entities in 2009 greater than the income tax expense?

Balance Sheet

    e. Why do accounts receivable appear net of allowance for doubtful accounts? Identify the events or transactions that cause the allowance account to increase or decrease.

    f. Identify the depreciation method(s) that Nike uses for its buildings and equipment. Does Nike's choice of depreciation method(s) seem appropriate?

EXHIBIT 1.31

Consolidated Balance Sheet for Nike
(amounts in millions)
(Case 1.2)

As of Fiscal Year-End May 31	2007	2008	2009
ASSETS			
Current Assets			
Cash and equivalents	$ 1,856.7	$ 2,133.9	$ 2,291.1
Short-term investments	990.3	642.2	1,164.0
Accounts receivable	2,494.7	2,795.3	2,883.9
Inventories	2,121.9	2,438.4	2,357.0
Prepaid expenses and other assets	393.2	602.3	765.6
Deferred income taxes, net	219.7	227.2	272.4
Total Current Assets	$ 8,076.5	$ 8,839.3	$ 9,734.0
Property and equipment, gross	3,619.1	4,103.0	4,255.7
Accumulated depreciation	(1,940.8)	(2,211.9)	(2,298.0)
Property and equipment, net	$ 1,678.3	$ 1,891.1	$ 1,957.7
Identifiable intangible assets	409.9	743.1	467.4
Goodwill	130.8	448.8	193.5
Deferred income taxes and other assets	392.8	520.4	897.0
Total Assets	$10,688.3	$12,442.7	$13,249.6
LIABILITIES AND STOCKHOLDERS' EQUITY			
Current Liabilities			
Current portion of long-term debt	$ 30.5	$ 6.3	$ 32.0
Notes payable	100.8	177.7	342.9
Accounts payable	1,040.3	1,287.6	1,031.9
Accrued liabilities	1,303.4	1,761.9	1,783.9
Income taxes payable	109.0	88.0	86.3
Total Current Liabilities	$ 2,584.0	$ 3,321.5	$ 3,277.0
Long-term debt	409.9	441.1	437.2
Deferred taxes and other long-term liabilities	668.7	854.5	842.0
Total Liabilities	$ 3,662.6	$ 4,617.1	$ 4,556.2
Redeemable preferred stock	$ 0.3	$ 0.3	$ 0.3
Common Shareholders' Equity			
Common stock	2.8	2.8	2.8
Capital in excess of stated value	1,960.0	2,497.8	2,871.4
Retained earnings	4,885.2	5,073.3	5,451.4
Accumulated other comprehensive income	177.4	251.4	367.5
Total Common Shareholders' Equity	$ 7,025.4	$ 7,825.3	$ 8,693.1
Total Liabilities and Shareholders' Equity	$10,688.3	$12,442.7	$13,249.6

EXHIBIT 1.32

Consolidated Income Statement for Nike
(amounts in millions except per share figures)
(Case 1.2)

Fiscal Years Ended May 31:	2007	2008	2009
Revenues	$16,325.9	$ 18,627.0	$ 19,176.1
Cost of sales	(9,165.4)	(10,239.6)	(10,571.7)
Gross Profit	$ 7,160.5	$ 8,387.4	$ 8,604.4
Selling and administrative expenses	(5,028.7)	(5,953.7)	(6,149.6)
Restructuring charges	—	—	(195.0)
Goodwill impairment	—	—	(199.3)
Intangible and other asset impairment	—	—	(202.0)
Other income (expenses)	0.9	(7.9)	88.5
Operating Income	$ 2,132.7	$ 2,425.8	$ 1,947.0
Interest and other income	116.9	115.8	49.7
Interest expense	(49.7)	(38.7)	(40.2)
Income before income taxes	$ 2,199.9	$ 2,502.9	$ 1,956.5
Provision for income taxes	(708.4)	(619.5)	(469.8)
Net Income	$ 1,491.5	$ 1,883.4	$ 1,486.7
Net income per share			
Basic	$ 2.96	$ 3.80	$ 3.07
Diluted	$ 2.93	$ 3.74	$ 3.03

g. Nike includes identifiable intangible assets on its balance sheet as an asset. Does this account include the value of the Nike name and Nike's "swoosh" trademark? Explain.

h. Nike includes deferred income taxes among current assets, noncurrent assets, and noncurrent liabilities. Under what circumstances will deferred income taxes give rise to an asset? To a liability?

i. Nike reports accumulated other comprehensive income of $367.5 million at the end of 2009 and $251.4 million at the end of 2008, implying that other comprehensive income items amounted to $116.1 million during 2009. Why is this "income" reported as part of shareholders' equity and not part of net income in the income statement?

Statement of Cash Flows

j. Why does the amount of net income differ from the amount of cash flow from operations?

k. Why does Nike add depreciation expense back to net income when calculating cash flow from operations?

l. Why does Nike subtract deferred income taxes from net income when calculating cash flow from operations for 2009?

m. Why does Nike subtract increases in accounts receivable to net income when calculating cash flow from operations for 2009?

EXHIBIT 1.33

Consolidated Statement of Cash Flows for Nike
(amounts in millions)
(Case 1.2)

Fiscal Years Ended May 31:	2007	2008	2009
OPERATING ACTIVITIES:			
Net income	$ 1,491.5	$ 1,883.4	$1,486.7
Depreciation	269.7	303.6	335.0
Deferred income taxes, net	34.1	(300.6)	(294.1)
Stock-based compensation	147.7	141.0	170.6
Impairments of goodwill, intangibles and other assets	—	—	401.3
Gain on divestiture	—	(60.6)	—
Amortization and other	0.5	17.9	48.3
Changes in operating assets and liabilities:			
Increase in accounts receivable	(39.6)	(118.3)	(238.0)
Decrease (increase) in inventories	(49.5)	(249.8)	32.2
Decrease (increase) in prepaid expenses	(60.8)	(11.2)	14.1
(Decrease) increase in payables and accrued liabilities	85.1	330.9	(220.0)
Cash Provided by Operations	$ 1,878.7	$ 1,936.3	$1,736.1
INVESTING ACTIVITIES:			
Purchases, sales, maturities of investment securities	$ 382.4	$ 380.4	$ (518.7)
Net additions to property, plant, and equipment	(285.2)	(447.3)	(423.7)
Acquisition of subsidiary, net of cash acquired	—	(571.1)	—
Proceeds from divestiture	—	246.0	—
Other investing activities	(4.3)	(97.8)	144.3
Cash Used in (Provided by) Investing Activities	$ 92.9	$ (489.8)	$ (798.1)
FINANCING ACTIVITIES:			
Proceeds from notes payable	$ 52.6	$ 63.7	$ 177.1
Net (payments on) proceeds from long-term debt	(213.9)	(35.2)	(6.8)
Proceeds from exercise of stock options	322.9	343.3	186.6
Excess tax benefit from exercise of stock options	55.8	63.0	25.1
Repurchases of common equity shares	(985.2)	(1,248.0)	(649.2)
Dividends—common and preferred	(343.7)	(412.9)	(466.7)
Cash Used by Financing Activities	$(1,111.5)	$(1,226.1)	$ (733.9)
Effects of exchange rate changes on cash	$ 42.4	$ 56.8	$ (46.9)
Net Change in Cash and Cash Equivalents	$ 902.5	$ 277.2	$ 157.2
Beginning Cash and Cash Equivalents	954.2	1,856.7	2,133.9
Ending Cash and Cash Equivalents	$ 1,856.7	$ 2,133.9	$2,291.1

EXHIBIT 1.34

Excerpts from Notes to Consolidated Financial Statements for Nike
(amounts in millions)
(Case 1.2)

Summary of Significant Accounting Policies

Recognition of Revenues: Nike recognizes wholesale revenues when the risks and rewards of ownership have passed to the customer, based on the terms of sale. This occurs upon shipment or upon receipt by the customer depending on the country of the sale and the agreement with the customer. Nike recognizes revenue at time of retail sales to its customers. Provisions for sales discounts and returns are made at the time of sale.

Allowance for Uncollectible Accounts Receivable: Accounts receivable consists principally of amounts receivable from customers. Nike makes ongoing estimates relating to the collectability of our accounts receivable and maintains an allowance for estimated losses resulting from the inability of our customers to make required payments. The allowance for uncollectible accounts receivable was $110.8 million and $78.4 million at May 31, 2009 and 2008, respectively.

Inventory Valuation: Inventories appear at lower of cost or market. Nike determines cost using the first-in, first-out (FIFO) method.

Property, Plant, and Equipment and Depreciation: Property, plant, and equipment are recorded at acquisition cost. Nike computes depreciation using the straight-line method. Estimated useful lives are over 2 to 40 years for buildings and leasehold improvements; over 2 to 15 years for machinery and equipment; and over 3 to 10 years for computer software.

Identifiable Intangible Assets and Goodwill: This account represents the excess of the purchase price of acquired businesses over the market values of identifiable net assets, net of amortization to date on assets with limited lives.

Foreign Currency Translation: Adjustments resulting from translating foreign functional currency financial statements into U.S. dollars and gains and losses from derivatives that Nike uses to hedge changes in exchange rate are included in accumulated other comprehensive income.

Income Taxes: Nike provides deferred income taxes for temporary differences between income before taxes for financial reporting and tax reporting. Income tax expense includes the following:

	2007	2008	2009
Currently Payable	$674.1	$920.1	$763.9
Deferred	34.3	(300.6)	(294.1)
Income Tax Expense	$708.4	$619.5	$469.8

Stock Repurchases: Nike repurchases outstanding shares of its common stock each year and retires them. Any difference between the price paid and the book value of the shares appears as an adjustment of retained earnings.

n. Why does Nike adjust net income by subtracting increases in inventory and adding decreases in inventory when calculating cash flow from operations?

o. When calculating cash flow from operations, why does Nike adjust net income by adding increases and subtracting decreases in accounts payable and other current liabilities?

p. Nike recognized a gain from the divestiture of the subsidiary for the Bauer line of hockey apparel and equipment in 2008. Why does Nike subtract the gain on the

EXHIBIT 1.35

Common-Size and Percentage Change Income Statements for Nike (Case 1.2)

Fiscal Years Ended May 31:	Common-Size Income Statements			Percentage Change Income Statements			
	2007	2008	2009	2008	2009	Compound Growth	
Revenues	100.0%	100.0%	100.0%	14.1%	2.9%	8.4%	
Cost of sales	(56.1%)	(55.0%)	(55.1%)	11.7%	3.2%	7.4%	
Gross Profit	43.9%	45.0%	44.9%	17.1%	2.6%	9.6%	
Selling and administrative expenses	(30.8%)	(32.0%)	(32.1%)	18.4%	3.3%	10.6%	
Restructuring charges	0.0%	0.0%	(1.0%)	n.m.	n.m.	n.m.	
Goodwill impairment	0.0%	0.0%	(1.0%)	n.m.	n.m.	n.m.	
Intangible and other asset impairment	0.0%	0.0%	(1.1%)	n.m.	n.m.	n.m.	
Other income (expenses)	0.0%	0.0%	0.5%	n.m.	n.m.	n.m.	
Operating Income	13.1%	13.0%	10.2%	13.7%	(19.7%)	(4.5%)	
Interest and other income	0.7%	0.6%	0.3%	(0.9%)	(57.1%)	(34.8%)	
Interest expense	(0.3%)	(0.2%)	(0.2%)	(22.1%)	3.9%	(10.1%)	
Income before income taxes	13.5%	13.4%	10.3%	13.8%	(21.8%)	(5.7%)	
Provision for income taxes	(4.4%)	(3.3%)	(2.5%)	(12.5%)	(24.2%)	(18.6%)	
Net Income	9.1%	10.1%	7.8%	26.3%	(21.1%)	(0.2%)	

EXHIBIT 1.36

Common-Size and Percentage Change Balance Sheets for Nike
(Case 1.2)

As of Fiscal Year End May 31	Common-Size Balance Sheets			Percentage Change Balance Sheets		Compound Growth
	2007	2008	2009	2008	2009	
ASSETS						
Current Assets						
Cash and equivalents	17.4%	17.1%	17.3%	14.9%	7.4%	11.1%
Short-term investments	9.3%	5.2%	8.8%	(35.2%)	81.3%	8.4%
Accounts receivable	23.3%	22.5%	21.8%	12.0%	3.2%	7.5%
Inventories	19.9%	19.6%	17.8%	14.9%	(3.3%)	5.4%
Prepaid expenses and other assets	3.7%	4.8%	5.8%	53.2%	27.1%	39.5%
Deferred income taxes, net	2.0%	1.8%	2.0%	3.4%	19.9%	11.3%
Total Current Assets	75.6%	71.0%	73.5%	9.4%	10.1%	9.8%
Property and equipment, gross	33.9%	33.0%	32.1%	13.4%	3.7%	8.4%
Accumulated depreciation	(18.2%)	(17.8%)	(17.3%)	14.0%	3.9%	8.8%
Property and equipment, net	15.7%	15.2%	14.8%	12.7%	3.5%	8.0%
Identifiable intangible assets	3.8%	6.0%	3.5%	81.3%	(37.1%)	6.8%
Goodwill	1.2%	3.6%	1.4%	243.1%	(56.9%)	21.6%
Deferred income taxes and other assets	3.7%	4.2%	6.8%	32.5%	72.4%	51.1%
Total Assets	100.0%	100.0%	100.0%	16.4%	6.5%	11.3%

(Continued)

EXHIBIT 1.36 (Continued)

As of Fiscal Year End May 31	Common-Size Balance Sheets			Percentage Change Balance Sheets		
	2007	2008	2009	2008	2009	Compound Growth
LIABILITIES AND STOCKHOLDERS' EQUITY						
Current Liabilities						
Current portion of long-term debt	0.3%	0.1%	0.2%	(79.3%)	407.9%	2.4%
Notes payable	1.0%	1.4%	2.6%	76.3%	93.0%	84.4%
Accounts payable	9.7%	10.3%	7.8%	23.8%	(19.9%)	(0.4%)
Accrued liabilities	12.2%	14.2%	13.4%	35.2%	1.2%	17.0%
Income taxes payable	1.0%	0.7%	0.7%	(19.3%)	(1.9%)	(11.0%)
Total Current Liabilities	24.2%	26.7%	24.7%	28.5%	(1.3%)	12.6%
Long-term debt	3.8%	3.5%	3.3%	7.6%	(0.9%)	3.3%
Deferred taxes and other long-term liabilities	6.3%	6.9%	6.4%	27.8%	(1.5%)	12.2%
Total Liabilities	34.3%	37.1%	34.4%	26.1%	(1.3%)	11.5%
Redeemable preferred stock	0.0%	0.0%	0.0%	0.0%	0.0%	0.0%
Common Shareholders' Equity						
Common stock	0.0%	0.0%	0.0%	0.0%	0.0%	0.0%
Capital in excess of stated value	18.3%	20.1%	21.7%	27.4%	15.0%	21.0%
Retained earnings	45.7%	40.8%	41.1%	3.9%	7.5%	5.6%
Accumulated other comprehensive income	1.7%	2.0%	2.8%	41.7%	46.2%	43.9%
Total Common Shareholders' Equity	65.7%	62.9%	65.6%	11.4%	11.1%	11.2%
Total Liabilities and Shareholders' Equity	100.0%	100.0%	100.0%	16.4%	6.5%	11.3%

divestiture from the operating activities? Why does Nike include the proceeds from the divestiture as an investing activity?

q. Given that notes payable appear on the balance sheet as a current liability, why does Nike include increases in this liability as a financing activity rather than as an operating activity?

Relations between Financial Statement Items

r. Compute the amount of cash collected from customers during 2009.

s. Compute the amount of cash payments made to suppliers of merchandise during 2009.

t. Prepare an analysis that accounts for the change in the property, plant, and equipment account and the accumulated depreciation account during 2009. You will have to plug certain amounts if Nike does not disclose them.

u. Identify the reasons for the change in retained earnings during 2009.

Interpreting Financial Statement Relationships

v. Exhibit 1.35 presents common-size and percentage change income statements for Nike for 2007, 2008, and 2009. What are the likely reasons for the higher net income/sales revenue percentages for Nike between 2007 and 2008? What are the likely reasons for the lower net income/sales revenue percentages for Nike between 2008 and 2009?

w. What are the likely reasons for the decrease in the cost of goods sold to sales percentages between 2007 and 2009?

x. What are the likely reasons for the increase in the selling and administrative expenses to sales percentages between 2007 and 2009?

y. Exhibit 1.36 presents common-size and percentage change balance sheets for Nike at the end of 2007, 2008, and 2009. What is the likely explanation for the relatively small percentages for property, plant, and equipment?

z. What is the likely explanation for the relatively small percentages for notes payable and long-term debt?

aa. What is the likely explanation for the small decreases in property, plant, and equipment for Nike for 2008 and 2009?

bb. Refer to the statement of cash flows for Nike in Exhibit 1.33. Cash flow from operations exceeded net income during all three years. Why?

cc. How has Nike primarily financed its acquisitions of property, plant, and equipment during the three years?

dd. What are the likely reasons for the repurchases of common stock during the three years?

ee. The dividends paid by Nike increased each year ($343.7 million in 2007, $412.9 million in 2008, and $466.7 million in 2009). Given that Nike repurchased its stock each year, what is the likely explanation for the increasing amount of dividends?

Chapter 4

Profitability Analysis

Learning Objectives

1 Evaluate firm profitability using the primary measure of firm performance—net income—as well as profitability analysis techniques including per share analysis, common-size analysis, percentage change analysis, and alternative measures of income.

2 Analyze and interpret levels of and changes in the profitability of a firm using the rate of return on assets and its components: profit margin and total assets turnover.

3 Become comfortable linking the effects of economic and strategic factors to the interpretation of the rate of return on assets and its components.

4 Examine other measures of operating performance that supplement the rate of return on assets in assessing profitability, including the integration of nonfinancial and financial measures.

5 Analyze and interpret levels of and changes in the rate of return on common shareholders' equity, including the conditions when a firm uses financial leverage successfully to increase the return to common shareholders.

The primary objective in most financial statement analysis is to value a firm's equity securities. As Chapters 10–14 make clear, the value of an equity security relates to the future *profitability* an investor anticipates relative to the *risk* involved. However, even if the objective is not valuation, but simply performance assessment, financial statement analysis examines aspects of a firm's *profitability* and its *risk*. Examining the profitability of a firm in the recent past provides information that helps the analyst project the firm's future profitability and the expected return from investing in the firm's equity securities. Evaluations of risk involve judgments about a firm's success in managing various dimensions of risk in the past and its ability to manage risks in the future.

This chapter describes several commonly used financial statement analysis techniques for analyzing profitability. Chapter 5 explores the use of financial statements in assessing risk. Both chapters apply these tools of analysis to the financial statements of PepsiCo, which appear in Appendix A. These financial statements also appear as Exhibits 1.9 (balance sheet), Exhibit 1.11 (income statement), and Exhibit 1.14 (statement of cash flows) in Chapter 1. We recommend that you trace the calculation of each financial ratio discussed in this chapter and the next chapter to these financial statements to ensure that you understand the source of the amounts used. The analytical tools discussed in Chapters 4 and 5 provide the framework for the discussion of alternative accounting principles and other data issues in Chapters 6–9 and the valuation of firms in Chapters 10–14. Although we will make some preliminary interpretations of the analytical results for PepsiCo in Chapters 4 and 5, a deeper understanding requires consideration of accounting issues relating to PepsiCo's financial statements, discussed in later chapters.

Our analysis examines changes in the financial ratios for PepsiCo over time, a process referred to as *time-series analysis*, which allows the analyst to address questions about changes over time. Is PepsiCo becoming more or less profitable over time? Is it becoming more or less risky? Are changes in PepsiCo's strategy, economic conditions, competition, or other factors causing its profitability and risk to change? How is management responding to external economic forces? Time-series analysis helps answer these questions.

It also is useful to compare the financial ratios for PepsiCo with those of its competitors, a process referred to as *cross-sectional analysis*. PepsiCo's principal competitor is The Coca-Cola Company (Coca-Cola). We might compare our analysis of PepsiCo with the corresponding financial ratios for Coca-Cola to gain a cross-sectional perspective on the profitability of the two firms. Profitability sometimes appears similar for two firms, but cross-sectional analysis of components of profitability may reveal that similar profitability is driven by different factors across firms. Similarly, we also might compare the results for PepsiCo with average industry ratios, such as those published by Moody's, Robert Morris Associates, Dun & Bradstreet, and others. Appendix D contains averages and other descriptive statistics for the most common ratios across time for 48 industries.

As discussed in Chapter 1, we view financial statement analysis as a three-legged stool (see Exhibit 1.1), which requires the analyst to understand the economics of a firm's industry and markets, the firm's specific strategy within its industry, and the information captured in its financial statements. The analysis of profitability includes, among other things, the analysis of various financial ratios based on numbers from the financial statements. We will discuss many ratios in this chapter. An important concept at this point is that ratios are not metrics to be memorized, but are useful tools that analysts may construct in different ways to capture information relevant to their particular task. Although in this text we demonstrate the most common and theoretically sound approaches to computing and interpreting ratios, some analysts use these ratios somewhat differently. (For example, analysts may vary whether they include gross or net sales or beginning or average asset balances in a ratio.) In particular, ratios differ across industries, especially as analysts following specific industries create and use specialized ratios designed to capture important elements of profitability and risk within that industry (such as revenues per passenger seat mile for airlines and loan loss allowances over total loans among banks). When confronted with ratios prepared by others, you need to understand how those ratios were defined and computed. Although differences in ratio definitions do not always generate substantive differences, sometimes they do.

Chapter 1 introduced the economic characteristics of the beverage industry and the strategy of PepsiCo to compete in this industry. We incorporate this information and other information provided by PepsiCo in its management discussion and analysis, or MD&A (Appendix B), into our interpretations of PepsiCo's financial ratios. Appendix C provides a printout for PepsiCo of FSAP (Financial Statement Analysis Package) available with this book, containing financial ratios computed for PepsiCo. Finally, Appendix D provides descriptive data for the distribution of commonly used financial rations, which provides a useful benchmark for many of the ratios we discuss in this chapter.

OVERVIEW OF PROFITABILITY ANALYSIS

Profitability analysis evaluates whether managers are effectively executing a firm's strategy. With this in mind, we view financial statement analysis as a form of hypothesis testing. For example, knowing that PepsiCo is a leading manufacturer of beverages, snack foods and breakfast foods with well-recognized brands and an international presence, we might hypothesize that PepsiCo is more profitable than the average firm. We can obtain data from the financial statements for PepsiCo and comparable firms to see if this hypothesis is descriptive of PepsiCo's performance. Because there are numerous ways to measure profitability, it is important to approach the many tools for analyzing profitability in an organized manner. In this chapter, using PepsiCo as an example, we discuss the analysis of profitability as a step-by-step examination of different layers of financial information.

Although firms must report comprehensive income, net income, or earnings, remains the key measure of profitability. Dhaliwal, Subramanyam, and Trezevant (1999) examined the association between stock returns and comprehensive income and its components.[1] With the exception of firms in the financial industry, net income is more strongly associated with stock returns than comprehensive income. Our purpose in analyzing profitability is to generate an understanding of a firm's performance to enable forecasts of future performance. Other comprehensive income amounts exhibit a very low level of persistence. Thus, we focus on net income as our primary measure of profitability, with the caveat that components of other comprehensive income for certain firms should not be automatically dismissed.[2] Different approaches to analyzing a firm's profitability are aimed at generating a deeper understanding of net income. The emphasis in this chapter is on the conceptual framework for analyzing net income in the context of a firm's overall financial statements. Obviously, Chapters 2 and 3 have laid important foundations of understanding how assets and liabilities and income are measured and how net income and cash flows differ. In addition, accounting method choices will affect the financial statements and the measurement of net income, topics discussed in Chapters 6–9. This chapter will address some accounting measurement effects on profitability, with later chapters providing more comprehensive discussion of these effects.

Exhibit 4.1 provides a diagram of the approaches to analyzing net income. The diagram begins with net income, which is the summary measure of profits from the income statement. From net income, two branches represent alternative approaches to better understanding firms' net income. On the left, the approach is to analyze alternative transformations of measured net income. The next four sections discuss the following approaches: earnings per share analysis, common-size analysis, percentage change analysis, and alternative definitions of profits. These are straightforward approaches to understand, so the majority of this chapter will focus on the right side of the diagram, which frames profitability in terms of rate of return metrics. Rates of return integrate information from the income statement and the balance sheet to compute various profitability metrics, the most common being ROA (return on total assets) and ROCE (return on common equity). Most of this chapter will focus on understanding how to interpret ROCE and ROA, as these are key metrics in the discussions of accounting quality in Chapters 6–9 and forecasting and valuation in Chapters 10–14. As Exhibit 4.1 shows, ROA and ROCE can be decomposed into measures of margin, turnover,

---

[1]Dan Dhaliwal, K. R. Subramanyam, and Robert Trezevant, "Is Comprehensive Income Superior to Net Income as a Measure of Firm Performance?" *Journal of Accounting and Economics* Vol. 26, Issues 1–3 (January 1999) pp. 43–67.

[2]For example, one possibility for the findings that components of other comprehensive income do not correlate strongly with stock prices is that investors are inappropriately downplaying the importance of these components. Indeed, a subsequent study confirmed that items of other comprehensive income are treated as transitory by investors, which leads to investors pricing the value of other comprehensive income on a dollar-for-dollar basis. See Dennis Chambers, Thomas J. Linsmeier, Catherine Shakespeare, and Theodore Sougiannis, "An Evaluation of SFAS No. 130 Comprehensive Income Disclosures." *Review of Accounting Studies* Vol. 12, No. 4 (December 2007).

EXHIBIT 4.1

Diagram of Alternative Approaches to Analyzing Net Income

Net Income

Alternative computations or measures of profits

Rate of return analysis

Per-share analysis

Common-size analysis

Percentage change analysis

Alternative definitions of profits

Return on total assets (ROA)

Return on common equity (ROCE)

Margin × Turnover × Leverage

Various expense ratios

Various asset utilization ratios

Operating vs. financial leverage

---

and leverage, which facilitate a deeper understanding of how a firm is generating wealth for its shareholders. The dashed lines for the decomposition of ROCE into margin (and leverage) highlight that there are differences in the decompositions for ROA and ROCE, as will be discussed later (under the section "Relating ROA to ROCE"). The primary difference is that profit margins for ROA and ROCE are computed based on different measures of income in the numerator. Finally, the measures of margin, turnover, and leverage can be further dissected by means of various financial ratios prepared from different line items in the financial statements. Later sections in the chapter discuss ROA and ROCE, including the decomposition into components and various explanatory ratios. However, note that the two branches of analysis of net income displayed in Exhibit 4.1 are interrelated, especially the use of common-size analysis and alternative definitions of profits. Both of these can be incorporated into rate of return analysis, as we will do later in the chapter.

EARNINGS PER SHARE (EPS)

One of the most frequently used measures of profitability is EPS (earnings per common share). As Chapter 14 discusses more fully, analysts and investors frequently use multiples of EPS, referred to as *price-earnings ratios,* to value firms. EPS is the only financial ratio that GAAP requires firms to disclose on the face of the income statement and is covered explicitly by the opinion of the independent auditor.[3] This section briefly describes the calculation of EPS and discusses some of its uses and limitations.

---

[3]Financial Accounting Standards Board, *Statement of Financial Accounting Standards No. 128,* "Earnings per Share" (1997), *FASB Codification Topic 260.* International Accounting Standards Board, *International Accounting Standard No. 33,* "Earnings Per Share" (2003).

Calculating EPS

Simple Capital Structure: Basic EPS

Firms that do not have (1) outstanding convertible bonds or convertible preferred stock that holders can exchange for shares of common stock or (2) options or warrants that holders can use to acquire common stock have *simple* capital structures. For such firms, the accountant calculates basic EPS as follows:

$$\frac{\text{Basic EPS}}{\text{(Simple Capital Structure)}} = \frac{\text{Net Income} - \text{Preferred Stock Dividends}}{\substack{\text{Weighted Average Number of} \\ \text{Common Shares Outstanding}}}$$

The deduction of preferred stock dividends from net income yields income available to common shareholders, the residual claimants on a firm's profits. The numerator of basic EPS is adjusted for preferred stock dividends because the denominator includes only common shares outstanding. The denominator is a daily weighted average of common shares outstanding during the period, reflecting new stock issues, treasury stock acquisitions, and similar transactions.

Example 1. Cat Corporation had the following capital structure during its most recent year:

	January 1	December 31
Preferred Stock, $20 Par Value, 500 Shares Issued and Outstanding	$ 10,000	$ 10,000
Common Stock, $10 Par Value, 4,000 Shares Issued	40,000	40,000
Additional Paid-In Capital	50,000	50,000
Retained Earnings	80,000	85,600
Treasury Shares—Common (1,000 shares)	—	(30,000)
Total Shareholders' Equity	$180,000	$155,600

Retained earnings changed during the year as follows:

Retained Earnings, January 1	$ 80,000
Plus Net Income	7,500
Less Dividends:	
Preferred Stock	(500)
Common Stock	(1,400)
Retained Earnings, December 31	$ 85,600

The preferred stock is not convertible into common stock. The firm acquired 1,000 shares of treasury stock on July 1. No stock options or warrants are outstanding. The calculation of basic earnings per share for Cat Corporation follows:

$$\text{Basic EPS} = \frac{\$7,500 - \$500}{(0.5 \times 4,000) + (0.5 \times 3,000)} = \frac{\$7,000}{3,500} = \$2 \text{ per share}$$

Complex Capital Structure: Diluted EPS

Firms that have convertible securities and/or stock options or warrants outstanding have *complex* capital structures. Such firms must present two EPS amounts: basic EPS and diluted EPS. Diluted EPS reflects the dilution potential of convertible securities, options, and warrants. Dilution refers to the reduction in basic EPS that would result if holders of convertible securities exchanged them for shares of common stock or if holders of stock options or warrants exercised them. Firms include in diluted EPS calculations only those securities, options, and warrants that would reduce EPS; income and share dilution effects of equity instruments are excluded from both the numerator and denominator if their conversion would increase EPS (such securities would be referred to as "out of the money" and their effect on EPS as "antidilutive"). Accordingly, diluted EPS will always be less than (or equal to) basic EPS. This section describes the calculation of diluted EPS in general terms.

$$\text{Diluted EPS (Complex Capital Structure)} = \frac{\text{Net Income} - \text{Preferred Stock Dividends} + \text{Adjustments for Dilutive Securities}}{\text{Weighted Average Number of Common Shares Outstanding} + \text{Weighted Average Number of Shares Issuable from Dilutive Securities}}$$

Adjustments for dilutive securities and the adjustment to weighted average number of shares outstanding presumes that the dilutive securities are converted to common shares *as of the beginning of the year*. To calculate diluted EPS, the accountant assumes the conversion of convertible bonds and convertible preferred stock and the exercise of stock options and warrants if their effect would be dilutive. The accountant adds back any interest expense (net of taxes) on convertible bonds and dividends on convertible preferred stock the firm subtracted in computing net income to common shareholders. Consistency would suggest that the accountant also add back to net income any compensation expense recognized on the employee stock options. However, U.S. GAAP and IFRS do not stipulate such an addback, but instead require firms to incorporate any unamortized compensation expense on those options into the calculation of the denominator of diluted EPS, as discussed next.

The diluted EPS computation adds common shares issuable on conversion of bonds and preferred stock and exercise of stock options and warrants to the denominator. The computation of the additional shares to be issued on the exercise of stock options assumes that the firm would repurchase common shares on the open market using an amount equal to the sum of (1) any cash proceeds from such exercise, (2) any unamortized compensation expense on those options, and (3) any tax benefits that would be credited to additional paid-in capital.[4] Only the net incremental shares issued (shares issued under options minus assumed shares repurchased) enter the computation of diluted EPS.

---

[4]Understanding the rationale for including unamortized compensation expense in the computation of the incremental shares issuable requires an understanding of the accounting for stock options, which is discussed in Chapter 6. In general terms, U.S. GAAP and IFRS view the value of stock options as a substitute for cash compensation. Firms expense this value over the expected period of benefit, which usually begins in the year firms grant the options and continues until the vesting date. The assumption underlying diluted EPS is that employees have exercised the options and the firm realizes a pseudo cash savings equal to the value of options not yet recognized, or amortized.

Example 2. Assume that Dawg Corporation has the same capital structure as Cat Corporation, except the preferred stock of Dawg Corporation is convertible into 1,000 shares of common stock. Also assume that Dawg Corporation has stock options outstanding that holders can currently exchange for 300 incremental shares of common stock.[5] The calculation of diluted EPS is as follows:

$$\text{Diluted EPS} = \frac{\$7,500 - \$500 + \$500}{(0.5 \times 4,000) + (0.5 \times 3,000) + (1.0 \times 1,000) + (1.0 \times 300)} = \frac{\$7,500}{4,800}$$

$$= \$1.56$$

The calculation assumes the conversion of the convertible preferred stock into common stock as of January 1. If conversion had taken place, the firm would not have paid preferred dividends during the year. Thus, the accountant adds back to the numerator of fully diluted earnings per share the $500 of preferred dividends, which the accountant subtracted in computing net income available to common stock when calculating basic earnings per share. The weighted average number of shares in the denominator increases for the 1,000 common shares the firm would issue on conversion of the preferred stock. The weighted average number of shares in the denominator also increases for the incremental shares issuable under stock option plans.

Refer to the income statement of PepsiCo in Appendix A. PepsiCo reports basic EPS of $3.26 and diluted EPS of $3.21 for 2008. PepsiCo's Note 11, "Net Income per Common Share" (Appendix A), shows the calculation of its EPS amounts. Basic EPS shows a subtraction from net income for preferred dividends. It also shows a subtraction for the redemption premium that PepsiCo paid when it redeemed some of the outstanding preferred stock.[6] Note 11 also indicates that the numerator of diluted EPS shows an addition for ESOP convertible preferred stock, which is dilutive; so the preferred dividends and redemption premium are added back to the numerator before calculating diluted EPS (based on the beginning-of-year conversion assumption). PepsiCo also reports the additional common shares issuable under stock option plans and from the convertible ESOP convertible preferred stock.

Criticisms of EPS

Critics of EPS as a measure of profitability point out that it does not consider the amount of assets or capital required to generate a particular level of earnings. Two firms with the same earnings and EPS are not equally profitable if one firm requires twice the amount of assets or capital to generate those earnings compared to the other firm. Also, the number of shares of common stock outstanding serves as a poor measure of the amount of capital in use. The number of shares outstanding usually relates to a firm's attempts to achieve a desirable trading range for its common stock. Suppose a firm has an aggregate market value for its common shares of $10 million. If the firm has 500,000 shares outstanding, the shares will sell for $20 per share. If the firm has 1 million shares outstanding, the shares will sell for $10 per share. The amount of capital in place is the same in both instances, but the number of shares outstanding (and therefore EPS) are different. A comparison of the EPS of PepsiCo and Coca-Cola is an example of how different EPS figures are not comparable. For 2008, Coca-Cola

---

[5]We are simplifying this example with the assumption of 300 *incremental* shares. An actual calculation would require separate computation of the proceeds from exercise, unamortized compensation expense, and associated tax benefits.

[6]The treatment of redemption premia in calculating basic EPS occurs infrequently and is beyond the scope of this book.

reported net income of $5.8 billion, higher than PepsiCo's $5.1 billion; however, PepsiCo reported higher basic EPS of $3.26 versus $2.51 for Coca-Cola because the two firms have very different numbers of shares outstanding. The comparison of EPS is not definitive about the relative performance of these two companies. Two firms can have identical earnings, common shareholders' equities, and ROCEs, but their EPSs will differ if they have different numbers of shares outstanding. Also, EPS is an ambiguous measure of changes in profitability over time because changes in shares outstanding over time can have disproportionate effects on the numerator and denominator. For example, a firm can experience reduced earnings during the year but report a higher EPS than it did the previous year if it repurchased sufficient shares during the period. When assessing earnings performance, the analyst must separate the impact of these two factors on EPS.

Despite these criticisms of EPS as a measure of profitability, it remains one of the focal points of the quarterly earnings announcement season and analysts frequently use it in valuing firms. The reason for its ubiquity is the direct comparability to firms' share prices. Chapter 14 discusses the use of EPS in valuation.

COMMON-SIZE ANALYSIS

A simple way of creating greater comparability across firms and for the same firm through time is common-size analysis. Common-size analysis is most frequently utilized in the analysis of profitability (the income statement), but it also can be used in the analysis of financial position (the balance sheet). Common-size income statements express all line items scaled by revenues (generally the largest line item on the income statement and the driver of many expenses); common-size balance sheets express all line items scaled by total assets (generally the largest line item on the balance sheet and reflective of resources used to generate returns to all providers of capital). Through the use of a common denominator, the common scaling enables figures across firms and across time (for the same firm) to be more comparable. For example, suppose a firm has ten times the sales of a competitor. The profitability of the two firms can be compared more meaningfully by scaling net income and the individual expense line items to a common denominator (each firm's total revenues) to remove the large discrepancy in the size of the two firms' operations.

Chapter 1 introduced common-size financial statements and examined PepsiCo and Coca-Cola (both a cross-sectional and a time-series analysis) for 2004–2008. Refer to Exhibits 1.18 and 1.20. The 2008 common-size figures scaled by revenues suggest that Coca-Cola shows a more favorable gross profit of 64 percent of revenues, relative to 53 percent for PepsiCo. Selling, general, and administrative expenses are similar for both companies, both being approximately 37 percent of revenues. Other line items contribute relatively limited differences, and the substantial difference in gross profits contributes to higher common-size net income for Coca-Cola relative to PepsiCo. Common-size analysis is a simple but powerful approach to understanding profitability. For example, the analyses in Exhibits 1.18 and 1.20 suggest that Coca-Cola realizes substantially higher profitability per dollar of sales than PepsiCo. However, to more deeply understand this comparison, an analyst must perform additional analysis to understand that a primary explanation for the higher gross profit at Coca-Cola is substantially greater presence and profitability in international beverage markets, despite PepsiCo's domestic operations being more profitable than those of Coca-Cola.

The common-size analysis of profitability across firms can be extended to time-series analysis as well. For example, Exhibits 1.18 and 1.20 show income statement data for five years for PepsiCo and Coca-Cola, respectively. Examining the time series for each company may suggest the direction in which various expenses are going. As noted previously, the primary difference between PepsiCo's and Coca-Cola's profitability in 2008 is due to the higher gross profit margins for Coca-Cola. Examining the trend in gross profit over the period 2004–2008 indicates that Coca-Cola's gross profit has varied from 64–66 percent, with no apparent trend. In contrast, PepsiCo's gross profit has ranged between 53 and 57 percent, with a monotonic downward trend. This suggests that PepsiCo's input costs are rising at a higher rate than increases in sales revenue or that the prices it is charging for products is declining or that it is shifting its revenue mix to lower margin products and markets. The MD&A suggests that pricing is generally increasing, so input prices must be the explanation. As discussed later in the chapter, PepsiCo reports that a primary driver of the decreased gross profit margin is higher commodity costs that could not be passed through to customers via price increases (for example, cooking oil and fuel).

Common-size analysis requires the analyst to be aware that percentages can change because of:

- changes in expenses in the numerator independent of changes in sales (for example, an increase in employee compensation levels),
- changes in sales independent of changes in expenses (for example, because the expense being examined is fixed for the period),
- interaction effects between the numerator and denominator (an increase in advertising expenses leads to an increase in sales), or
- coincident but independent changes in the numerator and denominator (that is, combinations of the other three possibilities).

Thus, although common-size analysis is useful, to fully understand patterns it reveals, the analyst must dig deeper into the economics of the firm's environment and the firm's strategy during the period being analyzed, as well as conduct further financial analysis using finer partitions of data. **That is why the six-step analytical framework of this book begins with an analysis of the firm's economic environment and strategy.** Note that FSAP performs the task of computing common-size financial statements automatically.

PERCENTAGE CHANGE ANALYSIS

Another way to analyze financial data is to compute percentage changes in individual line items, which also can be compared across firms or across time. Common-size analysis is useful because the process of dividing all line items on a financial statement by a common measure standardizes financial data such that the analyst can then compare different firms or the same firm across time. Percentage change analysis also permits the analyst to compare financial data because the transformations into percentage changes are comparable across firms or across time as well. However, the focus is not on the financial data themselves, but on the changes in individual line items through time. Percentage change analysis was introduced briefly in Chapter 1 along with common-size analysis. In addition to common-size figures, Exhibits 1.17 and 1.19 (balance sheets) and Exhibits 1.18 and 1.20 (income statements) also provide percentage change figures for PepsiCo and Coca-Cola, respectively, over 2005–2008. Note the loss of one year of data relative to common-size analysis, which simply reflects that financial data for 2004–2008 are required for computing changes; thus, five years of data yields four changes.

In the common-size analysis discussed above, we noted significant differences in the gross profit percentages between PepsiCo and Coca-Cola. The analyst might be further interested in whether there are trends in gross profits as a percentage of sales for PepsiCo relative to Coca-Cola. An increasing difference between the two companies would indicate that PepsiCo's performance is declining relative to Coca-Cola's; a decreasing difference would indicate the opposite. Examining percentage change analysis is helpful in further understanding differences revealed in common-size analysis. Refer to Exhibits 1.18 and 1.20, which show four-year percentage change analyses for PepsiCo and Coca-Cola, respectively. During 2005–2006, PepsiCo's revenue growth exceeded that of Coca-Cola, but this reversed in 2007–2008. More importantly, the percentage change of PepsiCo's cost of sales exceeds the percentage change in revenues for each year, which results in the decreased gross profits highlighted in the common-size analysis above. In addition, PepsiCo shows double-digit increases in SG&A expenses in every year except 2006. Chapter 10 discusses forecasting, and a helpful starting point is to examine prior percentage changes (and common-size data) to identify trends that may persist in the future. However, a limitation of percentage change analysis is that nonrecurring items or changes in "other" categories can be associated with extreme percentage changes. This can be seen for PepsiCo and Coca-Cola for a number of line items, including "Other operating charges," "Restructuring and impairment," and "Other income (loss)."

ALTERNATIVE DEFINITIONS OF PROFITS

When the analyst assesses the profitability of a firm in the recent past, the concern is with all revenues, expenses, gains, and losses that affected the economic value of the firm. However, when the analyst uses measures of past profitability to forecast the firm's future profitability, the emphasis is on those revenues, expenses, gains, and losses that are expected to persist. If net income in the recent past includes nonrecurring gains from sales of assets or nonrecurring losses from unusual asset impairment or restructuring charges, the analyst might decide to eliminate those items from past earnings when using past earnings to forecast future earnings. For purposes of valuation, the analyst strives to forecast the sustainable earnings of a firm. The famous investment text by Benjamin Graham and David Dodd refers to this concept as "earnings power."[7] Sustainable earnings, or earnings power, is the level of earnings and the growth in the level of earnings expected to persist in the future. Nonrecurring gains and losses may occur in future periods, but the analyst cannot anticipate their occurrence, their timing, or their amount with sufficient precision to include them in sustainable earnings. Thus, a key to developing forecasts that are useful for valuation is to identify components of bottom-line earnings that are recurring.

Comprehensive Income

Most financial statement users analyze net income as a summary bottom-line measure of performance. However, both U.S. GAAP and IFRS require presentation of comprehensive income, which is defined as "The change in equity (net assets) of a business entity during a period from transactions and other events and circumstances from nonowner sources. It includes all changes in equity during a period except those resulting from investments by owners and distributions to owners."[8] Thus, items included as part of "other comprehensive income" are added to or deducted from net income. Under U.S. GAAP, presentation of comprehensive income can be at the bottom of the income statement, can be a separate statement, or can be included in the statement of changes in shareholders' equity; IFRS permits all alternatives except the statement of changes in shareholders' equity. The presentation of comprehensive income is required only if the company has items that qualify as other comprehensive income. Such items include certain foreign currency translation items, defined benefit pension plan and other postretirement plan adjustments, certain unrealized gains and losses on investment securities and derivatives, and other adjustments.

---

[7]Benjamin Graham and David Dodd, *Security Analysis* (New York: McGraw-Hill), 1934.

[8]*FASB Codification 220-10-20.*

The overriding objective of reporting items of other comprehensive income is to present an *all-inclusive* picture of a company's economic events during a period, where items included as other comprehensive income are generally more likely to be *temporary* in nature and may likely reverse prior to ultimate realization of the currently recognized gains and losses. As with net income, reliance on comprehensive income as a summary measure of performance is not emphasized as much as an understanding of the components. The primary interest in examining the components is to assess situations in which certain components are likely to persist.

Operating Income, EBIT, EBITDA, and Other Profit Measures

Another factor driving the analysis of different aggregations of income statement line items is that firms have different organizational and capital structures. As a consequence, it is sometimes helpful to examine profitability prior to considering a variety of expenses that vary depending on different organizational or capital structures. Thus, analysts are sometimes interested in analyzing different levels of profitability. Examples include gross profit, operating income, EBIT, EBITDA, EBITDAR, NOPAT, EBIAT, and earnings excluding any number of recognized expenses.[9] For example, gross profit for manufacturing firms (revenues less cost of goods sold) is a key measure of profitability because it captures the amount of profits generated by the sale of primary products that are available to cover other firm costs, such as salaries, general and administrative expenses, interest payments, and taxes. Larger gross profits may reflect a price premium advantage due to brand assets or patents or may be due cost efficiencies due to low-cost supplier relationships or technological advantages. Thus, analysts frequently start with an income statement as reported by a firm and selectively create measures of profits that aggregate various components of revenues and expenses. As we saw in the common-size income statement analysis in Exhibits 1.18 and 1.20, gross profits is a key component of profitability when comparing PepsiCo and Coca-Cola, but PepsiCo's income statement (in Appendix A) does not report a separate line item for gross profit. Thus, the analyst should be adept at reconfiguring income statements to suit different purposes, especially cross-sectional comparisons. Similarly, measures of profitability farther down the income statement are also common, especially EBITDA. Unfortunately, many analysts and investors confuse EBITDA as a proxy for a firm's cash flows, as discussed in Chapter 3. If the objective of analyzing EBITDA is that it is a proxy for a firm's cash flows, it does not make sense to use EBITDA in lieu of operating cash flows, which are easily found on the statement of cash flows. Each metric identified above can be informative, but none should be viewed as the single indicator of financial performance.

Segment Profitability

Many firms consist of more than one operating segment. Both U.S. GAAP and IFRS require that companies provide measures of profitability and certain additional information for each segment. The definition of segments follows the "management approach," which leaves the identification of operating segments up to managers based on how they manage the operations of the company. For example, PepsiCo discloses three operating segments

---

[9]The acronyms mentioned are as follows: EBIT = earnings before interest and taxes; EBITDA = earnings before interest, taxes, depreciation, and amortization; EBITDAR = earnings before interest, taxes, depreciation, amortization, and rent; NOPAT = net operating profits after tax; EBIAT = earnings before interest after tax.

(Americas foods, Americas beverages, and international) and PepsiCo further partitions the foods and international segments into smaller segments determined by geography (see discussion later in this chapter). Most often, disclosure of segment profitability data is presented in the footnotes to the financial statements. Given the open-ended management approach to these required disclosures, there is generally wide variation in the details provided across firms, which makes cross-sectional comparisons of segments challenging. However, firms are required to reconcile revenues and other disclosed items presented for segments to the corresponding totals for the firm. Firms often do not allocate all general and administrative expenses to individual segments, so it also is challenging to compare performance of a segment within a multisegment firm to that of a pure-play firm, for which such costs are included on the income statement.

Pro Forma, Adjusted, or Street Earnings

Although it is useful to examine alternative levels and sources of profits in the income statement, the analyst should know that managers of firms have incentives to classify certain expenses as one-time or nonrecurring because the managers are aware that analysts are most interested in sustainable earnings. This is frequently accomplished with the earnings release disclosures that accompany earnings announcements. Managers frequently discuss specific computations of "earnings" that exclude certain line items and refer to such earnings as "pro forma" or "adjusted" earnings; collectively, such presentations of earnings, which are widely followed on Wall Street, are called "Street" earnings. Research Director Chuck Hill commented on the practice, "What companies are trying to do is entice analysts into excluding certain charges and value them only on that basis."[10] Exhibit 4.2 shows a hypothetical approach to computing pro forma earnings by sequentially arguing that certain line items on the income statement are nonrecurring or are not relevant to the assessment of current profitability. The example shows revenues of $100, total expenses of $50, and net income of $50. Consider a manager who argues that Expense 5 is a one-time expense, such as severance payments to workers from a closed plant. The manager would report pro forma earnings of $60 after

EXHIBIT 4.2

Pro Forma Earnings Example

		GAAP	Pro Forma 1	Pro Forma 2	Pro Forma 3	Pro Forma 4	Pro Forma 5
Revenues		$100	$100	$100	$100	$100	$100
− Expenses:	*Expense 1*	(10)	(10)	(10)	(10)	(10)	—
	Expense 2	(10)	(10)	(10)	(10)	—	—
	Expense 3	(10)	(10)	(10)	—	—	—
	Expense 4	(10)	(10)	—	—	—	—
	Expense 5	(10)	—	—	—	—	—
= Earnings		$ 50	$ 60	$ 70	$ 80	$ 90	$100

---

[10]Elizabeth MacDonald, "Varied Profit Reports by Firms Create Confusion," *The Wall Street Journal* (August 24, 1999), p. C1.

excluding this charge (Pro Forma 1 in Exhibit 4.2). Expense 4 might be for an expenditure such as advertising or R&D (research and development); so a manager might claim that these expenditures generate assets and are not relevant for assessing current performance. Excluding Expense 4 yields pro forma earnings of $70 (Pro Forma 2 in Exhibit 4.2). The manager also might claim that expenses such as depreciation and amortization should be ignored and not deducted in the measurement of "earnings" simply because such expenses do not involve cash outflows in the current period. If Expense 3 in Exhibit 4.2 represents depreciation and amortization, the manager might report and discuss Pro Forma 3, which reports earnings of $80. A scheming manager even might be inclined to argue against including *all* expenses, ending up reporting pro forma earnings equal to revenues without including any expenses (Pro Forma 5 in Exhibit 4.2). This may seem far-fetched, but it is what Internet firms did during the growth of this sector in the late 1990s. Managers of such firms argued that the key to assessing performance was the level of and growth in revenues, which reflected first-mover advantages to gain market share and growth in customers who would secure the firm's profitability in the future. Needless to say, most market observers agree that the valuation of such firms reached irrational levels and resulted in a subsequent stock market crash, partially attributable to the temporary disregard for profitability measured to include operating expenses.

An empirical research study by Bradshaw and Sloan (2002) revealed a significant increase in the trend of managers reporting pro forma earnings higher than bottom-line net income, primarily by excluding certain charges and expenses from reported "pro forma" earnings.[11] Exhibit 4.3 shows results from the study. The widening gap between plots in the graph makes it clear that firms increasingly excluded expenses from reported pro forma earnings beginning as far back as the late 1980s. In a study of how managers highlight nonrecurring gains

EXHIBIT 4.3

Pro Forma versus U.S. GAAP Annual Earnings Per Share (scaled by price) for 1985–1999

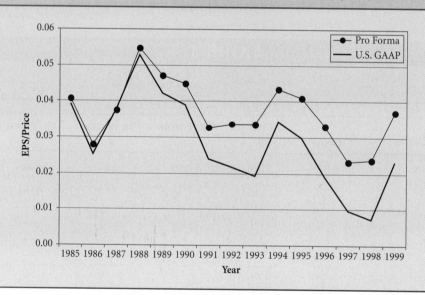

[11]Mark T. Bradshaw and Richard G. Sloan, "GAAP versus the Street: An Empirical Assessment of Two Alternative Definitions of Earnings," *Journal of Accounting Research*, Vol. 40, No. 1 (March 2002), pp. 41–66.

and losses, Schrand and Walther (2000) discovered that managers tend to highlight unusual or one-time expenses or losses during the quarter in which they occur.[12] However, when that quarter is used as a benchmark for the announcement of the same quarter's earnings in the next year, managers tend not to remind investors that the previous year included an unusual or one-time expense or loss. This makes the earnings announcement at that time appear more favorable in terms of year-to-year improvement in profitability.

In reaction to perceived abuses in the reporting of profits, the U.S. Securities and Exchange Commission (SEC) became concerned that the emphasis placed on pro forma earnings by managers risked misleading the average investor. The SEC issued Regulation G in 2003, which deals with what the SEC calls "non-GAAP" earnings, otherwise known in the investment community as pro forma earnings. Regulation G prohibits firms from placing more emphasis on pro forma earnings relative to bottom-line GAAP earnings or from identifying an amount as nonrecurring or unusual when such amounts have occurred in the past or are likely to recur in the future. Nevertheless, the reporting of non-GAAP (or pro forma) earnings is not prohibited outright, so investors must be diligent in understanding the composition of alternative measures of profits. For example, firms often include financial highlights in their annual reports but use small fonts for footnotes indicating that certain charges have been excluded from the figures presented. However, many firms now make it easier for investors to understand how management views nonrecurring or unusual charges with separate disclosures. For example, in PepsiCo's MD&A (Appendix B), the company includes a section titled "Reconciliation of GAAP and Non-GAAP Information," which shows various measures of profitability for PepsiCo, after excluding various charges such as mark-to-market losses and restructuring and impairment charges. The next section discusses whether and how to adjust measures of profitability such as ROA for nonrecurring or unusual charges.

RATE OF RETURN ON ASSETS (ROA)

The right-hand branch of Exhibit 4.1 relates to analysis of profitability using rate of return measures. Rate of return measures presume that a certain amount of investment generates economic profits. A simple example is interest earned on a savings account. A straightforward computation of the rate of return on such an investment is the interest income earned divided by the amount deposited. Conceptually, the analysis of returns to creditors and equity shareholders is similar. In the analysis of financial statements, the two most common measures of rate of return are ROA (return on assets) and ROCE. Our discussion of rate of return analysis begins with ROA. The next section builds on this discussion, transitioning to an examination of ROCE.

The rate of ROA measures a firm's success in using assets to generate earnings independent of the financing of those assets. ROA takes as given the particular set of environmental factors and strategic choices that a firm makes (such as product markets, operating decisions, and financing policies) and focuses on how well a firm has used its assets to generate earnings in a particular period. Most importantly, ROA ignores the means and costs of financing the firm's net assets (that is, the proportion of debt versus equity financing and the costs of those forms of capital).

The analyst calculates ROA as follows:

$$\text{ROA} = \frac{\text{Net Income} + (1 - \text{Tax Rate})(\text{Interest Expense}) + \text{Minority Interest in Earnings}}{\text{Average Total Assets}}$$

---

[12]Catherine M. Schrand and Beverly R. Walther, "Strategic Benchmarks in Earnings Announcements: The Selective Disclosure of Prior-Period Earnings Components," *The Accounting Review*, Vol. 75, No. 2 (April 2000), pp. 151–177.

The numerator of ROA adjusts net income to exclude the effects of any financing costs. Thus, as discussed in the previous section on alternative definitions of profitability, the measure of profits pertinent to ROA is net income *before* financing costs. If a firm has income from discontinued operations or extraordinary gains or losses, the analyst might exclude those items and start with net income from continuing operations instead of net income if the objective is to measure a firm's sustainable profitability.

Because accountants subtract interest expense when computing net income, the analyst must add it back when computing ROA. However, firms can deduct interest expense in measuring taxable income. Therefore, the *incremental* effect of interest expense on net income equals one minus the marginal tax rate times interest expense.[13] That is, the analyst adds back the full amount of interest expense to net income and then subtracts, or eliminates, the tax savings from that interest expense.

The tax savings from interest expense depends on the statutory tax rate in the tax jurisdiction where the firm raises its debt. As of the date this text was written, the statutory federal tax rate is 35 percent in the United States. Firms must disclose in a note to the financial statements why the average income tax rate (defined as income tax expense divided by net income before income taxes) differs from the federal statutory tax rate of 35 percent. The statutory federal rate will differ from a firm's average tax rate because of (1) state, local, and foreign tax rates that differ from 35 percent (Chapter 8 provides a discussion of these effects) and (2) revenues and expenses that firms include in accounting income but that do not impact taxable income (that is, permanent differences as described in Chapter 2). The analyst can approximate the combined statutory federal, state, local, and foreign tax rate applicable to tax savings from interest expense using 35 percent plus or minus the amounts disclosed related to (1) above. Permanent differences in (2) usually do not relate to interest expense and therefore should not affect the statutory tax rate applicable to interest expense deductions. To simplify the calculations, we will follow the common practice of using the *statutory* federal tax rate of 35 percent in the computations of the tax savings from interest in the numerator of ROA throughout this book. Because accountants do not subtract dividends on preferred and common stocks in measuring net income, calculating the numerator of ROA requires no adjustment for dividends.[14]

The rationale for adding back the minority interest in earnings relates to attaining consistency in the numerator and the denominator of ROA. The denominator of ROA includes all assets of the consolidated entity, not just the parent company's share. Net income in the numerator, however, represents the parent's earnings plus the parent's share of the earnings of consolidated subsidiaries. The accountant computes consolidated earnings by combining the earnings of the parent and consolidated subsidiaries and then subtracting the minority interest's claim on the earnings of consolidated subsidiaries. Consistency with the inclusion of all of the assets of the consolidated entity in the denominator of ROA requires that the numerator include all of the earnings of the consolidated entity, not just the parent's share. The addback of the minority interest in earnings accomplishes this objective. Most publicly traded corporations, including PepsiCo, do not disclose the minority interest in earnings because its amount, if any, is usually immaterial. Thus, the analyst makes this adjustment only for significant minority interests.

---

[13]The marginal tax rate times interest expense is the *interest tax shield*. An interest tax shield is the reduction in taxes payable for firms that deduct interest expense in the computation of income tax liability.

[14]One could argue that the analyst should exclude returns from short-term investments of excess cash (that is, interest revenue) from the numerator of ROA and the short-term investments from the denominator of ROA under the view that such investments are negative financings (that is, savings rather than borrowings). We do not make this adjustment when computing ROA, although we consider the effect of such short-term investments in the discussion of valuation in Chapters 10–14.

Calculating the numerator is usually accomplished most easily by starting with net income, as listed above, and that will be our approach. Equivalently, however, one could start with earnings before interest and taxes and deduct taxes applicable to pretax profits. For example, the numerator could also be stated as follows:

Revenues − Cost of Goods Sold − All Other Expenses (Excluding Interest Expense) − Adjusted Taxes

The difficulty with this specification is that "adjusted taxes" means taxes on the profits of the firm before deducting interest expense, which is not equal to income tax expense on the income statement. The difference is the tax savings associated with the interest deductible on tax returns, which is approximated as the marginal tax rate times interest expense. We label the numerator as in the first equation above, but analysts occasionally refer to this construct by acronyms such as NOPAT (net operating profit after taxes) or EBIAT (earnings before interest after taxes).[15]

Because net income before financing costs in the numerator of ROA reports the results for a period of time, the optimal denominator uses a measure of average assets in use during that same period. This computation aligns the income measure in the numerator with the average assets in place during the period. Using average total assets is not mandatory, however, in the sense that using beginning total assets is not necessarily wrong. (In fact, if total assets have not changed significantly during the period, there will be little difference between the beginning amount and the average.) The use of average total assets is a simple way to account for the changing level of investments in total assets upon which profits are judged. Thus, for a nonseasonal business, an average of assets at the beginning and end of the year is usually satisfactory. For a seasonal business, the analyst might use an average of assets at the end of each quarter.

Refer to the financial statements for PepsiCo in Appendix A. Also refer to the ROA and other ratio computations in the Analysis worksheet in FSAP, which are presented in Appendix C. The calculation of ROA for 2008 is as follows:

$$\text{ROA} = \frac{\begin{array}{c}\text{Net Income from} \\ \text{Continuing Operations}\end{array} + \begin{array}{c}(1 - \text{Tax Rate}) \times \\ (\text{Interest Expense})\end{array} + \begin{array}{c}\text{Minority Interest} \\ \text{in Earnings}\end{array}}{\text{Average Total Assets}}$$

$$15.2\% = \frac{\$5,142 + (1 - 0.35)(\$329) + \$0}{0.5(\$35,994 + \$34,628)}$$

As noted earlier in the chapter, the analyst should consider whether reported net income includes any unusual or nonrecurring items that might affect assessments of a firm's ongoing profitability. The notes to the financial statements and the MD&A provide information for making these assessments. PepsiCo includes a section in its MD&A (Appendix B) labeled "Items Affecting Comparability." PepsiCo lists several items affecting net income that the analyst might consider unusual or nonrecurring (such as mark-to-market fair value adjustments and restructuring and impairment charges). If the objective is to measure the sustainable profitability of PepsiCo, the analyst might decide to adjust the reported amounts for such items. Chapter 9 discusses and illustrates these adjustments more fully.

---

[15]Often analysts calculate EBIAT by deducting tax expense from the income statement, not including the adjustment for taxes on interest. For firms with limited amounts of interest-bearing debt, usually this is not a material omission. However, as with any ratio or financial computation, analysts should know whether trade-offs are being made for computational ease but at the expense of deviating from a theoretically correct construct.

In preparing a time-series analysis of ROA for 2006–2008, analysts should consider adjusting PepsiCo's reported net income for the following five items, all highlighted by PepsiCo in its MD&A. The following subsections discuss adjustments for each of these items in more detail.

1. For 2008, PepsiCo reports $543 million of pretax impairment and restructuring charges ($408 million after taxes) related to the closure of six plants under the company's Productivity for Growth program. For 2007, restructuring and impairment charges are $102 million ($70 million after tax); for 2006, such charges are $67 million ($43 million after tax).

2. For 2008, PepsiCo reports negative $346 million of mark-to-market adjustments (negative $223 million after taxes) related to commodity derivatives, for which gains and losses must be recognized immediately in income. For 2007, the mark-to-market adjustment is a positive $19 million ($12 million after tax); for 2006, the mark-to-market adjustment is negative $18 million (negative $12 million after tax).

3. For 2007, PepsiCo reports $129 million of tax benefits relative to favorable resolution of certain foreign tax matters; for 2006, PepsiCo recognized tax benefits of $602 million from favorable resolution of domestic tax matters.

4. For 2008, PepsiCo reports an after-tax charge of $114 million in bottling equity income ($138 million pre-tax charge), representing PepsiCo's share of Pepsi Bottling Group's (PBG's) impairment charges related to business in Mexico.

5. For 2006 only, PepsiCo reports an after-tax benefit of $18 million ($21 million pre-tax bottling equity income) related to PepsiCo's share of a favorable tax settlement from the conclusion of an audit by the Internal Revenue Service (IRS) of PBG's income tax returns for 1999–2000.

Impairment and Restructuring Charges

The first and fourth items in the preceding list of possible adjustments result from the closing of plants or impairment charges. PepsiCo closed manufacturing plants and other facilities, which required the firm to write off or write down the amounts appearing on the balance sheet for these plants and other facilities and to provide severance payments to employees; similarly, PBG began a restructuring initiative, triggering charges in 2008 related to operations in Mexico. PepsiCo recognized restructuring or impairment charges for the three recent years, and such charges are common going further back in time. When deciding whether to eliminate these charges as part of assessing sustainable profitability, the analyst will likely consider whether the plant closures are complete or will likely continue. PepsiCo does not disclose specific information about its plans in this regard, so the analyst must predict based on events of the recent past and knowledge of the firm's strategy and industry. The existence of PepsiCo's Productivity for Growth Program and recent history suggest that such charges will continue, supporting an analyst's decision to leave them in earnings when assessing profitability. Moreover, one could argue that "if it is not one thing, it will be another" and implicitly acknowledge that nonrecurring or unusual charges are more common than the nomenclature implies.

On the other hand, PepsiCo will not likely continue to close manufacturing facilities indefinitely. Also, closing such plants is not central to PepsiCo's ongoing activities, which include manufacturing and distributing foods and beverages. Thus, the analyst could decide in this case to eliminate such charges. A third approach is to leave the charges in earnings but de-emphasize them when contextually analyzing ongoing profitability, which is a fairly common approach.

We follow the second approach and eliminate the charges in 2006–2008 based on their peripheral nature to PepsiCo's central operations and the assumption that the closing of manufacturing facilities is largely complete. (We view the decision whether to eliminate the charges in this case as very close to call and could easily have concluded not to eliminate them based on their recurring nature in the recent past. In Chapter 10, we project future financial statements for PepsiCo based on the assumption that these charges will not be recurring.) Our decision to eliminate the charges is also due in part to the benefits of describing the elimination procedure, which we demonstrate later in this section.

Mark-to-Market Accounting Adjustments

The second item results from fluctuations in commodity derivatives, which PepsiCo's corporate finance group manages on behalf of all divisions. Prices of commodity derivatives are notoriously volatile, so it is not surprising that PepsiCo realizes adjustments in all three years. The question for the analyst is whether to cleanse reported earnings of such charges when analyzing profitability. The argument to exclude them is that they are tangential to core operations and that price movements of commodities are unpredictable. However, because the commodity derivatives cover "energy, fruit and other raw materials," it seems compelling that these are primary inputs into PepsiCo's core operations and hence not tangential. Thus, we do *not* exclude these charges from reported income during 2006–2008.

Tax Benefits

The third and fifth items are for the settlement of income taxes for PepsiCo and PBG for ongoing businesses in 2006 and 2007. The tax benefits do not appear to relate to earnings of current years, but to those of earlier years (for example, the $602 million benefit recognized in 2006 related to tax returns for 1998–2002 and the $18 million benefit related to PBG's tax returns for 1999–2000). Because PepsiCo continues to operate these businesses, we eliminate the tax benefits realized in 2006 and 2007 because the amounts are part of a negotiated settlement with taxing authorities, which is inherently unpredictable.

In summary, we adjust net income for all items listed above, except for the second item relating to mark-to-market adjustments of commodity derivative contracts. All adjustments should be net of income tax effects. If firms disclose the income tax effect, we use the reported amounts. Otherwise, we assume that the current marginal federal tax rate applies. PepsiCo discloses the pretax and after-tax amounts for each of these items in the section of the MD&A labeled "Items Affecting Comparability." The adjustments to net income appear in Exhibit 4.4. It is important to carefully consider the sign of the adjustments in Exhibit 4.4. Income-reducing charges such as impairments and restructuring charges are *added back* to income before income taxes, which is intuitive. The adjustment for tax effects is less intuitive, however. For example, because impairments and restructuring charges are associated with reduced income tax expense (to the extent that such amounts are tax deductible), removing these charges from the computation of income before taxes requires an adjustment to *increase* the level of tax expense; hence, the adjustments in Exhibit 4.4 must be added back to income tax expense. Similarly, tax benefits from settlements with taxing authorities reduced reported income tax expense, so adjusting net income to remove the effects of these settlements requires that such amounts also be added back to income tax expense.

The adjusted ROA for PepsiCo for 2008 is as follows:

$$16.7\% = \frac{\$5,664 + (1 - 0.35)(\$329) + \$0}{0.5(\$35,994 + \$34,628)} = \frac{\$5,878}{\$35,311}$$

We make similar adjustments for impairment and restructuring charges in 2007 and 2006 and the tax benefits in 2007 and 2006. As shown in Exhibit 4.4, adjusted net income is

EXHIBIT 4.4

Adjustments to Reported Net Income for Unusual and Nonrecurring Items for PepsiCo
(amounts in millions)

	2008	2007	2006
Reported Income before Income Taxes	$7,021	$7,631	$6,989
Impairment and Restructuring Charges: (PepsiCo + PBG)	681	102	67
Adjusted Income from Continuing Operations before Income Taxes	$7,702	$7,733	$7,056
Reported Income Tax Expense	$1,879	$1,973	$1,347
Tax Effects of Impairment and Restructuring Charges:			
2008: $681 − $408 − $114	159	—	—
2007: $102 − $70	—	32	—
2006: $67 − $43	—	—	24
Tax Benefits from Settlements with Taxing Authorities:	—	129	602
	—	—	18
Adjusted Income Tax Expense	$2,038	$2,134	$1,991
Adjusted Net Income	$5,664	$5,599	$5,065
Reported Net Income	$5,142	$5,658	$5,642

higher than reported net income for 2008, but in 2007 and 2006, adjusted income is lower than reported net income.

Calculations for both unadjusted and adjusted ROA are shown for all three years in Exhibit 4.5. Note that the numerator of ROA based on as-reported net income declines from $5,804 million in 2007 to $5,356 million in 2008, but the numerator based on adjusted net income increases in 2008 relative to 2007 (from $5,745 million to $5,878 million), largely due to the purging of large restructuring and impairment charges in 2008. ROA based on reported net income is 15.2 percent, 18.0 percent, and 18.8 percent in 2008, 2007, and 2006, respectively. Analyzing the time series of PepsiCo's ROA based on reported net income, performance in 2008 appears well below that in previous years. However, adjusting net income for nonrecurring items that we hypothesize affect comparability across years, ROA for 2008 appears more in line with recent ROA (16.7 percent versus 16.9–17.8 percent). Refer to the Analysis worksheet in the FSAP model for a five-year time series of these and other ratios computed based on as-reported and adjusted figures (also presented in Appendix C).

Two Comments on the Calculation of ROA

First, some analysts subtract average non-interest-bearing liabilities (such as accounts payable and accrued liabilities) from average total assets in the denominator of ROA, the argument being that these items are sources of indirect financing. An alternative argument for reducing total assets by non-interest-bearing liabilities is that ROA is better characterized as a return on invested capital when items that are not directly invested capital (such

EXHIBIT 4.5

Calculations of Unadjusted and Adjusted ROA for PepsiCo
(Data for total assets from Appendix C
and adjusted net income data from Exhibit 4.4.)

	2008	2007	2006
Total assets—Beginning of year	$34,628	$29,930	$31,727
Total assets—End of year	$35,994	$34,628	$29,930
Average total assets	$35,311	$32,279	$30,829
Net income	$ 5,142	$ 5,658	$ 5,642
Adjusted net income	$ 5,664	$ 5,599	$ 5,065
Interest expense	$ 329	$ 224	$ 239
Net income + (1 − 0.35) × Interest expense	$ 5,356	$ 5,804	$ 5,797
Adjusted net income + (1 − 0.35) × Interest expense	$ 5,878	$ 5,745	$ 5,220
ROA (unadjusted)	15.2%	18.0%	18.8%
ROA (adjusted)	16.7%	17.8%	16.9%

as accounts payable) are purged from total assets. Economics suggests that when liabilities do not provide for *explicit* interest charges, the creditor charges *implicit* interest by adjusting the terms of the contract, such as offering discounts for those who do pay immediately or setting higher prices for those who do not pay immediately. The numerator of the ROA calculation is a measure of income before deducting financing costs; therefore, an alternative approach would be to adjust net income for both explicit and implicit financing costs. Unfortunately, it is difficult to reliably estimate the implicit interest charges associated with non-interest-bearing liabilities such as accounts payable and accrued liabilities and to reclassify the implicit increments for financing charges in cost of goods sold and selling, general and administrative expenses to interest expense (which is added back to net income). Adjusting prefinancing income this way would increase the measure of operating income in the numerator, increasing calculated ROA. (An alternative of reducing the denominator by subtracting non-interest-bearing liabilities from total assets also would increase calculated ROA.) Despite the logic of adjusting income in the ROA calculation to account for implicit interest or adjusting total assets for indirectly invested capital, in all but extreme cases, the materiality of such theoretically correct adjustments is questionable and the degree of precision in estimating such amounts is low. Consequently, the examples and problems in this book follow the conventional practice of using average total assets in the denominator of ROA, making no adjustment for non-interest-bearing liabilities.

Second, it is important to note that although we adjusted the numerator of ROA for unusual or nonrecurring items, we did not adjust the denominator. This implicitly states that the effects of the unusual or nonrecurring items on profits are not persistent but that their effects on total assets are persistent. For example, consider the non-cash impairment charges that were added back to net income. These impairment charges reduced the carrying value of assets. Thus, our adjustment added back to net income the effect of the write-down but included the effect in the ending balance of total assets, which will be lower because of the write-down. Thus, our adjustment to the numerator (increase) paired with the impact of the unadjusted balance sheet write-down in the denominator (decrease) leads to an upward bias in current period ROA. The logic behind this seemingly inconsistent treatment is motivated by a desire to compute sustainable ROA. The current period restructuring charges will not persist in future periods, but the asset write-downs are permanent (those assets are worthless); thus, the adjusted ROA provides a better indicator of the ROA we might expect to observe next period even though it is a biased measured of the current period's ROA. Again, our approach reflects conventional practice, but the astute analyst should understand that blindly ignoring negative charges on the income statement but allowing them to affect the balance sheet can affect adjusted performance. This caveat echoes the cautionary discussion earlier in the chapter regarding the potentially misleading practice of managers emphasizing pro forma earnings.

Disaggregating ROA

The analyst obtains further insight into the behavior of ROA by disaggregating it into profit margin for ROA and total assets turnover (also simply referred to as *assets turnover*) components as follows:

$$\frac{\text{ROA}}{\begin{array}{c}\text{Net Income} + \text{Interest} \\ \text{Expense (net of taxes)} \\ + \text{Minority Interest} \\ \text{in Earnings} \\ \hline \text{Average Total Assets}\end{array}} = \frac{\begin{array}{c}\textbf{Profit Margin for ROA} \\ \text{Net Income} + \text{Interest} \\ \text{Expense (net of taxes)} \\ + \text{Minority Interest} \\ \text{in Earnings} \\ \hline \text{Sales}\end{array}}{} \times \frac{\textbf{Assets Turnover}}{\begin{array}{c} \\ \\ \\ \text{Sales} \\ \hline \text{Average Total Assets}\end{array}}$$

The profit margin for ROA indicates the ability of a firm to generate earnings for a particular level of sales.[16] Assets turnover indicates the ability to manage the level of investment in assets for a particular level of sales or, to put it another way, the ability to generate sales from a particular level of investment in assets. The assets turnover ratio indicates the firm's ability to use assets to generate sales, and the profit margin for ROA indicates the firm's ability to use sales to generate profits.

The disaggregation of ROA for PepsiCo for 2008, after adjusting for nonrecurring items, is as follows:

$$\begin{array}{ccccc}
\textbf{ROA} & = & \textbf{Profit Margin for ROA} & \times & \textbf{Assets Turnover} \\
\dfrac{\$\ 5,878}{\$35,311} & = & \dfrac{\$\ 5,878}{\$43,251} & \times & \dfrac{\$43,251}{\$35,311} \\
16.7\% & = & 13.6\% & \times & 1.22
\end{array}$$

Exhibit 4.6 summarizes ROA, profit margin for ROA, and assets turnover for PepsiCo for 2006–2008. PepsiCo's profit margin for ROA has been declining steadily. However, PepsiCo has increased assets turnover. After exploring economic and strategic factors underlying ROA and its components in the next section, we return to analyzing the profit margin for ROA and assets turnover of PepsiCo in greater depth.

---

[16]One might argue that the analyst should use total *revenues*, not just *sales*, in the denominator because assets generate returns in forms other than sales (for example, interest revenue and equity in earnings of affiliates). However, interpretations of various expense ratios (discussed later in this chapter) are usually easier when we use sales in the denominator.

EXHIBIT 4.6

ROA, Profit Margin, and Assets Turnover for PepsiCo: 2006–2008 (adjusted data)

	2008	2007	2006
ROA	16.7%	17.8%	16.9%
Profit Margin for ROA	13.6%	14.6%	14.9%
Assets Turnover	1.22	1.22	1.14

Economic and Strategic Factors in the Interpretation of ROA[17]

ROA and its components differ across industries depending on their economic characteristics and across firms within an industry depending on the design and implementation of their strategies. This section explores economic and strategic factors that impact the interpretation of ROA and its components.

Exhibit 4.7 depicts graphically the 15-year average of the median annual ROAs, profit margins for ROA, and assets turnovers of 23 industries for 1990–2004. The two isoquants

EXHIBIT 4.7

Median ROA, Profit Margin for ROA, and Assets Turnover for 23 Industries for 1990–2004

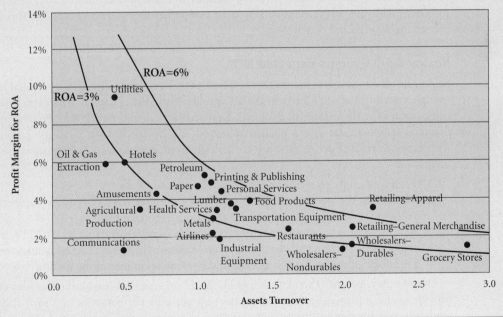

reflect ROAs of 3 percent and 6 percent. The isoquants show the various combinations of profit margin for ROA and assets turnover that yield an ROA of 3 percent and 6 percent. For instance, an ROA of 6 percent results from any of the following profit margins for ROA × assets turnover combinations: 6% × 1.0, 3% × 2.0, 2% × 3.0, 1% × 6.0.

The data for ROA, profit margin for ROA, and assets turnover underlying the plots in Exhibit 4.7 reflect aggregated amounts across firms and across years. Financial statement analysis focuses on the ROAs of specific firms (or even segments of specific firms) for particular years (or even quarters). However, we can obtain useful insights about the behavior of ROA at the segment or firm level by examining the average industry-level data, particularly the following:

1. What factors explain the consistently high or consistently low ROAs of some industries relative to the average of all industries? (That is, what are the reasons for differences in the distribution of industries in the inner left area versus the outer right area of Exhibit 4.7?)
2. What factors explain the fact that certain industries have high profit margins and low assets turnovers while other industries experience low profit margins and high assets turnovers? (That is, what are the reasons for differences in the distribution of industries in the upper left area versus the lower right area of Exhibit 4.7?)

The microeconomics and business strategy literature provides useful background for interpreting the behavior of ROA, profit margin, and assets turnover. As a prelude to the discussion that follows, consider the two extreme industries in Exhibit 4.7. Utilities show the highest profit margins in Exhibit 4.7, which can be explained by significant barriers to entry (both regulatory and enormous fixed costs). Barriers to entry permit existing firms to realize higher profit margins due to limited competition. On the other hand, grocery stores show the highest assets turnover in Exhibit 4.7. Given lower barriers to entry and significant competition, this industry survives not based on profit margins, but on the ability of firms in the industry to run efficient operations and generate substantial asset turnover, consistent with the perpetual efforts by such companies to generate foot traffic through ever-changing sales and promotions.

Realized ROA versus Expected ROA

Economic theory suggests that higher levels of perceived risk in any activity should lead to higher levels of expected return if that activity is to attract capital. The extra return compensates for the extra risk assumed. Realized rates of return (ROAs) derived from financial statement data for a particular period will not necessarily correlate perfectly with expected returns or with the level of risk involved in an activity as economic theory suggests if

1. Faulty assumptions were used in deriving expected ROAs.
2. Changes in the environment after expectations are formed (such as an unexpected recession) cause realized ROAs to deviate from expectations.
3. ROA is an incomplete measure of economic rates of return (that is, rates of return that include all changes in economic value) because GAAP relies on acquisition costs for reliable measurement of assets and conservatism in measuring income.

Despite these potential weaknesses, ROAs based on reported financial statement data provide useful information for tracking the past periodic performance of a firm and its segments and for developing expectations about future earnings potential. Three elements of risk help in understanding differences across firms and changes over time in ROAs: (1) operating leverage, (2) cyclicality of sales, and (3) product life cycles.

Operating Leverage. Firms operate with different mixtures of fixed and variable costs in their cost structures. Firms in the utilities, communications, hotel, petroleum, and chemical industries are capital-intensive. Depreciation and many operating costs are more or less fixed for any given period. Most retailers and wholesalers, on the other hand, have high proportions of variable costs in their cost structures. Firms with high proportions of fixed costs experience significant increases in operating income as sales increase, a phenomenon known as *economies of scale*. The increased income occurs because the firms spread fixed costs over a larger number of units sold, resulting in a decrease in average unit cost. Likewise, when sales decrease, these firms experience sharp decreases in operating income, the result of *diseconomies of scale*. Economists refer to this process of operating with high proportions of fixed costs as *operating leverage*. Firms with high levels of operating leverage experience greater variability in their ROAs than firms with low levels of operating leverage. All else being equal (see the discussion of cyclicality of sales in the next section), firms with high levels of operating leverage incur more risk in their operations and should earn higher rates of return.

Measuring the degree of operating leverage of a firm or its segments requires information about the fixed and variable cost structure. The top panel of Exhibit 4.8 shows the total revenue and total cost functions of two stylized firms, A and B. The graphs assume that the two firms are the same size and have the same total revenue functions (the line labeled "Total Revenue: A or B") and the same break-even points (the point where the total revenue line intersects with each firm's cost function line). These assumptions simplify the discussion of operating leverage but are not necessary when comparing actual companies.

Firm B has a higher level of fixed costs than Firm A does, as indicated by the intersection of the firm's total cost line on the y-axis above that for Firm A in the top panel of

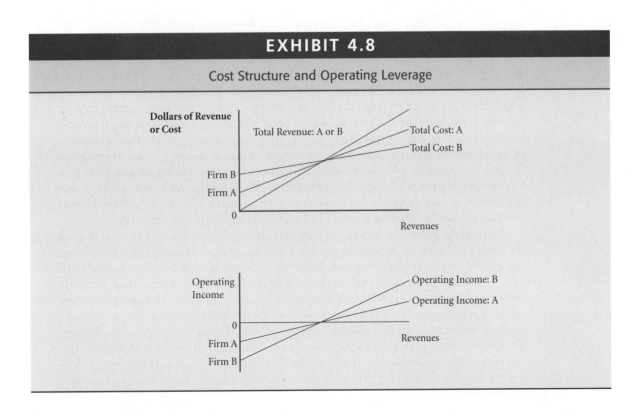

EXHIBIT 4.8

Cost Structure and Operating Leverage

Exhibit 4.8. Firm A has a higher level of variable costs than Firm B does, as indicated by the steeper slope of Firm A's total cost function as revenues increase above zero. The lower panel nets the total revenue and total cost functions to derive the operating income function (that is, revenue minus cost). Operating income is negative in an amount equal to fixed costs when revenues are zero and operating income is zero at break-even revenues. We use the slope of the operating income line as a measure of the extent of operating leverage. Firm B, with its higher fixed-cost and lower variable-cost mix, has more operating leverage. As revenues increase, its operating income increases more sharply than that of Firm A. On the downside, however, income decreases more sharply for Firm B as revenues decrease.

Unfortunately, firms do not publicly disclose information about their fixed and variable cost structures. To examine the influence of operating leverage on the behavior of ROA for a particular firm or its segments, the analyst must estimate the fixed versus variable cost structure. One approach to such estimation is to study the various cost items of a firm and attempt to identify items that are likely to behave as fixed costs. Firms incur some costs in particular amounts, referred to as *committed fixed costs,* regardless of the actual level of activity during the period. Examples include depreciation, amortization, and rent. Firms can alter the amount of other costs, referred to as *discretionary fixed costs,* in the short run in response to operating conditions, but in general, these costs do not vary directly with the level of activity. Examples include research and development, maintenance, advertising, and central corporate staff expenses. Whether the analyst should classify these latter costs as fixed costs or as variable costs in measuring operating leverage depends on their behavior in a particular firm. Given sufficient time-series data, an analyst also could estimate the level of fixed costs by estimating a regression of an operating expense on a variable that drives the variable component of the operating expense. For example, to estimate the fixed component of cost of goods sold, the analyst could estimate the following regression:

$$\text{Cost of Goods Sold}_t = \alpha + \beta * \text{Sales}_t + \varepsilon_t$$

The estimated intercept, α, would be the analyst's best estimate of the fixed component of cost of goods sold. Although ideal in theory, to obtain a sufficient number of observations to estimate the above model, the analyst would need to use data from past quarters or years, which likely are outdated given changes in the firm's current operating structure. As an example of a simpler approach for assessing the relative contribution of fixed versus variable costs—continuing with the cost of goods sold example—an analyst can test for the existence of significant fixed costs by examining the percent change in cost of goods sold relative to the percent change in sales. Firms with substantial fixed costs will behave like Firm B in Exhibit 4.8 and show percentage changes in cost of goods sold that are less than the percentage changes in sales. (Chapter 10 provides more discussion of how to estimate fixed versus variable costs and use that information in forecasting future expenses and income.)

Cyclicality of Sales. The sales of certain goods and services are sensitive to conditions in the economy. Examples include construction services, industrial equipment, computers, automobiles, and other durable goods. When the economy is in an upswing (healthy GNP growth, low unemployment, and low interest rates), customers purchase these relatively high-priced items, and sales of these firms grow accordingly. When the economy enters a recession, customers curtail their purchases, and the sales of these firms decrease significantly. Contrast these cyclical sales patterns with those of grocery stores, food processors, nonfashion clothing, and electric utilities. Those industries sell products that most consumers consider necessities. Also, their products tend to carry lower per-unit costs, reducing the benefits of delaying purchases to realize cost savings. Firms with cyclical sales patterns incur more risk than firms with noncyclical sales.

One means of reducing the risk inherent in cyclical sales is to strive for a high proportion of variable cost in the cost structure. Examples of variable-cost strategies include paying employees an hourly wage instead of a fixed salary and renting buildings and equipment under short-term cancelable leases instead of purchasing them. Cost levels should change proportionally with sales, thereby maintaining stable profit margin percentages and reducing risk. Of course, this depends on whether the firm can make timely adjustments to cost structures in response to changes in demand, such as the ability to furlough workers or return leased equipment to lessors.

The nature of the activities of some firms is such that they must carry high levels of fixed costs (that is, operating leverage). Examples include capital-intensive service firms such as airlines and railroads. Firms in these industries may attempt to transform the cost of their physical capacity from a fixed cost to a variable cost by engaging in short-term leases. However, lessors then bear the risk of cyclical sales and demand higher returns (that is, rents). Thus, some firms are especially risky because they bear a combination of operating leverage and cyclical sales risks.

A noncyclical sales pattern can compensate for high operating leverage and effectively neutralize this element of risk. Electric utilities, for example, carry high levels of fixed costs. However, their dominant positions in most service areas reduce their operating risks and permit them to achieve stable profitability.

Product Life Cycle. A third element of risk that affects ROA relates to the stage and length of a firm's product life cycle, a concept discussed in Chapter 3 with regard to relations between cash flows from operating, investing, and financing activities. Products move through four identifiable phases: introduction, growth, maturity, and decline. During the introduction and growth phases, a firm focuses on product development (product R&D spending) and capacity enlargement (capital spending). The objective is to gain market acceptance and market share. Considerable uncertainty may exist during these phases regarding the market viability of a firm's products. Products that have survived into the maturity phase have gained market acceptance. Also, firms have probably been able to cut back capital expenditures on new operating capacity. During the maturity phase, however, competition becomes more intense and the emphasis shifts to reducing costs through improved capacity utilization (economies of scale) and more efficient production (process R&D spending aimed at reducing manufacturing costs through better utilization of labor and materials). During the decline phase, firms exit the industry as sales decline and profit opportunities diminish.

Exhibit 4.9 depicts the behavior of revenues, operating income, investment, and ROA that corresponds to the four phases of the product life cycle. During the introduction and early growth phases, expenditures on product development and marketing, coupled with relatively low sales levels, lead to operating losses and negative ROAs. As sales accelerate during the high-growth phase, operating income and ROAs turn positive. Extensive product development, marketing, and depreciation expenses during this phase moderate operating income, while heavy capital expenditures to build capacity for expected higher future sales increase the denominator of ROA. Thus, ROA does not grow as rapidly as sales. ROA increases significantly during the maturity phase due to benefits of economies of scale and learning curve phenomena and to curtailments of capital expenditures. ROA deteriorates during the decline phase as operating income decreases, but ROA may remain positive or even increase for some time into this phase (particularly if the depreciable assets have been largely depreciated). Thus, as products move through their life cycles, their ROAs should move to the upper right area in Exhibit 4.9, peak during the maturity stage, and then move to the lower left area as the decline phase sets in. This movement in ROA appears negatively correlated with the level of risk. Risks are probably greatest in the introduction and growth stages, when ROA is low or negative, and least in the maturity phase, when ROA is high.

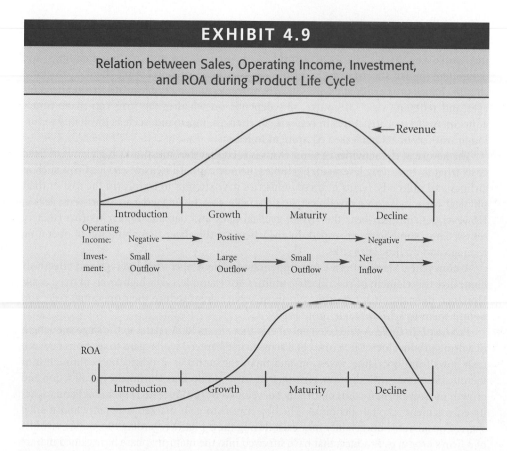

EXHIBIT 4.9

Relation between Sales, Operating Income, Investment, and ROA during Product Life Cycle

Recall, though, that ROA measures realized accounting returns in a given period, whereas the usual risk-return trade-off refers to expected returns and expected risks. Taking a weighted average of ROAs over several years will reflect more accurately the economic returns generated by high-growth firms.

Note that the product life cycle theory focuses on individual products. We can extend the theory to an industry level by examining the average stage in the product life cycle of all products in that industry. For instance, products in the computer industry range from the introduction to the decline phases, but the overall industry is probably in the latter part of the high-growth phase. The beverage and food-processing industries, the primary markets of PepsiCo, are mature, although PepsiCo and its competitors continually introduce new products. We might view the steel industry, at least in the United States, as in the early decline phase, although some companies have modernized production sufficiently to stave off the decline.[18]

In addition to the stage in the product life cycle, the length of the product life cycle also is an element of risk. Products with short product life cycles require more frequent expenditures to develop replacement or new products, thereby increasing risks. The product life cycles of most computer products run one to two years. Most pharmaceutical products experience product life cycles of approximately seven years. In contrast, the life cycles of PepsiCo's soft drinks, branded food products, and some toys (for example, Barbie® dolls and Matchbox® cars) are much longer.

[18]Empirical support for a link between life cycle stage, sales growth, capital expenditure growth, and stock market reaction appears in Joseph H. Anthony and K. Ramesh, "Association between Accounting Performance Measures and Stock Prices: A Test of the Life Cycle Hypothesis," *Journal of Accounting and Economics* 15 (1992), pp. 203–227.

Refer again to the average industry ROAs in Exhibit 4.7. The location of several industries is consistent with their incurring one or more of these elements of risk. The relatively high ROAs of the utilities and petroleum industries are consistent with high operating leverage. Paper, petroleum, and transportation equipment experience cyclical sales, and apparel retailers face the risk of their products becoming obsolete.

Some of the industry locations in Exhibit 4.7 appear inconsistent with these elements of risk. Oil and gas extraction, agricultural production, and communications are capital-intensive, yet their ROAs are the lowest of the 23 industries. One might view these positions as disequilibrium situations. Generating such low ROAs will not likely attract capital over the longer term.

The ROA locations of several industries appear to be affected by GAAP. A principal resource of food products firms such as General Mills and Campbell's Soup is the value of their brand names. Yet GAAP requires these firms to immediately expense advertising and other costs incurred to develop these brand names. Thus, their asset bases are understated and their ROAs are overstated.[19] Likewise, the publishing industry does not recognize the value of copyrights or authors' contracts as assets, resulting in an overstatement of ROAs. A similar overstatement problem occurs for service firms, for which the value of their employees does not appear as an asset.

Trade-Offs between Profit Margin and Assets Turnover

In addition to the differences in ROA depicted in Exhibit 4.7, we also must examine reasons for differences in the relative mix of profit margin and assets turnover. Explanations come from the microeconomics and business strategy literature.

Microeconomic Theory. Exhibit 4.10 sets out some important economic factors that constrain certain firms and industries to operate with particular combinations of profit

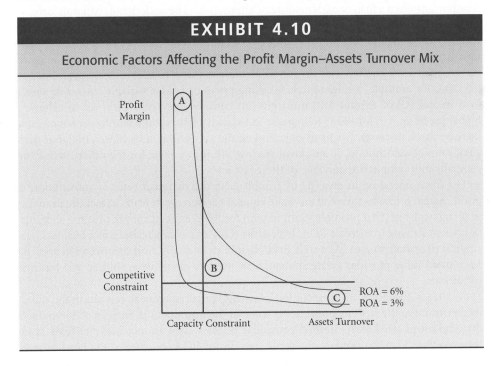

EXHIBIT 4.10

Economic Factors Affecting the Profit Margin–Assets Turnover Mix

---

[19]The immediate expensing of advertising costs understates net income as well, but the difference between the amount expensed and amortization of amounts from the current and prior periods that perhaps should have been capitalized results in less distortion of net income than of total assets.

margins and assets turnovers. Firms and industries characterized by heavy fixed capacity costs and lengthy periods required to add new capacity operate under a capacity constraint. There is an upper limit on the size of assets turnover achievable. To attract sufficient capital, these firms must generate a relatively high profit margin. Therefore, such firms operate in the area of Exhibit 4.10 marked (A). The firms usually achieve the high profit margin through some form of entry barrier. The entry barrier may take the form of large required capital outlays, high risks, or regulation. Such factors help explain the profit margin–assets turnover mix of utilities, oil and gas extraction, communications, hotels, and amusements in Exhibit 4.7.

Firms whose products are commodity-like where there are few entry barriers and where competition is intense operate under a competitive constraint. There is an upper limit on the achievable level of profit margin for ROA. To attract sufficient capital, these firms must strive for high assets turnovers. Therefore, such firms will operate in the area of Exhibit 4.10 marked (C). Firms achieve the high assets turnovers by keeping costs as low as possible (for example, minimizing fixed overhead costs, purchasing in sufficient quantities to realize discounts, and integrating vertically or horizontally to obtain cost savings). These firms match such actions to control costs with aggressively low prices to gain market share and drive out marginal firms. Most retailers and wholesalers operate in the low profit margin–high assets turnover area of Exhibit 4.7.

Firms that operate in the area of Exhibit 4.10 marked (B) are not as subject to capacity or competitive constraints as severe as those that operate in the tails of the ROA curves. Therefore, they have more flexibility to take actions that will increase profit margin for ROA, assets turnover, or both to achieve a higher ROA.

The notion of flexibility in trading off profit margin for assets turnover (or vice versa) is important when a firm considers strategic alternatives. The underlying economic concept is the marginal rate of substitution. First, consider a firm with a profit margin–assets turnover combination that puts it in area (A) of Exhibit 4.10. Such a firm will have to give up a significant amount of profit margin for ROA to obtain a meaningful increase in assets turnover. To increase ROA, this firm should emphasize actions that increase profit margin for ROA; for example, it might increase selling prices or reduce variable costs. Likewise, a firm in area (C) of Exhibit 4.10 must give up considerable assets turnover to achieve a higher profit margin for ROA. To increase ROA, such a firm should emphasize actions that increase assets turnover. For firms operating in the tails of the ROA curves, the poor marginal rates of substitution do not favor trading off one variable for the other. Such firms generally must emphasize only one of these factors.

For firms operating in area (B) of Exhibit 4.10, the marginal rates of substitution of profit margin for assets turnover are more equal. Therefore, such firms have more flexibility to design strategies that promote profit margin for ROA, assets turnover, or some combination when striving to increase ROA. Unless the economic characteristics of a business constrain it to operate in area (A) or (C), firms should strive to position themselves in area (B). Such positioning provides greater potential to adapt to changing economic and business conditions.

As already suggested, firms operating in area (A) might attempt to reposition the capacity constraint to the right by outsourcing some of their production. Such an action reduces the amount of fixed assets needed per dollar of sales (that is, increases the fixed assets turnover) but likely will reduce the profit margin for ROA (because of the need to share some of the margin with the outsourcing company). Firms operating in area (C) might add products with a higher profit margin for ROA. Grocery stores, for example, have added fresh flowers, salad bars, fresh bakery products, and pharmaceutical prescription services to their product offerings in recent years in an effort to increase their profit margin for ROA and advance beyond the competitive constraint common for grocery products.

In summary, the economic concepts underlying the profit margin–assets turnover mix are as follows:

Area in Exhibit 4.10	Capital Intensity	Competition	Likely Strategic Focus
A	High	Monopoly	Profit Margin for ROA
B	Medium	Oligopolistic or Monopolistic Competition	Profit Margin for ROA, Assets Turnover, or some combination
C	Low	Pure Competition	Assets Turnover

Business Strategy. Hall[20] and Porter[21] suggest that firms have two generic alternative strategies for a particular product: product differentiation and low-cost leadership. The thrust of the product differentiation strategy is to differentiate a product in such a way as to obtain market power over revenues and, therefore, profit margins. The differentiation could relate to product capabilities, product quality, service, channels of distribution, or some other factor. The thrust of the low-cost leadership strategy is to become the lowest-cost producer, thereby enabling the firm to charge the lowest prices and to achieve higher sales volumes. Such firms can achieve the low-cost position through economies of scale, production efficiencies, outsourcing, or similar factors or by asset parsimony (maintaining strict controls on investments in receivables, inventories, and capital expenditures).[22]

In terms of Exhibit 4.10, movements in the direction of area (A) from any point along the ROA curves focus on product differentiation. Likewise, movements in the direction of area (C) from any point along the ROA curves focus on low-cost leadership. For an example, look at the average profit margins for ROA and assets turnovers for three types of retailers.

	Profit Margin for ROA	Assets Turnover
Specialty Retailers	2.97%	2.21
General Merchandise Stores	2.38%	2.02
Grocery Stores	1.43%	2.82

In the retailing industry, specialty retailers have differentiated themselves by following a niche strategy and have achieved a higher profit margin for ROA than the other two segments. Competition severely constrains the profit margin for ROA of grocery stores, and they must pursue more low-cost leadership strategies. Thus, a firm does not have to be in the tails of the ROA curves to be described as a product differentiator or a low-cost leader. The appropriate basis of comparison is not other industries, but other firms in the same industry. Remember, however, that the relative location along the ROA curve affects a firm's flexibility to trade off

[20]W. K. Hall, "Survival Strategies in a Hostile Environment," *Harvard Business Review* (September–October 1980), pp. 78–85.

[21]M. E. Porter, *Competitive Strategy: Techniques for Analyzing Industries and Competitors* (New York: Free Press), 1998. Porter suggests that firms also might pursue a niche strategy. Because a niche strategy essentially represents differentiation within a market segment, we include it here under product differentiation strategy.

[22]Research in business strategy suggests that firms can simultaneously pursue product differentiation and low-cost leadership because product differentiation is revenue-oriented (output) and low-cost leadership is more expense-oriented (input).

profit margin (product differentiation) for assets turnover (low-cost leadership). More importantly, note that in any industry, firms are dispersed among the profit margin and asset turnover dimensions. For example, within grocery stores, Kroger has higher asset turnover and lower profit margin, whereas Whole Foods has higher profit margin but lower asset turnover.

Summarizing, differences in the profit margin for ROA–assets turnover mix relate to economic factors external to a firm (such as degree of competition, extent of regulation, entry barriers, and similar factors) and to internal strategic choices (such as product differentiation and low-cost leadership). The external and internal factors are, of course, interdependent and dynamic.

PepsiCo's Positioning Relative to the Consumer Foods Industry

PepsiCo is part of the consumer foods industry. The median ROA, profit margin for ROA, and assets turnover for the consumer foods industry and the average amounts for PepsiCo for 2006–2008 are as follows:

	Consumer Foods Industry	PepsiCo
ROA	8.4%	17.1%
Profit Margin for ROA	6.0%	14.3%
Assets Turnover	1.4	1.2

Note that the average ROA of PepsiCo significantly exceeds that for the consumer foods industry because of higher profit margins for ROA earned by PepsiCo. Possible economic or strategic explanations for the higher profit margin for ROA include (1) more value to PepsiCo's brand names than to other food products companies, (2) greater pricing power because of PepsiCo's and Coca-Cola's domination of the beverage industry, (3) greater pricing power because of PepsiCo's influence over its bottlers, and (4) greater efficiencies due to PepsiCo's size or quality of management. The next section explores this higher profit margin for ROA more fully.

Analyzing the Profit Margin for ROA

Profit margin for ROA captures the overall profitability of a firm's operations and is measured as the amount of after-tax profit generated (before financing costs) as a percentage of sales. Thus, the analysis of profit margin focuses on all expenses (other than interest expense) that reduce sales to after-tax profit. Using unadjusted income, ROA for PepsiCo declined steadily from 2006–2008, but adjusted ROA fluctuated somewhat, rising from 16.9 percent in 2006 to 17.8 percent in 2007 and then dropping back to 16.7 percent in 2008. The disaggregation of ROA into the profit margin for ROA and assets turnover components in Exhibit 4.6 (using adjusted ROA) reveals that the fluctuation in ROA results from steadily declining profit margins for ROA offset by a significant increase in assets turnover in 2007, followed by a small increase in 2008. One might liken this disaggregation to peeling an onion. ROA is the outer layer. Peeling away that layer reveals the profit margin for ROA and assets turnover. We can peel the onion an additional layer by examining the components of the profit margin for ROA and the components of assets turnover.

Appealing to the usefulness of common-size analysis discussed earlier in the chapter, we express each revenue and expense amount as a percentage of sales to identify reasons for changes in the profit margin for ROA. Exhibit 4.11 presents these revenue and expense percentages for PepsiCo. We maintain consistency with our earlier decision to adjust reported income for various items and show these effects separately in Exhibit 4.11.

EXHIBIT 4.11

Analysis of the Profit Margin for PepsiCo: 2006–2008

	2008	2007	2006
Net Revenue	100.0%	100.0%	100.0%
Bottling equity income	0.9%	1.4%	1.6%
Interest income	0.1%	0.3%	0.5%
Cost of sales	(47.1%)	(45.7%)	(44.9%)
Selling, general, and administrative expenses	(36.8%)	(36.0%)	(36.2%)
Amortization of intangible assets	(0.1%)	(0.1%)	(0.5%)
Adjustments (from Exhibit 4.6)	1.6%	0.3%	0.2%
Provision for income taxes (adjusted)	(5.0%)	(5.6%)	(5.9%)
Profit margin for ROA	13.6%	14.6%	14.9%

Note from Exhibit 4.11 that PepsiCo's profit margin for ROA decreases because of the following factors:

- Decreases in bottling equity income relative to sales
- Decreases in interest income relative to sales
- Increases in the cost of sales as a percentage of sales
- Increases in selling, general, and administrative expenses relative to sales
- Decreases in the provision for income taxes relative to sales, which offsets the effects of the above items

The above summary contains a degree of measurement error relating to the adjustments made earlier because the restructuring and impairment charges that we added back to reported income are scattered across several of the line items in Exhibit 4.11, including cost of sales and selling, general, and administrative expenses. As discussed in Note 3, "Restructuring and Impairment Charges" (Appendix A), of PepsiCo's $543 million restructuring charge, $455 million is included in selling, general, and administrative expenses and $88 million is included in cost of sales. Thus, unfavorable trends in both of these line items are not quite as negative as suggested if we adjust individual line items rather than the aggregate restructuring and impairment charges.

The task for the financial analyst is to identify reasons for the changes in these revenue and expense percentages. The MD&A provides information for interpreting the changes in these profitability percentages. Firms vary with respect to the informativeness of these discussions. Some firms give specific reasons for changes in various financial ratios. Other firms simply indicate the amount or rate of increase or decrease without providing explanations for the changes. Even when firms provide explanations, the analyst should assess their reasonableness in light of conditions in the economy and the industry, as well as the firm's stated strategy and the results for the firms' competitors. The analyst also should be cautious when a firm does not provide discussion or an explanation for a significant shift in a financial ratio; it implies that the firm is not being forthcoming with useful information.

We use information provided by PepsiCo in its MD&A (Appendix B) to identify reasons for changes in the profit margin for ROA.

Bottling Equity Income

Note 8, "Noncontrolled Bottling Affiliates" (Appendix A), indicates that PepsiCo owns approximately 40 percent of the common stock of some of its bottlers. Because PepsiCo does not own more than 50 percent of the common stock of these bottlers, it does not consolidate the financial statements of the bottlers. Instead, PepsiCo accounts for these investments using the equity method, which Chapter 7 discusses more fully. Firms using the equity method recognize as income each period their share of the net income or net loss of the investees. Thus, bottling equity income for PepsiCo represents its share of the net income of its noncontrolled bottling companies. PepsiCo discloses in its MD&A (Appendix B) that bottling equity income also includes gains and losses from selling shares of its bottlers. Bottling equity income as a percent of sales is as follows (in millions):

2006: $553/$35,137 = 1.57%
2007: $560/$39,474 = 1.42%
2008: $374/$43,251 = 0.86%

The above percentages are not very meaningful because the bottling equity income is not directly related to PepsiCo's sales revenue. Thus, a better ratio to use to evaluate the bottling investments' profitability is bottling equity income as a percentage of the average investments balance. Bottling equity income as a percentage of the average balance in Investments in Noncontrolled Affiliates is as follows (in millions)[23]:

2006: $553/$3,588 = 15.4%
2007: $560/$4,022 = 13.9%
2008: $374/$4,119 = 9.1%

PepsiCo discloses that it sold 8.8 million shares of PBG stock in 2008 and 9.5 million shares in 2007. Thus, PepsiCo has been decreasing its ownership stake in PBG. Over the same period, the profitability of the PBG investments have been decreasing as well, as a percentage of PepsiCo's sales and as a percentage of the investments in noncontrolled affiliates balance. PepsiCo does not provide sufficient information to determine how much of the bottling equity income represents its share of the income of the bottlers and how much represents gains or losses on sales of common stock in the bottlers. However, as discussed earlier, PepsiCo does highlight the fact that the decline in bottling equity income during 2008 is due primarily to PepsiCo's share of PBG's restructuring and impairment charges. PepsiCo's pretax share of this charge is $138 million, or $114 million after tax; thus, adjusting the numerator of the above computations for 2008 results in bottling equity income as a percentage of sales of 1.18% [($374 + $138)/$43,251] and 12.4 percent as a percentage of the average balance in Investments in Noncontrolled Affiliates [($374 + $138)/$4,119]. Even with this adjustment, the profitability of these investments is declining. Thus, we might infer that PepsiCo's decision to decrease investments in PBG is related to the declining profitability of these affiliates.

Bottling equity income is more central to PepsiCo's core operations. The analyst should evaluate with caution the increases in profitability of these bottlers. These bottlers derive most of their income by purchasing concentrate or syrup from PepsiCo, processing it into consumable beverages, placing it in bottles or other containers, and then selling and shipping the product. A principal cost to these bottlers is the amount it pays PepsiCo for the concentrate or syrup. Thus, PepsiCo's pricing policies in selling to the bottlers directly impacts the profitability of the bottlers. In addition, large brand-name consumer goods

---

[23]PepsiCo's current annual report has only two balance sheets but Exhibit 1.9 includes balance sheets for the previous five years. We need more balance sheets than income statements for this ratio because we are using an average balance in the denominator.

companies such as PepsiCo typically provide substantial amounts of marketing, advertising, and administrative support to key noncontrolled affiliates such as PepsiCo's bottlers. Also affecting the income of the bottlers is their control over other manufacturing, selling, and administrative costs. Firms seldom provide the information necessary for the analyst to identify how much of any changes in profitability results from pricing actions by the investor company (change in the investor company's share of marketing and support costs) and how much results from the affiliate's better management of other costs.

Interest Revenue

PepsiCo earns interest on cash balances and short-term investments. Interest revenue as a percentage of the average balance in cash and short-term investments during 2006–2008 are as follows (in millions):

> 2006: \$173/\$3,852 = 4.5%
> 2007: \$125/\$2,652 = 4.7%
> 2008: \$41/\$2,379 = 1.7%

Thus, the decreased interest revenue to sales percentage results from declining average balances in cash and short-term investments and decreases in the yield.

Firms with temporarily excess cash should invest the cash in income-yielding securities, as PepsiCo has done, instead of allowing the cash to remain idle. However, analysts generally do not view interest revenue as an important source of profitability for most manufacturing and retailing firms (except retailing or other firms that offer their own credit cards). To have the greatest impact on share value, firms should derive most of the increases in profitability from their core operations, which in PepsiCo's case is manufacturing and selling consumer foods and beverages. A buildup of excess cash and marketable securities may suggest that a firm has few opportunities to invest in its core operations. The proportion of assets comprising cash and short-term investments for PepsiCo averaged approximately 6–9 percent of total assets during the most recent three years.

Cost of Goods Sold

Interpreting changes in the cost of goods sold to sales percentage is often difficult because explanations might relate to sales revenue only, to cost of goods sold only, or to common factors affecting both the numerator and the denominator. Consider, for example, the following possible explanations for a decrease in the cost of goods sold to sales percentage for a firm:

1. An increase in demand for products in excess of available capacity in an industry will likely result in an increase in selling prices. Even though the cost of manufacturing the product does not change, the cost of goods sold percentage will decrease.
2. As a result of product improvements or effective advertising, a firm's market share for its product increases. The firm allocates the fixed cost of manufacturing the product over a larger volume of production, thereby lowering its per-unit cost. Even though selling prices do not change, the cost of goods sold to sales percentage will decrease.
3. A firm lowers the price for its product to gain a larger market share. It lowers its manufacturing cost per unit by purchasing raw materials in larger quantities to take advantage of quantity discounts. Cost of goods sold per unit declines more than selling price per unit, causing the cost of goods sold to sales percentage to decline.
4. A firm sells multiple products with different cost of goods sold to sales percentages. The product mix shifts toward products with higher profit margins, thereby lowering the overall cost of goods sold to sales percentage.

Thus, the analyst must consider changes in selling prices, manufacturing costs, and product mix when interpreting changes in the cost of goods sold percentage.

Exhibit 4.11 indicates that PepsiCo's cost of goods sold to sales percentage has increased steadily during the three-year period, from 44.9 percent in 2006 to 47.1 percent in 2008. Management's discussion of the results of operations (Appendix B) indicates that PepsiCo encountered higher commodity costs, particularly for cooking oil and fuel in both 2007 and 2008.

Selling, General, and Administrative Expenses

Most firms combine selling, general, and administrative expenses on the income statement. Combining these expense items is unfortunate from an analysis perspective because different factors tend to drive these expenses. Selling expenses include sales commissions, advertising, and promotion materials, which usually vary with the level of sales. General expenses include overhead expenses such as rent, utilities, communications, and insurance, whereas administrative expenses include top management's salaries and the cost of operating staff departments such as information systems, legal services, and R&D. These costs tend not to vary with the level of sales.

PepsiCo's selling, general, and administrative expenses to sales percentages were level between 2006 and 2007 (36.2 percent to 36.0 percent), but they increased to 36.8 percent in 2008. Sales increased 12.3 percent between 2006 and 2007, so the spreading of relatively fixed administrative costs over a larger sales base might explain the decrease from 36.2 percent to 36.0 percent in 2007. Sales increased during 2008, but at a lower rate of 9.6 percent, while selling, general, and administrative expense increased 11.9 percent. Management's discussion of operations (Appendix B) does not give sufficient information to ensure an understanding of the detailed breakdown of selling, general, and administrative expenses, but management does discuss that "other corporate unallocated expenses decreased." However, this decrease was more than offset by the $346 million mark-to-market adjustment discussed earlier, which is classified as a separate corporate unallocated expense. Additionally, Note 3, "Restructuring and Impairment Charges," indicates that $455 million of the $543 million restructuring and impairment charges discussed earlier is included within selling, general, and administrative expenses (with the remainder affecting cost of goods sold). The impact of these two amounts on selling, general, and administrative expenses in Exhibit 4.11 is 1.85 percent [= ($346 + $455 million)/$43,251 million]. Adjusting selling, general and administrative expenses in Exhibit 4.11 for these effects results in a lower percentage of sales (34.95 percent), which is an improvement relative to the levels in 2006 and 2007.

Income Taxes

Exhibit 4.11 indicates that income taxes as a percentage of sales declined from 5.9 percent in 2006 to 5.0 percent in 2008. Note that the computations for the provision for income taxes are adjusted for the tax impact of the adjustments made to the numerator of the adjusted ROA calculation. As discussed earlier, the income tax adjustments include increases for the restructuring and impairment charges and adjustments for tax benefits from settlements with taxing authorities. Further, tax expense is not based on sales (the denominator in Exhibit 4.11), but on pretax profits. A more relevant computation of common-size income taxes is income tax expense as a percentage of pretax operating profit (in millions):

As reported:	Adjusted income tax expense (from Exhibit 4.4):
2006: $1,347/$6,989 = 19.3%	$1,991/$7,056 = 28.2%
2007: $1,973/$7,631 = 25.9%	$2,134/$7,733 = 27.6%
2008: $1,879/$7,021 = 26.8%	$2,038/$7,702 = 26.5%

The comparison of as-reported figures suggests an increasing tax rate, with a marked jump in tax rates in 2007 relative to 2006. Again, the explanation pertains to "unusual" adjustments.

The adjustments to compute adjusted ROA shown in Exhibit 4.4 include tax adjustments totaling $620 million in 2006, reflecting (1) a settlement with the IRS of $602 million of tax filings for 1998–2002 and (2) PepsiCo's portion of PBG's $18 million settlement for 1999–2000. Excluding only these adjustments, the tax rate in 2006 is 28.1 percent [($1,347 + $620)/$6,989]. The adjusted income tax rate, based on adjusted tax expense from Exhibit 4.4, suggests a more stable tax rate of between 28 and 29 percent. Thus, income taxes play a minor role in explaining the overall decrease in the profit margin for ROA.

Firms must disclose in notes to the financial statements their average tax rate and the reasons this rate differs from the statutory federal tax rate. Note 5, "Income Taxes," to PepsiCo's financial statements (Appendix A) presents this information. The figures disclosed under "Tax rate reconciliation" correspond to those based on as-reported figures above. Although the adjusted income tax rate calculations above show a relatively stable tax rate, the reconciliation suggests that one item that is affecting PepsiCo's net income tax rate positively is a favorable decrease in the taxes of foreign results. This suggests an analysis of foreign versus U.S. results, which is discussed next.

Segment Data

The aggregate results in the common-size income statements for PepsiCo examined in Exhibit 4.11 mask potentially important differences in profitability in different product lines or geographic markets. Fortunately, as highlighted earlier in the chapter, both U.S. GAAP and IFRS require firms to provide financial data for their operating segments, products and services, and major customers.[24] Note 1, "Basis of Presentation and Our Divisions," to PepsiCo's financial statements (Appendix A) presents these segment data for 2006–2008. PepsiCo reports product segment data for three large divisions: PepsiCo Americas Foods, PepsiCo Americas Beverages, and PepsiCo International. Within these divisions, PepsiCo further partitions the first and third divisions into segments, with PepsiCo Americas Foods broken out by Frito-Lay North America, Quaker Foods North America, and Latin American Foods, and PepsiCo International broken out into two geographic segments, the United Kingdom & Europe, and the Middle East, Africa, & Asia. Geographic segment data also are reported for the United States, Mexico, Canada, the United Kingdom, and all other countries combined.

The segment disclosures permit the analyst to examine ROA, profit margin, and assets turnover at an additional level of depth, in effect peeling the onion one more layer. Firms such as PepsiCo report revenues, operating profits, and other aggregate information by segment, but to avoid disclosure of sensitive information, firms, unfortunately, do not generally report cost of goods sold and selling, general, and administrative expenses for each segment. That means we cannot reconcile changes in segment profit margins to changes in the overall levels of these two expense percentages. Firms also report segment data pretax, meaning that the segment ROAs and profit margins exceed those for the overall company to a considerable extent.

Exhibit 4.12 presents sales mix data for PepsiCo. PepsiCo's sales mix has shifted during the three years from its North America food and beverage segments to international segments, with international growth in Latin America Foods, United Kingdom & Europe, and All Other Countries segments. (Chapter 10 also utilizes this information data to develop financial statement forecasts.) An important insight that is conveyed by the common-size analysis in Exhibit 4.12 is that the three segments comprising PepsiCo Americas Foods

[24]Financial Accounting Standards Board, *Statement of Financial Accounting Standards No. 131*, "Disclosures about Segments of an Enterprise and Related Information" (1997); *FASB Codification No. 280*; International Accounting Standards Board, *International Financial Reporting Standards No. 8*, "Operating Segments" (November 2006).

EXHIBIT 4.12

Sales Mix Data for PepsiCo

	2008	2007	2006
Product/Geographic Segments			
PepsiCo Americas Foods			
Frito-Lay North America	28.9%	29.4%	30.9%
Quaker Foods North America	4.4%	4.7%	5.0%
Latin America Foods	13.6%	12.3%	11.3%
PepsiCo Americas Beverages	25.3%	28.1%	29.5%
PepsiCo International			
United Kingdom & Europe	14.9%	13.9%	13.5%
Middle East, Africa, & Asia	12.9%	11.6%	9.8%
Total	100.0%	100.0%	100.0%
Country-Level Sales Mix			
United States	52.1%	55.7%	59.2%
Mexico	8.6%	8.9%	9.2%
Canada	4.9%	5.0%	4.8%
United Kingdom	4.9%	5.0%	5.2%
All other countries	29.5%	25.4%	21.6%
	100.0%	100.0%	100.0%

account for almost half of PepsiCo's total sales. Food sales also are included in the PepsiCo International segments. Together, these data suggest that, contrary to the popular belief that PepsiCo is a beverage company, for those determined to categorize the company along a product line, PepsiCo may more accurately be deemed to be a food company than a beverage company (especially because the highest profit margins and asset turnovers reside in the foods segments, as we will see next).

Exhibit 4.13 presents ROAs, profit margins, and assets turnovers for each of PepsiCo's segments. Note that our methods of computation here differ from those we performed previously for PepsiCo consolidated. First, we compute segment ROAs and assets turnover using assets at the *end of the period* to simplify the calculations. The difficulty the analyst often encounters with using average segment assets is that firms frequently change their definition of segments over time and firms report the three most recent years of segment asset data in their current annual report. The analyst would need to access asset data for the fourth year back in order to compute average assets for the three years and hope that the firm maintained its definition of segments. Firms that have changed their segment definitions within the last year will not consistently show assets with current segment definitions. For a stable, mature company such as PepsiCo, the use of assets at the end of the period instead of the average for the period will affect the level of the ROAs and the asset turnover ratios but will not likely have a material effect on the trend of these segment ratios over time unless the firm made a significant corporate acquisition or divestiture during one of the years. Second, note that the numerator of our profitability calculations is based on pretax operating profits rather than net income adjusted for after-tax interest expense. This decision also is made for

EXHIBIT 4.13

Product Segment Pretax Profitability Analysis for PepsiCo

| ROA |

	2008	2007	2006
PepsiCo Americas Foods			
Frito–Lay North America	47.1%	45.4%	43.8%
Quaker Foods North America	56.2%	56.7%	55.2%
Latin America Foods	29.7%	23.2%	30.2%
PepsiCo Americas Beverages	26.4%	32.0%	32.5%
PepsiCo International			
United Kingdom & Europe	9.4%	10.9%	11.9%
Middle East, Africa, & Asia	16.8%	13.7%	13.5%

| Profit Margin for ROA | | | Assets Turnover | | |

	2008	2007	2006	2008	2007	2006
PepsiCo Americas Foods						
Frito–Lay North America	23.7%	24.6%	24.1%	1.99	1.85	1.82
Quaker Foods North America	30.6%	30.5%	31.3%	1.84	1.86	1.76
Latin America Foods	15.2%	14.7%	16.5%	1.95	1.58	1.83
PepsiCo Americas Beverages	18.5%	22.4%	22.3%	1.43	1.43	1.45
PepsiCo International						
United Kingdom & Europe	12.6%	14.1%	14.7%	0.75	0.77	0.81
Middle East, Africa, & Asia	12.0%	11.7%	11.7%	1.41	1.17	1.16

simplicity. Financing policies and activities frequently reside with the corporate division; thus, they are not allocated to operating segments. As with our use of end-of-period total assets, this simplifying procedure is not likely to prevent an analyst from gaining objective insight into the relative profitability and efficiency of the segments being analyzed. The primary limitation of these assumptions is that we cannot precisely reconcile the segment calculations with those for the consolidated results of PepsiCo. Data availability and practicality frequently drive financial analysis decisions and techniques, which further emphasizes our earlier cautionary note that the astute analyst does not memorize ratios, but understands the rationale for how to interpret various measures.

The top portion of Exhibit 4.13 indicates that the segments with the highest ROAs are Frito-Lay North America and Quaker Foods North America. Overall, the foods division is more profitable than the beverages or international division. The lower portion of Exhibit 4.13 shows the decomposition of ROA into profit margin and assets turnover. The profit margins generally mirror the distribution of ROA in the upper portion of Exhibit 4.13, with PepsiCo Americas Foods showing the highest profit margins. Similarly, this division also has the highest assets turnover, followed by PepsiCo Americas Beverages and PepsiCo International. The overall higher level of profitability and asset utilization for PepsiCo Americas Foods and PepsiCo Americas Beverages is consistent with our discussions of life cycle theory in Chapter 3 (Exhibit 3.1) and earlier in this chapter (Exhibit 4.9). The Americas segments are older and more mature than the International segments, so it is understandable that the Americas divisions are more profitable and efficient. Growth segments such as PepsiCo International are not as profitable due to required investments in growing sales volume and refining production and distribution operations to levels comparable to more mature segments. If PepsiCo proves as successful internationally as it has been in the Americas, profit margin and asset turnover for these segments should improve in the future. Because of this regularity, segment disclosures are frequently most helpful in the forecasting part of financial statement analysis and valuation, which we will return to in Chapter 10.

A caveat of segment reporting analysis relates to the data used. Note that the information in Note 1 of PepsiCo's footnotes is the basis of calculations for Exhibits 4.12 and 4.13. Exhibit 4.12 is based on sales that reconcile to the total for consolidated results for PepsiCo; that is, the total sales of all six segments adds up to the total sales for PepsiCo consolidated. However, Exhibit 4.13 is based on operating profits that do not reconcile with consolidated total operating profit for PepsiCo. As indicated in Note 1 of PepsiCo's footnotes, the difference between total operating profit of $6,935 million in 2008 and the $7,942 million sum of the operating profits of the individual operating segments is caused by corporate unallocated expenses of $1,007 million. Total corporate unallocated expenses increased 33.7 percent from $753 million in 2007, while total sales increased only 9.6 percent. PepsiCo includes these expenses in selling, general, and administrative expenses in its income statement but does not allocate them to its operating segments when disclosing segment data. Following are the corporate unallocated expenses as a percentage of sales for the three years (in millions):

2006: $738/$35,137 = 2.1%
2007: $753/$39,474 = 1.9%
2008: $1,007/$43,251 = 2.3%

The analyst must exert caution when interpreting segment profit margins and ROAs. Changes in the amount of expenses allocated versus not allocated to segments, a choice made by management, affect these ratios. PepsiCo discloses that the increase in corporate unallocated expenses in 2008 relates primarily to $346 million in mark-to-market adjustments for commodity derivative hedges, which we discussed above and chose not to adjust in our analyses.

Summary of Profit Margin Analysis

We noted at the beginning of this section that PepsiCo's profit margin for ROA fluctuated between 16.7 and 17.8 percent during 2006 through 2008. This reflected a declining profit margin for ROA (from 14.9 percent in 2006 to 13.6 percent in 2008) and increasing assets turnover. We used common-size analysis to identify the primary contributions to the observed profit margins and analyzed each item to better understand the factors contributing to the overall profit margin. The summary of our findings for the analysis of profit margins is as follows:

- Bottling equity income decreased in 2008, due primarily to PepsiCo's pretax share of a $138 million restructuring charge by PBG.

- Interest revenue declined due to declining balances of cash and short-term investments and declining yields.
- Cost of sales increased due to higher commodity costs, including cooking oil and fuel.
- Selling, general, and administrative expenses increased in 2008, due primarily to a $346 million mark-to-market adjustment for derivative hedges.
- Income tax expense increased relative to sales, but this was due primarily to a large favorable settlement in the benchmark year of 2006.
- Segment analysis suggested that the growth in sales is occurring in international markets, where margins are lower than in more mature markets such as the Americas.

Having examined the first component of ROA—profit margin—we examine next the other component—total assets turnover.

Analyzing Total Assets Turnover

Total assets turnover captures how efficiently assets are being utilized to generate revenues. Higher sales generated with a given level of assets indicates more efficient use of those assets. Exhibit 4.6 showed that PepsiCo's total assets turnover increased between 2006 and 2007 from 1.14 to 1.22 and stayed at that level for 2008. Unlike the analysis of profit margin, where we decomposed the numerator by examining different expenses that determined operating profit, the analysis of total assets turnover can best be achieved by decomposing the denominator. We can gain greater insight into changes in the total assets turnover by examining turnover ratios for particular classes of assets. Analysts frequently calculate the following three turnover ratios:

- Accounts receivable turnover
- Inventory turnover
- Fixed assets turnover

Management's discussion and analysis of operations usually provides detailed explanations for operating profits, but it does not include explanations for changes in asset turnovers; so the analyst must search for possible clues. This is unfortunate because small changes in assets turnover can have enormous effects on the overall profitability of a firm (that is, ROA and ROCE).

Accounts Receivable Turnover

The rate at which accounts receivable turn over indicates the average time until firms collect them in cash. The analyst calculates accounts receivable turnover by dividing net sales on account by average accounts receivable. Most sales transactions between businesses are on account, not for cash. Except for retailers and restaurants that deal directly with consumers, the assumption that all sales are on account is usually reasonable. The calculation of the accounts receivable turnover for 2008 for PepsiCo, assuming that it makes all sales on account, is as follows (in millions):

$$\frac{\text{Accounts Receivable}}{\text{Turnover}} = \frac{\text{Net Sales on Account}}{\text{Average Accounts Receivable}}$$

$$9.5 = \frac{\$43,251}{0.5\ (\$4,683 + \$4,389)}$$

PepsiCo's accounts receivable turnover was 9.7 in 2007 and 10.1 in 2006.

The analyst often expresses the accounts receivable turnover in terms of the average number of days receivables are outstanding before firms collect them in cash. The calculation divides 365 days by the accounts receivable turnover.[25] The average number of days that accounts receivable were outstanding was 38.4 days (= 365/9.5) during 2008, 37.6 days (= 365/9.7) during 2007, and 36.1 days (= 365/10.1) during 2006. One also could calculate the days sales included in the *ending* accounts receivable balance, in which case the calculation would be ending accounts receivable divided by average daily sales (= sales/365). Given an increased accounts receivable balance during 2008, this computation would yield slightly higher days sales for the ending receivables [$4,683/($43,251/365) = 39.5].

The interpretation of the average collection period depends on the terms of sale. These computations clearly indicate that PepsiCo is collecting accounts receivable more slowly. Assuming that customers must pay within 45 days, it appears that although they are paying more slowly, most of PepsiCo's customers pay within the required period. If the terms of sale are, for example, 15 days, on average, PepsiCo does not collect within the required period. Many firms transact business with credit sales terms of 30 days.

The interpretation of changes in the accounts receivable turnover and average collection period also relates to a firm's credit extension policies. Firms often use credit terms as a means of stimulating sales. For example, in an effort to stimulate sales, firms might permit customers to delay making payments on purchases of lawn mowers until after the summer and on snowmobiles until after the winter. Such actions would lead to a decrease in the accounts receivable turnover and an increase in the number of days receivables are outstanding. The changes in these accounts receivable ratios would not necessarily signal negative news if the increase in net income from the additional sales exceeded the cost of carrying accounts receivable for the extra time. Firms also can use credit policy to provide implicit financing to support affiliated companies, such as credit extended by automobile manufacturers to dealerships, producers to closely related distributors (such as PepsiCo and Coca-Cola to affiliated bottlers), and restaurant chains to franchisees or licensees (such as McDonald's to franchisees and Starbucks to licensees).

Retailing firms, particularly department store chains such as Sears and JCPenney, offer their own credit cards to customers. They use credit cards to stimulate sales and to earn interest revenue from customers' installment payments. Interpreting an increase in the number of days accounts receivable are outstanding involves two conflicting signals. The increase might suggest greater risk of uncollectibility, but it also provides additional interest revenues. Some firms price their products to obtain a relatively low gross margin from the sale and depend on interest revenue as a principal source of earnings. Thus, the analyst must consider a firm's credit strategy and policies when interpreting the accounts receivable turnover and days receivable outstanding ratios.

PepsiCo does not explain the slower accounts receivable turnover. A significant proportion of PepsiCo's accounts receivable likely relates to amounts owed PepsiCo by its bottlers and grocery retailers. PepsiCo might have intentionally granted more favorable repayment terms to support its bottlers and grocery retailers during the recessionary economy in 2007 and 2008. Another possibility is that repayment terms in other countries may differ from those in the United States. An increased percentage of sales from countries with longer repayment times might account for the slower accounts receivable turnover. In any case, the increase in the number of days it takes to collect accounts receivable from 36.1 days in 2006 to 38.4 days in 2008 does not seem to be a major concern. However, the trend has been increasing for several years going back prior to 2006. Assuming that PepsiCo borrowed

---

[25]Some analysts use 360 days in calculations like this. Although this choice introduces slight measurement error biasing toward faster turnover, as long as it is used consistently in all calculations, it is unlikely to have a significant effect on inferences.

short-term debt at 4 percent interest to finance the greater number of days receivables were outstanding, it would have cost PepsiCo approximately \$1.1 million [= ({38.4 − 36.1}/365) × 0.04 × 0.5(\$4,683 + \$4,389)] during 2008. PepsiCo's interest expense for 2008 was \$329 million. Under these assumptions, the increase in collection period increased interest expense only 0.3 percent (= \$1.1/\$329).

Inventory Turnover

The rate at which inventories turn over indicates the length of time needed to produce, hold, and sell inventories. The analyst calculates the inventory turnover by dividing cost of goods sold by the average inventory during the period. The calculation of inventory turnover for PepsiCo for 2008 is as follows (in millions):

$$\frac{\text{Inventory}}{\text{Turnover}} = \frac{\text{Cost of Goods Sold}}{\text{Average Inventories}}$$

$$8.5 = \frac{\$20,351}{0.5(\$2,522 + \$2,290)}$$

Thus, PepsiCo's inventory was on hand for an average of 42.9 days (= 365/8.5) during 2008. PepsiCo's inventory turnover was 8.6 (42.4 days) in 2007 and 8.7 (42.0 days) in 2006. Thus, the inventory turnover slowed by 0.9 days during the three-year period.

PepsiCo does not explain the slower inventory turnover. One possibility is that worldwide economic conditions led to reduced purchases of premium snacks or beverages, which could have led to reduced inventory turnover. The CEO's letter to shareholders (Appendix B) attributes sales declines for PepsiCo Americas Beverages to weakness in the U.S. economy. The MD&A (Appendix B) provides more details on the effect of the U.S. economy on beverage sales, indicating that carbonated soft drink volume declined 4 percent, largely due to lower sales of Pepsi and Sierra Mist, offset by increases in sales of Mountain Dew. Another possibility is that PepsiCo experienced a shift in sales mix due to its expansion in international markets with different consumer preferences. Unfortunately, the analyst cannot assess the latter possibility without a breakout of the various products by segment.

The interpretation of the inventory turnover figure involves two opposing considerations. A firm would like to sell as many goods as possible with a minimum of capital tied up in inventories. Moreover, inventory is subject to obsolescence or spoilage, especially in the case of food products. An increase in the rate of inventory turnover between periods would seem to indicate more profitable use of the investment in inventory and lowering costs for financing and carrying inventory. On the other hand, a firm does not want to have so little inventory on hand that shortages result and the firm misses sales opportunities. An increase in the rate of inventory turnover in this case may mean a loss of sales opportunities, thereby offsetting any cost savings achieved by a decreased investment in inventory. Firms must make trade-offs in deciding the optimum level of inventory and thus the desirable rate of inventory turnover.

The analyst often gains insight into changes in the inventory turnover by simultaneously examining changes in the inventory turnover and the cost of goods sold to sales percentage. Consider the following scenarios and possible interpretations:

- **Increasing cost of goods sold to sales percentage, coupled with an increasing inventory turnover.** The firm lowers prices to sell inventory more quickly. The firm shifts its product mix toward lower-margin, faster-moving products. The firm outsources the production of a higher proportion of its products, requiring it to share profit margin with the outsourcer but reducing the amount of raw materials and work-in-process inventories.

- **Decreasing cost of goods sold to sales percentage, coupled with a decreasing inventory turnover.** The firm raises prices to increase its gross margin, but inventory sells more slowly. The firm shifts its product mix toward higher-margin, slower-moving products. The firm produces a higher proportion of its products instead of outsourcing, thereby capturing more of the gross margin but requiring the firm to carry raw materials and work-in-process inventories.
- **Increasing cost of goods sold to sales percentage, coupled with a decreasing inventory turnover.** Weak economic conditions lead to reduced demand for the firm's products, necessitating price reductions to move goods. Despite price reductions, inventory builds up.
- **Decreasing cost of goods sold to sales percentage, coupled with an increasing inventory turnover.** Strong economic conditions lead to increased demand for the firm's products, allowing price increases. An inability to replace inventory as fast as the firm sells it leads to an increased inventory turnover. The firm implements a just-in-time inventory system, reducing storage costs, product obsolescence, and the amount of inventory held.

Some analysts calculate the inventory turnover ratio by dividing sales, rather than cost of goods sold, by the average inventory. As long as there is a reasonably constant relation between selling prices and cost of goods sold, the analyst can identify changes in the trend of the inventory turnover using either measure. It is inappropriate to use sales in the numerator if the analyst wants to use the inventory turnover ratio to calculate the average number of days inventory is on hand until sale or if the analyst wants to compare inventory turnover across firms with different markups and gross profit margins.

The cost-flow assumption (FIFO, LIFO, or weighted average) for inventories and cost of goods sold can significantly affect both the inventory turnover ratio and the cost of goods sold to sales percentage. Chapter 8 discusses the impact of the cost-flow assumption and illustrates adjustments the analyst might make to deal with these effects.

Fixed Assets Turnover

The fixed assets turnover ratio measures the relation between sales and the investment in property, plant, and equipment. The analyst calculates the fixed assets turnover by dividing sales by average fixed assets (net of accumulated depreciation) during the year. The fixed assets turnover ratio for PepsiCo for 2008 is as follows:

$$\frac{\text{Fixed Assets}}{\text{Turnover}} = \frac{\text{Sales}}{\text{Average Fixed Assets}}$$

$$3.8 = \frac{\$43,251}{0.5(\$11,663 + \$11,228)}$$

The fixed assets turnover for PepsiCo also was 3.8 in 2007 and 2006. Increasing the fixed assets turnover ratio generally indicates greater efficiency in the use of existing fixed assets, but if a firm has excess capacity, it can indicate increasing utilization of that capacity. With this information in mind, the analyst must carefully interpret changes in the fixed assets turnover ratio. Firms invest in fixed assets in anticipation of higher production and sales in future periods. Thus, a temporarily low or decreasing rate of fixed assets turnover may signal an expanding firm preparing for future growth. On the other hand, a firm may reduce its capital expenditures if the near-term outlook for its products is poor. Such an action could lead to an increase in the fixed assets turnover ratio.

In recent years, many firms have increased the proportion of production outsourced to other manufacturers. This action allows firms to achieve the same (or increasing) sales levels with less fixed assets, thereby increasing the fixed assets turnover.

Other Asset Turnover Ratios

Although turnover ratios are most common for the assets discussed above (receivables, inventory, and fixed assets), any asset can be examined as a turnover ratio as long as the appropriate numerator is used in the calculation. For example, firms maintain varying levels of cash and analysts are often interested in the efficiency with which cash is managed. Thus, an investor can gauge the strategic maintenance of cash balances by a cash turnover ratio. The cash turnover ratio is computed by dividing sales by the average cash balance during the year. The cash turnover ratio for PepsiCo for 2008 is as follows:

$$\frac{\text{Cash}}{\text{Turnover}} = \frac{\text{Sales}}{\text{Average Cash and Cash Equivalents}}$$

$$29.1 = \frac{\$43,251}{0.5(\$2,064 + \$910)}$$

Thus, PepsiCo turns over its cash balance approximately 29 times per year; equivalently, PepsiCo maintains a cash balance of approximately 12.5 days sales ($= 365/29.1$). Calculated with *sales* in the numerator, this implies that PepsiCo replenishes its cash balance every 12.5 days, which assumes that all sales are in cash. Alternatively, an analyst could view cash as a means of funding other working capital (inventory, for example). With this perspective, the analyst might calculate the cash turnover ratio with cost of goods sold in the numerator. The computations are similar to those above, but the interpretation is different.

Similarly, the analyst might want an overall metric for the efficiency with which all current assets are managed (rather than individually). Accordingly, the analyst would compute a current asset turnover ratio by dividing sales by the average current assets during the year. The current assets turnover ratio for PepsiCo for 2008 is as follows:

$$\frac{\text{Current Assets}}{\text{Turnover}} = \frac{\text{Sales}}{\text{Average Current Assets}}$$

$$4.1 = \frac{\$43,251}{0.5(\$10,806 + \$10,151)}$$

Thus, PepsiCo turns over its current assets approximately every fiscal quarter. The current assets turnover ratio conveys information similar to that for individual asset turnover ratios for cash, receivables, or inventory. However, the current assets turnover ratio is often more representative because the volatility of total current assets is less than the volatility of an individual current asset. For example, stronger-than-expected end-of-year sales might result in ending receivables being temporarily above normal levels and inventory being temporarily below current levels. This would cause the receivables turnover ratio to be deflated but the inventory turnover ratio to be inflated. All else equal, however, the current assets turnover ratio would be less likely to be affected because the volatilities in receivables balances and inventory levels tend to offset each other.

The analysis of working capital turnovers also will be important in Chapter 5 when we discuss the use of financial analysis to assess short-term liquidity risks.

Summary of Assets Turnover Analysis

PepsiCo's total assets turnover was steady between 2007 and 2008. We examined the three primary asset turnover ratios: accounts receivable, inventory, and fixed assets. Both accounts receivable turnover and inventory turnover decreased slightly, while fixed assets turnover held constant. Accounts receivable make up approximately 13 percent of total assets, and inventories make up approximately 7 percent of total assets. (See the common-size balance sheet percentages in Exhibit 1.17.) However, fixed assets make up 32 percent of total assets. Thus, one would expect that the pattern in fixed assets turnover would dominate among these three, especially given only small changes in accounts receivable and inventory turnovers. However, other assets beside receivables, inventories, and fixed assets affect the total assets turnover computation with which we began our analysis. The utilization of other assets could be examined to supplement our analysis of only three asset classes that collectively account for just over half of total assets. For example, the percentage of total assets represented by intangible assets fell from 20.8 percent in 2007 to 19.3 percent in 2008. Note 4, "Property, Plant, and Equipment and Intangible Assets," in PepsiCo's 2008 Annual Report (Appendix A) indicates that the relative decrease in intangibles is due to scheduled amortization of amortizable intangible assets combined with negative currency translation adjustments for goodwill and brands at PepsiCo's various non-U.S. segments. In addition, Investments in Noncontrolled Affiliates fell from 12.6 percent of total assets to 10.8 percent in 2008. As discussed under "Bottling Equity Income" in our analysis of profit margin earlier in the chapter, PepsiCo has been reducing its level of investments in PBG, which explains the decrease.

Summary of ROA Analysis

Recalling the analogy of decomposing profitability to peeling back layers of an onion, our analysis of operating profitability involves four levels of depth:

Level 1: ROA for the firm as a whole

Level 2: Disaggregation of ROA into profit margin for ROA and assets turnover for the firm as a whole

Level 3a: Disaggregation of profit margin into expense ratios for various cost items

Level 3b: Disaggregation of assets turnover into turnovers for individual assets

Level 4: Analysis of profit margins and asset turnovers for the segments of a firm

Exhibit 4.14 summarizes this analysis in a format used throughout the remainder of this book. **This layered approach to analyzing financial statements provides a disciplined approach that can be applied to any firm.**

Supplementing ROA in Profitability Analysis

ROA uses average total assets as a base for assessing a firm's effectiveness in using resources to generate earnings. For some firms and industries, total assets may not serve an informative role for this purpose because, as Chapter 2 discusses, accounting practices (1) do not assign asset values to certain valuable resources (technological knowledge and human capital) and (2) report assets at acquisition costs instead of current market values (forests for forest products companies and land for railroads). To supplement straightforward financial statement analysis, analysts often supplement ROA by relating sales, expenses, and earnings to *nonfinancial* attributes when evaluating profitability. This section discusses techniques for assessing profitability unique to several industries. The discussion is not intended to be exhaustive of all industries, but to provide a flavor for the types of supplemental measures used.

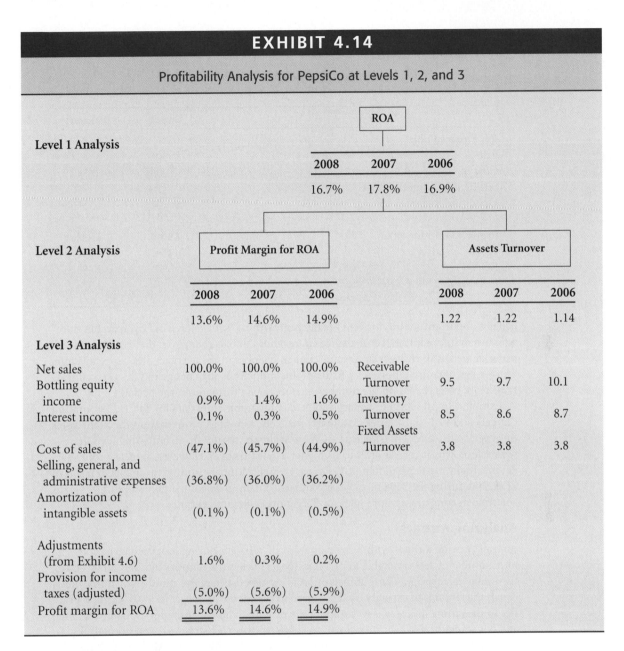

EXHIBIT 4.14

Profitability Analysis for PepsiCo at Levels 1, 2, and 3

Level 1 Analysis

ROA

2008	2007	2006
16.7%	17.8%	16.9%

Level 2 Analysis

Profit Margin for ROA			Assets Turnover		
2008	2007	2006	2008	2007	2006
13.6%	14.6%	14.9%	1.22	1.22	1.14

Level 3 Analysis

	2008	2007	2006		2008	2007	2006
Net sales	100.0%	100.0%	100.0%	Receivable Turnover	9.5	9.7	10.1
Bottling equity income	0.9%	1.4%	1.6%	Inventory Turnover	8.5	8.6	8.7
Interest income	0.1%	0.3%	0.5%	Fixed Assets Turnover	3.8	3.8	3.8
Cost of sales	(47.1%)	(45.7%)	(44.9%)				
Selling, general, and administrative expenses	(36.8%)	(36.0%)	(36.2%)				
Amortization of intangible assets	(0.1%)	(0.1%)	(0.5%)				
Adjustments (from Exhibit 4.6)	1.6%	0.3%	0.2%				
Provision for income taxes (adjusted)	(5.0%)	(5.6%)	(5.9%)				
Profit margin for ROA	13.6%	14.6%	14.9%				

Analyzing Retailers

A key resource of retailers is their retail space. Some retailers own their stores, while others lease their space. The analyst can constructively capitalize the present value of operating lease commitments to ensure that total assets include store buildings under operating leases. (Chapter 6 discusses this adjustment.) An alternative approach when analyzing retailers is to express sales, operating expenses, and operating income on a per-store basis or per square foot of retail selling space. This supplemental base for evaluating profitability circumvents the issue of whether firms own or lease their space. It also eliminates the effects on the denominator of ROA of using different depreciation methods and depreciable lives and having fixed assets with different ages. However, it does not eliminate the effect of different depreciation methods or depreciable lives on income in the numerator. An

EXHIBIT 4.15

Profitability Ratios for Target and Walmart

	Target	Walmart
Per Square Foot:		
Sales	$ 302	$ 454
Cost of Goods Sold	(205)	(342)
Selling and Administrative	(76)	(86)
Operating Income	$ 21	$ 26
Profit Margin for ROA	4.30%	3.82%
Assets Turnover	1.47	2.45
ROA	6.3%	9.4%
Comparable Store Sales Change	(2.9)%	3.5%

equally important metric for retail firms is growth in "same store" or "comparable store" sales. Analysts are interested in changes in revenues due to changes in the number of retail stores as well as in changes in revenues due to changes in the average sales per retail store. Thus, a key measure reported by firms in this industry is the change in sales on a comparable store basis (based on the number of stores open throughout the period).

Exhibit 4.15 presents per-square-foot and comparable store data for Target Corporation (Target) and Wal-Mart Stores (Walmart) for 2008, as well as profit margin for ROA, assets turnover, and ROA. The superior ROA of Walmart results from much higher sales per square foot, which corresponds to its higher assets turnover. However, Target's profit margin is actually higher than that of Walmart. Overall, Walmart is more profitable in terms of ROA, and during the 2008 fiscal year, Walmart actually grew comparable stores sales versus a decline in comparable store sales for Target over the same period.

Analyzing Airlines

Aircraft provide airlines with a fixed amount of capacity during a particular period. The total number of seats available to carry passengers times the number of miles flown equals the available capacity. The number of seats occupied times the number of miles flown equals the amount of capacity used (referred to as *revenue passenger miles*). Common practice in the airline industry is to compute the revenues and expenses per available seat mile and per revenue passenger mile flown to judge pricing, cost structure, and profitability.

Exhibit 4.16 presents selected profitability data for American Airlines, JetBlue, and Airtran for 2008. American operates both domestic and international routes, while JetBlue and Airtran provide primarily domestic services. The employees of American and Airtran are unionized, while those of JetBlue are not. All three airlines are publicly owned. The first three columns present revenues, expenses, and operating income before income taxes per available seat mile, and the last three columns present the same income items per revenue passenger mile flown.

The costs of an airline (such as depreciation and compensation) are largely fixed for a particular year. Thus, the operating expenses per available seat mile indicate the costs of operating each airline. Fuel costs were significant for all airlines, but JetBlue had the lowest cost; American had the highest. Compensation costs also were highest at American, as were all other operating expenses. This resulted in a significant operating loss for American in

EXHIBIT 4.16

Profitability Ratios for American, JetBlue, and Airtran

	Per Available Seat Mile			Per Revenue Passenger Mile		
	American	**JetBlue**	**Airtran**	**American**	**JetBlue**	**Airtran**
Operating Revenues	14.53¢	10.44¢	10.72¢	18.04¢	13.00¢	13.47¢
Fuel	(5.51)	(4.17)	(5.02)	(6.84)	(5.19)	(6.30)
Compensation	(4.07)	(2.14)	(1.99)	(5.05)	(2.66)	(2.51)
Other Operating Expenses	(6.11)	(3.79)	(4.01)	(7.58)	(4.73)	(5.04)
Operating Income	(1.16¢)	0.34¢	(0.30¢)	(1.43¢)	0.42¢	(0.38¢)
Profitability Decomposition:						
Profit Margin for ROA				(8.7%)	2.2%	(8.7%)
Assets Turnover				0.68	0.58	1.24
ROA				(5.9%)	1.3%	(10.8%)

2008, despite also having the highest revenue per seat mile. Airtran had lower costs than American, but because operating revenues on a per-mile basis were lower, it also realized an operating loss in 2008. In contrast, JetBlue had the lowest operating revenue on a per-mile basis, but due to low fuel, compensation, and other costs, it was profitable in 2008. The profit margins were similar (and negative) for American and Airtran but were positive for JetBlue. The assets turnover for Airtran was highest, which combined with the negative profit margin to yield Airtran's negative ROA. Given similar profit margins, the difference in ROA between Airtran and American is driven by assets turnover differences. The explanation for the higher assets turnover for Airtran relative to American is that Airtran leases 100 of 136 aircraft, versus 220 out of 892 for American (not shown in Exhibit 4.16). JetBlue had the lowest assets turnover, but it had a positive profit margin, which produced a positive but low ROA.

The analyst can apply similar metrics to other firms with fixed capacity. The analysis of hospitals often focuses on income data per available bed or per patient day. The analysis of hotels uses income data per room. The analysis of cable and telecommunications companies examines income data per subscriber or customer. For-profit education firms are judged based on income data per student.

Analyzing Service Firms

Using ROA to analyze the profitability of firms that provide services can result in misleading conclusions because their most important resources, their employees who deliver the services, do not appear on the balance sheet as assets under GAAP. One approach to deal with this omission is to express income on a per-employee basis. However, the analyst must use these data cautiously because of differences among firms in their use of full- versus part-time employees and their mix of direct service providers versus support personnel.

Exhibit 4.17 presents profitability data for three service firms. VisionChina Media is one of China's largest mobile TV advertising networks, with extensive coverage in public transportation facilities (<500 employees). Monster Worldwide is an online recruitment firm that links employers with people seeking employment (approximately 7,000 employees). Accenture is a multinational management consulting firm (>175,000 employees). VisionChina has the highest operating revenues per employee, followed by Monster, then Accenture. This is due to

EXHIBIT 4.17

Profitability Data for VisionChina Media, Monster Worldwide, and Accenture

Per Employee:	VisionChina Media	Monster Worldwide	Accenture
Operating Revenues	$ 220,044	$193,328	$130,909
Compensation	(5,619)	(78,168)	(92,259)
Administrative and Other Expenses	(126,293)	(90,706)	(23,713)
Operating Income before Income Taxes	$ 88,132	$ 24,454	$ 14,937
Profitability Decomposition:			
Profit Margin for ROA	45.1%	9.4%	7.5%
Assets Turnover	0.44	0.67	1.88
ROA	19.8%	6.3%	14.1%

the combined exclusivity of VisionChina's network throughout China and the fact that the service it provides—advertising via mobile video terminals—does not rely on people to provide the service. In sharp contrast, Accenture's services are provided almost exclusively by employees. Also, compensation expense is highest for Accenture, followed by Monster and VisionChina, with VisionChina having the lowest compensation costs per employee.[26] Administrative and other expenses are highest for VisionChina, which incurs substantial costs for media equipment (essentially cost of sales) and other media under certain agreements, which Monster and Accenture do not report. This difference in business models can be seen with the significantly lower assets turnover for VisionChina, which actually maintains substantial investments in assets, as it is not purely a "service" firm. Assets turnover is highest for Accenture, which maintains limited fixed assets and possesses brand recognition and an extensive professional network. Operating revenues and operating income before taxes per employee are lowest at Accenture (with the largest workforce), but Accenture generates a very high ROA due to the high assets turnover. Monster's operating revenues and operating income before taxes per employee are between those of Accenture and VisionChina, but its ROA is lowest.

Per-employee data might usefully supplement traditional financial ratios for numerous other industries, including investment banking, temporary help firms, engineering firms, advertising firms, professional sports teams, information technology, and other service firms. The use of per-employee data also might supplement the analysis of firms that use fixed assets in the provision of services, such as airlines, health care providers, and hotels.

Analyzing Technology-Based Firms

ROA can be an even more misleading ratio for analyzing technology-based firms than for analyzing service firms if the two most important resources of technology firms do not appear in their assets: (1) their people and (2) their technologies. Employees contribute to the creation of technologies, but the most important resource not recognized is the value of the

---

[26]The individual line items require judgment, as neither company separately discloses an income statement line item for salaries and benefits. So the analyst must examine additional disclosures when available to best prepare cross-sectionally comparable expense classifications.

technologies (when those technologies have been internally generated rather than acquired). GAAP requires firms to expense R&D costs in the year incurred. Thus, both assets and net income are understated during periods in which firms invest heavily in R&D. Subsequently, after R&D has led to the introduction of successful, profitable new products, assets are understated but income is overstated because the firms have already expensed investments in R&D.

Research by Lev and Sougiannis documents the value of technologies that might provide a basis for recognizing a technology asset on the balance sheet and recomputing net income each year.[27] The authors propose a methodology that involves studying the relationship between R&D expenditures in a particular year and revenues of subsequent years. The technology "asset" equals the present value of the future revenue stream net of the R&D expenditure during the year. The analyst would then amortize this "asset" over the future periods of benefit based on the projected stream of revenues. Traditional financial ratio analysis works reasonably well for established technology firms that have products in all stages of their life cycles. Traditional financial ratio analysis does not work as well for start-up firms and firms with most of their products in the early high-growth stages of their life cycles. Thus, many analysts take as-reported income statement and balance sheets for such companies and recast them to allow for the capitalization of technology assets (and subsequent amortization), similar to the study by Lev and Sougiannis. This further emphasizes the need for analysts to understand financial statements and business operations rather than memorize ratio formulas or scripted analysis techniques.

RATE OF RETURN ON COMMON SHAREHOLDERS' EQUITY

ROA measures the profitability of operations before considering the effects of financing. That is, ROA ignores the proportion of debt versus equity financing that a firm uses to finance the assets and the cost of debt financing. ROA is important for analysts interested in the profitability and efficiency of the firm's core operations. ROCE, on the other hand, measures the return to common shareholders after subtracting from revenues not only operating expenses (such as cost of goods sold, selling and administration expenses, and income taxes), but also the costs of financing debt and preferred stock that are senior to the common stock. The latter includes interest expense on debt and dividends on preferred stock (if any). Thus, ROCE incorporates the results of a firm's operating, investing, and financing decisions.

The analyst calculates ROCE as follows:

$$\text{ROCE} = \frac{\text{Net Income} - \text{Preferred Stock Dividends}}{\text{Average Common Shareholders' Equity}}$$

The numerator measures the amount of net income for the period available to the common shareholders after subtracting all amounts allocable to senior claimants. The accountant subtracts interest expense on debt in measuring net income, so the calculation of the numerator of ROCE requires no adjustment for creditors' claims on earnings. However, the analyst must subtract dividends paid or payable on preferred stock from net income to obtain income attributable to the common shareholders.[28]

---

[27]Baruch Lev and Theodore Sougiannis, "The Capitalization, Amortization and Value-Relevance of R&D," *Journal of Accounting and Economics* (1996), pp. 107–138.

[28]Chapter 14 indicates that for purposes of valuation, the analyst might compute ROCE using comprehensive income available to common shareholders, not net income available to common shareholders. Recall from Chapter 2 that comprehensive income equals net income plus or minus changes in the value of certain assets and liabilities that GAAP requires firms to include in Other Comprehensive Income until realized.

The denominator of ROCE measures the average amount of total common shareholders' equity in use during the period. An average of the total common shareholders' equity at the beginning and end of the year is appropriate unless a firm made a significant new common stock issue or buyback during the year. If the latter occurred, the analyst should use an average of the common shareholders' equity at the end of each quarter to better reflect the outstanding common shareholders' equity during the year.

Common shareholders' equity equals total shareholders' equity minus the minority interest in the net assets of consolidated subsidiaries minus the par value of preferred stock. Because net income to common shareholders in the numerator reflects a subtraction for the minority interest in earnings of consolidated subsidiaries, the denominator should exclude the minority interest in net assets (if any). Firms seldom issue preferred stock significantly above par value, so the analyst can assume that the amount in the additional paid-in capital account relates to common stock.[29]

PepsiCo reports no minority interest in its income statement or balance sheet, although it does have preferred stock outstanding. The calculation of the ROCE of PepsiCo for 2008, using the *reported* amounts of net income, which is shown on the "Analysis" worksheet of FSAP, is as follows (in millions):

$$ROCE = \frac{\text{Net Income} - \text{Preferred Stock Dividends}}{\text{Average Common Shareholders' Equity}}$$

$$34.8\% = \frac{\$5,142 - \$8}{0.5(\$12,203 + \$17,325)}$$

The calculation of the ROCE of PepsiCo for 2008, using the *adjusted* amounts of net income discussed previously and displayed in Exhibit 4.4, is as follows (in millions):

$$ROCE = \frac{\text{Adjusted Net Income} - \text{Preferred Stock Dividends}}{\text{Average Common Shareholders' Equity}}$$

$$38.3\% = \frac{\$5,664 - \$8}{0.5(\$12,203 + \$17,325)}$$

The amount for the preferred stock dividends appears in Note 11, "Net Income per Common Share from Continuing Operations" (Appendix A).[30] For purposes of our analysis of PepsiCo in this chapter, we demonstrate how to calculate net income available to common shareholders using the full preferred stock dividends, including a redemption premium.[31] Adjusting net

---

[29]Some analysts use the acronym ROCE to refer to "return on capital employed." The numerator of return on capital employed is net income before interest expense (net of tax savings) on long-term debt. The denominator is the average amount of long-term debt and shareholders' equity during the year. The rate of return on capital employed generally falls between ROA and ROCE as we have defined these ratios. We do not use return on capital employed in this book, but it is important to realize the confusion that blind adherence to acronyms can cause. Indeed, ROE is probably more common than ROCE, but we use the latter to emphasize that the construct we want is return on *common* shareholders' equity, not to be confused with total equity, which includes preferred equity for firms that issue preferred stock.

[30]The $8 million amount for preferred dividends in the numerator is actually a preferred dividend of $2 million and a redemption premium on preferred stock of $6 million. The SEC requires firms that redeem preferred stock for more than its book, or carrying, value to subtract the excess from net income when computing net income available to common shareholders in the computation of earnings per share. See Securities and Exchange Commission, *EITF Abstracts,* Topic No. D 42, "The Effect on the Calculation of Earnings per Share for the Redemption or Induced Conversion of Preferred Stock" (1994); *FASB Codification Topic 260.* To maintain consistency in the calculation of ROCE and earnings per share, we subtract the redemption premium in the numerator of both ratios. Analysts will likely encounter such redemption premiums infrequently.

[31]However, users of FSAP should note that due to the rarity of this item and its relative immateriality, FSAP follows the standard approach of adjusting only for the preferred stock dividend and treats the redemption premium as other expense. The alternative exposition in the chapter is intended to highlight the judgment required when analyzing financial statements, particularly when firms engage in unusual or nonrecurring transactions.

income for the preferred stock dividends and redemption premium, the ROCE of PepsiCo was 34.1 percent in 2007 and 34.0 percent in 2006, consistent with an upward trend in ROCE, in contrast to the fluctuating trend in ROA discussed earlier in the chapter.

Benchmarks for ROCE

Having computed (adjusted) ROCE for PepsiCo of 38.3 percent in 2008, the question arises as to whether this is "good" or "bad." One benchmark is the average ROCE of other firms. The average ROCE for the cross-section of publicly traded firms in the United States is approximately 10–12 percent, so PepsiCo is well above the average ROCE; hence, 38.3 percent is certainly "good."[32] Also, the ROCE of a similar firm such as Coca-Cola also can serve as a benchmark. For 2008, Coca-Cola had an ROCE of 27.5 percent, which also supports the inference that PepsiCo generates a substantially above average ROCE.

A more direct benchmark against which to judge ROCE is the return demanded by common shareholders for a firm's use of their capital. Because common shareholders are the residual claimants of the firm, accountants do not treat the cost of common shareholders' equity capital as an expense when computing net income. On the other hand, a firm that earns less than the cost of common equity capital destroys value for shareholders, whereas a firm that generates ROCE that exceeds the cost of capital creates value. ROCE measures the return to the common shareholders but does not indicate whether this rate of return exceeds or falls short of the cost of common equity capital.

To illustrate, PepsiCo's ROCE for 2008 as computed above is 38.3 percent. If the cost of common equity capital of PepsiCo is, for example, 8 percent, PepsiCo generated an excess return of 30.3 percent (= 38.3% − 8.0%). If the cost of common equity capital is, for example, 40 percent, PepsiCo did not generate a return sufficient to cover the cost of common equity capital.[33]

Conceptually, the cost of common equity capital is the rate of return the common shareholders demand as compensation for forgoing consumption and bearing the risk of investing in a firm. Measuring the cost of common equity capital is more difficult than measuring the cost of debt because debt instruments typically specify an interest rate, which occasionally differs from the effective rate, but typically by only small amounts. The dividend on common stock is not an accurate measure of the cost of common equity capital because managers and boards of directors determine dividend payout policies, whereas equity investors determine the cost of equity capital. Chapter 11 discusses the computation of the cost of equity capital, and Chapters 11–14 incorporate it into various valuation methods.

Chapter 13 describes a measure known as *residual income* (also called *abnormal earnings*). The principal difference between net income available to common shareholders, the numerator of ROCE, and residual income is that residual income includes a subtraction for the cost of common shareholders' equity capital, as follows:

Residual Income = Net Income Available to Common Shareholders
          − (Cost of Equity Capital × Beginning Common Shareholders' Equity)

The analyst might view residual income as a measure of the wealth a firm generates for its common shareholders in a period beyond the required return on their investment in the

---

[32]Average ROCEs depend on many factors, including the period of measurement, samples of firms used, and definitions of accounting data used in the numerator and denominator of the ROCE calculation.

[33]PepsiCo's cost of common equity capital is likely closer to 8 percent than to 40 percent. Chapter 11 discusses PepsiCo's cost of equity capital more fully, where we estimate it to be 8.5 percent.

firm. In recent years, the financial press and some corporate managers have given considerable attention to a measure called *economic value added* (EVA)®. Stern Stewart & Co., a management consulting firm, has taken the lead in promoting this measure.[34] Similar to but not identical to residual income, EVA likewise includes a subtraction for the cost of common shareholders' equity capital.[35] The concept behind EVA is that a firm does not create value unless it earns more than the cost of all of its capital, including common shareholders' equity capital. Chapter 13 describes how forecasts of residual income can be used to value a firm, equivalent to values obtained from using dividends or free cash flows as valuation model inputs. The intuition under this approach is that valuations are higher as firms generate future ROCE higher than the cost of equity capital. This same intuition is relevant in any analysis of ROCE.

As will be discussed further on the topic of the implications of market-based ratios in Chapter 14, ROCE is subject to the same life cycle and competitive pressures discussed earlier in the chapter. For example, Bernard (1994) examined the behavior of ROCE across time, conditional on the base year ROCE.[36] Exhibit 4.18 plots results from his study, which

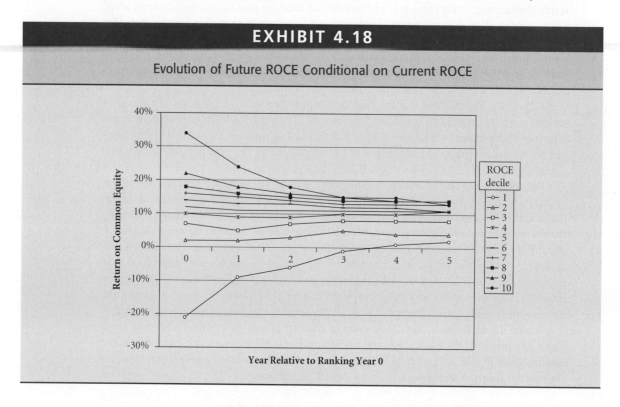

EXHIBIT 4.18

Evolution of Future ROCE Conditional on Current ROCE

[34]Other consulting firms promote similar measures, such as HOLT Value Associates' *cash flow return on investment* (CFROI), L.E.K. Consulting's *shareholder value added* (SVA), Marakon's *discounted economic profits* (EP), and KPMG's *economic value management* (EVM).

[35]The precise computation of EVA involves other accounting adjustments to net income that we do not consider here. See G. Bennett Stewart, III, *The Quest for Value* (New York: HarperCollins Publishers), 1999. Young and O'Bryne (2001) discuss that although close to 200 accounting adjustments have been discussed, most applications involve around ten adjustments. See David S. Young and Stephen F. O'Byrne, *EVA and Value-Based Management—A Practical Guide to Implementation* (New York: McGraw-Hill), 2001.

[36]See Victor L. Bernard, "Accounting-Based Valuation Methods, Determinants of Market-to-Book Ratios, and Implications for Financial Statement Analysis." Unpublished manuscript, University of Michigan Business School, Kresge Library (January 1994).

partitioned firms into deciles based on beginning ROCE and then tracked the average ROCE for each decile over subsequent years. The graph indicates that the initial spread in ROCE is very large, with the most profitable firms generating ROCEs in excess of 30 percent and the least profitable firms generating returns below negative 20 percent. However, competitive pressures erode the abnormally high ROCEs of the most profitable firms, and survival (or bankruptcy or an acquisition) results in the poorest performing firms increasing ROCE to positive levels. This does not imply that all firms with above-average ROCEs will realize lower ROCEs in the future, but it is the dominant pattern. A few companies with sustainable strategic advantages and/or substantial off-balance assets and equity (such as PepsiCo's valuable brand names) can generate ROCEs well above the average for extended numbers of years.

Relating ROA to ROCE

ROA measures operating performance independent of financing, while ROCE explicitly considers the cost of debt and preferred stock financing. Exhibit 4.1 diagrams the relation between ROA and ROCE and shows that both can be decomposed into margin, turnover, and leverage (although differences are highlighted with dashed lines). An expanded diagram of the relation between ROA and ROCE is as follows:[37]

Return on Assets	**Return to Creditors**	**Return to Preferred Shareholders**	**Return to Common Shareholders**
$\dfrac{\text{Net Income + Interest Expense Net of Taxes}}{\text{Average Total Assets}}$	$\dfrac{\text{Interest Expense Net of Taxes}}{\text{Average Total Liabilities}}$	$\dfrac{\text{Preferred Dividends}}{\text{Average Preferred Shareholders' Equity}}$	$\dfrac{\text{Net Income to Common}}{\text{Average Common Shareholders' Equity}}$

The analyst allocates each dollar of return generated from using assets to the various providers of capital. Creditors receive their return first in the form of interest payments. The cost of this capital to the firm is interest expense net of the income tax benefit derived from deducting interest in calculating taxable income. Many other liabilities, such as accounts payable and salaries payable, carry no explicit interest cost.

The preferred stock carries a cost equal to the preferred dividend amount. Historically, firms could not deduct preferred dividends when calculating taxable income, but in recent years, firms have been successful in structuring preferred stock issues so that they qualify for tax deductibility of dividends paid. In those cases, the analyst should adjust preferred dividends for the related tax savings.

The portion of net income that is *not* allocated to creditors or preferred shareholders is available for the common shareholders as the residual claimants. Likewise, the portion of a firm's assets not financed with capital provided by creditors or preferred shareholders represents the capital provided by the common shareholders.[38]

---

[37]Note that the relation does not appear as an equation. We use an arrow instead of an equal sign to indicate that the return on assets gets allocated to the various suppliers of capital. To express the relation as an equality requires that we weight each rate by the proportion of each type of capital in the capital structure.

[38]If a firm does not own 100 percent of the common stock of a consolidated subsidiary, the accountant must allocate a portion of the ROA to the minority shareholders. Thus, a fourth term would appear on the right-hand side of the arrow: minority interest in earnings/average minority interest in net assets.

Now consider the relation between ROA and ROCE. Under what circumstances will ROCE exceed ROA? Under what circumstances will ROCE be less than ROA? The key to answering those questions lies in understanding how the use of financing from sources other than common shareholders can harm or benefit common shareholders.

ROCE will exceed ROA whenever ROA exceeds the cost of capital provided by creditors and preferred shareholders. If a firm can generate a higher return on capital provided by creditors and preferred shareholders than the cost of those sources of capital, the excess return belongs to the common shareholders.

To illustrate, recall that PepsiCo generated an ROA of 16.7 percent during 2008 (adjusted for unusual items). The after-tax cost of capital provided by creditors during 2008 was 1.04 percent $[=(1-0.35)(\$329)/0.5(\$23,888 + \$17,394)]$.[39] The difference between the 1.04 percent cost of creditor capital and the 16.7 percent ROA generated on assets financed with debt capital belongs to the common shareholders. The preferred shareholders received a dividend of $2 million and PepsiCo paid a redemption premium of $6 million when it redeemed preferred stock during 2008. PepsiCo paid this dividend on the $41 million of outstanding preferred stock. However, PepsiCo repurchased preferred stock for more than it initially issued the stock, resulting in a negative net amount for preferred stock on the balance sheet. The average amount of preferred stock equity is a negative $94 million $[= 0.5(\$41 - \$138 + \$41 - \$132)]$. Therefore, the calculated cost of preferred equity capital is negative 8.5 percent $(= \$8/-\$94)$. Although showing a negative preferred shareholders' equity is mathematically correct, it is not conceptually sound. The excess in an economic sense reduces *common* shareholders' equity. However, we follow PepsiCo's treatment of the repurchased preferred stock as an element of preferred stock equity, not common stock equity.

The common shareholders also have a full claim on the 16.7 percent ROA generated on the assets financed with the equity capital they provided. Thus, the ROCE of PepsiCo for 2008 comprises the following. (Calculations use rates of return taken to more decimal points than the three shown, such as ROA = 0.1665.)

Excess Return on Capital Provided by Creditors:	
$[0.167 - 0.010][0.5(\$23,888 + \$17,394)]$	$3,222
Deficient Return on Negative Capital Provided by Preferred Shareholders:	
$[0.167 - (-0.085)][0.5(\$41 - \$138 + \$41 - \$132)]$	(24)
Return on Capital Provided by Common Shareholders:	
$[0.167][0.5(\$12,203 + \$17,325)]$	2,458
Total Return to Common Shareholders	$5,656
ROCE: $5,656/$[0.5(\$12,203 + \$17,325)]$	38.3%

Common business terminology refers to the practice of using lower-cost creditor and preferred stock capital to increase the return to common shareholders as *financial leverage* or *capital structure leverage*. To clarify the concept, consider the following simple example: Suppose a firm has one common equity investor who invests $100 to fund a firm that generates an ROA of 10 percent. At the end of the year, income available to the common equity investor is $10, reflecting the ROA of 10 percent (= $10 income ÷ $100 investment). Alternatively, the single equity investor could have invested only $10 and borrowed $90 to

---

[39]The amounts in the denominator for PepsiCo equal total assets minus total shareholders' equity, or equivalently, total liabilities. The after-tax cost of creditor capital seems low, but recall that many liabilities do not carry an explicit interest cost.

have the same amount to invest ($100) and generate the same return (10 percent). Suppose creditors provide the $90 loan at an after-tax interest cost to the firm of 5 percent. At the end of the year, the firm would have generated the same income of $10, but the after-tax cost of financing would be $4.50 (= $90 debt × 5 percent), leaving income available to the common shareholder of $5.50. Thus, a much smaller investment of $10 (rather than $100) combined with debt financing of $90 enables the common equity investor to realize a substantially higher rate of return. In this case, rather than a 10 percent return on equity, the equity investor would have realized a 55 percent return on equity (= $5.50 income ÷ $10 investment). This example demonstrates the advantages of the strategic use of financial leverage to increase returns to equity investors: deploying assets that generate 10 percent but partially financing through capital that costs only 5 percent generates "abnormal" returns. Of course, increased leverage triggers greater risk, which we will discuss in Chapter 5.

Regarding debt and preferred shareholders' equity combined, PepsiCo's financial leverage worked to the advantage of its common shareholders in 2006–2008 because its ROA exceeded the cost of all non-common equity financing. This resulted in ROCE exceeding ROA. We can measure the incremental effect of financial leverage beyond ROA by computing the ratio of ROCE divided by ROA. The ratios for PepsiCo are as follows:

> 2008: 38.3%/16.7% = 2.29
> 2007: 34.1%/17.8% = 1.92
> 2006: 34.0%/16.9% = 2.01

Thus, financial leverage worked very well during 2008 relative to the previous two years. Next, we explore the possible reasons for this increased effectiveness.

Disaggregating ROCE

We can disaggregate ROCE into several components to aid in its interpretation, much as we did with ROA. The disaggregated components of ROCE are profit margin for ROCE, assets turnover, and capital structure leverage. Note the distinction between profit margin for ROA and profit margin for ROCE is simply the different numerator used. The numerator of profit margin for ROCE is net income available to common shareholders, and the numerator for profit margin for ROA is net income with after tax interest expense and minority interest added back, which yields a measure of profits before deduction of financing costs.

ROCE	=	Profit Margin for ROCE	×	Assets Turnover	×	Capital Structure Leverage
$\dfrac{\text{Net Income to Common}}{\text{Average Common Shareholders' Equity}}$	=	$\dfrac{\text{Net Income to Common}}{\text{Sales}}$	×	$\dfrac{\text{Sales}}{\text{Average Total Assets}}$	×	$\dfrac{\text{Average Total Assets}}{\text{Average Common Shareholders' Equity}}$

The profit margin for ROCE indicates the earnings allocable to the common shareholders after subtracting from revenues all operating expenses and all financing costs of capital senior to the common shareholders. Note that the profit margin for ROA, used in the disaggregation of ROA, is measured *before* financing costs. The profit margin for ROCE is measured *after* financing costs for debt and preferred stock capital. Assets turnover is identical to that used to disaggregate ROA. The capital structure leverage ratio measures the degree to which a firm utilizes financial leverage to finance assets. The difference between the numerator and the denominator of the capital structure leverage ratio is the amount of liabilities (and preferred shareholders' equity, if any) in the capital structure. The larger the amount of capital obtained from these sources, the smaller the amount of capital obtained from common shareholders and therefore the larger the capital structure leverage ratio. Another way to interpret the capital structure leverage ratio is as follows:

$$\frac{\text{Total Assets}}{\substack{\text{Common} \\ \text{Shareholders'} \\ \text{Equity}}} = \frac{\substack{\text{Debt + Preferred Equity} \\ \text{+ Common Shareholders' Equity}}}{\substack{\text{Common} \\ \text{Shareholders'} \\ \text{Equity}}} = 1 + \frac{\text{Debt + Preferred Equity}}{\substack{\text{Common} \\ \text{Shareholders'} \\ \text{Equity}}}$$

Thus, capital structure leverage is simply one plus the debt-to-equity ratio for a firm with no preferred stock or one plus the ratio of debt plus preferred equity to common shareholder equity for a firm with preferred stock.

Before proceeding with a disaggregation of PepsiCo's ROCE, we note that there are many more ways to disaggregate ROA or ROCE than are discussed in this chapter. We will explore one alternative method of decomposing ROCE in the next chapter, which will high light the importance of benchmarking the returns generated by the firm's assets against the cost of borrowing from creditors. The decomposition of ROCE to be discussed in Chapter 5 requires the analyst to partition the income statement and balance sheet into operating and financing components. Then the analyst computes ROCE as follows:

$$\text{ROCE} = \text{RNOA} + \text{Leverage} \times (\text{RNOA} - \text{Net Borrowing Cost}),$$

where RNOA is "return on net operating assets." As will be discussed in Chapter 5, RNOA captures the returns generated by the operating activities of the firm, Leverage captures the extent to which the firm uses creditor financing, and the term (RNOA − Net Borrowing Cost) is the relative spread between the operating returns and the effective cost of creditor financing. The intuition is that when the firm's assets generate sufficiently high returns to cover the cost of borrowing (that is, the last term in the preceding equation), financial leverage can be strategically used to boost returns to common shareholders.

The disaggregation of ROCE for PepsiCo for 2008 under the basic decomposition discussed in this chapter is as follows:

ROCE	=	Profit Margin for ROCE	×	Assets Turnover	×	Capital Structure Leverage
$\dfrac{\$5,664 - \$8}{0.5(\$12,203 + \$17,325)}$	=	$\dfrac{\$5,664 - \$8}{\$43,251}$	×	$\dfrac{\$43,251}{0.5(\$35,994 + \$34,628)}$	×	$\dfrac{0.5(\$35,994 + \$34,628)}{0.5(\$12,203 + \$17,325)}$
38.3%	=	13.1%	×	1.22	×	2.39

Exhibit 4.19 presents the disaggregation of ROCE of PepsiCo for 2006–2008. The increasing ROCE of PepsiCo results from the net effect of (1) decreasing profit margins over 2006–2008, (2) an increase in assets turnover in 2007, and (3) a marked increase in capital structure leverage in 2008. The decreasing profit margin for ROCE mirrors that discussed previously for ROA. The calculation of assets turnover is the same in the decomposition of ROA and ROCE, so it also mirrors the previous discussion about the decomposition of

EXHIBIT 4.19

Disaggregation of ROCE of PepsiCo: 2006–2008

	ROCE	=	Profit Margin for ROCE	×	Total Assets Turnover	×	Capital Structure Leverage
2008	38.3%	=	13.1%	×	1.22	×	2.39
2007	34.1%	=	14.2%	×	1.22	×	1.97
2006	34.0%	=	14.4%	×	1.14	×	2.07

ROA. The primary difference between the ROA and ROCE decompositions is the capital structure leverage component. We must examine changes in PepsiCo's capital structure by examining changes in each source of financing. The change in preferred equity on the balance sheet is minimal, so it cannot explain the increased leverage. (See Appendix A.) The balance sheet does indicate changes in liabilities (which increased from $17,394 million to $23,888 million) and common shareholders' equity (which decreased from $17,325 million to $12,203 million).

The statement of cash flows and Note 9, "Debt Obligations and Commitments," indicate that PepsiCo issued $1,750 million and $2,000 million of senior unsecured notes in the second and fourth quarters of 2008, respectively, accounting for an additional $3,750 million of long-term debt obligations, netted by scheduled payments of long-term debt and other activity for short-term borrowings. Also, other liabilities increased from $4,792 million to $7,017 million. PepsiCo does not specifically discuss this change in other liabilities, but Note 7, "Pension, Retiree Medical, and Savings Plans," shows that PepsiCo's U.S. pension plan assets declined in value $1,434 billion during 2008, resulting in an underfunded status of the pension plans in the United States of $2,243 million, of which $2,183 million was included in other liabilities (relative to only $672 million at the end of 2007). The decline in value of pension fund assets is consistent with the sharp decline in the financial markets during 2008.

The statement of common shareholders' equity (see Appendix A) provides an explanation for why common shareholders' equity declined, with components summarized as follows (in millions):

	2008	2007	Change
Common stock	$ 30	$ 30	$ 0
Paid-in capital	351	450	(99)
Retained earnings	30,638	28,184	2,454
Accumulated other comprehensive loss	(4,694)	(952)	(3,742)
Treasury stock	(14,122)	(10,387)	(3,735)
Common Shareholders' Equity	$12,203	$17,325	$(5,122)

The net decrease in common shareholders' equity reflects the net of three large changes. First, retained earnings increased, reflecting primarily net income of $5,142 million less common dividends of $2,589 million, preferred dividends of $2 million, and restricted stock unit (RSU) dividends of $8 million. Second, PepsiCo's accumulated other comprehensive loss increased $3,742 million. This reflects primarily two changes. Currency translation adjustments turned unfavorable, reducing common shareholders' equity by $2,484 million, and net pension plan assets suffered declines of $1,376 million. Both amounts are commensurate with the global economic crisis during 2008 and sharp declines in the financial markets.

A moderate increase in liabilities—along with a significant decrease in shareholders' equity—caused PepsiCo's common shareholder leverage to increase from 1.97 to 2.39 in 2008. The $5,122 million net decrease in common shareholders' equity includes a large amount of other comprehensive loss, one can view the net of changes in retained earnings and treasury stock as net changes in common shareholders' equity due to management's decisions regarding capital structure. This change equates to a net decrease in the net of shareholders' equity and treasury stock of $1,281 million (= $2,454 − $3,735) reflecting a return of capital to shareholders in excess of what was generated during 2008. In addition, PepsiCo issued $3,750 million in debt during the year. The combination of the $1,281 decrease in common equity (exclusive of accumulated other comprehensive income) and $3,750 million increase in debt results in a deliberate net increase in leverage by PepsiCo management. During periods when equity prices fall, managers of profitable firms often repurchase common shares on the open market and seek needed financing through the debt markets (rather than issue shares at potentially deflated prices). The adjustments of $3,742 million for accumulated other comprehensive loss further reduced common shareholders' equity at the end of 2008, making a significant contribution to the overall increased leverage. The rationale for allowing adjustments for accumulated other comprehensive income to reside temporarily in shareholders' equity is that such adjustments are expected to be temporary. If the adjustments reverse and PepsiCo makes no further capital structure changes, PepsiCo's leverage will decline from current levels. The analyst will want to better understand these adjustments to gauge the likelihood and timing of any such adjustments. For example, losses in pension plan assets that are more likely to be permanent indicate a substantial future drag on shareholders' income to remedy the underfunded pension fund status. We will discuss pension plans in more detail in Chapter 8.

INTERPRETING FINANCIAL STATEMENT RATIOS

Financial ratios are easy to compute, and there are many sources of financial data that do the computing for investors, including free websites such as Yahoo! Finance and Smartmoney.com. The most important and valuable step, however, is *interpreting and gleaning key insights from a financial ratio*. To do this successfully, the analyst must know how a ratio was computed. For example, was ROA computed correctly such that the numerator includes net profits after taxes but before interest, or is the analyst using someone else's calculation that simply uses EBIT in the numerator? Differences in computations do not always create significant differences in ratio calculations, but the astute analyst must be aware of the underlying data embedded in ratios. The second, and most crucial, aspect of interpreting ratios is doing so with an understanding of the firm's economic environment and business strategy. As noted earlier in the chapter, an analyst must understand a firm's industry, organizational structure, and strategy to develop hypotheses about what to expect in terms of financial position, profitability, risk, and growth.

Analyzing financial statement ratios is the forensic part of the process of investigating for insights and answers to questions about how the firm is performing. In this step, the analyst must dig deep to understand why ratios are what they are. How do the ratios reflect the economics of the industry and the specific strategy of the firm? Do the ratios suggest that a firm is performing better or worse compared to its peers or is performing better or worse through time? Are there accounting choices that hinder the ability to productively use ratios to better understand the firm? In summary, the first three steps of the six-step process discussed in Chapter 1 (that is, (1) identify economic characteristics of the industry, (2) identify company strategies, and (3) assess the quality of the financial statements) link directly to the use of ratios to validate an analyst's understanding of the profitability and risk of a firm and to generate new insights not discovered in the first three steps.

The analyst can compare financial ratios for a particular firm with similar ratios for the same firm for earlier periods (time-series analysis), as we did in this chapter for PepsiCo, or with those of other firms for the same period (cross-sectional analysis), as we did for PepsiCo versus Coca-Cola and several other sets of firms in this chapter. The next section discusses some of the general issues involved in making such comparisons.

Comparisons with Earlier Periods

A time-series analysis of a particular firm's financial statement ratios permits a historical tracking of the trends and variability in the ratios over time. A firm's past financial ratios serve as a benchmark for interpreting its financial ratios during the current period. The analyst can draw useful insights by comparing a firm with itself over time. The analyst can study the impact of economic conditions (recession and inflation), industry conditions (shift in regulatory status and new technology), and firm-specific conditions (shift in corporate strategy and new management) on the time-series pattern of these ratios.

Some questions the analyst should raise before using ratios of past financial statement data as a basis for interpreting ratios for the current period are as follows:

1. Has the firm made a significant change in its product, geographic, or customer mix that affects the comparability of financial statement ratios over time?

2. Has the firm made a major acquisition or divestiture?

3. Has the firm changed its methods of accounting over time? For example, does the firm now consolidate a previously unconsolidated entity?

4. Are there any unusual or nonrecurring amounts that impair a comparable analysis of financial results across years?

Analysts should not use past performance as a basis for comparison without considering the level of past and current performance. For example, prior performance might have been at an unsatisfactory level. Improvement during the current year may still leave the firm at an undesirable level. An improved profitability ratio may mean little if the firm still ranks last in its industry in terms of profitability in all years. Similarly, if the firm's prior performance was exceptional but declined in the current period, the firm still may have performed well in the current period. An analyst may be less concerned about a decline in profitability if the firm ranks as the most profitable firm in its industry.

Another concern involves interpreting the relative rate of change in a ratio over time. The analyst's interpretation of a 10 percent increase in profit margin for ROA differs depending on whether other firms in the industry experienced a 15 percent versus a 5 percent increase. Comparing a particular firm's ratios with those of similar firms lessens the concerns discussed here.

Careful time-series analyses of a firm's financial ratios will not only yield key insights about how and why the firm's profitability has been changing over time, but also will provide valuable information about trends. Chapter 10 discusses techniques for building detailed and careful forecasts of financial statements, and we rely heavily on the information and trends gathered from time-series analysis of ratios. In that chapter, we project future financial statements for PepsiCo for the next five years, and the information in the current and past financial ratios provides valuable insights to help us make more reliable forecasts.

Comparisons with Other Firms

The major task confronting the analyst in performing a cross-sectional analysis is identifying the other firms to use for comparison. The objective is to select firms with similar products and strategies and similar size and age. Few firms may meet these criteria, and no firms will meet these criteria perfectly. Coca-Cola, for example, is a logical comparison firm for PepsiCo. However, Coca-Cola derives virtually all of its revenues from beverages, whereas PepsiCo derives revenues from beverages and food products, which makes the comparison less than perfect. However, comparable firms are never perfectly comparable. Even the comparison of similar firms such as Target and Walmart (discussed earlier in the chapter) gets complicated because Target's operations include a segment for its branded credit card and Walmart's operations include the Sam's Club warehouse store chain. The analyst must accept the fact that cross-sectional comparisons of ratios between firms will require subjective judgment about how the differences across firms in business model, strategy, and accounting affect the ratios.

An alternative approach uses average industry ratios, such as those published by Moody's, Dun & Bradstreet, and Robert Morris Associates, or ratios derived from computerized databases such as Compustat. These average industry ratios provide an overview of the performance of an industry, aiming to capture the commonalities across many firms.

The analyst should consider the following issues when using industry ratios:

1. **Definition of the industry:** Publishers of industry average ratios generally classify diversified firms into the industry of their major product. PepsiCo, for example, appears as a "beverage" company even though it generates a large percentage of its revenues from consumer foods. The industry may also exclude privately held and foreign firms if data are not available for those firms. If these types of firms are significant for a particular industry, the analyst should recognize the possible impact of their absence from the published data.
2. **Calculation of industry average:** Is the published ratio a simple (unweighted) average of the ratios of the included firms, or is it weighted by size of firm? Is the weighting based on sales, assets, market value, or some other factor? Is the median of the distribution used instead of the mean?
3. **Distribution of ratios around the mean:** To interpret a deviation of a particular firm's ratio from the industry average requires information on the distribution around the mean. The analyst interprets a ratio that is 10 percent larger than the industry mean differently depending on whether the standard deviation is 5 percent versus 15 percent greater or less than the mean. Useful sources of industry ratios give either the quartiles or the range of the distribution.
4. **Definition of financial statement ratios:** The analyst should examine the definition of each published ratio to ensure that it is consistent with that calculated by the analyst. For instance, is the rate of ROCE based on average or beginning-of-the-period common shareholders' equity? Are any adjustments made to reported net income, such as for nonrecurring or unusual charges?

Average industry ratios serve as a useful basis of comparison as long as the analyst recognizes their possible limitations. To assist the reader, Appendix D presents data on the distribution of the most common financial statement ratios across time for 48 industries.

SUMMARY

This chapter introduces the fourth step of the six-step process of financial statement analysis, which is to analyze profitability and risk. (See Exhibit 1.2.) We examined various financial statement ratios useful for assessing profitability in this chapter; analysis of risk is covered in Chapter 5. The large number of financial ratios discussed may be overwhelming at this point. Enhanced understanding of these financial ratios results from using and interpreting the ratios, *not from memorizing them.* The FSAP software available with this book facilitates calculation of the ratios and permits the analyst to devote more time to interpretations. As noted in the chapter, however, it cannot be emphasized enough how important the *interpretation* of financial statement ratios is. This is a necessarily qualitative and intellectual process, which requires the analyst to have understood the firm's specific strategy in the context of the industry *and* to be aware of any underlying accounting choices that affect the data used in the computation of the financial ratios being examined.

In this chapter, we highlighted alternative methods for examining profitability. The first part of the chapter focused on simple approaches, such as earnings-per-share, common-size, and percentage change analysis, as well as subjective redefinition of profits. However, the majority of the chapter focused on how to interpret different levels of profitability ratios. Exhibit 4.20 summarizes many of the key profitability ratios discussed in this chapter. Profitability analysis proceeds through four levels of depth. Level 1 involves measures of profitability for a firm as a whole: the rate of ROA and the rate of ROCE. Level 2 disaggregates ROA and ROCE into important components. ROA disaggregates into profit margin for ROA and assets turnover. ROCE disaggregates into profit margin for ROCE, assets turnover,

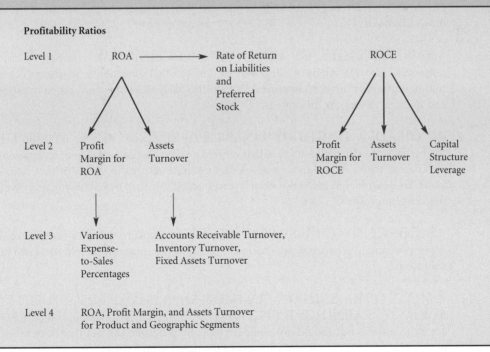

EXHIBIT 4.20

Summary of Profitability Ratios

and capital structure leverage components. Level 3 disaggregates the profit margin into various expense-to-sales percentages and disaggregates assets turnover into individual asset turnovers. Level 4 uses product and geographic segment data to study ROA, profit margin, and assets turnover more fully.

QUESTIONS, EXERCISES, PROBLEMS, AND CASES

Questions and Exercises

4.1 COMMON-SIZE ANALYSIS. Common-size analysis is a simple way to make financial statements of different firms comparable. What are possible shortcomings of comparing two different firms using common-size analysis?

4.2 EARNINGS PER SHARE. Firm A reports an increase in earnings per share; Firm B reports a decrease in earnings per share. Is this unconditionally informative about each firm's performance? If not, why is earnings per share so commonly discussed in the financial press?

4.3 PRO FORMA EARNINGS. Firms often provide supplemental disclosures that report and discuss income figures that do not necessarily equal bottom-line net income from the income statement. Discuss the merits and shortcomings of this managerial practice.

4.4 PROFIT MARGIN FOR ROA VERSUS ROCE. Describe the difference between the profit margin for ROA and the profit margin for ROCE. Explain why each profit margin is appropriate for measuring the rate of ROA and the rate of ROCE, respectively.

4.5 CONCEPT AND MEASUREMENT OF FINANCIAL LEVERAGE. Define financial leverage. Explain how financial leverage works to the benefit of the common shareholders.

4.6 ADVANTAGES OF FINANCIAL LEVERAGE. A company president remarked, "The operations of our company are such that we can take advantage of only a minor amount of financial leverage." Explain the likely reasoning the company president had in mind to support this statement.

4.7 DISADVANTAGES OF FINANCIAL LEVERAGE. The intuition behind the benefits of financial leverage is that a firm can borrow funds that bear a certain interest rate but invest those funds in assets that generate returns in excess of that rate. Why would firms with high ROAs not keep leveraging up their firm by borrowing and investing the funds in profitable assets?

4.8 CONCEPT OF RESIDUAL INCOME. Explain the intuition of residual income. Distinguish between net income available to the common shareholders and residual income.

4.9 RATE OF RETURN ON COMMON SHAREHOLDERS' EQUITY VERSUS BASIC EARNINGS PER COMMON SHARE. Analysts can compare ROCEs across companies but should not compare basic EPSs despite the fact that both ratios use net income to the common shareholders in the numerator. Explain.

4.10 CALCULATING ROA AND ITS COMPONENTS. Nucor, a steel manufacturer, reported net income for 2008 of $1,831 million on sales of $23,663 million. Interest expense for 2008 was $135 million, and minority interest was $314 million for 2008. The income tax rate is 35 percent. Total assets were $9,826 million at the beginning of 2008 and $13,874 million at the end of 2008. Compute the rate of ROA for 2008 and disaggregate ROA into profit margin for ROA and asset turnover components.

4.11 CALCULATING ROCE AND ITS COMPONENTS. Phillips-Van Heusen, an apparel manufacturer, reported net income (amounts in thousands) for Year 4 of $58,615 on sales of $1,460,235. It declared preferred dividends of $21,122. Preferred shareholders' equity totaled $264,746 at both the beginning and end of Year 4. Common shareholders' equity totaled $296,157 at the beginning of Year 4 and $364,026 at the end of Year 4. Phillips-Van Heusen had no minority interest in its equity. Total assets were $1,439,283 at the beginning of Year 4 and $1,549,582 at the end of Year 4. Compute the rate of ROCE for Year 4 and disaggregate it into profit margin for ROCE, assets turnover, and capital structure leverage ratio components.

4.12 CALCULATING BASIC AND DILUTED EPS. TJX, Inc., an apparel retailer, reported net income (amounts in thousands) of $609,699 for Year 4. The weighted average of common shares outstanding during Year 4 was 488,809 shares. TJX, Inc., subtracted interest expense net of tax saving on convertible debt of $4,482. If the convertible debt had been converted into common stock, it would have increased the weighted average common shares outstanding by 16,905 shares. TJX, Inc., has outstanding stock options that, if exercised, would increase the weighted average of common shares outstanding by 6,935 shares. Compute basic and diluted earnings per share for Year 4, showing supporting computations.

4.13 RELATING ROA AND ROCE. Boston Scientific, a medical device manufacturer, reported net income (amounts in millions) of $1,062 on sales of $5,624 during Year 4. Interest expense totaled $64. The income tax rate was 35 percent. Average total assets were $6,934.5, and average common shareholders' equity was $3,443.5. The firm did not have preferred stock outstanding or minority interest in its equity.

   a. Compute the rate of ROA. Disaggregate ROA into profit margin for ROA and assets turnover components.
   b. Compute the rate of ROCE. Disaggregate ROCE into profit margin for ROCE, assets turnover, and capital structure leverage ratio components.
   c. Calculate the amount of net income to common shareholders derived from the excess return on creditors' capital and the amount from the return on common shareholders' capital.

4.14 RELATING ROA AND ROCE. Valero Energy, a petroleum company, reported net income of $1,803.8 on revenues of $54,618.6 for Year 4. Interest expense totaled $359.7, and preferred dividends totaled $12.5. Average total assets for Year 4 were $17,527.9. The income tax rate is 35 percent. Average preferred shareholders' equity totaled $204.3, and average common shareholders' equity totaled $6,562.3. All amounts are in millions.

   a. Compute the rate of ROA. Disaggregate ROA into profit margin for ROA and assets turnover components.
   b. Compute the rate of ROCE. Disaggregate ROCE into profit margin for ROCE, assets turnover, and capital leverage ratio components.
   c. Calculate the amount of net income to common shareholders derived from the excess return on creditors' capital, the excess return on preferred shareholders' capital, and the return on common shareholders' capital.

Problems and Cases

4.15 ANALYZING OPERATING PROFITABILITY. Exhibit 4.21 presents selected operating data for three retailers for a recent year. Macy's operates several department store chains selling consumer products such as brand-name clothing, china, cosmetics, and bedding and has a large presence in the bridal and formalwear markets (under store names Macy's and Bloomingdale's). Home Depot sells a wide range of building materials and home improvement products, which includes lumber and tools, riding lawn mowers, lighting fixtures, and kitchen cabinets and appliances. Supervalu operates grocery stores under numerous brands (including Albertsons, Cub Foods, Jewel-Osco, Shaw's, and Star Market).

   a. Compute the rate of ROA for each firm. Disaggregate the rate of ROA into profit margin for ROA and assets turnover components. Assume that the income tax rate is 35 percent for all companies.
   b. Based on your knowledge of the three retail stores and their respective industry concentrations, describe the likely reasons for the differences in the profit margins for ROA and assets turnovers.

4.16 CALCULATING AND INTERPRETING ACCOUNTS RECEIVABLE TURNOVER RATIOS. Microsoft Corporation (Microsoft) and Oracle Corporation (Oracle) engage in the design, manufacture, and sale of computer software. Microsoft sells and licenses a wide range of systems and application software to businesses, computer hardware manufacturers, and consumer retailers. Oracle sells software for information management almost exclusively to businesses. Exhibit 4.22 presents selected data for the two firms for 2006–2008.

Required

   a. Calculate the accounts receivable turnover ratio for Microsoft and Oracle for 2006, 2007, and 2008.
   b. Suggest possible reasons for the differences in the accounts receivable turnovers of Microsoft and Oracle during the three-year period.
   c. Suggest possible reasons for the changes in the accounts receivable turnover for the two firms over the three-year period.

EXHIBIT 4.21

Selected Data for Three Retailers
(amounts in millions)
(Problem 4.15)

	Macy's	Home Depot	Supervalu
Sales	$24,892	$71,288	$44,564
Cost of Goods Sold	15,009	47,298	34,451
Interest Expense	588	624	633
Net Income	(4,803)	2,260	(2,855)
Average Inventory	4,915	11,202	2,743
Average Fixed Assets	10,717	26,855	7,531
Average Total Assets	24,967	42,744	19,333

EXHIBIT 4.22

Selected Data for Microsoft and Oracle
(amounts in millions)
(Problem 4.16)

	2008	2007	2006
Microsoft			
Sales	$58,437	$60,420	$51,122
Average Accounts Receivable	12,391	12,464	10,327
Change in Sales from Previous Year	−3.3%	+18.2%	+15.5%
Oracle			
Sales	$23,252	$22,430	$17,996
Average Accounts Receivable	4,430	5,799	4,589
Change in Sales from Previous Year	+3.7%	+24.6%	+25.2%

4.17 CALCULATING AND INTERPRETING INVENTORY TURNOVER RATIOS. Dell produces computers and related equipment on a made-to-order basis for consumers and businesses. Sun Microsystems designs and manufactures higher-end computers that function as servers and for use in computer-aided design. Sun Microsystems sells primarily to businesses. It also provides services to business customers in addition to product sales of computers. Selected data for each firm for 2007–2009 appear in Exhibit 4.23. (Dell's fiscal year-end is in January; Sun's fiscal year-end is in June. As of the writing of this text, an acquisition of Sun by Oracle is pending.)

EXHIBIT 4.23

Selected Data for Dell and Sun Microsystems
(amounts in millions)
(Problem 4.17)

	2009	2008	2007
Dell			
Cost of Goods Sold	$49,375	$48,855	$47,433
Average Inventories	1,024	920	618
Change in Sales from Previous Year	+1.1%	+3.0%	+4.1%
Sun Microsystems			
Cost of Goods Sold	$ 5,948	$ 6,639	$ 6,778
Average Inventories	623	602	532
Change in Sales from Previous Year	−10.4%	−2.1%	+3.7%

Required

   a. Calculate the inventory turnover ratio for each firm for 2007–2009.

   b. Suggest reasons for the differences in the inventory turnover ratios of these two firms.

   c. Suggest reasons for the changes in the inventory turnover ratios during the three-year period.

4.18 CALCULATING AND INTERPRETING ACCOUNTS RECEIVABLE AND INVENTORY TURNOVER RATIOS.

Nucor and AK Steel are steel manufacturers. Nucor produces steel in mini-mills. Mini-mills transform scrap ferrous metals into standard sizes of rolled steel, which Nucor then sells to steel service centers and distributors. Its steel falls on the lower end in terms of quality (strength and durability). AK Steel is an integrated steel producer, transforming ferrous metals into rolled steel and then into various steel products for the automobile, appliance, construction, and other industries. Its steel falls on the higher end in terms of quality. Exhibit 4.24 sets forth various data for these two companies for 2007 and 2008.

Required

   a. Calculate the accounts receivable turnovers for Nucor and AK Steel for 2007 and 2008.

   b. Describe the likely reasons for the differences in the accounts receivable turnovers for these two firms.

   c. Describe the likely reasons for the trend in the accounts receivable turnovers of these two firms during the two-year period.

   d. Calculate the inventory turnovers for Nucor and AK Steel for 2007 and 2008.

EXHIBIT 4.24

Selected Data for Nucor and AK Steel
(amounts in millions)
(Problem 4.18)

	2008	2007
Nucor		
Sales	$23,663	$16,593
Cost of Goods Sold	19,612	13,035
Average Accounts Receivable	1,420	1,340
Average Inventories	2,005	1,371
Change in Sales from Previous Year	+42.6%	+12.5%
AK Steel		
Sales	$ 7,644	$ 7,003
Cost of Goods Sold	6,479	5,904
Average Accounts Receivable	572	686
Average Inventories	607	752
Change in Sales from Previous Year	+9.2%	+15.3%

e. Describe the likely reasons for the differences in the inventory turnovers of these two firms.

f. Describe the likely reasons for the trend in the inventory turnovers of these two firms during the two-year period.

4.19 CALCULATING AND INTERPRETING FIXED ASSETS TURNOVER RATIOS.
Texas Instruments (TI) designs and manufactures semiconductor products for use in computers, telecommunications equipment, automobiles, and other electronics-based products. The manufacturing of semiconductors is highly capital-intensive. Hewlett-Packard Corporation (HP) manufactures computer hardware and various imaging products, such as printers and fax machines. Exhibit 4.25 presents selected data for TI and HP for 2006–2008.

Required

a. Compute the fixed assets turnover for each firm for 2006, 2007, and 2008.
b. Suggest reasons for the differences in the fixed assets turnovers of TI and HP.
c. Suggest reasons for the changes in the fixed assets turnovers of TI and HP during the three-year period.

4.20 CALCULATING AND INTERPRETING THE RATE OF RETURN ON COMMON SHAREHOLDERS' EQUITY AND ITS COMPONENTS.
JCPenney operates a chain of retail department stores, selling apparel, shoes, jewelry, and home furnishings. It also offers most of its products through catalog distribution. During fiscal Year 5, it sold Eckerd Drugs, a chain of retail drugstores, and used the cash proceeds,

---

EXHIBIT 4.25

Selected Data for Texas Instruments and Hewlett-Packard
(amounts in millions)
(Problem 4.19)

	2008	2007	2006
Texas Instruments			
Sales	$ 12,501	$ 13,835	$ 14,255
Cost of Goods Sold	6,256	5,432	5,775
Capital Expenditures	763	686	1,272
Average Fixed Assets	3,457	3,780	3,925
Percentage Fixed Assets Depreciated	54.9%	52.3%	49.0%
Percentage Change in Sales	−9.6%	−3.0%	+6.4%
Hewlett-Packard			
Sales	$114,552	$118,364	$104,286
Cost of Goods Sold	86,351	87,065	76,965
Capital Expenditures	3,695	2,990	3,040
Average Fixed Assets	11,050	9,318	7,331
Percentage Fixed Assets Depreciated	74.7%	72.4%	87.0%
Percentage Change in Sales	−3.2%	+13.5%	+13.8%

EXHIBIT 4.26			
Selected Data for JCPenney (amounts in millions) (Problem 4.20)			

	Year Ended January 31:		
	Year 5	**Year 4**	**Year 3**
Sales	$18,424	$17,786	$17,633
Net Income (Loss)	524	(928)	405
Interest Expense	279	271	245
Preferred Stock Dividend	12	25	27
Income Tax Rate	35%	35%	35%

January 31:	**Year 5**	**Year 4**	**Year 3**	**Year 2**
Total Assets	$14,127	$18,900	$17,787	$18,048
Preferred Stock	0	304	333	363
Total Common Shareholders' Equity	4,856	5,121	6,037	5,766

in part, to repurchase shares of its common stock. Exhibit 4.26 presents selected data for JCPenney for fiscal Year 3, Year 4, and Year 5.

Required

a. Calculate the rate of ROA for fiscal Year 3, Year 4, and Year 5. Disaggregate ROA into the profit margin for ROA and total assets turnover components. The income tax rate is 35 percent.

b. Calculate the rate of ROCE for fiscal Year 3, Year 4, and Year 5. Disaggregate ROCE into the profit margin for ROCE, assets turnover, and capital structure leverage components.

c. Suggest reasons for the changes in ROCE over the three years.

d. Compute the ratio of ROCE to ROA for each year.

e. Calculate the amount of net income available to common stockholders derived from the use of financial leverage with respect to creditors' capital, the amount derived from the use of preferred shareholders' capital, and the amount derived from common shareholders' capital for each year.

f. Did financial leverage work to the advantage of the common shareholders in each of the three years? Explain.

4.21 INTERPRETING THE RATE OF RETURN ON COMMON SHARE-HOLDERS' EQUITY AND ITS COMPONENTS. Selected financial data for Georgia-Pacific Corporation, a forest products and paper firm, appear in Exhibit 4.27.

EXHIBIT 4.27					
Selected Data for Georgia-Pacific Corporation (Problem 4.22)					
	Year 4	**Year 3**	**Year 2**	**Year 1**	**Year 0**
ROCE	10.8%	6.5%	(4.2%)	(9.1%)	7.4%
ROA	4.8%	3.7%	1.5%	0.8%	3.3%
Profit Margin for ROA	5.8%	4.6%	1.7%	0.9%	3.3%
Profit Margin for ROCE	3.2%	1.6%	(0.9%)	(1.9%)	1.6%
Assets Turnover	0.8	0.8	0.9	0.9	1.0
Capital Structure Leverage	4.1	4.9	5.4	5.3	4.8
Growth Rate in Sales	0.0%	(13.5%)	(9.2%)	13.4%	24.1%

Required

a. In which years did financial leverage work to the advantage of the common shareholders? In which years did it work to their disadvantage? Explain.

b. Identify possible reasons for the changes in the capital structure leverage ratio during the five-year period.

4.22 CALCULATING AND INTERPRETING THE RATE OF RETURN ON COMMON SHAREHOLDERS' EQUITY AND EARNINGS PER COMMON SHARE. Selected data for General Mills for 2007, 2008, and 2009 appear below (amounts in millions).

	2009	**2008**	**2007**
Net Income	$1,304.4	$1,294.7	$1,144.0
Weighted Average Number of Common Shares Outstanding	331.9	333.0	346.5
Average Common Shareholders' Equity	$5,695.3	$5,767.4	$5,545.5

Required

a. Compute the rate of ROCE for 2007, 2008, and 2009.
b. Compute basic EPS for 2007, 2008, and 2009.
c. Interpret the changes in ROCE versus EPS over the three-year period.

4.23 CALCULATING AND INTERPRETING PROFITABILITY RATIOS.
Hasbro is a leading firm in the toy, game, and amusement industry. Its promoted brands group includes products from Playskool, Tonka, Milton Bradley, Parker Brothers, Tiger, and Wizards of the Coast. Sales of toys and games are highly variable from year to year depending on whether the latest products meet consumer interests. Hasbro also faces increasing competition from electronic and online games. Hasbro develops and promotes its core brands and manufactures and distributes products

created by others under license arrangements. Hasbro pays a royalty to the creator of such products. In recent years, Hasbro has attempted to reduce its reliance on license arrangements, placing more emphasis on its core brands. Hasbro also has embarked on a strategy of reducing fixed selling and administrative costs in an effort to offset the negative effects on earnings of highly variable sales. Exhibit 4.28 presents the balance sheets for Hasbro for the years ended December 31, Year 1 through Year 4. Exhibit 4.29 presents the income statements and Exhibit 4.30 presents the statements of cash flows for Year 2 through Year 4.

EXHIBIT 4.28

Hasbro
Balance Sheets
(amounts in millions)
(Problem 4.23)

	December 31:			
	Year 4	Year 3	Year 2	Year 1
ASSETS				
Cash	$ 725	$ 521	$ 496	$ 233
Accounts receivable	579	607	555	572
Inventories	195	169	190	217
Prepayments	219	212	191	346
Total Current Assets	$1,718	$1,509	$1,432	$1,368
Property, plant, and equipment, net	207	200	213	236
Other assets	1,316	1,454	1,498	1,765
Total Assets	$3,241	$3,163	$3,143	$3,369
LIABILITIES AND SHAREHOLDERS' EQUITY				
Accounts payable	$ 168	$ 159	$ 166	$ 123
Short-term borrowing	342	24	223	36
Other current liabilities	639	747	578	599
Total Current Liabilities	$1,149	$ 930	$ 967	$ 758
Long-term debt	303	687	857	1,166
Other noncurrent liabilities	149	141	128	92
Total Liabilities	$1,601	$1,758	$1,952	$2,016
Common stock	$ 105	$ 105	$ 105	$ 105
Additional paid-in capital	381	398	458	455
Retained earnings	1,721	1,567	1,430	1,622
Accumulated other comprehensive income (loss)	82	30	(47)	(68)
Treasury stock	(649)	(695)	(755)	(761)
Total Shareholders' Equity	$1,640	$1,405	$1,191	$1,353
Total Liabilities and Shareholders' Equity	$3,241	$3,163	$3,143	$3,369

EXHIBIT 4.29

Hasbro
Income Statements
(amounts in millions)
(Problem 4.23)

	For the Year Ended December 31:		
	Year 4	Year 3	Year 2
Sales	$ 2,998	$ 3,139	$ 2,816
Cost of goods sold	(1,252)	(1,288)	(1,099)
Selling and administrative expenses:			
Advertising	(387)	(364)	(297)
Research and development	(157)	(143)	(154)
Royalty expense	(223)	(248)	(296)
Other selling and administrative	(687)	(799)	(788)
Interest expense	(32)	(53)	(78)
Income tax expense	(64)	(69)	(29)
Net Income	$ 196	$ 175	$ 75

EXHIBIT 4.30

Hasbro
Statements of Cash Flows
(amounts in millions)
(Problem 4.23)

	For the Year Ended December 31:		
	Year 4	Year 3	Year 2
OPERATIONS			
Net income	$196	$ 175	$ 75
Depreciation and amortization	146	164	184
Addbacks and subtractions, net	17	68	(67)
(Increase) Decrease in accounts receivable	76	(13)	34
(Increase) Decrease in inventories	(16)	35	39
(Increase) Decrease in prepayments	29	8	185
Increase (Decrease) in accounts payable and other current liabilities	(90)	17	23
Cash Flow from Operations	$358	$ 454	$ 473
INVESTING			
Property, plant, and equipment acquired	$(79)	$ (63)	$ (59)
Other investing transactions	(6)	(2)	(3)
Cash Flow from Investing	$(85)	$ (65)	$ (62)

(Continued)

EXHIBIT 4.30 (Continued)

	For the Year Ended December 31:		
	Year 4	Year 3	Year 2
FINANCING			
Increase in common stock	$ 3	$ 40	$ 3
Decrease in short-term borrowing	(7)	—	(15)
Decrease in long-term borrowing	(58)	(389)	(127)
Acquisition of common stock	—	(3)	—
Dividends	(37)	(21)	(21)
Other financing transactions	7	9	12
Cash Flow from Financing	$(69)	$(364)	$(148)
Change in Cash	$204	$ 25	$ 263
Cash—Beginning of year	521	496	233
Cash—End of Year	$725	$ 521	$ 496

Required

a. Exhibit 4.31 presents profitability ratios for Hasbro for Year 2 and Year 3. Calculate each of these financial ratios for Year 4. The income tax rate is 35 percent.

EXHIBIT 4.31

Hasbro
Financial Statement Ratio Analysis
(Problem 4.23)

	Year 4	Year 3	Year 2
Profit Margin for ROA		6.7%	4.5%
Assets Turnover		1.0	0.9
ROA		6.6%	3.9%
Profit Margin for ROCE		5.6%	2.7%
Capital Structure Leverage		2.4	2.6
ROCE		13.5%	5.9%
Cost of Goods Sold/Sales		41.0%	39.0%
Advertising Expense/Sales		11.6%	10.5%
Research and Development Expense/Sales		4.6%	5.5%
Royalty Expense/Sales		7.9%	10.5%
Other Selling and Administrative Expense/Sales		25.4%	28.0%
Income Tax Expense (excluding tax effects of interest expense)/Sales		2.8%	2.0%
Accounts Receivable Turnover		5.4	5.0
Inventory Turnover		7.2	5.4
Fixed Assets Turnover		15.2	12.5

b. Analyze the changes in ROA and its components for Hasbro over the three-year period, suggesting reasons for the changes observed.

c. Analyze the changes in ROCE and its components for Hasbro over the three-year period, suggesting reasons for the changes observed.

4.24 CALCULATING AND INTERPRETING PROFITABILITY RATIOS.

Abercrombie & Fitch sells casual apparel and personal care products for men, women, and children through retail stores located primarily in shopping malls. Its fiscal year ends January 31 of each year. Financial statements for Abercrombie & Fitch for fiscal years ending January 31, Year 3, Year 4, and Year 5 appear in Exhibit 4.32 (balance sheets), Exhibit 4.33

EXHIBIT 4.32

Abercrombie & Fitch
Balance Sheets
(amounts in millions)
(Problem 4.24)

	January 31:			
	Year 5	Year 4	Year 3	Year 2
ASSETS				
Cash	$ 350	$ 56	$ 43	$ 188
Marketable securities	—	465	387	51
Accounts receivable	26	7	10	21
Inventories	248	201	169	130
Prepayments	28	24	20	15
Total Current Assets	$ 652	$ 753	$ 629	$ 405
Property, plant, and equipment, net	1,560	1,342	1,172	947
Other assets	8	1	1	—
Total Assets	$2,220	$2,096	$1,802	$1,352
LIABILITIES AND SHAREHOLDERS' EQUITY				
Accounts payable	$ 84	$ 58	$ 79	$ 32
Short-term borrowing	54	33	—	—
Other current liabilities	276	220	193	132
Total Current Liabilities	$ 414	$ 311	$ 272	$ 164
Long-term debt	872	713	629	581
Other noncurrent liabilities	265	214	165	12
Total Liabilities	$1,551	$1,238	$1,066	$ 757
Common stock	$ 1	$ 1	$ 1	$ 1
Additional paid-in capital	140	139	143	141
Retained earnings	1,076	906	701	520
Treasury stock	(548)	(188)	(109)	(67)
Total Shareholders' Equity	$ 669	$ 858	$ 736	$ 595
Total Liabilities and Shareholders' Equity	$2,220	$2,096	$1,802	$1,352

EXHIBIT 4.33

Abercrombie & Fitch
Income Statements
(amounts in millions)
(Problem 4.24)

	For the Year Ended January 31:		
	Year 5	Year 4	Year 3
Sales	$2,021	$1,708	$1,596
Cost of goods sold	(1,048)	(936)	(893)
Selling and administrative expenses	(562)	(386)	(343)
Interest expense	(63)	(54)	(48)
Interest income	5	4	4
Income tax expense	(137)	(131)	(121)
Net Income	$ 216	$ 205	$ 195

(income statements), and Exhibit 4.34 (statements of cash flows). These financial statements reflect the capitalization of operating leases in property, plant, and equipment and long-term debt, a topic discussed in Chapter 6. Exhibit 4.35 (see page 322) presents financial statement ratios for Abercrombie & Fitch for Year 3 and Year 4. Selected data for Abercrombie & Fitch appear here.

	Year 5	Year 4	Year 3
Number of Stores	788	700	597
Square Feet of Retail Space (in thousands)	5,590	5,016	4,358
Number of Employees	48,500	30,200	22,000
Growth Rate in Sales	18.3%	7.0%	16.9%
Comparable Store Sales Increase	2.0%	(9.0%)	5.0%

Required

a. Calculate the ratios in Exhibit 4.35 for Year 5. The income tax rate is 35 percent.
b. Analyze the changes in ROA for Abercrombie & Fitch during the three-year period, suggesting possible reasons for the changes observed.
c. Analyze the changes in ROCE for Abercrombie & Fitch during the three-year period, suggesting possible reasons for the changes observed.

4.25 INTERPRETING PROFITABILITY RATIOS IN A CROSS-SECTIONAL SETTING. Coca-Cola Company is the principal competitor of PepsiCo in the soft drink beverage business. Coca-Cola engages almost exclusively in beverages, whereas, in addition to beverages, PepsiCo also engages in the manufacture and distribution of packaged foods such as chips, salsas, and cereals.

EXHIBIT 4.34

Abercrombie & Fitch
Statements of Cash Flows
(amounts in millions)
(Problem 4.24)

| | For the Year Ended January 31: | | |
	Year 5	Year 4	Year 3
OPERATIONS			
Net income	$ 216	$ 205	$ 195
Depreciation and amortization	106	90	76
Addbacks and subtractions, net	13	56	49
(Increase) Decrease in inventories	(34)	(27)	(34)
Increase (Decrease) in current liabilities	125	19	60
Cash Flow from Operations	$ 426	$ 343	$ 346
INVESTING			
Property, plant, and equipment acquired	$ (185)	$ (160)	$ (146)
Marketable securities sold	4,779	3,771	2,419
Marketable securities purchased	(4,314)	(3,849)	(2,729)
Other investing transactions	—	—	5
Cash Flow from Investing	$ (280)	$ (238)	$ (451)
FINANCING			
Increase in short-term borrowing	$ 20	$ 4	$ 4
Increase in common stock	49	20	—
Acquisition of common stock	(435)	(116)	(43)
Dividends	(46)	—	—
Cash Flow from Financing	$ (412)	$ (92)	$ (39)
Change in Cash	$ 294	$ 13	$ (144)
Cash—Beginning of year	56	43	188
Cash—End of Year	$ 350	$ 56	$ 43

The value chain for beverages involves the following steps:

1. Manufacturing concentrate and syrup to be used in the beverages
2. Mixing syrup, water, and other ingredients and placing the finished beverage in a container (can or bottle), a relatively capital-intensive process
3. Distributing packaged beverages to food distributors, retail establishments, and restaurant chains, also a capital-intensive process

Coca-Cola and PepsiCo are engaged primarily in the manufacture of concentrate and syrup (Step 1). They both rely heavily on other entities to perform Steps 2 and 3.

EXHIBIT 4.35

Abercrombie & Fitch
Financial Statement Ratio Analysis
(Problem 4.24)

	Year 5	Year 4	Year 3
Profit Margin for ROA		14.1%	14.2%
Assets Turnover		0.9	1.0
ROA		12.3%	14.3%
Profit Margin for ROCE		12.0%	12.2%
Capital Structure Leverage		2.4	2.4
ROCE		25.7%	29.3%
Cost of Goods Sold/Sales		54.8%	56.0%
Selling and Administrative Expense/Sales		22.6%	21.5%
Interest Revenue/Sales		0.2%	0.3%
Income Tax Expense (excluding tax effects of interest expense)/Sales		8.8%	8.6%
Accounts Receivable Turnover		200.9	103.0
Inventory Turnover		5.1	6.0
Fixed Assets Turnover		1.4	1.5
Sales per Store		$2,440,000	$2,673,367
Sales per Square Foot		$ 340.51	$ 366.22
Sales per Employee		$ 56,556	$ 72,545

The value chain for packaged foods involves the following steps:

1. Combining ingredients, cooking as appropriate, and packaging the finished food products
2. Distributing packaged food products to food distributors and retail establishments

Exhibit 4.36 presents ROA and its disaggregated components for Coca-Cola and PepsiCo for 2006–2008. Exhibit 4.37 (see page 324) presents ROCE and its disaggregated components, and Exhibit 4.38 (see page 324) presents segment data for these two companies. The ratio amounts for PepsiCo correspond to those discussed in the chapter but appear next to those for Coca-Cola to ease interpretation. No adjustments for unusual or nonrecurring items have been made for Coca-Cola. To ease computations, the segment computations of ROA and asset turnover use asset amounts at the end of the year instead of average assets during the year. (See the discussion under "Segment Data" in the chapter for an explanation of the use of end-of-year assets.) The segment profit margins and ROA are based on operating income before interest and income taxes. Thus, the aggregate profit margins and ROAs for the segments exceed those for the companies as a whole because the segment data do not subtract corporate-level overhead expenses. The segment data disclosed by each company have been categorized in three geographic segments, but there may be slight deviations from the actual segment data because of differences in the way each company defines its segments.

EXHIBIT 4.36

ROA and Its Disaggregated Components for Coca-Cola and PepsiCo
(Problem 4.25)

ROA		
2008	**2007**	**2006**

	2008	2007	2006
Coca-Cola	14.5%	17.1%	17.6%
PepsiCo	16.7%	17.8%	16.9%

Profit Margin for ROA			Assets Turnover		
2008	**2007**	**2006**	**2008**	**2007**	**2006**

	2008	2007	2006	2008	2007	2006
Coca-Cola	19.1%	21.8%	21.7%	0.76	0.79	0.81
PepsiCo	13.6%	14.6%	14.9%	1.22	1.22	1.14

	Coca-Cola			PepsiCo		
	2008	**2007**	**2006**	**2008**	**2007**	**2006**
Net Revenue	100.0%	100.0%	100.0%	100.0%	100.0%	100.0%
Bottling equity income	(2.7)	2.3	0.4	0.9	1.4	1.6
Interest income	1.0	0.8	0.8	0.1	0.3	0.5
Cost of sales	(35.6)	(36.1)	(33.9)	(47.1)	(45.7)	(44.9)
Selling, general, and administrative expenses	(36.9)	(37.9)	(39.2)	(36.8)	(36.0)	(36.2)
Amortization of intangible assets, other charges	(1.2)	(0.3)	0.0	(0.1)	(0.1)	(0.5)
Adjustments (from Exhibit 4.6)	—	—	—	1.6	0.3	0.2
Provision for income taxes (adjusted for PepsiCo)	(5.1)	(6.6)	(6.2)	(4.7)	(5.4)	(5.7)
Less: 0.35 × interest expense	(0.5)	(0.6)	(0.3)	(0.3)	(0.2)	(0.2)
Profit margin for ROA	19.1%	21.8%	21.7%	13.6%	14.6%	14.9%
Receivables turnover	10.0	9.8	9.9	9.5	9.7	10.1
Inventory turnover	5.2	5.4	5.4	8.5	8.6	8.7
Fixed assets turnover	3.8	3.7	3.8	3.8	3.8	3.8

Required

a. PepsiCo has shown a higher ROA than Coca-Cola for the last two years, but Coca-Cola has historically generated higher ROA than PepsiCo. Explain the current differences in ROA between PepsiCo and Coca-Cola.

b. Why might PepsiCo have a higher cost of sales than Coca-Cola?

EXHIBIT 4.37
ROCE and Its Disaggregated Components for Coca-Cola and PepsiCo
(Problem 4.25)

	ROCE		
	2008	**2007**	**2006**
Coca-Cola	27.5%	30.9%	30.5%
PepsiCo	38.3%	34.1%	34.0%

	Profit Margin for ROCE			Asset Turnover			Capital Structure Leverage		
	2008	**2007**	**2006**	**2008**	**2007**	**2006**	**2008**	**2007**	**2006**
Coca-Cola	18.2%	20.7%	21.1%	0.76	0.79	0.81	2.0	1.9	1.8
PepsiCo	13.1%	14.2%	14.4%	1.22	1.22	1.14	2.4	2.0	2.1

EXHIBIT 4.38
Geographic Segment Data for Coca-Cola and PepsiCo
(Problem 4.25)

	Coca-Cola			PepsiCo		
	2008	**2007**	**2006**	**2008**	**2007**	**2006**
Sales Mix						
Americas	59.8%	59.1%	56.4%	72.2%	74.5%	76.7%
UK & Europe	18.2%	18.3%	19.0%	14.9%	13.9%	13.5%
Middle East, Africa & Asia	22.0%	22.6%	24.6%	12.9%	11.6%	9.8%
	100.0%	100.0%	100.0%	100.0%	100.0%	100.0%
Profit Margin						
Americas	8.4%	15.9%	14.3%	20.7%	22.5%	22.8%
UK & Europe	54.9%	52.8%	52.0%	12.6%	14.1%	14.7%
Middle East, Africa & Asia	37.7%	36.2%	38.0%	12.0%	11.7%	11.7%
Assets Turnover						
Americas	0.65	0.57	0.73	1.73	1.62	1.66
UK & Europe	1.93	1.77	1.77	0.75	0.77	0.81
Middle East, Africa & Asia	2.93	2.62	3.00	1.41	1.17	1.16
ROA						
Americas	5.5%	9.1%	10.5%	35.9%	36.5%	37.7%
UK & Europe	105.6%	93.3%	91.9%	9.4%	10.9%	11.9%
Middle East, Africa & Asia	110.3%	94.8%	114.1%	16.8%	13.7%	13.5%

c. What are the likely reasons PepsiCo's inventory turnover ratio exceeds that for Coca-Cola? (Hint: Incorporate information from Exhibit 4.13 regarding PepsiCo's disclosed segments.)

d. For which firm is financial leverage helping the common shareholders more? Explain in such a way as to demonstrate your understanding of financial leverage.

4.26 ANALYZING THE PROFITABILITY OF A SERVICE FIRM. Kelly Services (Kelly) places employees at clients' businesses on a temporary basis. It segments its services into (1) commercial, (2) professional and technical, and (3) international. Kelly recognizes revenues for the amount billed to clients. Kelly includes the amount it pays to temporary employees in cost of services sold. It includes the compensation paid to permanent employees that administer its offices in selling and administrative expenses. The latter expense also includes data processing costs relating to payroll records for all employees, rent, taxes, and insurance on office space. Amounts receivable from clients appear in accounts receivable, and amounts payable to permanent and temporary employees appear in current liabilities.

The temporary personnel business offers clients flexibility in adjusting the number of workers to meet changing capacity needs. Temporary employees are typically less costly than permanent workers because they have fewer fringe benefits. However, temporary workers generally are not as well trained as permanent workers and have less loyalty to clients.

Barriers to entry in the personnel supply business are low. This business does not require capital for physical facilities (most space is rented), does not need specialized assets (most temporary employees do not possess unique skills; needed data processing technology is readily available), and operates with little government regulation. Thus, competition is intense and margins tend to be thin.

Exhibit 4.39 presents selected profitability ratios and other data for Kelly Services, the largest temporary personnel supply firm in the United States. Note that the data in Exhibit 4.39 reflect the capitalization of operating leases in property, plant, and equipment and long-term debt, a topic discussed in Chapter 6.

Required

Analyze the changes in the profitability of Kelly Services during the three-year period in as much depth as permitted by the data provided.

4.27 ANALYZING THE PROFITABILITY OF TWO HOTELS. Starwood Hotels (Starwood) owns and operates many hotel properties under well-known brand names, including Sheraton, W, Westin, and St. Regis. Starwood focuses on the upper end of the lodging industry. Choice Hotels (Choice) is a primarily a franchisor of several hotel chains, including Comfort Inn, Sleep Inn, Clarion, EconoLodge, and Rodeway Inn. Choice properties represent primarily the midscale and economy segments of the lodging industry. Exhibit 4.40 (see page 327) presents selected profitability ratios and other data for Starwood, and Exhibit 4.41 (see page 327) presents data for Choice. (Note that ROCE is not meaningful for Choice because of negative common shareholders' equity due to open market share repurchases, not accumulated deficits. As of the end of 2008, Choice had repurchased over one-third of all common shares issued: 34,640,510 out of 95,345,362 shares.) One of the closely followed metrics in the lodging industry is occupancy rate, which gives an indication of the capacity utilization of available hotel rooms. A second measure is the ADR (average daily rate), which measures the amount actually collected for an average room per night. Finally, REVPAR (revenue per available room) also is an important measure, which measures period-to-period growth in revenues per room for comparable properties (adjusted for properties sold or closed or otherwise not comparable across years). The interaction of occupancy rate and ADR is REVPAR.

EXHIBIT 4.39

Profitability Ratios and Other Data for Kelly Services
(Problem 4.26)

	Year 4	Year 3	Year 2
Profit Margin for ROA	0.6%	0.3%	0.6%
Assets Turnover	3.8	3.5	3.5
ROA	2.2%	0.9%	2.1%
Profit Margin for ROCE	0.4%	0.1%	0.4%
Capital Structure Leverage	2.1	2.0	1.9
ROCE	3.3%	0.8%	2.9%
Revenues	100.0%	100.0%	100.0%
Compensation of Temporary Employees/Revenues	84.0%	83.9%	82.9%
Selling and Administrative Expense/Revenues	15.1%	15.7%	16.1%
Income Tax Expense/Revenues	0.3%	0.2%	0.4%
Accounts Receivable Turnover	7.2	7.1	7.3
Fixed Assets Turnover	16.0	14.0	12.9
Sales Mix Data:			
Commercial	46.7%	49.3%	51.9%
Professional and Technical	20.7	20.7	21.4
International	32.6	30.0	26.7
Total	100.0%	100.0%	100.0%
Segment Profit Margin:			
Commercial	5.1%	4.4%	5.6%
Professional and Technical	6.0%	5.9%	5.8%
International	0.8%	0.0%	0.5%
Number of Offices	2,600	2,500	2,400
Number of Permanent Employees	8,400	7,900	8,200
Number of Temporary Employees, approximate	700,000	700,000	700,000
Growth Rate in Revenues	15.2%	6.9%	(4.7%)
Per-Office Data:			
Revenues	$1,916,923	$1,730,000	$1,690,417
Net Income	$ 8,077	$ 2,000	$ 7,500
Permanent Employees	3.2	3.2	3.4
Temporary Employees	269	280	292
Per-Permanent-Employee Data:			
Revenues	$ 593,333	$ 547,468	$ 494,756
Net Income	$ 2,500	$ 633	$ 2,195
Temporary Employees	83.3	88.6	85.4
Per-Temporary-Employee Data:			
Revenues	$ 7,120	$ 6,177	$ 5,796
Net Income	$ 30	$ 7	$ 26

EXHIBIT 4.40

Profitability Ratios and Other Data for Starwood Hotels
(Problem 4.27)

	2008	2007	2006
Sales Growth	(4.0%)	2.9%	0.0%
Profit Margin for ROA	7.8%	10.4%	19.8%
Assets Turnover	0.61	0.65	0.55
ROA	4.8%	6.8%	10.9%
Profit Margin for ROCE	5.6%	8.8%	17.4%
Capital Structure Leverage	5.23	3.72	2.65
ROCE	17.8%	21.3%	25.4%
Number of Hotels	942	925	871
Number of Rooms	285,000	282,000	266,000
Rooms/Hotel	303	305	305
Occupancy Rate	71.1%	72.7%	71.2%
Revenue/Available Room Night	$168.93	$171.01	$136.33
Average Daily Rate	$237.45	$235.18	$191.56

EXHIBIT 4.41

Profitability Ratios and Other Data for Choice Hotels
(Problem 4.27)

	2008	2007	2006
Sales Growth	4.2%	14.0%	13.1%
Profit Margin for ROA	16.7%	19.6%	22.6%
Assets Turnover	1.95	1.95	1.90
ROA	32.6%	38.2%	42.9%
Profit Margin for ROCE	15.6%	18.1%	20.9%
Capital Structure Leverage	(2.23)	(2.88)	(2.48)
ROCE	n.m.	n.m.	n.m.
Number of Hotels	4,716	4,445	4,211
Number of Rooms	373,884	354,139	$339,441
Rooms/Hotel	79	80	81
Occupancy Rate	55.3%	57.9%	58.4%
Revenue/Available Room Night	$ 40.98	$ 41.75	$ 40.13
Average Daily Rate	$ 74.11	$ 72.07	$ 68.71

n.m.: not meaningful due to negative common shareholders' equity

Required

Analyze the changes and the differences in the profitability of these two hotel chains to the deepest levels available given the data provided. Compare and contrast the ROAs and ROCEs of both companies. Do the results match your prior expectations given the type of lodging for which each company specializes?

4.28 ANALYZING THE PROFITABILITY OF TWO RESTAURANT CHAINS. Analyzing the profitability of restaurants requires consideration of their strategies with respect to ownership of restaurants versus franchising. Firms that own and operate their restaurants report the assets and financing of those restaurants on their balance sheets and the revenues and operating expenses of the restaurants on their income statements. Firms that franchise their restaurants to others (that is, franchisees) often own the land and buildings of franchised restaurants and lease them to the franchisees. The income statement includes fees received from franchisees in the form of license fees for using the franchiser's name; rent for facilities and equipment; and various fees for advertising, menu planning, and food and paper products used by the franchisee. The revenues and operating expenses of the franchised restaurants appear on the financial statements of the franchisees.

Exhibit 4.42 presents profitability ratios and other data for Brinker International, and Exhibit 4.43 presents similar data for McDonald's. Brinker operates chains of specialty

---

EXHIBIT 4.42

Profitability Ratios and Other Data for Brinker International (Problem 4.28)

	Year 4	Year 3	Year 2
Profit Margin for ROA	5.1%	6.2%	6.5%
Assets Turnover	1.4	1.3	1.3
ROA	7.1%	8.4%	8.8%
Profit Margin for ROCE	4.1%	5.1%	5.2%
Capital Structure Leverage	2.5	2.3	2.3
ROCE	14.1%	15.8%	16.1%
Cost of Goods Sold/Revenues	81.2%	80.9%	81.0%
Selling and Administrative Expenses/Revenues	10.9%	9.8%	9.1%
Income Tax Expense (excluding tax effects of interest expense)/ Revenues	2.8%	3.1%	3.4%
Accounts Receivable Turnover	100.2	106.0	101.3
Inventory Turnover	97.1	115.5	95.5
Fixed Assets Turnover	1.7	1.6	1.6
Revenues per Restaurant (000's)	$ 2,516	$ 2,343	$ 2,277
Operating Income per Restaurant (000's)	$ 129	$ 145	$ 148
Fixed Assets per Restaurant (000's)	$ 1,476	$ 1,493	$ 1,506
Percentage of Restaurants Owned and Operated	80.1%	81.7%	81.9%
Growth in Revenues	12.8%	13.8%	16.7%
Growth in Number of Restaurants	5.3%	10.6%	10.9%

EXHIBIT 4.43

Profitability Ratios and Other Data for McDonald's
(Problem 4.28)

	Year 4	Year 3	Year 2
Profit Margin for ROA	15.1%	12.2%	10.0%
Assets Turnover	0.6	0.5	0.5
ROA	8.5%	6.7%	5.3%
Profit Margin for ROCE	12.0%	8.8%	6.4%
Capital Structure Leverage	2.6	2.8	2.9
ROCE	17.4%	13.5%	9.8%
Cost of Goods Sold/Revenues	65.8%	66.7%	66.7%
Selling and Administrative Expenses/Revenues	12.6%	14.4%	17.0%
Income Tax Expense (excluding tax effects of interest expense)/Revenues	6.5%	6.7%	6.3%
Accounts Receivable Turnover	25.7	21.6	17.7
Inventory Turnover	90.9	94.8	94.2
Fixed Assets Turnover	0.7	0.6	0.6
Revenues per Restaurant (000's)	$ 605	$ 551	$ 495
Operating Income per Restaurant (000's)	$ 91	$ 67	$ 50
Fixed Assets per Restaurant (000's)	$ 881	$ 856	$ 795
Percentage of Restaurants Owned and Operated	29.2%	28.8%	28.9%
Growth in Revenues	11.2%	11.3%	3.6%
Growth in Number of Restaurants	1.4%	0.1%	3.4%

sit-down restaurants in the United States under the names of Chili's, Romano's Macaroni Grill, On the Border, Maggiano's Little Italy, and Corner Bakery Cafe. Its restaurants average approximately 7,000 square feet. Brinker owns and operates approximately 81 percent of its restaurants. McDonald's operates chains of fast-food restaurants in the United States and other countries under the names of McDonald's, Boston Market, Chipotle Mexican Grill, and Donatos Pizza. Its restaurants average approximately 2,800 square feet. McDonald's owns and operates approximately 29 percent of its restaurants. It also owns approximately 25 percent of the restaurant land and buildings of franchisees. The financial ratios and other data in Exhibits 4.42 and 4.43 reflect the capitalization of operating leases in property, plant, and equipment and long-term debt, a topic discussed in Chapter 6.

Required

    a. Suggest reasons for the changes in the profitability of Brinker during the three-year period.

    b. Suggest reasons for the changes in the profitability of McDonald's during the three-year period.

    c. Suggest reasons for differences in the profitability of Brinker and McDonald's during the three-year period.

INTEGRATIVE CASE 4.1

STARBUCKS

Part A

Integrative Case 1.1 introduced the industry economics of coffee shops and the business strategy of Starbucks to compete in this industry. Exhibit 1.26 presents balance sheets for Starbucks for the years ending 2005–2008. Exhibit 1.27 presents its income statements and Exhibit 1.28 presents the statement of cash flows for fiscals 2005, 2006, 2007, and 2008. Exhibit 1.29 presents common-size balance sheets and Exhibit 1.30 presents common-size income statements for Starbucks. Before beginning preparation of Integrative Case 4.1, we recommend that you review Integrative Case 1.1 in Chapter 1.

Part A of Integrative Case 4.1 analyzes changes in the profitability of Starbucks for fiscal 2006–2008.

Required

a. Exhibit 4.44 presents profitability ratios for Starbucks for fiscals 2006 and 2007. Using the financial statement data in Exhibits 1.26 and 1.27, compute the values of these ratios for fiscal 2008. The income tax rate is 35 percent. For accounts receivable turnover, use only specialty revenues for the numerator, because the accounts

---

EXHIBIT 4.44

Starbucks
Financial Statement Ratio Analysis
(Integrative Case 4.1, Part A)

	2008	2007	2006
Profit Margin for ROA		7.4%	7.3%
Assets Turnover		1.93	1.96
ROA		14.3%	14.3%
Profit Margin for ROCE		7.1%	7.2%
Capital Structure Leverage		2.17	1.84
ROCE		29.8%	26.1%
Cost of Sales/Revenues		42.5%	40.8%
Store Operating Expenses/Revenues		34.2%	34.5%
Nonretail Operating Expenses/Revenues		3.1%	3.3%
Depreciation and Amortization Expense/Revenues		5.0%	5.0%
General and Administrative Expense/Revenues		5.2%	6.2%
Restructuring Charge/Revenues		0.0%	0.0%
Income from Equity Investees/Revenues		1.1%	1.2%
Interest Revenue/Revenues		0.4%	0.3%
Income Tax Expense (excluding tax effects of interest expense)/ Revenues		4.2%	4.2%
Accounts Receivable Turnover		5.5	5.8
Inventory Turnover		6.0	5.4
Fixed Assets Turnover		3.6	3.8

receivable are primarily related to licensing and food service operations, not the retail operations. Use cost of sales, including occupancy costs, for the numerator of the inventory turnover because Starbucks does not disclose separately the cost of products sold (the appropriate numerator) and occupancy costs.

b. What are the most important reasons Starbucks' ROA decreased during the three-year period? Analyze the financial ratios to the maximum depth possible with the information given. Using the nomenclature from the schematic in Exhibit 4.20, Exhibit 4.45 provides information for analyzing profitability at Level 1, Level 2, and Level 3. Exhibit 4.45 presents additional information for Starbucks at a business segment level to permit analysis at Level 4. Corporate-level expenses not allocated to domestic or international operations, which include depreciation, amortization, general, and administrative expenses, as a percentage of total revenues were 3.3 percent for fiscal 2008, 3.6 percent for fiscal 2007, and 4.3 percent for fiscal 2006.

c. What are the most important reasons Starbucks' ROCE decreased during the three-year period?

Part B

Part B of Integrative Case 4.1 compares the profitability of Starbucks with Panera Bread Company. Although Starbucks and Panera Bread Company are not direct competitors in terms of the principal food products offered, they compete in the sense of offering a relaxed café experience. Whereas the products of Starbucks center on coffee and related beverages, Panera Bread Company emphasizes freshly baked bread and pastries. Panera Bread Company also sells sandwiches, soups, and similar lunch and light dinner products that build on their bread offerings, as well as coffee and other beverages. The average size of a Panera Bread Company retail outlet is typically larger than that of Starbucks. Both Starbucks and Panera Bread Company own some of their retail stores and franchise or license rights to use their names and products to other parties that own and operate other retail stores. Panera Bread Company prepares fresh dough daily in various regional facilities to use in company-owned stores and to sell to franchisees. Unlike Starbucks, it has not expanded beyond the United States.

Exhibit 4.46 (see page 333) presents profitability ratios for Panera Bread Company for 2006–2008, and Exhibit 4.47 (see pages 333–334) presents segment profitability and other data. The format of Exhibit 4.46 is similar to that of Exhibit 4.44. However, due to less detailed disclosures by Panera, Exhibit 4.47 does not contain specific cost structures for Panera's operating segments, similar to what was available from Starbucks and presented in Exhibit 4.45. The proportions of general and administrative expenses not allocated to divisions for Panera Bread Company are similar to the corresponding percentages for Starbucks (suggesting they are not material enough to specifically factor into the analysis).

Required

a. Panera's ROA has typically been below that of Starbucks prior to 2008. What are the likely reasons for the relative levels of ROA between Panera and Starbucks? Analyze the data to the maximum depth permitted by the information given and speculate on economic explanations for what the analysis indicates.

b. Panera's ROCE also has typically been below that of Starbucks, but by a large margin. Why?

EXHIBIT 4.45

Starbucks Segment Profitability Data (Integrative Case 4.1, Parts A and B)

	United States			International			Global Consumer Products Group		
	2008	2007	2006	2008	2007	2006	2008	2007	2006
Total Revenue Mix	76.0%	78.1%	79.3%	20.3%	18.0%	16.7%	3.8%	3.9%	3.9%
Net Revenues:									
Company-operated retail	88.7%	89.3%	88.9%	84.3%	84.7%	83.5%	0.0%	0.0%	0.0%
Licensing	6.4%	6.0%	6.0%	13.1%	13.0%	14.3%	0.0%	0.0%	0.0%
Foodservice and other	4.9%	4.7%	5.1%	2.6%	2.2%	2.2%	100.0%	100.0%	100.0%
Total net revenues	100.0%	100.0%	100.0%	100.0%	100.0%	100.0%	100.0%	100.0%	100.0%
Cost of sales including occupancy costs	42.8%	40.2%	38.4%	50.1%	48.6%	48.0%	55.9%	59.6%	58.7%
Store operating expenses	39.1%	36.5%	36.9%	31.6%	31.3%	31.3%	0.0%	0.0%	0.0%
Other operating expenses	2.8%	2.8%	3.1%	4.2%	4.1%	3.9%	5.6%	5.3%	4.0%
Depreciation and amortization	5.1%	4.7%	4.6%	5.2%	5.0%	5.1%	0.0%	0.0%	0.0%
General and administrative expenses	0.9%	1.2%	1.5%	5.4%	5.5%	6.0%	1.6%	1.7%	2.1%
Restructuring charges	2.7%	0.0%	0.0%	0.9%	0.0%	0.0%	0.0%	0.0%	0.0%
Total operating expense	93.3%	85.4%	84.5%	97.3%	94.6%	94.3%	63.2%	66.7%	64.8%
Income (loss) from equity investees	0.0%	0.0%	0.0%	2.6%	2.7%	2.6%	15.5%	16.8%	19.4%
Segment Profit Margin	6.7%	14.6%	15.5%	5.2%	8.1%	8.3%	52.3%	50.1%	54.6%
Segment Asset Turnover	2.5	2.5	2.5	2.6	2.5	2.9			
Segment ROA	17.0%	35.8%	39.0%	13.3%	20.6%	24.0%			
Stores Owned	7,238	6,793	5,728	1,979	1,743	1,435			
Stores Licensed	4,329	3,891	3,168	3,134	2,615	2,170			
Total Stores	11,567	10,684	8,896	5,113	4,358	3,605			
Revenues[a]/Stores Owned	$966,800	$965,832	$959,358	$896,513	$824,670	$758,118			
Revenues[b]/Stores Licensed	$116,470	$112,850	$116,509	$ 87,683	$ 84,474	$ 85,714			
Total Revenues/Total Stores	$681,854	$687,851	$694,526	$411,383	$389,215	$361,415			
Operating Income/Total Stores	$ 45,656	$100,197	$107,374	$ 21,514	$ 31,597	$ 30,097			
Assets/Total Stores	$267,995	$279,914	$274,966	$161,314	$153,258	$125,659			
Total Revenues Increase	7.3%	18.9%	21.2%	24.0%	30.2%	27.4%			
Comparable Stores Sales Increase[c]	(5.0%)	4.0%	7.0%	2.0%	7.0%	8.0%			

[a] Revenues represent sales from company-operated retail stores.
[b] Revenues represent fees and other revenues from licensees.
[c] Comparable stores represent stores open at least two full years.

EXHIBIT 4.46

Panera Bread Company
Financial Statement Ratio Analysis
(Integrative Case 4.1, Part B)

	2008	2007	2006
Sales growth	21.8%	28.7%	29.5%
Profit Margin for ROA	5.4%	5.4%	7.1%
Assets Turnover	1.89	1.72	1.69
ROA	10.2%	9.2%	12.0%
Profit Margin for ROCE	5.2%	5.4%	7.1%
Capital Structure Leverage	1.46	1.47	1.37
ROCE	14.3%	13.6%	16.5%
Cost of Sales/Revenues	34.0%	34.2%	34.1%
Store Operating Expenses/Revenues	34.4%	34.2%	31.3%
Nonretail Operating Expenses/Revenues	11.3%	11.4%	11.1%
Depreciation and Amortization Expense/Revenues	5.2%	5.4%	5.3%
General and Administrative Expense/Revenues	6.5%	6.5%	7.2%
Income Tax Expense (excluding tax effects of interest expense)/Revenues	3.2%	3.0%	4.1%
Accounts Receivable Turnover	64.4	48.3	44.5
Inventory Turnover	37.8	36.2	35.2
Fixed Assets Turnover	3.1	2.7	2.7

EXHIBIT 4.47

Panera Bread Company
Segment Profitability Data
(Integrative Case 4.1, Part B)

	2008	2007	2006
Net Revenues:			
Company-operated retail	85.2%	83.9%	80.4%
Franchising	5.8%	6.3%	7.4%
Foodservice and other	9.1%	9.8%	12.2%
Total net revenues	100.0%	100.0%	100.0%
Operating profit:			
Company-operated retail	14.1%	13.6%	14.9%
Franchising	5.0%	5.5%	6.5%
Foodservice and other	0.7%	1.1%	1.9%
Segment Asset Turnover:			
Company-operated retail	2.2	1.7	1.8
Franchising	12.6	10.9	16.5
Foodservice and other	4.2	3.2	2.7

(*Continued*)

EXHIBIT 4.47 (Continued)

	2008	2007	2006
Segment ROA:			
Company-operated retail	36.5%	28.3%	33.0%
Franchising	1,092.3%	955.0%	1,448.1%
Foodservice and other	18.1%	21.2%	25.6%
Stores Owned	562	532	391
Stores Franchised	763	698	636
Total Stores	1,325	1,230	1,027
Revenues/Stores Owned	$1,968,496	$1,682,147	$1,703,685
Revenues/Stores Franchised	$ 98,034	$ 96,258	$ 96,747
Total Revenues/Total Stores	$ 980,266	$ 867,228	$ 807,177
Operating Income/Total Stores	$ 82,044	$ 72,268	$ 90,240
Assets/Total Stores	$ 508,617	$ 568,091	$ 528,344
Total Revenues Increase	31.8%	28.7%	29.5%
Comparable Stores Sales Increase	5.8%	1.9%	3.9%

CASE 4.2

PROFITABILITY AND RISK ANALYSIS OF WAL-MART STORES

Part A

Wal-Mart Stores (Walmart) is the world's largest retailer. It employs an "everyday low price" strategy and operates stores as three business segments: Wal-Mart Stores U.S., International, and Sam's Club.

1. **Wal-Mart Stores U.S.:** This segment represented 63.7 percent of all 2008 sales and operates stores in three different formats: Discount stores (approximately 108,000 square feet), Supercenters (approximately 186,000 square feet), and Neighborhood Markets (approximately 42,000 square feet). Each format carries a variety of clothing, housewares, electronic equipment, pharmaceuticals, health and beauty products, sporting goods, and similar items, and Supercenters including a full-line supermarket.[40] Wal-Mart U.S. Stores are in all 50 states, Discount stores are in 47 states, Supercenters are in 48 states, and Neighborhood Markets are in 16 states. Customers also can purchase many items through the company's website at http://www.walmart.com.

2. **International:** The International segment includes wholly owned subsidiaries in Argentina, Brazil, Canada, Japan, Puerto Rico, and the United Kingdom; majority-owned subsidiaries in five countries in Central America, Chile, and Mexico; and joint ventures in India and China. The merchandising strategy for the International segment is similar to that of the Walmart U.S. segment.

3. **Sam's Clubs:** Sam's Clubs are membership club warehouses that operate in 48 states. The average Sam's Club is approximately 133,000 square feet, and customers can purchase

---

[40]Walmart's fiscal year ends at the end of January of each year. Despite Walmart's convention of referring to its year ending January 31, 2009, as its fiscal 2009, we follow the common practice of referring to it as 2008 because 11 of the 12 months fall within 2008. This same convention holds true for Carrefour and Target in Part B of this case.

many items through the company's website at http://www.samsclub.com. These warehouses offer bulk displays of brand name merchandise, including hardgoods, some softgoods, institutional-size grocery items, and certain private-label items. Gross margins for Sam's Clubs stores are lower than those of the U.S. and International segments.

Walmart uses centralized purchasing through its home office for substantially all of its merchandise. It distributes products to its stores through regional distribution centers. During fiscal 2008, the proportion of merchandise channeled through its regional distribution centers was as follows:

Walmart Stores, Supercenters, and Neighborhood Markets	81%
Sam's Club (non-fuel)	65%
International	74%

Exhibit 4.48 sets out various operating data for Walmart for its most recent three years. Exhibit 4.49 presents segment data. Exhibit 4.50 presents comparative balance sheets for Walmart for 2005–2008 (an extra year to enable average balance computations when necessary), Exhibit 4.51 (see page 338) presents comparative income statements for 2006–2008, and Exhibit 4.52 (see page 339) presents comparative statements of cash flows for 2006–2008. Exhibit 4.53 (see page 340) presents selected financial statement ratios for Walmart for 2006–2008. The statutory income tax rate is 35 percent.

EXHIBIT 4.48

Operating Data for Wal-Mart Stores
(Case 4.2, Part A)

	Fiscal Year:		
	2008	**2007**	**2006**
Walmart Discount Stores, Supercenters, and			
Neighborhood Markets (U.S.)			
Number	3,656	3,550	3,443
Square Footage (millions)	589.3	566.6	540.4
Sales per Square Foot	$ 433.98	$ 422.75	$ 418.75
Operating Income per Square Foot	$ 31.84	$ 30.91	$ 30.76
International			
Number	3,615	3,098	2,734
Square Footage (millions)	251.8	222.6	188.4
Sales per Square Foot	$ 391.76	$ 406.20	$ 383.04
Operating Income per Square Foot	$ 19.62	$ 21.23	$ 18.76
Sam's Club (Domestic)			
Number	602	591	579
Square Footage (millions)	79.9	78.2	76.3
Sales per Square Foot	$ 586.41	$ 567.23	$ 544.98
Operating Income per Square Foot	$ 20.15	$ 20.69	$ 19.40
Domestic Comparable Store Sales Increase	3.5%	1.6%	2.0%

EXHIBIT 4.49

Segment Profitability Analysis for Wal-Mart Stores
(Case 4.2, Part A)

	Fiscal Year:		
	2008	2007	2006
Sales Mix			
Walmart Discount Stores, Supercenters, and Neighborhood Markets	63.7%	64.0%	65.6%
International	24.6	24.1	22.3
Sam's Club	11.7	11.9	12.1
	100.0%	100.0%	100.0%
Walmart Discount Stores, Supercenters, and Neighborhood Markets			
Operating Profit Margin	7.3%	7.3%	7.3%
Assets Turnover	3.0	2.8	2.9
ROA	22.2%	20.8%	21.0%
International			
Operating Profit Margin	5.0%	5.2%	5.5%
Assets Turnover	1.6	1.5	1.4
ROA	8.2%	7.6%	7.8%
Sam's Club			
Operating Profit Margin	3.4%	3.6%	3.6%
Assets Turnover	3.8	3.8	3.6
ROA	13.0%	13.8%	12.9%

EXHIBIT 4.50

Wal-Mart Stores
Balance Sheets
(amounts in millions)
(Case 4.2, Part A)

	2008	2007	2006	2005
ASSETS				
Cash and cash equivalents	$ 7,275	$ 5,492	$ 7,373	$ 6,193
Marketable securities				
Accounts receivable—Net	3,905	3,642	2,840	2,575
Inventories	34,511	35,159	33,685	31,910
Prepaid expenses and other current assets	3,063	2,760	2,690	2,468
Current assets of discontinued segments	195	967	—	679
Current Assets	$ 48,949	$ 48,020	$ 46,588	$ 43,825

EXHIBIT 4.50 (Continued)

	2008	2007	2006	2005
Long-term investments	—	—	—	1,884
Property, plant, & equipment—At cost	131,161	127,992	115,190	100,929
Accumulated depreciation	(35,508)	(31,125)	(26,750)	(23,064)
Goodwill and nonamortizable intangibles	18,827	18,627	16,165	14,613
Total Assets	$163,429	$163,514	$151,193	$138,187
LIABILITIES AND EQUITIES				
Accounts payable—Trade	$ 28,849	$ 30,344	$ 28,090	$ 25,101
Current accrued liabilities	18,112	15,725	14,675	13,274
Notes payable and short-term debt	1,506	5,040	2,570	3,754
Current maturities of long-term debt	6,163	6,229	5,713	4,879
Income taxes payable	760	1,140	706	1,817
Current Liabilities	$ 55,390	$ 58,478	$ 51,754	$ 48,825
Long-term debt	34,549	33,402	30,735	30,096
Deferred tax liabilities—Noncurrent	6,014	5,087	4,971	4,630
Total Liabilities	$ 95,953	$ 96,967	$ 87,460	$ 83,551
Minority interest	$ 2,191	$ 1,939	$ 2,160	$ 1,465
Common stock + paid-in capital	4,313	3,425	3,247	3,013
Retained earnings	63,660	57,319	55,818	49,105
Accum. other comprehensive income (loss)	(2,688)	3,864	2,508	1,053
Common Shareholders' Equity	$ 65,285	$ 64,608	$ 61,573	$ 53,171
Total Liabilities and Equities	$163,429	$163,514	$151,193	$138,187

Required

a. What are the likely reasons for the changes in Walmart's rate of ROA during the three-year period? Analyze the financial ratios to the maximum depth possible.

b. What are the likely reasons for the changes in Walmart's rate of ROCE during the three-year period?

Note: Parts c and d require coverage of material from Chapter 5.

c. How has the short-term liquidity risk of Walmart changed during the three-year period?

d. How has the long-term solvency risk of Walmart changed during the three-year period?

Part B

Part A of Case 4.2 analyzed the profitability and risk of Wal-Mart Stores for its fiscals 2006, 2007, and 2008. Part B of this case compares the profitability and risk ratios of Walmart and two other leading discount retailers, Carrefour and Target, for their 2006–2008 fiscal years.

Carrefour

Carrefour, headquartered in France, is Europe's largest retailer and the second-largest retailer in the world. Sales in 2008 totaled €86,967 million (approximately $118,000 million).

EXHIBIT 4.51

Wal-Mart Stores
Income Statements
(amounts in millions)
(Case 4.2, Part A)

	2008	2007	2006
Revenues	$ 405,607	$ 378,476	$ 348,368
Cost of goods sold	(306,158)	(286,350)	(263,979)
Gross Profit	$ 99,449	$ 92,126	$ 84,389
Selling, general, and administrative expenses	(76,651)	(70,174)	(63,892)
Operating Profit	$ 22,798	$ 21,952	$ 20,497
Interest income	284	309	280
Interest expense	(2,184)	(2,103)	(1,809)
Income Before Tax	$ 20,898	$ 20,158	$ 18,968
Income tax expense	(7,145)	(6,889)	(6,354)
Minority interest in earnings	(499)	(406)	(425)
Income (loss) from discontinued operations	146	(132)	(905)
Net Income (Computed)	$ 13,400	$ 12,731	$ 11,284
Other comprehensive income items	(6,552)	1,356	1,575
Comprehensive Income	$ 6,848	$ 14,087	$ 12,859

Carrefour is organized by geographic region (France, Europe excluding France, Asia, and Latin America). Each segment is organized according to store formats, which include the following (2008 number of stores and sales mix percentages in parentheses):

Hypermarkets (203; 62%): Offer a wide variety of household and food products at competitively low prices under the Carrefour store brand

Supermarkets (590; 22%): Sell traditional grocery products under the Champion, Norte, GS, and GB supermarkets and other store brands

Hard Discount Stores (842; 11%): Offer a limited variety of food products in smaller stores than those of hypermarkets and supermarkets at aggressively low prices under the Dia, Ed, and Minipreco store brands

Other activities (9; 5%): Includes convenience stores and wholesale stores, the latter targeted at business customers, under the SHOPI, Marche Plus, 8 A Huit, express, Contact, and Proxi store brands

Carrefour derived approximately 44 percent of its 2008 sales in France, 37 percent in Europe excluding France, 12 percent in Latin America, and 7 percent in Asia.

Target

Target Corporation, headquartered in the United States, operates two reportable segments: retail and credit card. The retail segment includes all merchandising operations, including large-format general merchandise and food discount stores as well as an online business at

EXHIBIT 4.52

Wal-Mart Stores
Statements of Cash Flows
(amounts in millions)
(Case 4.2, Part A)

STATEMENT OF CASH FLOWS	2008	2007	2006
Net income	$ 13,400	$ 12,731	$ 11,284
Add back depreciation and amortization expenses	6,739	6,317	5,459
Deferred income taxes	581	(8)	89
(Increase) Decrease in accounts receivable	(101)	(564)	(214)
(Increase) Decrease in inventories	(220)	(775)	(1,274)
Increase (Decrease) in accounts payable	(410)	865	2,132
Increase (Decrease) in other current liabilities	2,036	1,034	588
Other addbacks to net income			
Other subtractions from net income	(146)	132	860
Other operating cash flows	1,268	910	1,311
Net Cash Flows from Operations	**$ 23,147**	**$ 20,642**	**$ 20,235**
Proceeds from sales of property, plant, and equipment	$ 714	$ 957	$ 394
Property, plant, and equipment acquired	(11,499)	(14,937)	(15,666)
Investments sold	781		267
Investments acquired		(95)	
Other investment transactions	(1,576)	(1,338)	(68)
Other	838	(257)	610
Net Cash Flows from Investing Activities	**$(10,742)**	**$(15,670)**	**$(14,463)**
Increase in short-term borrowing		$ 2,376	
Decrease in short-term borrowing	$ (3,745)		$ (1,193)
Increase in long-term borrowing	6,566	11,167	7,199
Decrease in long-term borrowing	(5,739)	(9,066)	(6,098)
Share repurchases—Treasury stock	(3,521)	(7,691)	(1,718)
Dividend payments	(3,746)	(3,586)	(2,802)
Other financing transactions	267	(622)	(510)
Net Cash Flows from Financing Activities	**$ (9,918)**	**$ (7,422)**	**$ (5,122)**
Effects of exchange rate changes on cash	(781)	252	97
Net Change in Cash	**$ 1,706**	**$ (2,198)**	**$ 747**
Cash and Cash Equivalents, Beginning of Year *	**$ 5,492**	**$ 7,373**	**$ 6193**

* The amounts do not reconcile with the balance sheet presentation because Walmart reclassified cash and equivalents applicable to discontinued operations.

http://www.target.com. Target stores offer a wide variety of clothing, household, electronics, sports, toys, and entertainment products at discount prices. Target stores attempt to differentiate themselves from Walmart's discount stores by pushing trendy merchandising with more brand-name products. Target emphasizes customer service, referring to its customers as "guests" and focusing on the theme of "Expect More, Pay Less." Target Corporation

EXHIBIT 4.53

Wal-Mart Stores
Financial Ratio Analysis
(Case 4.2, Part A)

	Fiscal Year:		
	2008	**2007**	**2006**
Profitability Ratios			
ROA	9.3%	9.3%	9.5%
Profit Margin for ROA	3.7%	3.9%	4.0%
Assets Turnover	2.5	2.4	2.4
Cost of Goods Sold/Sales	75.5%	75.7%	75.8%
Selling and Administrative Expense/Sales	18.9%	18.5%	18.3%
Interest Expense (net of taxes)/Sales	0.3%	0.4%	0.3%
Income Tax Expense (excluding tax effects of interest expense)/Sales	2.0%	2.0%	2.0%
Accounts Receivable Turnover	107.5	116.8	128.7
Inventory Turnover	8.8	8.3	8.0
Fixed Assets Turnover	4.2	4.1	4.2
ROCE	20.4%	20.4%	21.2%
Profit Margin for ROCE	3.3%	3.4%	3.5%
Capital Structure Leverage	2.5	2.4	2.4
Risk Ratios			
Current Ratio	0.88	0.82	0.90
Quick Ratio	0.20	0.16	0.20
Accounts Payable Turnover	10.3	9.9	10.0
Cash Flow from Operations to Current Liabilities Ratio	40.7%	37.5%	40.2%
Long-Term Debt Ratio	34.6%	34.1%	33.3%
Total Liabilities/Total Assets Ratio	58.7%	59.3%	57.8%
Cash Flow from Operations to Total Liabilities Ratio	24.0%	22.4%	23.7%
Interest Coverage Ratio	10.6	10.5	11.0

attempts to differentiate itself from competitors by providing wider aisles and a less cluttered store appearance. At the end of fiscal 2008, Target Corporation operated 1,682 stores and 34 distribution centers. The credit card segment offers branded proprietary credit cards under the names Target Visa and the Target Card. For 2008, total revenues were $64,948, consisting of retail sales of 62,884 and credit card revenues of $2,064.

Exhibits 4.54 and 4.55 (see page 342) present profitability ratios for Carrefour, Target, and Walmart for their 2006–2008 fiscal years. Exhibit 4.56 (see page 343) presents risk ratios for the three firms. Exhibit 4.57 (see page 344) presents selected other data for these firms. The financial statements include the present value of commitments under all leases in property, plant, and equipment and in long-term debt.

EXHIBIT 4.54

Cross-Section ROA Profitability Analysis for Carrefour, Target, and Walmart (Case 4.2, Part B)

	ROA		
	2008	**2007**	**2006**
Carrefour	3.0%	4.4%	4.5%
Target	6.0%	7.8%	8.6%
Walmart	9.3%	9.3%	9.5%

	Profit Margin for ROA			Assets Turnover		
	2008	**2007**	**2006**	**2008**	**2007**	**2006**
Carrefour	1.8%	2.6%	2.8%	1.7	1.7	1.6
Target	4.2%	5.2%	5.4%	1.4	1.5	1.6
Walmart	3.7%	3.9%	4.0%	2.5	2.4	2.4

	Carrefour			Target			Walmart		
	2008	**2007**	**2006**	**2008**	**2007**	**2006**	**2008**	**2007**	**2006**
Sales	100.0%	100.0%	100.0%	100.0%	100.0%	100.0%	100.0%	100.0%	100.0%
Other Revenues	1.4	1.4	1.3	3.3	2.1	2.8	1.1	1.1	1.0
Cost of Goods Sold	(79.0)	(78.6)	(78.6)	(70.2)	(69.8)	(69.7)	(76.3)	(76.5)	(76.6)
Selling and Administrative	(19.2)	(18.7)	(18.6)	(26.1)	(24.7)	(24.3)	(19.1)	(18.7)	(18.5)
Income Taxes	(0.9)	(1.0)	(1.1)	(2.1)	(2.9)	(3.0)	(1.8)	(1.8)	(1.8)
Profit Margin for ROA[*]	1.8%	2.6%	2.8%	4.2%	5.2%	5.4%	3.7%	3.9%	4.0%
Receivable Turnover	27.4	23.3	21.7	7.8	8.6	9.8	107.5	116.8	128.7
Inventory Turnover	10.0	10.0	9.9	6.5	6.6	6.7	8.8	8.3	8.0
Fixed Assets Turnover	5.9	5.8	5.7	2.5	2.7	2.9	4.2	4.1	4.2

[*]Amounts do not sum because Profit Margin for ROA is reduced by taxes on operating profits, which do not equal total taxes reported on the income statement.

EXHIBIT 4.55

Cross-Section ROCE Profitability Analysis for Carrefour, Target, and Walmart (Case 4.2, Part B)

	ROCE		
	2008	**2007**	**2006**
Carrefour	14.8%	24.6%	27.2%
Target	15.3%	18.4%	18.7%
Walmart	20.4%	20.4%	21.2%

	Profit Margin for ROCE			**Assets Turnover**			**Capital Structure Leverage**		
	2008	**2007**	**2006**	**2008**	**2007**	**2006**	**2008**	**2007**	**2006**
Carrefour	1.8%	3.0%	3.2%	1.7	1.7	1.6	5.0	4.9	5.2
Target	3.5%	4.6%	4.8%	1.4	1.5	1.6	3.1	2.6	2.4
Walmart	3.3%	3.4%	3.5%	2.5	2.4	2.4	2.5	2.5	2.5

Required

a. Walmart and Target follow somewhat different strategies. Walmart consistently has a higher ROA compared to Target. Using information in Exhibits 4.54 and 4.57, suggest reasons for these differences in operating profitability.

b. Walmart and Carrefour follow similar strategies. Walmart consistently outperforms Carrefour on ROA. Using information in Exhibits 4.54 and 4.57, suggest reasons for these differences in operating profitability.

c. Refer to Exhibit 4.55. Which firm appears to have used financial leverage most effectively in enhancing the rate of ROCE? Explain your reasoning.
   Note: Parts d and e require coverage of material from Chapter 5.

d. Refer to Exhibit 4.56. Rank-order these firms in terms of their short-term liquidity risk. Do any of these firms appear unduly risky as of the end of fiscal 2008? Explain.

e. Refer to Exhibit 4.56. Rank-order these firms in terms of their long-term liquidity risk. Do any of these firms appear unduly risky as of the end of fiscal Year 4? Explain.

EXHIBIT 4.56

Cross-Section Risk Analysis for Carrefour, Target, and Walmart
(Case 4.2, Part B)

	Carrefour			Target			Walmart		
	2008	2007	2006	2008	2007	2006	2008	2007	2006
Short-Term Liquidity									
Current Ratio	0.70	0.65	0.66	1.66	1.60	1.32	0.88	0.82	0.90
Quick Ratio	0.39	0.36	0.37	0.85	0.89	0.63	0.20	0.16	0.20
Cash Flow from Operations/ Average Current Liabilities	14.1%	14.2%	13.1%	39.7%	36.0%	47.0%	40.7%	37.5%	40.2%
Days Receivable	24	27	29	47	48	49	3	3	3
Days Inventory	37	39	37	55	58	57	42	44	45
Days Payable	92	95	99	52	56	59	35	37	37
Long-Term Solvency									
Long-Term Debt Ratio	46.5%	41.3%	41.8%	56.1%	49.7%	35.7%	34.6%	34.1%	33.3%
Total Liabilities/ Total Assets Ratio	79.0%	77.3%	77.9%	68.9%	65.6%	58.1%	58.7%	59.3%	57.8%
Cash Flow from Operations/ Average Total Liabilities	9.9%	10.2%	9.4%	14.9%	16.2%	22.9%	24.0%	22.4%	23.7%
Interest Coverage Ratio	6.4	8.4	9.1	5.9	9.6	10.0	10.6	10.5	11.0

EXHIBIT 4.57

Selected Other Financial Data for Carrefour, Target, and Walmart (Case 4.2, Part B)

	2008	2007	2006
Growth Rate in Sales			
Carrefour	5.9%	6.8%	5.2%
Target	2.3%	6.2%	12.9%
Walmart	9.4%	7.2%	8.6%
Number of Stores			
Carrefour	15,430	14,991	12,547
Target	1,682	1,591	1,488
Walmart	7,873	7,239	6,756
Square Footage (000's)			
Carrefour	192,801	181,900	164,350
Target	222,588	207,945	192,064
Walmart	921,000	867,400	805,100
Sales per Square Foot			
Carrefour	€451	€452	€468
Target	$283	$296	$301
Walmart	$440	$436	$433
Sales per Store			
Carrefour	€5,636,215	€5,479,855	€6,127,919
Target	$37,386,445	$38,636,706	$38,896,505
Walmart	$51,518,735	$52,282,912	$51,564,239
Square Feet per Store			
Carrefour	12,495	12,134	13,099
Target	132,335	130,701	129,075
Walmart	116,982	119,823	119,168
Fixed Assets per Square Foot			
Carrefour	€77	€81	€84
Target	$116	$116	$112
Walmart	$104	$112	$110
Sales per Employee			
Carrefour	€175,589	€167,636	€168,503
Target	$179,157	$167,954	$164,426
Walmart	$193,146	$180,227	$183,352
Exchange Rate:			
U.S. Dollars per Euro (€)	$1.4097	$1.4728	$1.3200

Chapter 5

Risk Analysis

Learning Objectives

1. Utilize the information that U.S. GAAP and IFRS require firms to disclose about their risk exposures and risk management activities.

2. Understand the concept of *financial flexibility* and use an innovative decomposition of return on common equity to assess financial flexibility.

3. Apply analytical tools to assess working capital management and *short-term liquidity risk*.

4. Evaluate the benefits and risks of financial leverage and apply analytical tools for assessing *long-term solvency risk*.

5. Use risk analysis tools in assessing *credit risk*.

6. Apply predictive statistical models to assess *bankruptcy risk*.

7. Understand the distinction between *firm-specific risks*, as measured by various financial statement ratios, and *systematic risk*, as measured by market equity beta, and relationships between these types of risks.

8. Examine factors that may lead firms to manipulate reported financial statement amounts and apply tools for analyzing the *fraudulent financial reporting risk*.

Equity investors make investment decisions based on the *expected return* from equity investments relative to the *risks* of realizing those returns. Similarly, lenders make lending decisions based on the *expected return* in the form of interest revenue relative to the *risks* of the borrower defaulting on repayments. The analysis of risk is central to any decision to commit economic resources to a project or an investment. This chapter describes disclosures required by U.S. GAAP and IFRS to inform financial statement users about how certain risks can affect a firm and how the firm manages those risks. The chapter also explores the analysis of various types of risk using financial statement ratios, predictive statistical models, and other analytical tools.

DISCLOSURES REGARDING RISK AND RISK MANAGEMENT

The sources and types of risk a firm faces are numerous and often interrelated. They include the following:

Source	Type or Nature
Firm-Specific	Ability to attract, retain, and motivate employees
	Dependence on one or few customers
	Dependence on one or few suppliers
	Employee relations
	Litigation
	Environmental or political scrutiny
Industry	Technology
	Competition
	Regulation
	Availability and price of raw materials or other production inputs
	Labor wages and supply
Domestic	Recessions
	Inflation or deflation
	Interest rate volatility
	Demographic shifts
	Political environment
International	Exchange rate changes
	Host government regulations and posturing
	Political unrest or asset expropriation

Most of these risks are inevitable, and firms must continually monitor each one to ensure that appropriate actions are taken to minimize the impact of detrimental events or changes in circumstances. The focus in this chapter, however, is on how to assess the financial consequences of these types of risk using disclosures and data from financial reports. Various financial reporting standards and financial market regulations require firms to discuss in notes to the financial statements or in regulatory filings how important elements of risk affect a particular firm and the actions the firm takes to manage these risks. Some of the more important disclosures are discussed below. Later chapters discuss more fully the accounting procedures for more complex and risky assets and liabilities. We use the disclosures available in PepsiCo's 10-K under "Item 1A. Risk Factors," a required disclosure for all companies under the purview of the SEC. We also use disclosures in Note 10, "Risk Management" (Appendix A), and the discussion under the heading "Market Risks" in PepsiCo's MD&A (Appendix B) to illustrate information that firms provide about risk.

Firm-Specific Risks

Like all companies, PepsiCo is subject to numerous firm-specific risks that are driven by the nature of the business, competition, supplier relationships, customers, and overall firm strategy. For Forms 10-K filed with the SEC, a candid discussion of such risks is required as Item 1A. For non-U.S. companies that list securities in the United States, a required

Form 20-F includes "Item 3D. Risk Factors." Capital market regulators generally require companies around the world to file similar reports in their local jurisdictions. For example, in France, companies file a Registration Document annually with the Autorité des Marchés Financiers (AMF) and in Singapore, companies file an Annual Return and Audited Accounts with the Accounting and Corporate Regulatory Authority (ACRA).

Within Item 1A of Form 10-K, PepsiCo identifies the following risks related to its business:

- *Demand for our products may be adversely affected by changes in consumer preferences and tastes or if we are unable to innovate or market our products effectively.*
- *Our operating results may be adversely affected by increased costs, disruption of supply or shortages of raw materials and other supplies.*
- *If we are not able to build and sustain proper information technology infrastructure, successfully implement our ongoing business transformation initiative or outsource certain functions effectively our business could suffer.*
- *Any damage to our reputation could have an adverse effect on our business, financial condition and results of operations.*
- *Trade consolidation, the loss of any key customer, or failure to maintain good relationships with our bottling partners could adversely affect our financial performance.*
- *If we are unable to hire or retain key employees or a highly skilled and diverse workforce, it could have a negative impact on our business.*
- *Changes in the legal and regulatory environment could limit our business activities, increase our operating costs, reduce demand for our products or result in litigation.*
- *Disruption of our supply chain could have an adverse impact on our business, financial condition and results of operations.*
- *Unstable political conditions, civil unrest or other developments and risks in the countries where we operate may adversely impact our business.*

Although many of the disclosures PepsiCo provides are general and applicable to any company, each is discussed in more detail in the company's Form 10-K. For example, PepsiCo gives more detail on the second risk factor, listed above, relating to input prices with the following discussion:

> We and our business partners use various raw materials and other supplies in our business, including aspartame, cocoa, corn, corn sweeteners, flavorings, flour, grapefruits and other fruits, juice and juice concentrates, oats, oranges, potatoes, rice, seasonings, sucralose, sugar, vegetable and essential oils, and wheat. Our key packaging materials include PET resin used for plastic bottles, film packaging used for snack foods, aluminum used for cans, glass bottles and cardboard. Fuel and natural gas are also important commodities due to their use in our plants and in the trucks delivering our products.

The identification and discussion of firm-specific risks provides a useful bridge between understanding a company's industry, business strategy, and profitability and identifying specific risks that may have an impact on the company's ability to grow, be profitable, and ultimately create value for debt and equity stakeholders. Of the firm-specific risks identified above, some are quantifiable and subject to required disclosures in the footnotes to financial statements. The remaining discussion in this section focuses on examples of such disclosures.

Commodity Prices

Firms purchase raw materials to use in manufacturing products. Changes in the prices of those raw materials affect future profitability unless the firm can pass along price increases to customers, engage in fixed-price contractual arrangements with suppliers, or purchase commodity futures contracts. For example, some firms manage this risk by engaging in a purchase commitment with suppliers to purchase certain quantities at a specified price over a particular period of time. Alternatively, the firm might acquire a futures contract or another hedging instrument to neutralize the risk of changes in prices. Chapter 8 discusses the accounting for such hedging instruments.

PepsiCo discloses the following with respect to commodity price risk in Note 10, "Risk Management" (Appendix A):

> We are subject to commodity price risk because our ability to recover increased costs through higher pricing may be limited in the competitive environment in which we operate. This risk is managed through the use of fixed-price purchase orders, pricing agreements, geographic diversity and derivatives. We use derivatives, with terms of no more than three years, to economically hedge price fluctuations related to a portion of our anticipated commodity purchases, primarily for natural gas and diesel fuel. For those derivatives that qualify for hedge accounting, any ineffectiveness is recorded immediately. However, such commodity cash flow hedges have not had any significant ineffectiveness for all periods presented. We classify both the earnings and cash flow impact from these derivatives consistent with the underlying hedged item. During the next 12 months, we expect to reclassify net losses of $64 million related to cash flow hedges from accumulated other comprehensive loss into net income. Derivatives used to hedge commodity price risks that do not qualify for hedge accounting are marked to market each period and reflected in our income statement.

In the MD&A section (Appendix B) and Note 10, "Financial Instruments" (Appendix A), PepsiCo provides the following information about the extent of hedging on commodity prices and the effect on pretax earnings if commodity prices declined:

> Our open commodity derivative contracts that qualify for hedge accounting had a face value of $303 million at December 27, 2008 and $5 million at December 29, 2007. These contracts resulted in net unrealized losses of $117 million at December 27, 2008 and net unrealized gains of less than $1 million at December 29, 2007. At the end of 2008, the potential change in fair value of commodity derivative instruments, assuming a 10% decrease in the underlying commodity price, would have increased our net unrealized losses in 2008 by $19 million.

It is unclear whether the $303 million of open derivative contracts at the end of 2008 relate to accounts payable and other current liabilities of $8,273 million or to purchasing commitments of $3,273 million. (See the balance sheet and Note 9, "Debt Obligations and Commitments," in Appendix A.) Regardless, the amount of open contracts is small compared to either base. PepsiCo uses a 10 percent decline in commodity prices to illustrate the sensitivity of earnings to hedged commodity price changes, which would be a loss on these contracts of $19 million. This amount is 0.3 percent of income before income taxes for 2008 (= $19/$7,021).

In addition to the above derivative contracts that qualify for hedge accounting, Note 10 also discloses a greater exposure for contracts that do not qualify for hedge accounting. These totaled $626 million at December 27, 2008 (relative to $105 million at December 29, 2007). Because these contracts did not qualify for hedge accounting, losses on these contracts of $343 million in 2008 are included in net income. This amount constitutes the bulk of the $346 million of mark-to-market impacts discussed in Chapter 4 as part of making adjustments to rate of return on assets calculations.

Foreign Exchange

Changes in foreign exchange rates can affect a firm in multiple ways:

- The prices a firm pays to acquire raw materials from suppliers abroad
- The prices a firm charges for products sold to customers abroad
- The amount of cash a firm receives when it collects an account receivable, a loan receivable, or another receivable denominated in a currency other than its own
- The amount of cash a firm pays when it settles an account payable, a loan payable, or another payable denominated in a currency other than its own
- The amount of cash a firm collects when it receives remittances from a foreign branch or dividends from a foreign subsidiary
- The cash-equivalent value of assets invested abroad and liabilities borrowed abroad in the event the firm liquidates the foreign unit

Firms often use foreign exchange contracts to hedge some or all of these risks. Chapter 7 discusses the effect of exchange rate changes on reporting the operations of foreign units, and Chapter 8 discusses forward contracts used to hedge such risks.

PepsiCo states the following in Note 10, "Financial Instruments" (Appendix A):

> Our operations outside of the U.S. generate 48% of our net revenue, with Mexico, Canada and the United Kingdom comprising 19% of our net revenue. As a result, we are exposed to foreign currency risks. On occasion, we enter into hedges, primarily forward contracts with terms of no more than two years, to reduce the effect of foreign exchange rates. Ineffectiveness of these hedges has not been material.

In its MD&A (Appendix B), PepsiCo discloses that foreign currency derivatives had a face value of $1.4 billion at the end of 2008, considerably more than the amount of commodity derivatives. A 10 percent unfavorable change in exchange rates would have resulted in a pre-tax loss of $70 million for 2008. This amount is 1.0 percent of income before income taxes (= $70/$7,021), a larger amount than for commodity derivatives and a larger amount than that for 2007.

Interest Rates

Changes in interest rates can affect firms in various ways:

- The value of investments in bonds or other investment securities with fixed interest rates
- The value of liabilities with fixed interest rates
- The returns a firm generates from pension fund investments

Firms often use interest rate swaps to hedge, or neutralize, the risk of interest rate changes. As Chapter 8 discusses, locking in a fixed rate insulates the principal amount from interest rate changes, but it exposes the fair value of the principal. Locking in a variable rate protects the fair value of the principal but induces risk (volatility) in the cash flows for interest payments. Firms, particularly financial institutions, also hedge some interest rate risk by matching investments in fixed-interest-rate assets with fixed-rate liabilities of equivalent amounts and duration.

PepsiCo discloses the following in Note 10, "Financial Instruments" (Appendix A):

> We centrally manage our debt and investment portfolios considering investment opportunities and risks, tax consequences and overall financing strategies. We may use interest rate and cross currency interest rate swaps to manage our overall interest expense and foreign exchange risk. These instruments effectively change the interest rate and currency of specific debt issuances. Our 2008 and 2007 interest rate swaps

were entered into concurrently with the issuance of the debt that they modified. The notional amount, interest payment and maturity date of the swaps match the principal, interest payment and maturity date of the related debt.

The MD&A (Appendix B) indicates that an increase in interest rates of 1-percentage-point would have increased net interest expense by $21 million for 2008, which is approximately 6.4 percent of realized interest expense (= $21/$329).

Other Risk-Related Disclosures

The particular elements of risk that firms include in their risk management disclosures depend on the types of risks to which a firm is exposed, and many of the financial statement footnotes include qualitative discussions or quantitative indicators of such risks. For example, PepsiCo discloses in Note 7, "Pension, Retiree Medical and Savings Plans," the effect that a 1-percentage-point change in the assumed health care cost trend rate would have on service cost and interest cost components of retiree medical expense and the associated benefit liability. The required disclosures in Note 6, "Stock-Based Compensation," enable financial statement users to assess the impact of different assumptions underlying the valuation of stock options. Similarly, information in Note 5, "Income Taxes," indicates that in determining the income tax provision, the company assesses the risk of a tax position being sustained on audit based on the technical merits of the position. Finally, Note 9, "Debt Obligations and Commitments," indicates that PepsiCo is the guarantor on $2.3 billion of long-term debt of Bottling Group, LLC, which highlights that the company is exposed not only to its own firm-specific financial risks, but also to those of affiliated companies.

Firms now disclose considerably more information for the analyst to use in assessing the effect of various risks on a firm. Increasingly, standard setters and regulators have required firms to disclose the sensitivity of reported amounts to changes in various variables and assumptions. One would expect the information value of these disclosures to increase even more as analysts and other users of financial statements become more familiar with them.

FINANCIAL STATEMENT ANALYSIS OF RISK

In addition to using information about risk disclosed in the notes to the financial statements and in the MD&A, analysts typically assess many dimensions of risk using ratios of various items in the financial statements. In addition to the balance sheet and income statement, the statement of cash flows (discussed in Chapter 3), which reports the net amount of cash generated or used by operating, investing, and financing activities, also is an important source of information for studying risk. In this chapter, we discuss how to use the collective information in the three primary financial statements to examine risk. We demonstrate financial statement analysis techniques to assess the following types of risk:

- Financial flexibility
- Short-term liquidity risk
- Long-term solvency risk
- Credit risk
- Bankruptcy risk
- Market equity risk
- Financial reporting manipulation risk

Many firms use financial leverage to increase returns to equity shareholders. When firms obtain funds from borrowing and invest those funds in assets that generate a higher return than the after-tax cost of the borrowing, the common shareholders benefit. Therefore, capital structure leverage enhances the return to the common shareholders, but it involves risk.

The impact of leverage on returns to common shareholders is part of the disaggregation of ROCE (return on common equity) discussed in Chapter 4. Therefore, the analysis of profitability discussed in that chapter is linked to the analysis of risk discussed in this chapter by an examination of *financial flexibility*. Financial flexibility is the ability of a firm to obtain debt financing conditional on its current leverage and profitability of its operating assets.

The risk associated with leverage arises because satisfying future debt retirements requires cash payments. Exhibit 5.1 relates the factors affecting a firm's ability to generate cash with its need to use cash. Many financial statement analysis techniques designed to assess risk focus on a comparison of the supply of cash and the demand for cash. For example, risk analysis using financial statement information can examine *short-term liquidity risk,* which is the near-term ability to generate cash to meet working capital needs and debt service requirements, as well as *long-term solvency risk,* which is the longer-term ability to generate cash internally or externally to satisfy plant capacity and debt repayment needs.

The field of finance identifies two closely related types of firm-specific risk: *credit risk* and *bankruptcy risk,* both of which can be evaluated using financial statement information. Credit risk concerns a firm's ability to make ongoing interest and principal payments on borrowings as they come due. Bankruptcy risk, on the other hand, relates to the likelihood that a firm will ultimately be forced to file for bankruptcy and perhaps subsequently liquidate due to a combination of insufficient profitability and cash flows and high debt service costs. Analysts view these two types of risk as states of financial distress that fall along a continuum of increasing gravity from (1) failing to make a required interest payment on time to (2) restructuring debt to (3) defaulting on a principal payment on debt to (4) filing for bankruptcy to (5) liquidating a firm. Analysts concerned with the economic loss of a portion of or the entire amount lent to or invested in a firm would examine a firm's position on this financial distress continuum. We demonstrate how analysts can use tools of short-term liquidity and long-term solvency risk in assessing credit risk and bankruptcy risk.

Less than 5 percent of publicly traded firms experience financial distress as defined by one of the five states listed previously. The other 95 percent of firms that are reasonably financially healthy utilize borrowings to finance future expansion or unforeseen investment opportunities, which is captured by the notion of financial flexibility described earlier. Thus, while examination of liquidity, solvency, credit, and bankruptcy risk is sometimes very important, analysts are more often interested in the financial flexibility of a firm to strategically utilize leverage through borrowing to enhance the returns to the firm's common equity investors.

EXHIBIT 5.1

Framework for Financial Statement Analysis of Risk

Activity	Ability to Generate Cash	Need to Use Cash	Financial Statement Analysis Performed
Operations	Profitability of goods and services sold	Working capital requirements	Short-term liquidity risk
Investing	Sales of existing plant assets or investments	Plant capacity requirements	Long-term solvency risk
Financing	Borrowing capacity	Debt service requirements	

The preceding types of risk do not encompass the full range of risks that equity investors must consider as the residual risk bearers of firms. Therefore, to value firms, investors also assess elements of risk inherent in investing in common shares of a firm relative to the risks that are common to all firms. For example, investors consider systematic (nondiversifiable) risk and use it to explain differences in expected rates of return on common stocks. Economic theory teaches that differences in risk relate to differences in expected returns. Studies of this risk/return relation use market equity beta as one measure of *market equity risk*. Market equity beta measures the covariability of a firm's returns with an index of returns of all securities in the equity capital market. Research and practice show that market equity betas are increasing in financial leverage. We briefly discuss the research relating financial statement data and market equity beta later in this chapter but elaborate on it more fully in Chapters 11–14. The discussion included in this chapter is intended to emphasize that market risk is related to the other risks discussed.

In conducting financial statement analysis, the presumption is that a firm adheres to its designated accounting standards in preparing its financial statements, which permits the analyst to use the reported amounts to assess each type of risk. In some cases, however, firms intentionally manipulate the financial statements in an effort to portray a more profitable or less risky profile than is appropriate. If the financial statements are manipulated, they are not useful—or worse, are misleading—as the basis for analyzing various risks. Thus, assessing *financial reporting manipulation risk* is an integral part of using financial statement data as the basis of risk analysis.

As will become clear, all seven of these elements of risk are interrelated. Firms use financial flexibility and leverage to achieve higher returns for equity investors, but doing so involves financial risk. Analysts evaluate short-term liquidity and long-term solvency risk and assess both credit risk and bankruptcy risk. Some of the factors affecting long-term solvency risk and financial flexibility also affect market equity risk. Financial reporting manipulation risk affects all of the other risks because such risk detracts from the usefulness of the financial statements as a basis for risk assessment.

We illustrate the analyses of various dimensions of risk using the financial statements of PepsiCo in Appendix A. As we did in Chapter 4, we compare financial ratios for PepsiCo for 2008 with the corresponding ratios for 2006 and 2007. Additional insights are often attained through comparison of the ratios for PepsiCo with average industry ratios or with those of PepsiCo's competitors (for example, Coca-Cola).

ANALYZING FINANCIAL FLEXIBILITY: ALTERNATIVE APPROACHES TO DISAGGREGATE ROCE

Firms that borrow funds and invest those funds in assets that generate a higher return than the after-tax cost of the borrowing create value for the common shareholders. Common shareholders benefit with increasing proportions of debt in the capital structure as long as the firm maintains an excess rate of return on assets over the after-tax cost of the debt. Therefore, financial leverage can enhance the return to common shareholders. The impact of leverage on returns to common shareholders is part of the disaggregation of ROCE discussed in Chapter 4. The disaggregation of ROCE into components of profit margin for ROCE (assets turnover and capital structure leverage) is as follows:

$$\text{ROCE} = \frac{\text{Net Income to Common}}{\text{Average Common Equity}}$$

$$= \frac{\text{Net Income to Common}}{\text{Sales}} \times \frac{\text{Sales}}{\text{Average Total Assets}} \times \frac{\text{Average Total Assets}}{\text{Average Common Equity}}$$

$$= \text{Profit Margin for ROCE} \times \text{Assets Turnover} \times \text{Capital Structure Leverage}$$

The disaggregation of ROCE provides insight about the degree to which common equity shareholders benefit from using leverage. Higher leverage generally suggests greater financial risk, as discussed in the following sections on short-term liquidity risk, long-term solvency risk, credit risk, and bankruptcy risk. The risk is primarily attributable to the costs of borrowing, reflected by interest expense for long-term debt and the requirement to make debt payments in cash when they come due. The disaggregation of ROCE suggests that common equity shareholders benefit from increasing leverage (that is, the third term in the ROCE disaggregation). However, there are two offsetting effects of increasing leverage. First, increasing leverage assumes that the firm can deploy the financing proceeds into assets that maintain the current levels of profitability and turnover (that is, the first and second terms), which depends on the firm's ability to scale up operations without experiencing diminishing returns, market saturation, and other strategic roadblocks. Second, increasing leverage increases interest expense, which reduces profit margins (that is, the first term in the disaggregation). Thus, increasing leverage has potential benefits and risks.

A shortcoming of the standard disaggregation of ROCE is the inability to directly gauge the extent to which a firm can strategically increase leverage to increase returns to common shareholders without offsetting profitability. We refer to this as *financial flexibility*. A better way to represent a firm's financial flexibility is to disaggregate ROCE to capture operating and financing impacts separately on returns to common shareholders. The alternative disaggregation discussed next requires that we reformulate the balance sheet and income statement into operating and financing components.[1]

Exhibit 5.2 presents the standard balance sheet equation in which assets are equal to liabilities plus equity. Each of these amounts is decomposed into primary components.

- Assets = Current Assets + Noncurrent Assets
- Liabilities = Current Liabilities + Noncurrent Liabilities + Short-Term Debt
                + Long-Term Debt + Preferred Equity + Minority Interest
- Equity = Common Equity

EXHIBIT 5.2

Reformulation of Standard Balance Sheet into Net Operating Assets, Financing Obligations, and Common Equity Components

Assets   =   Liabilities   +   Equity

Current Assets (CA) + Noncurrent Assets (NCA) = Current Liabilities (CL) + Noncurrent Liabilities (NCL) + S.T. Debt + L.T. Debt + Preferred Equity + Minority Interest + Common Equity

CA − CL + NCA − NCL = S.T. Debt + L.T. Debt + Preferred Equity + Minority Interest + Common Equity

Sources of Debt and Equity Financing that Generate Financing Costs

Net Operating Assets   Financing Obligations   Common Equity

---

[1] This alternative disaggregation of ROCE is sometimes referred to as the "Penman decomposition," following pioneering work by Stephen H. Penman in articulating the operating and financing activities of firms. For a more detailed discussion, see Chapter 11 of Stephen H. Penman, *Financial Statement Analysis and Security Valuation* (New York: McGraw-Hill Irwin), 2004.

These components are rearranged to group operating components together and financing components separately, which are then aggregated back into a reformulated balance sheet equation. We treat minority interest as preferred equity (that is, a financing obligation), consistent with the treatment of minority interest in accounting standards for business combinations. However, some analysts make the argument that minority interest should be netted against operating assets. Either approach can be justified so long as consistent treatment is used for minority interest on the income statement (discussed below).

The reformulated balance sheet equation is as follows:

$$\text{Net Operating Assets} = \text{Financing Obligations} + \text{Common Equity}$$

The primary change of this financial statement reformulation is that operating liabilities—both current and noncurrent—are netted against operating assets, leaving pure financing obligations and common equity on the right-hand side of the equation. Also, minority interest and preferred equity are included in financing obligations to be distinct from common equity. The equation still balances, but the totals differ from the standard balance sheet equation.

For ease of exposition, we assume that firms have no financial assets. However, most firms maintain some financial assets, which include cash, marketable equity securities, and short-term investments. Such financial assets should be netted against financing obligations, which yield net financing obligations (similar to how operating liabilities are netted against operating assets to yield net operating assets). This necessarily involves making judgments based on the purpose of the financial assets. Some financial assets are held for liquidity (marketable securities), strategic purposes (investments in noncontrolling interests of other firms), or financing (bond sinking funds). A more challenging determination is how to treat cash. Some cash is necessary as part of working capital, but firms can hold *excess cash*. There is no magic formula for computing excess cash, and any estimation of excess cash must consider possible reasons a firm holds what appears to be excess cash.

For example, in 2004, investors criticized Microsoft for holding excess cash. At the end of 2004, cash and short-term investments amounted to over $60 billion, relative to total assets of $94 billion. Microsoft subsequently paid a $3 per share special dividend, totaling $33 billion, and announced a plan to buy back up to $30 billion of outstanding common stock. It was difficult to quantify how much excess cash Microsoft held in 2004, but any approximation would have resulted in negative net financing obligations for Microsoft (which had no short- or long-term debt). Negative net financing obligations does not present a problem as long as the partition of the income statement, discussed below, is done consistently with the allocation of assets and liabilities to operating and financing components.

The reformulated balance sheet for PepsiCo is shown in Exhibit 5.3. Assuming that PepsiCo holds no financial assets intended for financing purposes (such as a bond sinking fund), we classify PepsiCo's cash and cash equivalents and short-term investments as operating assets. Thus, PepsiCo's operating assets are the same as total assets. Current and noncurrent liabilities are netted against operating assets, resulting in net operating assets of $20,333 million for 2008. Note that total assets as reported (Appendix A) are $35,994 million for 2008.

The reformulated balance sheet isolates operating assets (net of operating liabilities) and direct sources of financing.[2] To be consistent, we do the same for the income statement.

---

[2] As discussed in the previous section, we can view accounts payable as a source of financing. However, the objective here is to classify as financing only those obligations that have direct costs of capital associated with them.

EXHIBIT 5.3

Reformulated Balance Sheets for PepsiCo
(amounts in millions)

	2008	2007	2006	2005
OPERATING ASSETS				
Cash and cash equivalents	$ 2,064	$ 910	$ 1,651	$ 1,716
Short-term investments	213	1,571	1,171	3,166
Accounts and notes receivable, net	4,683	4,389	3,725	3,261
Inventories	2,522	2,290	1,926	1,693
Prepaid expenses and other current assets	1,324	991	657	618
Property, plant, and equipment, net	11,663	11,228	9,687	8,681
Amortizable intangible assets, net	732	796	637	530
Goodwill	5,124	5,169	4,594	4,088
Other nonamortizable intangible assets	1,128	1,248	1,212	1,086
Investments in noncontrolled affiliates	3,883	4,354	3,690	3,485
Other assets	2,658	1,682	980	3,403
LESS: OPERATING LIABILITIES				
Accounts payable and other current liabilities	(8,273)	(7,602)	(6,496)	(5,971)
Income taxes payable	(145)	(151)	(90)	(546)
Other liabilities	(7,017)	(4,792)	(4,624)	(4,323)
Deferred income taxes	(226)	(646)	(528)	(1,434)
Net Operating Assets	$20,333	$21,437	$18,192	$19,453
FINANCING OBLIGATIONS				
Short-term obligations	$ 369	$ 0	$ 274	$ 2,889
Current maturities of long-term debt	0	0	0	0
Long-term debt obligations	7,858	4,203	2,550	2,313
Preferred stock, no par value	41	41	41	41
Repurchased preferred stock	(138)	(132)	(120)	(110)
Financing Obligations	$ 8,130	$ 4,112	$ 2,745	$ 5,133
COMMON EQUITY				
Common stock, par value	$ 30	$ 30	$ 30	$ 30
Capital in excess of par value	351	450	584	614
Retained earnings	30,638	28,184	24,837	21,116
Accumulated other comprehensive loss	(4,694)	(952)	(2,246)	(1,053)
Treasury stock	(14,122)	(10,387)	(7,758)	(6,387)
Common Equity	$12,203	$17,325	$15,447	$14,320
Total Financing Obligations and Common Equity	$20,333	$21,437	$18,192	$19,453

EXHIBIT 5.4

Reformulated Income Statements for PepsiCo
(amounts in millions)

	2008	2007	2006
Net revenue	$43,251	$39,474	$35,137
Cost of sales	(20,351)	(18,038)	(15,762)
Selling, general, and administrative expenses	(15,901)	(14,208)	(12,711)
Other operating charges	(64)	(58)	(162)
Operating Profit	$ 6,935	$ 7,170	$ 6,502
Bottling equity income	374	560	553
Interest income	41	125	173
Adjusted Income Before Income Taxes	$ 7,350	$ 7,855	$ 7,228
Provision for income taxes at effective rate	(1,967)	(2,031)	(1,393)
Net Operating Profit After Tax (NOPAT)	$ 5,383	$ 5,824	$ 5,835
FINANCING EXPENSE			
Interest expense $\times$ (1 – Effective tax rate)	$ (241)	$ (166)	$ (193)
Preferred dividends	(8)	(12)	(11)
Net Financing Expense (After Tax)	$ (249)	$ (178)	$ (204)
Net Income to Common	$ 5,134	$ 5,646	$ 5,631
Effective Tax Rate	26.8%	25.9%	19.3%

Exhibit 5.4 demonstrates the straightforward identification of costs associated with financing for PepsiCo, including primarily interest expense and preferred dividends. All other amounts are elements of operating profit.[3] Operating profits are reduced by a provision for income taxes, generating the revised measure of profitability—NOPAT (Net Operating Profit After Taxes). Finance texts sometimes refer to this construct as EBIAT (Earnings Before Interest After Tax), which is the same as NOPAT with consistent treatment of operating and financing activities and proper treatment of taxes (discussed next).[4]

Note how the provision for income taxes from PepsiCo's as-reported income statement (Appendix A) is allocated to operating and financing activities. For 2008, PepsiCo's provision was $1,879 million (Appendix A), but Exhibit 5.4 indicates a provision on adjusted income before income taxes of $1,967 million. The higher provision in Exhibit 5.4 is due to the removal of financing expense from income before income taxes. The tax benefit of interest expense reduces the effective interest expense from $329 million (Appendix A) to $241 million, as shown in Exhibit 5.4. Preferred dividends are not tax-deductible, so no tax adjustment is necessary. The difference in the provision for income taxes on adjusted income before

---

[3] Chapter 4 emphasized that judgment could be exercised in the preparation of profitability ratios. The exposition there used adjusted net income based on a subjective assessment of nonrecurring components of reported profitability. For purposes here, we revert to the amounts reported in the 2008 financial statements. Further, we deliberately use net income available to common, which requires that preferred dividends be deducted from net income as shown on the income statement in Appendix A.

[4] NOPAT is more common than EBIAT. A simple online search of each term indicates approximately four times as many results for NOPAT. Further, many search results for EBIAT relate to last names, not the profitability construct.

income taxes in Exhibit 5.4 and the provision for income taxes as reported (Appendix A) equals the difference between gross interest expense as reported (Appendix A) and the after-tax interest expense shown in Exhibit 5.4 ($1,967 − $1,879 = $329 − $241 = $88). This difference of $88 million is equal to interest expense of $329 million times the effective tax rate of 26.8 percent (= $1,879/$7,021 from the income statement).

Also note the following:

$$\frac{\begin{array}{l} \text{NOPAT} \\ - \text{ Net Financing Expense (after tax)} \end{array}}{= \text{ Net Income Available to Common}}$$

If we had categorized PepsiCo's short-term investments as a financing asset, this asset would have been netted against PepsiCo's financing obligations in Exhibit 5.3. Accordingly, to be consistent with the treatment on the balance sheet, interest revenues (after tax) pertaining to the short-term investments would have been netted against interest expense (after tax) to compute net financing expense (after tax) in Exhibit 5.5. The reformulated balance sheets would still balance, with different totals, and the reformulated income statements would still reflect the same net income available to common. The same argument holds true for the treatment of minority interest for applicable companies. If the analyst treats minority interest as part of financing obligations (as we do in Exhibit 5.2), minority interest from the income statement would be included in net financing expense.

With these new financial statement classifications, Exhibit 5.5 demonstrates the algebraic disaggregation of ROCE into operating and financing components. The algebra is simple and easy to follow. The result is an alternative disaggregation of ROCE:

$$\text{ROCE} = \text{Operating ROA} + (\text{Leverage} \times \text{Spread})$$

Operating ROA is the rate of return the firm generates on its *net* operating assets. Operating ROA is the rate of return available to *all* sources of financing, including debt, preferred equity, and common equity. It is different from the definition of ROA discussed in Chapter 4, primarily because the denominator is net operating assets (as opposed to total assets).[5]

In addition to operating ROA, the right-hand side of the new ROCE equation consists of two other factors: leverage and spread. As noted in Exhibit 5.5, leverage is simply the total financial obligations divided by common equity, which is commensurate with the standard debt-to-equity ratio, except that preferred equity and minority interest are included in financial obligations. Spread is the difference between operating ROA and the net borrowing rate, which is the combined effective rate of interest and preferred dividends. Thus, the intuition of the new ROCE equation is that returns to common equity shareholders increase by the following:

- Increases in the rate of return on the firm's net operating assets
- Increases in leverage
- Decreases in the after-tax cost of debt and preferred equity

---

[5] An easy way to understand how the classification of financial statement amounts can vary while still resulting in components that combine mathematically to ROCE is to consider reformulated financial statements where all assets and all liabilities are categorized as operating. Thus, short- and long-term debt, preferred stock (if any), and minority interest are netted against assets to compute net operating assets. By definition, this equals common equity. Then to be consistent with this treatment in reformulation of the income statement, all interest expense, preferred dividends, and minority interest would be categorized as operating items. The result would be net income available to common. The alternative disaggregation of ROCE into Operating ROA + (Leverage × Spread) would reduce to ROCE = Operating ROA, where Operating ROA = Net Income Available to Common/Common Equity. This would not accomplish much, but the point of the exercise is to emphasize the mathematical equivalence of this ROCE decomposition regardless of how assets or liabilities are reformulated.

EXHIBIT 5.5

Algebra Demonstrating the Disaggregation of Return on Common Equity (ROCE)

$$\text{ROCE} = \frac{\text{Net Income Available to Common}}{\text{Common Equity}}$$

$$= \frac{\text{NOPAT} - \text{Net Financing Expense (after tax)}}{\text{Common Equity}}$$

$$= \frac{\text{NOPAT}}{\text{Net Operating Assets}} \times \frac{\text{Net Operating Assets}}{\text{Common Equity}} - \frac{\text{Net Financing Expense (after tax)}}{\text{Financing Obligations}} \times \frac{\text{Financing Obligations}}{\text{Common Equity}}$$

$$= \frac{\text{NOPAT}}{\text{Net Operating Assets}} \times \frac{\text{Common Equity} + \text{Financing Obligations}}{\text{Common Equity}} - \frac{\text{Net Financing Expense (after tax)}}{\text{Financing Obligations}} \times \frac{\text{Financing Obligations}}{\text{Common Equity}}$$

$$= \frac{\text{NOPAT}}{\text{Net Operating Assets}} \times \left(1 + \frac{\text{Financing Obligations}}{\text{Common Equity}}\right) - \frac{\text{Net Financing Expense (after tax)}}{\text{Financing Obligations}} \times \frac{\text{Financing Obligations}}{\text{Common Equity}}$$

$$= \text{Operating ROA} \times \left(1 + \frac{\text{Financing Obligations}}{\text{Common Equity}}\right) - \frac{\text{Net Financing Expense (after tax)}}{\text{Financing Obligations}} \times \frac{\text{Financing Obligations}}{\text{Common Equity}}$$

$$= \text{Operating ROA} + \left[\text{Operating ROA} \times \frac{\text{Financing Obligations}}{\text{Common Equity}}\right] - \left[\frac{\text{Net Financing Expense (after tax)}}{\text{Financing Obligations}} \times \frac{\text{Financing Obligations}}{\text{Common Equity}}\right]$$

$$= \text{Operating ROA} + \left[\text{Operating ROA} - \frac{\text{Net Financing Expense (after tax)}}{\text{Financing Obligations}}\right] \times \frac{\text{Financing Obligations}}{\text{Common Equity}}$$

$$= \text{Operating ROA} + [\text{Leverage}] \times (\text{Operating ROA} - \text{Net Borrowing Rate})$$

$$= \text{Operating ROA} + \text{Leverage} \times \text{Spread}$$

Incidentally, note that similar to ROA, operating ROA can be further disaggregated simply by dividing and multiplying by sales:

$$\text{Operating ROA} = \frac{\text{NOPAT}}{\text{Average Net Operating Assets}}$$

$$= \frac{\text{NOPAT}}{\text{Sales}} \times \frac{\text{Sales}}{\text{Average Net Operating Assets}}$$

Operating ROA is thus the product of profit margin for operating ROA and net operating asset turnover in the same way that ROA is the product of profit margin for ROA and total assets turnover.

Spread is the key to understanding financial flexibility. As stated, incremental increases in leverage are likely associated with increased borrowing costs. For example, second mortgages on properties generally carry higher interest rates than first mortgages. Increases in the cost of debt or preferred equity increase the net borrowing rate, which decreases spread, lowering the incremental benefits of increasing leverage. Nevertheless, firms with a large spread probably face strategic roadblocks in deploying capital that leads to diminishing rates of return, which dominates any increasing cost of debt or preferred equity. Thus, firms that generate very high operating ROA relative to the cost of borrowing can likely increase the level of borrowings—with either debt or preferred equity—and thus are characterized as having greater financial flexibility. Financial flexibility also is associated with lower short-term and long-term solvency risk, discussed in the next two sections.

To illustrate the disaggregation of ROCE into operating ROA, leverage, and spread, Exhibit 5.6 uses the amounts from the financial statements in Exhibits 5.3 and 5.4 to compute ROCE. For comparison, Exhibit 5.6 presents the standard and alternative decompositions of ROCE. Of course, both computations produce the same ROCE.

The alternative ROCE decomposition reveals that PepsiCo generates a significant spread between operating ROA and the net borrowing rate. For 2006, 2007, and 2008, Operating ROA is 31.0, 29.4, and 25.8 percent, respectively. PepsiCo's operations clearly utilize the operating assets very profitably. The net borrowing rates were 4.1 percent in 2008 and 5.1 percent in both 2007 and 2006 (not tabulated in Exhibit 5.6). Therefore, PepsiCo's spread was 21.7 percent in 2008 (= 25.8 percent operating ROA − 4.1 percent net borrowing rate), 24.2 percent in 2007, and 25.8 percent in 2006. An interpretation of PepsiCo's spread in 2008 is that for every dollar PepsiCo currently borrows and deploys in operating assets, it generates 25.8¢ in operating profit, whereas the borrowing triggers only 4.1¢ in net borrowing costs (after tax), resulting in 21.7¢ accruing to common equity shareholders. This is the essence of strategic use of leverage by equity investors.

The large spread generated by PepsiCo indicates that the company enjoys a high level of financial flexibility. Creditors are relatively comfortable lending money to companies that generate rates of returns on assets that far exceed debt service costs. However, the trends shown in Exhibit 5.6 suggest that PepsiCo is increasing its leverage significantly. PepsiCo's leverage was only 0.26 in 2006 and 0.21 in 2007, but it jumped to 0.41 in 2008.

Therefore, the alternative ROCE decomposition reveals that PepsiCo's ROCE in 2008 of 34.8 percent is the result of an operating ROA of 25.8 percent plus leverage of 0.41 times the spread of 21.7 percent [34.8% = 25.8% + (0.41 × 21.7%)]. In comparison to 2007, this decomposition reveals that PepsiCo's operating ROA and spread fell dramatically in 2008, but ROCE increased slightly because of a dramatic increase in leverage.

Both approaches to the decomposition of ROCE indicate decreases in margins, increases in turnover, and increases in leverage from 2006 to 2008. However, the alternative ROCE decomposition provides additional insights about the nature of the change in leverage that

EXHIBIT 5.6

Computations of ROCE Decomposition Using Standard and Alternative Approaches for PepsiCo 2006–2008 (dollar amounts in millions)

Standard ROCE decomposition		Calculation for 2008	2008	2007	2006
Profit Margin for ROCE	Net Income to Common/Sales	$5,134/$43,251	11.9%	14.3%	16.0%
× Assets Turnover	Sales/Average Total Assets	$43,251/ 0.5($35,994 + $34,628)	1.22	1.22	1.14
× Capital Structure Leverage	Average Total Assets/ Average Common Equity	0.5($35,994 + $34,528)/ 0.5($12,203 + $17,325)	2.39	1.97	2.07
= ROCE	Net Income to Common/ Average Common Equity	$5,134/ 0.5($12,203 + $17,325)	34.8%	34.5%	37.8%

Alternative ROCE decomposition			2008	2007	2006
Net Margin for Operating ROA	NOPAT/Sales	$5,383/$43,251	12.4%	14.8%	16.6%
× Net Operating Assets Turnover	Sales/Average Net Operating Assets	$43,251/ 0.5($20,333 + $21,437)	2.07	1.99	1.87
= Operating ROA	NOPAT/Average Net Operating Assets	$5,383/ 0.5($20,333 + $21,437)	25.8%	29.4%	31.0%
+ Leverage	Average Financing Obligations/ Average Common Equity	0.5($8,130 + $4,112)/ 0.5($12,203 + $17,325)	0.41	0.21	0.26
× Spread	Operating ROA – Net Borrowing Rate (=Net Financing Expense (after tax)/Average Financing Obligations	25.8% – 4.1%	21.7%	24.2%	25.8%
= ROCE	Operating ROA + (Leverage × Spread)	25.8% + (0.41 × 21.7%)	34.8%	34.5%	37.8%
Net Borrowing Rate	Net Financing Expense (after tax)/ Average Financing Obligations	[$249]/ 0.5($8,130 + $4,112)]	4.1%	5.2%	5.2%

are masked in the traditional ROCE decomposition at the top of Exhibit 5.6. For the alternative ROCE decomposition in the bottom part of Exhibit 5.6, the increase in leverage is more dramatic, especially between 2007 and 2008 when it nearly doubled from 0.21 to 0.41; under the standard ROE decomposition, capital structure leverage increases from 1.97 to 2.39 between 2007 and 2008. Recall that under the standard approach to disaggregating ROCE, leverage is defined as follows:

$$\text{Capital Structure Leverage} = \frac{\text{Total Assets}}{\text{Common Equity}}$$

$$= \frac{\text{Total Liabilities} + \text{Common Equity}}{\text{Common Equity}}$$

$$= 1 + \frac{\text{Total Liabilities}}{\text{Common Equity}}$$

Thus, the standard approach treats *all* liabilities as leverage, not just those that generate borrowing costs. If non-interest-bearing liabilities are significant, including such amounts can mask the true leverage attributable to interest-bearing debt. Indeed, Appendix A shows that total liabilities are $23,888 million at the end of 2008, but only $8,227 million are actually interest-bearing financing obligations (= $369 million short-term obligations + $7,858 million long-term debt obligations). The other liabilities treated as leverage in the standard decomposition of ROCE include accounts payable of $8,273 million and other liabilities of $7,017 million, neither of which are leverage in the sense that matters in terms of long-term solvency risk.

Summary of Financial Flexibility

Financial flexibility represents the ability of a firm to strategically use creditor financing to increase the returns to common shareholders. We discussed an alternative decomposition of ROCE that requires the analyst to reformulate financial statements into operating and financing components, which highlights the benefits available to common shareholders through the use of leverage. Firms with large spreads—return on net operating assets minus the net after-tax borrowing rate—stand to benefit from leverage. PepsiCo generates large returns on net operating assets and has a large degree of financial flexibility. The analysis of financial flexibility provides a natural link between profitability analysis discussed in the previous chapter and the analysis of numerous risks, discussed next.

ANALYZING SHORT-TERM LIQUIDITY RISK

The analysis of short-term liquidity risk requires an understanding of the operating cycle of a firm, introduced in Chapter 1. Consider a typical manufacturing firm. It acquires raw materials on account, promising to pay suppliers within 30–60 days. The firm then combines the raw materials, labor services, and other inputs to produce a product. It pays for some of these costs at the time of incurrence and delays payment of other costs. At some point, the firm sells the product to a customer, probably on account. It then collects the customer's account and pays suppliers and others for purchases on account.

If a firm (1) can delay all cash outflows to suppliers, employees, and others until it receives cash from customers and (2) receives more cash than it must disburse, the firm will not likely encounter short-term liquidity problems. Most firms, however, cannot time their cash inflows and outflows precisely, especially firms in the start-up or growth phase. Employees may require weekly or semimonthly payments, whereas customers may delay payments for 30 days or more. Firms may experience rapid growth and need to produce more units of product than they sell during a period. Even if perfectly timed, the cash outflows to support the higher level of production in this period can exceed customers' cash inflows this period from the lower level of sales of prior periods. Firms that operate at a net loss for a period often find that the completion of the operating cycle results in a net cash outflow instead of a net cash inflow. As an extreme example, consider a Scotch whiskey distillery that incurs significant cash outflows for grains and other ingredients, distills the whiskey, and then ages it in wooden barrels for many years before finally generating cash inflows from sales to customers.

Short-term liquidity problems also can arise from a high degree of longer-term leverage. For example, a firm may assume a relatively high percentage of debt in its capital structure. This level of debt usually requires periodic interest payments and may require repayments of principal as well. For some firms, especially financial, real estate, and energy firms, interest expense is one of the largest single costs. The operating cycle must generate sufficient cash not only to supply operating working capital needs, but also to service debt.

Financially healthy firms frequently close temporary cash flow gaps in their operating cycles with short-term borrowing. Such firms may issue commercial paper on the market or obtain three- to six-month bank loans. Most firms maintain lines of credit with their banks so they can obtain cash quickly for working capital needs. The notes to the financial statements usually disclose the amount of the line of credit and the level of borrowing used on that line during the year, as well as any financial covenant restrictions imposed by the line of credit agreements. PepsiCo, for example, discloses the following in Note 9, "Debt Obligations and Commitments" (Appendix A):

> Additionally, in the fourth quarter of 2008, we entered into a new 364-day unsecured revolving credit agreement which enables us to borrow up to $1.8 billion, subject to customary terms and conditions, and expires in December 2009. This agreement replaced a $1 billion 364-day unsecured revolving credit agreement we entered into during the third quarter of 2008. Funds borrowed under this agreement may be used to repay outstanding commercial paper issued by us or our subsidiaries and for other general corporate purposes, including working capital, capital investments and acquisitions. This line of credit remained unused as of December 27, 2008.
>
> This 364-day credit agreement is in addition to our $2 billion unsecured revolving credit agreement. Funds borrowed under this agreement may be used for general corporate purposes, including supporting our outstanding commercial paper issuances. This agreement expires in 2012. This line of credit remains unused as of December 27, 2008.

Note 9 indicates that PepsiCo's outstanding short-term debt totaled $369 million and its long-term debt totaled $7,858 million at the end of 2008. Thus, PepsiCo has the ability to increase borrowing approximately 46.2 percent [= ($1,800 + $2,000)/($369 + $7,858)] at the end of 2008 by drawing on its existing lines of credit. It is important to note available but untapped borrowing capacity when assessing the overall financial risk profile of a firm. These amounts represent potential increases in financial risk, but at the same time, they provide the firm with beneficial financial flexibility (as discussed in the previous section).

A simple way to quickly grasp short-term liquidity issues is to examine common-size balance sheets, as discussed in Chapter 1. Common-size balance sheets provide a basic quantification of the relative amount of cash tied up in non-cash assets, and the relative amount of liabilities across several categories. We discuss seven financial statement ratios for assessing short-term liquidity risk: (1) current ratio, (2) quick ratio, (3) operating cash flow to current liabilities ratio, (4) accounts receivable turnover, (5) inventory turnover, (6) accounts payable turnover, and (7) revenues to cash ratio.

Current Ratio

The current ratio equals current assets divided by current liabilities. It indicates the amount of cash available at the balance sheet date plus the amount of other current assets the firm expects to turn into cash within one year of the balance sheet date (from collection of receivables and sale of inventory) relative to obligations coming due during that period. Large current ratios indicate the substantial amounts of cash and near-cash assets available to repay obligations coming due within the next year. Small ratios, on the other hand, indicate that current levels of cash and near-cash assets may not be sufficient to repay short-term obligations.

The current ratio for PepsiCo at the end of 2008 is as follows:

$$\text{Current Ratio} = \frac{\text{Current Assets}}{\text{Current Liabilities}}$$

$$1.23 = \frac{\$10,806}{\$8,787}$$

The current ratio for PepsiCo was 1.31 at the end of 2007 and 1.33 at the end of 2006. Thus, PepsiCo experienced a decreasing current ratio during the three years.

Banks, suppliers, and others that extend short-term credit to a firm generally prefer a current ratio in excess of 1.0. They typically evaluate the appropriate level of a firm's current ratio based on the length of the firm's operating cycle, the expected cash flows from operations, the extent to which the firm has noncurrent assets that could be used for liquidity if necessary, the extent to which the firm's current liabilities do not require cash outflows (such as liabilities for deferred revenues), and similar factors. Prior to the 1980s, the average current ratios for most industries exceeded 2.0. As interest rates increased in the early 1980s, firms attempted to stretch their accounts payable and use suppliers to finance a greater portion of their working capital needs (that is, receivables and inventories). Also, firms increasingly instituted just-in-time inventory systems that reduced the amount of raw materials and finished goods inventories. As a consequence of these two factors, current ratios began moving in the direction of 1.0. Current ratios hovering around this level, or even just below 1.0, are now common. Although this directional movement suggests an increase in short-term liquidity risk, most investors view this level of risk as tolerable. Recall that accountants report inventories, a major component of current assets for many firms, at acquisition cost. The cash that firms expect to generate from selling inventories is larger than the amount used in calculating the current ratio. PepsiCo, for example, has a cost of goods sold to sales percentage of approximately 47 percent. Thus, inventories have selling prices of 2.1 (= 1.00/.47) times the amount appearing on the balance sheet. Therefore, a current ratio slightly greater than 1.0 at the end of 2006 through 2008 is not a major concern for PepsiCo.

Analysts should consider several additional interpretive issues when evaluating the current ratio:

- An increase of equal amounts in current assets and current liabilities (for example, purchasing inventory on account) results in a decrease in the current ratio when the ratio is greater than 1.0 before the transaction but an increase in the current ratio when it is less than 1.0 before the transaction. Similar interpretive difficulties arise when current assets and current liabilities decrease by equal amounts. With current ratios for many firms now in the neighborhood of 1.0, this concern with the current ratio has greater significance.

- A very high current ratio may accompany poor business conditions, whereas a low or decreasing ratio may accompany profitable operations. For example, during a recession, firms may encounter difficulties in selling inventories and collecting receivables, causing the current ratio to increase to higher levels due to the growth in receivables and inventory. In a boom period, just the reverse can occur.
- The current ratio is susceptible to window dressing; that is, management can take deliberate steps leading up to the balance sheet date to produce a better current ratio than is the normal or average ratio for the period. For instance, toward the end of the period, a firm may accelerate purchases of inventory on account (if the current ratio is less than 1.0) or delay such purchases (if the current ratio is greater than 1.0) in an effort to improve the current ratio. Alternatively, a firm may collect loans previously made to officers, classified as noncurrent assets, and use the proceeds to reduce current liabilities.

Despite these interpretive issues with the current ratio, the analyst will find widespread use of the current ratio as a measure of short-term liquidity risk. Empirical studies of bond default, bankruptcy, and other conditions of financial distress have found that the current ratio has strong predictive power for costly financial outcomes. A later section of this chapter discusses this empirical research more fully.

Quick Ratio

A variation of the current ratio is the quick ratio, also called the acid test ratio. The analyst computes the quick ratio by including in the numerator only those current assets the firm could convert *quickly* into cash, often interpreted as within 90 days. The numerator customarily includes cash, marketable securities, and receivables. However, the analyst should study the facts in each case before deciding whether to include receivables and exclude inventories. Some businesses can convert their inventory of merchandise into cash more quickly (for example, a retail chain such as Walmart) than other businesses can collect their receivables (for example, an equipment manufacturer such as John Deere that provides long-term financing for its customers' purchases).

Assuming that we include accounts receivable but exclude inventories, the quick ratio of PepsiCo at the end of 2008 is as follows:

$$\text{Quick Ratio} = \frac{\text{Cash} + \text{Marketable Securities} + \text{Accounts Receivable}}{\text{Current Liabilities}}$$

$$0.79 = \frac{\$2,064 + \$213 + \$4,683}{\$8,787}$$

The quick ratio for PepsiCo was 0.89 at the end of 2007 and 0.95 at the end of 2006. Unless inventory turnovers have changed dramatically, the comparative trends in the quick ratio and the current ratio correlate highly. That is, the analyst obtains similar information about improving or deteriorating short-term liquidity risk by examining either ratio. Note that the current and quick ratios for PepsiCo follow the same downward trend. However, the decline in the quick ratio is more pronounced. In 2008, current assets increased 6 percent, whereas current liabilities increased 13 percent. On the other hand, the sum of cash, marketable securities, and accounts receivable increased only 1 percent in 2008, leading to the decline in these amounts relative to current liabilities. Thus, the discrepancy between the current ratio and quick ratio for PepsiCo is due to changes in less liquid current assets. The balance sheet indicates that PepsiCo increased prepaid expenses and other current assets by 34 percent in 2008.

The quick ratio is subject to some of the same interpretive issues as the current ratio. With quick ratios typically less than 1.0, equal increases in the numerator and denominator increase the ratio and equal decreases in the numerator and denominator decrease the ratio. The quick ratio also is susceptible to year-end window dressing or temporary increases in cash on hand.

Operating Cash Flow to Current Liabilities Ratio

In addition to using current assets measured at a point in time as an indicator of a firm's ability to generate cash in the near term, the analyst also can use cash flow from operations. Cash flow from operations, reported on the statement of cash flows, indicates the amount of cash the firm derived from (or used in) operations after funding working capital needs. Because the numerator of this ratio uses amounts for a period of time, the denominator typically uses an average of current liabilities for the same period. This ratio for PepsiCo for 2008 is as follows:

$$\text{Operating Cash Flow to Current Liabilities Ratio} = \frac{\text{Cash Flow from Operations}}{\text{Average Current Liabilities}}$$

$$0.85 = \frac{\$6,999}{0.5(\$8,787 + \$7,753)}$$

The ratio was 0.95 for 2007 and 0.75 for 2006. An empirical study utilizing the operating cash flow to current liabilities ratio found that a ratio of 0.40 or more was common for a typical healthy manufacturing or retailing firm.[6] PepsiCo consistently has an operating cash flow to current liabilities ratio well in excess of 0.40. Thus, PepsiCo does not display much short-term liquidity risk in terms of operating cash flows relative to current liabilities.

Working Capital Turnover Ratios

The analyst uses three measures of the rate of activity in working capital accounts to study the cash-generating ability of operations and the short-term liquidity risk of a firm:

$$\text{Accounts Receivable Turnover} = \frac{\text{Sales}}{\text{Average Accounts Receivable}}$$

$$\text{Inventory Turnover} = \frac{\text{Cost of Goods Sold}}{\text{Average Inventories}}$$

$$\text{Accounts Payable Turnover} = \frac{\text{Purchases}}{\text{Average Accounts Payable}}$$

Chapter 4 discussed the accounts receivable and inventory turnovers, which are components of *total* assets turnover, as measures of profitability. These same ratios are used here as measures of the speed with which firms sell inventories and turn accounts receivable into cash. The accounts payable turnover indicates the speed at which a manufacturing or retailing firm pays for purchases of raw materials or inventories on account. Firms typically do not disclose the amount of raw materials or inventory purchases, but

---

[6] Cornelius Casey and Norman Bartczak, "Cash Flow—It's Not the Bottom Line," *Harvard Business Review* (July–August 1984), pp. 61–66.

this amount can be easily computed. Recall that the inventory account primarily reflects the following:

$$\text{Ending Inventory} = \text{Beginning Inventory} + \text{Purchases} - \text{Cost of Goods Sold.}$$

The analyst can approximate purchases as follows:[7]

$$\text{Purchases} = \text{Cost of Goods Sold} + \text{Ending Inventory} - \text{Beginning Inventory.}$$

Note that Purchases is used to generically capture retailing firms' purchase of inventory or manufacturing firms' purchase of raw materials and production costs.

The analyst often expresses the preceding three ratios in terms of the number of days each balance sheet item (that is, receivables, inventories, and accounts payable) is outstanding. To do so, divide 365 days by the turnover metrics. More intuitively stated, divide the balance sheet item by the appropriate flow variable converted to a daily average amount (that is, divided by 365). For example, the days sales outstanding in accounts receivable can be calculated equivalently as 365/Accounts Receivable Turnover or, more intuitively, as Accounts Receivable/(Sales/365).

Exhibit 5.7 presents the calculation of these three turnover ratios and the related number of days for PepsiCo for 2008. PepsiCo combines accounts payable and other current liabilities on its balance sheet. Note 14, "Supplemental Financial Information" (Appendix A), disaggregates this combined amount into its various elements and reports the amounts for accounts payable separately. We use the amounts for accounts payable from Note 14 to compute the accounts payable turnover. For example, of the $8,273 million total accounts payable and other current liabilities at the end of 2008, only $2,846 million relate to accounts payable; the remainder includes accrued marketplace spending, accrued compensation, dividends payable, and other current liabilities.

EXHIBIT 5.7

Working Capital Activity Ratios for PepsiCo for 2008

Accounts Receivable Turnover

$$\frac{\$43,251}{0.5(\$4,683 + \$4,389)} = 9.5 \text{ times per year}$$

Days Receivables Outstanding

$$\frac{365}{9.5} = 38 \text{ days}$$

Inventory Turnover

$$\frac{\$20,351}{0.5(\$2,522 + \$2,290)} = 8.5 \text{ times per year}$$

Days Inventory Held

$$\frac{365}{8.5} = 43 \text{ days}$$

Accounts Payable Turnover

$$\frac{\$20,351 + \$2,522 - \$2,290}{0.5(\$2,846 + \$2,562)} = 7.6 \text{ times per year}$$

Days Accounts Payable Outstanding

$$\frac{365}{7.6} = 48 \text{ days}$$

---

[7] The accounts payable turnover ratio will be skewed upward if cost of goods sold includes a high proportion of costs (such as depreciation and labor) that do not flow through accounts payable. This bias is more of a concern for manufacturing firms than for retailing firms and is more of an issue in cross-sectional comparisons than in time-series analyses.

The number of days firms hold inventory until sale plus the number of days firms hold accounts receivable until collection indicates the total number of days from the production or purchase of inventory until collection of cash from the sale of inventory to customers. This combined number of days indicates the length of time for which the firm must obtain financing for its primary working capital assets. The number of days accounts payable are outstanding indicates the working capital financing the firm obtained from suppliers. The difference between the total number of days for which the firm requires financing for its working capital and the number of days for which it obtained financing from suppliers indicates the additional days for which it must obtain financing. This difference is known as the cash-to-cash cycle (also known as the cash operating cycle), and it quantifies the length of time between cash outlays that ultimately result in cash collections. The offset for the days outstanding in accounts payable reflects the benefit of suppliers delaying the time before the firm is required to remit cash. We depict these relations here.

Days of Working Capital Financing Required:

Days Inventory Held	Days Accounts Receivable Outstanding

Days of Working Capital Financing Provided:

Days Account Payable Outstanding	Days of Working Capital Financing Needed from Other Sources

Exhibit 5.8 shows the net number of days of financing needed from other sources for PepsiCo for 2006, 2007, and 2008. PepsiCo's days accounts payable is slightly higher than its days inventory, indicating that it has strategically utilized supplier financing for its inventory. The net days financed from other sources approximates the days accounts receivable were outstanding. Like most companies, PepsiCo used short-term borrowing to finance part of the net days of needed financing.

In general, the shorter the number of days of needed financing, the larger the cash flow from operations to average current liabilities ratio. A small number of net days indicates

EXHIBIT 5.8

Net Number of Days of Working Capital Financing Needed from Other Sources for PepsiCo

Year	Days Accounts Receivable Outstanding	+	Days Inventory Held	−	Days Accounts Payable Outstanding	=	Days Other Financing Required
2006	36		42		(45)		33
2007	38		43		(46)		35
2008	38		43		(48)		33

relatively little need to finance accounts receivable and inventories (that is, the firm sells inventory quickly and receives cash from customers soon after sale) or aggressive use of suppliers to finance these current assets (that is, the firm delays paying cash to suppliers). Both scenarios enhance cash flow from operations in the numerator of this ratio. Furthermore, firms with a shorter number of days of financing required from other sources need not engage in as much short-term borrowing from banks and other financing institutions. Such borrowing increases current liabilities in the denominator of the operating cash flow to current liabilities ratio, thereby lowering this ratio.

As an example of a company with extreme favorable working capital requirements, Exhibit 5.9 shows the working capital financing investments for Amazon, a well-known large online retailer of books, electronic media, and numerous other products. Due to low levels of accounts receivable and inventory and extended accounts payable, Amazon has a *negative* value for days of other financing required. Not surprisingly, Amazon does not require any short-term debt financing. The only other liabilities Amazon has at the end of 2009 are (1) accrued expenses of $1,759 million, (2) long-term debt of $109 million, and (3) other long-term liabilities of $1,083 million (relative to total assets of $13,813 million).

Revenues to Cash Ratio

Firms ultimately collect revenues in cash and pay operating costs and current liabilities with cash. The amount of cash on the balance sheet reflects the net effect of operating, investing, and financing activities on cash, as well as management's judgments about the desired level of cash. A ratio that incorporates the amount of cash on the balance sheet helps the analyst evaluate short-term liquidity. To aid comparability across time and across firms, we must relate the amount of cash to some measure of operating activity.

EXHIBIT 5.9

Net Number of Days of Working Capital Financing Needed from Other Sources for Amazon, 2005–2009
(amounts in millions)

	2005	2006	2007	2008	2009
Sales	$8,490	$10,711	$14,835	$19,166	$24,509
Cost of Goods Sold	$6,451	$ 8,255	$18,978	$14,896	$11,482
Purchases	$6,537	$ 8,566	$19,301	$15,095	$12,254
Accounts Receivable	$ 274	$ 399	$ 705	$ 827	$ 988
Inventory	$ 566	$ 877	$ 1,200	$ 1,399	$ 2,171
Accounts Payable	$1,366	$ 1,816	$ 2,795	$ 3,594	$ 5,605
Days Receivables Outstanding	10.2	11.5	13.6	14.6	13.5
Days Inventory Held	29.6	31.9	20.0	31.8	56.7
Days Accounts Payable Outstanding	(70.0)	(67.8)	(43.6)	(77.2)	(137.0)
Days Other Financing Required	(30.2)	(24.4)	(10.0)	(30.8)	(66.8)

Either revenues or cash operating expenses may serve as the measure of activity, but we use revenues. The revenues to cash ratio for PepsiCo for 2008 is as follows:

$$\text{Revenues to Cash Ratio} = \frac{\text{Revenues}}{\text{Average Cash Balance}}$$

$$29.1 = \frac{\$43,251}{0.5(\$2,064 + \$910)}$$

The revenues to cash flow ratio was 30.8 for 2007 and 20.9 for 2006. Interpreting the revenues to cash ratio requires caution. From the viewpoint of short-term liquidity risk, lenders prefer a smaller revenues to cash ratio (that is, more cash in the denominator) and a larger number of days revenue available as cash on hand. However, management may prefer to avoid maintaining excess idle cash. Further, unless managers focus on window-dressing the balance sheet, the amount of cash on hand is expected to fluctuate with the timing of cash receipts and outflows.

Days Revenues Held in Cash

One can view the revenues to cash ratio as a cash turnover ratio, analogous to the accounts receivable turnover ratio described previously. We can express the revenues to cash ratio in terms of the number of days of revenue held in cash by dividing 365 days by the revenues to cash ratio. That ratio for PepsiCo is as follows:

2006: 365/20.9 = 17.5 days
2007: 365/30.8 = 11.9 days
2008: 365/29.1 = 12.5 days

The intuition of the days revenues held in cash measure is that it quantifies the number of days sales the firm has on hand as available cash. This measure will prove useful when analysts forecast financial statements because the forecast of the cash balance can be defined as a function of revenues. Furthermore, as the number of days revenues held in cash becomes high, this ratio may identify firms that are carrying excess cash and thus are more vulnerable to agency problems or takeover.

One variation in this ratio is to include not only the amount of cash, but also the amount of marketable securities. Firms typically invest in marketable securities when they have temporary excess cash, then sell the securities when they need cash. The classification of marketable securities as a current asset suggests that firms could easily sell the securities if they needed cash. Including cash and marketable securities in the denominator results in a revenues to cash and marketable securities ratio of 18.2 [= $43,251/0.5($2,064 + $213 + $910 + $1,571)] for 2008 and 20.1 days (= 365/18.2) of revenues held in cash and marketable securities.

Another variation of this ratio uses cash operating expenses instead of revenues in the numerator. The rationale is that firms generally need cash to pay operating expenses. The analyst can approximate cash operating expenses by summing cost of goods sold and selling and administrative expenses and subtracting depreciation and amortization. Refer to the income statement of PepsiCo in Appendix A. PepsiCo reports amortization expense separately. However, it includes depreciation expense in cost of sales and selling, general, and administrative expenses. Note 4, "Property, Plant, and Equipment and Intangible Assets" (Appendix A), indicates that depreciation expense for 2008 is $1,422 million. Thus, cash operating expenses, excluding impairment and restructuring charges, total $34,830 million

(= \$20,351 + \$15,901 − \$1,422). The ratio of cash operating expenses to average cash and marketable securities for 2008 is 14.6 [= \$34,830/(.5{\$2,064 \$213 + \$910 + \$1,571})], and the days of cash and marketable securities held for paying operating expenses is 25.0 days (= 365/14.6). This ratio is a variant of the *defensive interval*[8] or *run rate*, which indicates the number of days a firm could continue to operate without injections of additional cash. The defensive interval has intuitive merit, but note that we use the ratio of revenues to cash in this book instead of these variations in the ratio.

Summary of Short-Term Liquidity Risk

The short-term liquidity risk ratios suggest that PepsiCo has relatively little short-term liquidity risk. Although the current ratio is slightly above 1, the quick ratio is just below 1; in addition, the operating cash flow to current liabilities ratio equals or exceeds 0.75 in all years. PepsiCo has an established brand name and dominates (along with Coca-Cola) the soft drink beverage industry, generating substantial amounts of positive cash flow from operating activities. Chapter 4 discussed PepsiCo's healthy profitability profile, suggesting that it could obtain short-term financing if needed. Moreover, it maintains two revolving credit agreements that totaled \$3.8 billion at the end of 2008. Neither revolving credit agreement had been used as of the end of the year. The availability of such revolving credit agreements is consistent with PepsiCo enjoying financial flexibility, which was discussed in the preceding section. We turn to long-term solvency risk next.

ANALYZING LONG-TERM SOLVENCY RISK

As described in the section on financial flexibility, financial leverage enhances the return to common shareholders when firms borrow funds and invest those funds in assets that generate a higher return than the after-tax cost of borrowing. Common shareholders benefit with increasing proportions of debt in the capital structure as long as the firm maintains an excess rate of return on assets over the after-tax cost of the debt. However, increasing the proportion of debt in the capital structure increases the risk that the firm cannot pay interest and repay the principal on the amount borrowed. That is, credit and bankruptcy risk increases, and the incremental cost of borrowing also is likely to increase. Analysts use measures of long-term solvency risk to examine a firm's ability to make interest and principal payments on long-term debt and similar obligations as they come due.

Perhaps the best indicator for assessing long-term solvency risk is a firm's ability to generate earnings over a period of years. Profitable firms generate sufficient cash from operations or obtain needed cash from creditors or owners. Therefore, the measures of profitability discussed in Chapter 4 apply to this purpose as well. Also, firms must survive in the short term if they are to survive in the long term. Thus, analysis of long-term solvency risk must begin with an assessment of the level of and trends in financial flexibility and with an analysis of short-term liquidity risk. Having discussed these analyses, we turn to three measures used in examining long-term solvency risk: (1) debt ratios, (2) interest coverage ratios, and (3) the operating cash flow to total liabilities ratio.

---

[8] See George H. Sorter and George Benston, "Appraising the Defensive Position of a Firm: The Interval Measure," *Accounting Review* 35 (October 1960), pp. 633–640. The denominator of their defensive interval measure included marketable securities and accounts receivable in addition to cash. See the discussion of bankruptcy risk later in this chapter.

Debt Ratios

Analysts use debt ratios to measure the amount of liabilities, particularly long-term debt, in a firm's capital structure. The higher this proportion, the greater the long-term solvency risk. The capital structure leverage ratio discussed in Chapter 4, one of the disaggregated components of ROCE, is one version of a debt ratio, as is the alternative computation of leverage used in the alternative decomposition of ROCE discussed earlier in this chapter. Several additional variations in debt ratios exist. Four commonly encountered measures are as follows:

$$\text{Liabilities to Assets Ratio} = \frac{\text{Total Liabilities}}{\text{Total Assets}}$$

$$\text{Liabilities to Shareholders' Equity Ratio} = \frac{\text{Total Liabilities}}{\text{Total Shareholders' Equity}}$$

$$\frac{\text{Long-Term Debt to}}{\text{Long-Term Capital Ratio}} = \frac{\text{Long-Term Debt}}{\text{Long-Term Debt} + \text{Total Shareholders' Equity}}$$

$$\text{Long-Term Debt to Shareholders' Equity Ratio} = \frac{\text{Long-Term Debt}}{\text{Total Shareholders' Equity}}$$

The debt ratios for PepsiCo at the end of 2008 are as follows:

$$\text{Liabilities to Assets Ratio} = \frac{\$23,888}{\$35,994} = 0.664$$

$$\text{Liabilities to Shareholders' Equity Ratio} = \frac{\$23,888}{\$12,106} = 1.973$$

$$\text{Long-Term Debt to Long-Term Capital Ratio} = \frac{\$7,858}{\$7,858 + \$12,106} = 0.394$$

$$\text{Long-Term Debt to Shareholders' Equity Ratio} = \frac{\$7,858}{\$12,106} = 0.649$$

Exhibit 5.10 shows the debt ratios for PepsiCo at the end of 2006, 2007, and 2008. The debt ratios involving total liabilities increased during the three-year period, but not as significantly as the long-term debt ratios over the same period. This is consistent with the insights generated in the previous discussion of trends in financial flexibility for PepsiCo.

EXHIBIT 5.10

Debt Ratios for PepsiCo at the End of 2006–2008

	2006	2007	2008
Liabilities to Assets Ratio	0.487	0.502	0.664
Liabilities to Shareholders' Equity Ratio	0.948	1.009	1.973
Long-Term Debt to Long-Term Capital Ratio	0.142	0.196	0.394
Long-Term Debt to Shareholders' Equity Ratio	0.166	0.244	0.649

Note the high correlations between changes in the two debt ratios involving total liabilities over time and in the two long-term debt ratios over time. These results are not surprising because they use overlapping financial statement data. Generally, the analyst can select one of these ratios and use it consistently over time. Because different debt ratios exist, the analyst should use caution when reading financial periodicals and discussing debt ratios with others to be sure of the particular version of the debt ratio used. A liabilities to shareholders' equity ratio greater than 1.0 (that is, more liabilities than shareholders' equity) is not unusual, but a liabilities to assets ratio or a long-term debt to long-term capital ratio greater than 1.0 is highly unusual (because it requires a negative shareholders' equity).

In addition to computing debt ratios, the analyst should study the note to the financial statements on long-term debt. The note includes information on the types of debt a firm has issued and the interest rates and maturity dates of the debt. The analyst also should examine the debt contract for each debt issue to assess whether the firm is nearing violation of any debt covenants.

Refer to Note 9, "Debt Obligations and Commitments" (Appendix A), for PepsiCo. PepsiCo indicates that it classifies a portion of its short-term borrowing as a noncurrent liability even though the amounts are due within the next year. PepsiCo states the following:

> As of December 27, 2008, we have reclassified $1.3 billion of short-term debt to long-term based on our intent and ability to refinance on a long-term basis.

GAAP permits PepsiCo and other firms to reclassify short-term debt in this way. PepsiCo's reclassification of $1.3 billion in additional short-term borrowing is similar to a reclassification at the end of 2007 totaling $1.4 billion.

Note 9 also provides information about the increase in long-term debt from $4.2 billion to $7.9 billion between 2007 and 2008. PepsiCo issued two tranches of senior unsecured 10-year notes during the year, which totaled $3.75 billion, accounting for almost all of the change in long-term obligations. For both issuances, PepsiCo indicates that the proceeds were used for "general corporate purposes, including the repayment of outstanding short-term indebtedness." Further, as discussed in the previous section, the interest rate on the incremental debt issuances is higher. The $1.75 billion issued in the second quarter of 2008 carried a 5 percent fixed rate, while the $2.0 billion issued in the fourth quarter carried a 7.9 percent rate. PepsiCo entered into an interest rate swap to convert the 5 percent fixed rate on the $1.75 billion of debt to a variable rate based on LIBOR. This is relevant for solvency risk analysis because swaps like this hedge the fair value of the debt but create cash flows risk.

In an effort to appear less risky and to lower their cost of financing or perhaps to avoid violating debt covenants in existing borrowing arrangements, firms often attempt to structure financing in a manner that keeps debt off the balance sheet. Chapter 6 discusses some of the avenues available under GAAP (for example, accounting for leases as operating leases instead of capital leases) to minimize reported long-term debt. The analyst should recognize the possibility of such actions when interpreting debt ratios and perhaps adjust the reported amounts, as illustrated for leases in Chapter 6.

Interest Coverage Ratios

Interest coverage ratios indicate the number of times a firm's income or cash flows could cover interest charges. For example, one common approach to the interest coverage ratio divides net income before interest expense and income taxes by interest expense. This income-based interest coverage ratio for PepsiCo, using the amounts reported for net income and income tax expense for 2008, is as follows:[9]

$$\text{Interest Coverage Ratio (Net Income Basis)} = \frac{\begin{array}{c}\text{Net Income} + \text{Interest Expense} \\ + \text{ Income Tax Expense} + \text{Minority Interest in Earnings}\end{array}}{\text{Interest Expense}}$$

$$22.3 = \frac{\$5,142 + \$329 + \$1,879 + \$0}{\$329}$$

The interest coverage ratio for PepsiCo was 35.1 in 2007 and 30.2 in 2006. PepsiCo's reported profitability decreased slightly during the three-year period (see the discussion in Chapter 4) while its debt levels increased, resulting in a decreasing interest coverage ratio. Analysts typically view coverage ratios of less than approximately 2.0 as risky situations. Thus, by this measure, PepsiCo exhibits very low long-term solvency risk. Sometimes firms are able to capitalize interest as part of the cost basis of tangible assets. The analyst should be aware of significant interest capitalization when examining net borrowing costs.

If a firm must make other required periodic payments (such as pensions or leases), the analyst could include these amounts in the calculation as well. If so, the ratio is referred to as the *fixed charges coverage ratio*.

One criticism of the interest and the fixed charges coverage ratios as measures of long-term solvency risk is that they use earnings rather than cash flows in the numerator. Firms pay interest and other fixed charges with cash, not earnings. The analyst can create cash-flow-based variations of these coverage ratios by using cash flow from operations (before interest and income taxes) in the numerator. When the value of the ratio based on earnings in the numerator is relatively low (that is, less than approximately 2.0), the analyst should use cash flow from operations before interest and income taxes in the numerator to calculate coverage ratios.

To illustrate, cash flow from operations for PepsiCo for 2008 was $6,999 million. Note 14, "Supplemental Financial Information" (Appendix A), indicates that PepsiCo paid $359 million for interest and $1,477 million for income taxes during 2008. The calculation of the interest coverage ratio using cash flows is as follows:

$$\text{Interest Coverage Ratio (Cash Flow Basis)} = \frac{\begin{array}{c}\text{Cash Flow from Operations} + \\ \text{Payments for Interest and Income Taxes}\end{array}}{\text{Cash Payments for Interest}}$$

$$24.6 = \frac{\$6,999 + \$359 + \$1,477}{\$359}$$

Operating Cash Flow to Total Liabilities Ratio

Standard debt ratios such as the Liabilities to Assets Ratio give no recognition to the ability of a firm to generate cash flow from operations to service debt. The ratio of cash flow from operations to average total liabilities overcomes this deficiency. This cash flow ratio is similar to the one used in assessing short-term liquidity, but here the denominator includes all liabilities (current and noncurrent).

---

[9] Increased precision suggests that the denominator include total interest cost for the year, not just the amount recognized as interest expense. If a firm self-constructs fixed assets, it must capitalize a portion of its interest cost each year and add it to the cost of the self-constructed assets. The analyst probably should apply this refinement of the interest coverage ratio only to electric utilities, which engage in heavy borrowing to construct their capital-intensive plants.

The operating cash flow to total liabilities ratio for 2008 for PepsiCo is as follows:

$$\text{Operating Cash Flow to Total Liabilities Ratio} = \frac{\text{Cash Flow from Operations}}{\text{Average Total Liabilities}}$$

$$0.34 = \frac{\$6,999}{0.5(\$23,888 + \$17,394)}$$

The ratio for PepsiCo was 0.43 in 2007 and 0.38 in 2006. A ratio of 0.20 or more is common for a financially healthy company.[10] Thus, by this measure, PepsiCo appears to have low long-term solvency risk.

Summary of Long-Term Solvency Risk

The debt, interest coverage, and cash flow ratios indicate that PepsiCo has low long-term solvency risk. PepsiCo is profitable and generates the needed cash flow to service its debt. However, the trends indicate increasing use of leverage, which calls for the analyst to monitor future changes to ensure that PepsiCo's current low solvency risk persists. Similarly, decreases in financial flexibility (discussed earlier in the chapter) could be an early indicator of potential liquidity and solvency problems.

ANALYZING CREDIT RISK

Potential lenders to a firm, whether short- or long-term, assess the likelihood that the firm will pay periodic interest and repay the principal amount lent. To assess credit risk, lenders use the short-term liquidity and long-term solvency ratios already presented in the chapter. Lenders also consider other factors when deciding whether to extend credit. Common practice uses the following checklist as factors a creditor might consider when making lending decisions. The list is neither an exhaustive catalog of the factors that lenders consider in assessing credit risk nor a mandatory list of factors that must be examined.

1. Circumstances Leading to Need for the Loan

The reason a firm needs to borrow affects the riskiness of the loan and the likelihood of repayment. Consider the following examples.

Example 1

W. T. Grant Company, a discount retail chain, filed for bankruptcy in 1975. Its bankruptcy has become a classic example of how poorly designed and implemented controls can lead a firm into financial distress. (See Case 3.3 in Chapter 3.) Between 1968 and 1975, Grant experienced increasing difficulty collecting accounts receivable from credit card customers. To finance the buildup of its accounts receivable, Grant borrowed short-term funds from commercial banks. However, Grant failed to fix the credit extension and cash collection problems with its receivables. The bank loans simply kept Grant in business in an ever-worsening credit situation. Lending to satisfy cash-flow needs related to an unsolved problem or difficulty can be highly risky.

---

[10] Casey and Bartczak, *op. cit.*

Example 2

Toys"R"Us purchases toys, games, and other entertainment products in September and October in anticipation of heavy demand during the end-of-the-year holiday season. It typically pays its suppliers within 30 days for these purchases but does not collect cash from customers until December, January, or later. To finance its inventory, Toys"R"Us borrows short term from its banks. It repays these loans with cash collected from customers. Lending to satisfy cash-flow needs related to ongoing seasonal business operations is generally relatively low risk. Toys"R"Us has an established brand name and predictable demand. Although some risk exists that the products offered will not meet customer preferences in a particular year, Toys"R"Us offers a sufficiently diverse product line that failure to collect sufficient cash to repay the bank loan is low. Despite being profitable, Toys"R"Us suffered declines in market share relative to rivals such as Walmart. As a result, Toys"R"Us was acquired by an investment group formed by Bain Capital, LLC; Kohlberg Kravis Roberts & Co.; and Vornado Realty Trust. The company continues to follow the same seasonal purchasing pattern.

Example 3

Wal-Mart Stores has grown the number of its stores during each of the last five years. (See Case 4.2 in Chapter 4.) The fastest growth is in its international segment, which now represents approximately 25 percent of total sales. Walmart borrows a large portion of the funds needed to construct new stores using 20- to 25-year loans. (Walmart also enters into leases for a portion of the space needed for its new stores.) Such loans are relatively low-risk given the operating success of Walmart in the past and the existence of land and buildings that serve as collateral for the loans.

Example 4

National Semiconductor designs and manufactures semiconductors for use in computers and other electronic products. Its principal competitors include well-known companies such as Intel, Analog Devices, Linear Technology, Maxim Integrated Products, and Texas Instruments. National Semiconductor has continued to lose market share in recent years. Assume that National Semiconductor wants to develop new semiconductors and needs to borrow funds to finance the design and development effort. Such a loan would likely be relatively high-risk. Technological change occurs rapidly in semiconductors, which would make obsolete any semiconductors developed by National Semiconductor. In addition, expenditures on design and development of semiconductors would not likely result in assets that could serve as collateral for the loan.

In sum, lending to established firms for ongoing operating needs and capital expenditures presents the lowest credit risk. Lending to firms experiencing operating problems, lending to emerging businesses, and lending to support investments in intangible assets typically carry higher risks. Lenders should be wary of borrowers that are unclear as to how they intend to use the proceeds of a loan.

2. Credit History

Lenders like to see that a firm has borrowed in the past and successfully repaid the loans. Young firms sometimes shy away from borrowing to avoid constraints that such borrowing may impose. However, such firms often find that an inadequate credit history precludes them from borrowing later when they need to do so. On the other hand, developing a poor credit history early on can doom a firm to failure because of the difficulty of overcoming initial impressions.

3. Cash Flows

Lenders prefer that firms generate sufficient cash flows to pay interest and repay principal (collectively referred to as *debt service)* on a loan rather than having to rely on selling the collateral. Tools for studying the cash-generating ability of a firm include examining the statement of cash flows for recent years, computing various cash flow financial ratios, and studying cash flows in projected financial statements.

Statement of Cash Flows

An examination of a firm's statement of cash flows for the most recent three or four years will indicate whether a firm is experiencing potential cash flow problems. We discussed cash flows in detail in Chapter 3. Some of the indicators of potential cash flow problems, if observed for several years in a row, include:

- Growth in accounts receivable and inventories that exceeds the growth rate in sales.
- Increases in accounts payable or other liabilities that routinely exceed the increase in inventories or sales.
- Persistent negative cash flow from operations because of net losses or substantial increases in net working capital (current assets minus current liabilities).
- Capital expenditures that substantially exceed cash flow from operations. Although the analyst should expect such an excess for a rapidly growing, capital-intensive firm, the negative excess cash flow (cash flow from operations minus capital expenditures) indicates a firm's continuing need for external financing to sustain that growth.
- Reductions in capital expenditures over time. Although such reductions conserve cash in the near term, they might signal that a firm expects declines in future sales, earnings, and operating cash flows.
- Sales of marketable securities in excess of purchases of marketable securities. Such sales provide cash immediately but might signal the inability of a firm's operations to provide adequate cash flow to finance working capital and long-term investments. Firms sell the marketable securities to obtain the cash needed for these purposes. Such sales, however, may not indicate cash flow problems if the firm temporarily invested excess cash that it now plans to use to make a corporate acquisition or to acquire fixed assets.
- A reduction or elimination of dividend payments or stock repurchases. Although such actions conserve cash in the near term, dividend reductions or omissions and cessation of share repurchase plans can provide a negative signal about a firm's future prospects.
- A full use of available revolving lines of credit. Full utilization of letters of credit might suggest that a firm's cash flows have become insufficient for operating purposes.

Although none of these indicators by themselves represents conclusive evidence of cash flow problems, they do signal the need to obtain explanations from management to see whether an emerging cash flow problem does exist. Just as analysts must understand a firm's industry and strategy to effectively analyze profitability, lenders must follow the same analysis steps.

Cash Flow Financial Ratios

Previous sections of this chapter discussed two cash flow ratios that may signal a cash flow problem: (1) operating cash flow to current liabilities ratio and (2) operating cash flow to total liabilities ratio.

Cash Flows in Projected Financial Statements

Projected financial statements represent forecasted income statements, balance sheets, and statements of cash flows for some number of years in the future. Lenders may require potential borrowers to prepare such statements (which are rarely made publicly available) to demonstrate the borrower's ability to repay the loan with interest as it comes due. The credit analyst should question each of the important assumptions (such as sales growth, cost structure, or capital expenditures plans) underlying these projected financial statements. The credit analyst also should assess the sensitivity of the projected cash flows to changes in key assumptions. For example, suppose sales grow by 4 percent instead of the 6 percent projected. Suppose raw materials costs increase 5 percent instead of the 3 percent projected. Suppose additional plant expenditures are necessary because a firm reaches capacity limits with a higher-than-expected sales increase. What impact will each of these changed assumptions have on cash flow from operations? Chapter 10 illustrates the preparation of projected, or forecasted, financial statements.

4. Collateral

A fourth consideration when assessing credit risk is the availability and value of collateral for a loan. If a company's cash flows are insufficient to pay interest and repay the principal on a loan, the lender has the right to take possession of any collateral pledged in support of the loan. Depending on the nature of the collateral pledged, the analyst might examine the following:

Marketable Securities

Chapter 7 discusses the accounting for marketable securities. Marketable equity securities representing less than a 20 percent ownership appear on the balance sheet at market value. The analyst can assess whether the market value of securities pledged as collateral exceeds the unpaid balance of a loan. Marketable securities representing 20 percent or more of another entity generally appear on the balance sheet using the equity method. Determining whether the market value of such securities adequately covers the unpaid balance of a loan is more difficult. The analyst might examine the amount reported as equity in earnings of affiliates in recent years to assess the level and changes in profitability of the investee.

Accounts Receivable

A lender should assess whether the current value of accounts receivable is sufficient to cover the unpaid portion of a loan collateralized by accounts receivable. Determining whether the book value of accounts receivable accurately reflects their market value involves an examination of changes in the provision for uncollectible accounts relative to sales, the balance in allowance for uncollectible accounts relative to gross accounts receivable, the amount of accounts written off as uncollectible relative to gross accounts receivable, and the number of days receivables that are outstanding. Deterioration in the days receivables outstanding can suggest decreasing collectability or lowering of customer credit standards.

Inventories

Inventory represents valuable collateral to a lender only if it is salable for sufficient cash flows in the event of the borrower's distress. The analyst should examine changes in the inventory turnover ratio; in the cost of goods sold to sales percentage; and in the mix of raw materials, work-in-process, and finished goods inventories to identify possible inventory obsolescence problems. The analyst should remember that the market value of inventories are likely to differ more from their book value for a firm using LIFO than for a firm using FIFO. Firms using LIFO must report the excess of market or FIFO value over LIFO cost, permitting the analyst to assess the adequacy of LIFO inventories to cover the unpaid balance on a loan collateralized by inventories. (See the discussion of inventories in Chapter 8.)

Property, Plant, and Equipment

Firms often pledge fixed assets as collateral for long-term borrowing. Determining the market values of such assets is difficult using reported financial statement information because of the use of acquisition cost valuations. Market values of unique firm-specific assets are particularly difficult to ascertain. Clues indicating market value declines include restructuring charges, asset impairment charges, and recent sales of such assets at a loss. (See the discussion of property, plant, and equipment in Chapter 7.)

Intangibles

Intangibles generally do not serve well as collateral for borrowing because lenders cannot easily repossess the intangible (that is, sever it from all other assets or capabilities of the firm) in the event of a loan default. For example, the value of a newspaper or magazine publisher's customer list is closely tied to its writers and reporters and its production and distribution capability. The value of a brand name of a consumer foods product is closely tied to the firm's manufacturing quality control and marketing expertise. On the other hand, in some limited situations, intangibles can serve as collateral for borrowing. Rights owned by airlines to landing and gate slots at airports can be transferred to lenders in the event of loan default and resold to cover unpaid balances on a loan.

Some lending occurs on a nonsecured basis; that is, the borrower pledges no specific collateral in support of the loan. In these cases, the lender should study the notes to the financial statements to ascertain how much of the borrower's assets, if any, are not already pledged or otherwise restricted. The liquidation value of such assets represents the available resources of a firm to repay unsecured creditors. For smaller family-owned businesses, an additional source of collateral may be the personal assets of management or major shareholders. Has management or the shareholders pledged their personal residence, debt or equity securities owned, or other assets to serve as additional collateral for a business loan?

5. Capacity for Debt

Closely related to a firm's cash-generating ability and available collateral is a firm's capacity to assume additional debt. The cash flows and the collateral represent the means to repay the debt. Most firms do not borrow up to the limit of their debt capacity. Lenders want to make sure a margin of safety exists. Although no precise methodology exists to measure debt capacity, the analyst can study various financial statement ratios when assessing debt capacity. Capacity for debt is related to the discussion earlier in the chapter for financial flexibility. Moreover, footnote disclosures highlight the amount of unused credit lines, which provide additional, direct evidence of capacity for debt, especially if the firm exhibits a history of maintaining unused lines of credit.

Debt Ratios

An earlier section described several ratios that relate the amount of long-term debt or total liabilities to shareholders' equity or total assets as measures of the proportion of liabilities in the capital structure. In general, the higher the debt ratios, the higher the credit risk and the lower the unused debt capacity of the firm. When measuring debt ratios, the analyst must be careful to consider possible off-balance-sheet obligations (such as operating lease commitments or underfunded pension or health care benefit obligations). The analyst can compare a particular firm's debt ratios with those of similar firms in the same industry.

Interest Coverage Ratio

As discussed earlier, the number of times interest payments are covered by operating income before interest and income taxes serves as a gauge of the margin of safety provided by operations to service debt. When firms make heavy use of operating leases for their fixed assets, as is common for airlines and retail stores, the analyst might convert the operating leases to capital leases for the purpose of computing the interest coverage ratio. (See the discussion of leases in Chapter 6.) When computing cash flows from operations, the analyst adds back the lease payments (that is, rent expense) to net income in the numerator of this ratio and includes the lease payments in the denominator. When the interest coverage ratio falls below approximately 2, the credit risk is generally considered high. Interest coverage ratios that exceed 4 or 5 usually suggest a capacity to carry additional debt.

6. Contingencies

The credit standing of a firm could change abruptly in the future if current uncertainties turn out negatively for the firm. Questions the analyst might ask include the following:

- Is the firm a defendant in a major lawsuit involving its principal products, its technological advantages, its income tax returns, or other core endeavors that could change its profitability and cash flows in the future? Consider, for example, the uncertainty currently confronting the tobacco and asbestos industries with the unsettled status of lawsuits in the United States. Most large firms are continually engaged in lawsuits as a normal part of their business. Most of their losses are insured. Negative legal judgments are likely to have a more pronounced effect on smaller firms, however, because they have less of a resource base with which to defend themselves and to sustain such losses and may not carry adequate insurance.
- Has the firm sold receivables with recourse or served as guarantor on a loan by a subsidiary, joint venture, special-purpose entity, or corporate officer that, if payment is required, will consume cash flows otherwise available to service other debt obligations?
- Is the firm exposed to making payments related to derivative financial instruments that could adversely affect future cash flows if interest rates, exchange rates, or other prices change significantly in an unexpected direction? (See the discussion of derivatives in Chapter 8.)
- Is the firm dependent on one or a few key employees, contracts or license agreements, or technologies, the loss of which could substantially affect the viability of the business?

Obtaining answers to such questions require the analyst to read the notes to the financial statement carefully and to ask astute questions of management, attorneys, and others.

7. Character of Management

An intangible that can offset to some extent otherwise weak signals about the creditworthiness of a firm is the character of its management. Has the management team successively weathered previous operating problems and challenges that could have bankrupted most firms? Has the management team delivered in the past on projections regarding sales levels, cost reductions, new product development, and similar operating targets? Does the firm have a reputation for honest and fair dealings with suppliers, customers, bankers, and others? Lenders also are more comfortable lending to firms in which management has a substantial portion of its personal wealth invested in the firm's common equity. Managers wanting to increase the value of their equity holdings have incentives to operate the firm profitably and avoid defaulting on debt.

8. Communication

Developing relations with lenders requires effective communication at the outset and on an ongoing basis. If lenders are unfamiliar with the business or its managers, efforts must be directed at communicating the nature of the firm's products and services and the strategies the firm pursues to gain competitive advantage. The firm's managers must demonstrate their knowledge of the business, including principal competitors, role of technological change, extent of government regulation, and similar factors. Inviting lenders to an office or plant visit provides visual evidence of an ongoing business.

Throughout the term of a loan, the borrowing firm should communicate regularly with lenders. If lenders required projected financial statements at the outset, communicating the extent to which the firm meets its projections is desirable. Alerting lenders to unexpected problems that may arise demonstrates that the firm's managers are on top of the problem and are dealing with it. Lenders do not like surprises and need to receive transparent information throughout the term of the loan.

9. Conditions or Covenants

Lenders often place restrictions, or constraints, on a firm to protect their interests. Such restrictions might include minimum or maximum levels of certain financial ratios. For example, the current ratio cannot fall below 1.2 and the long-term debt to shareholders' equity ratio cannot exceed 75 percent. Firms also may be precluded from paying dividends, repurchasing common stock, or taking on new financing with rights senior to existing lenders in the event of bankruptcy. Violation of these debt constraints, or covenants, could result in the need to repay loans immediately, higher interest rates, or other burdensome restrictions. Although these covenants can protect the interest of senior collateralized lenders, they can place less senior lenders in jeopardy if the firm must quickly liquidate assets to repay debt. Thus, debt covenants are a double-edged sword from the viewpoint of credit risk. They provide protection against undue deterioration in the financial condition of a firm but increase the likelihood of default or bankruptcy if the constraints are too tight.

Summary of Credit Risk Analysis

The analysis of credit risk is a multifaceted endeavor. The financial statements and notes provide evidence of a firm's cash-generating ability, extent of collateralized assets, amount of unused debt capacity, and constraints imposed by existing borrowing agreements. Although the financial statements might provide some clues, the credit analyst must search beyond the financial statements for information on the credit history of the borrower, the market value of collateral, contingencies confronting the firm, and the character of management. Existing lenders should monitor a firm's credit risk on an ongoing basis, maintaining communications throughout the process. New lenders should assess how their loan will incrementally affect the firm's credit risk.

ANALYZING BANKRUPTCY RISK

This section discusses the analysis of bankruptcy risk by using information in the financial statements.

The Bankruptcy Process

During the recession of 2008–2009, a staggering number of large, well-known firms filed for bankruptcy, including IndyMac Bancorp (July 2008), Lehman Brothers (September 2008),

Washington Mutual (September 2008), Circuit City (November 2008), Tribune Group (December 2008), Saab Automobile (February 2009), Chrysler (April 2009), General Motors (June 2009), Eddie Bauer (June 2009), The Jolt Company (September 2009), and Simmons Bedding (November 2009). Most firms that file for bankruptcy in the United States file under Chapter 11 of the National Bankruptcy Code. Under Chapter 11, firms have six months in which to present a plan of reorganization to the court. After that period elapses, creditors, employees, and others can file their plans of reorganization. One such plan might include immediately selling the assets of the business and paying creditors the amounts due. The court decides which plan provides the fairest treatment for all parties concerned. While the firm is in bankruptcy, creditors cannot demand payment of their claims. The court oversees the execution of the reorganization. When the court determines that the firm has executed the plan of reorganization successfully and appears to be a viable entity, the firm is released from bankruptcy.

A Chapter 7 filing entails an immediate sale, or liquidation, of the firm's assets and a distribution of the proceeds to the various claimants in order of priority.

Firms typically file for bankruptcy when they have insufficient cash to pay creditors' claims coming due. If such firms did not file for bankruptcy, creditors could exercise their right to take possession of any collateral pledged to secure their lending and effectively begin liquidation of the firm. In an effort to keep assets intact and operating activities functioning and to allow time for the firm to reorganize, the firm files for bankruptcy. In recent years, some firms have filed for bankruptcy for reasons other than insufficient liquid resources to pay creditors. Some firms have filed for bankruptcy to avoid labor contracts or retirement obligations because the firms considered them too costly. Other firms facing potentially costly litigation have filed for bankruptcy as a means of forcing the contending party to negotiate a settlement.

Models of Bankruptcy Prediction

Empirical studies of bankruptcy attempt to distinguish the financial characteristics of firms that file for bankruptcy from those that do not, a dichotomous outcome. The objective is to develop a model that predicts which firms will likely file for bankruptcy one or more years before the filing. These models use financial statement ratios and other data.

Univariate Bankruptcy Prediction Models

Early research on bankruptcy prediction in the mid-1960s used univariate analysis. Univariate models examine the relation between a particular financial statement ratio and bankruptcy. Multivariate models, discussed next, combine several financial statement ratios to determine whether the set of ratios together can improve bankruptcy prediction. Beaver[11] studied 29 financial statement ratios for the five years preceding bankruptcy using a sample of 79 bankrupt and 79 nonbankrupt firms. The objective was to identify the ratios that best differentiated between these two groups of firms and to determine how many years prior to bankruptcy the differences in the ratios emerged. The six ratios with the best discriminating power (and the nature of the risk that each ratio measures) were as follows:

1. Net Income plus Depreciation, Depletion, and Amortization/Total Liabilities (long-term solvency risk)[12]
2. Net Income/Total Assets (profitability)

---

[11] William Beaver, "Financial Ratios as Predictors of Failure," *Empirical Research in Accounting: Selected Studies, 1966,* supplement to *Journal of Accounting Research* (1966), pp. 71–102.

[12] This ratio is similar to the operating cash flow to total liabilities ratio discussed earlier in this chapter except that the numerator of Beaver's ratio does not include changes in working capital accounts. Published "funds flow" statements at the time of Beaver's study defined funds as working capital (instead of cash).

3. Total Debt/Total Assets (long-term solvency risk)
4. Net Working Capital/Total Assets (short-term liquidity risk)
5. Current Assets/Current Liabilities (short-term liquidity risk)
6. Cash, Marketable Securities, Accounts Receivable/Operating Expenses Excluding Depreciation, Depletion, and Amortization (short-term liquidity risk)[13]

Note that this list includes profitability, short-term liquidity risk, and long-term solvency risk ratios. Beaver's best predictor was net income before depreciation, depletion, and amortization divided by total liabilities. Exhibit 5.11 summarizes for each of the five years preceding bankruptcy the success of this ratio in correctly predicting firms that go bankrupt. The predictive accuracy increased as bankruptcy approached, but was close to 80 percent for as early as five years preceding bankruptcy.

The error rates deserve particular attention, however. A Type I error is classifying a firm as nonbankrupt when it ultimately goes bankrupt. A Type II error occurs when a firm is classified as bankrupt and ultimately survives. A Type I error is more costly to an investor because of the likelihood of losing the full amount invested. A Type II error costs the investor the opportunity cost of funds invested. Note in Exhibit 5.11 that the Type I error rates are much higher than the Type II error rates in Beaver's study. When the net income before depreciation, depletion, and amortization to total liabilities ratio is used to predict bankruptcy four years prior to bankruptcy, 47 percent of the predictions that firms would be nonbankrupt turned out to be incorrect, whereas only 3 percent of the predictions that firms would be bankrupt turned out to be incorrect.

Because univariate analysis helps identify factors related to bankruptcy, it is a useful step in the initial development of predictors of bankruptcy risk. However, in the assessment of risk, univariate analysis does not provide a means of measuring the relative importance of individual financial statement ratios or of combining them. For example, does a firm with a high current ratio and a high debt-to-assets ratio have more bankruptcy risk than a firm with a low current ratio and a low debt-to-assets ratio? The analyst also must subjectively judge the level of each financial ratio that signals a high probability of bankruptcy.

EXHIBIT 5.11

Classification Accuracy and Error Rates for Bankruptcy Prediction based on Net Income before Depreciation, Depletion, and Amortization/Total Liabilities

Years Prior to Bankruptcy	Proportion Correctly Classified	Error Rate	
		Type I	Type II
5	78%	42%	4%
4	76%	47%	3%
3	77%	37%	8%
2	79%	34%	8%
1	87%	22%	5%

Source: William Beaver, "Financial Ratios as Predictors of Failure," *Empirical Research in Accounting: Selected Studies,* 1966, supplement to *Journal of Accounting Research* (1966), p. 90. Reprinted by permission of Wiley-Blackwell.

---

[13] This ratio, referred to as the *defensive interval,* indicates the proportion of a year that a firm could continue to operate by paying cash operating expenses with cash and near-cash assets. See the discussion earlier in this chapter in the section on the revenues to cash ratio.

Bankruptcy Prediction Models Using Multiple Discriminant Analysis (MDA)

During the late 1960s and throughout the 1970s, deficiencies of univariate analysis led researchers to use MDA, a multivariate statistical technique, to develop bankruptcy prediction models. Researchers typically selected a sample of bankrupt firms and matched them with healthy firms of approximately the same size in the same industry. This matching procedure attempts to control factors for size and industry so the researcher can examine the impact of other factors that might explain bankruptcy. The researcher then calculates a large number of financial statement ratios expected a priori to explain bankruptcy. Using these financial ratios as inputs, an MDA model selects the subset (usually four to six ratios) that best discriminates between bankrupt and nonbankrupt firms. The resulting MDA model includes a set of coefficients that, when multiplied by the particular financial statement ratios and then summed, yields a multivariate score that is the basis of predicting the likelihood of a firm going bankrupt. The researcher then examines the pattern of Type I and Type II errors and chooses a cutoff that distinguishes firms with a high probability of bankruptcy from those with a low probability. Researchers usually develop the MDA model on an estimation sample and apply the resulting model to a separate holdout, or prediction, sample to check on the general applicability and predictability of the model.

Perhaps the best-known MDA bankruptcy prediction model is Altman's Z-score.[14] Altman used data for manufacturing firms to develop the model. Following is the calculation of the Z-score:

$$\text{Z-score} = 1.2 \left[\frac{\text{Net Working Capital}}{\text{Total Assets}} \right] + 1.4 \left[\frac{\text{Retained Earnings}}{\text{Total Assets}} \right]$$

$$+ 3.3 \left[\frac{\text{Earnings before Interest and Taxes}}{\text{Total Assets}} \right] + 0.6 \left[\frac{\text{Market Value of Equity}}{\text{Book Value of Liabilities}} \right]$$

$$+ 1.0 \left[\frac{\text{Sales}}{\text{Total Assets}} \right]$$

Each ratio captures a different dimension of profitability or risk as follows:

1. Net Working Capital/Total Assets: The proportion of total assets comprising relatively liquid net current assets (current assets minus current liabilities). This ratio serves as a measure of short-term liquidity risk.
2. Retained Earnings/Total Assets: Accumulated profitability and relative age of a firm.
3. Earnings before Interest and Taxes/Total Assets: A variant of ROA. This ratio measures current profitability.
4. Market Value of Equity/Book Value of Liabilities: A form of the debt-to-equity ratio but it incorporates the market's assessment of the value of the firm's shareholders' equity. Therefore, this ratio measures long-term solvency risk and the market's overall assessment of the profitability and risk of the firm.
5. Sales/Total Assets: Similar to the total assets turnover ratio discussed in Chapter 4. This ratio indicates the ability of a firm to use assets to generate sales.

In applying this model, Altman found that Z-scores of less than 1.81 indicated a high probability of bankruptcy, while Z-scores higher than 3.00 indicated a low probability of bankruptcy. Scores between 1.81 and 3.00 were in the gray area.

---

[14] Edward Altman, "Financial Ratios, Discriminant Analysis, and the Prediction of Corporate Bankruptcy," *Journal of Finance* (September 1968), pp. 589–609.

We can convert the Z-score into a more intuitive probability of bankruptcy using the normal density function in Excel.[15] A Z-score of 3.00 translates into a probability of bankruptcy of 2.75 percent. A Z-score of 1.81 translates into a probability of bankruptcy of 20.90 percent. Thus, Z-scores that correspond to probabilities of less than 2.75 percent indicate low probability of bankruptcy, probabilities between 2.75 percent and 20.90 percent are in the gray area, and probabilities above 20.90 percent are in the high probability area. These probabilities levels cannot be interpreted in the usual way. Altman had to trade off Type I and Type II errors when specifying the cutoff points for ranges of low probability, gray area, and high probability.

Altman obtained a 95 percent correct prediction accuracy rate one year prior to bankruptcy, with a Type I error rate of 6 percent and a Type II error rate of 3 percent. The correct prediction rate two years before bankruptcy was 83 percent, with a Type I error rate of 28 percent and a Type II error rate of 6 percent. As with Beaver's study, the more costly Type I error rate is larger than the Type II error rate.

Exhibit 5.12 shows the calculation of Altman's Z-score for PepsiCo for 2008. We use the originally reported amounts for PepsiCo instead of the adjusted amounts that eliminate nonrecurring items because Altman developed his model using originally reported amounts. If Altman had adjusted the earnings numbers to eliminate nonrecurring items, the coefficients would likely have been different; the financial ratios with the most discriminating power might have been different as well. Not surprisingly, PepsiCo's Z-score of 5.2709 clearly indicates a low probability of bankruptcy. FSAP computes Altman's Z-scores and the corresponding probabilities of bankruptcy (Appendix C).

The principal strengths of MDA are as follows:

1. It incorporates multiple financial ratios simultaneously.
2. It provides the appropriate coefficients for combining the independent variables.
3. It is easy to apply once the initial model has been developed.

EXHIBIT 5.12

Altman's Z-Score for PepsiCo

Net Working Capital/Total Assets 1.2[($10,806 − $8,787)/$35,994]	0.0673
Retained Earnings/Total Assets 1.4[$30,638/$35,994]	1.1917
Earnings before Interest and Taxes/Total Assets 3.3[($5,142 + $329 + $1,879)/$35,994]	0.6739
Market Value of Equity/Book Value of Liabilities 0.6[($54.77 × 1,553)/$23,888]	2.1364
Sales/Total Assets 1.0[$43,251/$35,994]	1.2016
Z-Score	5.2709

---

[15] The formula in Excel is =NORMSDIST(1–Z score). Altman developed his model so that higher positive Z-scores mean lower probability of bankruptcy; thus, computing the probability of bankruptcy requires that the normal density function be applied to 1 minus the Z-score. The website for this book (www.cengage.com/accounting/wahlen) contains an Excel spreadsheet for computing Altman's Z-score and the probability of bankruptcy. FSAP also computes these values.

The principal criticisms of MDA are as follows:

1. As in univariate applications, the researcher cannot be sure that the MDA model includes all relevant discriminating financial ratios. Most early studies, for example, used only accrual-basis income statement and balance sheet data and did not augment those data with cash flow data. MDA selects the best ratios from those provided, but that set does not necessarily provide the best explanatory power.

2. As in univariate applications, the researcher must subjectively judge the value of the cutoff score that best distinguishes bankrupt from nonbankrupt firms, taking into consideration the levels and costs of Type I and Type II errors.

3. The development and application of the MDA model requires firms to disclose the information needed to compute each financial ratio. Firms excluded because they do not provide the necessary data may bias the MDA model.

4. MDA assumes that each of the financial ratios for bankrupt and nonbankrupt firms is normally distributed. Firms experiencing financial distress often display unusually large or small ratios that can skew the distribution away from normal. In addition, the researcher cannot include dummy variables (for example, 0 if financial statements are audited and 1 if they are not audited). Dummy variables are not normally distributed.

5. MDA requires that the variance-covariance matrix of the explanatory variables be the same for bankrupt and nonbankrupt firms.[16]

Bankruptcy Prediction Models Using Logit Analysis

A third stage in the methodological development of bankruptcy prediction research was the move during the 1980s and early 1990s to using logit analysis instead of MDA. Logit does not require that the data display the underlying statistical properties described previously for MDA.

The use of logit analysis to develop a bankruptcy prediction model follows a procedure that is similar to that of MDA: (1) initial calculation of a large set of financial ratios, (2) reduction of the set of financial ratios to a subset that best predicts bankrupt and nonbankrupt firms, and (3) estimation of coefficients for each included variable.

The logit model defines the probability of bankruptcy as follows:

$$\text{Probability of Bankruptcy for a Firm} = \frac{1}{1 + e^{-y}}$$

where e equals approximately 2.718282. The exponent y is a multivariate function that includes a constant and coefficients for a set of explanatory variables (that is, financial statement ratios that discriminate bankrupt and nonbankrupt firms).

Ohlson[17] and Zavgren[18] used logit analysis to develop bankruptcy prediction models. Their models use different financial statement ratios than Altman's model does, and they are somewhat more complex to apply. We do not discuss their models in depth here, but interested readers can consult the research cited. Despite the shortcomings of discriminant models, Altman's Z-score model is still the most widely referenced and the one emphasized in this chapter.

---

[16] For an elaboration of these criticisms, see James A. Ohlson, "Financial Ratios and the Probabilistic Prediction of Bankruptcy," *Journal of Accounting Research* (Spring 1980), pp. 109–131, and Mark E. Zmijewski, "Methodological Issues Related to the Estimation of Financial Distress Prediction Models," *Journal of Accounting Research,* Supplement (1984), pp. 59–82.

[17] Ohlson, *op. cit.*.

[18] Christine V. Zavgren, "Assessing the Vulnerability to Failure of American Industrial Firms: A Logistic Analysis," *Journal of Business Finance and Accounting* (Spring 1985), pp. 19–45.

Application of Altman's Bankruptcy Prediction Model to W. T. Grant Company

W. T. Grant Company (Grant), one of the largest retailers in the United States at the time, filed for bankruptcy in October 1975. Case 3.3 in Chapter 3 includes financial statement data for Grant for its fiscal years ended January 31, 1967 through 1975. Exhibit 5.13 shows the calculation of Altman's Z-score for each of these fiscal years using amounts from Exhibits 3.38 and 3.39 of Case 3.3.

Altman's model shows a low probability of bankruptcy prior to the 1973 fiscal year, a move into the gray area in 1973 and 1974, and a high probability of bankruptcy in 1975. The absolute levels of these Z-scores are inflated because Grant was a retailer, whereas Altman developed the model using manufacturing firms. Retailing firms typically have a faster assets turnover than do manufacturing firms. In this case, the trend of the Z-score is more meaningful than its absolute level. Note that the Z-score declined steadily beginning in the 1970 fiscal year. With a few exceptions in individual years, each of the five components also declined steadily.[19]

Other Methodological Issues in Bankruptcy Prediction Research

Bankruptcy prediction research has addressed several other methodological issues.

1. **Equal Sample Sizes of Bankrupt and Nonbankrupt Firms.** The proportion of bankrupt firms in the economy is substantially smaller than the proportion of nonbankrupt firms. The matched-pairs research design common in most studies overfits the MDA and logit models toward the characteristics of bankrupt firms. This overfitting is not necessarily a problem if the objective is to identify characteristics of bankrupt firms. However, it will likely result in classifying too many nonbankrupt firms as bankrupt (a Type II error) when the model is applied to the broader population of firms. Researchers (such as Ohlson in the study cited previously) have addressed this criticism by using a proportion of nonbankrupt firms that more closely reflects the population of firms.

2. **Matching Bankrupt and Nonbankrupt Firms on Size and Industry Characteristics.** This matching precludes consideration of either of these factors as possible explanatory variables for bankruptcy. Yet compared to larger firms, small firms may experience greater difficulty obtaining needed funds. Industry membership, particularly for cyclical industries, may be an important factor in explaining bankruptcy. Some researchers select a random sample of nonbankrupt firms. Another approach is to develop the MDA or logit models for each industry. Platt,[20] for example, developed models for 16 two-digit SIC industries. The explanatory variables and their coefficients varied across the industries. Platt and Platt[21] normalized the financial ratios of each firm by relating them to the corresponding average industry ratio of the firm's industry. They found that normalized financial ratios increased the classification accuracy of their sample to 90 percent, versus 78 percent based on a model of non-normalized ratios.

3. **Use of Accrual versus Cash Flow Variables.** Until the mid-1980s, most bankruptcy research used accrual-basis balance sheet and income statement ratios or ratios from

---

[19] The solution to the Grant case indicates that prior to its 1975 fiscal year, Grant failed to provide adequately for uncollectible accounts. The effect of this action was to overstate the net working capital/assets, retained earnings/assets, and EBIT/assets components of the Z-score; understate the sales/assets component; and probably overstate the overall Z-score.

[20] Harlan D. Platt, "The Determinants of Interindustry Failure," *Journal of Economics and Business* (1989), pp. 107–126.

[21] Harlan D. Platt and Marjorie B. Platt, "Development of a Class of Stable Predictive Variables: The Case of Bankruptcy Prediction," *Journal of Business, Finance, and Accounting* (Spring 1990), pp. 31–51.

EXHIBIT 5.13

Application of Altman's Bankruptcy Prediction Models to W. T. Grant

Fiscal Year:	1968	1969	1970	1971	1972	1973	1974	1975
Altman's Z-Score Model								
Net Working Capital/Assets	0.54353	0.51341	0.44430	0.37791	0.44814	0.36508	0.38524	0.19390
Retained Earnings/Assets	0.43738	0.42669	0.41929	0.38511	0.34513	0.31023	0.25712	0.04873
EBIT/Assets	0.41358	0.44611	0.44228	0.38848	0.27820	0.26029	0.25470	(0.63644)
Market Value Equity/Book Value Liabilities	0.86643	1.01740	0.95543	0.89539	0.69788	0.50578	0.10211	0.01730
Sales/Assets	1.77564	1.76199	1.71325	1.67974	1.57005	1.58678	1.54797	1.62802
Z-Score	4.03656	4.16560	3.97455	3.72663	3.33940	3.02816	2.54714	1.25151
Probability of Bankruptcy Range	Low	Low	Low	Low	Low	Gray	Gray	High
Probability of Bankruptcy	0.12%	0.07%	0.15%	0.32%	0.97%	2.13%	6.09%	40.07%

the "funds flow" statement, which defined funds as working capital. The transition to a cash definition of funds in the statement of cash flows led researchers to add cash flow variables to bankruptcy prediction models. Casey and Bartczak,[22] among others, found that adding cash flow from operations/current liabilities and cash flow from operations/total liabilities did not significantly add explanatory power to models based on accrual basis amounts. However, other researchers have found contrary results, suggesting that the use of cash flow variables may enhance bankruptcy prediction.[23]

4. **Stability in Bankruptcy Prediction Models over Time.** A final methodological issue in bankruptcy prediction research concerns the stability of the bankruptcy prediction models over time with regard to the explanatory variables included and their coefficients. Bankruptcy laws and their judicial interpretation change over time. The frequency of bankruptcy filings changes as economic conditions change. Changes occur in the mix of industry concentration of firms. New financing vehicles emerge (for example, redeemable preferred stock or debt and equity securities with various option rights) that previous MDA or logit models did not consider in their formulation. To apply these models in practical settings, the analyst should update them periodically.

Begley, Ming, and Watts[24] applied Altman's MDA model and Ohlson's logit model to a sample of bankrupt and nonbankrupt firms in the 1980s, a later period than that used by Altman and Ohlson. Begley, Ming, and Watts found that the Type I and Type II error rates increased substantially relative to those in the original studies. They then reestimated the coefficients for each model using data for a portion of their 1980s sample. The coefficients on the liquidity ratios increased and the coefficients on the debt ratio decreased relative to those in the original studies. When they applied the original and reestimated coefficients to the 1980s sample, they observed a reduction in Type II errors but no improvement in Type I errors for the Altman model. For the Ohlson model, they found that a reduction in Type II errors was offset by an equal increase in Type I errors. Thus, the revised coefficients result in fewer errors in classifying nonbankrupt firms as bankrupt, but similar or worse errors occur in classifying bankrupt firms as nonbankrupt.

Synthesis of Bankruptcy Prediction Research

The preceding sections of this chapter discussed bankruptcy prediction models. Similar streams of research relate to commercial bank lending,[25] bond ratings,[26] corporate restructurings,[27] corporate liquidations,[28] and earnings management.[29] Although the statistical models and relevant financial statement ratios vary among the numerous studies,

---

[22] Casey and Bartczak, *op. cit.*

[23] For a summary of this research, see Michael J. Gombola, Mark E. Haskins, J. Edward Ketz, and David D. Williams, "Cash Flow in Bankruptcy Prediction," *Financial Management* (Winter 1987), pp. 55–65.

[24] Joy Begley, Jin Ming, and Susan Watts, "Bankruptcy Classification Errors in the 1980s: An Empirical Analysis of Altman's and Ohlson's Models," *Review of Accounting Studies* 1, No. 4 (1996), pp. 267–284.

[25] Edward Altman, *Corporate Financial Distress and Bankruptcy,* 2nd ed., (New York: John Wiley & Sons, 1993), pp. 245–266.

[26] George E. Pinches and Kent A. Mingo, "A Multivariate Analysis of Industrial Bond Ratings," *Journal of Finance* (March 1973), pp. 1–18.

[27] James E. Seward, "Corporate Restructuring and Reorganization" in *Handbook of Modern Finance,* ed. Dennis Logue, (New York: Warren, Gorham & Lamont, 1993), pp. E8–1 to E8–36.

[28] Cornelius J. Casey, Victor McGee, and Clyde P. Stickney, "Discriminating between Reorganized and Liquidated Firms in Bankruptcy," *Accounting Review* (April 1986), pp. 249–262.

[29] Messod D. Beneish, "Detecting GAAP Violation: Implications for Assessing Earnings Management among Firms with Extreme Financial Performance," *Journal of Accounting and Public Policy* (1997), pp. 271–309.

certain commonalities do appear. This section summarizes the factors that explain bankruptcy most consistently across various studies.

Investment Factors

The following two factors relate to the asset side of the balance sheet:

1. Relative Liquidity of a Firm's Assets. The probability of financial distress decreases as the relative liquidity of a firm's assets increases. Firms with relatively large proportions of current assets tend to experience less financial distress than firms with fixed assets or intangible assets as the dominant assets. Greater asset liquidity means that the firm has or will soon generate the necessary cash to meet creditors' claims. Note that the expected return from more liquid assets (for example, cash, marketable securities, and accounts receivable) is usually less (reflecting lower risk) than the expected return from fixed and intangible assets. Thus, firms must balance their mix of assets to obtain the desired return/risk profile. This chapter has described a number of ratios that analysts typically use to measure relative liquidity—cash/total assets, current assets/total assets, and net working capital/total assets; analysts use ratios such as fixed assets/total assets to measure relative illiquidity.

2. Rate of Asset Turnover. The returns from investment of funds in any asset are ultimately realized in cash. Firms acquire fixed assets or create intangibles to produce a salable product (inventory) or to create a desired service. Goods or services are often sold on account (accounts receivable) and later collected in cash. The faster assets turn over, the more quickly they generate cash. Thus, a retailer may have the same proportion of fixed assets to total assets as a manufacturing firm. The other assets of the retailer (that is, accounts receivable and inventories) likely turn over more quickly and thus are more liquid. Commonly used financial ratios for this factor are total assets turnover, accounts receivable turnover, and inventory turnover. The working capital turnover ratio [= sales/(current assets minus current liabilities)] and fixed assets turnover ratio (= sales/fixed assets) have not generally shown statistical significance in studies of financial distress.

Financing Factors

The following two factors relate to the liability side of the balance sheet:

1. Relative Proportion of Total Debt in the Capital Structure. Firms experience bankruptcy because they are unable to pay liabilities as they come due. The higher the proportion of total liabilities in the capital structure, the higher the probability that firms will experience bankruptcy. Firms with lower proportions of debt tend to have unused borrowing capacity that they can use in times of difficulty. Some measure of the proportion of debt in the capital structure appears in virtually all bankruptcy prediction models. Commonly used ratios include total liabilities/total assets and total liabilities/shareholders' equity.

2. Relative Proportion of Short-Term Debt in the Capital Structure. This factor has a similar rationale to that described previously except that the earlier maturity of short-term debt increases the risk of bankruptcy. Thus, considering only the financing side of the balance sheet, a retailer using extensive short-term bank and creditor financing will likely have a greater risk of bankruptcy than a manufacturer with a similar proportion of total liabilities but whose liabilities are primarily long-term debt. A commonly used ratio for this factor is current liabilities/total assets.

Operating Factors

The following two factors relate to the operating activities of a firm:

1. Relative Level of Profitability. Profitable firms ultimately generate positive cash flows. Also, compared to unprofitable firms, profitable firms are usually able to borrow funds more easily. Firms with low or negative profitability must often rely on available cash or additional borrowing to meet financial commitments as they come due. Research has demonstrated that most bankruptcies initiate with one or several consecutive years of poor operating performance. Firms with unused debt capacity can often borrow for a year or two until the operating difficulties reverse. A combination of weak profitability and high debt ratios usually triggers financial distress. Commonly used financial ratios for profitability are net income/assets, income before interest and taxes/assets, net income/sales, and cash flow from operations/assets. The second profitability measure (income before interest and taxes/assets) identifies profitability problems in the core input/output markets of a firm before debt service costs and income taxes are considered. The third measure (net income/sales) appears in bankruptcy distress prediction models because profit margin, not assets turnover, is usually the driving force behind return on assets. The fourth measure (cash flow from operations/assets) substitutes cash flow from operations for net income in measuring profitability on the premise that cash pays the bills, not earnings.

2. Variability of Operations. Firms that experience variability in their operations (for example, from cyclical sales patterns) exhibit a greater likelihood of bankruptcy than do firms with low variability. During the down times in the cycle, such firms often struggle to obtain financing to meet financial commitments and maintain operating levels. The risk of bankruptcy in these cases relates to the unknown length of the down portion of the cycle. For how many years can a firm hold on until the cycle reverses? Researchers typically use the change in sales or the change in net income from the previous year to measure variability, although a longer period seems more reasonable.

Other Possible Explanatory Variables

Three other factors examined in bankruptcy research warrant discussion.

1. Size. Studies of bankruptcy, particularly since the early 1980s, have increasingly identified size as an important explanatory variable. Larger firms generally have access to a wider range of financing sources and more flexibility to redeploy assets than do smaller firms. Until recently, larger firms experienced very low probabilities of bankruptcy. Most studies measure size using total assets.

2. Growth. Studies of bankruptcy often include some measure of growth (for example, growth in sales, assets, or net income) as a possible explanatory variable. The statistical significance of growth as an independent variable has varied considerably across studies. Therefore, it is difficult to conclude much about its relative importance. The mixed results may relate in part to ambiguity in how growth relates to bankruptcy. Rapidly growing firms often need external financing to cover cash shortfalls from operations and to permit acquisitions of fixed assets. These firms often display financial ratios typical of a firm in financial difficulty (that is, high debt ratios and weak profitability). Yet their growth potential provides access to capital that allows them to survive. Firms in the late maturity or early decline phase of their life cycle may experience slow (or negative) growth and display healthy financial ratios, but prospects are sufficiently poor that the probability of future financial difficulty is high.

3. Qualified Audit Opinion. Several studies have examined the information value of a qualified audit opinion in predicting bankruptcy. Hopwood, McKeown, and Mutchler compared the predictive accuracy of a qualified audit opinion versus models that include only financial ratios in predicting bankruptcy.[30] They found that the qualified audit opinion had similar predictive accuracy to that of the models based on financial ratios. This

---

[30] William Hopwood, James C. McKeown, and Jane F. Mutchler, "A Reexamination of Auditor versus Model Accuracy within the Context of the Going-Concern Opinion Decision," *Contemporary Accounting Research* (Spring 1994), pp. 409–431.

result is not surprising if auditors use bankruptcy prediction models in deciding whether to issue a qualified opinion. Chen and Church found that the negative stock price reaction at the time of a bankruptcy filing was less for firms that had previously had a qualified audit opinion than for firms that had only clean audit opinions, suggesting that the audit opinion had information content.[31]

Some Final Thoughts

Bankruptcy prediction research represents an effort to integrate traditional financial statement analysis with statistical modeling. This area of research evolved between the mid-1960s and mid-1980s from relatively simple univariate models to multivariate models. The models developed by Altman, Ohlson, and Zavgren rely on data that are decades old and are based on business activities and bankruptcy laws that differ from those currently encountered. Nevertheless, security analysts and academic researchers continue to use these models and they appear relatively robust despite the numerous limitations discussed previously.[32]

MARKET EQUITY BETA RISK

Firms face additional risks besides credit and bankruptcy risk. Recessions, inflation, changes in interest rates, foreign currency fluctuations, rising unemployment, and similar economic factors affect all firms, but in varying degrees depending on the nature of their operation. The investor in a firm's common stock must consider these dimensions of risk when making investment decisions. Economic theory teaches that differences in expected rates of return between investment alternatives should relate to differences in risk. Thus, we can turn to equity markets to obtain a broader measure of risk. Then we will relate this market measure of risk to financial statement information.

Studies of market rates of return have traditionally used the CAPM (capital asset pricing model). The research typically regresses the rate of returns on a particular firm's common shares [dividends plus (minus) capital gains (losses)/beginning-of-period share price] over some period of time on the excess of the returns of all common stocks over the risk-free rate. The regression takes the following form:

$$
\begin{array}{l}\text{Returns on Common Stock} \\ \text{of a Particular Firm}\end{array} = \begin{array}{l}\text{Risk-Free} \\ \text{Interest Rate}\end{array} + \begin{array}{l}\text{Market} \\ \text{Beta}\end{array} \times \left[\begin{array}{l}\text{Market} \\ \text{Return}\end{array} - \begin{array}{l}\text{Risk-Free} \\ \text{Interest Rate}\end{array}\right] + \text{Error}
$$

The beta coefficient measures the covariability of a firm's returns with the returns of a diversified portfolio of all shares traded on the market (in excess of the risk-free interest rate). Firms with a market beta of 1.0 experience covariability in returns equal to the average covariability of the stock market as a whole. Firms with a beta greater than 1.0 experience greater covariability than the average. Firms with a beta less than 1.0 experience less covariability than the average firm. A beta of 1.20 suggests 20 percent greater covariability. A beta of .80 suggests 20 percent less covariability.

---

[31] Kevin C. W. Chen and Bryan K. Church, "Going Concern Opinions and the Market's Reaction to Bankruptcy Filings," *Accounting Review* (January 1996), pp. 117–128.

[32] A recent study models bankruptcy prediction as an option pricing valuation using market values. The authors compare the prediction accuracy of this market-based model with the Altman and Ohlson models and find that their model has better prediction accuracy. However, using either the Altman or Ohlson model in addition to the option pricing model adds to the prediction accuracy. See Stephen A. Hillegeist, Donald P. Cram, Elizabeth K. Keating, and Kyle G. Lundstedt, "Assessing the Probability of Bankruptcy," *Review of Accounting Studies* (March 2004), pp. 5–34.

Beta is a measure of the *systematic* (or *nondiversifiable*) *risk* of the firm. The market, through the pricing of a firm's shares, rewards shareholders for bearing systematic risk. Elements of risk that are not systematic are referred to as nonsystematic risk. Nonsystematic risk factors include firm-specific risks such as product obsolescence; labor strike; loss of a product liability lawsuit; and damages from fire, weather, or natural disaster. By constructing a diversified portfolio of securities, the investor can eliminate the effects of nonsystematic risk on the returns to the portfolio as a whole. Thus, market pricing should provide no returns for the assumption of nonsystematic risk.

Studies of the determinants of market beta have identified the following three principal explanatory variables:[33]

1. Degree of operating leverage
2. Degree of financial leverage
3. Variability of sales

Each of these factors causes the earnings of a particular firm to vary over time.

Operating leverage refers to the extent of fixed operating costs in the cost structure. Costs such as depreciation and amortization do not vary with the level of sales. Other costs, such as insurance and executive and administrative salaries and benefits, may vary somewhat with the level of sales, but they remain relatively fixed for any particular period. The presence of fixed operating costs leads to variations in operating earnings as sales increase and decrease. Likewise, the presence of debt in the capital structure adds a fixed cost for interest and creates the potential for causing earnings to increase or decrease as sales vary.

The presence of these fixed costs does not necessarily lead to earnings fluctuations over time. A firm with stable or growing sales may be able to adjust the level of fixed assets and related financing (for example, through leasing) to the level of sales, in effect converting fixed costs into variable costs. Firms with high fixed costs from operating and financial leverage, such as electric utilities, historically have had a regulated form of monopoly power to price their services to cover costs regardless of demand. Such firms likewise have not experienced wide variations in earnings. Operating and financial leverage create variations in earnings when sales vary and firms cannot alter their level of fixed costs. Thus, we would expect capital-intensive firms in cyclical industries to experience wide variations in earnings over the business cycle.

Research has shown a link between changes in earnings and changes in stock prices.[34] Thus, operating leverage, financial leverage, and variability of sales should result in fluctuations in the market returns for a particular firm's common shares. The average returns for all firms in the market should reflect the average level of operating leverage, financial leverage, and sales variability of these firms. Therefore, the market beta for a particular firm reflects its degree of variability relative to the average firm. Chapters 11 and 14 discuss more fully the relation between financial statement information and market beta and the use of market beta in the valuation of firms.

---

[33] Robert S. Hamada, "The Effect of a Firm's Capital Structure on the Systematic Risk of Common Stocks," *Journal of Finance* (May 1972), pp. 435–452; Barr Rosenberg and Walt McKibben, "The Prediction of Systematic and Specific Risk in Common Stocks," *Journal of Financial and Quantitative Analysis* (March 1973), pp. 317–333; James M. Gahlon and James A. Gentry, "On the Relationship between Systematic Risk and Degrees of Operating and Financial Leverage," *Financial Management* (Summer 1982), pp. 15–23.

[34] Ray Ball and Philip Brown, "An Empirical Evaluation of Accounting Income Numbers," *Journal of Accounting Research* (Autumn 1968), pp. 159–178.

FINANCIAL REPORTING MANIPULATION RISK

Enron, Parmalat, WorldCom, Global Crossing, Ahold, Sunbeam, AIG, Fannie Mae, Tyco, Societe General, Allied Irish, Satyam, and other companies have been the subject of SEC and other government regulatory investigations and negative media coverage in recent years for allegedly preparing financial statements outside the limits of permissible accounting standards. The firms violated accounting standards in an effort to portray themselves in a more favorable light. As a consequence, because they cannot rely on misleading financial statements when assessing profitability and risk, analysts must be vigilant in order to gain comfort that financial statements are not misleading. This section explores the characteristics of firms accused of falsifying their financial statements and describes tools for assessing this type of risk.

At the outset, we need to recognize a distinction between earnings manipulation and earnings management. *Earnings manipulation,* which refers to reporting amounts outside the limits of U.S. GAAP or IFRS, is the subject of this section. *Earnings management* refers to choices made within the limits of U.S. GAAP or IFRS or may refer to actual operating decisions that affect reported earnings. Not all financial economists or accountants agree with this distinction between earnings manipulation and earnings management, but it is important to at least appreciate the continuum from innocuous attempts to window-dress earnings to flagrant disregard for financial reporting rules. Chapter 9 discusses less egregious forms of earnings management. The focus of this discussion is on the more flagrant violations of accounting standards and regulations promulgated by oversight bodies such as the FASB, IASB, and SEC.

Motivations for Earnings Manipulation

A firm might manipulate earnings for the following reasons:

1. To influence stock prices positively (or delay stock price declines) by meeting or beating the market's expectations for earnings
2. To increase management bonuses based on earnings or stock prices
3. To obtain debt financing at a lower cost by appearing more profitable or less risky
4. To avoid violation of debt covenants or influence the effects of other binding constraints from accounting-based contracts
5. To influence the outcomes of transactions that affect corporate control, such as proxy fights, takeovers, initial public offerings, seasoned equity offerings, and share repurchases
6. To avoid regulatory intervention or adverse political consequences

Empirical Research on Earnings Manipulation

Dechow, Sloan, and Sweeney[35] examined the governance characteristics of firms subject to accounting and auditing enforcement actions by the SEC. They found that such firms have weak corporate governance structures, including the absence of an audit committee within their board of directors, the appointment of the founder of the company as the CEO (chief executive officer), the appointment of the CEO as chairperson of the board, and the domination of the board by insiders (employees, consultants, or individuals otherwise closely associated with the firm). The SEC enforcement actions led to a 9 percent reduction in

---

[35] Patricia M. Dechow, Richard G. Sloan, and Amy P. Sweeney, "Causes and Consequences of Earnings Manipulation: An Analysis of Firms Subject to Enforcement Actions by the SEC," *Contemporary Accounting Research* (Spring 1996), pp. 1–36.

stock price on average, an increase in the bid-ask spread, less analyst consensus on earnings forecasts, and increased short interest, each of which likely increases the firm's cost of capital. Nevertheless, governance is neither a solution nor a well-defined concept. For example, the World Council for Corporate Governance awarded Satyam its Golden Peacock Award for Corporate Governance in 2008, shortly before it was uncovered in January 2009 that the company had perpetrated one of the largest financial reporting frauds in corporate history.

Given the importance of identifying financial reporting risk, Beneish developed a probit model to identify the financial characteristics of firms likely to engage in earnings manipulation. Beneish developed both a twelve-factor model[36] and an eight-factor model.[37] The twelve-factor model relies on a combination of financial statement items and changes in stock prices for a firm's shares. The eight-factor model uses only financial statement items. Beneish developed the models using data for firms subject to SEC enforcement actions related to fraudulent accounting reports.

Developing these models involves identifying characteristics of firms likely to manipulate earnings, selecting financial statement ratios or other measures of these characteristics, and then using probit regressions to select the significant factors and the appropriate coefficient for each factor (similar to the MDA and logit approaches for identifying predictors of bankruptcy, described earlier in this chapter). Applying the coefficient to the value of each factor for a particular firm yields a score that becomes the value of y.

Unlike logit models, which convert the value of y into a probability based on a logistical distribution using the somewhat nonintuitive metric, $\frac{1}{1 + e^{-y}}$, probit converts y into a probability using a standardized normal distribution and a specified prior probability of earnings manipulation. The command NORMSDIST in Excel, when applied to a particular value of y, converts it to the appropriate probability value.[38] Positive coefficients increase the probability of earnings manipulation.

Beneish's eight factors and the rationale for their inclusion are as follows:

1. *Days Sales in Receivables Index (DSRI).* This index relates the ratio of accounts receivable at the end of the current year as a percentage of sales for the current year to the corresponding amounts for the preceding year. A large increase in accounts receivable as a percentage of sales might indicate an overstatement of accounts receivable and sales during the current year to boost earnings. Such an increase also might result from a change in the firm's credit policy (for example, liberalizing credit terms).

2. *Gross Margin Index (GMI).* This index relates gross margin (that is, sales minus cost of goods sold) as a percentage of sales last year to the gross margin as a percentage of sales for the current year. A decline in the gross margin percentage will result in an index greater than 1.0. Firms with weaker profitability this year are more likely to engage in earnings manipulation.

3. *Asset Quality Index (AQI).* Asset quality refers to the proportion of total assets comprising assets other than (1) current assets; (2) property, plant, and equipment; and (3) investments in securities. The remaining assets include intangibles for which future

---

[36] Beneish, *op. cit.* For an instructional case applying this model to an actual company, see Christine I. Wiedman, "Instructional Case: Detecting Earnings Manipulation," *Issues in Accounting Education* (February 1999), pp. 145–176. Also see Messod D. Beneish, "A Note on Wiedman's (1999) Instructional Case: Detecting Earnings Manipulation," *Issues in Accounting Education* (May 1999), pp. 369–370.

[37] Messod D. Beneish, "The Detection of Earnings Manipulation," *Financial Analyst Journal* (September/October 1999), pp. 24–36.

[38] In contrast to Altman's Z-score model, Beneish set up his model so that larger positive values increase the probability of earnings manipulation. Thus, one can simply apply the normal density function directly to the value of y to compute the probability of earnings manipulation.

benefits are less certain than for current assets and property, plant, and equipment. The AQI equals the proportion of these potentially lower-quality assets during the current year relative to the preceding year. An increase in the proportion might suggest an increased effort to capitalize and defer costs the firm should have expensed.

4. **Sales Growth Index (SGI).** This index equals sales of the current year relative to sales of the preceding year. Growth does not necessarily imply manipulation. However, growing companies usually rely on external financing more than mature companies do. The need for low-cost external financing might motivate managers to manipulate sales and earnings. Growing companies are often young and tend to have less developed governance practices to monitor managers' manipulation efforts.

5. **Depreciation Index (DEPI).** This index equals depreciation expense as a percentage of net property, plant, and equipment before depreciation for the preceding year relative to the corresponding percentage for the current year. A ratio greater than 1.0 indicates that the firm has slowed the rate of depreciation, perhaps by lengthening depreciable lives, thereby increasing earnings.

6. **Selling and Administrative Expense Index (SAI).** This index equals selling and administrative expenses as a percentage of sales for the current year to the corresponding percentage for the preceding year. An index greater than 1.0 might suggest increased marketing expenditures that would lead to increased sales in future periods. Firms not able to sustain the sales growth might be induced to engage in earnings manipulation. An alternative interpretation is that an index greater than 1.0 suggests that the firm has not taken advantage of capitalizing various costs; instead, it has expensed them. Firms attempting to manipulate earnings would defer costs, and the index value would be less than 1.0. If this latter explanation is descriptive, the coefficient on this variable will be negative. Thus, the interpretation of this component of Beneish's fraud model is conditional.

7. **Leverage Index (LVGI).** This index equals the proportion of total financing comprising current liabilities and long-term debt for the current year relative to the proportion for the preceding year. An increase in the proportion of debt likely subjects a firm to a greater risk of violating debt covenants and the need to manipulate earnings to avoid the violation.

8. **Total Accruals to Total Assets (TATA).** Total accruals equals the difference between income from continuing operations and cash flow from operations. Dividing total accruals by total assets at the end of the year scales total accruals across firms and across time. Beneish used this variable as an indicator of the extent to which earnings result from accruals instead of from cash flows. A large excess of income from continuing operations over cash flow from operations indicates that accruals play a large part in measuring income. Accruals can serve as a means of manipulating earnings.

Beneish developed a weighted probit model that takes the proportion of earnings manipulations into account and an unweighted probit model. We illustrate the unweighted model in this section and FSAP uses the unweighted model to compute Beneish's Manipulation Index and the corresponding probabilities of earnings manipulation. The unweighted model tends to classify more nonmanipulating firms as manipulators (higher Type II error), but lowers the most costly Type I error rate. The value of y is as follows:

$$y = -4.840 + 0.920\,(\text{DSRI}) + 0.528\,(\text{GMI}) + 0.404\,(\text{AQI}) + 0.892\,(\text{SGI}) + 0.115\,(\text{DEPI})$$
$$-\,0.172\,(\text{SAI}) - 0.327\,(\text{LVGI}) + 4.670\,(\text{TATA})$$

The coefficient on SAI is negative, suggesting that a lower selling and administrative expense to sales percentage in the current year relative to the preceding year increases the likelihood that the firm engaged in earnings manipulation to boost earnings. The coefficient on the leverage variable also is negative. A decrease in the proportion of debt in the capital structure may suggest decreased ability to obtain funds from borrowing and the need to engage in earnings manipulation to portray a healthier firm. The coefficients on the SAI and LVGI variables were not statistically significant. However, one cannot interpret the sign or statistical significance of a coefficient in a multivariate model independent of the other variables in the model; so these factors must be included.

Application of Beneish's Model to Sunbeam Corporation

We illustrate the application of Beneish's probit model to the financial statements of Sunbeam Corporation (Sunbeam). Sunbeam manufactures countertop kitchen appliances and barbecue grills. Its sales growth and profitability slowed considerably in the mid-1990s, and the firm experienced market price declines for its common stock. The firm hired Al Dunlap in mid-1996 as CEO. Known as "Chainsaw Al," he had developed a reputation for dispassionately cutting costs and strategically redirecting troubled companies. Dunlap laid off half the workforce, closed or consolidated more than half of Sunbeam's factories, and divested several businesses in 1996 and 1997. He also announced major growth initiatives centering on new products and corporate acquisitions.

The reported results for 1997 showed significant improvement over 1996. Sales increased 18.7 percent while gross margin increased from 8.5 percent to 28.3 percent. The stock price more than doubled between the announcement of Dunlap's hiring in mid-1996 and the end of 1997.

The turnaround appeared to proceed according to plan until the firm announced earnings for the first quarter of 1998, seven quarters into the turnaround effort. To the surprise of analysts and the stock market, Sunbeam reported a net loss for the quarter. Close scrutiny by analysts and the media suggested that Sunbeam might have manipulated earnings in 1997. The SEC instituted a formal investigation into this possibility in mid-1997. Sunbeam responded in October 1998 by restating its financial statements from the fourth quarter of 1996 to the first quarter of 1998. The restatements revealed that Sunbeam had engaged in various actions that boosted earnings for 1997. The actions included the following:

- Sunbeam instituted "early buy" and "bill and hold" programs in 1997 to encourage retailers to purchase inventory from Sunbeam during the last few months of 1997. Sunbeam did not adequately provide for returns and canceled transactions, resulting in an overstatement of sales and net income for 1997.
- Sunbeam overstated a restructuring charge in the fourth quarter of 1996 for expenses that should have appeared in the income statement for 1997.
- Sunbeam understated bad debt expense for 1997.

Exhibit 5.14 shows the application of Beneish's earnings manipulation model to the originally reported financial statement amounts and the restated amounts for 1996 and 1997.[39]

Selecting the cutoff probability that signals earnings manipulation involves trade-offs between Type I and Type II errors, in a manner similar to that of Beaver's bankruptcy prediction tests discussed earlier. A Type I error involves failing to identify a firm as an income

---

[39] The website for this book (www.cengage.com/accounting/whalen) contains an Excel spreadsheet called Beneish's Manipulation Index for use in calculating the probability of earnings manipulation using Beneish's probit model. This spreadsheet is adapted from one prepared by Professor Christine I. Wiedman (see Wiedman 1999, *op. cit.*). FSAP also computes Beneish's Manipulation Index and the corresponding probability of earnings manipulation.

EXHIBIT 5.14

Application of Beneish's Earnings Manipulation Model to Sunbeam Corporation

Value of Variable before Applying Coefficient	Originally Reported		Restated	
	1996	**1997**	**1996**	**1997**
Days in Receivables Index	1.020	1.167	1.020	0.982
Gross Margin Index	2.403	0.300	2.303	0.393
Asset Quality Index	0.912	0.928	0.912	0.919
Sales Growth Index	0.968	1.187	0.968	1.090
Depreciation Index	0.752	1.284	0.752	1.290
Selling and Administrative Expense Index	1.608	0.516	1.665	0.632
Leverage Index	1.457	0.795	1.457	0.917
Total Accruals/Total Assets	(0.196)	0.117	(0.208)	0.055
Beneish's Manipulation *y* Value	(2.983)	(1.827)	(3.101)	(2.388)
Probability of Manipulation	0.143%	3.386%	0.096%	0.848%

Note: The amounts in this table are rounded to three decimal places.

manipulator when it turns out to be one. A Type II error involves identifying a firm as an income manipulator when it turns out not to be one. The Type I error is more costly to the investor than a Type II error is. The cutoff probability depends on the analyst's view of the relative cost of the Type I error compared to a Type II error. That is, how much more costly is it to classify an actual earnings manipulator as a nonmanipulator than to classify an actual nonmanipulator as a manipulator? A Type I error can result in an investor losing *all* of the investment in a firm when the manipulation comes to light. In contrast, misclassifying an actual nonmanipulator results only in a forgone investment opportunity, the amount being the return that could have been earned had an investment been made in the firm. However, the investor presumably invested the funds in another firm. Thus, as with bankruptcy prediction, the Type I error is more costly. If a particular investment makes up a small proportion of an investor's diversified portfolio of investments, a Type I error is less costly than if the investment comprises a more significant proportion of a less diversified portfolio of investments. The cutoff probabilities for various relative mixtures of Type I and Type II error costs follow.

Cost of Type I Error Relative to Type II Error	Cutoff Probability
10:1	6.85%
20:1	3.76%
30:1	3.76%
40:1 or higher	2.94%

Exhibit 5.14 indicates that the probability of manipulation for Sunbeam for 1996 is 0.143 percent based on its originally reported amounts. This probability level falls well below the cutoff probabilities listed previously for all mixtures of Type I and Type II errors;

therefore, it does not suggest earnings manipulation. On the other hand, the probability for 1997 jumps to 3.386 percent. (See Exhibit 5.14.) Under the assumption of a 40:1 Type I to Type II cost relation, you would conclude that Sunbeam is a manipulator. An examination of changes in the individual variables between 1996 and 1997 signals the nature of the manipulation that might have occurred. TATA increased significantly. Sunbeam reported a significant increase in income from continuing operations from a net loss of $196.7 million in 1996 to a net profit of $123.1 million 1997, but cash flow from operations turned from $13.3 million in 1996 to a negative $8.2 million in 1997. Buildups of accounts receivable and inventories are major reasons for the negative cash flow from operations in 1997. The days receivable index increased between these two years, consistent with the buildup of receivables related to the early buy-and-bill and hold programs. The SGI also increased, consistent with the aggressive recognition of revenues. The depreciation index variable increased between the two years, but the firm's financial statements and notes provide no obvious explanation to suggest manipulation. The gross margin improved significantly between the two years, moderating the increased probability of earnings manipulation. However, this improvement is misleading because of failure to provide adequately for returns and canceled transactions.

Exhibit 5.14 indicates that the probabilities of manipulation based on the restated data are below the cutoff points for 1996 and 1997. The most important difference between the reported and restated probabilities arises for 1997. The downward restatement of income from continuing operations results in fewer accruals, moderating the influence of this variable on the manipulation index. Interestingly, the model would not indicate that Sunbeam was an earnings manipulator if it had reported accurately to begin with (that is, reported the restated data). Initially reporting the restated data, however, would likely have decreased Sunbeam's stock price, which Dunlap presumably wanted to avoid.

Summary of Earnings Manipulation Risk

The recent revelations of corporate reporting abuses add to the importance of assessing whether firms have intentionally manipulated earnings. Academic research on earnings manipulation is at an early stage of development. The data in the studies discussed previously deal with reporting violations prior to the mid-1990s. The business environment since that time has changed dramatically, particularly for technology-based companies. Additional research in this area might be expected in coming years. Also, the analyst should note that the assessment of earnings manipulation risk is not restricted to the construction of financial ratios. Also relevant are qualitative factors that might change the incentives of managers to incur the potential costs of manipulating earnings, such as an increase in compensation based on stock options, an expectation of growth, or extensive related party transactions.

SUMMARY

An effective analysis of risk requires the analyst to consider a wide range of factors (for example, government regulatory status, industry competition, technological change, management's health, competitors' actions, profitability, and financial reporting risk). This chapter examines those dimensions of risk that have financial consequences and impact the financial statements.

This chapter began with a discussion of financial flexibility, which is an extension of profitability analysis, but with an emphasis on partitioning the firm's financial statements into operating and financing components. With an understanding of how leverage can be strategically used to increase returns available to shareholders, we then examined the analysis of financial risk associated with the use of leverage along the following four dimensions:

1. *With respect to time frame:* We examined the analysis of a firm's ability to pay liabilities coming due the next year (short-term liquidity risk analysis) and its ability to pay liabilities coming due over a longer term (long-term solvency risk analysis). The financial ratios examined a firm's need for cash and other liquid resources relative to amounts coming due within various time frames.

2. *With respect to the degree of financial distress:* We emphasized the need to consider risk as falling along a continuum from low risk to high risk of financial distress. Firms with a great deal of financial flexibility fall on the low side of this continuum. Most credit analysis occurs on the low- to medium-risk side of this continuum. Most bankruptcy risk analysis occurs on the medium- to high-risk side of this continuum.

3. *With respect to covariability of returns with other securities in the market:* We briefly highlighted the use of market equity beta as an indicator of systematic risk with the market, which is affected by the types of risk analyzed in this chapter.

4. *With respect to financial reporting:* We described various motives that induce managers to manipulate and report earnings numbers and other accounting data outside the bounds of GAAP and illustrated a model that estimates the likelihood of financial reporting manipulation.

Analysts and academic researchers refer to the first two dimensions of risk as nonsystematic, or firm-specific, risk. They refer to the third dimension of risk as systematic risk. They sometimes refer to the fourth dimension of risk as information risk. Common factors come into play in all four settings of risk analysis. Fixed costs related to operations or to financing constrain the flexibility of a firm to adapt to changing economic, business, and firm-specific conditions. The profitability and cash-generating ability of a firm allow it to operate within its constraints or to change the constraints in some desirable direction. If the constraints are too high or the capabilities to adapt are too low, a firm faces the risk of financial distress. Firms facing potential financial distress are more likely to manipulate earnings and accounting information.

QUESTIONS, EXERCISES, PROBLEMS, AND CASES

Questions and Exercises

5.1 INTERPRETING THE ALTERNATIVE DECOMPOSITION OF ROCE WITH NEGATIVE NET FINANCIAL OBLIGATIONS. Suppose an analyst reformulates financial statements to prepare the alternative decomposition of ROCE for a firm with no debt. The analyst determines that the company holds excess cash as large marketable equity securities. The result will be net financial obligations that are negative. Assume that operating ROA is positive and large. How will this affect the decomposition of ROCE = Operating ROA + (Leverage × Spread)? How do you interpret the net borrowing rate for this firm?

5.2 RELATION BETWEEN CURRENT RATIO AND OPERATING CASH FLOW TO CURRENT LIABILITIES RATIO. A firm has experienced an increasing current ratio but a decreasing operating cash flow to current liabilities ratio during the last three years. What is the likely explanation for these results?

5.3 RELATION BETWEEN CURRENT RATIO AND QUICK RATIO. A firm has experienced a decrease in its current ratio but an increase in its quick ratio during the last three years. What is the likely explanation for these results?

5.4 RELATION BETWEEN WORKING CAPITAL TURNOVER RATIOS AND CASH FLOW FROM OPERATIONS. While a firm's sales and net income have been steady during the last three years, the firm has experienced a decrease in its accounts receivable and inventory turnovers and an increase in its accounts payable turnover. What is the likely direction of change in cash flow from operations? How would your answer be different if sales and net income were increasing?

5.5 EFFECT OF TRANSACTIONS ON DEBT RATIOS. A firm had the following values for the four debt ratios discussed in the chapter:

Liabilities to Assets Ratio: less than 1.0
Liabilities to Shareholders' Equity Ratio: equal to 1.0
Long-Term Debt to Long-Term Capital Ratio: less than 1.0
Long-Term Debt to Shareholders' Equity Ratio: less than 1.0

a. Indicate whether each of the following independent transactions increases, decreases, or has no effect on each of the four debt ratios.
(1) The firm issued long-term debt for cash.
(2) The firm issued short-term debt and used the cash proceeds to redeem long-term debt (treat as a unified transaction).
(3) The firm redeemed short-term debt with cash.
(4) The firm issued long-term debt and used the cash proceeds to repurchase shares of its common stock (treat as a unified transaction).
b. The text states that analyst need not compute all four debt ratios each year because the debt ratios are highly correlated. Does your analysis in Part a support this statement? Explain.

5.6 INTEREST COVERAGE RATIO AS A MEASURE OF LONG-TERM SOLVENCY RISK. Identify the assumptions underlying the interest coverage ratio needed to make it an appropriate measure for analyzing long-term solvency risk.

5.7 INTEREST COVERAGE RATIO AS A MEASURE OF SHORT-TERM LIQUIDITY RISK. In what sense is the interest coverage ratio more a measure for assessing short-term liquidity risk than it is a measure for assessing long-term solvency risk?

5.8 INTERPRETING OPERATING CASH FLOW TO CURRENT AND TOTAL LIABILITIES RATIOS. Empirical research cited in the text indicates that firms with an operating cash flow to current liabilities ratio exceeding 0.40 portray low short-term liquidity risk. Similarly, firms with an operating cash flow to total liabilities ratio exceeding 20 percent portray low long-term solvency risk. What do these empirical results suggest about the mix of current and noncurrent liabilities for a financially healthy firm? What do they suggest about the mix of liabilities versus shareholders' equity financing?

5.9 INTERPRETING ALTMAN'S Z-SCORE BANKRUPTCY PREDICTION MODEL. Altman's bankruptcy prediction model places a coefficient of 3.3 on the earnings before interest and taxes divided by total assets variable but a coefficient of only 1.0 on the sales to total assets variable. Does this mean that the earnings variable is 3.3 times as important in predicting bankruptcy as the asset turnover variable? Explain.

5.10 MARKET EQUITY BETA IN RELATION TO SYSTEMATIC AND NONSYSTEMATIC RISK. Market equity beta measures the covariability of a firm's returns with all shares traded on the market (in excess of the risk-free interest rate). We refer to the degree of covariability as systematic risk. The market prices securities so that the expected returns should compensate the investor for the systematic risk of a particular stock. Stocks carrying a market equity beta of 1.20 should generate a higher return than stocks carrying a market equity beta of 0.90. Nonsystematic risk is any source of risk that does not affect the covariability of a firm's returns with the market. Some writers refer to nonsystematic risk as firm-specific risk. Why is the characterization of nonsystematic risk as firm-specific risk a misnomer?

5.11 COMPARISON OF ALTMAN'S BANKRUPTCY PREDICTION MODEL AND BENEISH'S EARNINGS MANIPULATION RISK MODEL.

Altman's bankruptcy risk model utilizes the values of the variables at a particular point in time (balance sheet variables) or for a period of time (income statement values). For the most part, Beneish's earnings manipulation risk model utilizes changes in variables from one period to the next. Why might the levels of values in Altman's model be more appropriate for predicting bankruptcy and changes in values in Beneish's model be more appropriate for identifying earnings manipulation?

Problems and Cases

5.12 CALCULATING AND INTERPRETING RISK RATIOS. Refer to the financial statement data for Hasbro in Problem 4.23 in Chapter 4. Exhibit 5.15 presents risk ratios for Hasbro for Year 2 and Year 3.

EXHIBIT 5.15

Risk Ratios for Hasbro
(Problem 5.12)

	Year 4	Year 3	Year 2
Revenues to Cash Ratio		6.2	7.7
Days Revenues Held in Cash		59	47
Current Ratio		1.6	1.5
Quick Ratio		1.2	1.1
Operating Cash Flow to Average Current Liabilities Ratio		0.479	0.548
Days Accounts Receivable		68	73
Days Inventory		51	68
Days Accounts Payable		47	49
Net Days Working Capital		72	91
Liabilities to Assets Ratio		0.556	0.621
Liabilities to Shareholders' Equity Ratio		1.251	1.639
Long-Term Debt to Long-Term Capital Ratio		0.328	0.418
Long-Term Debt to Shareholders' Equity Ratio		0.489	0.720
Operating Cash Flow to Total Liabilities Ratio		0.245	0.238
Interest Coverage Ratio		5.6	2.3

Required

   a. Calculate the amounts of these ratios for Year 4.

   b. Assess the changes in the short-term liquidity risk of Hasbro between Year 2 and Year 4 and the level of that risk at the end of Year 4.

   c. Assess the changes in the long-term solvency risk of Hasbro between Year 2 and Year 4 and the level of that risk at the end of Year 4.

5.13 CALCULATING AND INTERPRETING RISK RATIOS. Refer to the financial statement data for Abercrombie & Fitch in Problem 4.24 in Chapter 4. Exhibit 5.16 presents risk ratios for Abercrombie & Fitch for fiscal Year 3 and Year 4.

Required

   a. Compute the amounts of these ratios for fiscal Year 5.

   b. Assess the changes in the short-term liquidity risk of Abercrombie & Fitch between fiscal Year 3 and fiscal Year 5 and the level of that risk at the end of fiscal Year 5.

   c. Assess the changes in the long-term solvency risk of Abercrombie & Fitch between fiscal Year 3 and fiscal Year 5 and the level of that risk at the end of fiscal Year 5.

EXHIBIT 5.16

Risk Ratios for Abercrombie & Fitch
(Problem 5.13)

	Year 5	Year 4	Year 3
Revenues to Cash Ratio		34.5	13.8
Days Revenues in Cash		11	26
Current Ratio		2.4	2.3
Quick Ratio		1.7	1.6
Operating Cash Flow to Current Liabilities Ratio		1.177	1.587
Days Accounts Receivable		2	4
Days Inventory		72	61
Days Accounts Payable		26	22
Net Days Working Capital		48	43
Liabilities to Assets Ratio		0.591	0.592
Liabilities to Shareholders' Equity Ratio		1.443	1.448
Long-Term Debt to Long-Term Capital Ratio		0.454	0.461
Long-Term Debt to Shareholders' Equity Ratio		0.831	0.855
Operating Cash Flow to Total Liabilities Ratio		0.298	0.380
Interest Coverage Ratio		7.2	7.6

5.14 INTERPRETING RISK RATIOS. Refer to the profitability ratios of Coca-Cola in Problem 4.25 in Chapter 4. Exhibit 5.17 presents risk ratios for Coca-Cola for 2006-2008. As we did within the chapter for PepsiCo, we utilize Coca-Cola's footnote disclosures

EXHIBIT 5.17

Risk Ratios for Coca-Cola
(Problem 5.14)

	2008	2007	2006
Revenues to Cash Ratio	6.9	8.4	6.5
Days Revenues in Cash	53	44	56
Current Ratio	0.9	0.9	0.9
Quick Ratio	0.6	0.6	0.6
Operating Cash Flow to Average Current Liabilities Ratio	0.578	0.647	0.636
Days Accounts Receivable	37	37	37
Days Inventory	71	68	68
Days Accounts Payable	44	38	40
Net Days Working Capital	64	67	65
Liabilities to Assets Ratio	0.495	0.497	0.435
Liabilities to Shareholders' Equity Ratio	0.979	0.990	0.771
Long-Term Debt to Long-Term Capital Ratio	0.120	0.131	0.072
Long-Term Debt to Shareholders' Equity Ratio	0.136	0.151	0.078
Operating Cash Flow to Average Total Liabilities Ratio	0.364	0.414	0.456
Interest Coverage Ratio	17.0	17.3	29.9

to extract the amount of trade accounts payable included within the line item accounts payable and accrued expenses.

Required

a. Assess the changes in the short-term liquidity risk of Coca-Cola between 2006 and 2008.

b. Assess the changes in the long-term solvency risk of Coca-Cola between 2006 and 2008.

c. Compare the short-term liquidity ratios of Coca-Cola with those of PepsiCo discussed in the chapter. Which firm appears to have more short-term liquidity risk? Explain.

d. Compare the long-term solvency ratios of Coca-Cola with those of PepsiCo discussed in the chapter. Which firm appears to have more long-term solvency risk? Explain.

5.15 COMPUTING AND INTERPRETING RISK AND BANKRUPTCY PREDICTION RATIOS FOR A FIRM THAT DECLARED BANKRUPTCY.

Delta Air Lines is one of the largest airlines in the United States. It has operated on the verge of bankruptcy for several years. Exhibit 5.18 presents selected financial data for Delta Air Lines for each of the five years ending December 31, 2000, to December 31, 2004. Delta Air Lines filed for bankruptcy on September 14, 2005. We recommend that you create an Excel spreadsheet to compute the values of the ratios and the Altman's Z-score in Parts a and b, respectively.

EXHIBIT 5.18

Financial Data for Delta Air Lines
(amounts in millions except per share amounts)
(Problem 5.15)

Year Ended December 31:	2004	2003	2002	2001	2000
Sales	$15,002	$14,087	$13,866	$13,879	$15,657
Net Income (Loss) before					
Interest and Taxes	$(3,168)	$ (432)	$(1,337)	$(1,365)	$ 1,829
Interest Expense	$ 824	$ 757	$ 665	$ 499	$ 380
Net Income (Loss)	$(5,198)	$ (773)	$(1,272)	$(1,216)	$ 828
Current Assets	$ 3,606	$ 4,550	$ 3,902	$ 3,567	$ 3,205
Total Assets	$21,801	$25,939	$24,720	$23,605	$21,931
Current Liabilities	$ 5,941	$ 6,157	$ 6,455	$ 6,403	$ 5,245
Long-Term Debt	$12,507	$11,040	$ 9,576	$ 7,781	$ 5,797
Total Liabilities	$27,320	$26,323	$23,563	$19,581	$16,354
Retained Earnings					
(Deficit)	$(4,373)	$ 844	$ 1,639	$ 2,930	$ 4,176
Shareholders' Equity	$(5,519)	$ (384)	$ 1,157	$ 4,024	$ 5,577
Cash Flow Provided					
by Operations	$(1,123)	$ 142	$ 225	$ 236	$ 2,898
Common Shares					
Outstanding	139.8	123.5	123.4	123.2	123.0
Market Price per Share	$ 7.48	$ 11.81	$ 12.10	$ 29.26	$ 50.18

Required

a. Compute the value of each the following risk ratios.
  (1) Current Ratio (at the end of 2000–2004)
  (2) Operating Cash Flow to Current Liabilities Ratio (for 2001–2004)
  (3) Liabilities to Assets Ratio (at the end of 2000–2004)
  (4) Long-Term Debt to Long-Term Capital Ratio (at the end of 2000–2004)
  (5) Operating Cash Flow to Total Liabilities Ratio (for 2001–2004)
  (6) Interest Coverage Ratio (for 2000–2004)
b. Compute the value of Altman's Z-score for Delta Air Lines for each year from 2000–2004.
c. Using the analyses in Parts a and b, discuss the most important factors that signaled the likelihood of bankruptcy of Delta Air Lines in 2005.

5.16 COMPUTING AND INTERPRETING RISK AND BANKRUPTCY PREDICTION RATIOS FOR A FIRM THAT WAS ACQUIRED. Sun

Microsystems develops, manufactures, and sells computers for network systems. Exhibit 5.19 presents selected financial data for Sun Microsystems for each of the five years ending June 30, 2005, to June 30, 2009. The company did not go bankrupt, but instead was acquired in 2010 by Oracle. We recommend that you create an Excel spreadsheet to compute the values of the ratios and the Altman's Z-score in Parts a and b, respectively.

EXHIBIT 5.19

Financial Data for Sun Microsystems
(amounts in millions except per share amounts)
(Problem 5.16)

Year Ended June 30:	2009	2008	2007	2006	2005
Sales	$11,449	$13,880	$13,873	$13,086	$11,070
Net Income (Loss) before					
Interest and Taxes	$(2,166)	$ 640	$ 622	$ (620)	$ (150)
Interest Expense	$ 17	$ 30	$ 39	$ 55	$ 34
Net Income (Loss)	$(2,234)	$ 403	$ 473	$ (864)	$ (107)
Current Assets	$ 6,864	$ 7,834	$ 9,328	$ 8,460	$ 7,191
Total Assets	$11,232	$14,340	$15,838	$15,082	$14,190
Current Liabilities	$ 5,621	$ 5,668	$ 5,451	$ 6,165	$ 4,766
Long-Term Debt	$ 695	$ 1,265	$ 1,264	$ 575	$ 1,123
Total Liabilities	$ 7,927	$ 8,752	$ 8,659	$ 8,738	$ 7,516
Retained Earnings	$(2,055)	$ 430	$ 189	$ (257)	$ 1,387
Shareholders' Equity	$ 3,305	$ 5,588	$ 7,179	$ 6,344	$ 6,674
Cash Flow Provided by Operations	$ 457	$ 1,329	$ 958	$ 567	$ 279
Common Shares Outstanding	752	752	884	876	$ 852
Market Price per Share	$ 9.22	$ 10.88	$ 20.76	$ 16.60	$ 14.92

Required

a. Compute the value of each of the following risk ratios.
  (1) Current Ratio (at the end of 2005–2009)
  (2) Operating Cash Flow to Current Liabilities Ratio (for 2006–2009)
  (3) Liabilities to Assets Ratio (at the end of 2005–2009)
  (4) Long-Term Debt to Long-Term Capital Ratio (at the end of 2005–2009)
  (5) Operating Cash Flow to Total Liabilities Ratio (for 2006–2009)
  (6) Interest Coverage Ratio (for 2005–2009)
b. Compute the value of Altman's Z-score for Sun Microsystems for each year from 2005–2009.
c. Using the analyses in Parts a and b, discuss the most important factors that signal the likelihood of bankruptcy of Sun Microsystems in 2010.

5.17 COMPUTING AND INTERPRETING BANKRUPTCY PREDICTION RATIOS.
Exhibit 5.20 presents selected financial data for Best Buy and Circuit City for fiscal 2008 and 2007. Best Buy and Circuit City operate as specialty retailers offering a wide range of consumer electronics, service contracts, product repairs, and home installation. Competition from Walmart, Costco, and Internet retailers has put downward pressure on prices and margins. In November 2008, Circuit City filed Chapter 7 bankruptcy. In the media, Circuit City's bankruptcy is largely blamed on its poor treatment of employees. In early 2007, Circuit City laid off 3,400 high-paid salespersons, or approximately 8 percent of its workforce, which left inexperienced, low-paid workers in charge of customer service. Customer service plummeted, which was especially harmful for the

EXHIBIT 5.20

Financial Data for Best Buy and Circuit City
(amounts in thousands except per share amounts)
(Problem 5.17)

| | Best Buy | | Circuit City | |
| | Year-End 3/1 | | Year-End 2/28 | |
	2008	2007	2008	2007
Sales	$40,023	$35,934	$11,744	$12,430
Net Income (Loss) before				
Interest and Taxes	$ 2,290	$ 2,161	$ (352)	$ 22
Net Income (Loss)	$ 1,407	$ 1,377	$ (321)	$ (10)
Current Assets	$ 7,342	$ 9,081	$ 2,440	$ 2,884
Total Assets	$12,758	$13,570	$ 3,746	$ 4,007
Current Liabilities	$ 6,769	$ 6,301	$ 1,606	$ 1,714
Total Liabilities	$ 8,274	$ 7,369	$ 2,243	$ 2,216
Retained Earnings	$ 3,933	$ 5,507	$ 981	$ 1,336
Common Shares Outstanding	411	481	169	171
Market Price per Share	$ 42.00	$ 44.97	$ 4.38	$ 18.47

company that previously provided higher levels of customer satisfaction for their expensive electronic items, warranty products, and installation services.

Required

a. Compute Altman's Z-score for Best Buy and Circuit City for 2007 and 2008.
b. How did the bankruptcy risk of Best Buy change between 2007 and 2008? Explain.
c. How did the bankruptcy risk of Circuit City change between 2007 and 2008? Explain.
d. As noted, Circuit City filed Chapter 7 bankruptcy in November 2008. Using the analysis from Parts b and c, would you have predicted Circuit City or Best Buy to file bankruptcy in 2008? Explain.

5.18 APPLYING AND INTERPRETING BANKRUPTCY PREDICTION MODELS. Exhibit 5.21 presents selected financial data for Harvard Industries and Marvel Entertainment for fiscal Year 5 and Year 6. Harvard Industries manufactures automobile components that it sells to automobile manufacturers. Competitive conditions in the automobile industry in recent years have led automobile manufacturers to put pressure on suppliers such as Harvard Industries to reduce costs and selling prices. Marvel Entertainment creates and sells comic books, trading cards, and other youth entertainment products and licenses others to use fictional characters created by Marvel Entertainment in their products. Youth readership of comic books and interest in trading cards have been declining steadily in recent years. Marvel Entertainment recognized a significant asset impairment charge in fiscal Year 6.

Required

a. Compute Altman's Z-score for Harvard Industries and Marvel Entertainment for fiscal Year 5 and Year 6.

EXHIBIT 5.21

Financial Data for Harvard Industries and Marvel Entertainment (amounts in thousands except per share amounts) (Problem 5.18)

	Harvard Industries		Marvel Entertainment	
	Year 6	Year 5	Year 6	Year 5
Sales	$ 824,835	$ 631,832	$ 745,400	$ 828,900
Net Income (Loss) before				
Interest and Taxes	$ (11,012)	$ 40,258	$(370,200)	$ 25,100
Net Income (Loss)	$ (68,712)	$ 6,921	$(464,400)	$ (48,400)
Current Assets	$ 156,226	$ 195,417	$ 399,500	$ 490,600
Total Assets	$ 617,705	$ 662,262	$ 844,000	$1,226,310
Current Liabilities	$ 163,384	$ 176,000	$ 345,800	$ 318,100
Total Liabilities	$ 648,934	$ 624,817	$ 999,700	$ 948,100
Retained Earnings	$(184,308)	$(115,596)	$(350,300)	$ 114,100
Common Shares Outstanding	7,014	6,995	101,810	101,703
Market Price per Share	$ 85.00	$ 100.50	$ 1.625	$ 10.625

b. How did the bankruptcy risk of Harvard Industries change between fiscal Year 5 and Year 6? Explain.

c. How did the bankruptcy risk of Marvel Entertainment change between Year 5 and Year 6? Explain.

d. Which firm is more likely to file for bankruptcy during fiscal Year 7? Explain using the analyses from Part b.

5.19 APPLYING AND INTERPRETING BANKRUPTCY PREDICTION MODELS. Exhibit 5.22 presents selected financial data for Tribune Company and Washington Post for fiscal 2006 and 2007. The Washington Post Company is an education and media company. It owns, among others, Kaplan, Inc.; Cable ONE Inc.; *Newsweek* magazine; and Washington Post Media. The Tribune Company is a media and entertainment company, which also is diversified, owning the *Chicago Tribune*, the *Los Angeles Times*, television and radio affiliates such as The CW Network and WGN, and the Chicago Cubs. The Tribune Company filed for bankruptcy in December 2008.

Required

a. Compute Altman's Z-score for Tribune Company and Washington Post for fiscal 2006 and 2007.

b. How did the bankruptcy risk of Tribune Company change between fiscal 2006 and 2007? Explain.

c. How did the bankruptcy risk of Washington Post change between fiscal 2006 and 2007? Explain.

d. The Tribune Company filed Chapter 7 bankruptcy in December 2008. Using the analysis from Parts b and c, would you have predicted the Tribune Company or the Washington Post Company to file bankruptcy? Explain.

EXHIBIT 5.22

Financial Data for Tribune Company and Washington Post
(amounts in millions except per share amounts)
(Problem 5.19)

	Tribune Company		Washington Post	
	2007	2006	2007	2006
Sales	$ 5,063	$ 5,444	$ 4,180	$ 3,905
Net Income (Loss) before				
Interest and Taxes	$ 619	$ 1,085	$ 505	$ 544
Net Income (Loss)	$ 87	$ 594	$ 289	$ 324
Current Assets	$ 1,385	$ 1,346	$ 995	$ 935
Total Assets	$13,150	$13,401	$ 6,005	$ 5,381
Current Liabilities	$ 2,190	$ 2,549	$ 1,013	$ 812
Total Liabilities	$16,664	$ 9,081	$ 2,543	$ 2,222
Retained Earnings (Deficit)	$(3,474)	$ 3,138	$ 4,330	$ 4,120
Common Shares Outstanding	239	307	10	10
Market Price per Share	$ 45.04	$ 58.69	$759.25	$711.53

EXHIBIT 5.23

Financial Statement Data for Enron Corporation
(amounts in millions)
(Problem 5.20)

	2000	1999	1998	1997
Accounts Receivable	$ 10,396	$ 3,030	$ 2,060	$ 1,697
Current Assets	30,381	7,255	5,933	4,669
Property, Plant, and Equipment, net	11,743	10,681	10,657	9,170
Total Assets	65,503	33,381	29,350	23,422
Current Liabilities	28,406	6,759	6,107	4,412
Long-Term Debt	8,550	7,151	7,357	6,254
Sales	100,789	40,112	31,260	20,273
Cost of Goods Sold	94,517	34,761	26,381	17,311
Selling and Administrative Expenses	3,184	3,045	2,473	1,406
Income from Continuing Operations	979	1,024	703	105
Cash Flow from Operations	4,779	1,228	1,640	501
Depreciation Expense	485	565	563	480

**5.20 APPLYING AND INTERPRETING THE EARNINGS MANIPULA-
TION MODEL.** Exhibit 5.23 presents selected financial statement data for Enron
Corporation for 1997, 1998, 1999, and 2000. These data reflect amounts from the financial
statements as originally reported for each year. In 2001, Enron restated its financial statements for earlier years because it reported several items beyond the limits of GAAP.

Required

a. Use Beneish's earnings manipulation model to compute the probability that Enron engaged in earnings manipulation for 1998, 1999, and 2000.

b. Identify the major reasons for the changes in the probability of earnings manipulation during the three-year period.

5.21 REFORMULATING FINANCIAL STATEMENTS, PREPARING AN ALTERNATIVE DECOMPOSITION OF ROCE, AND ASSESSING FINANCIAL FLEXIBILITY. Exhibit 5.24 presents balance sheets for 2007 and 2008 for Whole Foods; Exhibit 5.25 presents income statements for 2006–2008.

Required

a. Prepare the standard Dupont decomposition of ROCE. Use average balances for balance sheet amounts.

b. Assume that all cash is operating cash (that is, no excess cash). Also assume that deferred lease liabilities are operating. Prepare the alternative decomposition of ROCE by computing NOPAT, Net Financing Expense (after tax), Operating Profit

---

EXHIBIT 5.24

Balance Sheets for Whole Foods
(amounts in thousands)
(Problem 5.21)

	2008	2007
ASSETS		
Cash and cash equivalents	$ 31,151	$ 2,310
Accounts receivable and other receivables	115,424	270,263
Merchandise inventories	327,452	288,112
Prepaid expenses and other current assets	68,150	40,402
Deferred income taxes	80,429	66,899
Total Current Assets	$ 622,606	$ 667,986
Property and equipment, net of accumulated depreciation and amortization	1,900,117	1,666,559
Goodwill	659,559	668,850
Intangible assets, net of accumulated amortization	78,499	97,683
Deferred income taxes	109,002	104,877
Other assets	10,953	7,173
Total Assets	$3,380,736	$3,213,128
LIABILITIES AND SHAREHOLDERS' EQUITY		
Current installments of long-term debt and capital lease obligations	$ 380	$ 24,781
Accounts payable	183,134	225,728
Accrued payroll, bonus and other benefits due team members	196,233	181,290
Other current liabilities	286,430	340,551
Total Current Liabilities	$ 666,177	$ 772,350

(Continued)

EXHIBIT 5.24 (Continued)		
	2008	**2007**
Long-term debt and capital lease obligations, less current installments	$ 928,790	$ 736,087
Deferred lease liabilities	199,635	152,552
Other long-term liabilities	80,110	93,335
Total Liabilities	$1,874,712	$1,754,324
Common stock, no par value, 300,000 shares authorized; 140,286 and 143,787 shares issued, 140,286 and 139,240 shares outstanding in 2008 and 2007, respectively	$1,066,180	$1,232,845
Common stock in treasury, at cost	—	(199,961)
Accumulated other comprehensive income	422	15,722
Retained earnings	439,422	410,198
Total Shareholders' Equity	$1,506,024	$1,458,804
Total Liabilities and Shareholders' Equity	$3,380,736	$3,213,128

EXHIBIT 5.25		
Income Statements for Whole Foods (amounts in thousands) (Problem 5.21)		
	2008	**2007**	**2006**
---	---	---	---
Sales	$7,953,912	$6,591,773	$5,607,376
Cost of goods sold and occupancy costs	5,247,207	4,295,170	3,647,734
Gross Profit	$2,706,705	$2,296,603	$1,959,642
Direct store expenses	2,107,940	1,711,229	1,421,968
General and administrative expenses	270,428	217,743	181,244
Pre-opening expenses	55,554	59,319	32,058
Relocation, store closure and lease termination	36,545	10,861	5,363
Operating Income	$ 236,238	$ 297,451	$ 319,009
Interest expense	(36,416)	(4,208)	(32)
Investment and other income	6,697	11,324	20,736
Income before income taxes	$ 206,519	$ 304,567	$ 339,713
Provision for income taxes	91,995	121,827	135,885
Net Income	$ 114,524	$ 182,740	$ 203,828

Margin, Net Operating Assets Turnover, Operating ROA, Leverage, and Spread for 2008. Use average balances for balance sheet amounts.

c. Use the same assumptions as in Part b, except that all cash is a financing asset (that is, all cash is excess cash) and deferred lease liabilities are a financing obligation. Prepare the alternative decomposition of ROCE by computing NOPAT, Net Financing Expense (after tax), Operating Profit Margin, Net Operating Assets Turnover, Operating ROA, Leverage, and Spread for 2008. Use average balances for balance sheet amounts.

d. Does the different treatment of financial assets and liabilities affect inferences you draw from the decomposition of ROCE? Explain.

INTEGRATIVE CASE 5.1

STARBUCKS

Exhibit 5.26 presents risk ratios for Starbucks for 2006 and 2007. Exhibits 1.26, 1.27, and 1.28 in Chapter 1 present the financial statements for Starbucks.

EXHIBIT 5.26

Risk Ratios for Starbucks
(Integrative Case 5.1)

	2008	2007	2006
Revenues to Cash Ratio		31.7	32.0
Days Revenues Held in Cash		11.5	11.4
Current Ratio		0.79	0.79
Quick Ratio		0.34	0.35
Operating Cash Flow to Average Current Liabilities Ratio		65.1%	71.6%
Days Accounts Receivable		66	63
Days Inventory		61	68
Days Accounts Payable		33	31
Net Days Working Capital		94	100
Liabilities to Assets Ratio		0.573	0.497
Liabilities to Shareholders' Equity Ratio		1.340	0.987
Long-Term Debt to Long-Term Capital Ratio		0.194	0.001
Long-Term Debt to Shareholders' Equity Ratio		0.241	0.001
Operating Cash Flow to Average Total Liabilities Ratio		0.506	0.625
Interest Coverage Ratio		28.7	106.8
Altman's Z-Score		6.72	9.95
Probability of Bankruptcy		0.0%	0.0%
Beneish's Earnings Manipulation Score		−2.84	−2.89
Probability of Earnings Manipulation		0.23%	0.19%

Required

a. Compute the values of each of the ratios in Exhibit 5.26 for Starbucks for 2008. Starbucks had 735.5 million common shares outstanding at the end of 2008, and the market price per share was $14.17. For days accounts receivable, use only specialty revenues in your calculations, because accounts receivable are primarily related to licensing and food service operations, not the retail operations. Use cost of sales, including occupancy costs, in the numerator of the GMI in the Beneish earnings manipulation model.

b. Interpret the changes in Starbucks risk ratios during the three-year period, indicating areas of concern.

CASE 5.2

MASSACHUSETTS STOVE COMPANY—BANK LENDING DECISION

Massachusetts Stove Company manufactures wood-burning stoves for the heating of homes and businesses. The company has approached you, as chief lending officer for the Massachusetts Regional Bank, seeking to increase its loan from the current level of $93,091 as of January 15, Year 12, to $143,091. Jane O'Neil, chief executive officer and majority stockholder of the company, indicates that the company needs the loan to finance the working capital required for an expected 25 percent annual increase in sales during the next two years, to repay suppliers, and to provide funds for expected nonrecurring legal and retooling costs.

The company's woodstoves have two distinguishing characteristics: (1) the metal frame of the stoves includes inlaid soapstone, which increases the intensity and duration of the heat provided by the stoves and enhances their appearance as an attractive piece of furniture, and (2) a catalytic combuster, which adds heating potential to the stoves and reduces air pollution.

The company manufactures wood-burning stoves in a single plant in Greenfield, Massachusetts. It purchases metal castings for the stoves from foundries in Germany and Belgium. The soapstone comes from a supplier in Canada. These purchases are denominated in U.S. dollars. The catalytic combuster is purchased from a supplier in the United States. The manufacturing process is essentially an assembly operation. The plant employs an average of eight workers. The two keys to quality control are structural airtightness and effective operation of the catalytic combuster.

The company rents approximately 60 percent of the 25,000-square-foot building it uses for manufacturing and administrative activities. This building also houses the company's factory showroom. The remaining 40 percent of the building is not currently rented.

The company's marketing of woodstoves follows three channels:

1. Wholesaling of stoves to retail hardware stores. This channel represents approximately 20 percent of the company's sales in units.
2. Retail direct marketing to individuals in all 50 states. This channel utilizes (a) national advertising in construction and design magazines and (b) the sending of brochures to potential customers identified from personal inquiries. This channel represents approximately 70 percent of the company's sales in units. The company is the only firm in the industry with a strategic emphasis on retail direct marketing.
3. Retailing from the company's showroom. This channel represents approximately 10 percent of the company's sales in units.

The company offers three payment options to retail purchasers of its stoves:

1. **Full payment:** Check, money order, or charge to a third-party credit card is used to pay in full.
2. **Layaway plan:** Monthly payments are made over a period not exceeding one year. The company ships the stove after receiving the final payment.
3. **Installment financing plan:** The company has a financing arrangement with a local bank to finance the purchase of stoves by credit-approved customers. The company is liable if customers fail to repay their installment bank loans.

The imposition of strict air emission standards by the Environmental Protection Agency (EPA) has resulted in a major change in the woodstove industry. By December 31, Year 9, firms were required by EPA regulations to demonstrate that their woodstoves met or surpassed specified air emission standards. Besides these standards being stricter than industry practices at the time, firms had to engage in numerous company-sponsored and independent testing of their stoves to satisfy EPA regulators. As a consequence, the number of firms in the woodstove industry decreased from more than 200 in the years prior to Year 10 to approximately 35 by December 31, Year 11.

The company received approval for its Soapstone Stove I in Year 11, after incurring retooling and testing costs of $63,001. It capitalized these costs in the Property, Plant, and Equipment account. It depreciates these costs over the five-year EPA approval period. A second stove, Soapstone Stove II, is currently undergoing retooling and testing. For this stove, the company incurred costs of $19,311 in Year 10 and $8,548 in Year and has received preliminary EPA approval. It anticipates additional design, tooling, and testing costs of approximately $55,000 in Year 12 and $33,000 in Year 13 to obtain final EPA approval.

The company holds an option to purchase the building in which it is located for $608,400. The option also permits the company to assume the unpaid balance on a low-interest-rate loan on the building from the New England Regional Industrial Development Authority. The interest rate on this loan is adjusted annually and equals 80 percent of the bank prime interest rate. The unpaid balance on the loan exceeds the option price and will result in a cash transfer to the company from the owner of the building at the time of transfer. The company exercised its option in Year 9, but the owner of the building refused to comply with the option provisions. The company sued the owner. The case has gone through the lower court system in Massachusetts and is currently under review by the Massachusetts Supreme Court. The company incurred legal costs totaling $68,465 through Year 11 and anticipates additional costs of approximately $45,000 in Year 12. The lower courts have ruled in favor of the company's position on all of the major issues in the case. The company expects the Massachusetts Supreme Court to concur with the decisions of the lower courts when it renders its final decision in the spring of Year 12. The company has held discussions with two prospective tenants for the building's 10,000 square feet that Massachusetts Stove Company does not use in its operations.

Jane O'Neil owns 51 percent of the company's common stock. The remaining stockholders include John O'Neil (chief financial officer and father of Jane O'Neil), Mark Forest (vice president of manufacturing), and four independent local investors.

To assist in the loan decision, the company provides you with financial statements (see the first three columns of Exhibits 5.27–5.29 on pages 414–416) and notes for the three years ending December 31, Year 9, Year 10, and Year 11. These financial statements were prepared by John O'Neil, chief financial officer, and are not audited. The company also provides you with projected financial statements for Year 12 and Year 13 (see the last two columns of Exhibits 5.27–5.29) to demonstrate its need for the loan and its ability to repay. The loan requested involves an increase in the current loan amount from

EXHIBIT 5.27

Massachusetts Stove Company
Income Statements
(Case 5.2)

	Actual			Projected	
	Year 9	**Year 10**	**Year 11**	**Year 12**	**Year 13**
Sales	$ 665,771	$ 783,754	$ 955,629	$1,194,535	$1,493,170
Cost of goods sold	(460,797)	(474,156)	(514,907)	(609,213)	(731,653)
Selling and administrative	(177,631)	(290,719)	(390,503)	(489,760)	(612,200)
Legal (Note 1)	(28,577)	(30,092)	(9,796)	(45,000)	—
Interest	(25,948)	(24,122)	(23,974)	(26,510)	(26,510)
Income tax (Note 2)	—	—	—	—	—
Net Income (Loss)	$ (27,182)	$ (35,335)	$ 16,449	$ 24,052	$ 122,807

$93,091 to $143,091. The company will pay monthly interest and repay the $50,000 additional amount borrowed by December 31, Year 13. Exhibit 5.30 (see page 417) presents financial statement ratios for the company.

The assumptions underlying the projected financial statements are as follows:

Sales: Sales are projected to increase 25 percent annually during the next two years, after increasing 17.7 percent in Year 10 and 21.9 percent in Year 11. The increase reflects continuing market opportunities related to the company's strategic emphasis on retail direct marketing and to the expected continuing contraction in the number of competitors in the industry.

Cost of Goods Sold: Most manufacturing costs vary with sales. The company projects cost of goods sold to equal 51 percent of sales in Year 12 and 49 percent of sales in Year 13, having declined from 69.2 percent of sales in Year 9 to 53.9 percent of sales in Year 11. The reductions resulted from a higher proportion of retail sales in the sales mix (which have a higher gross margin than wholesale sales), a more favorable pricing environment in the industry (fewer competitors), a switch to lower-cost suppliers, and more efficient production.

Selling and Administrative Expenses: The company projects these costs to equal 41 percent of sales, having increased from 26.7 percent of sales in Year 9 to 40.9 percent of sales in Year 11. The increases resulted from a heavier emphasis on retail sales, which require more aggressive marketing than wholesale sales.

Legal Expenses: The additional $45,000 of legal costs represents the best estimate by the company's attorneys.

Interest Expense: Interest expense has averaged approximately 6 percent of short- and long-term borrowing during the last three years. The projected income statement assumes a continuation of the 6 percent average rate.

Income Tax Expense: The company has elected to be taxed as a Subchapter S corporation, which means that the net income of the firm is taxed at the level of the individual shareholders, not at the corporate level. Thus, the pro forma financial statements include no income tax expense. The firm has operated at a net loss for tax purposes for several years

EXHIBIT 5.28

Massachusetts Stove Company
Balance Sheets
(Case 5.2)

December 31:	Actual				Projected	
	Year 8	Year 9	Year 10	Year 11	Year 12	Year 13
ASSETS						
Cash	$ 3,925	$ 11,707	$ 8,344	$ 37,726	$ 11,289	$ 6,512
Accounts receivable	94,606	54,772	44,397	31,964	40,035	49,964
Inventories	239,458	208,260	209,004	225,490	291,924	329,480
Total Current Assets	$ 337,989	$ 274,739	$ 261,745	$ 295,180	$ 343,248	$ 385,956
Property, plant, and equipment, at cost	$ 258,870	$ 316,854	$ 362,399	$ 377,784	$ 440,284	$ 487,784
Accumulated depreciation	(205,338)	(228,985)	(250,189)	(274,347)	(302,502)	(333,694)
Property, plant, and equipment, net	$ 53,532	$ 87,869	$ 112,210	$ 103,437	$ 137,782	$ 154,090
Other assets	17,888	17,888	17,594	17,006	17,006	17,006
Total Assets	$ 409,409	$ 380,496	$ 391,549	$ 415,623	$ 498,036	$ 557,052
LIABILITIES AND SHAREHOLDERS' EQUITY						
Accounts payable	$ 148,579	$ 139,879	$ 189,889	$ 160,905	$ 198,206	$ 176,915
Notes payable—Banks (Note 3)	152,985	140,854	125,256	93,091	143,091	93,091
Other current liabilities (Note 4)	13,340	11,440	23,466	62,440	33,500	41,000
Total Current Liabilities	$ 314,904	$ 292,173	$ 338,611	$ 316,436	$ 374,797	$ 311,006
Long-term debt (Note 3)	248,000	269,000	268,950	298,750	298,750	298,750
Total Liabilities	$ 562,904	$ 561,173	$ 607,561	$ 615,186	$ 673,547	$ 609,756
Common stock	$ 2,000	$ 2,000	$ 2,000	$ 2,000	$ 2,000	$ 2,000
Additional paid-in capital	435,630	435,630	435,630	435,630	435,630	435,630
Accumulated deficit	(591,125)	(618,307)	(653,642)	(637,193)	(613,141)	(490,334)
Total Shareholders' Equity	$(153,495)	$(180,677)	$(216,012)	$(199,563)	$(175,511)	$(52,704)
Total Liabilities and Shareholders' Equity	$ 409,409	$ 380,496	$ 391,549	$ 415,623	$ 498,036	$ 557,052

EXHIBIT 5.29

Massachusetts Stove Company
Statements of Cash Flows
(Case 5.2)

	Actual			Projected	
	Year 9	Year 10	Year 11	Year 12	Year 13
OPERATIONS					
Net income (loss)	$(27,182)	$(35,335)	$ 16,449	$ 24,052	$122,807
Depreciation and amortization	23,647	21,204	24,158	28,155	31,192
(Increase) Decrease in accounts receivable	39,834	10,375	12,433	(8,071)	(9,929)
(Increase) Decrease in inventories	31,198	(744)	(16,486)	(66,434)	(37,556)
Increase (Decrease) in accounts payable	(8,700)	50,010	(28,984)	37,301	(21,291)
Increase (Decrease) in other current liabilities	(1,900)	12,026	38,974	(28,940)	7,500
Cash Flow from Operations	$ 56,897	$ 57,536	$ 46,544	$(13,937)	$ 92,723
INVESTING					
Fixed assets acquired	$(57,984)	$(45,545)	$(15,385)	$(62,500)	$(47,500)
Other investing	—	294	588	—	—
Cash Flow from Investing	$(57,984)	$(45,251)	$(14,797)	$(62,500)	$(47,500)
FINANCING					
Increase (Decrease) in short-term borrowing	$(12,131)	$(15,598)	$(32,165)	$ 50,000	$(50,000)
Increase (Decrease) in long-term borrowing	21,000	(50)	29,800	—	—
Cash Flow from Financing	$ 8,869	$(15,648)	$ (2,365)	$ 50,000	$(50,000)
Change in Cash	$ 7,782	$ (3,363)	$ 29,382	$(26,437)	$ (4,777)
Cash—Beginning of year	3,925	11,707	8,344	37,726	11,289
Cash—End of Year	$ 11,707	$ 8,344	$ 37,726	$ 11,289	$ 6,512

prior to Year 11, primarily because of losses of a lawn products business that it acquired ten years ago. The company discontinued the lawn products business in Year 10.

Cash: The projected amounts for cash represent a plug to equate projected assets with projected liabilities and shareholders' equity. Projected liabilities include the requested loan during Year 12 and its repayment at the end of Year 13.

Accounts Receivable: Days accounts receivable outstanding, calculated on the average accounts receivable balances, will be 11 days in Year 12 and Year 13.

Inventories: Days inventory held, calculated on the average inventory balances, will be 155 days in Year 12 and Year 13.

EXHIBIT 5.30

Massachusetts Stove Company
Profitability and Risk Ratios
(Case 5.2)

	Actual			Projected	
	Year 9	Year 10	Year 11	Year 12	Year 13
Profit Margin for ROA	(0.2%)	(1.4%)	4.2%	4.2%	10.0%
Assets Turnover	1.7	2.0	2.4	2.6	2.8
Return on Assets	(0.3%)	(2.9%)	10.0%	11.1%	28.3%
Cost of Goods Sold/Sales	69.2%	60.5%	53.9%	51.0%	49.0%
Selling and Administrative/Sales	26.7%	37.1%	40.9%	41.0%	41.0%
Legal Expense/Sales	4.3%	3.8%	1.0%	3.8%	—
Interest Expense/Sales	3.9%	3.1%	2.5%	2.2%	1.8%
Days Accounts Receivable	41	23	15	11	11
Days Inventory	177	161	154	155	155
Days Accounts Payable	122	127	122	96	89
Fixed Assets Turnover	9.4	7.8	8.9	9.9	10.2
Current Ratio	0.9	0.8	0.9	0.9	1.2
Quick Ratio	0.2	0.2	0.2	0.1	0.2
Operating Cash Flow to Current Liabilities Ratio	0.187	0.182	0.142	(0.040)	0.270
Liabilities to Assets Ratio	1.475	1.552	1.480	1.352	1.095
Long-Term Debt to Total Assets Ratio	0.707	0.687	0.719	0.600	0.536
Operating Cash Flow to Total Liabilities Ratio	0.101	0.098	0.076	(0.022)	0.145
Interest Coverage Ratio	0.0	(0.5)	1.7	1.9	5.6

Property, Plant, and Equipment: Capital expenditures for Year 12 include a $55,000 cost for retooling the Soapstone Stove II and $7,500 for other equipment; for Year 13, they include $33,000 for retooling the Soapstone Stove II and $14,500 for other equipment. The projected balance excludes the cost of acquiring the building, its related debt, the cash received at the time of transfer, and rental revenues from leasing the unused 40 percent of the building to other businesses.

Accumulated Depreciation: This is continuation of the historical relation between depreciation expense and the cost of property, plant, and equipment.

Other Assets: A new financial reporting standard no longer requires amortization of intangibles after Year 11.

Accounts Payable: Days accounts payable outstanding, based on the average accounts payable balances, will be 97 days in Year 12 and 89 days in Year 13. The decrease in days payable reflects the ability to pay suppliers more quickly with the proceeds of the increased bank loan.

Notes Payable: Notes payable is projected to increase by the amount of the bank loan in Year 12 and to decrease by the loan repayment at the end of Year 13.

Other Current Liabilities: The large increase at the end of Year 11 resulted from a major promotional offer in the fall of Year 11, which increased the amount of deposits by customers. The projected amounts for Year 12 and Year 13 represent more normal expected levels of deposits.

Long-Term Debt: Long-term borrowing represents loans from shareholders to the company. The company does not plan to repay any of these loans in the near future.

Retained Earnings: The change each year represents net income or net loss from operations. The company does not pay dividends.

Statement of Cash Flows: Amounts are taken from the changes in various accounts on the actual and projected balance sheets.

Notes to Financial Statements

Note 1: The company has incurred legal costs to enforce its option to purchase the building used in its manufacturing and administrative activities. The case is under review by the Massachusetts Supreme Court, with a decision expected in the spring of Year 12.

Note 2: The company is not subject to income tax because it has elected Subchapter S tax status.

Note 3: The notes payable to banks are secured by machinery and equipment, shares of common stock of companies traded on the New York Stock Exchange owned by two shareholders, and personal guarantees of three shareholders. The long-term debt consists of unsecured loans from three shareholders.

Note 4: Other current liabilities include the following:

	Year 8	Year 9	Year 10	Year 11
Customer Deposits	$11,278	$ 9,132	$20,236	$59,072
Employee Taxes Withheld	2,062	2,308	3,230	3,368
	$13,340	$11,440	$23,466	$62,440

Required

Would you make the loan to the company in accordance with the stated terms? Explain. In responding, consider the reasonableness of the company's projections, positive and negative factors affecting the industry and the company, and the likely ability of the company to repay the loan. (Excel spreadsheet for this case is available at www.cengage.com/accounting/wahlen.)

CASE 5.3

FLY-BY-NIGHT INTERNATIONAL GROUP: CAN THIS COMPANY BE SAVED?

Douglas C. Mather, founder, chair, and chief executive of Fly-by-Night International Group (FBN), lived the fast-paced, risk-seeking life that he tried to inject into his company. Flying the company's Learjets, he logged 28 world speed records. Once he throttled a company plane to the top of Mount Everest in three and a half minutes.

These activities seemed perfectly appropriate at the time. Mather was a Navy fighter pilot in Vietnam and then flew commercial airlines. In the mid-1970s, he started FBN as a pilot training school. With the defense buildup beginning in the early 1980s, Mather branched out into government contracting. He equipped the company's Learjets with radar jammers and other sophisticated electronic devices to mimic enemy aircraft. He then contracted his "rent-an-enemy" fleet to the Navy and Air Force for use in fighter pilot training. The Pentagon liked the idea, and FBN's revenues grew to $55 million in the fiscal year ending April 30, Year 14. Its common stock, issued to the public in Year 9 at $8.50 a share, reached a high of $16.50 in mid-Year 13. Mather and FBN received glowing write-ups in *Business Week* and *Fortune*.

EXHIBIT 5.31

Fly-by-Night International Group
Comparative Balance Sheets
(amounts in thousands)
(Case 5.3)

April 30:	Year 14	Year 13	Year 12	Year 11	Year 10	Year 9
ASSETS						
Cash	$ 159	$ 583	$ 313	$ 142	$ 753	$ 192
Notes receivable	—	—	—	1,000	—	—
Accounts receivable	6,545	4,874	2,675	1,490	1,083	2,036
Inventories	5,106	2,514	1,552	602	642	686
Prepayments	665	829	469	57	303	387
Net assets of discontinued businesses	—	—	—	—	1,926	—
Total Current Assets	$ 12,475	$ 8,800	$ 5,009	$ 3,291	$ 4,707	$ 3,301
Property, plant, and equipment	$106,529	$76,975	$24,039	$17,809	$37,250	$17,471
Less accumulated depreciation	(17,231)	(8,843)	(5,713)	(4,288)	(4,462)	(2,593)
Net	$ 89,298	$68,132	$18,326	$13,521	$32,788	$14,878
Other assets	$ 470	$ 665	$ 641	$ 1,112	$ 1,566	$ 1,278
Total Assets	$102,243	$77,597	$23,976	$17,924	$39,061	$19,457
LIABILITIES AND SHAREHOLDERS' EQUITY						
Accounts payable	$ 12,428	$ 6,279	$ 993	$ 939	$ 2,285	$ 1,436
Notes payable	—	945	140	1,021	4,766	—
Current portion of long-term debt	60,590	7,018	1,789	1,104	2,774	1,239
Other current liabilities	12,903	12,124	2,423	1,310	1,845	435
Total Current Liabilities	$ 85,921	$26,366	$ 5,345	$ 4,374	$11,670	$ 3,110
Long-term debt	—	41,021	9,804	6,738	20,041	9,060
Deferred income taxes	—	900	803	—	1,322	1,412
Other noncurrent liabilities	—	—	226	—	248	—
Total Liabilities	$ 85,921	$68,287	$16,178	$11,112	$33,281	$13,582
Common stock	$ 34	$ 22	$ 21	$ 20	$ 20	$ 20
Additional paid-in capital	16,516	5,685	4,569	4,323	3,611	3,611
Retained earnings	(29)	3,802	3,208	2,469	2,149	2,244
Treasury stock	(199)	(199)	—	—	—	—
Total Shareholders' Equity	$ 16,322	$ 9,310	$ 7,798	$ 6,812	$ 5,780	$ 5,875
Total Liabilities and Shareholders' Equity	$102,243	$77,597	$23,976	$17,924	$39,061	$19,457

In mid-Year 14, however, FBN began a rapid descent. Although still growing rapidly, its cash flow was inadequate to service its debt. According to Mather, he was "just dumbfounded. There was never an inkling of a problem with cash."

In the fall of Year 14, the board of directors withdrew the company's financial statements for the year ending April 30, Year 14, stating that there appeared to be material misstatements that needed investigation. In December of Year 14, Mather was asked to step aside as manager and director of the company pending completion of an investigation of certain transactions between Mather and the company. On December 29, Year 14, NASDAQ (over-the-counter stock market) discontinued quoting the company's common shares. In February, Year 15, following its investigation, the board of directors terminated Mather's employment and membership on the board.

Exhibits 5.31–5.33 present the financial statements and related notes of FBN for the five years ending April, Year 10, through April, Year 14. The financial statements for Year 10 to Year 12 use the amounts originally reported for each year. The amounts reported on the statement of cash flows for Year 10 (for example, the change in accounts receivable) do not precisely reconcile to the amounts on the balance sheet at the beginning and end of the year because certain items classified as relating to continuing operations on the balance sheet at the end of Year 9 were reclassified as relating to discontinued operations on the balance sheet at the end of Year 10. The financial statements for Year 13 and Year 14 represent the restated financial statements for those years after the board of directors completed its investigation of suspected material misstatements that caused it to withdraw the originally issued financial statements for fiscal Year 14. Exhibit 5.34 (see page 422) lists the members of the board of directors. Exhibit 5.35 (see page 422) presents profitability and risk ratios for FBN.

EXHIBIT 5.32

Fly-by-Night International Group
Comparative Income Statements
(amounts in thousands)
(Case 5.3)

For the Year Ended April 30:	Year 14	Year 13	Year 12	Year 11	Year 10
CONTINUING OPERATIONS					
Sales	$54,988	$36,597	$20,758	$19,266	$31,992
EXPENSES					
Cost of services	$38,187	$26,444	$12,544	$ 9,087	$22,003
Selling and administrative	5,880	3,020	3,467	2,989	4,236
Depreciation	9,810	3,150	1,703	2,798	3,003
Interest	5,841	3,058	1,101	2,743	2,600
Income taxes	(900)	379	803	671	74
Total Expenses	$58,818	$36,051	$19,618	$18,288	$31,916
Income—Continuing operations	$(3,830)	$ 546	$ 1,140	$ 978	$ 76
Income—Discontinued Operations	—	47	(400)	(659)	(171)
Net Income	$(3,830)	$ 593	$ 740	$ 319	$ (95)

EXHIBIT 5.33

Fly-by-Night International Group
Comparative Statements of Cash Flows
(amounts in thousands)
(Case 5.3)

For the Year Ended April 30:	Year 14	Year 13	Year 12	Year 11	Year 10
OPERATIONS					
Income—Continuing operations	$ (3,830)	$ 546	$ 1,140	$ 978	$ 76
Depreciation	9,810	3,150	1,703	2,798	3,003
Other adjustments	1,074	1,817	1,119	671	74
Changes in Working Capital:					
(Increase) Decrease in receivables	(1,671)	(2,199)	(1,185)	(407)	403
(Increase) Decrease in inventories	(2,592)	(962)	(950)	40	19
(Increase) Decrease in prepayments	164	(360)	(412)	246	36
Increase (Decrease) in accounts payable	6,149	5,286	54	(1,346)	359
Increase (Decrease) in other current liabilities	779	9,701	1,113	(535)	596
Cash Flow from Continuing Operations	$ 9,883	$ 16,979	$ 2,582	$ 2,445	$ 4,566
Cash flow from discontinued operations	—	(77)	(472)	(752)	(335)
Net Cash Flow from Operations	$ 9,883	$ 16,902	$ 2,110	$ 1,693	$ 4,231
INVESTING					
Sale of property, plant, and equipment	$ 259	$ 3	$ 119	$ 18,387	$ 12
Acquisition of property, plant, and equipment	(33,035)	(52,960)	(6,573)	(2,424)	(20,953)
Other	(1,484)	78	1,017	(679)	30
Net Cash Flow from Investing	$(34,260)	$(52,879)	$(5,437)	$ 15,284	$(20,911)
FINANCING					
Increase in short-term borrowing	$ —	$ 805	$ —	$ —	$ 4,766
Increase in long-term borrowing	43,279	42,152	5,397	5,869	14,739
Issue of common stock	12,266	191	428	—	—
Decrease in short-term borrowing	(945)	—	(881)	(3,745)	—
Decrease in long-term borrowing	(30,522)	(7,024)	(1,647)	(19,712)	(2,264)
Acquisition of common stock	—	(198)	—	—	—
Other	(125)	321	201	—	—
Net Cash Flow from Financing	$ 23,953	$ 36,247	$ 3,498	$(17,588)	$ 17,241
Change in Cash	$ (424)	$ 270	$ 171	$ (611)	$ 561
Cash—Beginning of year	583	313	142	753	192
Cash—End of Year	$ 159	$ 583	$ 313	$ 142	$ 753

EXHIBIT 5.34

Fly-by-Night International Group
Members of the Board of Directors
(Case 5.3)

Charles A. Barry, USAF (Ret.), Executive Vice President of Wicks and Associates, Inc., a management consulting firm
Thomas P. Gilkey, Vice President, Marketing
Lawrence G. Hicks, Secretary and General Counsel
Michael S. Holt, Vice President, Finance, and Chief Financial Officer
Gordon K. John, Executive Vice President and Chief Operating Officer
Douglas C. Mather, Chair of the Board, President and Chief Executive Officer
Edward F. O'Hara, President of the O'Hara Companies, which manufactures aircraft products
E. William Shapiro, Professor of Law, Emory University

EXHIBIT 5.35

Profitability and Risk Ratios for FBN
(Case 5.3)

	Year 14	Year 13	Year 12	Year 11	Year 10
Profit Margin for ROA	(0.1%)	6.9%	9.0%	14.5	5.6%
Assets Turnover	0.6	0.7	1.0	0.7	1.1
ROA	0.0%	5.0%	8.9%	9.8%	6.1%
Cost of Goods and Services/Sales	69.4%	72.3%	60.4%	47.2%	68.8%
Selling and Administrative/Sales	10.7%	8.3%	16.7%	15.5%	13.2%
Depreciation Expense/Sales	17.8%	8.6%	8.2%	14.5%	9.4%
Income Tax Expense (excluding tax effects of interest)/Sales	2.1%	4.0%	5.7%	8.3%	3.0%
Interest Expense/Sales	10.6%	8.4%	5.3%	14.2%	8.1%
Days Accounts Receivable	38	38	37	24	18
Days Accounts Payable	84	48	26	65	31
Fixed Assets Turnover	0.7	0.8	1.3	0.8	1.3
Profit Margin for ROCE	(7.0%)	1.5%	5.5%	5.1%	0.2%
Capital Structure Leverage	7.0	5.9	2.9	4.5	5.0
ROCE	(29.9%)	6.4%	15.6%	15.5%	1.3%
Current Ratio	0.2	0.3	0.9	0.8	0.4
Quick Ratio	0.1	0.2	0.6	0.6	0.2
Operating Cash Flow to Current Liabilities Ratio	0.176	1.071	0.531	0.305	0.618
Liabilities to Assets Ratio	0.840	0.880	0.675	0.620	0.852
Long-Term Debt to Long-Term Capital Ratio	0.000	0.815	0.557	0.497	0.776
Operating Cash Flow to Total Liabilities Ratio	0.128	0.402	0.189	0.112	0.195
Interest Coverage Ratio	0.2	1.3	2.8	1.6	1.1

Required

Study these financial statements and notes and respond to the following questions:

a. What evidence do you observe from analyzing the financial statements that might signal the cash flow problems experienced in mid-Year 14?

b. Can FBN avoid bankruptcy during Year 15? What changes in the design or implementation of FBN's strategy would you recommend? To compute Altman's Z-score, use the low-bid market price for the year to determine the market value of common shareholders' equity.

Notes to Financial Statements

1. Summary of Significant Accounting Policies

Consolidation. The consolidated financial statements include the accounts of the company and its wholly owned subsidiaries. The company uses the equity method for subsidiaries that are not majority owned (50 percent or less) and eliminates significant intercompany transactions and balances.

Inventories. Inventories, which consist of aircraft fuel, spare parts, and supplies, appear at lower of FIFO cost or market.

Property and Equipment. Property and equipment appear at acquisition cost. The company capitalizes major inspections, renewals, and improvements, while it expenses replacements, maintenance, and repairs that do not improve or extend the life of the respective assets. The company computes depreciation of property and equipment using the straight-line method.

Contract Income Recognition. Contractual specifications (such as revenue rates, reimbursement terms, and functional considerations) vary among contracts; accordingly, the company recognizes guaranteed contract income (guaranteed revenue less related direct costs) as it logs flight hours or on a straight-line monthly basis over the contract year, whichever method better reflects the economics of the contract. The company recognizes income from discretionary hours flown in excess of the minimum guaranteed amount each month as it logs such discretionary hours.

Income Taxes. The company recognizes deferred income taxes for temporary differences between financial and tax reporting amounts.

2. Transactions with Major Customers

The company provides contract flight services to three major customers: the U.S. Air Force, the U.S. Navy, and the Federal Reserve Bank System. These contracts have termination dates in Year 16 or Year 17. Revenues from all government contracts as a percentage of total revenues were as follows: Year 14, 62 percent; Year 13, 72 percent; Year 12, 73 percent; Year 11, 68 percent; and Year 10, 31 percent.

3. Segment Data

During Year 10, the company operated in the following five business segments:

Flight Operations—Business. Provides combat readiness training to the military and nightly transfer of negotiable instruments for the Federal Reserve Bank System, both under multiyear contracts.

Flight Operations—Transport. Provides charter transport services to a variety of customers.

Fixed-Base Operations. Provides ground support operations (fuel and maintenance) to commercial airlines at several major airports.

Education and Training. Provides training for nonmilitary pilots.

Aircraft Sales and Leasing. Acquires aircraft that the company then resells or leases to various firms.

The company discontinued the Flight Operations—Transport and Education and Training segments in Year 11. It sold most of the assets of the Aircraft Sales and Leasing segment in Year 11.

Segment revenue, operating profit, and asset data for the various segments are as follows (amounts in thousands):

April 30:	Year 14	Year 13	Year 12	Year 11	Year 10
Revenues					
Flight Operations—Business	$ 44,062	$31,297	$16,026	$11,236	$10,803
Flight Operations—Transport	—	—	—	—	13,805
Fixed-Base Operations	9,597	4,832	4,651	3,911	3,647
Education and Training	—	—	—	—	542
Aircraft Sales and Leasing	1,329	468	81	4,119	3,195
Total	$ 54,988	$36,597	$20,758	$19,266	$31,992
Operating Profit					
Flight Operations—Business	$ 5,707	$ 4,863	$ 3,455	$ 2,463	$ 849
Flight Operations—Transport	—	—	—	—	(994)
Fixed-Base Operations	(2,041)	1,362	1,038	174	332
Education and Training	—	—	—	—	12
Aircraft Sales and Leasing	1,175	378	(15)	1,217[b]	2,726[a]
Total	$ 4,841	$ 6,603	$ 4,478	$ 3,854	$ 2,925
Assets					
Flight Operations—Business	$ 85,263	$64,162	$17,738	$11,130	$13,684
Flight Operations—Transport	—	—	—	—	1,771
Fixed-Base Operations	16,544	13,209	5,754	5,011	4,784
Education and Training	—	—	—	—	1,789
Aircraft Sales and Leasing	436	226	438	1,262	18,524
Total	$102,243	$77,597	$23,930	$17,403	$40,552

[a]Includes a gain of $2.6 million on the sale of aircraft
[b]Includes a gain of $1.2 million on the sale of aircraft

4. Discontinued Operations

Income from discontinued operations consists of the following (amounts in thousands):

Year 13

Income from operations of Flight Operations—Transport ($78),
  net of income taxes of $31 $ 47

Year 12

Loss from write-off of airline operations certificates in
  Flight Operations—Transport business $(400)

Year 11

Loss from operations of Flight Operations—Transport
  ($1,261) and Education and Training ($172) segments,
  net of income tax benefits of $685 $(748)

Gain on disposal of Education and Training business, net
  of income taxes of $85   89
  Total $(659)

Year 10

Loss from operations of Charter Tour business, net of
  income tax benefits of $164 $(171)

5. Related-Party Transactions

On April 30, Year 11, the company sold most of the net assets of the Aircraft Sales and Leasing segment to Interlease, Inc., a Georgia corporation wholly owned by the company's majority stockholder, whose personal holdings at that time represented approximately 75 percent of the company.

Under the terms of the sale, the sales price was $1,368,000, of which the buyer paid $368,000 in cash and gave a promissory note for the remaining $1,000,000. The company treated the proceeds received in excess of the book value of the net assets sold of $712,367 as a capital contribution due to the related-party nature of the transaction. FBN originally acquired the assets of the Aircraft Sales and Leasing segment during Year 10.

On September 29, Year 14, FBN's board of directors established a Transaction Committee to examine certain transactions between the company and Douglas Mather, FBN's chair, president, and majority stockholder. These transactions appear here.

Certain Loans to Mather. In early September, Year 13, the board of directors authorized a $1 million loan to Mather at the company's cost of borrowing plus $1/_8$ percent. On September 19, Year 13, Mather tendered a $1 million check to the company in repayment of the loan. On September 22, Year 13, at Mather's direction, the company made an additional $1 million loan to him, the proceeds of which Mather apparently used to cover his check in repayment of the first $1 million loan. The Transaction Committee concluded that the board of directors did not authorize the September 22, Year 13, loan to Mather, nor was any director other than Mather aware of the loan at the time. The company's Year 13 Proxy Statement, dated September 27, Year 13, incorrectly stated that "as of September 19, Year 13, Mather had repaid the principal amount of his indebtedness to the company." Mather's $1 million loan remained outstanding until it was canceled in connection with the ESOP (employee stock ownership plan) transaction discussed next.

ESOP Transaction. On February 28, Year 14, the company's ESOP acquired 100,000 shares of the company's common stock from Mather at $14.25 per share. FBN financed the purchase. The ESOP gave the company a $1,425,000 unsecured demand note. To complete the transaction, the company canceled a $1,000,000 promissory note from Mather and paid the remaining $425,000 in cash. The Transaction Committee determined that the board of directors did not authorize the $1,425,000 loan to the ESOP, the cancellation of Mather's $1,000,000 note, or the payment of $425,000 in cash.

Eastwind Transaction. On April 27, Year 14, the company acquired four Eastwind aircraft from a German company. FBN subsequently sold these aircraft to Transreco, a corporation owned by Douglas Mather, for a profit of $1,600,000. In late September and early October, Transreco sold these four aircraft at a profit of $780,000 to unaffiliated third parties. The Transactions Committee determined that none of the officers or directors of the company were aware of the Eastwind transaction until late September, Year 14.

On December 12, Year 14, the company announced that Mather had agreed to step aside as chair and director and take no part in management of the company pending resolution of the matters presented to the board by the Transactions Committee. On February 13, Year 15, the company announced that it had entered into a settlement agreement with Mather and Transreco resolving certain of the issues addressed by the Transactions Committee. Pursuant to the agreement, the company will receive $211,000, the bonus paid to Mather for fiscal Year 14, and $780,000, the gain recognized by Transreco on the sale of the Eastwind aircraft. Also pursuant to the settlement, Mather will resign all positions with the company and waive his rights under his employment agreement to any future compensation or benefits to which he might otherwise have a claim.

6. Long-Term Debt

Long-term debt consists of the following (amounts in thousands):

April 30:	Year 14	Year 13	Year 12	Year 11	Year 10
Notes Payable to Banks:					
Variable Rate	$44,702	$30,495	$ 2,086	$2,504	$ 3,497
Fixed Rate	13,555	14,679	6,292	3,562	1,228
Notes Payable to Finance Companies:					
Variable Rate	—	—	1,320	1,667	10,808
Fixed Rate	—	—	—	—	325
Capitalized Lease Obligations	2,333	2,865	1,295	—	5,297
Other	—	—	600	39	1,660
Total	$60,590	$48,039	$11,593	$7,842	$22,815
Less Current Portion	(60,590)	(7,018)	(1,789)	(1,104)	(2,774)
Net	$ —	$41,021	$ 9,804	$6,738	$20,041

Substantially all of the company's property, plant, and equipment serve as collateral for this debt. The borrowings from bank and finance companies contain restrictive covenants, the most restrictive of which appear in the following table:

	Year 14	Year 13	Year 12	Year 11	Year 10
Liabilities/Tangible Net Worth	<2.5	<3.0	<4.2	<5.5	<6.7
Tangible Net Worth	>$20,000	>$5,800	>$5,400	>$5,300	>$5,100
Working Capital	>$5,000	—	—	—	—
Interest Coverage Ratio	>1.15	—	—	—	—

As of April 30, Year 14, the company is in default of its debt covenants. It is also in default with respect to covenants underlying its capitalized lease obligations. As a result, lenders have the right to accelerate repayment of their loans. Accordingly, the company has classified all of its long-term debt as a current liability.

The company has entered into operating leases for aircraft and other equipment. The estimated present value of the minimum lease payments under these operating leases as of April 30 of each year is as follows:

Year 14:	$2,706
Year 13:	$3,142
Year 12:	$3,594
Year 11:	$3,971
Year 10:	$4,083

7. Income Taxes

Income tax expense consists of the following:

		Year Ended April 30			
	Year 14	Year 13	Year 12	Year 11	Year 10
Current					
Federal	$ —	$ —	$ —	$—	$ —
State	—	—	—	—	—
Deferred					
Federal	$(845)	$380	$685	$67	$(85)
State	(55)	30	118	4	(5)
Total	$(900)	$410	$803	$71	$(90)

The cumulative tax loss and tax credit carryovers as of April 30 of each year are as follows:

April 30:	Tax Loss	Tax Credit
Year 14	$10,300	$250
Year 13	5,200	280
Year 12	1,400	300
Year 11	2,100	450
Year 10	4,500	750

The deferred tax provision results from temporary differences in the recognition of revenues and expenses for income tax and financial reporting. The sources and amounts of these differences for each year are as follows:

	Year 14	Year 13	Year 12	Year 11	Year 10
Depreciation	$ —	$ 503	$ 336	$(770)	$ 778
Aircraft Modification Costs	—	1,218	382	982	703
Net Operating Losses	(900)	(1,384)	290	—	(1,729)
Other	—	73	(205)	(141)	158
Total	$(900)	$ 410	$ 803	$ 71	$ (90)

A reconciliation of the effective tax rate with the statutory tax rate is as follows:

	Year 14	Year 13	Year 12	Year 11	Year 10
Federal Taxes at Statutory Rate	(35.0)%	35.0%	34.0%	34.0%	(34.0)%
State Income Taxes	(2.5)	3.0	3.0	3.0	(3.0)
Effect of Net Operating Loss and Investment Credits	16.5	—	(7.2)	(29.9)	—
Other	2.0	2.9	22.2	11.1	(12.0)
Effect Tax Rate	(19.0)%	40.9%	52.0%	18.2%	(49.0)%

8. Market Price Information

The company's common stock trades on the NASDAQ National Market System under the symbol FBN. Trading in the company common stock commenced on January 10, Year 10. High- and low-bid prices during each fiscal year are as follows:

Fiscal Year	High Bid	Low Bid
Year 14	$16.50	$9.50
Year 13	$14.63	$6.25
Year 12	$11.25	$3.25
Year 11	$ 4.63	$3.00
Year 10	$ 5.25	$3.25

On December 29, Year 14, the company announced that NASDAQ had decided to discontinue quoting the company's common stock because of the company's failure to comply with NASDAQ's filing requirements.

Ownership of the company's stock at various dates appears here.

April 30:	Year 14	Year 13	Year 12	Year 11	Year 10
Douglas Mather	42%	68%	72%	75%	75%
Public	48	23	24	25	25
Company ESOP	10	9	4	—	—
	100%	100%	100%	100%	100%
Common Shares Outstanding (000's)	3,357.5	2,222.8	2,095.0	2,000.0	2,000.0

CASE 5.4

MILLENNIAL TECHNOLOGIES: APOCALYPSE NOW

Millennial Technologies, a designer, manufacturer, and marketer of PC cards for portable computers, printers, telecommunications equipment, and equipment diagnostic systems, was the darling of Wall Street during Year 6. Its common stock price was the leading gainer for the year on the New York Stock Exchange. Its bubble burst during the third quarter of Year 7 when revelations about seriously misstated financial statements for prior years became known. This case seeks to identify signals of the financial shenanigans and to assess the likelihood of the firm's future survival.

Industry and Products

Digital computing and processing have expanded beyond desktop computing systems in recent years to include a broad array of more mobile applications, including portable computers, cell phones, digital cameras, and medical and automobile diagnostic equipment. A PC card is a rugged, lightweight, credit-card-sized device inserted into a dedicated slot in these products that provides programming, processing, and storage capabilities normally provided on hard drives and floppy disks in conventional desktop computers. The PC card has a high shock and vibration tolerance, low power consumption, a small size, and a high access speed. The market for PC cards is one of the fastest-growing segments of the electronics industry.

Millennial Technologies designs PC cards for four principal industries: (1) communications (routers, cell phones, and local-area networks), (2) transportation (vehicle diagnostics and navigation), (3) mobile computing (handheld data collection terminals and notebook computers), and (4) medical (blood gas analysis systems and defibrillators). The firm targets its engineering and product development, all of which it conducts in-house, to these four industry groups. It works closely with original equipment manufacturers (OEMs) to design PC cards that meet specific needs of products aimed at these four industries. Its customers include Lucent Technologies, Philips Electronics, 3Com Corporation, and Bay Networks. Millennial Technologies also conducts its manufacturing in-house, which allows it to respond quickly to changing requirements and schedules of these OEMs. The firm markets its products using its own sales force.

In Year 4, Millennial Technologies was incorporated in Delaware as the successor of M. Millennial, a Massachusetts corporation. The firm made its initial public offering of common stock (1 million shares) on April 19, Year 4, at a price of $5.625 per share. Each common share issued included a redeemable common stock purchase warrant that permitted the holder to purchase one share of the firm's common stock for $7.20. Prior to its initial public offering, Millennial Technologies obtained a $550,000 bridge loan during Year 4, which it repaid with proceeds from the initial public offering. Holders of the stock purchase warrants exercised their options during Year 5 and Year 6. The firm obtained equity capital during Year 5 as a result of a private placement of its common stock at $5.83 a share. It issued additional shares to the public during Year 6 at $18 a share. Its stock price was $5.25 on June 30, Year 4; $22.625 on June 30, Year 5; $29.875 on June 30, Year 6; and $52 on December 31, Year 7.

Millennial Technologies maintained a line of credit throughout Year 4 to Year 6 with a major Boston bank to finance its accounts receivables and inventories. The borrowing was at the bank's prime lending rate. Substantially all of the assets of the firm collateralized this borrowing.

The firm's chief executive officer, Manuel Pinoza, also is its major shareholder. The firm maintains an employment agreement with Pinoza under which it pays his compensation to a Swiss executive search firm, which then pays Pinoza.

Beginning in Year 6, Millennial Technologies made minority investments in five corporations engaged in technology development, four of which the firm accounts for using the cost method and one of which it accounts for using the equity method. Products developed by these companies could conceivably use PC cards. Millennial Technologies also advanced amounts to some of these companies using interest-bearing notes.

Exhibits 5.36–5.38 (see pages 430–432) present the financial statements for the fiscal years ended June 30, Year 4, Year 5, and Year 6, for Millennial Technologies based on the amounts originally reported for each year. Exhibit 5.39 (see page 433) presents selected financial statement ratios based on these reported amounts.

Financial Statement Irregularities

On February 10, Year 7, after receiving information regarding various accounting and reporting irregularities, the board of directors fired Pinoza and relieved the chief financial officer of his duties. The board formed a special committee of outside directors to investigate the purported irregularities, obtaining the assistance of legal counsel and the firm's independent accountants. On February 21, Year 7, the New York Stock Exchange

EXHIBIT 5.36

Balance Sheets for Millennial Technologies
As Originally Reported
(amounts in thousands)
(Case 5.4)

Year Ended June 30:	Year 6	Year 5	Year 4	Year 3
ASSETS				
Cash	$ 6,182	$ 970	$ 981	$ —
Marketable securities	4,932	—	—	—
Accounts receivable	12,592	3,932	1,662	730
Inventories	18,229	8,609	3,371	2,257
Other current assets	6,256	1,932	306	234
Total Current Assets	$48,191	$15,443	$6,320	$3,221
Investments in securities	2,472	—	—	—
Property, plant, and equipment, net	4,698	1,323	669	208
Other assets	421	1,433	601	666
Total Assets	$55,782	$18,199	$7,590	$4,095
LIABILITIES AND SHAREHOLDERS' EQUITY				
Accounts payable	$ 3,494	$ 3,571	$ 616	$1,590
Notes payable	4,684	1,153	—	980
Current portion of long-term debt	336	103	—	—
Other current liabilities	614	765	516	457
Total Current Liabilities	$ 9,128	$ 5,592	$1,132	$3,027
Long-term debt	367	162	—	—
Deferred tax liability	242	—	39	24
Total Liabilities	$ 9,737	$ 5,754	$1,171	$3,051
Common stock	$ 165	$ 110	$ 90	$ 60
Additional paid-in capital	38,802	10,159	5,027	146
Retained earnings	7,078	2,176	1,302	838
Total Shareholders' Equity	$46,045	$12,445	$6,419	$1,044
Total Liabilities and Shareholders' Equity	$55,782	$18,199	$7,590	$4,095

announced the suspension of trading in the firm's common stock. The stock was delisted on April 25, Year 7. On February 14, Year 7, the major Boston bank providing working capital financing notified the firm that the firm had defaulted on its line of credit agreement. Although this bank subsequently extended the line of credit through July 31, Year 7, it increased the interest rate significantly above prime. Millennial Technologies decided to seek a new lender.

The investigation by the board's special committee revealed the following accounting and reporting irregularities:

- Recording of invalid sales transactions: The firm created fictitious purchase orders from regular customers using purchase order forms from legitimate purchase transactions.

EXHIBIT 5.37

Income Statements for Millennial Technologies
As Originally Reported
(amounts in thousands)
(Case 5.4)

For the Year Ended June 30:	Year 6	Year 5	Year 4
Sales	$ 37,848	$12,445	$ 8,213
Other revenues	353	10	9
Cost of goods sold	(23,636)	(6,833)	(4,523)
Selling and administrative	(4,591)	(3,366)	(1,889)
Research and development	(1,434)	(752)	(567)
Interest	(370)	(74)	(495)[a]
Income taxes	(3,268)	(556)	(284)
Net Income	$ 4,902	$ 874	$ 464

[a]Includes the cost of factoring receivables and interest on bridge financing obtained and repaid during the year.

The firm then purportedly shipped empty PC card housings to these customers at bogus addresses. Pinoza apparently paid the accounts receivable underlying these sales with his personal funds.

- Recording of revenues from bill and hold transactions: The firm kept its books open beyond June 30 each year and recorded as sales of each year products that were shipped in July and should have been recorded as revenues of the next fiscal year.
- Manipulation of physical counts of inventory balances and inclusion of empty PC card housings in finished goods inventories.
- Failure to write down inventories adequately for product obsolescence.
- Inclusion of certain costs in property, plant, and equipment that the firm should have expensed in the period incurred.
- Inclusion in advances to other technology companies of amounts that represented prepaid license fees. The firm should have amortized these fees over the license period.
- Failure to provide adequately for uncollectible amounts related to advances to other technology companies.
- Failure to write down or write off investments in other technology companies when their market value was less than the cost of the investment.

Exhibits 5.40–5.42 (see pages 434–436) present the restated financial statements for Millennial Technologies for the fiscal years ending June 30, Year 4, Year 5, and Year 6, after correcting for the irregularities described previously. These exhibits also present the financial statements for the nine months ended March 30, Year 7. The firm decided during February of Year 7 to change its fiscal year to a March year-end. Exhibit 5.43 presents (see page 437) selected financial ratios based on the restated financial statements.

Required

a. Using information in the financial statements as originally reported in Exhibits 5.36–5.38, compute the value of Beneish's manipulation index for fiscal Year 5 and Year 6.

EXHIBIT 5.38

Statements of Cash Flows for Millennial Technologies
As Originally Reported
(amounts in thousands)
(Case 5.4)

For the Year Ended June 30:	Year 6	Year 5	Year 4
OPERATIONS			
Net income	$ 4,902	$ 874	$ 464
Depreciation	645	337	193
Other addbacks and subtractions, net	1,159	(5)	219
Working capital provided by operations	$ 6,706	$ 1,206	$ 876
(Increase) Decrease in accounts receivables	(8,940)	(2,433)	(981)
(Increase) Decrease in inventories	(9,620)	(5,238)	(1,115)
(Increase) Decrease in other current assets	(836)	(2,406)	(71)
Increase (Decrease) in accounts payable	(76)	2,955	(974)
Increase (Decrease) in other current liabilities	(152)	251	87
Cash Flow from Operations	$(12,918)	$(5,665)	$(2,178)
INVESTING			
Sale of investments	$ 3,981	$ —	$ —
Acquisition of fixed assets	(3,899)	(862)	(525)
Acquisitions of investments	(11,186)	—	—
Other investing transactions	(2,800)	—	—
Cash Flow from Investing	$(13,904)	$ (862)	$ (525)
FINANCING			
Increase in short-term borrowing	$ 3,531	$ 1,153	$ 550
Increase in long-term borrowing	691	320	—
Increase in common stock	28,064	5,099	4,663
Decrease in short-term borrowing	—	—	(1,529)
Decrease in long-term borrowing	(252)	(56)	—
Cash Flow from Financing	$ 32,034	$ 6,516	$ 3,684
Net Change in Cash	$ 5,212	$ (11)	$ 981
Cash—Beginning of year	970	981	—
Cash—End of Year	$ 6,182	$ 970	$ 981

b. Using information from Part a and the financial ratios in Exhibit 5.39, indicate possible signals that Millennial Technologies might have been manipulating its financial statements.

c. Describe the effect of each of the eight accounting irregularities on the balance sheet, income statement, and statement of cash flows.

EXHIBIT 5.39

Financial Ratios for Millennial Technologies Based on Originally Reported Amounts (Case 5.4)

	Year 6	Year 5	Year 4
Profit Margin for ROA	13.6%	7.4%	9.6%
Assets Turnover	1.0	1.0	1.4
ROA	13.9%	7.2%	13.5%
Profit Margin for ROCE	13.0%	7.0%	5.6%
Capital Structure Leverage	1.3	1.4	1.6
ROCE	16.8%	9.3%	12.4%
Cost of Goods Sold/Sales	62.4%	54.9%	55.1%
Selling and Administrative/Sales	12.1%	27.0%	23.0%
Research and Development/Sales	3.8%	6.0%	6.9%
Income Tax Expense (excluding tax effects of interest expense)/Sales	9.0%	4.7%	5.5%
Accounts Receivable Turnover	4.6	4.4	6.9
Inventory Turnover	1.8	1.1	1.6
Fixed Assets Turnover	12.6	12.5	18.7
Current Ratio	5.3	2.8	5.6
Quick Ratio	2.6	0.9	2.3
Days Accounts Payable	39	63	71
Operating Cash Flow to Current Liabilities Ratio	(1.755)	(1.685)	(1.047)
Long-Term Debt to Long-Term Capital Ratio	0.008	0.013	—
Liabilities to Assets Ratio	0.175	0.316	0.154
Operating Cash Flow to Total Liabilities Ratio	(1.668)	(1.636)	(1.032)
Interest Coverage Ratio	23.1	20.3	2.5

d. Using information in the restated financial statements in Exhibits 5.40–5.42, the financial ratios in Exhibit 5.43, and the information provided in this case, as a commercial banker, would you be willing to offer Millennial Technologies a line of credit as of July 31, Year 7? If so, provide the conditions that would induce you to offer such a line of credit.

e. Exhibit 5.44 (see page 438) presents the values of Altman's Z-score for fiscal Year 4, Year 5, and Year 6 based on the originally reported amounts and the restated amounts. Compute the value of Altman's Z-score for the fiscal year ended March 31, Year 7. Although this is not technically correct, use the income amounts for the nine-month period ending March 31, Year 7. Based on the amounts in the proposed settlement of the class-action lawsuits, the value of the common equity on March 31, Year 7, is $50,068,568.

f. Can Millennial Technologies avoid bankruptcy as of mid-Year 7? Explain. Why doesn't the Altman model signal the financial difficulties earlier?

EXHIBIT 5.40

Balance Sheets for Millennial Technologies
Using Restated Data
(amounts in thousands)
(Case 5.4)

	March 31:	June 30:			
	Year 7	Year 6	Year 5	Year 4	Year 3
ASSETS					
Cash	$ 57	$ 6,182	$ 970	$ 981	$ —
Marketable securities	—	4,932	—	—	—
Accounts receivable	5,571	11,260	2,802	1,280	730
Inventories	7,356	8,248	2,181	1,581	2,257
Other current assets	14,229	6,395	2,284	839	669
Total Current Assets	$ 27,213	$ 37,017	$ 8,237	$4,681	$3,656
Investments in securities	20,332	1,783	—	—	—
Property, plant, and equipment, net	3,087	2,033	923	399	243
Other assets	566	299	390	123	172
Total Assets	$ 51,198	$ 41,132	$ 9,550	$5,203	$4,071
LIABILITIES AND SHAREHOLDERS' EQUITY					
Accounts payable	$ 4,766	$ 3,025	$ 3,303	$ 772	$1,590
Notes payable	10,090	4,684	1,153	—	980
Current portion of long-term debt	671	336	103	—	—
Other current liabilities	7,117	811	562	116	457
Total Current Liabilities	$ 22,644	$ 8,856	$ 5,121	$ 888	$3,027
Long-term debt	—	367	162	—	—
Total Liabilities	$ 22,644	$ 9,223	$ 5,283	$ 888	$3,027
Common stock	$ 177	$ 165	$ 110	$ 90	$ 60
Additional paid-in capital	82,240	42,712	10,843	5,059	146
Retained earnings	(53,630)	(10,968)	(6,686)	(834)	838
Foreign currency adjustment	(233)	—	—	—	—
Total Shareholders' Equity	$ 28,554	$ 31,909	$ 4,267	$4,315	$1,044
Total Liabilities and Shareholders' Equity	$ 51,198	$ 41,132	$ 9,550	$5,203	$4,071

EXHIBIT 5.41

Income Statements for Millennial Technologies Using Restated Data (amounts in thousands) (Case 5.4)

	Nine Months Ended March 31:	Year Ended June 30:		
	Year 7	Year 6	Year 5	Year 4
Sales	$ 28,263	$ 33,412	$ 8,982	$ 7,801
Other revenues	67	353	10	9
Cost of goods sold	(24,453)	(29,778)	(11,575)	(6,508)
Selling and administrative	(7,318)	(3,803)	(2,442)	(2,083)
Research and development	(1,061)	(1,434)	(753)	(567)
Loss on investments	(14,096)[a]	(2,662)[a]	—	—
Investigation costs	(3,673)[b]	—	—	—
Provision for settlement of shareholder litigation	(20,000)[c]	—	—	—
Interest	(391)	(370)	(74)	(495)
Income taxes	—[d]	—[d]	—[d]	171
Net Income (Loss)	$(42,662)	$ (4,282)	$ (5,852)	$(1,672)

[a]Write-offs of advances (and write-downs or write-offs of investments) in technology companies.

[b]Legal, accounting, and related costs of investigating misstatements of financial statements.

[c]Estimated cost of class-action lawsuits arising from misstatements of financial statements. Millennial Technologies reached an agreement on June 18, Year 7, to pay the plaintiffs $1,475,000 in cash (included in accounts payable on the March 31, Year 7 balance sheet) and common stock of $18,525,000 (included in additional paid-in capital on the March 31, Year 7 balance sheet). The common stock portion of the settlement represents 37 percent of the common stock of Millennial Technologies.

[d]Millennial Technologies incurred net losses for income tax purposes and maintains a valuation allowance equal to the balance in deferred tax assets.

EXHIBIT 5.42

Statements of Cash Flows for Millennial Technologies
Using Restated Data
(amounts in thousands)
(Case 5.4)

	Nine Months Ended March 31:	Year Ended June 30:		
	Year 7	Year 6	Year 5	Year 4
OPERATIONS				
Net loss	$(42,662)	$ (4,282)	$(5,852)	$(1,672)
Depreciation and amortization	831	471	281	176
Other addbacks and subtractions, net	28,812	2,005	224	352
Working capital provided by operations	$(13,019)	$ (1,806)	$(5,347)	$(1,144)
(Increase) Decrease in accounts receivable	5,289	(8,883)	(1,693)	(599)
Increase (Decrease) in inventories	454	(6,067)	(600)	676
(Increase) Decrease in other current assets	(8,092)	(5,213)	(1,932)	(176)
Increase (Decrease) in accounts payable	6,572	(9)	3,072	(818)
Increase (Decrease) in other current liabilities	—	(20)	(96)	(340)
Cash Flow from Operations	$ (8,796)	$(21,998)	$(6,596)	$(2,401)
INVESTING				
Sale of investments	$ 32,182	$ 3,981	$ —	$ —
Acquisition of fixed assets	(2,074)	(1,459)	(583)	(332)
Acquisition of investments	(38,892)	(11,186)	—	—
Cash Flow from Investing	$ (8,784)	$ (8,664)	$ (583)	$ (332)
FINANCING				
Increase in short-term borrowing	$ 5,406	$ 3,531	$ 1,153	$ 550
Increase in long-term borrowing	250	691	320	—
Increase in capital stock	4,060	28,813	5,099	4,663
Decrease in short-term borrowing	—	—	—	(1,529)
Decrease in long-term borrowing	(282)	(252)	(56)	—
Proceeds from related-party transaction	2,021	3,091	652	30
Cash Flow from Financing	$ 11,455	$ 35,874	$ 7,168	$ 3,714
Change in Cash	$ (6,125)	$ 5,212	$ (11)	$ 981
Cash—Beginning of year	6,182	970	981	—
Cash—End of Year	$ 57	$ 6,182	$ 970	$ 981

EXHIBIT 5.43

Financial Ratios for Millennial Technologies Based on Restated Data (Case 5.4)

	Year 7[a]	Year 6	Year 5	Year 4
Profit Margin for ROA	(150.0%)	(12.1%)	(64.6%)	(17.2%)
Assets Turnover	0.6	1.3	1.2	1.7
ROA	(91.9%)	(15.9%)	(78.7%)	(29.0%)
Profit Margin for ROCE	(150.9%)	(12.8%)	(65.2%)	(21.4%)
Capital Structure Leverage	1.5	1.4	1.7	1.7
ROCE	(141.1%)	(23.7%)	(136.4%)	(62.4%)
Cost of Goods Sold/Sales	86.5%	89.1%	128.9%	83.4%
Selling and Administrative/Sales	25.9%	11.4%	27.2%	26.7%
Research and Development/Sales	3.8%	4.3%	8.4%	7.3%
Special Provisions/Sales	133.6%	8.0%	—	—
Accounts Receivable Turnover	3.4	4.8	4.4	7.8
Inventory Turnover	3.1	5.7	6.2	3.4
Fixed Assets Turnover	11.0	22.6	13.6	24.3
Current Ratio	1.2	4.2	1.6	5.3
Quick Ratio	0.3	2.5	0.7	2.6
Days Accounts Payable	60	32	61	74
Operating Cash Flow to Current Liabilities Ratio	(0.558)	(3.148)	(2.195)	(1.227)
Long-Term Debt to Long-Term Capital Ratio	—	0.011	0.037	—
Liabilities to Assets Ratio	0.442	0.224	0.553	0.171
Operating Cash Flow to Total Liabilities Ratio	(0.552)	(3.033)	(2.138)	(1.227)
Interest Coverage Ratio	(108.1)	(10.6)	(78.1)	(2.7)

[a]Amounts based on a nine-month fiscal year

EXHIBIT 5.44

Altman's Z-Score for Millennial Technologies
(Case 5.4)

	Originally Reported Data			Restated Data		
	Year 6	Year 5	Year 4	Year 6	Year 5	Year 4
Net Working Capital/Total Assets	0.8403	0.6496	0.8203	0.8216	0.3915	0.8748
Retained Earnings/Total Assets	0.1776	0.1674	0.2402	(0.3733)	(0.9801)	(0.2244)
Income Before Interest and Taxes/Total Assets	0.5052	0.2727	0.5404	(0.3139)	(1.9966)	(0.8550)
Market Value of Equity/Book Value of Liabilities	15.3089	13.1911	8.0700	16.1620	14.3672	10.6419
Sales/Total Assets	0.6785	0.6838	1.0821	0.8123	0.9405	1.4993
Z-Score	17.5105	14.9646	10.7530	17.1088	12.7225	11.9366

Chapter **6**

Financing Activities

Learning Objectives

1 Describe the financial statement reporting of investments by owners (equity issuances) and distributions to owners (dividends and share repurchases).

2 Explain the accounting for equity issued to compensate employees (stock options, stock appreciation rights, and restricted stock).

3 Separate financial reporting effects of transactions with non-owners into those that flow through the current income statement (net income) and those that do not (other comprehensive income).

4 Apply financial statement recognition principles to long-term and short-term debt (bonds, notes payable, leases, and troubled debt).

5 Explain the accounting for and financial reporting of hybrid securities.

6 Identify forms of off-balance-sheet financing and, when necessary, how to adjust the financial statements to recognize this financing.

7 Understand the effects of the accounting methods for operating and capital leases on the financial statements and make the adjustments required to convert operating leases to capital leases.

8 Identify the differences between U.S. GAAP and International Financial Reporting Standards in the area of equity and debt financing.

The previous five chapters demonstrated how to analyze a firm's strategy, performance, and financial position using financial statement ratios and analytical tools. This chapter and the next three describe the principles and practices of how the financial statements are prepared so that the analyst can more deeply understand the accounting procedures used by management to, hopefully, best represent the economics of the business. In this chapter, we examine the accounting issues related to financing activities—the right-hand side of the balance sheet. We focus on the financial statement information that conveys the results of raising capital from investors (equity capital) and creditors (debt capital). If the growth opportunities of a business cannot be satisfied using cash flows from current operations or if the terms of external capital are favorable, firms engage in financing activities to raise the capital necessary to engage in investing activities (the acquisition of productive and investment assets), which we cover in Chapter 7. Having deployed external capital into productive assets, firms engage in their primary operating activities, which we discuss in Chapter 8. Throughout Chapters 6–9, we identify the choices made by management and the rules promulgated by standard setters that lead to published financial statements. Because of the rapid pace with which accounting is moving toward common standards for financial reporting, we cover both U.S. generally accepted accounting principles (U.S. GAAP) and standards issued by the International Accounting Standards Board (International Financial Reporting Standards, or IFRS). Many of the accounting principles are similar under U.S. GAAP and IFRS. If a difference exists, we discuss U.S. GAAP and then IFRS differences.[1] Chapter 9 discusses how to evaluate the quality of financial statements and the implications of financial statement quality for forecasting future earnings. The final five chapters, Chapters 10–14, utilize the information derived from the financial ratios analyses and the firm's accounting to forecast future financial statements and to estimate firm value.

To preview the focus in this chapter on financing activities, refer to PepsiCo's December 27, 2008 Consolidated Balance Sheet (Appendix A). PepsiCo reports $35,994 million of total assets, virtually all of it used in operations. The primary claims against these assets are $23,888 million of creditor claims (that is, Total Liabilities), of which $7,858 million and $369 million are classified as Long-Term and Short-Term Debt Obligations, respectively, and $12,203 million in equity claims (that is, total common shareholders' equity). This chapter focuses on the balance sheet claims represented by Long-Term and Short-Term Debt Obligations, as well as residual claims represented by Shareholders' Equity. Chapter 8 covers all of the creditor claims that arise from operating activities such as transactions with suppliers, employees, and tax authorities, as opposed to transactions with shareholders, bondholders, banks, and other financial institutions.

We begin with equity financing activities, which include raising capital by issuing common stock and preferred stock, the return of capital to shareholders via dividends and share repurchases, and the use of equity (and equity appreciation) to compensate employees via stock options, stock appreciation rights, and restricted stock plans. Then we discuss the shareholders' equity effects of net income and other comprehensive income. The second section of the chapter deals with debt financing activities. After a review of the financial statement recognition principles relating to liabilities in general, we examine the specific accounting for and reporting of notes payable and bonds, troubled debt, and hybrid securities. The chapter concludes with a focus on risk analysis when potential liabilities are not reflected in financial statements (off-balance-sheet financing), including operating leases and their effective capitalization for cross-sectional comparability and risk analysis purposes.

EQUITY FINANCING

Corporations raise a substantial amount of cash by issuing shares of common stock and by deploying the funds received into profitable operations. The amount of shareholders' equity reported in the balance sheet (the *book value* of shareholders' equity) is the investment base for return on equity calculations used in profitability analysis (Chapter 4), the measure of owner financing in risk analysis (Chapter 5), and the measure of the value of net assets in place used in residual income-based equity valuation (Chapter 13). The three primary events that lead to changes in the book value of shareholders' equity are:

- Investments by shareholders, usually net cash received by the company at equity issue date.
- Distributions to shareholders, usually in the form of periodic cash dividend payments to investors and sometimes in the form of share repurchases.

---

[1]We refer to specific accounting standards by the FASB and IASB. Also, we provide codification numbers from the FASB's Codification Project, which represents authoritative guidance in the United States as of July 1, 2009.

- Profitable operating and investing activities. Net income is a large component of this increase. Chapters 6–9 will show that another part of this increase is designated as "other comprehensive income."

The following sections discuss the accounting and financial statement disclosures related to these events.[2]

Investments by Shareholders: Common Equity Issuance

The general rule of accounting for common equity issues is to record the equity claim on the balance sheet at the *fair value* of what the corporation initially receives from the investor. If the issuing firm cannot reliably measure fair value of what it receives, it will use the fair value of the equity issued to record the transaction. As long as the fair value of one side of the exchange is determinable, the fair value of the other side of the transaction is implied under the assumption that unrelated parties exchange equal fair values in arm's-length transactions.

Most commonly, an equity investor transfers cash to the corporation to secure an equity interest. However, the investor could transfer property to the corporation or perform services for the corporation in return for an equity interest. Instead of issuing common stock, the corporation could issue other types of equity interests: preferred stock, stock subscriptions, options to purchase common stock, or stock rights to the investor.[3] In any event, the fair value rule applies. The fair value received is split between two contributed capital accounts: common stock (par value) and additional paid-in capital (amount of fair value received that exceeds par value). Additional paid-in capital is generally referred to as *share premium* in many non-U.S. jurisdictions. The partition of proceeds into the par and additional paid-in capital accounts is not significant from an analysis viewpoint because par value is declared by the board of directors and has no economic meaning. In fact, some firms issue "no par" common stock.[4]

Common shareholders' equity is the residual interest in the corporation, which equals the assets remaining after all liabilities are paid. Because common shareholders bear both residual upside and downside risk, they generally have control as evidenced by the right to vote. However, contractual relationships between the firm and other parties can limit common shareholder control. For example, effective control can be obtained through contracts to acquire all of a firm's output or to use all of a firm's productive capacity or through rights

---

[2]*FASB Codification Topic 505* describes applicable U.S. GAAP on shareholders' equity accounting, and Financial Accounting Standards Board, *Statement of Financial Accounting Standards No. 129*, "Disclosure of Information about Capital Structure," (1979) describes U.S.GAAP relating to capital structure disclosure. Equity financing is a prime example of the scarcity of formal IFRS guidance. Other than standards on disclosure (International Accounting Standards Board, *International Accounting Standards 1*, "Presentation of Financial Statements," amended 2005) and share-based payment (International Accounting Standards Board, *International Financial Reporting Standard 2*, "Share-Based Payment"), international standards are basically silent on how to account for shareholders' equity transactions.

[3]Common shareholders normally possess a preemptive right that enables them to maintain a proportional ownership when the corporation issues additional stock. When a corporation issues stock rights, it receives nothing from investors in return (no effect on financial statements). The issuance of rights is nothing more than a formal recognition of a right that already existed. When investors exercise their stock rights, the resulting issuance of common stock is reported as an issue of stock for cash. Another type of stock right sometimes issued by a company as a takeover defense, stock purchase rights, allows current shareholders to purchase an additional number of shares in the event that an outside party acquires or attempts to acquire a substantial equity stake in the company.

[4]Generally, fair value is measured at the date on which common shares are issued. Under some circumstances (discussed in this and later chapters), the fair value might be measured at an earlier date when the first part of a two-part transaction occurs (for example, date of issue of warrants, convertible preferred stock, and stock options). Also, on occasion, individuals and governments donate assets to a corporation. Although the corporation issues nothing in return, existing shareholders have greater equity because of the donation. The basis for recording a donation is the fair value of the donated asset.

to obtain control of productive capacity through purchase at a later date. These types of contracts are common in the area of SPEs (special purpose entities), which are discussed in more detail later in this chapter and in Chapter 7. Also, to protect their claims on assets, debtholders often require firms to enter into debt covenants, which are contracts to restrict common shareholder control of certain operating and financing decisions such as expansion, dividend payment, and additional borrowings.

Corporations also issue *preferred stock.* Issuing preferred stock involves a trade-off between maintaining corporate control (preferred stock does not have voting rights) and creating a class of shareholders with preference in all asset distributions, including dividends. Accounting for the initial issue of preferred stock is no different than accounting for the issue of common stock. The fair value rule applies when a firm issues preferred stock. Preferred stock (at par) is normally reported before common stock in the shareholders' equity section because preferred shareholders have priority over common shareholders in corporate liquidations. Any additional paid-in capital on preferred stock usually is listed with additional paid-in capital amounts on common stock so that only one amount appears for additional paid-in capital. In addition to the preference in dividends and distribution, preferred stock dividends may accumulate if not declared and paid (the cumulative right). These *dividends in arrears* must be declared and paid before common stock dividends are declared and paid and must be disclosed in the notes to the financial statements. Preferred stock may be convertible into common shares (a positive feature for investors) or callable at scheduled dates or at the firm's discretion (a negative feature for investors). The call options that can exist on preferred stock raise the larger issue (discussed in a later section) of whether certain types of preferred stock should be designated as debt rather than equity.

Finally, to market shares in initial (and, less often, seasoned) public offerings, firms sometimes enter into agreements whereby the companies agree to issue shares in the future and potential buyers agree to pay for the shares in the future. The transaction, called a *subscription agreement,* results in a subscriptions receivable to the extent that cash is not collected when the subscription agreement is reached. The SEC (Securities and Exchange Commission) and IFRS (in IAS 1) require reporting of the fair value of the subscribed shares as common equity and the subscriptions receivable as contra-equity (an account that is subtracted in determining total shareholders' equity). Therefore, only the cash received from investors at subscription increases owners equity.

Example 1

Assume that a company raises capital through the following series of equity issues:

1. Issues 100,000 shares of $1 par value common stock for $5 per share.
2. Receives land in exchange for 28,000 shares of $1 par common stock. The equity investor purchased the land for $85,000. Similar land has recently sold for $150,000.
3. Issues 5,000 shares of $10 par value preferred stock for $75,000.
4. Receives subscriptions for the issue of 40,000 shares of $1 par value common stock. The share issue price is $6, of which 30 percent is received as a down payment. Subsequently, the remaining 70 percent is received.

Exhibit 6.1 summarizes the financial statement effects of the transactions. (Let APIC = Additional paid-in capital.) Dollar amounts indicate the effects of each transaction on the financial statement elements (that is, Assets; Liabilities; or sub-element of Shareholders' Equity: Contributed capital = CC; Accumulated other comprehensive income = AOCI; and Retained earnings = RE). The applicable journal entry follows each financial statement effect template entry and shows the effects of each transaction on specific accounts.

EXHIBIT 6.1: EXAMPLE 1 SOLUTION

	Assets		=	Liabilities	+	Shareholders' Equity		
						CC	AOCI	RE
1	Cash	+500,000				Common Stock +100,000 APIC +400,000		

Cash	500,000	
Common Stock		100,000
APIC		400,000

	Assets		=	Liabilities	+	Shareholders' Equity		
						CC	AOCI	RE
2	Land	+150,000				Common Stock +28,000 APIC +122,000		

Land	150,000	
Common Stock		28,000
APIC		122,000

	Assets		=	Liabilities	+	Shareholders' Equity		
						CC	AOCI	RE
3	Cash	+75,000				Preferred Stock +50,000 APIC +25,000		

Cash	75,000	
Preferred Stock		50,000
APIC		25,000

Down Payment

	Assets		=	Liabilities	+	Shareholders' Equity		
						CC	AOCI	RE
4	Cash	+72,000				Common Stock +40,000 APIC +200,000 Subscriptions Receivable −168,000		

Cash	72,000	
Subscriptions Receivable	168,000	
Common Stock		40,000
APIC		200,000

Receipt of Remaining Cash

	Assets		=	Liabilities	+	Shareholders' Equity		
						CC	AOCI	RE
4	Cash	+168,000				Subscriptions Receivable +168,000		

Cash	168,000	
Subscriptions Receivable		168,000

Shareholders' equity is increased by the fair value of the asset (cash) contributed to the corporation in Transaction 1. In Transaction 2, the fair value of the land contributed to the company is a readily determinable $150,000 (cash price of similar land), and this amount becomes the basis for measurement of the transaction. However, often non-cash asset (for example, land) fair values are harder to obtain and may require the corporation to rely on an estimate of the fair value of common shares issued (for example, share price in an active market if available). Note that contributed capital is divided into par value and additional paid-in capital amounts when preferred or common shares are issued (Transactions 1–3). In Transaction 4, the contra-equity account, Subscriptions Receivable, is used to set the net equity interest equal to the cash received as down payment. Because a down payment of only $72,000 is received, contributed capital increases only $72,000 (= $40,000 par value + $200,000 APIC – $168,000 subscription receivable contra-equity). When the remainder of the cash is received, the contra-equity account is reduced, which increases total contributed capital by the amount of cash received.

Cash flow effects of these financing activities are reported in the financing section of the statement of cash flows as sources of cash. The issue of stock for land is reported in a separate schedule of "significant investing and financing activities that do not affect cash" that accompanies the statement of cash flows.

Example 2

Refer to PepsiCo's Consolidated Balance Sheet (Appendix A). PepsiCo has issued 1,782 million shares of common stock (out of 3,600 million shares authorized for issue by the board of directors) with a par value of 1 2/3¢ per share. (1,782 million × 1 2/3¢ per share is approximately equal to $30 million.) The December 27, 2008 balance in capital in excess of par (that is, additional paid-in capital) implies that issue prices over time have exceeded par value by $351 million. PepsiCo reports $41 in preferred stock, but does not use a separate additional paid-in capital account because the preferred stock has no par value. PepsiCo reports in Note 12 that the preferred stock was issued for an employee stock ownership program established by its Quaker subsidiary. Each of the 266,253 shares outstanding as of December 27, 2008, is convertible into 4.9625 shares of PepsiCo common stock at the option of the holder. PepsiCo also may call the preferred shares at $78 per share plus accrued and unpaid dividends. We examine the financial statement effects of conversions and calls later in this chapter.

Distributions to Shareholders: Dividends

Net income is accumulated through time in retained earnings, which is reported as part of shareholders' equity in the balance sheet. Total shareholders' equity, which represents the shareholders' claims on assets, equals original capital contributed by shareholders plus the accumulation of net income (in retained earnings) and other comprehensive income (in accumulated other comprehensive income) less treasury stock. Dividend distributions are simply a transfer (usually in cash) to shareholders of a portion of what they already own: namely, the net assets of the firm. As a consequence, dividends reduce retained earnings. The portion of net income not paid out in dividends represents reinvestments by shareholders. As discussed in Chapter 12, retention of earnings by corporations effectively reflects additional equity investment by shareholders, which increases the earnings hurdle for the company.

The declaration of dividends is formalized by three important dates because of the administrative complexity of identifying shareholders of record at any given point in time. On the date on which the board of directors declares a dividend, the *date of declaration*, the firm incurs a legal liability to distribute the dividend to owners of the stock on a specific future date, the *date of record*. On the *date of payment*, the dividend distribution occurs. Typically, these three dates are several weeks apart.

Corporations generally pay dividends in cash. However, corporations can pay dividends with an interest-bearing promise to pay dividends (scrip dividends), investments in other corporations' stock (property dividends), or additional shares of the corporation's own stock

(stock dividends). For cash, scrip, and property dividends, the retained earnings component of shareholders' equity is reduced by the fair value of the item distributed on the date of declaration and a liability is recorded. Dividends decrease the net assets of a corporation, and this decrease is reported in the statement of shareholders' equity. The date of record has no impact on the corporation's accounting. No change in equity occurs on the date of payment because both assets (cash or property) and liabilities (dividends payable) decrease (that is, no change in *net* assets). If dividends are declared but not paid by year-end, a (non-operating) liability for dividends payable appears in the current liabilities section of the balance sheet.[5]

In many jurisdictions (especially non-U.S. countries), the balance of retained earnings represents the limit for dividend payments.[6] However, *liquidating dividends*, payments to shareholders that exceed the balance in retained earnings, can occur. Recall that the two primary components of shareholders' equity are contributed capital (common and preferred shares at par value plus additional paid-in capital accounts) and retained earnings. When equity capital is issued, the contributed capital accounts increase. As income is earned, retained earnings increases. Finally, when dividends are paid, retained earnings decreases. If the dividend is greater than the retained earnings balance, in most jurisdictions, the increment must be used to decrease contributed capital. A liquidating dividend is a return of the original investment by shareholders (that is, their original contribution to the firm when they purchased common shares).

Stock Dividends and Stock Splits

On occasion, corporations distribute shares of their own stock to investors. A *stock dividend* does not involve a transfer of assets to investors. Thus, unlike other dividends, stock dividends result in no change in total shareholders' equity. Also, because no change occurs in the assets of the corporation and proportional ownership is retained, investor wealth is unchanged by stock dividends, per se.

The effects of stock dividends and splits on retained earnings and contributed capital are determined by accounting rules and jurisdictional legal requirements.[7] In small stock dividends (distributions of less than 20–25 percent of common shares), the fair value of shares issued is transferred out of retained earnings and into contributed capital. U.S. GAAP is ambiguous with respect to midrange dividends (20–100 percent), and frequently, laws of the state of incorporation determine the accounting treatment. However, in most cases (and consistent with SEC guidance), midrange stock dividends are treated as a transfer of the par value of shares among shareholders' equity accounts (that is, from retained earnings to contributed capital or within contributed capital accounts).

Most large distributions that are greater than or equal to 100 percent are in the form of a *stock split*. Suppose a company wanted to double the number of shares outstanding and therefore halve the price of its stock. This could be accomplished by issuing a 100 percent stock dividend or a 2-for-1 stock split. Similar to midrange stock dividends, accounting for a large stock dividend depends on appropriate state law. Most of the time, the par value of the shares is transferred to common stock from either retained earnings or additional paid-in capital.

---

[5]IFRS (*IAS* 1) requires disclosure of proposed but not yet approved dividends and post-year-end declared dividends.

[6]Dividends also are often based on earnings calculated under statutory financial statements of a given country. For example, SAP reports in its 2008 Annual Report that "Under the German Stock Corporation Act (Aktiengesetz), the total amount of dividends available for distribution to SAP AG's shareholders is based on the earnings of SAP AG as reported in its statutory financial statements which are determined under the accounting rules stipulated by the German Commercial Code (Handelsgesetzbuch)."

[7]Committee on Accounting Procedure, *Accounting Research Bulletin No. 43*, "Restatement and Revision of Accounting Research Bulletins No. 1–42" (1953); *FASB Codification Topic 505*.

In a stock split, U.S. GAAP does not require an amount to be shifted from retained earnings to contributed capital, but state laws may allow an amount to be shifted from either retained earnings or additional paid-in capital to common stock. Accounting rules require that the par value of individual shares be adjusted so that the total par value after the stock split is the same as the total par value before the split. Therefore, in a 2-for-1 split of 50,000 shares of $10 par value stock, a company issues an additional 50,000 shares and reduces par value to $5 on all 100,000 shares.

From an analysis viewpoint, it is important to remember that the accounting for stock dividends and splits simply reallocates amounts *within* shareholders' equity. The total amount of shareholders' equity remains unchanged because assets have not been disbursed from the corporation (that is, cash has not been paid out), although increasing the number of shares outstanding does proportionately decrease per-share amounts for earnings, book value, and cash flow.

Example 3

Motorola, Inc., reports the following in its 2007 financial statements: common stock, $3 par, 2,263.1 million shares outstanding; average share price during 2007 was approximately $20; common dividends paid during 2007 were $.20 per share. Exhibit 6.2 shows the financial statement effects of the following events. (Assume the events are independent.)

1. Motorola's dividend declaration and payment (2,263.1 million shares × $.20 per share = $452.6 million). Assume that the dividends are declared and then paid at a later date.
2. Motorola distributes a property dividend by giving common shareholders common shares of another company that it carries as a short-term investment in marketable securities. The securities have a fair value of $2,000,000 and an original cost of $1,800,000. Motorola uses mark-to-market accounting for these securities and declares the dividend at some time after the securities have been marked to market.
3. Motorola distributes a 10 percent stock dividend (10% × 2,263.1 million shares outstanding = 226.3 million shares; 226.3 million shares × $3 = $678.9 million par value; 226.3 million shares × $20 market price = $4,526 million fair value).
4. Motorola distributes a 100 percent stock dividend (2,263.1 million additional shares; 2,263.1 × $3 = $6,789.3 million par value).
5. Motorola declares a 2-for-1 stock split.
6. Motorola declares a 1-for-2 reverse stock split.

All amounts in Exhibit 6.2 are in millions of dollars:

EXHIBIT 6.2: EXAMPLE 3 SOLUTION

Declaration

	Assets	=	Liabilities	+	Shareholders' Equity		
					CC	AOCI	RE
1			Dividends Payable +452.6				Retained Earnings −452.6
	Retained Earnings		452.6				
	Dividends Payable		452.6				

Payment

	Assets	=	Liabilities	+	Shareholders' Equity		
					CC	AOCI	RE
1	Cash −452.6		Dividends Payable −452.6				
	Dividends Payable		452.6				
	Cash		452.6				

(Continued)

EXHIBIT 6.2 (CONTINUED)

Assets	=	Liabilities	+	Shareholders' Equity		
				CC	AOCI	RE
2	Investments −2.0						Retained Earnings −2.0

Assets			=	Liabilities	+	Shareholders' Equity		
Retained Earnings				2.0				
Investments					2.0			

Assets	=	Liabilities	+	Shareholders' Equity		
				CC	AOCI	RE
3				Common Stock +678.9 APIC +3,847.1		Retained Earnings −4,526.0

Assets	=	Liabilities	+	Shareholders' Equity		
Retained Earnings		4,526.0				
Common Stock			678.9			
APIC			3,847.1			

Assets	=	Liabilities	+	Shareholders' Equity		
				CC	AOCI	RE
4				Common Stock +6,789.3		Retained Earnings −6,789.3

Assets	=	Liabilities	+	Shareholders' Equity		
Retained Earnings		6,789.3				
Common Stock			6,789.3			

5. Memorandum entry only to note number of shares outstanding doubles to 4,526.2 million, and par value decreases to $1.50 per share.
6. Memorandum entry only to note number of shares outstanding falls in half to 1,131.6 million, and par value doubles to $6 per share.

Note that dividends distributed in the form of assets (that is, cash and property; Transactions 1 and 2) decrease shareholders' equity (the sum of the last three columns). Dividends distributed in the form of common stock (Transactions 3 and 4) generate a rearrangement of shareholders' equity but no change in total shareholders' equity. Likewise, stock splits (Transactions 5 and 6) have no effect on total shareholders' equity or the balance of any account in shareholders' equity. Cash outflow for cash dividends is reported in the financing section of the statement of cash flows.[8]

Example 4

Refer to PepsiCo's 2008 Consolidated Statement of Common Shareholders' Equity. In the reconciliation from beginning to ending retained earnings, PepsiCo reports cash dividends declared in 2008 on common stock ($2,589 million), on preferred stock ($2 million), and on RSUs, restricted stock units ($8 million), yielding total reduction of retained earnings due to a dividend declaration of $2,599 million. PepsiCo's Consolidated Statement of Cash Flows reports $2,541 million cash dividends paid in the Financing Activities section. The excess of dividends declared over dividends paid as of the balance sheet date ($58 million) is reflected as an increase in the non-operating liability "Dividends payable." (See Example 3, Transaction 1.) Note 14, "Supplemental Financial Information" (Appendix A), disaggregates current liabilities and confirms the $58 million increase in dividends payable from $602 million at the end of 2007 to $660 million at the end of 2008.

---

[8]Transactions 3 and 4 in Example 3 assume that Motorola declares a stock dividend and distributes the dividend in the same period. If a financial statement reporting date intervenes, "Stock dividend distributable" will be reported as a contra-equity account instead of a reduction in retained earnings as shown in the template.

Distributions to Shareholders: Share Repurchases

For several reasons, corporations may distribute cash to shareholders and reduce share-holders' equity via *share repurchases*. For example, employee compensation plans often grant options to acquire common stock. To service the possible exercise of options, compa-nies may repurchase shares to have a supply of their own stock on hand or, alternatively, to offset the dilution of existing shareholders' proportional ownership from share issuances under the option exercises. Corporations also might repurchase stock simply to shift the mix of debt and equity financing or to signal to investors that corporate management believes the stock is undervalued because investors have underestimated potential future earnings or cash flows. Finally, fewer shares outstanding means less dilution of voting power. This may be particularly important if the firm is facing a takeover attempt.

When a firm engages in transactions like those above that reduce equity, the effects on the statement of cash flows are simple. Using cash to reduce equity is a cash outflow reported as a financing activity. Similarly, the effects on the income statement are simple: there are no effects. The reduction of equity is a distribution to owners, a transaction that does not affect income. Balance sheet effects of share repurchases depend on whether the shares of stock are retired or held as treasury stock for eventual reissue. If the shares are retired, the amounts originally recorded in the common stock (that is, par value) and the additional paid-in capital accounts are removed. The typical case is that the cash paid to retire the shares exceeds the amount at which the shares were originally issued. This excess is treated as a dividend, and like regular cash dividends, it is removed from retained earn-ings. Less typical is the case in which the amount paid to buy back the shares is less than the original issue price. In this case, additional paid-in capital is increased as if the share-holders left amounts in the firm as a permanent capital contribution.

If firms repurchase stock for reissue at a later date, the stock is referred to as *treasury stock*. Two acceptable methods are used to account for treasury stock: the cost method and the par method. Because the par method is rarely used, we focus our discussion on the cost method. The cost method was designed under the assumption that any treasury stock acquired would be reissued.

A cash disbursement to acquire stock to be held in the treasury decreases shareholders' equity. The treasury stock acquired is not an asset of the corporation. A corporation can-not own itself. The payment of cash to owners is a distribution to owners. Under the cost method, this distribution is shown as an increase in a contra-equity account called treasury stock. The increase in contra-equity is equivalent to a decrease in equity. Under the cost method, the treasury stock account is usually shown at the bottom of the shareholders' equity section. Subsequent treasury share reissues increase (or decrease) additional paid-in capital if the subsequent reissue price is greater than (less than) the cost of the treasury stock. No gain or loss is recorded because the reissue of treasury stock is, in concept, iden-tical to the original issue of common stock (cash invested, common stock issued).[9]

---

[9]The main difference between the cost and rarely used par methods is in how treasury stock is disclosed in the shareholders' equity sec-tion of the balance sheet. The amount of cash paid by a corporation to reacquire a share and hold it as treasury stock is intended to compensate the shareholder for his or her original contribution (par value of stock plus additional paid-in capital) plus his or her share of earnings not paid out in dividends (retained earnings). Therefore, the cost method discloses treasury stock as a subtraction from the totality of shareholders' equity. Under the par method, the cost of treasury stock would be broken up and allocated as reductions of the individual accounts in owners' equity. The portion of treasury stock cost related to par value would be subtracted from the common stock account. The portion related to originally contributed capital over par would be subtracted from the additional paid-in capital account. The portion related to earnings not paid out in dividends would be subtracted from retained earnings. Thus, the accounts in shareholders' equity would be reported net of the allocated portion of the treasury share purchase. The sole exception to this "netting" is that common stock would be reported at par value of shares issued and a contra-equity account, treasury stock, would be reported as a subtraction from common stock at an amount equal to par value as a means of disclosing the existence of treasury stock.

Example 5

Refer to the Common Shareholders' Equity section of PepsiCo's Consolidated Balance Sheet (Appendix A). PepsiCo reports a subtraction in the equity section for (in millions) "Repurchased common stock, at cost (229 and 177 shares, respectively)" of $14,122 million and $10,387 million at the ends of 2008 and 2007, respectively. Therefore, PepsiCo uses the cost method. PepsiCo's Consolidated Statement of Common Shareholders' Equity explains the change between years. Additional share repurchases total $4,720 million. This amount is a cash outflow to reduce equity capital, so it also is reported in the Financing Activities section of PepsiCo's Consolidated Statement of Cash Flows. In fact, it is the largest single cash flow for 2008. Treasury stock is often reissued when stock options are exercised, a topic discussed in the next section.

Equity Issued as Compensation: Stock Options

Firms develop compensation plans to attract, retain, and motivate employees. Many of these plans include cash compensation that is fixed or that varies with levels of employee performance, with performance defined by an accounting-based income measure (such as return on equity) or stock returns. In a typical compensation arrangement, firms give employees the right, or option, to acquire shares of common stock at a fixed price. If share prices increase over time, employees can exercise their option to purchase shares at a price that is less than the market price of the shares. These arrangements are referred to as *stock options*, and their use skyrocketed in the last 20 years. Firms in the technology sector, especially since the Internet boom of the 1990s, have used options as a dominant component of their employee compensation packages.[10]

Stock options permit employees to purchase shares of common stock at a price usually equal to the market price of the stock at the time the firm grants the stock option. Employees exercise these stock options at a later time if the stock price increases above the stock option exercise price. Corporations grant stock options because options have characteristics that align the interests of the employee with those of shareholders. Clearly, an increase in stock price benefits shareholders, which is the same way stock options reward employees. Unlike compensation in the form of salaries, however, stock options do not require firms to use cash during the period when they grant stock options to employees. In addition to the incentive feature of stock options, they also can be used to attract or retain employees. The ability of a corporation to attract employees is enhanced when firms offer equity incentives such as stock options as part of a sign-on or retention package. Likewise, corporations benefit by reduced employee turnover, as employees with unvested stock options face incentives to continue their employment with the company to realize the financial upside as the company's stock price appreciates.

Fair Value Method and Required Disclosures

An understanding of the accounting for stock-based compensation requires understanding several key parameters. The *grant date* is the date a firm gives a stock option to employees. The *vesting date* is the first date employees can exercise their stock options. Employees cannot exercise options before the vesting date or after the end of the option's life. To enhance employee retention and increase motivation during the vesting period, firms usually structure stock

---

[10]Due to more recent concerns about excessive executive compensation, the use of stock options has declined to some degree. However, many companies still use stock option plans for incentive compensation.

option plans so that a period of time elapses between the grant date and the vesting date. Firms may preclude employees from exercising the option for one or more years, or they may set an exercise price so high that employees would not want to exercise the option until the stock price increases. The *exercise date* is the date employees elect to exchange the option plus cash for shares of common stock. The *exercise price* is the price specified in the stock option contract for purchasing the common stock. The *market price* is the price of the stock as it trades in the market. In theory, the value of a stock option has two elements: (1) the benefit realized on the exercise date because the market price of the stock exceeds the exercise price (the *benefit element*) and (2) the length of the period during which the holder can exercise the option (the *time-value element*).

The amount of the benefit element is not known until the exercise date. In general, stock options with exercise prices less than the current market price of the stock (described as *in the money*) have a higher value than stock options with exercise prices exceeding the current market price of the stock (described as *out of the money*). The time-value element of an option results from the benefit it provides its holder if the market price of the stock increases during the exercise period. The greater the market price of the stock exceeds the exercise price during the exercise period, the greater the benefit to the option holder. This time-value element of an option will have more value the longer the exercise period, the more volatile the market price of the stock, the lower the dividend yield, and the lower the discount rate. Note that a stock option may have an exercise price that exceeds the current market price (zero value for the benefit element) but still have value because of the possibility that the market price will exceed the exercise price on the exercise date (positive value for the time-value element). As the expiration date of the option approaches, the value of the time-value element approaches zero.[11]

Statements No. 123 and *No. 123 (Revised 2004)* address accounting for stock options, and both were extremely controversial and followed decades of tumultuous arguments about how to reflect the cost of granting stock options to employees.[12] Before these standards, APB *Opinion No. 25* (released in 1972) accounted for stock-based compensation expense using the *intrinsic value method.* Under this method, the amount to be expensed under any option grant was deemed to be the intrinsic value of the option when it was granted, equal to the market value of the underlying share minus the exercise price of the option. Perhaps not surprisingly, companies converged to a practice whereby they granted options with the exercise price equal to the market price per share on the date of grant. Under the intrinsic value method of computing the value of a stock option, setting the exercise price equal to the market price on the date of grant yields an intrinsic value of zero. So stock-based compensation expense was zero, allowing firms to report higher earnings numbers.[13] The FASB revisited the topic in the 1990s, culminating in the board's issuing an exposure draft of a new reporting standard that would have required firms to recognize the cost of stock options as compensation expense on the date of the grant based on measurement of the option's fair value based on an option pricing model. This proposal was never adopted, however, because the business community lobbied various congressional interests so vigorously that some U.S. senators pressured the FASB to withdraw its proposal. The FASB eventually issued *Statement No. 123* in 1995, which reaffirmed the conclusions of *Opinion No. 25* but required only pro

---

[11]For an elaboration on the history of options pricing, see Fischer Black and Myron Scholes, "The Pricing of Options and Corporate Liabilities," *Journal of Political Economy* (May/June 1973), pp. 637–654.

[12]Financial Accounting Standards Board, *Statement No. 123,* "Accounting for Stock-Based Compensation" (1995); Financial Accounting Standards Board, *Statement No 123 (Revised 2004),* "Accounting for Share-Based Payment" (2004). *FASB Codification Topic 718.*

[13]Accounting Principles Board *Opinion No. 25,* "Accounting for Stock Issued to Employees" (1972). *Statements No. 123* and *123 (Revised 2004)* supersede *Opinion No. 25.*

forma *disclosures* in the notes to the financial statements about the impact of stock option grants on earnings if the company utilized the fair value method instead of the intrinsic value method. In contrast to the intrinsic value method, the fair value method of accounting for stock options computes the value of an option grant based on various option pricing models, all of which attach a positive value to stock options with exercise prices equal to or greater than the share price on the date of grant.

Subsequent to issuance of *Statement No. 123* in 1995 and, importantly, after the financial reporting and accounting scandals of the early 2000s, some firms began to voluntarily treat the cost of stock options given to employees as compensation expense based on an assessment of the option's fair value. These firms decided that the fair value approach is theoretically superior or that investors would view these firms more favorably for taking this voluntary action. Riding the growing movement of stock options being recognized as a form of compensation expense, as well as the view of many that the accounting scandals were partially the result of poor corporate governance and reporting, including reporting for stock options, the FASB revisited the topic. The result was *Statement No. 123 (Revised 2004)*, which requires firms to use the fair value method to value stock options and report the amounts as compensation expense in the income statement.[14]

As noted previously, under the fair value method, firms must measure the value of stock options on the date of grant. Because the value of employee stock options typically cannot be measured with an observable value established by trading in an active market, *Statement No. 123 (Revised 2004)* recognizes that most firms will use an option pricing model to estimate the value of the options. *Statement No. 123 (Revised 2004)* does not require a specific option pricing model, although the Black-Scholes model[15] or a lattice model (for example, the binomial model) are most commonly used. A detailed discussion of option valuation models can be found in the finance literature and is beyond the scope of this text. However, any model employed must incorporate a variety of factors, including the exercise price of the option, the term of the option, the current market price of each share of underlying stock, expected stock volatility, dividends, and the risk-free interest rate.[16]

Once the value of stock options is estimated using an acceptable option pricing model, firms must recognize this amount as compensation expense ratably over the period in which an employee provides services. This is commonly the vesting period of the stock options. *Statement No. 123 (Revised 2004)* requires disclosures regarding stock option grants, their effect on total compensation expense, the methodology (model) used to value the stock options, and the key assumptions made to estimate the value of the stock options.

Example 6

Assume that an Internet-based company decides to conserve cash and align upper management incentives with shareholders' incentives by compensating managers with 9,000 options to purchase $1 par value common stock any time during the next seven years for $10 per share. The current stock price is $10 per share. The vesting period is three years. Using an appropriate options pricing model, the company values the options at $2 each.

---

[14]The promulgation of FASB *Statement No. 123 (Revised 2004)* represents a convergence with international standards. International Accounting Standards Board, *International Financial Reporting Standard 2*, "Share-Based Payment."

[15]See footnote 9.

[16]A critique of the reliability of various valuation models can be found in American Accounting Association's Financial Accounting Standards Committee, "Response to the FASB's Exposure Draft on Share-Based Payment: An Amendment of FASB *Statements No. 123* and *No. 95*," *Accounting Horizons* (June 2005), pp. 101–114.

Exhibit 6.3 illustrates the financial statement effects of these transactions:

1. Grant date (the date options are granted to management)
2. Recognition of compensation expense for each of the three years in the vesting period
3. Exercise of a single option when a share of common stock is trading at $18
4. Expiration of a single option
5. Revocation of a single option early in the third year of the vesting period when a manager leaves the firm

The options' fair value is $2 per option × 9,000 options = $18,000. No financial statement effects occur at the grant date because the manager has yet to provide service to the firm. The $18,000 fair value is allocated over the three-year vesting period, $6,000 per year, as an increase in compensation expense (a decrease in net income, which is also a decrease in retained earnings). Rather than accepting cash compensation, the manager accepts an option to acquire an equity interest as evidenced by the stock options. APIC from stock options increases shareholders' equity. In Transaction 2, note that shareholders' equity in total (the sum of the last three columns) is not affected by the compensation allocation process because assets and liabilities do not change.[17]

Exercise of a single option (Transaction 3) involves a transfer of the stock option plus a $10 exercise price from the manager to the corporation. Through the effects on three shareholders' equity accounts, total shareholders' equity increases by $10, the fair value of the cash received. Note that the cash received is not equal to the fair value of the common equity, which is trading at $18. The amount reflected in the equity accounts after this transaction is posted is $1 in common stock and $11 in additional paid-in capital. Thus, common stock issued is recorded at $12, which equals the fair value of the cash surrendered ($10) plus the grant date estimate of the fair value of the option ($2).[18]

In a stock option expiration (Transaction 4), the capital contributed to the firm by the manager's employment is reclassified as a permanent contribution to shareholders' equity. If a manager fails to perform the three years of service, the option is revoked (Transaction 5). The amount of the compensation expense related to revoked options is removed from compensation expense of the current period. This treatment is an example of a change in estimate handled prospectively. The firm estimated that compensation expense was $6,000 per year based on the expected three-year service of employees. If an employee leaves the firm and an option is revoked, estimates must be revised *going forward*. Prior period adjustments to expenses are not made.[19]

Option events create two cash flows. The exercise of an option increases cash from equity issues and is reported as a financing activity. Although not shown in the preceding template, the corporation will receive a tax deduction at the date the manager exercises the option, equal to the market price at the exercise date minus the exercise price. (The manager will be taxed on this same amount because it is compensation.) Under a recent FASB rule, the tax savings is treated as a financing cash inflow.[20]

---

[17]The no longer accepted intrinsic value method assumes the options have no intrinsic value at the grant date because the exercise price equals the stock price. This approach ignored the time value of money element and assumed that managers are indifferent about using the option to acquire at $10 per share or just going out into the open market and acquiring the share for $10. Compensation expense under the intrinsic value method would have been zero.

[18]If previously acquired treasury shares rather than new shares are issued, treasury stock is reduced by the amount of the original acquisition cost and APIC is used to record the remainder of the equity increase.

[19]We assume that the forfeiture was unexpected. If forfeitures are expected, then the original estimate of compensation expense should be lower, and the treatment we show should be used for additional unexpected forfeitures. Also, we reduced compensation expense by the entire amount of the option (instead of the two-thirds already recognized as compensation expense) assuming that the last year's worth of the compensation expense allocation would be unaffected. An alternative would be to reduce compensation expense by $2 × 2/3 and reduce the $6,000 compensation expense for Year 3 by the same amount.

[20]Financial Accounting Standards Board, *Statement No 123 (Revised 2004),* "Accounting for Share-Based Payment" (2004).

EXHIBIT 6.3: EXAMPLE 6 SOLUTION

1. No entry at grant date. (The contract is executory.) However, the fair value of the options is measured at the grant date. Fair value = 9,000 options × $2 per option = $18,000.

Year 1

	Assets	=	Liabilities	+	Shareholders' Equity		
					CC	**AOCI**	**RE**
2					APIC—Stock Options +6,000		Compensation Expense −6,000

Year 2

	Assets	=	Liabilities	+	Shareholders' Equity		
					CC	**AOCI**	**RE**
2					APIC—Stock Options +6,000		Compensation Expense −6,000

Year 3

	Assets	=	Liabilities	+	Shareholders' Equity		
					CC	**AOCI**	**RE**
2					APIC—Stock Options +6,000		Compensation Expense −6,000

Each year:		
Compensation Expense	6,000	
APIC—Stock Options		6,000

Exercise

	Assets	=	Liabilities	+	Shareholders' Equity		
					CC	**AOCI**	**RE**
3	Cash +10				Common Stock +1 APIC +11 APIC—Stock Options −2		

Cash	10	
APIC—Stock Options	2	
Common Stock		1
APIC		11

Expiration

	Assets	=	Liabilities	+	Shareholders' Equity		
					CC	**AOCI**	**RE**
4					APIC—Expired Options +2 APIC—Stock Options −2		

APIC—Stock Options	2	
APIC—Expired Options		2

Revocation

	Assets	=	Liabilities	+	Shareholders' Equity		
					CC	**AOCI**	**RE**
5					APIC—Stock Options −2		Compensation Expense +2

APIC—Stock Options	2	
Compensation Expense		2

Alternative Share-Based Compensation: Restricted Stock and RSUs

Exercising stock options can create a cash flow problem for managers at the exercise date. The manager must pay the exercise price and may have to pay taxes on compensation in order to acquire the stock, which he or she may want to hold rather than sell. An alternative share-based compensation program eliminates a manager's need to pay the exercise price. At the grant date, the manager could be given shares of stock rather than options (far fewer shares than options because the fair value of a share is usually greater than the fair value of an option to purchase the stock), which cannot be traded until the vesting period is completed (*restricted stock*).[21] Or the manager could receive non-tradable rights for a number of shares of stock once the vesting period is completed (called *restricted stock units*, or RSUs). In concept, the accounting for stock options, restricted stock, and RSUs is similar except for the fact that stock is issued (or restrictions placed on trading already issued stock will be removed) once the vesting period ends. Accordingly, financial statements reflect the existence of the restricted stock or RSU at the grant date as illustrated in the following example.

Example 7

Assume that an Internet-based company decides to compensate managers by giving them 1,000 shares of $1 par value common stock when the stock price is $10 per share. The vesting period is two years, and the stock cannot be traded until the vesting period is over. Exhibit 6.4 illustrates the financial statement effects of the following transactions:

1. Grant date (the date restricted stock is granted to management)
2. Recognition of compensation expense at the end of each of the two years in the vesting period

Recall that no entry occurs at the grant date in the case of stock options. However, in the case of restricted stock (Transaction 1), the common stock has been issued, so an entry recognizes the existence of the common stock. Note that no change in net assets occurred, so total shareholders' equity does not change. During the vesting period, as managers earn the compensation under the restricted stock plan (Transaction 2), retained earnings is decreased by the net income effect of compensation expense and deferred compensation, a contra-equity account, is decreased. The net effect of the second transaction is a shift of amounts out of retained earnings in to contributed capital. Again, no change in assets or liabilities occurred, so no change in total shareholders' equity is recognized.

The decrease in stock option use in recent years has been offset by an increase in the use of restricted stock plans and cash settlement plans. Once the FASB disallowed the use of the intrinsic value method to value stock options (usually at $0), the primary benefit of using stock options for compensation—no expense on the income statement—disappeared. As a consequence, the use of restricted stock became more common, and although there are some tax ramifications to the employee, a primary benefit to the employee of restricted stock grants relative to option grants is that options can expire worthless but restricted stock almost always has a nonzero value.

---

[21]The descriptor *restricted* simply means that the stock granted is generally restricted from being traded until it vests. Generally, the shares are common shares approved by shareholders for such purposes.

EXHIBIT 6.4: EXAMPLE 7 SOLUTION

Grant Date

	Assets	=	Liabilities	+	Shareholders' Equity		
					CC	AOCI	RE
1					Common Stock +1,000 APIC +9,000 Deferred Compensation +10,000		

Deferred Compensation	10,000	
Common Stock		1,000
APIC		9,000

Year 1

	Assets	=	Liabilities	+	Shareholders' Equity		
					CC	AOCI	RE
2					Deferred Compensation +5,000		Compensation Expense −5,000

Year 2

	Assets	=	Liabilities	+	Shareholders' Equity		
					CC	AOCI	RE
2					Deferred Compensation +5,000		Compensation Expense −5,000

Each Year:		
Compensation Expense	5,000	
Deferred Compensation		5,000

Alternative Share-Based Compensation: Cash-Settled Share-Based Plans

The number, complexity, and diversity of share-based compensation plans do not permit a comprehensive treatment in any given textbook. However, the stock option, restricted stock, and RSU plans illustrated in this chapter represent the large majority of compensation plans settled by the conveyance of common stock to an employee.

In recent years, a number of firms have created compensation plans that provide cash compensation to employees based on share-price appreciation. These plans, often called *stock appreciation rights* plans, are cash-settled plans and, accordingly, do not result in increases in the contributed capital portion of shareholders' equity pursuant to a distribution of an option or a share of common stock. Conceptually, cash-settled share appreciation plans are similar to compensating employees with cash bonuses for output (for example, exceeding sales quotes or earnings targets). The key difference is that the firm relies on the stock market's assessment of the value of the firm to determine the amount of the cash payment.

The essence of the accounting for cash-settled compensation plans is an increase in an operating liability for the estimated cash payments to the employee and a corresponding increase in compensation expense. For example, SAP AG's IFRS-based financial statements describe the workings of its STAR plan and note that "As our STAR plans are settled in cash, rather than by issuing equity instruments, a liability is recorded for such plans based on the current fair value of the STAR awards at the reporting date."

Example 8

Note 6, "Stock-Based Compensation" (Appendix A), describes the stock options PepsiCo granted to employees and members of the company's board of directors. The PepsiCo LTIP (long-term incentive plan) is typical of plans offered by many firms. PepsiCo options generally have ten-year terms and three-year vesting periods. In a subsection of Note 6, "Stock-Based Compensation—Method of Accounting and Our Assumptions" (Appendix A), PepsiCo states, "We account for our employee stock options . . . under the fair value method of accounting using a Black-Scholes valuation model to measure stock option expense at the date of grant." The subsection describes the assumptions used in the Black-Scholes model. PepsiCo also uses RSUs to compensate executives. Stock-based compensation for 2008 ($238 million) is relatively small for PepsiCo when compared to its total expenses for 2008 of more than $36 billion, as shown on its Consolidated Income Statement. However, this is not the case for some firms, particularly technology-based firms.

PepsiCo reports four line items in its 2008 Consolidated Statement of Cash Flows that relate to share-based compensation arrangements. In the Financing Activities section, cash proceeds from the exercise of stock options totaled $620 million, which by any measure is a substantial increase in equity financing. The Financing Activities section also includes the tax benefits from the deduction afforded PepsiCo when employees exercise their options, $107 million in 2008. Because stock option-based compensation is an operating expense that reduces net income (and the tax savings increases net income), two line items exist in the Operating Activities section as well. Under the indirect method of preparing this section, stock-based compensation expense is a non-cash expense; thus, $238 million is added back to net income. Also, although the excess tax benefits are a source of cash, the source is not considered an operating activity by rule; thus, the $107 million tax benefits are deducted to arrive at operating cash flows.

Net Income, Retained Earnings, Accumulated Other Comprehensive Income, and Reserves

In addition to contributed capital, earned capital not distributed in dividends is available to finance investing and operating activities. The following sections describe the reporting of earned capital.

Net Income and Retained Earnings

The financing events examined so far—equity issues, share buybacks, and dividends—are transactions with shareholders in which net assets (that is, shareholders' equity) either increase or decrease. The use of capital obtained from financing activities to support profitable investing and operating activities also leads to increases in shareholders' equity via increases in net assets reported as net income on the income statement. Then, through the accounting closing process, net income is reflected as an increase in retained earnings on the statement of shareholders' equity, which supports the final balance in retained earnings reported on the balance sheet.

PepsiCo's 2008 Consolidated Statement of Shareholders' Equity reconciles the balance of retained earnings at the beginning of 2008 ($28,184 million) to its balance at the balance sheet date, December 27, 2008 ($30,638 million). Net income of $5,142 million causes retained earnings (and thus, shareholders' equity) to increase. Dividends declared on common stock, preferred stock, and RSUs decrease retained earnings. Note that PepsiCo adjusts the beginning balance of retained earnings in two of the years before performing the reconciliation. We address these "prior period adjustments" in Chapter 9.

Accumulated Other Comprehensive Income

Another component of shareholders' equity, *AOCI (accumulated other comprehensive income),* is a consequence of standard setters allowing certain asset and liability revaluations (called *other comprehensive income*) to bypass the income statement and be reported directly in shareholders' equity (as opposed to the treatment of items in net income, which first appear on the income statement and then are reflected as an increase in shareholders' equity via an increase in retained earnings).[22] Chapter 3 introduced the comprehensive income concept. This chapter provides brief examples, with subsequent chapters discussing the detailed accounting and reporting.

For example, other comprehensive income arises when firms experience unrealized fair value gains or losses on securities deemed available for sale (described in detail in Chapter 7). Each year, a firm will recognize in comprehensive income the net change in unrealized gains or losses on available-for-sale securities, which are reported cumulatively in AOCI. When the firm sells the securities, it eliminates the unrealized gain or loss account and recognizes a realized gain or loss in measuring net income.

Another example relates to foreign currency translation (discussed in Chapter 7). U.S. firms with foreign operations usually translate the financial statements of their foreign entities into U.S. dollars each period using the exchange rate at the end of the period. Changes in the exchange rate cause an unrealized foreign currency gain or loss. Firms do not recognize this gain or loss in measuring net income each period; instead, they increase or decrease accumulated other comprehensive income (through the Statement of Comprehensive Income). Presumably, using accumulated other comprehensive income to capture such unrealized gains and losses minimizes the impact of the volatility of foreign currency exchange rates on reported profits while reflecting current values of assets and liabilities. If exchange rates reverse or the firm disposes of the foreign unit, it eliminates the unrealized foreign currency adjustment from accumulated other comprehensive income and, in the case of a disposal, recognizes a gain or loss in net income.

IFRS permits periodic revaluations of fixed assets and intangible assets to their current market value (discussed in Chapter 7). Increased valuation of assets leads to an increase in a revaluation reserve account included in the shareholders' equity section of the balance sheet (similar to accumulated other comprehensive income). Depreciation or amortization of the revalued assets may appear fully on the income statement each period as an expense or may be split between the income statement (depreciation or amortization based on acquisition cost) and a reduction in the revaluation reserve (depreciation or amortization based on the excess of current market value over acquisition cost).

The analyst's concern with other comprehensive income is the appropriateness of revaluing the asset and delaying recognition of its income effect. Are the revaluations the free choice of the company's managers, or are they under the purview of the board of directors, the auditors, or other external parties? Total shareholders' equity is the same regardless of whether the unrealized gain or loss immediately affects net income or affects another shareholders' equity account and later affects net income. Because this treatment does not result in an effect on net income of the current period, the analyst may want to restate reported net income of the current period to incorporate other comprehensive income. We revisit this issue in Chapter 9.

---

[22]Financial Accounting Standards Board, *Statement of Accounting Standards No. 130,* "Reporting Comprehensive Income" (1997); *FASB Codification Topic 220;* International Accounting Standards Board, *International Accounting Standard 1,* "Presentation of Financial Statements."

Reserves

In the United States, major revenues, gains, expenses, and losses flow through the income statement. In some countries outside the United States, local country GAAP permits certain income items to bypass the income statement and, instead, increase or decrease a shareholders' equity account directly. A practice in some countries is to create a reserve account by reducing retained earnings. For example, a firm might decrease retained earnings and increase an account titled reserve for contingencies or retained earnings appropriated for contingencies. These reserve accounts appear among the shareholders' equity accounts. When firms later resolve the contingency, they charge the cost against the reserve account rather than include it in expenses. Therefore, these costs bypass the income statement and usually result in an overstatement of earnings. Note that this use of reserves does not misstate total shareholders' equity because all of the affected accounts (retained earnings, reserve accounts, and expense accounts) are components of shareholders' equity. Thus, the analyst's primary concern with these reserves is assessing whether the reported net income that excludes these items is an appropriate base for estimating future earnings. The analyst can study the shareholders' equity portion of the balance sheet to ascertain whether firms have used reserve accounts to avoid sending legitimate expenses through the income statement. Reserves of this type had been particularly common in the German home-country standards-based reporting system prior to the adoption of IFRS.[23]

Example 9

Refer to the Common Shareholders' Equity section of PepsiCo's Consolidated Balance Sheet (Appendix A). At December 27, 2008, PepsiCo reports retained earnings of $30,638 million and an accumulated other comprehensive loss of $4,694 million. The retained earnings balance represents accumulated (over the life of PepsiCo) increases in net assets of the company, *which were reported in net income*, minus dividends declared. The accumulated other comprehensive loss represents decreases in net assets of the company from asset and liability revaluations, *which were not reported in net income*. PepsiCo's Consolidated Statement of Common Shareholders' Equity describes how accumulated other comprehensive loss changed during 2008 from a beginning accumulated loss of $952 million to an ending accumulated loss of $4,694 million. This *change* in accumulated other comprehensive loss (that is, the current year's portion) is the difference between 2008 net income ($5,142 million) and 2008 comprehensive income ($1,349 million). PepsiCo shows this reconciliation in a statement of comprehensive income appearing at the bottom of the Consolidated Statement of Common Shareholders' Equity.[24] The losses that PepsiCo recognize in comprehensive income in 2008 are largely a consequence of a negative currency translation adjustment ($2,484 million) and net losses associated with pensions ($1,358 million). During 2007, comprehensive income was larger than net income because of a positive foreign currency translation adjustment and gains associated with pensions. One argument for recognizing such gains and losses in other comprehensive income and in the accumulated

---

[23]Also found in financial statements prepared under home-country GAAP is the use of a reserve account to designate that a portion of shareholders' equity is not available for dividends. Local laws or practices may dictate that firms transfer an amount from retained earnings, which is available for dividends, to a more permanent account that is not available for dividends. U.S. firms typically "capitalize" a portion of retained earnings when they issue a stock dividend. Several other countries require firms to report a certain amount of legal capital on the balance sheet. Such firms reduce retained earnings and increase an account titled Legal Capital or Legal Reserve. The implication of such disclosures is that assets equal to the amount of this legal capital are not available for dividends. This use of reserves has no effect on net income of the current period or future periods.

[24]IFRS (IAS 1) requires a separate schedule of other comprehensive income included in a note disclosure or included with net income in a statement of comprehensive income. U.S. GAAP also permits these two approaches.

other comprehensive income/loss account is that these types of revaluations of assets and liabilities tend to be transitory; that is, they have the potential to reverse over time. The analyst should examine the behavior of accumulated other comprehensive income through time to see whether including elements of other comprehensive income in current income would aid in the assessment of the risk of the firm and in the prediction of future income.

Summary and Interpretation of Equity

Common shareholders' equity represents the book value of equity investor claims. Dividing common shareholders' equity by the number of common shares outstanding yields *book value per share*. The economic meaning of this number is not clear because owners' equity is the difference between assets and liabilities, each measured using different attributes (for example, historical cost, present value, fair market value, or net realizable value). Reference to equity securities markets provides a *market price per share* of common stock that is created by the interaction of supply and demand for shares. This market price is the dollar amount that a common shareholder would receive from selling a share of owners' equity. The ratio of book and market value, called the *market-to-book ratio*, is as follows:

$$\text{Market-to-Book Ratio} = \text{Market Price per Share/Book Value per Share}$$

Market-to-book ratios are commonly greater than one for two primary reasons. First, the conservatism of accounting (as a result of accounting standards themselves or management's application of accounting standards) leads to book values of individual assets that are typically equal to or less than their fair values (but not greater than their fair values). For example, if a company's operations include a great deal of R&D (research and development) (expensed immediately under U.S. GAAP), the unrecorded economic assets created by such expenditures causes book value per share to be lower than fair value. Second, future growth opportunities increase market price per share but have not been reflected in accounting measurements of book value.

For book value to be recognized in financial statements, U.S. GAAP and IFRS require that transactions have taken place or that unresolved future events can be estimated reliably. Therefore, book value of shareholders' equity tends to lag market value. Chapter 13 describes a valuation approach that relates book value to market value through the expectations of future accounting earnings not yet embedded in book value.

Changes in shareholders' equity result from transactions with owners (issuances of stock and distributions such as dividends and share buybacks) and transactions with non-owners, which are reflected in one of the two parts of comprehensive income, either net income or other comprehensive income. Financing strategy drives the changes in shareholders' equity from transactions with owners. Operating strategies drive the changes in shareholders' equity from transactions with non-owners.

DEBT FINANCING

As discussed in Chapter 5, the use of debt to finance investments and operations levers up the return on common equity, which can benefit common shareholders. However, the use of debt also has its costs. The required return to common shareholders (that is, the cost of equity capital) is increasing in the amount of debt in a corporation's capital structure. Further, net income is reduced by the amount of interest charges on debt and long-term solvency risk is increasing in the amount of debt. Accordingly, the financial reporting and analysis of debt is critical to understanding the profitability and risk of a firm.

This section addresses the accounting for debt financing. Our discussion begins with the principles of liability recognition and the measurement and application of those principles. Liabilities arise from both operating and financing activities. Therefore, this chapter pertains to debt financing; operating liabilities (both short- and long-term) that arise from operating activities are discussed in Chapter 8. Then this chapter considers how financial statements report traditional financing activities, which receive balance sheet recognition (for example, the issue of long-term notes and bonds, debt reduction, accounting for troubled debt, and the issue and conversion of hybrid securities). The final part of the chapter discusses off-balance-sheet financing, giving special attention to lease financing and how an analyst can adjust financial statements to incorporate off-balance-sheet lease financing in the assessment of financial risk.

Principles of Liability Recognition

Financial reporting recognizes an obligation as a liability if it satisfies the following three criteria:

- The obligation involves a probable future sacrifice of economic benefits—a future transfer of cash, goods, or services; the forgoing of a future cash receipt; or the transfer of equity shares—at a specified or determinable date. The firm can measure with reasonable precision the cash-equivalent value of the resources needed to satisfy the obligation.
- The firm has a present obligation (not a possible future obligation) and little or no discretion to avoid the transfer.
- The transaction or event that gave rise to the obligation has already occurred. [25]

Principles of Liability Valuation

The general principles underlying the valuation of liabilities are as follows:

- Liabilities requiring future cash payments (such as the debt financing provided by bonds payable) appear at the present value of the required future cash flows discounted at an interest rate that reflects the uncertainty that the firm will be able to make the cash payments. The firm establishes the discount rate at the time it initially records a liability in the accounts (often referred to as the *historical interest rate*) and generally uses this interest rate in accounting for the liability in all future periods.
- Liabilities requiring the future delivery of goods or services (such as the operating liability for warranties) appear at the estimated cost of those goods and services.
- Liabilities representing cash advances from customers (such as the operating liabilities Rental Fees Received in Advance or Subscription Fees Received in Advance) appear at the amount of the cash advance.

The fair value of a liability may differ from the amount appearing on the balance sheet, particularly for long-term debt. Fair value reflects current interest rates and assessments of the firm's ability to make the required payments as opposed to historical rates in effect when the debt contracts were originally written. U.S. GAAP requires firms to disclose the fair values of financial instruments, whether or not these financial instruments appear as liabilities (or assets) in the notes to the financial statements. Also, recent standards issued

---

[25]Financial Accounting Standards Board, *Statement of Financial Accounting Concepts No. 6*, "Elements of Financial Statements" (1985). Financial Accounting Standards Board, *Statement of Financial Accounting Standards No. 150*, "Accounting for Certain Financial Instruments with Characteristics of both Liabilities and Equity," (2008) requires certain obligations settled in equity shares to be classified as liabilities; *FASB Codification Topic 480.*

by the FASB and IASB allow firms the option of valuing financial liabilities (and assets) at fair value in the financial statements.[26] Firms may choose to exercise this option on an instrument-by-instrument basis, but the choice, once made, is irrevocable for the life of the financial instrument. The choice is made upon first adoption of FASB *Statement No. 159* or IASB *IAS 39* or at the initial acquisition of a financial asset instrument or incurrence of a financial liability instrument.

Several exceptions exist with regard to the general rule of using the historical interest rate to report long-term liabilities on the balance sheet. For example, firms that have hedged the interest rate or foreign exchange risk in liabilities (discussed in Chapter 8) must report them at the present value of the cash flows using the current market interest rate. Also, for some liabilities due within the next year (such as the operating liabilities accounts payable, income taxes payable, and salaries payable), the difference between the amount of the future cash flows and their present value is sufficiently small that accounting ignores the discounting process and reports the liabilities at the amounts ultimately payable.

Application of Criteria for Liability Recognition

The criteria for liability recognition may appear straightforward and subject to unambiguous interpretation. Unfortunately, this is often not the case. Various obligations of an enterprise fall along a continuum with respect to how well they satisfy these criteria. Exhibit 6.5 classifies obligations into six groups.

Obligations with Fixed Payment Dates and Amounts

The obligations that most clearly satisfy the liability recognition criteria are those with fixed payment dates and amounts (typically set by contract). Most obligations arising from borrowing arrangements (classified as financing activities) fall into this category. A firm receives the benefit of having funds available for use. The borrowing agreement specifies the timing and amount of interest and principal payments.

Obligations with Fixed Payment Amounts but Estimated Payment Dates

Most current (operating) liabilities fall into this category. Oral agreements, written agreements, or legal statutes fix the amounts payable to suppliers, employees, and government agencies. Firms normally settle these obligations within a few months after incurring them. The firm can estimate the settlement date with sufficient accuracy to warrant recognizing a liability.

Obligations with Estimated Payment Dates and Amounts

Obligations in this group require estimation because the firm cannot identify the specific future recipients of cash, goods, or services at the time the obligation becomes a liability. In addition, the firm cannot precisely compute what amount of resources it will transfer in the future or when the transfer will occur. For example, when a firm sells products under a warranty agreement, it promises to replace defective parts or perform certain repair services for a specified period of time. At the time of sale, the firm can neither identify the specific customers who will receive warranty benefits nor ascertain the timing or amounts of customers' claims. Past experience, however, often provides the necessary information for

---

[26]Financial Accounting Standards Board, *Statement of Financial Accounting Standards No. 107*, "Disclosures about Fair Values of Financial Instruments" (1991); Financial Accounting Standards Board, *Statement of Financial Accounting Standards No. 159*, "The Fair Value Option for Financial Assets and Financial Liabilities" (2008); *FASB Codification Topic 825*; International Accounting Standards Board, *International Accounting Standard 39*, "Financial Instruments: Recognition and Measurement."

EXHIBIT 6.5

Classification of Accounting Liabilities by Degree of Uncertainty

Obligations with Fixed Payment Dates and Amounts	Obligations with Fixed Payment Amounts but Estimated Payment Dates	Obligations for which the Firm Must Estimate Both Timing and Amount of Payment	Obligations Arising from Advances from Customers on Unexecuted Contracts and Agreements	Obligations under Mutually Unexecuted Contracts	Contingent Obligations[a]
• Notes Payable • Interest Payable • Bonds Payable	• Accounts Payable • Salaries Payable • Taxes Payable	• Warranties Payable • Insurance Claims	• Rental Fees Received in Advance • Subscription Fees Received in Advance	• Purchase Commitments • Employment Commitments	• Unsettled Lawsuits • Financial Instruments with Off Balance-Sheet Risk • Loan Guarantees

Most Certain ←————————————————————————→ Least Certain

←———— Recognized as Accounting Liabilities ————→   Not Generally
←— Recognized as —→
Accounting Liabilities

[a]If an obligation meets certain criteria for a loss contingency, firms must recognize this obligation as a liability. See the discussion later in this chapter.

estimating the likely proportion of customers who will make claims and the probable average amount of their claims. As long as the firm can reasonably estimate the probable amount of the obligation, it satisfies the first criterion for a liability. The selling price of goods sold under warranty includes an explicit or implicit charge for the warranty services. Thus, the receipt of cash or the right to receive cash in the sales transaction benefits the firm and creates the warranty liability.

Obligations Arising from Advances from Customers on Unexecuted Contracts and Agreements

A firm sometimes receives cash from customers in advance for goods or services it will provide at a future time. For example, a rental firm may receive cash in advance of the rental period for rented property. A magazine publisher may receive subscription fees in advance of the subscription period. Organizations and associations may receive membership dues prior to the membership period. Airlines may receive cash for tickets prior to passenger travel. Retailers and restaurant chains may sell cash gift cards or certificates that are redeemable for future products and services. These firms generally cannot recognize revenue upon receipt of cash because revenue recognition usually requires that the firm deliver the goods or provide the services. In the case of advances from customers, all of the required transfer of resources (goods or services) will occur in the future. Thus, the receipt of cash in advance from customers creates a liability equal to the cash received. The firm might conceivably recognize a liability equal to the expected cost of delivering the promised goods or services, but doing so would result in recognizing the profit from the transaction before substantial performance had occurred.

Obligations under Mutually Unexecuted Contracts

Mutually unexecuted contracts arise when two entities agree to transfer resources but *neither* entity has yet made a transfer. For example, a firm may agree to purchase from its suppliers specified amounts of merchandise over the next two years. A baseball organization may agree to pay its "franchise" player a certain sum as compensation for services the player will render over the next five years. A bank may agree to provide lines of credit to its business customers in the event these firms need funds in the future. Both parties have exchanged promises, but neither party has transferred resources. Thus, no accounting liability arises at the time of the exchange of promises. A liability arises only when one party or the other transfers resources in the future. This category of obligation, called *executory contracts*, differs from the preceding two, in which the contracts or agreements are partially executed. With warranty agreements, a firm receives cash but has not fulfilled its warranty obligation. With advances from customers, a firm receives cash but has not provided the required goods or services.

GAAP generally does not require firms to recognize as accounting liabilities obligations under mutually unexecuted contracts. (Exceptions do occur for some leasing arrangements, discussed later in this chapter, and for derivatives, discussed in Chapter 8.) If the amounts involved are material, the firm must disclose the nature of the obligation and its amount in notes to the financial statements. The analyst might conclude, however, that these obligations create sufficient risk for the firm to justify adjusting the reported financial statements to include such obligations.

Contingent Obligations

An event whose future outcome is unknown may create an obligation for the future transfer of resources. For example, a firm may be a defendant in a lawsuit, the outcome of which depends on the results of legal proceedings. Or a firm may guarantee loans of a subsidiary, the outcome of which depends on the future solvency of the subsidiary. Or an insurer may promise to pay certain amounts or reimburse certain expenses if particular future events occur. Obligations such as these are *contingent* on future events.

Contingent obligations may or may not give rise to accounting liabilities. Financial reporting requires firms to recognize an estimated loss from a contingency (called a *loss contingency*) and a related liability only if both of the following conditions are met:

- Information available prior to the issuance of the financial statements indicates that it is probable that an asset has been impaired or that a liability has been incurred.
- The firm can estimate the amount of the loss with reasonable precision.[27]

The first criterion for recognition of a loss contingency rests on the probability, or likelihood, that an asset has been impaired or a liability has been incurred. Financial reporting does not

---

[27]Financial Accounting Standards Board, *Statement of Financial Accounting Standards No. 5*, "Accounting for Contingencies" (1975); *FASB Codification Topic 450*.

provide clear guidance as to what probability cutoff defines *likely* or *probable*. The FASB has stated that "probable is used with its usual general meaning, rather than in a specific accounting or technical sense, and refers to that which can be expected or believed on the basis of available evidence or logic but is neither certain or proved."[28]

The second criterion requires reasonable estimation of the amount of the loss. Again, financial reporting does not define *reasonably estimable* in precise terms. Instead, if the firm can narrow the amount of the loss to a reasonable range, however large, financial reporting presumes that the firm has achieved sufficient precision to justify recognition of a liability. The amount of the loss is the most likely estimate within the range. If no amount within the range is more likely than another, the firm should use the amount at the lower end of the range. As might be suspected, the estimates of contingent liabilities is fraught with measurement error, and possibly managerial bias.

Financial reporting refers to obligations meeting both of these criteria as loss contingencies. One example suggested by the FASB relates to a toy manufacturer that sold toys that were later found to present a safety hazard. The toy manufacturer concludes that the likelihood of having to pay damages is high. The firm meets the second criterion if experience or other information enables the manufacturer to make a reasonable estimate of the loss. The toy manufacturer recognizes a loss and a liability in this case. As another example, firms in the tobacco industry and in environmentally sensitive industries grapple with measuring loss contingencies related to litigation and draw on lawyers and others to facilitate quantifying the loss.

Closely related to the concept of a loss contingency is a *guarantee*. For example, one firm may guarantee the repayment of another entity's borrowing in the event the other entity cannot repay the loan at maturity. As another example, a firm may sell a portion of its accounts receivable to another entity, promising to reimburse the other entity if uncollectible accounts exceed a specified amount. The need to make a future cash payment is contingent on future events. U.S. GAAP requires firms to recognize the fair value of the guarantee as a liability.[29] Measuring this fair value involves estimating the likelihood, timing, and amount that might be payable. However, a guarantee can have a fair value even when the likelihood of making a future payment is low. A guarantee by a financially strong firm of a financially weaker firm's debt will reduce the weaker firm's cost of borrowing. The guarantor recognizes a receivable and a liability for the fair value of the benefit granted to the borrower by the grantor. The obligation to reimburse a purchaser of accounts receivable for excess uncollectibles likely increases the amount the buyer pays the seller for the receivables. Recognizing the fair value of this guarantee as a liability affects the amount of gain or loss the seller recognizes on the sale of the receivables. In addition to recognizing the fair value of guarantees as liabilities, firms must disclose the maximum amount that could become payable and any available collateral that the guarantor could recover in the event it must execute the guarantee. Note 9, "Debt Obligations and Commitments," of PepsiCo's 2008 financial statements (Appendix A) indicates that PepsiCo guarantees $2.3 billion of Bottling Group, LLC's long-term debt.

Financing with Long-Term Debt

As illustrated in Chapters 4 and 5, firms are able to use leverage to increase the rate of return on common equity. The primary source of leverage for most firms is the issuance of

---

[28]*Statement of Financial Accounting Concepts No. 6* (1985). Although the FASB has not defined *probable*, practice demands that firms and auditors define it. Currently, most firms and auditors appear to use *probable* to mean 80–85 percent or larger.

[29]Financial Accounting Standards Board, *Interpretation No. 45*, "Guarantor's Accounting and Disclosure Requirements for Guarantees, Including Indirect Indebtedness of Others" (2002); *FASB Codification Topic 460.*

long-term debt in the form of notes payable (primarily to banks and other financial institutions), bonds payable (to any type of bondholder, including open-market debt investors), and leases (entered into with property owners, equipment dealers, or finance companies). Debt issuance is evidenced by a bond indenture, promissory note, or lease agreement. These documents will specify promises to pay maturity amounts at specified dates; promises to pay cash interest (or in the case of leases, lease payments) of specified amounts at specified dates; call provisions; descriptions of property pledged as security; whether the debt is convertible to another claim and at what rate the conversion will occur; and covenants and restrictions that specify sinking fund requirements, working capital restrictions, dividend payment restrictions, restrictions on the issuance of new debt, and other restrictions. Bonds are issued almost exclusively for cash consideration. Notes also are issued for cash consideration, but they may be issued for non-cash consideration as well. Lease agreements result in a lessee receiving non-cash consideration, the use of property, plant, and equipment.

This section illustrates the accounting for long-term debt using notes payable. Accounting for bonds payable is similar except for the possibility that bonds may be traded in more active markets, thus having more readily determinable fair values. As discussed in the following sections, fair value of financial instruments is a required disclosure in the notes to the financial statements and an optional measurement for recognition in the financial statements. Lease accounting is discussed in a subsequent section about off-balance-sheet financing.

Example 10

Note 9, "Debt Obligations and Commitments" (Appendix A), indicates that PepsiCo uses both long-term interest-bearing and long-term non-interest-bearing (that is, "zero coupon") notes to raise capital. Assume that on January 1, 2010, PepsiCo borrows money from a bank by issuing a $100 million promissory note to the bank. The note matures in five years on January 1, 2015, and pays 5 percent interest once a year on January 1. The bank transfers $95.79 million (rounded) to PepsiCo.

PepsiCo's cash flows over the life of the note are as follows (in millions):

Cash inflow at issue		$ 95.79
Annual cash outflows (interest payments):		
Face amount of note	$100.00	
Coupon or stated interest rate	× 5%	
Annual cash interest payment	$ 5.00	
Years	× 5	
Total Interest Payments		(25.00)
Cash outflow at retirement date		(100.00)
Net cash outflow		$ (29.21)

The $29.21 net cash outflow represents the total interest cost on the note. Accrual accounting's goal is to recognize the interest cost on the note over the five-year period in an economically meaningful way.

By paying less than $100 million for the note, the bank will earn a return that is greater than the 5 percent stated interest rate. That is, this investment is sufficiently risky such that a yield or an effective rate of interest should be higher than 5 percent, and therefore, the bank "discounts" the note. For a bond or note, the *cash interest* is determined by the *coupon rate* or *stated rate* of interest, which may be negotiated in a note or private bond placement or simply presented to potential buyers in a public bond issuance, multiplied by the face value of the debt. Cash interest may or may not be a function of the risk characteristics of the transaction. *Effective interest,* also known as the *yield, yield-to-maturity,* or *rate of return,* is a function of the risk characteristics of the transaction. It is the economic return on the transaction to creditors and the economic cost to debtors.[30]

A number of factors determine the effective interest rate. A portion of any effective interest rate contains compensation for the use of the lender's funds. While the funds are on loan, alternative, possibly more profitable opportunities for lending may become available. Also, the effective interest rate will reflect expected inflation, which causes future dollars to have less purchasing power. In addition, if the loan is denominated in a foreign currency, relative changes in economic conditions across countries could result in an unfavorable transformation of foreign currency into the dollar. Finally, firm-specific liquidity and solvency risk (as discussed in Chapter 5) explains differences in effective interest rates.

Analysts solve for a loan's effective rate of return (i) using the following formula:

$$\text{Present Value} = \sum_{n=1}^{t} \frac{\text{Cash Interest}}{(1 + i)^n} + \frac{\text{Maturity Value}}{(1 + i)^t}$$

$$\$95.79 \text{ million} = \sum_{n=1}^{5} \frac{\$5 \text{ million}}{(1 + i)^n} + \frac{\$100 \text{ million}}{(1 + i)^5}$$

Solving for i results in a yield of 6 percent.[31]

PepsiCo must use the effective interest method to account for the note. The method can be best understood by referring to the effective interest amortization table in Exhibit 6.6, in which the cash interest column is obtained by multiplying the face value of the debt by the stated interest rate of 5 percent and the effective interest column is obtained by multiplying the beginning of the period book value of debt (previous row) by the 6 percent effective interest rate charged by the bank.

EXHIBIT 6.6

Example 10. Effective Interest Amortization Table
(amounts in millions)

Date	5% Cash Interest	6% Effective Interest Expense	Amortization	Book Value of Note
1/1/10				$ 95.79
12/31/10	$ 5.00	$ 5.75	$0.75	$ 96.54
12/31/11	$ 5.00	$ 5.79	$0.79	$ 97.33
12/31/12	$ 5.00	$ 5.84	$0.84	$ 98.17
12/31/13	$ 5.00	$ 5.89	$0.89	$ 99.06
12/31/14	$ 5.00	$ 5.94	$0.94	$100.00
	$25.00	$29.21		

[30]If the effective rate of interest and the stated rate of interest are equal, computing the present value of the note will yield a present value equal to the face value of the note. When the debtholder pays the face value to acquire a bond or note, the bond or note is said to be "issued at par."

[31]Using a financial calculator to solve for i involves setting n (number of annual interest payments) = 5, payment (annual cash interest payment) = $5 million, present value = $95.79 million, and future value = $100 million.

The beginning book value of $95.79 million represents the amount lent to PepsiCo on 1/1/10. In 2010, PepsiCo incurs a 6 percent interest charge on its $95.79 million initial borrowing, $5.75 million of effective interest expense. Essentially, the debt has grown by $5.75 million. Because PepsiCo pays only $5 million in cash interest to the bank, the difference between the effective interest expense and cash interest paid [shown in the amortization column ($0.75 million)] increases the book value of the debt. Note that the amount of effective interest expense increases each period. This occurs because the amount borrowed increases each period and PepsiCo incurs a constant 6 percent economic interest charge on the debt. The annual increase in the debt is paid off as part of the $100 million maturity payment.

Financial Reporting of Long-Term Debt

In the balance sheet, notes payable are reported at the present value of future cash flows using the historical effective rate of interest at the issue date. Note that the effective interest amortization table provides the book values of the note at each year-end. At December 31, 2014, the $100 million maturity value must be reclassified as a current liability because funds will be disbursed within one year of the balance sheet date (actually, the next day). A reclassification of a large note payable from long-term to current may have a material adverse impact on working capital (current assets minus current liabilities) and the current ratio (current assets divided by current liabilities). In practice, this potential adverse impact is alleviated two ways. First, a firm may set up a sinking fund in liquid assets (because of debt covenants or as part of the firm's cash management policy) to be used to repay the debt. The sinking fund and debt classifications will have countervailing effects on working capital.[32]

Another means of avoiding the reclassification of long-term debt to a current liability is to enter into a refinancing agreement. If management intends to refinance the debt on a long-term basis and the corporation demonstrates the ability to refinance the debt, GAAP allows the obligation to remain in the long-term classification at the balance sheet date. Auditors will investigate whether the ability to refinance is present by searching for a refinancing agreement with a lender or for evidence that actual refinancing has taken place before the financial statements are issued.[33] In Note 9, "Debt Obligations and Commitments" (Appendix A), PepsiCo reports $1,259 million reclassified from short-term to long-term debt. In the note, PepsiCo describes entering into two long-term borrowing agreements, part of which will be used to repay short-term debt.

The statement of cash flows reports the net proceeds of debt issues, interest payments, and maturity payments. Under both U.S. GAAP and IFRS, cash flows relating to principal amounts of debt are reported as financing activities. Under U.S. GAAP, interest expense is included as an operating cash outflow because interest expense reduces net income, which is reported as a source of cash flow from operating activities under the indirect method. Additional adjustments in the operating cash flow section include changes in interest payable and amortizations of bond discounts and premiums. (Although due to the use of the indirect method, which does not directly disclose cash payments for interest, many companies disclose cash interest payments in the notes to the financial statements or in a supplementary schedule provided with the cash flow statement. PepsiCo discloses cash paid for interest in Note 14.) Under IFRS, cash payments for interest can be reported as an operating or financing cash outflow. Under both U.S. GAAP and IFRS, the income statement reports interest expense as a non-operating charge.

---

[32]FASB No. 47 requires note disclosure of sinking fund and bond retirement payments for each of the next five years after the balance sheet date.

[33]Balance sheet classification intricacies of long-term debt are addressed in FASB *Statement of Financial Accounting Standards No. 6*, "Balance Sheet Classification of Short-Term Obligations Expected to Be Refinanced" (Stamford, CT: FASB 1975*); No. 47*, "Disclosure of Long-Term Obligations" (1981); and *No. 129*, "Disclosure of Information about Capital Structure" (1997).

Fair Value Disclosure and the Fair Value Option

Long-term notes and bonds are financial instruments; therefore, firms must disclose the fair values of such debt in the notes to the financial statements.[34] In referring back to Exhibit 6.6, the December 31, 2012, book value of the note payable is $98.17 million. This amount is referred to as *amortized cost* because it represents the original "cost" of the debt, $95.79 million, adjusted for the amortization of the bank's discount for 2010–2012. The amount also represents the present value of the remaining cash flows (two more $5 million interest payments and one final $100 million principal payment) at the historical 6 percent effective rate of interest.

$$\$98.17 \text{ million} = \sum_{n=1}^{2} \frac{\$5 \text{ million}}{(1 + 0.06)^n} + \frac{\$100 \text{ million}}{(1 + 0.06)^2}$$

If the market's required rate of interest has changed since the original signing date of the note, the fair value of the debt will change as well. Suppose the market requires a 7 percent return on PepsiCo's note at December 31, 2012.

$$\$96.38 \text{ million} = \sum_{n=1}^{2} \frac{\$5 \text{ million}}{(1 + 0.07)^n} + \frac{\$100 \text{ million}}{(1 + 0.07)^2}$$

PepsiCo would report the amortized cost of $98.17 million on the face of the balance sheet (probably in a group with other long-term debt) and the fair value of $96.38 million in the notes to the financial statements.

Recently, both the FASB and IASB passed a rule allowing firms the option of using fair value as the basis for balance sheet reporting of financial liabilities (and financial assets) instead of amortized cost.[35] If PepsiCo were to adopt the *fair value option* for this debt, it would report $96.38 million of notes payable on the face of the balance sheet and an unrealized gain on remeasurement of long-term debt equal to $98.17 million − $96.38 million = $1.79 million on the income statement. The standards are silent on how to recognize interest expense on this new long-term-debt basis. However, using the effective interest method (as described previously) with the new market rate and new book value would be consistent with current practice.

Example 11

Using the data in Example 10 and the remeasurement under the fair value option in the preceding paragraphs, Exhibit 6.7 summarizes the accounting for the long-term note payable through the remeasurement at December 31, 2012 (all amounts in millions of dollars).

Measuring Fair Value

The challenge that companies face in providing fair value disclosures is obtaining reliable data. Historically, standard setters have eschewed fair value measurement in favor

---

[34]Financial Accounting Standards Board, *Statement of Financial Accounting Standards No.107*, "Disclosures about Fair Value of Financial Instruments" (1991); *FASB Codification Topic 825*; International Accounting Standards Board, *International Financial Reporting Standard 7*, "Financial Instruments: Disclosures."

[35]Financial Accounting Standards Board, *Statement of Financial Accounting Standards No.159*, "The Fair Value Option for Financial Assets and Financial Liabilities" (2008); *FASB Codification Topic 825*; International Accounting Standards Board, *International Financial Reporting Standard 39*, "Financial Instruments: Recognition and Measurement."

EXHIBIT 6.7: EXAMPLE 11 SOLUTION

1/1/10 Signing

Assets	=	Liabilities	+	Shareholders' Equity		
				CC	AOCI	RE
Cash +95.79		Note Payable +95.79				

Cash 95.79
    Note Payable 95.79

12/31/10 Year-End Interest Accrual

Assets	=	Liabilities	+	Shareholders' Equity		
				CC	AOCI	RE
		Note Payable +0.75 Interest Payable +5.00				Interest Expense −5.75

Interest Expense 5.75
    Note Payable 0.75
    Interest Payable 5.00

1/1/11 Interest Payment Date

Assets	=	Liabilities	+	Shareholders' Equity		
				CC	AOCI	RE
Cash +5.00		Interest Payable −5.00				

Interest Payable 5.00
    Cash 5.00

12/31/11 Year-End Interest Accrual

Assets	=	Liabilities	+	Shareholders' Equity		
				CC	AOCI	RE
		Note Payable +0.79 Interest Payable +5.00				Interest Expense −5.79

Interest Expense 5.79
    Note Payable 0.79
    Interest Payable 5.00

1/1/12 Interest Payment Date

Assets	=	Liabilities	+	Shareholders' Equity		
				CC	AOCI	RE
Cash +5.00		Interest Payable −5.00				

Interest Payable 5.00
    Cash 5.00

12/31/12 Year-End Interest Accrual

Assets	=	Liabilities	+	Shareholders' Equity		
				CC	AOCI	RE
		Note Payable +0.84 Interest Payable +5.00				Interest Expense −5.84

Interest Expense 5.84
    Note Payable 0.84
    Interest Payable 5.00

(Continued)

EXHIBIT 6.7 (CONTINUED)

12/31/12 Year-End Remeasurement at Fair Value

| Assets | = | Liabilities | + | Shareholders' Equity | | |
				CC	AOCI	RE
		Note Payable −1.79				Unrealized Gain +1.79
Note Payable		1.79				
Unrealized Gain			1.79			

of reliable historical data obtained from arm's-length transactions between the company and outside parties. Recently, however, the alleged relevance of fair value data in decision making has been judged to outweigh potential measurement reliability issues, especially when the item being measured is a financial asset or financial liability and the company can provide information on the level of likely data reliability.

Authoritative guidance for fair value measurement (SFAS No. 157) identifies a hierarchy of inputs for fair value measurements, which were introduced in the discussion of fair value in Chapter 2.[36] Level 1 inputs provide the most reliable measure and should be used if possible, followed by Level 2 and then Level 3. The level used for each asset or liability measurement must be disclosed. If multiple levels are used for a measurement, the least reliable level having a significant influence on the measurement must be disclosed. The levels are as follows:

Level 1: Observable quoted market prices in active markets for identical assets or liabilities

Level 2: Observable market data (other than Level 1 market prices) serving as inputs into estimates of the market value of the asset or liability in question, including quoted market prices of similar assets or liabilities in active markets, quoted market prices of identical assets or liabilities in inactive markets, and inputs into present value-based measurements of fair value such as interest rates, foreign exchange rates, and default rates

Level 3: Unobservable inputs used by the reporting entity when modeling how the market would determine the fair value of the asset or liability in question

Exhibit 6.8 summarizes information in PepsiCo's Note 10 about fair value measurement. Notice that PepsiCo uses a Level 2 basis for determining the fair value of its long-term debt.

EXHIBIT 6.8

An Excerpt from PepsiCo's Note 10, "Financial Instruments," from Its December 27, 2008 Annual Report (Appendix A)

We adopted SFAS 157 at the beginning of our 2008 fiscal year and our adoption did not have a material impact on our financial statements. The fair value framework requires the categorization of assets and liabilities into three levels based on the assumptions (inputs) used to price the assets or liabilities. Level 1 provides the most reliable measure of fair value, whereas Level 3 generally requires significant management judgment. . . . Under SFAS 157, the fair value of our debt obligations as of December 27, 2008 was $8.8 billion, based upon prices of similar instruments in the market place. The fair value of our debt obligations as of December 29, 2007 was $4.4 billion.

---

[36]As of the writing of this text, the IASB is deliberating on guidance for fair value measurement.

While few question the relevance of fair value measurement, many worry about the reliability of Level 2 and Level 3 estimates of fair values. While the quoted market prices of Level 1 valuations have intuitive appeal, the reliability of a Level 1 valuation is compromised if the market from which it comes is not "orderly." The market for mortgage-backed securities in 2008–2009 exhibited a volatility that caused some to question its orderliness.

Reducing Debt

Outstanding debt can be reduced by waiting until maturity to pay off the maturity value. Alternatively, debt can be retired earlier through engagement in open-market purchase of traded debt, exercising call options if available, or through a forced conversion (if available). The difference between the amounts used to extinguish the debt and the book value of the debt at the time of extinguishment is reported as a realized gain or loss on the income statement. Cash flows used to reduce debt are reported as cash outflows from financing activities in the statement of cash flows. *In-substance defeasance* of debt, transferring or pledging assets to an irrevocable trust to satisfy debt while remaining contingently obligated, used to be another popular way of removing debt from the balance sheet. U.S. GAAP and IFRS (IAS 39) now prohibit de-recognition of debt via in-substance defeasance.

Accounting for Troubled Debt

The financial crisis of the late 2000s found many firms struggling to make debt payments. Many firms ended up declaring bankruptcy or renegotiating the terms of outstanding debt obligations. This section examines how the debtor accounts for the restructuring of troubled debt.[37] From the debtor's perspective, two situations exist for handling troubled debt: settlement and modification of terms.

The *settlement* of troubled debt results in an economic gain to the debtor because the creditor accepts less than the book value of the debt to settle the debt. If a non-cash asset is transferred to settle the debt (for example, a collateral asset), the non-cash asset must be adjusted to fair value prior to its transfer, with the resulting gain or loss reported in income. A gain on debt settlement is recognized as the difference between the book value of the debt settled (principal plus any accrued interest) and the fair market value of the non-cash asset or cash transferred to retire the debt. Alternatively, debt could be settled by issuing capital stock. In this case, the stock issue is recorded at its fair market value and the gain to the debtor is the excess of the book value of the debt relative to the fair value of the stock issued to settle the debt.

Instead of accepting an asset or common stock (a right of net asset ownership) to retire the debt, a creditor might *modify the terms* of the debt, hoping a debtor will be able to perform under less stringent debt service requirements. Under U.S. GAAP, if terms are modified, the debtor must compare the total (undiscounted) future cash flows of the restructured debt to the current book value of the debt. If the total restructured future cash flows remain greater than the book value of the debt, the debtor will make no adjustment to book value (that is, record no gain). Future recognition of interest expense will follow the effective interest method using a new interest rate that discounts the total restructured future cash flows to the current book value.

Alternatively, if the total undiscounted restructured future cash flows are less than the book value of the debt, the debtor will reduce the book value of the debt to equal the total of the new restructured future cash flows, recording a gain in the process. Future interest expense will not be recognized because all future cash flows represent the repayment of

---

[37]U.S. GAAP for the debtor is found in "Accounting by Debtors and Creditors for Troubled Debt Restructurings," FASB No. 15 (Norwalk, CT: FASB, 1977); *FASB Codification Topic 470.* We address creditor accounting for troubled debt in Chapter 7.

principal; that is, the discount rate is zero. This accounting is conservative because future cash flows must fall fairly far before the debtor can recognize a gain. The result of the conservative accounting is to minimize any gains recognized by debtors who experience difficulty and must restructure debt agreements. The existing conservative accounting rules for troubled debt are subject to frequent (and deserved) criticism because they ignore the present value of future restructured cash flows for determining book values of troubled debt and gains from debt restructuring, and they often result in subsequent recognition of interest expense based on an unrealistic interest rate assumption.

Under IFRS (IAS 39), the measurement and recognition rules are quite different from those under U.S. GAAP. The following example contrasts U.S. GAAP and IFRS treatment of troubled debt from the debtor's perspective.

Example 12

Assume that Tribune Co. owes Bank of America $2,000,000 on a 5-year, 8% note originally issued at par. After one year of making scheduled payments, the firm faces financial difficulty. At the end of the second year, Tribune owes Bank of America $2,000,000 plus $160,000 of accrued but unpaid interest. Bank of America restructures the note by forgiving the $160,000 interest payable, reducing the note principal to $1,800,000, and reducing the interest rate to 7 percent.

Under U.S. GAAP, Tribune compares the gross (that is, undiscounted) future cash outflows under the restructured debt to the current book value of the debt as follows:

Undiscounted future cash flows of restructured debt:

New principal	$1,800,000	
New interest ($1,800,000 × 7% × 3 remaining years)	378,000	$2,178,000

Current book value of debt:

Old principal	$2,000,000	
Old accrued interest	160,000	$2,160,000

Because undiscounted future cash flows exceed the current book value of the debt, Tribune does not record a gain. Future interest expense is accounted for using the effective interest method and an effective interest rate that equates the future cash flows with the present value (that is, current book value) of the debt.

$$\$2,160,000 = \sum_{n=1}^{3} \frac{\$126,000}{(1 + i)^n} + \frac{\$1,800,000}{(1 + i)^3}$$

Solving for i yields a very small interest rate of 0.0029 percent.

Instead, if Bank of America reduced the principle to $1,700,000, Tribune would make the following comparison:

Undiscounted future cash flows of restructured debt:

New principal	$1,700,000	
New interest ($1,700,000 × 7% × 3 remaining years)	357,000	$2,057,000

Current book value of debt:

Old principal	$2,000,000	
Old accrued interest	160,000	$2,160,000

Because undiscounted future cash flows are less than the current book value of debt, Tribune reduces the book value of the debt to $2,057,000 and records a gain of

$2,160,000 − 2,057,000 = \$103,000$. Future interest expense does not exist (that is, the effective rate is set equal to zero) because the future cash flows are now equal to the present value (that is, the reduced book value).

Under IFRS, Tribune would compare the present value of future cash flows under the restructured debt (instead of the undiscounted cash flows as under U.S. GAAP) to the book value of the debt. Return to the original example where Bank of America reduced the principal to $1,800,000. The present value calculation uses the historical effective interest rate of 8 percent as follows:

Present value of future cash flows (using a financial calculator:
  FV = \$1,800,000, PMNT − \$1,800,000 × 7%
  = \$126,000, i = 8%, n = 3): $\underline{\$1,753,612}$

Current book value of debt:
  Old principal   \$2,000,000
  Old accrued interest $\underline{160,000}$ $\underline{\$2,160,000}$

IFRS uses a "10 percent rule" to determine whether a gain is recognized. Because the present value of $1,753,612 is 23.2 percent below the book value of $2,160,000 (that is, greater than 10 percent below book value), Tribune recognizes a gain. The *amount* of the gain is equal to the amount by which the *fair value* of the debt is below the current book value. Computing fair value of the restructured debt's cash flows requires the use of a current market rate of interest instead of the historical rate of 8 percent. For example, because of Tribune's financial difficulties, assume that a more appropriate current rate of interest for Tribune is 12 percent. Discounting the same cash flows using a 12 percent rate yields a present value of $1,583,835. Therefore, Tribune would record a gain of $2,160,000 − 1,583,835 = \$576,165. Future interest expense would be recognized using the 12 percent effective interest rate so that the new book value (computed using the 12 percent rate) is correctly amortized to the new maturity value by the maturity date.

If the present value of the restructured cash flows at the historical rate is within 10 percent of the book value of the debt, Tribune does not recognize a gain. Income effects are similar to the effects under U.S. GAAP when no gain is recognized. Because IFRS uses the economically sound present value approach to determine the magnitude of the settlement and U.S. GAAP uses the more conservative undiscounted future cash flows approach, the magnitude of the new book value of the restructured debt will be lower and the gain recognition will be larger under IFRS.

Example 13

PepsiCo's Consolidated Balance Sheet (Appendix A) shows Long-Term Debt Obligations of $7,858 and $4,203 million at the end of 2008 and 2007, respectively. Note that PepsiCo reports Short-term Obligations (usually the currently due portion of long-term obligations) of $369 million at the end of 2008. Both of these liabilities are financing instead of operating liabilities. The financing activities section in the Consolidated Statement of Cash Flows shows that $3,719 million of long-term debt capital was raised in 2008 and $649 million was paid off. Also, short-term borrowings increased. Note 9, "Debt Obligations and Commitments" (Appendix A), reports the detail on the short- and long-term obligations. Note 9 also reports interest rate swaps, which we cover in Chapter 8.

ADDITIONAL ISSUES IN LIABILITY RECOGNITION AND DEBT FINANCING

In the following sections, we examine two additional issues in long-term liability reporting, the use of hybrid securities to obtain financing and the structure of financing arrangements to keep debt off of the balance sheet.

Hybrid Securities

Ambiguities arise in the measurement and classification of certain securities issued to raise capital because the securities have both debt and equity characteristics. These securities are referred to as *hybrid securities* or *compound financing instruments*. For example, firms often issue preferred stock that is subject to certain rights of redemption in either cash or common shares after some period of time.[38] The classification of preferred stock as debt or equity depends on who holds the power to trigger redemption and whether the firm reports under U.S. GAAP or IFRS. If redemption will occur at a specific time or upon a specific event (for example, death of the holder), both U.S. GAAP and IFRS treat the preferred stock as a liability. This situation is typically referred to as *mandatorily redeemable preferred stock*. If the redemption is at the option of the issuing firm (that is, the preferred stock is callable), U.S. GAAP and IFRS will treat the preferred stock as equity. If redemption is at the holder's discretion (that is, the preferred stock is "putable"), U.S. GAAP will require that the stock be disclosed between debt and equity (the so-called "mezzanine" disclosure) and IFRS will require disclosure as a liability.

Convertible preferred stock is similar to preferred stock except that the holder has the option to exchange the convertible preferred stock for common stock under some pre-agreed exchange ratio. For example, a holder of 1,000 shares of $100 par, 7% convertible preferred stock may have the right to exchange each share of convertible preferred for five shares of $10 par common stock. Convertible preferred stock is treated as preferred stock at the date of issue. (Equity increases by the fair value of the consideration received at the issue date.) If converted to common stock, the recorded amounts are simply shifted from preferred stock to common stock.

Convertible debt may, at the creditor's option, be converted into common shares at a pre-specified exchange rate. The creditor holds (1) debt with a stated interest rate and maturity date and (2) an option to exchange the debt for equity. However, the debt and option features do not trade separately in secondary markets. While holding the convertible debt, the creditor receives interest payments, a feature of debt. Also, the debtholder has the ability to exchange the debt for equity, an equity-like feature. Under U.S. GAAP, accountants have historically recorded convertible debt as a financial liability and recorded interest expense. The option to exchange the debt for equity is not valued and recorded. IFRS differs in that the debt and equity features are recorded separately to the extent that the separate components can be reliably estimated at fair value.

---

[38]The following discussion is based on Financial Accounting Standards Board, *Statement No. 150*, "Accounting for Certain Financial Instruments with Characteristics of Both Liabilities and Equity" (2003); Accounting Principles Board, *Opinion No. 14*, "Accounting for Convertible Debt and Debt Issued with Stock Purchase Warrants" (1969); *FASB Codification Topic 480*; Securities and Exchange Commission *Accounting Series Release No. 268*, "Presentation in Financial Statements of Redeemable Preferred Stock"; And International Accounting Standards Board, *International Accounting Standard 32*, "Financial Instruments: Presentation" (revised 2003).

Under both U.S. GAAP and IFRS, most companies use the *book value method* to record conversion. The book value method is based on the idea that the conversion is a culmination of the original transaction. Whatever amounts are recorded in debt (and in equity under IFRS) are simply shifted to shareholders' equity when the debt is converted into equity. Both U.S. GAAP and IFRS allow the use of the *market value method,* under which the market value of the common stock determines the basis of the conversion transaction. This approach is rarely used because it generates potentially large losses.

Example 14

The December 31, 2008, Consolidated Balance Sheet of Digital River, Inc., reports 1.25%, 20-year convertible senior notes originally issued in 2004 at a par value of $195 million. Each $1,000 of note principal may be converted into 22.6948 shares of Digital River $0.01 par value common stock, a conversion price of $44.063 per share. Exhibit 6.9

EXHIBIT 6.9: EXAMPLE 14 SOLUTION

U.S. GAAP

	Assets		=	Liabilities		+	Shareholders' Equity		
							CC	AOCI	RE
1	Cash	+195.00		Notes Payable	+195.00				

Cash	195.00	
Notes Payable		195.00

IFRS

	Assets		=	Liabilities		+	Shareholders' Equity		
							CC	AOCI	RE
1	Cash	+195.00		Notes Payable	+122.12		APIC—Notes Payable +72.88		

Cash	195.00	
Notes Payable		122.12
APIC—Notes Payable		72.88

U.S. GAAP

	Assets		=	Liabilities	+	Shareholders' Equity		
						CC	AOCI	RE
2	Cash	−2.4375						Interest Expense −2.4375

Interest Expense	2.4375	
Cash		2.4375

IFRS

	Assets		=	Liabilities		+	Shareholders' Equity		
							CC	AOCI	RE
2	Cash	−2.4375		Notes Payable	+2.4073				Interest Expense −4.8848

Interest Expense	4.8848	
Notes Payable		2.4073
Cash		2.4375

(Continued)

EXHIBIT 6.9 (CONTINUED)

U.S. GAAP

	Assets	=	Liabilities	+	Shareholders' Equity		
					CC	AOCI	RE
3a			Notes Payable −195.0000		Common Stock +0.0443 APIC +194.9557		
	Notes Payable			195.0000			
	Common Stock				0.0443		
	APIC				194.9557		

IFRS

	Assets	=	Liabilities	+	Shareholders' Equity		
					CC	AOCI	RE
3a			Notes Payable −124.5273		APIC—Notes Payable −72.8800 Common Stock +0.0443 APIC +197.3630		
	Notes Payable			124.5273			
	APIC—Notes Payable			72.8800			
	Common Stock				0.0443		
	APIC				197.3630		

U.S. GAAP

	Assets	=	Liabilities	+	Shareholders' Equity		
					CC	AOCI	RE
3b			Notes Payable −195.0000		Common Stock +0.0443 APIC +221.2300		Loss on Conversion −26.2743
	Notes Payable			195.0000			
	Loss on Conversion			26.2743			
	Common Stock				0.0443		
	APIC				221.2300		

IFRS

	Assets	=	Liabilities	+	Shareholders' Equity		
					CC	AOCI	RE
3b			Notes Payable −124.5273		APIC—Notes Payable −72.8800 Common Stock +0.0443 APIC +221.2300		Loss on Conversion −23.8670
	Notes Payable			124.5273			
	APIC—Notes Payable			72.8800			
	Loss on Conversion			23.8670			
	Common Stock				0.0443		
	APIC				221.2300		

shows the financial statement effects under both U.S. GAAP and IFRS of the following transactions:

1. Recording of the original issue. For the IFRS treatment, assume that Digital River would have borrowed at 4 percent if it did not offer a conversion privilege.
2. Recognition of one year's interest effect.
3. Conversion of the notes assuming a share of Digital River trades at $50
   a. Using the "book value method."
   b. Using the "market value method."

U.S. GAAP treats the entire convertible note issue proceeds of Transaction 1 as debt. Under IFRS, the proceeds are allocated between the fair values of the notes and the conversion options on the notes. If Digital would have paid 4 percent interest on the notes issued without the conversion option, the fair value of the notes could be approximated by discounting the notes' contractual cash flows at 4 percent. The present value of $195 million received 20 years hence and a contractual cash interest payment of $2.4375 million ($195 million × 1.25%) each period for 20 years equals $122.12 million. Thus, the note payable is recorded at $122.12 million and the remainder of the proceeds ($195 million − $122.12 million = $72.88 million) is classified as equity. The account Additional paid-in capital—Note payable would be reported in the shareholders' equity section as part of additional paid-in capital.

U.S. GAAP records the $2.4375 million annual payment as interest expense in Transaction 2. The cash interest and effective interest are equal because Digital River issued the notes payable at par. Under IFRS treatment, the notes were discounted at the effective interest rate of 4 percent. Therefore, the effective interest of $4.8848 million ($122.12 million beginning note book value times 4% effective interest rate) does not equal the contractual cash interest, and the note payable discount ($2.4073 million) is amortized.[39]

The book value method (Transaction 3a) is based on the idea that the conversion is a culmination of the original transaction. Whatever amounts recorded in debt are simply shifted to shareholders' equity when the debt is converted into equity. Under U.S. GAAP, the original issue was recorded as debt. Therefore, the $195 million is removed from notes payable. The common shares issued at conversion total 4,425,486, which is computed by multiplying the 22.6948 contractual conversion rate per $1,000 of note principal by $195 million divided by $1,000. The common stock account is increased by the par value of those shares ($0.01 × 4,425,486 shares), and the rest is treated as additional paid-in capital. Under IFRS, the original issue was treated as part debt (recorded in notes payable) and part equity (recorded in additional paid-in capital—notes payable). Upon conversion, amounts are shifted from these two accounts into common stock (at par) and additional paid-in capital. The amount shifted out of notes payable is equal to its original issue price from Transaction 1 plus the increase in notes payable from the amortization of the note in Transaction 2.

Transaction 3b shows how the market value method affects financial statements. Basically, the equity issued is recorded at the $50 current market value, split between common stock at par and additional paid-in capital. Because the increase in equity (what the corporation is giving) is greater than the decrease in debt (debt and equity under IFRS) surrendered by the claimholders, a loss on conversion is recorded. This loss would reduce net income and retained earnings.

Bonds issued with detachable warrants provide a good example of where debt and equity features may be more easily separated (and are separated under both U.S. GAAP and IFRS). Typically, after issuance, the bonds and detachable warrants are traded separately in secondary markets. When purchasing bonds with detachable warrants, an investor is buying a debt instrument (the bond) and the option to acquire equity at a fixed price (the stock warrants). Because the debt and equity features trade separately after issuance, accountants allocate the purchase price of the bond with detachable warrants between the bond and the stock warrants on the basis of the two instruments' relative fair market values. As a simple example, assume that bonds with a face value of $1,000,000 plus detachable warrants are issued for $975,000. Assume that immediately

---

[39]As is the case with any long-term debt, accrual of interest expense at the effective rate increases the amount owed by Digital River and contractual cash payments decrease the amount owed. Given that the effective interest is greater than the cash payment, Digital River's debt has increased as evidenced by the increase in notes payable.

after issue, the bonds trade for $900,000 and the warrants trade for $100,000. Accountants would allocate 90 percent ($900,000 value of the bonds/$1,000,000 value of bonds plus warrants) of the $975,000 value received to the bonds ($975,000 × 90% = $877,500) and 10 percent to the warrants ($975,000 × 10% = $97,500).

Off-Balance-Sheet Financing Arrangements

Investors and lenders often use the proportion of debt in a firm's capital structure as a measure of risk and therefore as a factor in establishing the cost of funds. (Chapter 5 discusses various ratios for measuring risk, and Chapter 11 describes techniques for using a firm's capital structure to compute the weighted average cost of capital.) Other things being equal, firms prefer to obtain funds without showing a liability on the balance sheet in the hope that future lenders or investors will ignore the risks associated with such financing. Firms sometimes structure innovative financing arrangements in ways that may not satisfy the criteria for the recognition of a liability. That is, firms structure financing in such a way that GAAP treats the obligation (if any) as an executory contract or a contingency. The principal aim of such arrangements is to reduce the amount shown as liabilities on the balance sheet. Although there is little empirical evidence to support the notion that lenders and investors ignore such financing in assessing a firm's risk, some firms act as if they do overlook such borrowing. Firms usually accomplish off-balance-sheet financing using one or a combination of two approaches: (1) sale of an existing asset and (2) use of another entity to obtain the financing.

Sale of an Existing Asset

A firm may use accounts receivable; inventories; property, plant, and equipment; and other assets as collateral for a loan. If the firm borrowed funds using the assets as collateral, The selling firm would increase cash and increase a liability. The notes to its financial statements would disclose that certain assets serve as collateral for the loan. Structuring the transaction in this way places debt on the balance sheet.

If, on the other hand, the firm sold the same asset to the provider of the funds, it would increase cash, reduce the asset transferred, and recognize a gain or loss for the difference. The selling firm would show cash but would not show a liability on the balance sheet. This is appropriate as long as the sale did not expose the selling firm to the risk of having to make payments to the purchaser in the future (for example, if the selling firm had to guarantee that the purchaser could resell the asset for a certain minimum amount). A similar transaction is a sale-leaseback. The firm sells a long-lived asset to a lessor, using the cash received from the sale to reduce any liabilities originally used to finance the asset purchase. The firm then leases the asset from the lessor under an operating lease that is not shown as a long-term liability. Later in this chapter, lease accounting is illustrated in more detail.

Use of Another Entity to Obtain Financing

The general theme of this approach to off-balance-sheet financing is that the firm obtains access to the asset that the funds finance, but neither the asset nor its financing appear on the firm's balance sheet. Instead, they appear on the balance sheet of another entity.

Suppose, for example, a firm needs additional manufacturing capacity but does not want to borrow funds to build the extra plant assets. Instead, it commits to purchase a certain amount of output from an unaffiliated company at a specified cost that covers operating and debt-service costs. The unaffiliated company takes the purchase commitment to a financial institution and obtains a loan. The unaffiliated company uses the loan proceeds to construct the needed capacity. The new plant assets and the loan appear on the balance sheet of the unaffiliated company. The purchase commitment is a mutually unexecuted contract of the firm initially needing the additional manufacturing capacity. Recall from the earlier discussion and Exhibit 6.5 that firms do not recognize mutually unexecuted contracts as liabilities.

Alternatively, the firm can accomplish the same result using an affiliated company, one over which the firm has a greater degree of influence than an unaffiliated one. The key to keeping debt off the balance sheet in this case is to ensure that the firm is not required to prepare consolidated financial statements with the affiliated company. Consolidated statements aggregate the separate financial statements of two or more entities under the control of one of the entities. The debt will appear on the consolidated balance sheet as long as it appears on the balance sheet of any one entity in the consolidated group. (Chapter 7 discusses consolidated financial statements more fully.) To avoid consolidation, the firm needing the financing must not effectively *control* the entity obtaining the financing.

One means of avoiding consolidation is to set up a joint venture with another entity, with each entity owning 50 percent of the common stock. In this case, neither firm controls the joint venture. GAAP currently does not require either firm to prepare consolidated financial statements with the joint venture.

Another means of avoiding consolidation is to set up an *SPE (special-purpose entity),* also known as a *VIE (variable interest entity).* The SPE obtains financing and either (1) constructs or acquires the asset desired by the firm attempting to keep debt off its balance sheet or (2) purchases the particular asset from this firm. In both cases, the asset held by the SPE serves as collateral for the loan. The lender to the SPE will likely require some commitment from the firm that sets up the SPE to ensure repayment of the loan. The commitment may take the form of a noncancelable purchase commitment or a loan guarantee. The key to avoiding consolidation is that effective control of the SPE must not reside primarily with the firm setting it up. The SPE must have economic substance of its own and other parties—the lender or other equity owners—must be the primary beneficiary of the SPE.

Central to the early 2000's bankruptcy of Enron was the misuse of SPEs to hold off-balance-sheet derivative instruments, securities, and other assets such as power plants in India and Nigeria initially acquired by Enron and to keep the related financing for these instruments and securities off the balance sheet. Enron did not consolidate these SPEs, maintaining that it did not control them. Later revelations showed that Enron had effective control, requiring Enron to restate its previously issued financial statements. The restatements increased assets and liabilities on the balance sheet and eliminated gains that Enron recognized on the "sale" of the assets to the SPEs. Chapter 7 discusses the accounting for SPEs.

The following sections describe several off-balance-sheet financing arrangements. In several cases, the FASB or IASB have issued an accounting standard that specifies how firms should treat such transactions for financial reporting purposes. In other cases, the standard-setting bodies have not issued a specific financial reporting standard and the accountant must apply the general criteria for liability recognition.

Sale of Receivables

Firms sometimes sell their receivables as a means of obtaining financing or use an SPE to issue securities backed by the receivables (for example, mortgage-backed securities issued by financial institutions or their SPEs). If collections from customers are not sufficient to repay the amount borrowed plus interest, the transferring firm may have to pay the difference; that is, the lender has recourse against the borrowing firm.

The question arises as to whether the recourse provision creates an accounting liability. Some argue that the arrangement is similar to a collateralized loan. The firm should leave the receivables on its books and recognize a liability in the amount of the cash received. Others argue that the firm has sold an asset; it should recognize a liability only if it is probable that collections from customers will be insufficient and the firm will be required to repay some portion of the amount received.

The FASB and IASB provide accounting rules to guide the decision of whether to classify a transfer of receivables as a sale or a loan.[40] For example, Statement of Financial Accounting Standards No. 140, "Accounting for Transfers and Servicing of Financial Assets and Extinguishments of Liabilities," requires that firms recognize transfers of receivables as sales only if the transferor surrenders control of the receivables. Firms surrender control only if all of the following conditions are met:

- The assets transferred (that is, receivables) have been isolated from the selling ("transferor") firm; that is, neither the transferor nor a creditor of the selling firm could access the receivables in the event of the seller's bankruptcy.
- The buying ("transferee") firm obtains the right to pledge or exchange the transferred assets, and no condition both constrains the transferee from taking advantage of its right and provides more than a trivial benefit to the transferor.
- The selling firm does not maintain effective control over the assets transferred through (a) an agreement that both entitles and obligates it to repurchase the assets or (b) the ability to unilaterally cause the transferee to return specific assets.

The principal refinement to the concept of an accounting liability brought out by Statement No. 140 relates to identifying the party involved in the transaction that controls the determination of which party enjoys the economic benefits and sustains the economic risk of the assets (receivables in this case). If the selling (borrowing) firm controls the economic benefits/risks, the transaction is a collateralized loan. If the arrangement transfers these benefits/risks to the buying (lending) firm, the transaction is a sale.

Example 15

Assume that Sears transfers $1,000,000 of installment receivables to a bank in exchange for $950,000. Sears is liable to the bank for uncollectible receivables (a "with recourse" transfer), and the estimated fair value of the recourse obligation is $20,000. Exhibit 6.10 shows the financial statement effects if reported as a borrowing and if reported as a sale.

EXHIBIT 6.10: EXAMPLE 15 SOLUTION

Borrowing

Assets		=	Liabilities		+	Shareholders' Equity		
						CC	AOCI	RE
Cash	+950,000		Loan Payable	+950,000				
Cash				950,000				
Loan Payable						950,000		

Sale

Assets		=	Liabilities		+	Shareholders' Equity		
						CC	AOCI	RE
Cash	+950,000		Recourse Liability	+20,000				Loss on Sale −70,000
Accounts Receivable	−1,000,000							
Cash				950,000				
Loss on Sale				70,000				
Accounts Receivable						1,000,000		
Recourse Liability						20,000		

[40]Financial Accounting Standards Board, *Statement of Financial Accounting Standards No. 140*, "Accounting for Transfers and Servicing of Financial Assets and Extinguishments of Liabilities" (2000); *FASB Codification Topic 860*; Financial Accounting Standards Board, *Statement of Financial Accounting Standards No. 156*, "Accounting for Servicing of Financial Assets" (2006); International Accounting Standards Board, *International Accounting Standard No. 39*, "Financial Instruments: Recognition and Measurement" (revised 2003).

In the "borrowing" transaction, Sears does not surrender control of the receivables (that is, does not meet the FASB's three conditions to record a sale). Therefore, Sears keeps the accounts receivable on its books and records the receipt of cash and the incurrence of a liability (loan payable). In the "sale" transaction, the accounts receivable are removed from Sears' balance sheet because Sears no longer controls the accounts receivable. Sears also records the expected cash outflow to satisfy the recourse provisions of the agreement should customers fail to pay. Because assets decrease in the net by $50,000 and liabilities increase by $20,000, Sears records a loss on sale of $70,000, which is reported on the income statement and reduces retained earnings.

Product Financing Arrangements

Product financing arrangements occur when a firm (sponsor) does either of the following:

- Sells inventory to another entity and, in a related transaction, agrees to repurchase the inventory at specified prices over specified times
- Arranges for another entity to purchase inventory items on the firm's behalf and, in a related transaction, agrees to purchase the inventory items from the other entity

The first arrangement is similar to the sale of receivables with recourse except that greater certainty exists that the inventory transaction will require a future cash outflow. The second arrangement is structured to appear as a purchase commitment. In this case, however, the sponsoring firm usually creates an SPE for the sole purpose of acquiring the inventory. The sponsoring firm usually guarantees the debt incurred by the SPE in acquiring the inventory.

Financial reporting requires that firms recognize product financing arrangements as liabilities if they meet two conditions:

- The arrangement requires the sponsoring firm to purchase the inventory, substantially identical inventory, or processed goods of which the inventory is a component at specified prices.
- The payments made to the other entity cover all acquisition, holding, and financing costs.[41]

The second criterion requires that the sponsoring firm recognize a liability whenever it incurs the economic risks (such as changing costs or interest rates) of purchasing and holding inventory, even though it may not physically control the inventory or have a legal obligation to the supplier of the inventory. Thus, as with sales of receivables with recourse, a firm recognizes a liability when it controls the determination of which party enjoys the economic benefits and incurs the economic risks of the asset involved. It also recognizes an asset of equal amount, usually inventory.

Research and Development Financing Arrangements

When a firm borrows funds to conduct R&D, it recognizes a liability at the time of borrowing and recognizes expenses as it incurs R&D costs. As the next example demonstrates, firms have engaged in innovative means of financing aimed at keeping liabilities off the balance sheet and effectively excluding R&D expenses from the income statement.

Example 16

Merck, a pharmaceutical company, forms joint ventures with another pharmaceutical company to develop, manufacture, and market new products. Because joint ventures are owned equally by the two entities in each case, Merck does not consolidate the financial statements

---

[41]Financial Accounting Standards Board, *Statement of Financial Accounting Standards No. 49*, "Accounting for Product Financing Arrangements" (1981); *FASB Codification Topic 470.*

of the joint ventures with its own financial statements; instead, it reports its share of ownership in the joint venture as an investment. Any liabilities of the joint ventures appear on the financial statements of the joint ventures, not on Merck's balance sheet. Likewise, the R&D expense of the joint ventures appears on the income statement issued by the joint ventures, not on Merck's income statement.

Firms can also use other arrangements besides joint ventures. Although the structures vary somewhat across firms, they generally operate as follows:

1. The sponsoring firm contributes either preliminary development work or rights to future products to a partnership in exchange for a general interest in the partnership. It obtains limited partners (often corporate directors or officers) who contribute cash for their partnership interests.
2. The sponsoring firm conducts R&D work for the partnership for a fee. The sponsoring firm usually performs the R&D on a best-efforts basis, with no guarantee of success. The sponsoring firm recognizes amounts received from the partnership for R&D services as revenues. The amount of revenue generally equals or exceeds the R&D costs it incurs.
3. The rights to any resulting products usually reside in the partnership. However, the partnership agreement usually constrains the returns and risks of the limited partners. The sponsoring firm can often acquire the limited partners' interests in the partnership if valuable products emerge. The sponsoring firm may have to guarantee certain minimum royalty payments to the partnership or agree to purchase the partnership's rights to the product.

In arrangements such as these, a primary objective of the sponsoring firm involves obtaining financing for its R&D work without having to recognize a liability. Criteria exist for when firms must recognize such financing arrangements as liabilities.[42] The sponsoring firm recognizes a liability under the following conditions:

- If the contractual agreement requires the sponsoring firm to repay any of the funds provided by the other parties regardless of the outcome of the R&D.
- If surrounding conditions indicate that the sponsoring firm bears the risk of failure of the R&D work even though the contractual agreement does not obligate it to repay the other parties. For example, if a sponsoring firm guarantees the debt of the partnership, must make minimum royalty payments to the partnership, or must acquire the partnership's interest in any product, the sponsoring firm will bear the risk of the R&D work.

The criteria require that, as with the off-balance-sheet financing arrangements involving receivables and inventories discussed previously, firms recognize liabilities when they bear the risk associated with the asset or product involved in the financing of a joint venture for R&D.[43]

The joint ventures formed by Merck and the other pharmaceutical company operate as independent entities, with broad oversight by the joint owners. The joint ventures retain the rights to products developed. Neither joint owner guarantees any debt of the joint ventures. Neither joint owner must pay the other joint owner any amounts if the research effort is nonproductive. Although the two joint owners ultimately bear the risk of failure of the

---

[42]Financial Accounting Standards Board, *Statement of Financial Accounting Standards No. 68*, "Research and Development Arrangements" (1982); *FASB Codification Topic 730*.

[43]A study of firms that conduct their research and development through limited partnerships found that the stock market appears to consider the call option that firms have on research findings in the valuation of the firm. The author calls for improved disclosure of these arrangements instead of recognition of a liability in the balance sheet. See Terry Shevlin, "The Valuation of R&D Firms with R&D Limited Partnerships," *Accounting Review* (January 1991), pp. 1–21.

joint venture, GAAP accounting for the Merck joint ventures requires only that the joint owners recognize their equity investment in the joint venture on the balance sheet.

Take-or-Pay or Throughput Contracts

A take-or-pay contract is an agreement in which a purchaser agrees to pay specified amounts periodically to a seller for products or services. A throughput contract is similar to a take-or-pay contract except that the "product" purchased is transportation or processing services.

To understand the rationale for such arrangements, consider the following case. Suppose two petroleum companies need additional refining capacity. If either company builds a refinery, it will record an asset and any related financing on its balance sheet. Suppose instead the two companies form a joint venture to construct a refinery. The joint venture, an entity separate from the two petroleum companies, obtains financing and constructs the refinery. To secure financing for the joint venture, the two petroleum companies sign take-or-pay contracts agreeing to make certain payments to the joint venture each period for refining services. The payments are sufficient to cover all of the refinery's operating and financing costs. The joint owners must make the payments even if they acquire no refinery services.

The economic substance of this arrangement is that each petroleum company owns half of the refinery and is obligated to the extent of half of the financing. The legal status of the arrangement is that the two firms have simply signed noncancelable purchase commitments (that is, executory contracts). Accounting likewise treats these arrangements as executory contracts. At the time of signing the contract, the firms have not yet received any benefits that obligate them to pay. As they receive benefits or incur obligations over time, a liability arises. If one or the other entity guarantees the debt of the partnership, the guarantee is a contingent obligation, which is not recognized as a liability until future events indicate that payment is probable.

Financial reporting requires firms to disclose take-or-pay and throughput commitments in the notes.[44] The analyst should examine disclosures of these commitments in notes to the financial statements to assess whether the firm incurs the risks and rewards of the arrangement and should therefore recognize a liability.

Example 17

Refer to Note 9, "Debt Obligations and Commitments," to PepsiCo's Consolidated Financial Statements (Appendix A). PepsiCo presents a subsection entitled "Long-Term Contractual Commitments" in which it lists cash payments due under noncancelable contracts, some of which are reflected in the balance sheet as liabilities and some that are not. Long-term debt payments totaling $6,599 million are reflected in the balance sheet at the present value of those payments. Interest on debt obligations is reflected as interest payable in the balance sheet to the extent incurred (as time passes) and not yet paid. Operating leases are not treated as liabilities, as you will learn in a later section of this chapter. Purchase commitments and marketing commitments are executory contracts not reflected as liabilities (hence, their required supplemental disclosure in Note 9). In a section entitled "Off-Balance-Sheet Arrangements," PepsiCo discloses that it guarantees $2.3 billion of Bottling Group, LLC's long-term debt and that its " . . . payment obligation would be triggered if Bottling Group, LLC failed to perform under these debt obligations. . . . "

---

[44]Financial Accounting Standards Board, *Statement of Financial Accounting Standards No. 47*, "Disclosure of Long-Term Obligations," 1981.

Summary of Off-Balance-Sheet Financing

The conventional accounting model based on historical cost is exchange or transaction oriented. Accounting recognizes events when an exchange takes place. The criteria for liability recognition discussed earlier in this chapter and in Exhibit 6.5 illustrate this exchange orientation. Accounting recognizes liabilities when a firm incurs an obligation to sacrifice resources in the future for benefits already received. Financial reporting has typically not recognized mutually unexecuted contracts as liabilities because the parties have merely exchanged promises to perform in the future. Financial reporting also does not generally require the recognition of contingent obligations as liabilities because some future obligating event must occur to establish the existence of a liability.

The evolving concept of an accounting liability recognizes that exchanges of promises can have economic substance even though a legal obligation to pay does not immediately arise. When a firm controls the determination of which party enjoys the economic benefits and/or incurs the economic risks from an asset, the firm should recognize the asset and its related financial obligations.

The FASB and IASB closely monitor reporting issues related to off-balance-sheet commitments of firms, but both boards continue to be challenged because of the ever-changing nature of business financing arrangements and the flexible and fluid organizational arrangements that firms create.[45]

LEASES

Many firms acquire rights to use assets through leases. For example, a company might agree to lease computer equipment for 3 years, an office suite for 5 years, or an entire building for 40 years, promising to pay a fixed periodic fee for the duration of the lease. Leasing provides benefits to lessees, the users of the leased assets, such as the following:

- Ability to shift the tax benefits from depreciation and other deductions from a lessee that has little or no taxable income (such as an airline) to a lessor, or owner of the asset, that has substantial taxable income. The lessee expects the lessor to share some of the benefits of these tax deductions by allowing lower lease payments.
- Flexibility to change capacity as needed without having to purchase or sell assets.
- Ability to reduce the risk of technological obsolescence, relative to outright ownership, by maintaining the flexibility to shift to technologically more advanced assets.
- Ability to finance the "acquisition" of an asset using lessor financing when alternative sources of financing are unavailable or more costly.

These potential benefits of leasing to lessees do not come without a cost. When the lessor assumes the risks of ownership, it requires the lessee to make larger lease payments than if the lessee faces these risks. Which party bears the risks is a matter of negotiation between lessor and lessee.

Promising to make an irrevocable series of lease payments commits the firm just as surely as a bond indenture or mortgage, and the accounting is similar in many cases.[46] This section examines two methods of accounting for long-term leases: the operating lease method and the capital (sometimes called finance) lease method.[47] The illustrations show

---

[45]Specific IFRS rules relating to off-balance-sheet financing are rare. However, guidelines may be found in IASB, *SIC Interpretation 12*, "Consolidating Special Purpose Entities" (1998).

[46]Lease disclosures often use the term *noncancelable leases* to capture the contractual lease commitments of the lessee. Under noncancelable leases, the lessee typically can cancel the lease only after incurring a severe penalty.

[47]Financial Accounting Standards Board, *Statement of Financial Accounting Standards No. 13*, "Accounting for Leases," (1975); *FASB Codification Topic 840*; International Accounting Standards Board, *International Accounting Standard 17*, "Leases" (revised 2003).

the accounting by the lessee, the user of the leased asset. Chapter 7 illustrates the accounting for the lessor, the owner of the asset.

Example 18

To illustrate these two methods, suppose Myers Company wants to acquire a computer that has a three-year life and could be purchased for $45,000. Also assume that Myers Company must pay 10 percent per year to borrow money for three years. The computer manufacturer is willing to sell the equipment for $45,000 or to lease it for three years. Myers Company is responsible for property taxes, maintenance, and repairs of the computer whether it leases or purchases the computer.

Assume that Myers Company signs a lease on January 1, Year 1, and must make payments on the lease on December 31, Year 1, Year 2, and Year 3. (In practice, lessees usually make lease payments in advance, but the assumption of year-end payments simplifies the computations.) The lessor sets the lease payments to return the $45,000 principal and 10 percent interest in three equal end-of-year payments. Similar to bond and note calculations, the payment is the amount that solves the following equation:

$$\$45,000 = \sum_{n=1}^{3} \frac{\text{Payment}}{(1 + 0.10)^n}$$

Solving this equation for the payment using a financial calculator ($i = .10$, $n = 3$, future value $= 0$, present value $= \$45,000$) yields an annual payment of $18,095.

Operating Lease Method

In an operating lease, the owner, or lessor, transfers only the rights to use the property to the lessee for specified periods of time. At the end of the lease period, the lessee returns the property to the lessor. For example, car rental companies lease cars by the day or week on an operating basis. In leasing arrangements in which the lessee neither assumes the risks nor enjoys the rewards of ownership, the lessee should treat the lease as an operating lease. Accounting gives no recognition to the signing of an operating lease. (That is, the lessee reports neither the leased asset nor a lease liability on its balance sheet; the lease is simply a mutually unexecuted contract). Over the life of the lease, the lessee recognizes rent expense in measuring net income each year. The effect on the financial statements of Myers Company each year (ignoring income taxes) if it treats the lease as an operating lease appears in Exhibit 6.11.

EXHIBIT 6.11: EXAMPLE 18 SOLUTION FOR OPERATING LEASES

12/31/Year 1

Assets		=	Liabilities	+	Shareholders' Equity		
					CC	AOCI	RE
Cash	−18,095						Rent Expense −18,095

Rent Expense				18,095			
Cash					18,095		

12/31/Year 2

Assets		=	Liabilities	+	Shareholders' Equity		
					CC	AOCI	RE
Cash	−18,095						Rent Expense −18,095

Rent Expense				18,095			
Cash					18,095		

(Continued)

EXHIBIT 6.11 (CONTINUED)

12/31/Year 3

Assets		=	Liabilities	+	Shareholders' Equity		
					CC	AOCI	RE
Cash	−18,095						Rent Expense −18,095
Rent Expense			18,095				
Cash					18,095		

Total income effect over three years = $54,285 decrease

The total income statement effect over the three years is the sum of the rent expense ($54,285), which also equals the total cash outflow from lease payments.

Capital Lease Method

In leasing arrangements in which the lessee assumes the risks and enjoys the rewards of ownership, the lease contract is considered a capital lease. In a capital lease, the lessee recognizes the signing of the lease as the simultaneous acquisition of a long-term asset and the incurring of a long-term liability for lease payments. Lessees recognize two expense items each year on capital leases. First, the lessee must depreciate the leased asset over the time period it uses the asset (that is, the least term or the asset's economic useful life if the asset is expected to remain with the lessee after the lease term expires). Assuming that Myers Company uses straight-line depreciation, it recognizes depreciation expense of $15,000 (= $45,000/3) each year. Second, as shown in the amortization schedule in Exhibit 6.12, the lease payment made each year is part interest expense on the lease liability and part reduction in the liability itself.

The effects of (1) the signing of the capital lease on January 1, Year 1, and the recognition of (2) depreciation and (3) interest for each year appear in Exhibit 6.13.

EXHIBIT 6.12

Example 18 Lease Amortization Table

Date	Payment	10% Effective Interest Expense	Amortization	Book Value of Lease Liability
1/1/Year 1				$45,000
12/31/Year 1	$18,095	$4,500	$13,595	$31,405
12/31/Year 2	$18,095	$3,141	$14,954	$16,451
12/31/Year 3	$18,095	$1,644	$16,451	$ 0
	$54,285	$9,285	$45,000	

EXHIBIT 6.13: EXAMPLE 18 SOLUTION FOR CAPITAL LEASES

1/1/Year 1 Signing

Assets		=	Liabilities		+	Shareholders' Equity		
						CC	AOCI	RE
Leased Asset	+45,000		Lease Liability	+45,000				
Leased Asset			45,000					
Lease Liability						45,000		

(Continued)

Exhibit 6.13 (Continued)

12/31/Year 1 Payment

Assets	=	Liabilities	+	Shareholders' Equity		
				CC	AOCI	RE
Cash −18,095		Lease Liability −13,595				Interest Expense −4,500

Interest Expense	4,500		
Lease Liability	13,595		
Cash		18,095	

12/31/Year 1 Depreciation

Assets	=	Liabilities	+	Shareholders' Equity		
				CC	AOCI	RE
Leased Asset (Net) −15,000						Depreciation Expense −15,000

Depreciation Expense	15,000	
Leased Asset (Net)		15,000

12/31/Year 2 Payment

Assets	=	Liabilities	+	Shareholders' Equity		
				CC	AOCI	RE
Cash −18,095		Lease Liability −14,954				Interest Expense −3,141

Interest Expense	3,141	
Lease Liability	14,954	
Cash		18,095

12/31/Year 2 Depreciation

Assets	=	Liabilities	+	Shareholders' Equity		
				CC	AOCI	RE
Leased Asset (Net) −15,000						Depreciation Expense −15,000

Depreciation Expense	15,000	
Leased Asset (Net)		15,000

12/31/Year 3 Payment

Assets	=	Liabilities	+	Shareholders' Equity		
				CC	AOCI	RE
Cash −18,095		Lease Liability −16,451				Interest Expense −1,644

Interest Expense	1,544	
Lease Liability	16,451	
Cash		18,095

12/31/Year 3 Depreciation

Assets	=	Liabilities	+	Shareholders' Equity		
				CC	AOCI	RE
Leased Asset (Net) −15,000						Depreciation Expense −15,000

Depreciation Expense	15,000	
Leased Asset (Net)		15,000

The leased asset and liability are shown on the balance sheet as of the signing of the lease. Then in each year, the effective interest method is used to account for the lease liability as was illustrated earlier for a note payable, and the leased asset is depreciated each year. Notice that in the capital lease method, the total expense over the three years is $54,285, comprising $45,000 (= $15,000 + $15,000 + $15,000) for depreciation expense and $9,285 (= $4,500 + $3,141 + $1,644) for interest expense. This total expense is the same as that recognized under the operating lease method described previously ($18,095 × 3 = $54,285). The capital lease method recognizes expenses sooner than the operating lease method does. But over sufficiently long time periods, total expense equals the cash expenditure. One difference between the operating lease method and the capital lease method is the timing of the expense recognition. The other difference is that the capital lease method recognizes both the asset and the liability on the balance sheet.[48]

Choosing the Accounting Method

When a lessee treats a lease as a capital lease, it recognizes both an asset and a liability, thereby increasing total liabilities and making the company appear riskier. Given a choice, most lessees prefer not to show the asset and a related liability on the balance sheet. Lessees prefer an operating lease to an installment purchase or a capital lease, for which both the asset and liability appear on the balance sheet. Lessees also prefer to recognize expenses for financial reporting later rather than sooner. These preferences have led a number of lessees to structure asset acquisitions so that the financing takes the form of an operating lease, thereby achieving off-balance-sheet financing.

U.S. GAAP provides detailed rules of accounting for long-term leases. The lessor and lessee must account for a lease as a capital lease if the lease meets any one of four conditions.[49] These conditions attempt to identify which party, the lessor or the lessee, bears most of the risk related to the asset under lease. When the lessor bears most of the risk, the lease is an operating lease. When the lessee bears most of the risk, the lease is a capital lease.

A lease is a capital lease if it meets any one of the following conditions:

- If it extends for at least 75 percent of the asset's total expected economic life (that is, the lessee uses the asset for most of its life).
- If it transfers ownership to the lessee at the end of the lease term (that is, the lessee bears the risk of changes in the residual value of the asset at the end of the lease term).
- If it seems likely the lessor will transfer ownership to the lessee because of a "bargain purchase" option (that is, the lessee again bears the residual value risk; a bargain purchase option gives the lessee the right to purchase the asset for a price less than the expected fair market value of the asset when the lessee exercises its option).
- The present value of the contractual minimum lease payments equals or exceeds 90 percent of the fair market value of the asset at the time of signing.[50]

The first three conditions are relatively easy to avoid in lease contracts if lessors and lessees prefer to treat a lease as an operating lease instead of a capital lease. The most difficult

---

[48]The fair value option is not allowed for assets and liabilities reported under capital leases.

[49]Financial Accounting Standards Board, *Statement of Financial Accounting Standards No. 13*, "Accounting for Leases" (1976); *FASB Codification Topic 840.*

[50]IFRS criteria are similar, although as is often the case with IFRS, the criteria do not provide "bright-line" percentages such as 75 or 90 percent. Instead, judgment is relied upon to implement the following: (1) Does ownership transfer from the lessor to the lessee at the end of the lease? (2) Is there a bargain purchase option? (3) Does the lease extend for the major portion of the asset's useful life? (4) Does the present value of the minimum lease payments equal substantially all of the asset's fair value? (5) Is the leased asset specialized for use by the lessee?

of the four conditions to avoid is the fourth. When the present value of the contractual minimum lease payments equal or exceed 90 percent of the fair market value of the asset at the time of signing, the lessor has less than or equal to 10 percent of the asset's value at risk to an uncertain residual value at the end of the lease term. Therefore, the lease transfers the major risks and rewards of ownership from the lessor (landlord) to the lessee. In economic substance, the lessee has acquired an asset and has agreed to pay for it under a long-term contract, which the lessee recognizes as a liability. When the present value of the minimum lease payments is less than 90 percent of the fair market value of the asset at the time of signing, the lessor bears the major risks and rewards of ownership and the lease is an operating lease.

Firms often report both operating and capital leases because certain lease agreements meet one or more of these conditions; other lease agreements meet none of the conditions.

Example 19

Airtran leases many of its aircraft and ground facilities. In the notes to its December 31, 2008 financial statements, Airtran Holdings, Inc., provides a schedule of capital and operating lease commitments, as reported in Exhibit 6.14 (in thousands). The firm also reports the present value of its capital lease commitments ($16,866 thousand on December 31, 2008, of which $16,031 thousand is long-term). Airtran reports other long-term debt of $940,569 thousand. Thus, the capitalized lease payments are not a large portion of Airtran's total long-term debt at the end of 2008. Airtran's commitments under operating leases (gross future cash flows of $3,125,518 thousand) are more substantial, representing an important off-balance-sheet cash flow commitment of the firm.

EXHIBIT 6.14

Excerpt from Airtran Holdings, Inc.'s December 31, 2008 Annual Report

Note 6 (partial). Total rental expense charged to operations for aircraft, facilities and office space for the years ended December 31, 2008, 2007 and 2006 was approximately $326.0 million, $315.6 million and $287.5 million, respectively. . . . The following schedule outlines the future minimum lease payments at December 31, 2008, under non-cancelable operating leases and capital leases with initial terms in excess of one year (in thousands):

	Capital leases	Operating leases
2009	$ 2,328	$ 288,031
2010	2,328	275,985
2011	2,328	263,684
2012	2,328	262,020
2013	2,328	256,901
Thereafter	15,904	1,778,897
Total minimum lease payments	$ 27,544	$3,125,518
Less: amounts representing interest	(10,678)	
Present value of future payments	$ 16,866	
Less: current obligations	(835)	
Long-term obligations	$ 16,031	

Converting Operating Leases to Capital Leases

Lease commitments by lessees accounted for as operating leases do not appear as assets or liabilities on the balance sheet and, if one believes these obligations are essentially financial commitments, can cause the analyst to understate the short-term liquidity or long-term solvency risk of the firm. In cross-sectional comparisons of different firms, the analyst also may want to treat all leases as capital leases with the objective of making all firms more comparable in terms of assets and liabilities. For this reason, the analyst may want to restate the financial statements of lessees to convert all operating leases into capital leases. Such a restatement provides a more conservative measure of total liabilities.

Example 20

To illustrate the procedure, refer to PepsiCo's operating lease disclosures in Note 9, "Debt Obligations and Commitments" (Appendix A). Exhibit 6.15 summarizes PepsiCo's information on operating lease commitments. The second column shows PepsiCo's commitments on noncancelable operating leases net of sublease revenues at December 27, 2008. PepsiCo reports aggregate payments for 2010–2011 and 2012–2013. We assume the payments are evenly distributed. To convert these operating lease cash payments to a capital lease, the analyst must express the lease commitments in present value terms. The discount rate the analyst should use is the lessee's incremental borrowing rate for secured debt with similar risk to that of the leasing arrangement. PepsiCo's interest expense (see the income statement) as a percentage of average short- and long-term borrowing for 2008 (see the balance sheet) is 5.3 percent [= $329/(0.5{\$0 + \$4,203 + \$369 + \$7,858})]. A 6 percent rate is assumed in this case to compute the present value of operating lease commitments.

Exhibit 6.15 illustrates the lease capitalization process. The present value of each cash flow equals the cash flow times a present value factor. Each factor in the column is obtained from a present value table or by the formula $1/(1 + i)^n$. For example, 2010's factor of $0.89000 = 1/(1 + 0.06)^2$. To select a present value factor for payments in 2014 and beyond, you need to know the years and amounts in which PepsiCo will pay the $268 million.

EXHIBIT 6.15

PepsiCo., Inc. Operating Lease Disclosures; Summarized from PepsiCo, Inc. December 27, 2008 Annual Report (amounts in millions)

Year	Operating Lease Commitments	Present Value Factor at 6%	Present Value
2009	$ 262.0	0.94340	$247.2
2010	179.5	0.89000	159.8
2011	179.5	0.83962	150.7
2012	99.5	0.79209	78.8
2013	99.5	0.74726	74.4
2014 and beyond	268.0	—	178.4*
	$1,088.0		$889.3

*Present value of an annuity of $89.3 million for three periods at 6 percent, then that present value discounted back five periods at 6 percent.

Presume that payments will continue at the same amount as the $99.5 million payment in 2013, in which case PepsiCo will pay the remaining $268 million in less than three periods ($268/$99.5 < 3). Given the decline in payments over the years shown in Exhibit 6.15, the remainder is spread over an assumed three periods, yielding a payment of $89.3 million per year ($268 million/3 years). The $178.4 million present value is obtained by computing the present value of an annuity of $89.3 million for three periods at 6 percent to yield a present value at the end of 2013 and then discounting that amount five additional periods at 6 percent. The present value of all of PepsiCo's operating lease payments is $889.3 million.

To approximate what leased asset and liability would have existed if capital lease treatment had been used, the analyst adds the $889.3 million lease to property, plant, and equipment; the $247.2 million present value of the 2009 lease payments to short-term debt; and the $652.1 million present value of lease payments in 2010 and beyond to long-term debt on the December 27, 2008 balance sheet. Certain ratios could be affected substantially by the operating lease capitalization. For example, PepsiCo's ratio of long-term debt to shareholders' equity based on reported amounts is $7,858/$12,203 = 64.4%. Adding the long-term portion of the capital lease liability of $652.1 million to the numerator of the ratio changes the ratio to ($7,858 + $652.1)/$12,203 = 69.7%. While this increase is substantial, greater increases are often found when the adjustment is made for retailers, restaurant chains, and airlines. For time-series analysis of PepsiCo, similar calculations would be necessary for at least two previous years.

If the analyst views the economic substance of this lease more as a means of financing the acquisition of long-term assets (that is, as a capital lease) than as a right to use such assets for a short period of time, the analyst also should convert the income statement from the operating to the capital lease method by eliminating rent expense but including depreciation expense on the capitalized asset and interest expense on the lease obligation. In general, if the average lease is in the first half of its life, total expenses under the capital lease method tend to exceed total expenses under the operating lease method; so adjusted income will tend to be less than reported income. If the average lease is in the last half of its life, total expenses under the capital lease method tend to be less than under the operating lease method; so adjusted income tends to be greater than reported income. The two expense amounts are approximately equal at the midlife point. The average operating lease for PepsiCo appears to be near the midpoint of its life. You reach this conclusion by comparing the operating lease payment in 2009 ($262 million), which would be treated as rent expense if the lease were operating, to the following rough approximations for expenses if the lease were capital:

$$\text{Depreciation Expense} = \$889.3 \text{ million asset/6.27 years remaining lease life}[51]$$
$$= \$141.83 \text{ million}$$

$$\text{Interest Expense} = \$889.3 \text{ million lease liability} \times 6\% = \$53.36 \text{ million}$$

The sum of depreciation expense and interest expense (capital lease treatment) is $195.19 million, which is less than but relatively close to the $262.0 million in rent

---

[51]We calculated the 6.27 years as a weighted average. If the rent payments are equal over the 2009–2016 period, it would be reasonable to assume that all leased assets are going to be used over the eight-year period. However, the rent payments decline, implying that some assets are used up and, thus, off-lease. Working backwards in the schedule, $89.3 million of cash flow appears in each year, $10.2 million additional cash flow ($89.3 + $10.2 = $99.5) in cash flow appears in the first five years, $80 million additional cash flow appears for the first three years ($99.5 + $80 = $179.5), and $82.5 million additional cash flow ($179.5 + $82.5 = $262) appears in 2009. Therefore 66 percent of the cash flows related to assets in use for eight years ($89.3 per year × 8 years = $714.4 out of a total of $1,087.9), 5 percent of the cash flows related to assets in use for five years ($10.2 per year × 5 years = $51 out of a total of $1,087.9), and so on. Weighting an eight-year life by 66 percent, a five-year life by 5 percent, and so on, yields an average useful life of 6.27 years.

expense (operating lease treatment). PepsiCo's Note 4, "Property, Plant, and Equipment and Intangible Assets" (Appendix A), shows that accumulated depreciation on depreciable property, plant, and equipment is about one-half of property, plant, and equipment, confirming the estimate that remaining asset lives are approximately at the midpoint of total useful life.

Therefore, constructive capitalization of the operating leases would increase net income by the difference between these two expenses ($66.81 million) times one minus the statutory tax rate, or $66.81 million $\times$ (1 − 0.35) = $43.42 million. This amount is less than 1 percent of PepsiCo's 2008 net income of $5,142 million.

Often, balance sheet restatements are more significant than income statement restatements. Consequently, the analyst usually can ignore restatements of the income statement, particularly if the analyst's emphasis is assessment of a firm's credit risk, as discussed in Chapter 5. However, note that even for firms with leases at the midlife point, where the income statement effect may be immaterial, the effect on the balance sheet can be substantial.[52]

The analyst could restate the statement of cash flows for the capitalization of operating leases. Under the operating lease method, the lease payment for the year is an operating use of cash. Its inclusion as a subtraction in computing net income results in reporting its negative cash flow effect in the operating section of the statement of cash flows. Under the capital lease method, a portion of the cash payment represents a repayment of the lease liability, a financing use of cash instead of an operating use of cash. The analyst should reclassify this portion of the cash payment from the operating section to the financing section of the statement of cash flows. The analyst also could reduce net income for depreciation expense on the capitalized lease assets, but this amount appears as an addback to net income for a non-cash expense. Thus, the net effect of depreciation expense on operating cash flows is zero.

It is clear from the discussion that note disclosures allow the financial analyst to capitalize operating leases effectively, but with error. A number of assumptions and estimates (sometimes rough) must be employed, and these assumptions may not be valid for all firms in all industries. As a result, credit rating agencies such as Moody's and Fitch have developed methodologies with the objectives of standardization and simplicity. For example, some analysts estimate the lease liability and leased asset to be capitalized simply using an "8X" rule. That is, a simple method of computing the capitalized liability and asset is to multiply the amount of annual rent expense times eight. Because this "8X" heuristic is based on specific assumptions (a 6 percent interest rate and an asset life of 15 years), Moody's uses a modified approach that takes into account industry differences in useful lives and the "seasoning" (that is, age) of the leased assets. Thus, for any given firm, a factor of 5X, 6X, 8X, or greater might be applied, with firms with long-lived assets such as airlines, shipping, and public utilities receiving the highest factor. Fitch also uses the 8X heuristic, a present value approach if sufficient data exists, and individual analysis about the validity of the approach for a given firm.[53]

---

[52]For an alternative procedure for converting operating leases into capital leases, see Eugene A. Imhoff, Jr., Robert C. Lipe, and David W. Wright, "Operating Leases: Impact of Constructive Capitalization," *Accounting Horizons* (March 1991), pp. 51–63. In this study, the authors found that capitalizing operating leases decreased the rate of return on assets 34 percent for high-lease firms and 10 percent for low-lease firms and increased the debt-to-equity ratio 191 percent for high-lease firms and 47 percent for firms.

[53]Moody's Approach to Global Standard Adjustments in the Analysis of Financial Statements for Non-Financial Corporations—Part I, *Standardized Adjustments to Enable Global Consistency for US and Canadian GAAP Issuers* (March 2005); "Capitalization of Operating Leases by Credit Rating Agencies," *ELT* (February 2007).

Impact of Accounting for Operating Leases as Capital Leases

Virtually all firms have some amount of commitment under operating leases. The change in debt ratios for some firms is relatively minor, as is the case for PepsiCo. For other firms, particularly airlines and retail stores, the effect can be significant. Even for firms for which the effect is relatively small, adding the effect of capitalizing operating leases to the effect of other off-balance-sheet obligations can result in a combined material effect. Thus, the analyst should examine the effect of leases when assessing the risk and accounting quality of a firm's financial statements. The analyst should also consider the effects of off-balance-sheet leases when determining capital structure weights and debt costs for the weighted average cost of capital calculations used in enterprise valuation.

SUMMARY

This chapter explores various accounting issues related to measuring the financing activities of the firm. Both profitability analysis and risk analysis are affected by management's choice between interest-bearing debt and shareholders' equity to finance the acquisition of operating capacity. The proper measurement and reporting of liabilities enables the analyst to understand the risk of investing in the firm's debt and equity instruments, and the existence of off-balance-sheet arrangements complicates the analysis.

Although we provide a broad description of liability recognition, this chapter focuses primarily on the set of liabilities arising from transactions with lending institutions that generate notes and bonds payable. Typically, these liabilities are generated to raise funds for investments in long-term assets used in operations. The next chapter (Chapter 7) examines the accounting issues surrounding these long-term assets. Chapter 8 returns to measuring and reporting liabilities generated from operating activities, such as accounts payable, provisions, deferred tax liabilities, and pension liabilities.

QUESTIONS, EXERCISES, PROBLEMS, AND CASES

Questions and Exercises

6.1 COMMON EQUITY TRANSACTIONS. Describe the directional effect (increase, decrease, or no effect) of each transaction on the components of the book value of common shareholders' equity shown in the chart on the next page.

- **a.** Issuance of $1 par value common stock at an amount greater than par value
- **b.** Donation of land by a governmental unit to a corporation
- **c.** Cash dividend declared
- **d.** Previously declared cash dividend paid
- **e.** Property dividend declared and paid
- **f.** Large stock dividend declared and issued
- **g.** Small stock dividend declared and issued
- **h.** 2-for-1 stock split announced and issue
- **i.** Stock options granted
- **j.** Recognition of compensation expense on stock options
- **k.** Stock options exercised
- **l.** Stock options expired
- **m.** Treasury stock acquired (company uses the cost method)

n. Treasury stock in Transaction m reissued at an amount greater than original acquisition price

o. Treasury stock in Transaction m reissued at an amount less than the original acquisition price

p. Restricted stock issued (grant date)

q. Recognition of compensation expense related to restricted stock

r. Granting of stock appreciation rights to be settled with cash

s. Recognition of compensation expense on stock appreciation rights

t. Reacquisition and retirement of common stock at an amount greater than original issue price

Item	Common Stock	Additional Paid-in Capital	Deferred Compensation	Retained Earnings (use * to indicate income statement effect)	Treasury Stock at Cost	Total Common Shareholders' Equity
a						
b						
c						
...						

6.2 COMMON EQUITY ISSUE.

Assume that a start-up manufacturing company raises capital through a series of equity issues.

a. Using the financial statement template below, summarize the financial statement effects of the following transactions. Identify the account affected and use plus and minus signs to indicate the increases and decreases in the specific element of the balance sheet (assets, liabilities, components of shareholders' equity).

(1) Issues 100,000 shares of $1 par value common stock for $10 per share.

(2) Receives land in exchange for 10,000 shares of $1 par common stock when the common stock is trading in the market at $15 per share. The land has no readily determinable market value.

(3) Receives subscriptions for the issue of 40,000 shares of $1 par value common. The share issue price is $20, of which 30 percent is received as a down payment. Subsequently, the remaining 70 percent is received.

Assets	=	Liabilities	+	Shareholders' Equity		
				CC	AOCI	RE
Journal entry:						

b. In each case, how does the company measure the transaction? What measurement attribute is used?

6.3 DIVIDENDS.

Following is the shareholders' equity section of All-Wood Doors on a day its common stock is trading at $130 per share.

Common stock ($2 par value, 40,000 shares issued and outstanding)	$	80,000
Additional paid-in capital on common stock		1,600,000
Retained earnings		3,000,000

a. Use the financial statement template below to show the financial statement effects of the following dividend events. (Assume that the events are independent.)
   (1) Cash dividend declaration and payment of $1 per share
   (2) Property dividend declaration and payment of shares representing a short-term investment in Screen Products, Ltd., with a fair value of $10,000
   (3) 10 percent stock dividend
   (4) 100 percent stock dividend
   (5) 3-for-1 stock split
   (6) 1-for-2 reverse stock split

Assets	=	Liabilities	+	Shareholders' Equity		
				CC	AOCI	RE
Journal entry:						

b. Which events changed the book value of common equity? Under what conditions will these events lead to future increases and decreases in ROE?

6.4 CASH FLOW EFFECTS OF EQUITY AND DEBT FINANCING.
Identify where the cash flow effect of each of the following transactions is reported in the statement of cash flows: operating, investing, or financing section. State the direction of each change. State *None* if there is no cash flow effect.

   a. Issuance of stock for cash
   b. Issuance of stock for land
   c. Acquisition of treasury stock
   d. Reissuance of treasury stock
   e. Declaration of a cash dividend
   f. Payment of a cash dividend previously declared
   g. Declaration and issuance of a large stock dividend
   h. Declaration and issuance of a small stock dividend
   i. Granting of stock options
   j. Exercise of stock options
   k. Granting of RSUs
   l. Issuance of long-term notes payable
   m. Issuance of convertible bonds
   n. Conversion of convertible bonds to common stock
   o. Payment of interest on bonds
   p. Retirement of bonds at book value
   q. Retirement of bonds at a gain
   r. Retirement of bonds at a loss

6.5 ACCOUNTING FOR A NOTE PAYABLE. Assume that on December 31, 2010, The Coca-Cola Company borrows money from a consortium of banks by issuing a

$900 million promissory note. The note matures in four years on December 31, 2014, and pays 3 percent interest once a year on December 31. The consortium transfers $867.331 million (rounded) to Coca-Cola, implying that the bank expects a 4 percent return on the note.

    a. Use the template below to show the financial statement effects of (1) the December 31, 2010 issue, (2) the December 31, 2011 interest payment and interest expense accrual, and (3) the December 31, 2012 interest payment and interest expense accrual.

Assets	=	Liabilities	+	Shareholders' Equity		
				CC	AOCI	RE
Journal entry:						

    b. Assume that events involving foreign operations have increased the risk of The Coca-Cola Company to the point where creditors expect a 5 percent return on the note as of December 31, 2012. What amounts would Coca-Cola report for long-term debt (1) on the face of its December 31, 2012 balance sheet and (2) in the notes to the financial statements?

    c. In addition to the information in Part b, assume that The Coca-Cola Company has chosen the fair value option for the reporting of this note. What amounts would Coca-Cola report for long-term debt (1) on the face of its December 31, 2012 balance sheet and (2) and on the income statement with respect to the note's fair value change?

6.6 ACCOUNTING FOR TROUBLED DEBT: SETTLEMENT. Assume that Circuit City owes Synovus Bank $1,000,000 on a 4-year, 7% note originally issued at par. After one year of making scheduled payments, Circuit City faces financial difficulty. At the end of the second year, Circuit City owes Synovus $1,000,000 plus $70,000 of accrued but unpaid interest. Circuit City settles the debt by paying $700,000 in cash and transferring investments to Synovus. Circuit City recently purchased the investments for $120,000 and carried them on the books at that amount. The investments are worth $135,000 at the date of the debt settlement. Use the template below to show the financial statement effects of the debt settlement.

Assets	=	Liabilities	+	Shareholders' Equity		
				CC	AOCI	RE
Journal entry:						

6.7 ACCOUNTING FOR TROUBLED DEBT: MODIFICATION OF TERMS. Assume that Great Beef Co. owes Bank of America $5,000,000 on a 3-year, 9% note originally issued at par. After one year of making scheduled payments, the firm faces financial difficulty. At the end of the second year, Great Beef owes Bank of America

$5,000,000 plus $450,000 of accrued but unpaid interest. (Assume that the financial difficulty has increased the riskiness of Great Beef Co. to the point where it would have to pay 15 percent to borrow money.)

a. Assume that Bank of America restructures the note by forgiving the $450,000 interest payable, reducing the note principal to $4,500,000, and reducing the interest rate to 6 percent. Show the financial statement effects at the date of restructuring using the template below assuming that Great Beef Co. uses
   (1) U.S. GAAP.
   (2) IFRS.

Assets	=	Liabilities	+	Shareholders' Equity		
				CC	AOCI	RE
Journal entry:						

b. Assume that Bank of America restructures the note by forgiving the $450,000 interest payable, reducing the note principal to $4,800,000, and reducing the interest rate to 7 percent. Show the financial statement effects at the date of restructuring using the template below assuming that Great Beef Co. uses
   (1) U.S. GAAP.
   (2) IFRS.

Assets	=	Liabilities	+	Shareholders' Equity		
				CC	AOCI	RE
Journal entry:						

c. Comment on the differences between the two systems. Which reporting system better represents the underlying economics of the debt restructuring? Will U.S. GAAP supplemental disclosures provide similar information? Explain.

6.8 REDEEMABLE PREFERRED STOCK. Determine and compare the financial reporting (debt versus equity classification) of redeemable preferred stock with the following characteristics under U.S. GAAP and IFRS.

a. Redemption will occur at a specific time or upon a specific event (for example, death of the holder).
b. Redemption is at the option of the issuing firm; that is, the preferred stock is "callable."
c. Redemption is at the holder's discretion; that is, the preferred stock is "putable."

6.9 CONVERTIBLE PREFERRED STOCK. Assume that John Deere Co. issues 2,000 shares of $100 par, 6% convertible preferred stock for $105 per share. Shareholders have the right to exchange each share of convertible preferred stock for five shares of

$10 par common stock. Use the template below to show the financial statement effects of the following events.

a. Issuance of the preferred stock.

b. Declaration and payment of the cash dividend on the preferred stock.

c. Conversion of the preferred stock to common stock when the market value of the common stock is $29 per share.

Assets	=	Liabilities	+	Shareholders' Equity		
				CC	AOCI	RE
Journal entry:						

6.10 CONVERTIBLE DEBT UNDER IFRS AND U.S. GAAP ARTL Company issued 3%, 10-year convertible bonds on January 1, 2010, at their par value of $500 million. Each $1,000 bond is convertible into 40 shares of ARTL's $1 par value common stock. Use the template below to show the financial statement effects under U.S. GAAP and IFRS of the following transactions.

a. Original issue. For the IFRS treatment, assume that ARTL would have borrowed at 8 percent if it did not offer a conversion privilege.

b. Recognition of one year's interest effect.

c. Conversion of the bonds when a share of ARTL common stock trades at $30.

(1) Using the "book value method"
(2) Using the "market value method"

Assets	=	Liabilities	+	Shareholders' Equity		
				CC	AOCI	RE
Journal entry:						

6.11 BONDS ISSUED WITH DETACHABLE WARRANTS. Assume that Motorola, Inc., issues bonds with a face value of $10,000,000 for $9,200,000. The bonds have detachable warrants that may be traded in for shares of common stock. Assume that immediately after issue, bonds with warrants detached trade for $9,000,000; the warrants, for $400,000. Use the template below to show the financial statement effects at the date of issue.

Assets	=	Liabilities	+	Shareholders' Equity		
				CC	AOCI	RE
Journal entry:						

6.12 ACCOUNTING FOR LOSS CONTINGENCIES. The text states that loss contingencies may or may not give rise to accounting liabilities. Financial reporting requires firms to recognize a loss contingency when two criteria are met. Describe the two criteria and provide an example in which applying the criteria would trigger booking the loss contingency as an accounting liability.

6.13 SECURITIZATION OF RECEIVABLES. Firms such as Deere & Company and Macy's, Inc., often sell their receivables as a means of obtaining financing. Should firms selling receivables remove the receivables from the balance sheet, or should the receivables remain on the balance sheet? Should the firms recognize a liability in the amount of the cash received for the receivables? Describe the applicable criteria to determine whether the transfer of receivables can be recorded as a sale.

6.14 EFFECT OF CAPITAL AND OPERATING LEASES ON THE FINANCIAL STATEMENTS. All leases for financial reporting purposes are treated as either capital (finance) leases or operating leases. The effects of the two reporting techniques on the financial statements differ substantially. From the perspective of the lessee, prepare a chart that lists the line items reported on the (a) income statement, (b) balance sheet, and (c) statement of cash flows under each reporting technique.

6.15 NATURE OF RESERVE ACCOUNTS. The use of the term *reserve* in the title of a financial statement account is not acceptable in the United States, primarily because its purpose is often too vague. However, informal use of the term by chief financial officers, analysts, and the media is common when they are discussing various aspects of *acceptable* accrual accounting techniques employed by U.S. firms. Provide several examples of financial statement accounts that are often loosely referred to as reserves. What is typically common about all financial statement accounts that are informally referred to as reserves?

6.16 ACCOUNTING FOR STOCK-BASED COMPENSATION. Historically, technology firms have been the most aggressive users of stock-based compensation in the form of stock options granted to almost all employees of the firms. What is the rationale for offering stock options as compensation? Why has this form of compensation been particularly popular with technology firms in the past?

Problems and Cases

6.17 ACHIEVING OFF-BALANCE-SHEET FINANCING (ADAPTED FROM MATERIALS BY R. DIETER, D. LANDSITTEL, J. STEWART, AND A. WYATT). Patrick Company wants to raise $50 million cash but for various reasons does not want to do so in a way that results in a newly recorded liability. The firm is sufficiently solvent and profitable, so its bank is willing to lend up to $50 million at the prime interest rate. Patrick Company's financial executives have devised six different plans, described in the following sections.

Transfer of Receivables with Recourse

Patrick Company will transfer to Credit Company its long-term accounts receivable, which call for payments over the next two years. Credit Company will pay an amount equal to the present value of the receivables, less an allowance for uncollectibles, as well as a discount, because it is paying now but will collect cash later. Patrick Company must repurchase from Credit Company at face value any receivables that become uncollectible in excess of the allowance. In addition, Patrick Company may repurchase any of the receivables not yet due at face value less a discount specified by formula and based on the prime rate at the time of the initial transfer. (This option permits Patrick Company to benefit if an unexpected drop in interest rates occurs after the transfer.) The accounting issue is whether the transfer is a sale (in which Patrick Company increases Cash, reduces Accounts Receivable, and recognizes expense or loss on transfer) or merely a loan collateralized by the receivables (in which Patrick Company increases Cash and increases Notes Payable at the time of transfer).

Product Financing Arrangement

Patrick Company will transfer inventory to Credit Company, which will store the inventory in a public warehouse. Credit Company may use the inventory as collateral for its own borrowings, whose proceeds will be used to pay Patrick Company. Patrick Company will pay storage costs and will repurchase the entire inventory within the next four years at contractually fixed prices plus interest accrued for the time elapsed between the transfer and later repurchase. The accounting issue is whether the inventory is sold to Credit Company, with later repurchases treated as new acquisitions for Patrick's inventory, or whether the transaction is merely a loan, with the inventory remaining on Patrick's balance sheet.

Throughput Contract

Patrick Company wants a branch line of a railroad built from the main rail line to carry raw material directly to its plant. It could, of course, borrow the funds and build the branch line itself. Instead, it will sign an agreement with the railroad to ship specified amounts of material each month for ten years. Even if Patrick Company does not ship the specified amounts of material, it will pay the agreed shipping costs. The railroad will take the contract to its bank and, using it as collateral, borrow the funds to build the branch line. The accounting issue is whether Patrick Company would increase an asset for future rail services and increase a liability for payments to the railroad. The alternative is to make no accounting entry except when Patrick makes payments to the railroad.

Construction Partnership

Patrick Company and Mission Company will jointly build a plant to manufacture chemicals that both need in their production processes. Each will contribute $5 million to the project, called Chemical. Chemical will borrow another $40 million from a bank, with Patrick being the only guarantor of the debt. Patrick and Mission are each to contribute equally to future operating expenses and debt service payments of Chemical, but in return for its guaranteeing the debt, Patrick will have an option to purchase Mission's interest for $20 million four years hence. The accounting issue is whether Patrick Company should recognize a liability for the funds borrowed by Chemical. Because of the debt guarantee, debt service payments ultimately will be Patrick Company's responsibility. Alternatively, the debt guarantee is a commitment merely to be disclosed in notes to Patrick Company's financial statements.

Research and Development Partnership

Patrick Company will contribute a laboratory and preliminary findings about a potentially profitable gene-splicing discovery to a partnership, called Venture. Venture will raise funds by selling the remaining interest in the partnership to outside investors for $2 million and borrowing $48 million from a bank, with Patrick Company guaranteeing the debt.

Although Venture will operate under the management of Patrick Company, it will be free to sell the results of its further discoveries and development efforts to anyone, including Patrick Company. Patrick Company is not obligated to purchase any of Venture's output. The accounting issue is whether Patrick Company would recognize the liability.

Hotel Financing

Patrick Company owns and operates a profitable hotel. It could use the hotel as collateral for a conventional mortgage loan. Instead, it considers selling the hotel to a partnership for $50 million cash. The partnership will sell ownership interests to outside investors for $5 million and borrow $45 million from a bank on a conventional mortgage loan, using the hotel as collateral. Patrick Company guarantees the debt. The accounting issue is whether Patrick Company would record the liability for the guaranteed debt of the partnership.

Required

Discuss the appropriate treatment of each proposed arrangement from the viewpoint of the auditor, who must apply GAAP in deciding whether the transaction will result in a liability to be recorded or whether footnote disclosure will suffice. Does GAAP reporting result in an accurate portrayal of the economics of the arrangement in each case? Explain.

6.18 ACCOUNTING FOR SECURITIZATION OF RECEIVABLES. Ford Motor Credit Company discloses the following information with respect to finance receivables (amounts in millions).

December 31:	Year 4	Year 3
Finance Receivables	$146,451	$152,276
Securitized Receivables Sold	$(35,600)	$(46,900)
Finance Receivables on Balance Sheet	$110,851	$105,376
Retained Interest in Securitized Receivables Sold	$ 9,166	$ 12,569

Notes to Financial Statements

The Company periodically sells finance receivables in securitization transactions to fund operations and to maintain liquidity. The securitization process involves the sale of interest-bearing securities to investors, the payment of which is secured by a pool of receivables. In many securitization transactions, the Company surrenders control over certain of its finance receivables by selling these assets to SPEs. SPEs then securitize the receivables by issuing certificates representing undivided interests in the SPEs' assets to outside investors and to the Company (retained interest). These certificates entitle the holder to a series of scheduled cash flows under present terms and conditions, the receipt of which is dependent upon cash flows generated by the related SPEs' assets. The cash flows on the underlying receivables are used to pay principal and interest on the debt securities as well as transaction expenses.

In each securitization transaction, the Company retains certain subordinated interests in the SPE, which are the first to absorb credit losses on the sold receivables. As a result, the credit quality of certificates held by outside investors is enhanced. However, the investors and the trusts have no recourse against the Company beyond the trust assets. The Company also retains the servicing rights to the sold receivables and receives a servicing fee. While servicing the sold receivables for the SPE, the Company applies the same servicing policies and procedures that it applies to its own receivables and maintains a normal relationship with its financing customers.

Required

    a. Applying the criteria for the sale of receivables from FASB *Statement No. 140,* justify Ford Motor Credit's treatment of the securitization of finance receivables on December 31, Year 3 and Year 4, as a sale instead of a collateralized loan.

    b. Assume that the receivables disclosed as securitized on December 31, Year 3, had been initially securitized on that day. Give the journal entry that Ford Motor Credit would have made to securitize these receivables, assuming that it securitized the receivables at no gain or loss.

    c. Assume that Ford Motor Credit decided to consolidate its receivables securitization structure in Year 4 and to start accounting for it as secured borrowings. Give the journal entry that the company would make on December 31, Year 4, to account for this change, assuming that it recognized no gain or loss on this event.

    d. Most firms prefer to report the securitization of receivables as a sale. The alternative is to view the arrangement as a collateralized loan with the receivables remaining on the firm's balance sheet. Speculate on why firms prefer to report the securitization of receivables as a sale.

6.19 ACCOUNTING FOR ATTEMPTED OFF-BALANCE-SHEET FINANCING ARRANGEMENTS.

    a. International Paper Company (IP) needs $100 million of additional financing, but because of restrictions in existing debt covenants, it cannot place any more debt on its balance sheet. To obtain the needed funds, it plans to transfer cutting rights to a mature timber tract to a newly created trust as of January 1, Year 8. The trust will use the cutting rights to obtain a $100 million, 5-year, 10% interest rate bank loan due in five equal installments, with interest on December 31 of each year.

        The timber will be harvested each year and sold to obtain funds to service the loan and pay operating costs. Based on current prices, 10 percent more standing wood is available for cutting than should be needed to service the loan and pay ongoing operating costs of the tract (including wind, fire, and erosion insurance). If the selling price of timber decreases in the future, the volume of timber harvested will be increased sufficiently to service the debt. If the selling price of timber increases in the future, the volume harvested will remain as originally anticipated, but any cash left over after debt service and coverage of operating costs will be invested by the trust to provide a cushion for possible future price decreases. The value of any cash or uncut timber at the end of five years will revert to IP.

        IP will not guarantee the debt. The bank, however, has the right to inspect the tract at any time and to replace IP's forest management personnel with managers of its own choosing if it believes the tract is being mismanaged.

Required

Discuss the appropriate accounting for this transaction by IP in light of other FASB pronouncements on off-balance-sheet financing.

    b. On June 24, Year 4, Delta Air Lines entered into a revolving accounts receivable facility (Facility) providing for the sale of $489 million of a defined pool of accounts receivable (Receivables) through a wholly owned subsidiary to a trust in exchange for a senior certificate in the principal amount of $300 million (Senior Certificate) and a subordinate certificate in the principal amount of $189 million (Subordinate Certificate). The subsidiary retained the Subordinate Certificate, and the company received $300 million in cash from the sale of the Senior Certificate to a third party. The principal amount of the Subordinate Certificate fluctuates daily depending on the volume of Receivables sold and is payable to the subsidiary only to the extent that the collections received on the Receivables exceed amounts due on the Senior Certificate. The full amount of the allowance for doubtful accounts related to the Receivables sold has been retained, as the company has substantially the same credit risk as if the Receivables had not been sold. Under the terms of the Facility, the company is obligated to pay fees that approximate the purchaser's cost of issuing a like amount of commercial paper plus certain administrative costs.

Required

Delta requests your advice on the appropriate accounting for this transaction. How would you respond?

c. In Year 2, a wholly owned subsidiary of Sun Company became a one-third partner in Belvieu Environmental Fuels (BEF), a joint venture formed for the purpose of constructing, owning, and operating a $220 million methyl tertiary butyl ether (MTBE) production facility in Mont Belviu, Texas. As of December 31, Year 3, BEF had borrowed $128 million against a construction loan facility of which the company guarantees one-third, or $43 million. The plant, which has a designed daily capacity of 12,600 barrels of MTBE, is expected to begin production in mid-Year 4. When production commences, the construction loan will be converted into a five-year, nonrecourse term loan with a first priority lien on all project assets.

To obtain a secure supply of oxygenates for the manufacture of reformulated fuels, Sun has entered into a ten-year take-or-pay agreement with BEF, which commences when the plant becomes operational. Pursuant to this agreement, Sun will purchase all MTBE production from the plant. The minimum per-unit price to be paid for the MTBE production while the nonrecourse term loan is outstanding will equal BEF's annual raw material and operating costs and debt service payments divided by the plant's annual designed capacity. Notwithstanding this minimum price, during the first three years of the off-take agreement, Sun has agreed to pay BEF a price that approximates prices included in current MTBE long-term sales agreements in the marketplace. This price is expected to exceed the minimum price required by the loan agreement. Sun will negotiate a new pricing arrangement with BEF for the remaining years the take-or-pay agreement is in effect. That pricing arrangement will be based on the expected market conditions existing at the time.

Required

How should Sun account for this transaction?

6.20 EFFECT OF CAPITALIZING OPERATING LEASES ON BALANCE SHEET RATIOS. Some retailing companies own their own stores or acquire their premises under capital leases. Other retailing companies acquire the use of store facilities under operating leases, contracting to make future payments. An analyst comparing the capital structure risks of retailing companies may want to adjust reported financial statement data to put all firms on a comparable basis.

Certain data from the financial statements of Gap Inc. and Limited Brands follow (amounts in millions).

Balance Sheet as of January 31, 2009	Gap Inc.	Limited Brands
Current liabilities	$2,158	$1,255
Long-term debt	0	2,897
Other noncurrent liabilities	1,019	946
Shareholders' equity	4,387	1,874
Total	$7,564	$6,972

Minimum Payments under Operating Leases		
2009	$1,069	$ 478
2010	927	455
2011	712	416
2012	520	373
2013	386	341
After 2013	1,080	1,334
Total	$4,694	$3,397

Required

a. Compute the present value of operating lease obligations using an 8 percent discount rate for Gap Inc. and Limited Brands as of January 31, 2009. Assume that all cash flows occur at the end of each year. Also assume that the minimum lease payment each year after 2013 equals $360 million per year for three years for Gap Inc. and $333.5 million for four years for Limited Brands. (This payment scheduling assumption can be obtained by assuming that the payment amount for 2013 continues until the aggregate payments after 2013 have been made, rounding the number of years upward, and then assuming level payments for that number of years. For Gap Inc.: $1,080/$386 = 2.8 years. Rounding up to three years creates a three-year annuity of $1,080/3 years = $360 million per year.)

b. Compute each of the following ratios for Gap, Inc. and Limited Brands as of January 31, 2009, using the amounts originally reported in their balance sheets for the year.
   (1) Liabilities to Assets Ratio = Total Liabilities/Total Assets
   (2) Long-Term Debt to Long-Term Capital Ratio = Long-Term Debt/(Long-Term Debt + Shareholders' Equity)

c. Repeat Part b but assume that these firms capitalize operating leases.

d. Comment on the results from Parts b and c.

6.21 STOCK-BASED COMPENSATION.

Exhibit 6.16 includes a footnote excerpt from the annual report of The Coca-Cola Company for Year 4. The beverage company offers stock options to key employees under plans approved by stockholders.

Required

Review Exhibit 6.16 and answer the following questions.

a. Coca-Cola reports both pretax and after-tax stock-based compensation in its notes to the financial statements. What is the tax savings for Year 2, Year 3, and Year 4 that Coca-Cola generates from the stock-based compensation provided to its employees? Speculate on what income statement line item includes this tax savings as well as what income statement line item includes the stock-based compensation expense. (The income statement is not provided in this problem.)

b. The average option price per share and market price per share at time of grant is equal each year ($44.69 for Year 2, $49.67 for Year 3, and $41.63 for Year 4). Discuss why Coca-Cola structured the stock option grants this way each year.

EXHIBIT 6.16

The Coca-Cola Company
Stock Option Disclosures
(Problem 6.21)

Note—Stock-Based Compensation (partial footnote disclosure)

Our Company currently sponsors stock option plans. Effective January 1, Year 2, our Company adopted the preferable fair value recognition provisions of Statement of Financial Accounting Standards ("SFAS") No. 123, "Accounting for Stock-Based Compensation." The fair values of the stock awards are determined using a single estimated expected life. The compensation expense is recognized on a straight-line basis over the vesting period. The total stock-based compensation expense, net of related tax effects, was $254 million in Year 4, $308 million in Year 3 and $267 million in Year 2.

	Year 4	Year 3	Year 2
Stock-Based Compensation Expense, pretax[a]	$ 345	$ 422	$ 365
Number of Options Granted[b]	31	24	29
Average Option Price per Share	$41.63	$49.67	$44.69
Average Market Price per Share at Time of Grant	$41.63	$49.67	$44.69
Fair Value of Option Granted per Share	$ 8.84	$13.49	$13.10
Vesting Period of Options Granted, years	1–4	1–4	1–4
Life of Options, years	10	10	10
Option Valuation Assumptions for Black-Scholes Model[b]			
Risk-Free Interest Rate	3.8%	3.5%	3.4%
Dividend Yield	2.5%	1.9%	1.7%
Stock Volatility	23.0%	28.1%	30.2%
Expected Option Life, years	6.0	6.0	6.0
Number of Options Exercised[a]	5	4	3
Average Option Exercise Price	$35.54	$26.96	$31.09

[a]Amounts in millions.
[b]Weighted averages.

c. What are the likely reasons that the fair value of options granted per share increased from Year 2 to Year 3 and then decreased from Year 3 to Year 4?

d. Coca-Cola does not report the market price of its stock at the time employees exercised options (3 million in Year 2, 4 million in Year 3, and 5 million in Year 4), but in each year the end-of-year market price is substantially higher than the average option exercise price reported in Exhibit 6.16 ($31.09 for Year 2, $26.96 for Year 3, and $35.54 for Year 4). Discuss why Coca-Cola is willing to sell shares of its stock to employees at a price (option exercise price) much lower than the firm could obtain for shares sold on the market (market price at time of exercise).

e. Coca-Cola employs the Black-Scholes valuation model for valuing stock option grants. Speculate on the directional effects of the key assumptions made in applying the Black-Scholes options pricing model. That is, which assumptions will result in a higher fair value for stock options and which will result in a lower fair value? Why?

6.22 STOCK-BASED COMPENSATION. Eli Lilly and Company produces pharmaceutical products for humans and animals. Exhibit 6.17 includes a footnote excerpt from the quarterly report of Lilly for the period ending March 31, Year 5. The firm first adopted *Statement No. 123 (Revised 2004)* reporting in this quarter.

Required

Review Exhibit 6.17 and answer the following questions.

a. Lilly's statement of cash flows (not provided in this problem) includes an addback for stock-based compensation in calculating cash flows from operations of $108.2 million for Year 5 and $25.2 million for Year 4. Why does Lilly add stock-based compensation back to net income?

EXHIBIT 6.17

Eli Lilly and Company
Stock Option Disclosures
(Problem 6.22)

Note—Stock-Based Compensation (partial footnote disclosure)

We adopted Statement of Financial Accounting Standards No. 123 (revised 2004), Share-Based Payment (SFAS 123R), effective January 1, Year 5. SFAS 123R requires the recognition of the fair value of stock-based compensation in net income. Stock options are granted to employees at exercise prices equal to the fair market value of our stock at the dates of grant. Generally, options fully vest three years from the grant date and have a term of 10 years. We recognize the stock-based compensation expense over the requisite service period of the individual grantees, which generally equals the vesting period.

We recognized compensation cost in the amount of $108.2 million and $25.2 million in the first quarter of Year 5 and Year 4, respectively, as well as related tax benefits of $32.8 million and $8.8 million, respectively.

Beginning with the Year 5 stock option grant, we utilized a lattice-based option valuation model for estimating the fair value of the stock options. The lattice model allows the use of a range of assumptions related to volatility, risk-free interest rate, and employee exercise behavior. Expected volatilities utilized in the lattice model are based on implied volatilities from traded options on our stock, historical volatility of our stock price, and other factors. Similarly, the dividend yield is based on historical experience and our estimate of future dividend yields. The risk-free interest rate is derived from the U.S. Treasury yield curve in effect at the time of grant. The model incorporates exercise and post-vesting forfeiture assumptions based on an analysis of historical data. The expected life of the Year 5 grants is derived from the output of the lattice model.

The weighted-average fair values of the options granted in the first quarter of Year 5 were $16.06 per option, determined using the following assumptions:

Dividend Yield	2.0%
Weighted-Average Volatility	27.8%
Range of Volatilities	27.6%–30.7%
Risk-Free Interest Rate	2.5%–4.5%
Weighted-Average Expected Life	7.2 years

As of March 31, Year 5, the total remaining unrecognized compensation cost related to non-vested stock options amounted to $397.5 million which will be amortized over the weighted-average remaining requisite service period of 2 years.

b. Refer to Part a. Lilly's statement of cash flows includes a cash inflow in the section on cash flows from financing activities of $12.5 million for Year 5 and $46.5 million for Year 4. The amounts are labeled "Issuance of common stock under stock plans." Who provided these cash inflows to Lilly? In general terms, how are the amounts determined?

c. Lilly states in the note: "Stock options are granted to employees at exercise prices equal to the fair market value of our stock at the dates of grant." Discuss why Lilly structured the stock option grants this way.

d. The note reports $397.5 million of remaining unrecognized compensation cost related to nonvested stock options. What portion of this amount will be reported as compensation expense in the second quarter ending June 30, Year 5? Does this amount represent total stock-based compensation expense for the quarter?

e. Prior to *Statement No. 123 (Revised 2004)*, firms were required to report pro forma earnings per share, taking into consideration stock-based compensation. As discussed in the chapter, *Statement No. 123 (Revised 2004)* requires stock-based compensation to be reported in the income statement, and thus included in the calculations of reported earnings per share. In addition to properly following GAAP (that is, *Statement No. 123 Revised 2004*), many firms present non-GAAP earnings numbers before deducting the effects of stock compensation as a supplemental disclosure in their annual reports (which is comparable to the old reported earnings number before 123R). Why do companies do this? Which earnings number is more meaningful, net income or this non-GAAP measure?

6.23 STOCK-BASED COMPENSATION–VESTING AND VALUATION MODELS. Exhibits 6.16 and 6.17 provide footnote excerpts to the financial reports of The Coca-Cola Company and Eli Lilly and Company that discuss the stock option grants given to the employees of the two firms. Each firm uses options extensively to reward employees for their performance.

Required

Review Exhibits 6.16 and 6.17 and answer the following questions.

a. Explain the concept of vesting. Discuss why firms typically include a vesting feature in the stock-based compensation plans that they offer to their employees.

b. What are the vesting characteristics of the two plans discussed in the exhibits? What effect do they have on stock-based compensation expense using the fair value method as required by *Statement No. 123 (Revised 2004)?*

c. For each firm, (1) what is the life of the options granted, (2) how does option life relate to the vesting period, and (3) why might the weighted-average *expected* life of the options be less than the full life of the options?

d. The Coca-Cola Company uses the Black-Scholes valuation model for estimating the fair value of the stock options, whereas Eli Lilly and Company utilizes a lattice-based option valuation model. Both valuation techniques are permitted by GAAP. Perform an Internet search to determine which valuation model is more commonly used by the largest publicly held firms. Speculate on why this is the case.

6.24 INTERPRETING STOCK OPTION DISCLOSURES. Exhibit 6.18 summarizes the information disclosed by General Electric Company (GE) regarding its stock option plans for Year 2 to Year 4. Assume an income tax rate of 35 percent.

EXHIBIT 6.18

General Electric Company
Stock Option Disclosures
(Problem 6.24)

	Year 4	Year 3	Year 2
Number of Options Granted[a]	27.141	8.261	46.928
Average Option Price per Share	$32.26	$31.19	$27.37
Average Market Price per Share at Time of Grant	$32.26	$31.19	$27.37
Fair Value of Option Granted per Share	$ 8.33	$ 9.44	$ 7.73
Vesting Period of Options Granted, years	1–5	1–5	1–5
Option Valuation Assumptions:			
Discount Rate	4.0%	3.5%	3.5%
Volatility	27.7%	34.7%	33.7%
Dividend Yield	2.5%	2.5%	2.7%
Expected Option Life, years	6.0	6.0	6.0
Number of Options Exercised[a]	43.110	43.829	29.146
Average Option Exercise Price	$10.54	$ 9.45	$ 9.45
Average Market Price at Time of Exercise	$32.68	$27.59	$31.86

[a]Amounts in millions.

Required

a. The average option price per share and market price per share at time of grant is equal in each year ($27.37 for Year 2, $31.19 for Year 3, and $32.26 for Year 4). Speculate on why GE structured the stock option grants this way in each year.

b. What are the likely reasons that the fair value of options granted per share increased from Year 2 to Year 3?

c. Compute the amount that GE received from the exercise of stock options each year versus the amount it would have received if it had issued the same number of shares on the market.

d. Refer to your answer to Part c. Discuss why GE is willing to sell shares of its stock to employees at a price (average option exercise price) much lower than the firm could obtain for shares sold on the market (average market price at time of exercise).

e. Refer again to your answer to Part c. Compute the effect of stock-based compensation on net income for each year, assuming that stock option compensation expense equaled the difference between the market price and the exercise price of options exercised.

f. Discuss the strengths and weaknesses of each of the following approaches to recognizing the cost of stock options: (1) no expense as long as the option price equals the market price on the date stock options are granted, (2) expense in the year of the grant equal to value of options granted, and (3) expense in the year of exercise equal to the benefit realized by employees from purchasing shares for less than market value.

INTEGRATIVE CASE 6.1

STARBUCKS

A common practice of fast-food and retail coffee shop chains such as Starbucks is to lease some or all of their retail space. Starbucks' Form 10-K filing states that the firm "leases retail store, roasting and distribution facilities and office space under operating leases."

Note 12 to Starbuck's Consolidated Financial Statements for the fiscal year ending September 28, 2008, provides the following future operating lease commitments of Starbucks as of the end of the fiscal year (amounts in millions).

Fiscal Year Ending in:	
2009	$ 741.0
2010	706.6
2011	660.7
2012	604.6
2013	546.4
Thereafter	1,838.8
Total Lease Payments	$5,098.1

Required

a. Compute the present value of operating lease obligations using a 6 percent discount rate for Starbucks at September 28, 2008. Assume that all cash flows occur at the end of each year. Also assume that the minimum lease payments after 2013 occur evenly over a four-year period.

b. Refer to Exhibit 1.26 (Chapter 1), which reports the fiscal 2008 comparative balance sheet for Starbucks. Compute each of the following ratios for Starbucks as of September 28, 2008, using the amounts as originally reported in its balance sheets for the year.

   (1) Liabilities to Assets Ratio = Total Liabilities/Total Assets

   (2) Long-Term Debt to Long-Term Capital Ratio = Long-Term Debt/(Long-Term Debt + Shareholders' Equity)

c. Repeat Part b but assume that Starbucks capitalizes operating leases and reports them as part of long-term debt.

d. Comment on the results from Parts b and c. To what extent does the capitalization of operating lease obligations affect your assessment of Starbucks' risk?

e. Refer to Exhibit 1.27 (Chapter 1), which reports the comparative income statement for Starbucks for Year 4. Note that the firm reports an expense labeled "Cost of Sales including Occupancy Costs." Speculate why Starbucks reports cost of sales and occupancy (operating lease payments) costs as a combined amount on the income statement.

Note: See Integrative Case 2.1 (Chapter 2), which addresses Starbucks' accounting for income taxes.

CASE 6.2

ORACLE CORPORATION: SHARE-BASED COMPENSATION EFFECTS/STATEMENT OF SHAREHOLDERS' EQUITY

A sales-based ranking of software companies provided by Yahoo! Finance on November 5, 2008, places Oracle Corporation third behind sales leaders Microsoft Corporation and IBM Software. Typical of high-tech companies in the software industry, Oracle Corporation uses share-based compensation plans extensively to motivate its employees. In Note 11 of its May 31, 2008 annual report, Oracle states that it settles employee stock options exercises primarily with newly issued common shares.

As indicated by the selected data from Oracle's May 31, 2008 Consolidated Balance Sheet in Exhibit 6.19, Oracle finances operations using substantially more common shareholder's equity than it does long-term debt. However, Oracle's long-term debt to shareholders' equity ratio of 44.5 percent is substantially larger than major U.S. competitor Microsoft Corporation and major foreign competitor SAP AG, both of which report almost no long-term financial debt. Exhibit 6.20 presents the most current year of the multiyear Consolidated Statement of Shareholders' Equity for Oracle. Exhibit 6.21 (see page 512) presents portions of financial statement notes 10 and 11 from Oracle's May 31, 2008 annual report.

Required

a. Compute Oracle's long-term debt to shareholders' equity ratio for May 31, 2008 and 2007. Identify the increases in shareholders' equity in 2008 from share-based compensation plans. Calculate the long-term debt to shareholders' equity ratio that would have occurred had Oracle not implemented the stock repurchase plan. Comment on the potential effect on future ROE of Oracle's financing strategy.

b. Retained earnings increases because of net income and decreases because of dividends declared. Why, then, did Oracle decrease retained earnings when it repurchased common stock?

EXHIBIT 6.19

Oracle Corporation May 31, 2008 Consolidated Balance Sheet (in millions of dollars)

	May 31,	
	2008	2007
Non-current notes payable and other non-current borrowings	$10,235	$ 6,235
Stockholders' equity		
Common stock, $0.01 par value and additional paid-in capital—authorized: 11,000 shares; outstanding: 5,150 shares and 5,107 shares as of May 31, 2008 and 2007	$12,446	$10,293
Retained earnings	9,961	6,223
Accumulated other comprehensive income	618	403
Total stockholders' equity	$23,025	$16,919

EXHIBIT 6.20

Oracle Corporation Consolidated Statements of Stockholders' Equity at May 31, 2008 (in millions of dollars)

| | Comprehensive Income | Common Stock and Additional Paid-in Capital | | Retained Earnings | Accumulated Other Comprehensive Income | Total |
		Number of Shares	Amount			
Balances as of May 31, 2007		5,107	$10,293	$6,223	$403	$16,919
Common stock issued under stock award plans		137	1,229			1,229
Common stock issued under stock purchase plans		3	59			59
Assumption of stock award in conjunction with acquisitions			240			240
Stock-based compensation			367			367
Repurchase of common stock		(97)	(214)	(1,786)		(2,000)
Tax benefits from stock plans			472			472
Adjustment to retained earnings upon adoption of FIN 48				3		3
Net unrealized loss on defined benefit plan assets, net of tax	$ (9)				(9)	(9)
Foreign currency translation	300				300	300
Net unrealized losses on derivative financial instruments, net of tax	(77)				(77)	(77)
Net unrealized gain on marketable securities, net of tax	1				1	1
Net income	5,521			5,521		5,521
Comprehensive income	$5,736					
Balances as of May 31, 2008		5,150	$12,446	$9,961	$618	$23,025

c. Of the first five changes listed in the shareholders' equity section, one of them, the common stock repurchase, clearly represents a cash outflow. Identify the cash flow effects of the other four items. Where will each cash flow effect be reported in the statement of cash flows?

d. Oracle engages in many transactions with non-owners (that is, customers, suppliers, and the government) that increase net assets. For example, Oracle's foreign subsidiaries perform services on credit with unrelated third-party customers. The

EXHIBIT 6.21

10. STOCKHOLDERS' EQUITY (partial)

Stock Repurchases

Our Board of Directors has approved a program for Oracle to repurchase shares of our common stock to reduce the dilutive effect of our stock option and stock purchase plans. In April 2007, our Board of Directors expanded our repurchase program by $4.0 billion and as of May 31, 2008, $2.2 billion was available for share repurchases pursuant to our stock repurchase program. We repurchased 97.3 million shares for $2.0 billion (including 1.1 million shares for $24 million that were repurchased but not settled), 233.5 million shares for $4.0 billion and 146.9 million shares for $2.1 billion in fiscal 2008, 2007 and 2006, respectively.

Our stock repurchase authorization does not have an expiration date and the pace of our repurchase activity will depend on factors such as our working capital needs, our cash requirements for acquisitions, our debt repayment obligations (as described above), our stock price, and economic and market conditions. Our stock repurchases may be affected from time to time through open market purchases or pursuant to a Rule 10b5-1 plan. Our stock repurchase program may be accelerated, suspended, delayed or discontinued at any time.

11. EMPLOYEE BENEFIT PLANS (partial)

Stock-based Compensation Plans

Stock Option Plans

... In connection with certain of our acquisitions, including PeopleSoft, BEA, Siebel and Hyperion, we assumed all of the outstanding stock options and other stock awards of each acquiree's respective stock plans. These stock options and other stock awards generally retain all of the rights, terms and conditions of the respective plans under which they were originally granted. As of May 31, 2008, options to purchase 77 million shares of common stock and 1 million shares of restricted stock were outstanding under these plans.

Tax Benefits from Option Exercises

We settle employee stock option exercises primarily with newly issued common shares and may, on occasion, settle employee stock option exercises with our treasury shares. Total cash received as a result of option exercises was approximately $1.2 billion, $873 million and $573 million for fiscal 2008, 2007 and 2006, respectively. The aggregate intrinsic value of options exercised was $2.0 billion, $986 million and $594 million for fiscal 2008, 2007 and 2006, respectively. In connection with these exercises, the tax benefits realized by us were $588 million, $338 million and $169 million for fiscal 2008, 2007 and 2006, respectively. The adoption of Statement 123(R) required us to change our cash flow classification of certain tax benefits received from stock option exercises beginning in fiscal 2007. Of the total tax benefits received, we classified excess tax benefits from stock-based compensation of $454 million and $259 million as cash flows from financing activities rather than cash flows from operating activities for fiscal 2008 and 2007, respectively.

Employee Stock Purchase Plan

We have an Employee Stock Purchase Plan (Purchase Plan). Starting with the April 1, 2005 semi-annual option period, we amended the Purchase Plan such that employees can purchase shares of common stock at a price per share that is 95% of the fair value of Oracle stock as of the end of the semi-annual option period. As of May 31, 2008, 81 million shares were reserved for future issuances under the Purchase Plan. During fiscal 2008, 2007 and 2006, we issued 3 million, 3 million and 6 million shares, respectively, under the Purchase Plan.

accounts receivable generated by the transactions are denominated in a foreign currency and thus are reported on the foreign subsidiaries balance sheet in that foreign currency. The consolidation process causes the subsidiary's accounts receivable to be added to the parent company's (Oracle's) accounts receivable and reported on Oracle's Consolidated Balance Sheet. Assuming that the foreign currency strengthens relative to the U.S. dollar, how does Oracle's Consolidated Statement of Shareholders' Equity capture the increases in accounts receivable described in this example transaction?

e. Using the foreign currency translation gain of $300 million as a context, present an argument for including the gain on Oracle's income statement and an argument for excluding the gain as Oracle does under GAAP.

f. Under Oracle's Employee Stock Purchase Plan, employees can purchase common shares at 95 percent of their fair values. Will Oracle report a loss on this transaction? Why or why not?

CASE 6.3

LONG-TERM SOLVENCY RISK: SOUTHWEST AND LUFTHANSA AIRLINES

The first decade of the 21st century witnessed a flurry of losses, bankruptcies, acquisitions, and strategic partnerships in the airline industry. The heavily levered firms in the industry are particularly susceptible to increases in fuel prices, economic changes that affect travel, and safety concerns. These conditions require the analyst to have a strong understanding of the long-term solvency risk of firms in the airline industry.

Two of the larger liabilities of airlines relate to promises to provide free flights to customers (frequent-flyer programs) and promises to make cash payments under flight equipment and ground facilities agreements. The former liability is captured in the total liabilities to assets ratio. The latter promise is captured in the total liabilities to assets ratio and in the long-term debt to shareholders' equity ratio, but only if the promises are treated as long-term debt.

Exhibits 6.22–6.27 (see pages 514–521) present the income statements, balance sheets, and other key information for U.S. airline Southwest, which prepares financial statements under U.S. GAAP, and German airline Lufthansa, which prepares financial statements under IFRS.

Required

a. Using the information in the exhibits, provide a comprehensive and detailed comparison of the long-term solvency risk of Southwest to Lufthansa as of December 31, 2008, and as of December 31, 2007. (Ignore tax effects. Deferred taxes are covered in Chapter 8 on operating activities.)

   (1) Consider the following ratios in your analysis:

   Liabilities to assets ratio = Total Liabilities/Total Assets

   Long-term debt to shareholders' equity ratio = Long-Term Debt/ Total Shareholders' Equity

   Operating cash flow to average total liabilities ratio = Operating Cash Flow/ Average Total Liabilities

   Interest coverage ratio (cash basis) = (Operating Cash Flow + Interest Paid + Taxes Paid)/Interest Paid

   (2) Compute the ratios using financial information (a) as reported and (b) after capitalization of operating leases. (Hint: Adjusting operating cash flow for assumed lease capitalization requires the removal of rent paid from operating cash flows

EXHIBIT 6.22

SOUTHWEST AIRLINES CO.
CONSOLIDATED BALANCE SHEET

	December 31	
	2008	**2007**
	(In millions, except share data)	
ASSETS		
Current assets:		
Cash and cash equivalents	$ 1,368	$ 2,213
Short-term investments	435	566
Accounts and other receivables	209	279
Inventories of parts and supplies, at cost	203	259
Fuel derivative contracts		1,069
Deferred income taxes	365	—
Prepaid expenses and other current assets	313	57
Total current assets	2,893	4,443
Property and equipment, at cost:		
Flight equipment	13,722	13,019
Ground property and equipment	1,769	1,515
Deposits on flight equipment purchase contracts	380	626
	15,871	15,160
Less allowance for depreciation and amortization	4,831	4,286
	11,040	10,874
Other assets	375	1,455
	$14,308	$16,772
LIABILITIES AND STOCKHOLDERS' EQUITY		
Current liabilities:		
Accounts payable	$ 668	$ 759
Accrued liabilities	1,012	3,107
Air traffic liability	963	931
Current maturities of long-term debt	163	41
Total current liabilities	2,806	4,838
Long-term debt less current maturities	3,498	2,050
Deferred income taxes	1,904	2,535
Deferred gains from sale and leaseback of aircraft	105	106
Other deferred liabilities	1,042	302
Commitments and contingencies		
Stockholders' equity:		
Common stock, $1.00 par value: 2,000,000,000 shares authorized; 807,611,634 shares issued in 2008 and 2007	808	808
Capital in excess of par value	1,215	1,207
Retained earnings	4,919	4,788
Accumulated other comprehensive income (loss)	(984)	1,241

EXHIBIT 6.22 (Continued)

	December 31	
	2008	**2007**
	(In millions, except share data)	
Treasury stock, at cost: 67,619,062 and 72,814,104 shares in 2008 and 2007, respectively	**(1,005)**	(1,103)
Total stockholders' equity	**4,953**	6,941
	$14,308	$16,772

See accompanying notes.

EXHIBIT 6.23

SOUTHWEST AIRLINES CO.
CONSOLIDATED STATEMENT OF INCOME

	Years Ended December 31,		
	2008	**2007**	**2006**
	(In millions, except per share amounts)		
OPERATING REVENUES:			
Passenger	**$10,549**	$9,457	$8,750
Freight	**145**	130	134
Other	**329**	274	202
Total operating revenues	**11,023**	9,861	9,086
OPERATING EXPENSES:			
Salaries, wages, and benefits	**3,340**	3,213	3,052
Fuel and oil	**3,713**	2,690	2,284
Maintenance materials and repairs	**721**	616	468
Aircraft rentals	**154**	156	158
Landing fees and other rentals	**662**	560	495
Depreciation and amortization	**599**	555	515
Other operating expenses	**1,385**	1,280	1,180
Total operating expenses	**10,574**	9,070	8,152
OPERATING INCOME	**449**	791	934
OTHER EXPENSES (INCOME):			
Interest expense	**10**	119	128
Capitalized interest	**(25)**	(50)	(51)
Interest income	**(26)**	(44)	(84)
Other (gains) losses, net	**92**	(292)	151
Total other expenses (income)	**171**	(267)	144
INCOME BEFORE INCOME TAXES	**278**	1,058	790
PROVISION FOR INCOME TAXES	**100**	413	291
NET INCOME	**$ 178**	$ 645	$ 499
NET INCOME PER SHARE, BASIC	**$ .24**	$ .85	$ .63
NET INCOME PER SHARE, DILUTED	**$ .24**	$ .84	$ .61

EXHIBIT 6.24

Additional Data from Southwest Airlines Co. December 31, 2008 10K Filing

From Consolidated Statement of Cash Flows (in millions):	2008	2007
Net cash provided by (used in) operating activities	$(1,521)	$2,845
Interest paid	$ 100	$ 63
Income taxes	$ 71	$ 94

From 2008 Note 8 (Leases)

. . . Total rental expense for operating leases, both aircraft and other, charged to operations in 2008, 2007, and 2006 was $527 million, $469 million, and $433 million, respectively. The majority of the Company's terminal operations space as well as 82 aircraft were under operating leases at December 31, 2008. Future minimum lease payments under capital leases and noncancelable operating leases with initial or remaining terms in excess of one year at December 31, 2008, are provided in the following table.

In millions	Capital Leases	Operating Leases
2009	$16	$ 376
2010	15	324
2011	12	249
2012	—	203
2013	—	152
After 2013	—	728
Total minimum lease payments	43	$2,032
Less amount representing interest	4	
Present value of minimum lease payments	39	
Less current portion	14	
Long-term portion	$25	

From 2007 Note 8 (Leases)

. . . Total rental expense for operating leases, both aircraft and other, charged to operations in 2007, 2006, and 2005 was $469 million, $433 million, and $409 million, respectively. The majority of the Company's terminal operations space as well as 86 aircraft were under operating leases at December 31, 2007. Future minimum lease payments under capital leases and noncancelable operating leases with initial or remaining terms in excess of one year at December 31, 2007, are provided in the following table.

In millions	Capital Leases	Operating Leases
2008	$16	$ 400
2009	17	335
2010	15	298
2011	12	235
2012	—	195
After 2012	—	876
Total minimum lease payments	60	$2,339
Less amount representing interest	8	
Present value of minimum lease payments	52	
Less current portion	13	
Long-term portion	$39	

and the inclusion of interest paid in operating cash flows. Use rent expense and interest expense to approximate rent paid and interest paid, respectively.

b. An analyst who compares the debt ratios of firms under U.S. GAAP and IFRS must consider key differences in the two sets of standards related to convertible debt and troubled debt restructurings. In general, which system would most likely yield lower debt and higher equity? Explain.

EXHIBIT 6.25

Lufthansa
Consolidated Balance Sheet as of 31 December 2008

Assets

in €m	Notes	31.12.2008	31.12.2007
Intangible assets with indefinite useful life*	17)	821	797
Other intangible assets	18)	261	252
Aircraft and reserve engines	19) 22)	8,764	8,380
Repairable spare parts for aircraft		669	586
Property, plant and other equipment	20) 22)	1,931	1,773
Investment property	21)	3	3
Investments accounted for using the equity method	23)	298	323
Other equity investments	24) 25)	790	777
Non-current securities	24) 25)	509	298
Loans and receivables	24) 26)	475	399
Derivative financial instruments	24) 27)	339	368
Accrued income and advance payments	30)	15	22
Effective income tax receivables	14)	72	79
Deferred claims for income tax rebates	14)	28	19
Non-current assets		**14,975**	**14,076**
Inventories	28)	581	511
Trade receivables and other receivables	24) 29)	3,015	3,448
Derivative financial instruments	24) 27)	213	481
Accrued income and advance payments	30)	119	110
Effective income tax receivables		130	62
Securities	24) 31)	1,834	1,528
Cash and cash equivalents	24) 32)	1,444	2,079
Assets held for sale	33)	97	25
Current assets		**7,433**	**8,244**
Total assets		**22,408**	**22,320**

*Incl. goodwill.

(Continued)

EXHIBIT 6.25 (Continued)

Shareholders' equity and liabilities

in €m	Notes	31.12.2008	31.12.2007
Issued capital	34) 35)	1,172	1,172
Capital reserve	36)	1,366	1,366
Retained earnings	36)	3,140	2,063
Other neutral reserves	36)	579	589
Net profit for the period		599	1,655
Equity attributable to shareholders of Deutsche Lufthansa AG		6,856	6,845
Minority interests		63	55
Shareholders' equity		**6,919**	**6,900**
Pension provisions	37)	2,400	2,461
Other provisions	38)	291	349
Borrowings	39) 40)	3,161	3,098
Other financial liabilities	41)	51	55
Advance payments received, accruals and deferrals and other non-financial liabilities	42)	64	66
Derivative financial instruments	27) 39)	118	371
Deferred income tax liabilities	14)	813	749
Non-current provisions and liabilities		**6,898**	**7,149**
Other provisions	38)	1,873	1,686
Borrowings	39) 40)	420	247
Trade payables and other financial liabilities	39) 43)	3,626	3,959
Liabilities from unused flight documents		1,693	1,546
Advance payments received, accruals and deferrals and other non-financial liabilities	44)	388	289
Derivative financial instruments	27) 39)	492	481
Actual income tax liabilities		99	51
Provisions and liabilities included in disposal groups	45)	—	12
Current provisions and liabilities		**8,591**	**8,271**
Total shareholders' equity and liabilities		**22,408**	**22,320**

EXHIBIT 6.26

Lufthansa
Consolidated Income Statement for the 2008 Financial Year

in €m	Notes	2008	2007
Traffic revenue	3)	19,998	17,568
Other revenue	4)	4,872	4,852
Total revenue		**24,870**	**22,420**
Changes in inventories and work performed by the enterprise and capitalised	5)	178	119
Other operating income	6)	1,969	1,571
Cost of materials and services	7)	−13,707	−11,553
Staff costs	8)	−5,692	−5,498
Depreciation, amortisation and impairment	9)	−1,289	−1,204
Other operating expenses	10)	−4,946	−4,269
Profit from operating activities		**+1,383**	**+1,586**
Result of equity investments accounted for using the equity method	11)	−22	+223
Result from other equity investments	11)	+42	+131
Interest income	12)	202	177
Interest expense	12)	−374	−371
Other financial items	13)	−427	−133
Financial result		**−579**	**+27**
Profit before income taxes		**+804**	**+1,613**
Income taxes	14)	−195	−356
Profit from continuing operations		**+609**	**+1,257**
Profit from the discontinued Leisure Travel segment	15)	—	**+503**
Profit after income taxes		**+609**	**+1,760**
Minority interests		−10	−105
Net profit attributable to shareholders of Lufthansa AG		**+599**	**+1,655**
Basic earnings per share in €	16)	1.31	+3.61
Diluted earnings per share in €	16)	1.30	+3.60

EXHIBIT 6.27

Additional Data from Lufthansa December 31, 2008 Annual Report

From Consolidated Statement of Cash Flows (In €m):	2008	2007
Net cash provided by (used in) operating activities	2,473	2,862
Net interest paid	172	194
Income taxes	123	274

12) Net interest

Net Interest

In €m	2008	2007
Income from other securities and financial loans	11	13
Other interest and similar income	191	164
Interest income	**202**	**177**
Interest expenses on pensions obligations	−119	−154
Interest expense on other provisions	−16	−9
Interest and other similar expenses	−239	−208
Interest expenses	**−374**	**−371**
	−172	**−194**

Operating leases

In addition to the finance leases, a large number of leases have been signed which, on the basis of their economic parameters, are qualified as operating leases, i.e. the leased asset is deemed to belong to the lessor. As well as 106 additional aircraft on operating leases, these are mainly aircraft leased as part of the Lufthansa Regional concept and leases for buildings.

The operating leases for aircraft have a term of between one and nine years. These agreements generally end automatically after the term has expired, but there is sometimes an option for extending the agreement.

The leases for buildings generaly run for up to 25 years. The fixtures at the airports in Frankfurt and Munich are leased for 30 years.

The following payments are due in the years ahead (amounts in millions; p.a. denotes per annum):

in €m	2009	2010–2013	from 2014
Aircraft	209	343	—
Various buildings	213	872	215 p.a.
Other leases	70	273	56 p.a.
	492	**1,488**	**271 p.a.**
Payments from sub-leasing	9	13	1 p.a.

EXHIBIT 6.27 (Continued)

In the previous year the following figures were given for operating leases:

in €m	2008	2009–2012	from 2013
Aircraft	196	418	—
Various buildings	236	920	227 p.a.
Other leases	80	306	65 p.a.
	512	**1,644**	**292 p.a.**
Payments from sub-leasing	14	13	2 p.a.

Chapter 7

Investing Activities

Learning Objectives

1 Describe the accounting for a firm's investments in tangible productive assets, including the initial decision to capitalize or expense and the use of choices and estimates to allocate costs through the depreciation process.

2 Describe the alternative ways that firms account for intangible assets, highlighting research and development expenditures, software development expenditures, and goodwill, including the exercise of judgment in the allocation of costs through the amortization process.

3 Review and apply the rules for testing the impairment of different categories of long-lived assets, including goodwill.

4 Describe the accounting and reporting of investments in securities, including the market value, equity, proportionate consolidation, and full consolidation methods.

5 Explain the accounting for variable-interest entities, commonly referred to as special-purpose entities, including the requirement to consolidate them with the firm identified as the primary beneficiary.

6 Prepare a set of translated financial statements using the all-current method and the monetary/nonmonetary method and describe the conditions under which each method best portrays the operating relationship between a U.S. parent firm and its foreign subsidiary.

In Chapter 6 we discussed the financial reporting for financing activities, which are the primary source of capital for investing and operating activities. In this chapter, we discuss the accounting, reporting, and analysis of investing activities. Once a firm obtains financing, it must invest the proceeds effectively to generate returns that cover the costs of the financing.

Investing activities include (1) the acquisition of long-term tangible and intangible assets in the operations of the business or financial assets for investment purposes and (2) the dispositions of those assets. The accounting for investing activities directly affects the analysis of the profitability of the firm. Investing activities significantly impact the denominator (assets) for ROA (return on assets) computations discussed in Chapters 4 and 5. Also, the profits that arise from using assets and the gains and losses that arise from holding assets create the numerator (net income before financing costs, adjusted for tax) used in the ROA computation. Finally, forecasted future financial statements depend heavily on forecasted investing activities, especially investments in operating assets such as property, plant, and equipment.

This chapter addresses accounting and reporting topics related to asset investments, which fall into two broad categories as follows:

- Investments in long-lived operating assets (which include long-lived tangible fixed assets such as land, building, and equipment; intangible assets such as patents, brand names, customer lists, and goodwill; and natural resources such as oil reserves and timberlands).
- Investments in the securities of other firms (including stock and bond investments). (Because a significant subset of stock investments are controlling investments in foreign subsidiaries, a third major section of the chapter deals with the translation of foreign subsidiary financial statements denominated in a foreign currency.)

Firms also make tactical and operating investments in net working capital. Because working capital assets (for example, accounts receivable and inventory) and working capital liabilities (for example, accounts payable and other current liabilities) are generated by and used in day-to-day normal revenue-generating activities, we consider these investments in working capital in the chapter about operating activities (Chapter 8).

For an illustration of the scope of this chapter, refer to the Assets section of PepsiCo's 2008 Consolidated Balance Sheet in Appendix A. This chapter focuses on the types of assets that PepsiCo shows as Short-term investments (in the Current Assets section) and all of the assets listed as noncurrent apart from other assets (that is, property, plant, and equipment, net; amortizable intangible assets, net; goodwill; other nonamortizable intangible assets; and investments in noncontrolled affiliates). Collectively, these assets sum to $22,743 million, or more than 63 percent of PepsiCo's $35,994 million total assets at December 27, 2008. Also, the fact the PepsiCo's statements are "consolidated" means that in all of its financial statements, PepsiCo includes the assets, liabilities, revenues, expenses, and cash flows of its subsidiaries.

Because this chapter is about a major portion of a company's assets, it is useful to revisit the definition of *assets* discussed in Chapter 1 prior to consideration of the two major classifications of assets created by investing activities. Currently, the FASB's *Statements of Accounting Concepts* (*Nos. 5* and 6) define an asset as having four characteristics (the first three form the definition of an asset and the fourth is a key characteristic for measurement): (1) probable future benefits, (2) obtained/controlled by the entity, (3) as a result of a past transactions and events, and (4) reliably measured (essentially at acquisition cost or fair value).[1] Practical application of the definition of an *asset* is guided by management's judgment and by rule. Remember that costs not judged to be assets are expensed in the current period and thus immediately reduce net income. Consideration given to acquire financial assets with contractual and other legal rights, such as investments in bonds or common stock of another company, clearly yields assets. Also, for many acquisitions of long-lived productive assets, such as a simple acquisition of a piece of machinery by sacrifice

---

[1] Financial Accounting Standards Board, *Statement of Financial Accounting Concepts No. 5*, "Recognition and Measurement in Financial Statements of a Business Enterprise," (1984); Financial Accounting Standards Board, *Statement of Financial Accounting Concepts No. 6*, "Elements of Financial Statements," (1985). Currently, the IFRS definition of an asset is very similar to the U.S. GAAP definition. As of the writing of this text, the FASB and IASB are in discussions about a new definition of assets that de-emphasizes past transactions and events and expected future benefits in favor of determining whether the entity has, at present, an economic resource that (a) is separable from the entity by sale, license, or another potential type of exchange or (b) is arising from a contractual or legal right. This definition is consistent with standard-setters' beliefs that more assets and liabilities should be measured at fair value. The separability of the asset and the contractual or legal right definitions directly permit or enhance the ability to measure an asset's fair value.

of cash or creation of a liability (for example, issuance of a note payable), determining whether the item acquired is an asset and measuring its cost are not difficult. However, some transactions are not as clear-cut. For example, as you will see in the following subsections relating to long-lived operating assets, certain costs might fail the probable future benefits test, such as certain costs related to research and development, marketing and brand-building activities, and exploration for natural resources. Also, as discussed in the second major part of the chapter, the control criterion will determine which assets are reported on the books of the investor in an intercompany investment and availability of reliable fair value information will drive the measurement for many financial assets.

INVESTMENTS IN LONG-LIVED OPERATING ASSETS

Example 1

Refer to PepsiCo's Note 4, "Property, Plant and Equipment and Intangible Assets" in Appendix A in which PepsiCo provides the detail to support the following long-lived operating assets reported in its Consolidated Balance Sheet at December 27, 2008:

- $11,663 million in property, plant and equipment, net
- $732 million in amortizable intangible assets, net
- $6,252 million in nonamortizable intangible assets (including goodwill)

The individual amounts in Note 4 provide a good summary of the accounting issues of interest to a financial statement analyst, as follows:

1. PepsiCo uses the first part of the note to explain the $11,663 million reported as its *tangible asset* property, plant and equipment. PepsiCo reports $22,552 million as the cost of acquiring the property, plant, and equipment, and accumulated depreciation is $10,889 million to date. The difference, the $11,663 million *net book value of the asset*, is reported on the balance sheet. The annual depreciation expenses (that sum over time to equal accumulated depreciation) are reflected each year in PepsiCo's net income. For 2008, PepsiCo reports $1,422 million of depreciation expense.

2. In the second part of the note, PepsiCo repeats this description of acquisition cost and accumulated amortization for a second type of long-lived operating asset, *amortizable intangible assets* with definite useful lives. PepsiCo recognizes amortization expense of $64 million in 2008 net income.

3. In the last part of the note, PepsiCo reconciles from the beginning to the ending balances of the components of a third type of long-lived operating asset, its *nonamortizable intangible assets*—perpetual brands and goodwill. Because these assets have been judged to have indefinite lives, they are not amortized, but instead are assessed annually for impairment. If impaired, the carrying amounts are written down to fair value. As a result, PepsiCo recognizes no amortization expense for these assets in net income in 2008.

Each of the following sections identifies an important issue in financial statement analysis and refers back to Note 4. The section headings are in the form of analysts' questions. It is important to understand that the answers to these questions are prescribed by accounting rule, are the result of managers' choice and judgment, or are some combination of rules and judgments. The answers determine accounting quality in the long-lived asset investments area. The chapter discusses how the answers affect an analyst's ability to conduct profitability and risk analysis and to forecast future financial statements.

Are the Acquisition Costs "Assets"?

The following subsections examine the practical application of rules and judgments to determine whether the costs of acquiring property, plant, and equipment; research and development costs; software development costs; subsequent expenditures to enhance or maintain property, plant, and equipment; costs of self-construction; costs of acquiring intangible assets; and costs of acquiring natural resources can be recognized as assets or whether they should receive expense treatment. The financial statement effects of the capitalization (asset treatment) versus immediate expensing decision are shown in Exhibit 7.1.

EXHIBIT 7.1: FINANCIAL STATEMENT EFFECTS OF CAPITALIZATION VERSUS EXPENSING

Assets	=	Liabilities	+	Total Shareholders' Equity		
				CC	AOCI	RE
Capitalization (initial acquisition costs):						
Cash consideration: Long-Lived Asset (net) +xx Cash −xx						
Liability incurred: Long-Lived Asset (net) +xx		Liability +xx				
Common stock consideration: Long-Lived Asset (net) +xx				Common Stock +xx APIC +xx		
Subsequent cost allocation to periods benefitted via depreciation, amortization, and depletion: Long-Lived Asset (net) −xx						Expense −xx
Capitalization (initial acquisition costs):						
Cash consideration: Long-Lived Asset (net) xx Cash xx						
Liability incurred: Long-Lived Asset (net) xx Liability xx						
Common stock consideration: Long-Lived Asset (net) xx Common Stock xx APIC xx						
Subsequent cost allocation to periods benefitted via depreciation, amortization, and depletion: Expense xx Long-Lived Asset (net) xx						
Expense treatment:						
Cash consideration: Cash −xx						Expense −xx
Liability incurred:		Liability +xx				Expense −xx
Common stock consideration:				Common Stock +xx APIC +xx		Expense −xx

(*Continued*)

EXHIBIT 7.1 (CONTINUED)

Expense treatment:		
Cash consideration:		
Expense	xx	
Cash		xx
Liability incurred:		
Expense	xx	
Liability		xx
Common stock consideration:		
Expense	xx	
Common Stock		xx
APIC		xx

Note: We use Long-Lived Asset (net) in all entries to link to the balance sheet presentation. However, most accountants use Long-Lived Asset for all acquisition and disposal entries to account for the original acquisition cost and the contra-asset account Accumulated Depreciation as the credit in the depreciation entry.

The effects on financial statements of the capitalization of initial acquisition costs depends on the consideration given (cash paid, liability incurred, or shares of stock issued). Subsequent cost allocation decreases the long-lived asset over its useful life, and the consumption of the cost is treated as an expense. The remaining book value of the asset (its *adjusted acquisition cost*) is reported on the balance sheet. If a cost is deemed to be an expense, the amount of consideration given will be expensed immediately and no balance sheet asset will exist. Therefore, the key difference between the capitalization and expense treatment is the timing of expense recognition.

Accounting for the Acquisition of Property, Plant, and Equipment: General Rule

In many cases, it is clear that costs have been incurred to acquire a piece of property, plant, and equipment that will yield future benefits; thus, asset recognition is warranted. The general rule for recording the acquisition of an asset is that it should be recorded at the fair value of what has been sacrificed to acquire and prepare the asset for its intended use. This sacrifice includes cash paid, the fair value of debt incurred, the fair value of lease payments under capital leases (as illustrated in Chapter 6), or the fair value of stock issued to acquire the asset, in addition to costs to ship, temporarily store, insure, set up, test, and calibrate (as in the case of machinery) an asset as it is prepared for operational use.

Cash used to acquire property, plant, and equipment is reported as a cash outflow in the investing activities section of the statement of cash flows. If property, plant, and equipment are acquired using long-term debt or equity (both of which are non-cash transactions), the investing activity will be reported as a significant non-cash investing and financing activity in a separate schedule accompanying the statement of cash flows. PepsiCo reports capital spending of more than $2 billion per year over the 2006–2008 period in its Consolidated Statement of Cash Flows (Appendix A), which represents a use of more than one-third of the more than $6 billion annually of net cash provided by operating activities.

In many other cases, it is less clear whether cost incurrence yields probable future benefits. The following sections address these cases.

Accounting for Research and Development Costs

R&D (research and development) is an important activity for many firms. However, U.S. GAAP requires firms to expense immediately all R&D costs incurred *internally* because of the inherent uncertainty in determining whether R&D activities will produce sufficient future economic benefits to warrant being capitalized as an asset.[2] Externally acquired R&D from purchasing patents or licenses can be capitalized because the arm's-length transaction between two market participants provides a reliable measure of acquisition cost and is an indicator of the existence of future economic benefits. For industries with high R&D expenditures, such as the research-intensive biotechnology industry, the U.S. GAAP requirement to expense rather than capitalize is especially troublesome because a major asset never appears on the balance sheet because standard-setters question whether expected future benefits will exist or are reliably measurable.

Consider the following three examples for biotechnology firms.

Example 2

Biogen Idec (formerly Biogen) is a biotech company with leading products and capabilities in oncology and immunology. Revenues for 2008 exceed $2.8 billion. Biogen Idec principally develops drug-related products *internally* in its research laboratories and is engaged in discovering and developing drugs for human health care through genetic engineering. Its two highest revenue-producing drugs on the market as of December 31, 2008, were Avonex® to treat multiple sclerosis and Rituxan® to treat rheumatoid arthritis and non-Hodgkin's lymphoma. In describing its accounting policy on R&D costs, Biogen Idec states that "research and development expenses consist of upfront fees and milestones paid to collaborators and expenses incurred in performing research and development activities including salaries and benefits, facilities expenses, overhead expenses, clinical trial and related clinical manufacturing expenses, contract services and other outside expenses. Research and development expenses are expensed as incurred."

The firm's R&D expense averaged slightly more than 40 percent of sales during the 2006–2008 period. In accordance with U.S. GAAP, the firm showed no asset on its balance sheet related to this in-house research activity.[3]

Example 3

Genzyme Corporation is a biotechnology and health care products firm engaged in the development of medical products and services. For 2008, revenues totaled $4.6 billion, with the firm's top products including Cerezyme® (Gaucher disease), Renagel® (end-stage renal disease), and Fabrazyme® (Fabry disease). The company follows a strategy of *internal* development of technology and *acquisition of other companies* involved in biotechnology research. Genzyme *expenses* the portion of the acquisition price of companies related to *in-process* technology, but it *capitalizes and subsequently amortizes* any portion of the price related to *completed* technologies.

Several years ago Genzyme made a large acquisition and, as a result, expensed a large amount of in-process R&D related to the acquisition. The R&D expense for internal R&D costs for the year was slightly more than 20 percent of sales. However, because of the acquisition, Genzyme also expensed the portion of the purchase price related to in-process technology. As a result, the total R&D expense/sales percentage for the year was almost 50 percent. A year later the total R&D expense/sales percentage was less than 25 percent because only a small portion of in-process technology was purchased and expensed.

---

[2] Financial Accounting Standards Board, *Statement of Financial Accounting Standards No. 2*, "Accounting for Research and Development Costs" (1974); *FASB Codification Topic 730*. Long-lived assets used in multiple R&D projects are initially capitalized; then the depreciation of the assets is assigned to R&D expense.

[3] Biogen Idec does report an intangible asset on its balance sheet for established core technologies and patent rights acquired in acquisitions.

Example 4

Amgen Inc. is a leading human therapeutics company in the biotechnology industry, generating over $15 billion in revenues in 2008 from a number of top-selling products, including Epogen® (Epoetin alfa), a recombinant version of a human protein that stimulates the production of red blood cells, and Aranesp®, which also stimulates red blood cell production and is used to treat anemia associated with chronic renal failure. The firm follows a strategy of *internal* development of biotechnology and *external* development through a series of joint ventures and partnerships. Amgen contributes preliminary research findings to obtain its interest in these joint ventures and partnerships. The other participants provide funding to continue development of this preliminary research.

In some cases, Amgen contracts with the joint venture or partnership to perform the continued development in its own laboratories. In this case, Amgen receives a fee each period in an amount approximately equal to the R&D costs incurred in conducting the research (resulting in no net R&D cost). In other cases, the joint venture or partnership entity conducts the research, in which case Amgen may show no R&D expense on its books. Amgen generally maintains a right of first refusal for any products developed, in which case it must pay the owners of the joint venture a periodic royalty.

Amgen's R&D expense for 2008 was 20.2 percent of sales, the lowest of the three firms for the most recent year. The company shows only minor amounts on its balance sheet for investments in joint ventures and partnerships, relating to cash advances. Because Amgen must expense initial development costs when incurred, its contribution of preliminary research findings for an interest in these joint ventures and partnerships does not increase an asset.

Summary of Examples 2–4

Examples 2–4 illustrate three different strategies that firms pursue in developing biotechnologies and highlight the problem with current R&D reporting rules. The different strategies that firms follow, especially when combined with the required accounting for R&D costs, complicate any cross-sectional analysis of firms' financial data. To the extent that the economic substance of these arrangements differ, different accounting treatments may be appropriate.

The economic characteristics of R&D arrangements suggest the following twofold approach that an analyst might use:

1. Modify as-reported financial statements by capitalizing and subsequently amortizing all expenditures on R&D that have future service potential, whether a firm incurs the R&D cost internally or purchases in-process or completed technology externally. Immediately expense all R&D costs that have no future service potential.

2. Consolidate the firm's share of the assets, liabilities, revenues, and expenses of R&D joint ventures or partnerships.

Unfortunately, the inherent uncertainty about future benefits that led accounting standard setters to require all R&D expenditures to be expensed creates difficulties for an analyst to judge future service potential from financial statement disclosures alone. Reliance on firm disclosures of scientific and other information outside the financial reporting model is necessary. Also, only some R&D joint venture data will be present in notes to the financial statements. Therefore, the consolidation of joint ventures also might prove to be difficult.

The analyst must be aware of the effects of the R&D expensing rule on profitability analysis. The effects on ROA are countervailing between numerator and denominator. Missing assets understate the denominator. The numerator of ROA, net income, is understated when all R&D is classified as current expense and is overstated when the amortization of an R&D asset is excluded. In the typical case of growing R&D expenditures, the numerator will be understated because current R&D expenses exceed the amortizations. A maturing firm may reach a steady state where current R&D expense equals the amortizations, which would have taken place if R&D had been capitalized. If that happens, the ROA numerator would be unaffected, but the denominator would still be understated due to the omission of the R&D asset.

In general, capitalization and amortization (relative to immediate expensing) results in a smoother income series and thus is an easier prediction of future net income. To yield improved predictions of future income and cash flows (illustrated in Chapter 10), the analyst should examine the past time series of R&D expenditures, looking for volatility and growth. Dealing with the potential effects of asset understatement and income understatement in valuation is addressed in Chapters 11–13.

IFRS rules on R&D mitigate the likely overstatement of ROA because research costs are expensed and product development costs (the costs incurred after the research yields a product or process that is technologically feasible) are capitalized.[4] Also, recent standards have changed the accounting for *in-process R&D* acquired as part of an acquisition. If the in-process R&D meets the criterion of separability discussed later in this chapter, it is capitalized at an amount equal to its fair value.[5]

Although managers and others view R&D as a necessary investing activity, statement of cash flow reporting treats R&D as an operating activity because it does not result in a balance sheet asset. R&D reduces current period net income and thus reduces current period cash flows from operating activities.

Accounting for Software Development Costs

U.S. GAAP treats the cost of developing computer software somewhat differently from R&D costs. Similar to IFRS treatment, firms must expense as incurred all costs incurred internally in developing computer software until such development achieves the "technological feasibility" of a product. Thereafter, the firm must capitalize and subsequently amortize additional development costs.[6] The FASB defines technological feasibility as "completion of a detailed program design or, in its absence, completion of a working model." Clearly, determining when a software development project achieves technological feasibility requires significant judgment by managers and other personnel. Another key issue in capitalizing software development costs is the treatment of costs to improve an existing product.

Example 5

Consider the software accounting policies of IBM, Adobe Systems, and Microsoft.

IBM is a world leader in providing software and consulting services. The firm includes the following note on its accounting for software development costs in a recent Form 10-K filing:

> **Software Costs.** Costs that are related to the conceptual formulation and design of licensed programs are expensed as incurred to R&D expense. Also for licensed programs, the company capitalizes costs that are incurred to produce the finished product

---

[4] International Accounting Standards Board, *International Accounting Standard 38*, "Intangible Assets" (1998).

[5] Financial Accounting Standards Board, *Statement of Financial Accounting Standards No. 141 (revised 2007)*, "Business Combinations"; *FASB Codification Topic 805*; International Accounting Standards Board, *International Financial Reporting Standard 3*, "Business Combinations" (2007).

[6] Financial Accounting Standards Board, *Statement of Financial Accounting Standards No. 86*, "Accounting for the Costs of Computer Software to Be Sold, Leased, or Otherwise Marketed" (1985); *FASB Codification Topic 985*. This standard does not apply to software created for internal use that is capitalized and amortized, similar to the treatment of long-lived tangible assets.

after technological feasibility has been established. Capitalized amounts are amortized using the straight-line method, which is applied over periods ranging up to three years. The company performs periodic reviews to ensure that unamortized program costs remain recoverable from future revenue. Costs to support or service licensed programs are charged to software cost as incurred.

As indicated here, IBM's R&D expense includes costs for conceptual formulation of software products as well as amortization of software costs previously capitalized for products that had reached the technological feasibility stage.

Adobe Systems also is a leading developer of graphics software. Its Acrobat® and Reader® products are well known because of their extensive use in the financial community. Adobe develops new software internally and through aggressive external acquisitions of other software companies. Adobe expenses initial software development costs incurred internally as R&D. Adobe capitalizes software development costs once the firm deems a graphics software program to have achieved technological feasibility. It also capitalizes the cost of software acquired in corporate acquisitions if the software has achieved technological feasibility. In both scenarios, however, Adobe indicates that the amount of software costs capitalized is immaterial to the financial statements. The firm states in a recent Form 10-K:

> Capitalization of software development costs begins upon the establishment of technological feasibility, which is generally the completion of a working prototype that has been certified as having no critical bugs and is a release candidate or when alternative future use exists. To date, software development costs incurred between completion of a working prototype and general availability of the related product have not been material and have not been capitalized.

Microsoft appears to capitalize a very small portion of the development costs of subsequent generations of Windows® or Office because of the lateness of the point at which it believes that technological feasibility has been reached. The following policy is taken from the notes to Microsoft's 2008 annual report:

> Research and development expenses include payroll, employee benefits, stock-based compensation, and other headcount-related expenses associated with product development. Research and development expenses also include third-party development and programming costs, localization costs incurred to translate software for international markets, the amortization of purchased software code and services content, and in-process research and development. We have determined that technological feasibility for our software products is reached shortly before the products are released to manufacturing. The amortization of these costs is included in cost of revenue over the estimated lives of the products.

Interpretation of the meaning of *technological feasibility* has created diversity in practice. The Software Publishers Association, a trade association for firms in the software development industry, has advocated expensing all software development costs when incurred, suggesting that expensing these costs eliminates the concerns of extremely shortened software product lives and uncertainty over realization of software assets. On the other hand, a study addressing this intriguing position of the association shows that in recent years, enhancing reported earnings through software capitalization schemes has diminished.[7] The researchers conclude that because software capitalization no longer provides an opportunity

---

[7] David Aboody and Baruch Lev, "The Value-Relevance of Intangibles: The Case of Software Capitalization," *Journal of Accounting Research* supplement (1998), pp. 161–191.

for earnings management, nothing is lost by restricting software producers to only one allowable reporting technique. In addition, the study addresses the more substantive issue of whether software capitalization is value-relevant to investors. For firms that capitalize software development costs (that is, report a cumulative software intangible asset on the balance sheet), the researchers find a significant association between these costs and future earnings, concluding that this finding supports capitalizing and amortizing product development costs, as permitted by U.S. GAAP and IFRS.

The flexibility available to firms applying software accounting standards should cause the analyst to proceed cautiously when analyzing computer software development companies. An added concern in this regard is the small size of many such companies and the rapid pace of technological change in this industry. The information technology industry, and particularly the software segment of the industry, has experienced an even greater rate of change over the past decade due to the surge of interest in the Internet and related services. The crash that many information technology industry stocks experienced several years ago is further reason to practice a healthy level of skepticism when analyzing firms in the industry.

Subsequent Expenditures for Enhancement or Improvements

Subsequent to acquiring long-lived operating assets, firms make additional expenditures to add to or improve them. Proper accounting is to capitalize (that is, add to the asset's book value) expenditures that increase the service life or potential (in either quantity or quality) of an asset beyond that originally anticipated. Firms should expense immediately expenditures for repairs and maintenance that merely maintain the originally expected service potential. For example, replacing tires on a delivery truck does not qualify as a capital expenditure because the original useful life was determined with the assumption that tires would be replaced regularly. However, if a refrigeration unit was added to the cargo area of the truck to add the capability to transport perishable cargo, the expenditure would be capitalized because the quality of service was improved beyond original estimates.

Example 6

American Airlines, one of the largest airlines in the world, follows a rigorous maintenance program for all of its aircraft. In a recent annual report, the firm provides the following information about its maintenance and repair costs:

> **Maintenance and Repair Costs.** Maintenance and repair costs for owned and leased flight equipment are charged to operating expense as incurred, except costs incurred for maintenance and repair under flight hour maintenance contract agreements, which are accrued based on contractual terms when an obligation exists.

Management judgment in the subsequent expenditures area creates ample opportunity for earnings management. Remember that the capitalization versus expensing choice has immediate effects on the income statement. One way to increase earnings is to (incorrectly) classify routine maintenance and repair costs as capital expenditures. Thus, investors must rely on management integrity and auditor monitoring as protection against self-interested managers manipulating earnings through biased application of the judgment necessary in many settings. Strong corporate governance and auditor reporting of internal control weaknesses assist the assessment of accounting quality.

Costs of Self-Construction

A company might choose to self-construct plant and equipment because it wants to save costs or because no external supplier is available. Wal-Mart Stores, Inc., for example, might construct its own stores. The cost of a self-constructed asset equals the fair value of all necessary costs incurred to produce it, including materials, labor, and overhead, both variable (that is, varies directly with production activity) and fixed. For example, self-construction projects frequently use existing equipment and do not create the need for additional expenditures on equipment, plant management supervision, and property taxes. But these fixed costs are necessary for the construction to occur, and both U.S. GAAP and IFRS require an allocation of part of the fixed overhead cost to self-construction costs. If internal expenditures exceed the cost of acquiring the asset externally, the amount recorded in the self-constructed asset's account will be limited to the cost of external purchase and the excess of costs incurred over the external fair value is recorded as a loss of the period under the conservatism principle. This process ensures that an asset is not recorded initially at an amount greater than its fair value.

Interest Incurred to Self-Construct Assets

As a general rule, interest costs on debt are treated as an expense of the period, as illustrated in Chapter 6. However, both U.S. GAAP and IFRS have an exception to this rule for interest cost incurred during the self-construction of a long-lived productive asset intended for the company's own use.[8] Interest on debt used to finance asset construction is a valid and often necessary cost of constructing an asset. By capitalizing interest on self-constructed assets, the firm better captures the fair value sacrificed to acquire the asset. The capitalized interest cost becomes part of the asset's historical cost (depreciation basis) and, hence, annual depreciation expense.

Avoidable interest is the term used to describe the amount of a company's annual interest cost that should be capitalized. To compute avoidable interest, expenditures linked to the self-construction project are weighted by the amount of time the expenditures were outstanding during the year. The weighted expenditures, called *average accumulated expenditures,* are multiplied by the interest rate on specific borrowings to fund the construction. If accumulated expenditures exceed specific construction borrowings, the excess average accumulated expenditures are multiplied by the weighted average interest cost of the company's other interest-bearing debt.[9] If the company has no debt, it has no avoidable interest.[10]

Example 7

Assume that Target Corporation obtained a $10,000,000 construction loan bearing a 5 percent interest rate and began construction of several warehousing facilities for a regional distribution center on January 1, 2010 (interest paid at the end of each year). Materials, labor, and overhead expenditures on the project are as follows:

January 1, 2010	$ 6,000,000
July 1, 2010	6,000,000
October 1, 2010	10,000,000
Total through December 31, 2010	$22,000,000

---

[8] Interest costs also may be capitalized on construction of certain types of inventory (discussed in Chapter 8). Financial Accounting Standards Board, *Statement of Financial Accounting Concepts No. 34,* "Capitalization of Interest Cost," (1979); *FASB Codification Topic 835*; International Accounting Standards Board, *International Accounting Standard 23 (revised 2007),* "Borrowing Costs."

[9] Alternatives exist in the application of SFAS No. 34 with respect to the assignment of interest rates to average accumulated expenditures other than the method provided in this text. For an analysis of these alternatives, see Kathryn Means and Paul Kazenski, "SFAS 34: Recipe for Diversity," *Accounting Horizons* (September 1998).

[10] Public utilities are an exception, however, because they are permitted by public utility commissions and specific industry accounting rules to impute interest on *equity* when capitalizing interest costs.

On December 31, 2010, the project was completed. In addition to the construction note, two other interest-bearing debts were outstanding during the construction period:

Bond payable (4%)	$20,000,000
Note payable (8%)	$40,000,000

The amount of avoidable interest to be capitalized in 2010 is computed as follows:

Average accumulated expenditures:

$ 6,000,000 × 12 months/12 months =	$ 6,000,000
6,000,000 × 6 months/12 months =	3,000,000
10,000,000 × 3 months/12 months =	2,500,000
$22,000,000	$11,500,000

Avoidable interest:

The average accumulated expenditures of $11,500,000 are greater than the $10,000,000 specific construction borrowing. Therefore, to compute avoidable interest, the specific borrowing's 5 percent interest rate is used for the first $10,000,000 of average accumulated expenditures and a weighted average interest rate on other borrowings is used for the excess accumulated expenditures:

$10,000,000 × 5.0% =	$500,000
1,500,000 × 6.7%* =	100,500
$11,500,000	$600,500

* The weighted interest rate on other interest bearing borrowings is as follows:
[$20 million/($20 million + $40 million) × 4%] + [$40 million/($20 million + $40 million) × 8%] = 6.7%

Avoidable interest cannot exceed actual interest:

Construction note	$10,000,000 × 5% =	$ 500,000
Bond payable	$20,000,000 × 4% =	800,000
Note payable	$40,000,000 × 8% =	3,200,000
Total actual interest		$4,500,000

The total recorded amount for the regional distribution center is obtained by adding the $22,000,000 expenditures to the $600,500 capitalized interest, yielding a depreciable fixed asset acquisition cost of $22,600,500.[11] The remainder of the $4,500,000 interest ($4,500,000 − 600,500 capitalized = $3,899,500) is charged to interest expense of the current period. The capitalized interest becomes an expense through the annual depreciation process.

---

[11] Temporary investments of funds not used in construction generate interest revenue and are not to be treated as offsets to capitalizable interest (Financial Accounting Standards Board *Statement of Financial Accounting Standards No. 62*, "Capitalization of Interest Cost in Situations Involving Certain Tax-Exempt Borrowings and Certain Gifts and Grants—an amendment of FASB Statement No. 34"). FASB Codification Topic 835. Under IFRS, the revenue is treated as an offset to borrowing costs. International Accounting Standards Board, *International Accounting Standard 23(Revised 2007)*, "Borrowing Costs."

Costs of Acquiring Natural Resources

Oil fields, timber tracts, and mineral deposits are examples of natural resources. Three types of costs incurred in connection with natural resources are as follows:

- Acquisition costs
- Exploration costs
- Development costs[12]

Acquisition Costs. Acquisition costs include the costs of acquiring the natural resources and the costs associated with returning the resource site to an acceptable condition after the resources have been obtained. Often, the natural resource is attached to land that is salvageable at the end of production. If that is the case, the initial cost is separated into two accounts, with the portion of cost attributable to land reported separately in a "land" or "property" account. All other costs of acquisition are capitalized as part of the "natural resources" account and reported in the property, plant, and equipment section with the other productive, operational assets.

Frequently, a natural resource asset is subject to *reclamation cost* or *restoration costs* at the end of the life of a project. For example, at the end of coal strip mine's productive life, the mine operator incurs substantial costs to fill in the mine and return the land to its original contour. The need to incur costs to reclaim a natural resource is an example of an *ARO (asset retirement obligation)*. The fair value of the obligation (usually determined by discounting expected future reclamation costs) is capitalized and amortized over the life of the related natural resource asset.[13]

Exploration Costs. Exploration costs are incurred to discover the existence and exact location of the natural resource. For example, a petroleum manufacturer acquires an oil field (acquisition cost) and then drills to discover oil. The costs of engaging in drilling activity, including supplies, labor, and machinery depreciation charges, are exploration costs. The accounting for exploration costs has emerged as one of the most controversial topics in accounting history. At the center of the controversy is the determination of whether the costs of unsuccessful exploration activities are assets or expenses. The following two schools of thought on that issue have emerged:

- *Successful efforts* (exploration costs of successful wells are capitalized as assets, but unsuccessful wells are expensed)
- *Full costing* (exploration costs of successful and unsuccessful wells are assets)

The *successful efforts* argument maintains that if six wells are drilled and only two strike oil, the exploration costs of the two successful wells are capitalized in the natural resources

---

[12] Financial Accounting Standards Board, *Statement of Financial Accounting Standards No. 19*, "Financial Accounting and Reporting by Oil and Gas Companies" (1977); *FASB Codification Topics 930 and 932;* International Accounting Standards Board, *International Financial Reporting Standard 6*, "Exploration for and Evaluation of Mineral Resources" (2004). IFRS cost classifications are slightly different from U.S. GAAP classifications. IFRS requires a clear and consistent accounting policy in the natural resource area involving judgment as to whether costs are capitalized or expensed. As of the writing of this text, the International Accounting Standards Board continues to consider natural resource accounting issues. Given that the U.S. GAAP rules described in this section yield asset measurements that can be justified by reasonable judgment and permit some choice in the capitalization versus expensing decision, one can conclude that U.S. GAAP and IFRS treatments are not likely to yield variations in natural resource valuations that are greater than the variations in valuations that occur in U.S. GAAP.

[13] Financial Accounting Standards Board, *Statement of Financial Accounting Standards No. 141*, "Accounting for Asset Retirement Obligations" (2001); *FASB Codification Topic 410;* International Accounting Standards Board, *International Accounting Standard 16*, "Property, Plant and Equipment" (1998).

account and the costs of the four unsuccessful wells are expensed. This argument is rational because only the successful wells yield probable future economic benefits (that is, the sale of oil) and, hence, should be called assets.

The *full costing* approach capitalizes exploration costs for all six wells as part of the natural resources account. The argument is that it was necessary to drill all of the wells in order to discover oil. The cost of exploring all six locations is deemed a necessary investment to generate future economic benefits. Therefore, all costs are capitalizable. This argument also is rational, and it has precedence in other areas of accounting. The costs of producing defective or spoiled output, for example, are included as part of the cost of producing good output if it is necessary to destroy or spoil some goods in the production of good output. For example, the rapid filling of beverage bottles involves some waste; however, the cost of the wasted beverage is capitalized as part of beverage inventory. An unexpected machine malfunction causing a material waste of the beverage is not necessary for successful beverage production and thus would be treated as an expense of the period.

Because reasonable arguments can be made to support successful efforts or full costing, both methods are used to account for natural resource exploration costs. Managers choose the method they believe is best for their company. Firms in the same industry frequently choose different approaches, and the resulting financial statements are not comparable across firms.

In the past, many financial statement users complained about the lack of comparability brought about by the availability of two such different accounting methods for the same transaction. At one time, the SEC (Securities and Exchange Commission) urged the accounting profession to decide on one method, and accounting policy makers chose the successful efforts method. Smaller companies then presented economic consequences arguments in favor of full costing for their firms. They argued that smaller companies would be less likely to raise capital with favorable terms because their income was not sufficiently large to absorb the expensing of unsuccessful wells. As an unfavorable consequence, oil exploration would decrease. In response to the political pressure from firms supporting full costing, the SEC rejected both the full costing and the successful efforts method in favor of a value-based measure, *RRA (reserve recognition accounting)*. RRA required the company to estimate the value of reserves which, in substance, required estimates of the magnitude of reserves and when the reserves would be extracted, how much it would cost to do so, when the goods would be sold, what the selling price would be, and what an appropriate interest rate would be to discount cash flows. Practical implementation problems eventually led the SEC to abandon RRA. Under intense political pressure, the FASB reversed its earlier position and once again allowed both the full costing and the successful efforts methods. Currently, the successful efforts method tends to be used by larger producers, while full costing tends to be used by smaller producers. Accordingly, the financial analyst should consider the differential treatment of exploration costs when comparing the profitability and risk of small and large firms in the extractive industry. Firms disclose their method choice in the accounting policies note to the financial statements.

Development Costs. Once the natural resource has been acquired and exploration has determined the location of deposits, the natural resource must be developed. Development costs are both tangible (for example, heavy equipment to drill and transport the resource) and intangible (for example, the costs of drilling wells and constructing mine shafts). Tangible development costs are capitalized as part of the equipment (or another property, plant, and equipment) account. Intangible development costs are capitalized as part of the natural resources account because the costs are not separable from the natural resource; for example, the costs associated with drilling a specific oil well cannot be moved to another well site.[14]

In summary, acquisition costs, exploration costs (of successful efforts or all efforts depending on the method used), and intangible development costs are capitalized as part of the natural resource account. Eventually, the costs are expensed as the natural resource is consumed. Depletion expense represents an estimate of the amount of consumption.

Costs of Acquiring Intangible Assets

Intangible assets include trade and brand names, trademarks, patents, copyrights, franchise rights, customer lists, and goodwill. Under both U.S. GAAP and IFRS, firms expense the cost of *internally* developing intangibles in the period incurred. The rationale for immediate expensing of such costs is the difficulty and uncertainty in ascertaining whether a particular expenditure results in a future benefit (that is, an asset) or not (an expense). Thus, although PepsiCo spends millions of dollars each year promoting its products, and brand names such as Pepsi and Frito-Lay® represent valuable economic "assets" of the firm, PepsiCo is not permitted to recognize an asset for the expenditures made to internally develop and maintain its brand names. The rationale for not recognizing the value of intangible assets such as brand names is that the error in estimating such valuations and management incentives to misuse discretion over the capitalization of such costs are so great as to offset the relevance of such estimates in the financial statements.

Firms capitalize as an asset the costs to acquire intangible assets from others because the existence of an external market transaction provides evidence of the existence of the intangible asset as well as a reliable measure of its value. The front matter in PepsiCo's 2008 Annual Report identifies 18 "mega-brands" controlled by PepsiCo, each generating more than $1 billion in annual sales. PepsiCo acquired many of these brands over the years through acquisitions. The third part of Note 4, "Property, Plant and Equipment and Intangible Assets" to PepsiCo's 2008 Financial Statements (Appendix A) shows that total capitalized brands equal $1,128 million. Using the same reasoning, in-process R&D is recorded at its fair value if arising from a corporate acquisition.

Because intangible assets, by definition, involve an inherently high degree of uncertainty regarding future economic benefits, most analysts prefer immediate expensing of all intangible assets.[15] Some analysts remove from the balance sheet any R&D costs, software development costs, and goodwill reported as assets before performing a financial analysis. By doing so, they argue that (1) quality of earnings information improves because the ability to manage earnings is reduced and (2) quality of balance sheet information improves because the balance sheet is cleansed of "soft" assets lacking physical substance. Some analysts also remove the costs of the intangible assets from retained earnings, as if intangible acquisition costs had been expensed over time. (Often the term *tangible equity* is used to describe the remaining shareholders' equity.) The financial analysis must be interpreted carefully, however, because the analyst may understate a firm's asset base by eliminating these assets—as is the case with PepsiCo's asset base because PepsiCo's balance sheet does not recognize brand names such as Pepsi and Frito-Lay® (among other important intangibles owned by the firm). Further, as discussed in more detail later in this chapter, many

---

[14] The accounting system captures costs incurred with respect to natural resources, including additional costs incurred to protect the environment. Some costs are incurred to minimize the environmental risk. For example, in the aftermath of the Exxon Valdez oil spill, double-hull oil tankers, which are more expensive to produce than single-hull tankers, are now used to transport Alaskan crude oil. The direct cost to Exxon to clean up the oil spill and indirect costs associated with tarnishing Exxon's reputation were substantial.

[15] For a stable or moderate-growth firm, the expense each year from immediate expensing is approximately the same as the expense from capitalizing expenditures and subsequently amortizing them.

intangibles acquired in a business combination receive balance sheet recognition because they have fair values accruing from a contractual right and may be separated and either leased or sold by the firm.

Goodwill

The most common setting for intangible asset recognition is in corporate acquisitions, where acquiring firms must allocate the purchase price to the assets acquired and liabilities assumed. Acquiring firms usually allocate the purchase price to the fair values of identifiable, tangible assets (inventories, land, and equipment) and liabilities first. They then allocate any excess purchase price to the fair values of specifically identifiable intangible assets such as patents, customer lists, and trade names, with the remainder allocated to goodwill. *Goodwill* is a residual and effectively represents all intangibles that are not specifically identifiable.

How should an analyst treat goodwill that appears on a firm's balance sheet? One approach is to follow financial reporting rules and view goodwill like any other productive asset in which the firm has invested (such as property, plant, and equipment). The justification for this approach is that the initial valuation of goodwill arose from an arm's-length investment in another corporate entity and simply represents valuable resources that accountants cannot identify and measure separately. The analyst should include these resources in the asset base on which management is expected to generate a reasonable return. If these valuable resources are not likely to last forever, amortization of their cost over some number of years is appropriate.

Another approach available to the analyst is to eliminate goodwill from assets and to subtract its amount from retained earnings or other common shareholders' equity accounts. The justification for this approach is based on an assumption that the amount allocated to goodwill from a corporate acquisition may occur simply because the firm paid too much and may not necessarily indicate the presence of resources with future service potential. Subtracting the amount allocated to goodwill from retained earnings suggests that the excess purchase price is a loss for the firm. Immediate subtraction of goodwill from retained earnings treats goodwill arising from an acquisition similar to goodwill developed internally. Later in this chapter, we discuss corporate acquisitions, and we address goodwill in more detail at that point.

What Choices Are Managers Making to Allocate Acquisition Costs to the Periods Benefited?

As discussed in the previous sections, some investing-like activities (R&D, pretechnological feasibility software costs, maintenance, and exploration costs) result in immediate recognition of expenses. However, most acquisition costs are capitalized and are subsequently expensed through the cost allocation processes of depreciation (for tangible fixed assets), amortization (for limited-life intangible assets), and depletion (for natural resources).

Managers make three primary choices and estimates when allocating acquisition costs of tangible assets and intangible assets to the periods benefited: they (1) choose an allocation method, (2) estimate useful life, and (3) estimate salvage value. Also, throughout the life of a long-lived asset, the book value must be tested for reasonableness relative to economic values, which may result in revaluing the asset for impairment (U.S. GAAP and IFRS) or appreciation (an option under IFRS). Such assessments often require a significant amount of judgment. Given the magnitude of long-lived assets on most balance sheets and the importance of understanding accounting judgments available to managers, the following subsections discuss these choices and estimates.

Useful Life for Long-Lived Tangible and Limited-Life Intangible Assets

Depreciation (amortization and depletion) is the process of allocating the historical cost of a long-lived asset less the estimate of its salvage value to the periods of its use in a rational and systematic manner. Both physical wear and tear and technological obsolescence affect the projection of the total useful life and salvage value. Because managers estimate expected useful lives, they have an opportunity to convey information to the firm's stakeholders about their expectations of the future usefulness of long-lived assets. However, the estimation process also provides an opportunity to introduce bias into reported earnings. For example, a manager wanting to report higher earnings could bias the estimated useful lives or salvage values of assets upward, which would result in lower annual depreciation expense.

Unfortunately, the disclosures that firms make about depreciable lives are usually not very helpful to the analyst in assessing a firm's aggressiveness in lengthening or shortening depreciable lives to manage earnings. The problems include the aggregated nature of the disclosures, the fact that firms usually disclose ranges of useful lives for asset categories, and the rare disclosure of expected salvage values.

Example 8

In this example, we demonstrate the process of estimating average lives for long-lived assets from note disclosures using PepsiCo financial disclosures. PepsiCo's Note 4, "Property, Plant and Equipment and Intangible Assets" (Appendix A), reports average useful lives of depreciable and amortizable assets, as follows:

Land and improvements	10–34 years
Buildings and improvements	20–44 years
Machinery and equipment, including fleet and software	5–14 years
Brands	5–40 years
Other identifiable intangibles	10–24 years

Because most firms in the U.S. use the straight-line depreciation method for financial reporting purposes, the analyst can estimate the average useful life of depreciable (and amortizable) assets by dividing average depreciable cost (gross, assuming zero salvage value) by depreciation expense for the year. The calculations for PepsiCo are as follows (amounts in millions):

	Property, plant, and equipment (excluding land and construction in progress)	Amortizable intangible assets
December 27, 2008	$19,911.0	$1,771.0
December 29, 2007	$19,048.0	$1,820.0
Average cost	$19,479.5	$1,795.5
Depreciation/amortization expense for 2008	$ 1,422.0	$ 64.0
Average total life = Average depreciable cost/ Annual depreciation or amortization expense	13.7 years	28.1 years

Even with such aggregated data, analysts can gain insight by comparing the average useful life of depreciable assets across firms. Firms with similar asset composition should have similar useful lives; if not, the analyst should assess why they differ. Analysts also need to question firms that report dramatic changes in the useful lives of depreciable assets over time.[16] Is the change because of assumption changes in the useful lives of the assets, has the composition of the firm's assets changed over time, or has the firm made the strategic decision to use assets differently? Firms choosing useful lives that accurately (and consistently) represent the period of time they expect to be able to use the assets report the highest-quality accounting data for depreciable assets.

Repeating the analysis for 2007 (using 2006 and 2007 data from PepsiCo's 2007 Annual Report) yields average total life estimates of 13.8 years for property, plant, and equipment and 29.3 years for amortizable intangible assets. Comparing these estimates to the estimates calculated for 2008 (13.7 and 28.1 years) shows the consistency of PepsiCo's total useful lives used in depreciation and amortization computations. The slight change in useful life for intangibles is immaterial. If PepsiCo had used 29.3 years life for the amortization computation in 2008, amortization expenses would have been $61.3 million (= $1,795.5/29.3) instead of $64.0 million reported in 2008. The $2.7 million pretax difference is less than four one-hundredths of one percent of the $7,021 million pretax income in 2008. The after-tax effect of this difference would have to be ten times higher to affect earnings per share by one cent.

Both U.S. GAAP and IFRS allow managers to classify certain intangible assets (such as perpetual brands and goodwill reported by PepsiCo in Note 4) as having an indefinite life; therefore, they are not amortized. These nonamortizable intangibles are assessed for impairment (discussed in a later section).

Cost Allocation (Depreciation/Amortization/Depletion) Method

Firms may allocate the acquisition costs over the useful life of the asset using *any* systematic and rational allocation method. The allocation of cost is charged to depreciation expense (for tangible fixed assets), amortization expense (for intangibles), or depletion expense (for natural resources) and is reported on the income statement.[17]

Most firms write off tangible long-lived assets evenly over their useful lives (straight-line method). Some firms write off larger amounts during the early years and smaller amounts in later years (accelerated depreciation methods). Nearly all firms amortize intangible assets using the straight-line method. Firms generally deplete natural resources using the straight-line method or in proportion to the amount of natural resource consumed (for example, number of board feet of lumber harvested relative to an estimate of the total amount of board feet of lumber in a forest). Regardless of the cost allocation method chosen, the total depreciation over an asset's life generally does not exceed acquisition costs (except in rare cases when firms revalue such assets to current fair values). Thus, the various depreciation methods differ only in the timing of expense, not in its total amount over time.

Virtually all firms in the U.S. use accelerated depreciation methods for tax reporting based on depreciable lives specified in the income tax law, which are usually shorter than the depreciable lives that firms use for financial reporting purposes. In countries where tax

---

[16] When a firm changes a useful life or salvage value estimate, it handles the change prospectively. That is, it simply depreciates the remaining book value over the remaining useful life. Financial Accounting Standards Board, *Statement of Financial Accounting Standards No. 154*, "Accounting Changes and Error Corrections" (2005*); FASB Codification Topic 250;* International Accounting Standards Board, *International Accounting Standard 16,* "Property, Plant and Equipment" (1998).

[17] If the long-lived asset is used in production, the depreciation is initially added to inventory as a product cost and then expensed as cost of goods sold when the inventory is sold.

laws heavily influence financial reporting (such as Germany, France, and Japan), many firms use accelerated depreciation methods for both financial and tax reporting. Thus, comparisons of U.S. firms with those of some other countries require the analyst to assess the effect of different depreciation methods and assumptions. To increases the comparability of firms across such different environments, the analyst must restate reported U.S. amounts to an accelerated basis or convert reported amounts for other countries to a straight-line basis.

The analyst can place U.S. firms on an accelerated depreciation basis using information in the income tax note. As Chapter 2 described, *Statement No. 109* requires firms to report in notes to the financial statements the portion of the deferred tax liability that is attributable to book versus tax depreciation timing differences at the beginning and end of the year.[18]

Example 9

In Note 5, "Income Taxes" (Appendix A), PepsiCo reports that the portion of its deferred tax liability attributable to property, plant, and equipment was $828.0 million on December 29, 2007, and $881.0 million on December 27, 2008. An increase in a deferred tax liability relating to differences in expensing procedure for book and tax purposes indicates that PepsiCo depreciated fixed assets faster for tax purposes than for book purposes. As a result, taxes are lower in the current period, but they will be higher in the future when depreciation for tax purposes falls below depreciation for financial reporting purposes (hence, the current period increase in the deferred tax liability). If the analyst wants to compare PepsiCo's profitability and risk to another company (foreign or otherwise) that uses accelerated methods of depreciation, he or she must convert key amounts for PepsiCo, including the asset PP&E (net) and net income, to an accelerated depreciation method basis or convert those amounts for the comparable firm to a straight-line basis. The following computations demonstrate the former approach, converting PepsiCo's amounts to an accelerated depreciation basis. (PepsiCo discloses a 35 percent federal statutory tax rate in Note 5. We use this rate in the computation that follows, which assumes that the depreciation differences arise primarily from U.S. operations.)

Conversion of PP&E (net) to an accelerated basis (amounts in millions):

PP&E (net) as reported at December 27, 2008, using book depreciation method		$11,663.0
Excess accumulated depreciation over time using tax method:		
Deferred tax liability related to excess depreciation (measured originally by multiplying the excess depreciation	$881.0	
by the tax rate) ÷ tax rate	÷ 0.35	(2,517.1)
PP&E (net) using tax depreciation method		$ 9,145.9

Because PepsiCo measures the deferred tax liability of $881.0 million by multiplying the excess tax depreciation over time by 35 percent, the excess accumulated tax depreciation over time ($2,517.1 million) can be obtained by dividing the deferred tax liability amount by 35 percent.

---

[18] Financial Accounting Standards Board, *Statement of Financial Accounting Standards No. 109*, "Accounting for Income Taxes" (1992); *FASB Codification Topic 740*. Chapter 2 provides an initial discussion of this statement.

Excess current depreciation expense using tax method:

Increase in deferred tax liability during the year ($881.0 − $828.0)	$ 53.0	
÷ tax rate	÷ 0.35	$ 151.4
Decrease in tax expense ($151.4 × 0.35)		(53.0)
Decrease in 2008 net income if tax depreciation method is used		$ 98.4

This latter computation relies on the idea that income is affected by the *change* in the deferred tax liability amount ($53.0 million), which, when divided by the tax rate, represents the excess tax depreciation expense if an accelerated method is used. If PepsiCo had used the tax method, it would have had a lower pretax income and, hence, a lower tax expense of $53.0 million. Thus, the effect of changing PepsiCo's book depreciation to a tax-based method is a decrease in 2008 net income of $98.4 million. This would represent an almost 2 percent decrease in 2008 net income.

Depreciation, amortization, and depletion also are reported as addbacks to net income in the operating section of the statement of cash flows because they reduce net income but are not cash outflows. In fact, for many firms, the depreciation addback is the largest single reconciling item between net income and cash flow from operations.

What Is the Relationship between the Book Values and Market Values of Long-Lived Assets?

Companies use the aforementioned depreciation choice and useful life and salvage value estimates to report long-lived operational assets at acquisition costs less the accumulated depreciation to date (adjusted acquisition cost). The use of acquisition-cost-based reporting rests on the presumption that such amounts are more objectively measurable than the fair values of fixed assets. Difficulties encountered in determining fair values include (1) the absence of active markets for many used fixed assets, particularly those specific to a particular firm's needs; (2) the need to identify comparable assets currently available in the market to value assets in place; and (3) the need to make assumptions about the effect of technological and other improvements when using the prices of new assets currently available on the market in the valuation process.

Nevertheless, accounting standards require firms to determine whether the net book values of long-lived assets reflect the economic reality of market values. In particular, accounting standards are concerned with how long-lived asset values must be tested for impairments and written down if impairment losses have occurred. The following sections examine the U.S. GAAP and IFRS standards related to reporting long-lived assets when book values and market values differ. To facilitate the discussion, the next three sections deal, in turn, with three basic types of long-lived operating assets: (1) long-lived assets subject to depreciation and amortization (land is in this category even though it is not depreciated), (2) intangible assets not subject to amortization because of indefinite lives, and (3) goodwill. Then, a fourth section addresses upward revaluations of long-lived assets under IFRS.

Impairment of Long-Lived Assets Subject to Depreciation and Amortization

The development of new technologies by competitors, changes in government regulations, changes in demographic trends, and other external factors may reduce the future benefits originally anticipated from long-lived assets. Firms are required to assess whether conditions exist implying that the carrying amounts of fixed assets are not recoverable, and if they are not, firms are to write down the assets to their fair values and recognize impairment losses in income from continuing operations.[19]

U.S. GAAP defines a carrying amount (that is, the book value at the moment of the impairment test) as not being recoverable if it is greater than the sum of the *undiscounted* cash flows expected from the asset's use and disposal. If an impairment charge is to be recorded because the asset's carrying amount is not recoverable, the charge equals the amount by which the carrying value exceeds the asset's fair value. Recognize that under U.S. GAAP, although the firm uses undiscounted future cash flows to decide whether an impairment charge is necessary, fair value is used to measure the actual impairment charge. Fair value is defined using the three-level FASB designation described in Chapters 2 and 6. Because of the difficulty of observing values of the same or similar assets in organized markets, firms often must estimate fair values by computing the present (*discounted*) value of expected cash flows from using the fixed asset (Level 3 inputs used in a valuation approach applying present value techniques).

In requiring firms to use undiscounted cash flows to test for impairment of long-lived tangible assets, U.S. standard setters reasoned that a loss had not occurred if the firm could recover in future cash flows an amount equal to or larger than the current book value. Accounting theorists and practitioners question the logic of using undiscounted, instead of discounted, cash flows in testing for impairment. In some cases, the economic value of the long-lived asset may decline below its carrying value but the firm would recognize no impairment because the *undiscounted* future cash flows from the asset exceed its carrying value.

IFRS uses rules that are more theoretically defensible. Firms are required to determine whether an impairment has occurred and to measure impairment by comparing the book value of the long-lived asset to the greater of (1) the fair value of the assets less estimated costs to *sell* the asset or (2) the value of the asset *in use* (which is the present value of estimated future cash flows from using the asset).

Example 10

Assume that a real estate company owns an apartment building that originally cost $20 million, with a current carrying amount of $15 million. The company originally expected to collect rents of $1.67 million each year for 30 years before selling the apartment complex for $8 million. Deteriorating neighborhood conditions, however, have caused the company to reassess the future rentals, especially given a recent appraisal that set a fair value for the apartment building at $10 million. The company now estimates that it will receive rentals of $1.35 million per year for 15 years and then will sell the building for $5 million. The company uses an 8 percent discount rate to compute the present value for this investment. Costs to sell are estimated at $300,000.

U.S. GAAP Treatment: Because total undiscounted future cash flows of $25.25 million [= ($1.35 × 15) + $5] exceed the carrying value of $15 million, the real estate company reports no impairment loss. In essence, the firm has suffered an economic loss but will not report any loss for financial reporting. If the total undiscounted future cash flows in this illustration were estimated to fall below the carrying value of $15 million, the real estate

---

[19] Financial Accounting Standards Board, *Statement of Financial Accounting Standards No. 144*, "Accounting for Impairment of Long-Lived Assets" (2001); *FASB Codification Topic 360;* International Accounting Standards Board, *International Accounting Standard 36*, "Impairment of Assets" (revised 2004).

company would compute an impairment loss as the difference between the carrying value and the fair market value of the apartment building (in this case, $10 million). The company would report the impairment loss of $5 million in income from continuing operations, and the apartment building would be recorded at the new carrying value of $10 million.

IFRS Treatment: Under IFRS, the greater of the asset's value in use and fair value from sale is identified first. Value in use is $13.1 million, obtained by using the 8 percent discount rate to compute the present value of a 15-year annuity of $1.35 million cash inflow plus the present value of $5 million received at the end of Year 15. The value from a sale is $9.7 million, the $10 million fair value less $0.3 million in disposal costs. The larger of the two, $13.1 million, is then compared to the carrying value of $15 million, and a $1.9 million impairment is recorded. The company would report an impairment loss of $1.9 million in income from continuing operations, and the apartment building would be recorded at the new carrying value of $13.1 million.

Impairment of Intangible Assets Not Subject to Amortization

For intangibles *not requiring* amortization (that is, intangible assets with an indefinite life), firms must test for asset impairment annually—or more frequently if events and circumstances indicate that the asset may be impaired. Unlike the impairment test for depreciable assets and amortizable intangible assets, U.S. GAAP defines impairment of intangible assets not subject to amortization as occurring when the fair value of the intangible asset is below its carrying amount. This approach is more defendable from a theoretical viewpoint because fair value is more closely related to discounted cash flows than to the undiscounted cash flows used in the impairment tests for limited-life assets. IFRS impairment tests for intangible assets not subject to amortization mirror its tests for depreciable and amortizable assets.

Impairment of Goodwill

The U.S. GAAP and IFRS goodwill impairment tests are similar. Both sets of standards view goodwill as not being separable from other assets and therefore require the impairment test to be conducted at the unit level, where several assets combine to produce future cash flows. U.S. GAAP (SFAS No. 142, FASB Codification Topic 350) defines a *reporting unit* as a segment or a component of a segment that is a business with separate financial information that management regularly reviews. IFRS (IAS 36) defines a *cash generating unit* as "the smallest identifiable group of assets that generates cash inflows that are largely independent of the cash inflows from other assets or groups of assets." The impairment test is basically a simulation of a transaction between the firm and an outsider in an organized market to reacquire the unit.

Example 11

Woods Co. acquires Golf Tech, Inc., on January 1, 2010, by paying $1,000,000 in cash. At the date of acquisition, the price is allocated as follows:[20]

Price paid	$1,000,000
Fair value of Golf Tech's long-lived tangible assets	(400,000)
Fair value of a brand name with an indefinite useful life	(100,000)
Goodwill	$ 500,000

---

[20] In an acquisition, the fair value transferred by the acquirer ($1,000,000 in this example) is assigned to the assets acquired, which are recorded at their fair values. The excess is recorded as goodwill. The acquisition process is discussed in greater detail later in the chapter.

One year later on December 31, 2010, Woods estimates the fair value of the Golf Tech unit to be $800,000. The fair value of Golf Tech's long-lived tangible assets is $400,000, and the fair value of the brand name is $70,000.

U.S. GAAP Treatment: Firms following U.S. GAAP would first apply impairment tests to its non-goodwill assets. The fair value of the brand name has declined by $30,000. Therefore, a $30,000 intangible asset impairment charge is reported by reducing the carrying value of the intangible asset to $70,000.

The second step in the process is to compare the carrying amount of the unit to the unit's fair value, as follows:

Fair value of Golf Tech unit at 12/31/09		$800,000
Carrying value of Golf Tech unit at 12/31/09		
Long-lived tangible assets	$400,000	
Brand name (after its reduction to fair value)	70,000	
Goodwill	500,000	$970,000

If the fair value of the unit exceeds the carrying amount, goodwill is deemed not to be impaired. However, in this example, the carrying value exceeds the fair value of the unit, so Wood's must measure the amount of goodwill impairment by simulating a reacquisition. The fair value of the unit is compared to the fair value of the identifiable assets to yield an implied goodwill, as follows:

Fair value of Golf Tech unit at 12/31/09		$800,000
Fair values of Golf Tech's assets other than goodwill at 12/31/09:		
Long-lived tangible assets	$400,000	
Brand name	70,000	(470,000)
Implied goodwill at 12/31/09		$330,000

Goodwill is written down from $500,000 to $330,000, and a $170,000 impairment loss is reflected in operating income. Exhibit 7.2 shows the brand name and goodwill impairment charges, which total $200,000.

EXHIBIT 7.2: SOLUTION TO EXAMPLE 11 ON GOODWILL IMPAIRMENT UNDER U.S. GAAP

Assets		=	Liabilities	+	Total Shareholders' Equity		
					CC	AOCI	RE
Brand Name	−30,000						Impairment
Goodwill	−170,000						Losses −200,000
Impairment Losses			200,000				
Brand Name					30,000		
Goodwill					170,000		

Note that the new carrying amounts for individual assets are as follows:

Long-lived tangible assets	$400,000
Brand name ($100,000 − $30,000 impairment)	70,000
Goodwill ($500,000 − $170,000 impairment)	330,000
Total new carrying value	$800,000

IFRS Treatment: Under IFRS, the recoverable amount of the assets is compared to their original carrying amounts. For long-lived tangible assets and brand names, the recoverable amount is the higher of fair value in use or from sale (less disposal costs). For goodwill, recoverable amount is the implied goodwill of $330,000 computed in the same way as previously illustrated for the U.S. GAAP treatment.

	Original Carrying Amount	Recoverable Amount
Long-lived tangible assets	$ 400,000	$400,000
Brand name	100,000	70,000
Goodwill	500,000	330,000
Total	$1,000,000	$800,000

The financial statement effects are the same as those shown in Exhibit 7.2. These amounts support the write-down of brand name and goodwill by $30,000 and $170,000, respectively.

It is clear from the example above that managers (and their valuation consultants) make several estimates of future cash flows or fair values to support a goodwill impairment charge. The analyst should consider several issues when assessing current profitability and predicting future earnings. First, the relatively unpredictable and volatile goodwill impairment charge has replaced the inherently certain and constant goodwill amortization charge. The analyst should examine a firm's past time series of goodwill impairment charges as well as the reasonableness of prices paid in recent acquisitions to forecast whether additional impairments are likely. Second, the analyst should attempt to determine whether the goodwill impairment charge is indicative of management performance or is due to uncontrollable external factors. Finally, the substantial estimation involved in goodwill impairments permits earnings management.

Example 12

The impairment of goodwill can occur shortly after an acquisition. In 2008, Nike acquired Umbro. Nike reports the following in its June 2009 10K:

Umbro Impairment

In accordance with FAS 142 "Goodwill and Other Intangible Assets," the Company performs annual impairment tests on goodwill and intangible assets with indefinite lives in the fourth quarter of each fiscal year, or when events occur or circumstances change that would, more likely than not, reduce the fair value of a reporting unit or intangible assets with an indefinite life below its carrying value. As a result of a significant decline in global consumer demand and continued weakness in the macroeconomic environment, as well as decisions by Company management to adjust planned investment in the Umbro brand, the Company concluded that sufficient indicators of impairment existed to require the performance of an interim assessment of Umbro's goodwill and indefinite lived intangible assets as of February 1, 2009. Accordingly, the Company performed the first step of the goodwill impairment assessment for Umbro by comparing the estimated fair value of Umbro to its carrying amount, and determined there was a potential impairment of goodwill as the carrying amount exceeded the estimated fair value. Therefore, the Company performed the second step of the assessment which compared the implied fair value of Umbro's goodwill to the book value of goodwill. The implied fair value of goodwill is determined by allocating the estimated fair value of Umbro to all of its assets and liabilities, including both recognized and unrecognized intangibles, in the same manner as goodwill was determined in the original business combination.

The Company measured the fair value of Umbro by using an equal weighting of the fair value implied by a discounted cash flow analysis and by comparisons with the market values of similar publicly traded companies. The Company believes the blended use of both models compensates for the inherent risk associated with either model if used on a stand-alone basis, and this combination is indicative of the factors a market participant would consider when performing a similar valuation. The fair value of Umbro's indefinite-lived trademark was estimated using the relief from royalty method, which assumes that the trademark has value to the extent that Umbro is relieved of the obligation to pay royalties for the benefits received from the trademark. The assessments of the Company resulted in the recognition of impairment charges of $199.3 million and $181.3 million related to Umbro's goodwill and trademark, respectively, during the third quarter ended February 28, 2009. A deferred tax benefit of $54.5 million was recognized as a result of the trademark impairment charge. In addition to the above impairment analysis, the Company determined an equity investment held by Umbro was impaired, and recognized a charge of $20.7 million related to the impairment of this investment. These charges are included in the Company's "Other" category for segment reporting purposes.

The discounted cash flow analysis calculated the fair value of Umbro using management's business plans and projections as the basis for expected cash flows for the next twelve years and a 3% residual growth rate thereafter. The Company used a weighted average discount rate of 14% in its analysis, which was derived primarily from published sources as well as our adjustment for increased market risk given current market conditions. Other significant estimates used in the discounted cash flow analysis include the rates of projected growth and profitability of Umbro's business and working capital effects. The market valuation approach indicates the fair value of Umbro based on a comparison of Umbro to publicly traded companies in similar lines of business. Significant estimates in the market valuation approach include identifying similar companies with comparable business factors such as size, growth, profitability, mix of revenue generated from licensed and direct distribution and risk of return on investment.

Holding all other assumptions constant at the test date, a 100 basis point increase in the discount rate would reduce the adjusted carrying value of Umbro's net assets by 12%.

Note that Nike uses a combination of models (discounted cash flow analysis and market comparables) because it argues that these models are used by market participants. Also note the assumptions to develop the projections used in the discounted cash flow analysis, the use of a weighted average discount rate, and the sensitivity analysis performed. Return to this example after studying financial statement forecasts and valuation covered in Chapters 10–14.

If a company reports an impairment of any kind, net income is reduced. However, impairments are not cash outflows. Accordingly, impairments, if any, are added back to net income in the operating section of the statement of cash flows.

IFRS Treatment of Upward Asset Revaluations

Under U.S. GAAP, upward revaluations of long-lived assets are not permitted. However, IFRS gives firms the option to revalue upward both intangible and tangible long-lived assets.[21] When fair value remains above original acquisition cost, upward and downward revaluations are reported as other comprehensive income and are accumulated in the shareholders' equity section of the balance sheet. The account typically used in the other comprehensive income classification is "Revaluation Surplus." If fair value is less than or equal to cost, reversals of previous downward revaluations (that were reported as losses on the income statement) are treated as gains on the income statement.

Example 13

Assume that a French company following IFRS has land originally costing €2,000,000. At the end of the next four years, the land is worth the following:

2009:	€2,500,000
2010:	€2,300,000
2011:	€1,900,000
2012:	€2,000,000

Exhibit 7.3 shows the effects of upward and downward revaluations of the asset.

Fair value increases above original acquisition cost in 2009, causing an upward revaluation of the land and an increase in comprehensive income (OCI) but not net income. The increase is recognized in accumulated other comprehensive income in the shareholders'

EXHIBIT 7.3: SOLUTION TO EXAMPLE 13 ON UPWARD ASSET REVALUATIONS UNDER IFRS

Assets		=	Liabilities	+	Total Shareholders' Equity		
					CC	AOCI	RE
2009:							
Land	+500,000					Unrealized Gains +500,000	
2010:							
Land	−200,000					Unrealized Gains −200,000	
2011:							
Land	−400,000					Unrealized Gains −300,000	Unrealized Losses −100,000
2012:							
Land	+100,000						Unrealized Gains +100,000

2009:			
Land		500,000	
Unrealized Gains (OCI)			500,000
2010:			
Unrealized Gains (OCI)		200,000	
Land			200,000
2011:			
Unrealized Gains (OCI)		300,000	
Unrealized Losses (NI)		100,000	
Land			400,000
2012:			
Land		100,000	
Unrealized Gains (NI)			100,000

---

[21] International Accounting Standards Board, *International Accounting Standard 16*, "Property, Plant and Equipment" (1998).

equity section. In 2010, the land is revalued downward, causing a partial reversal in the accumulated unrealized gains. Such reversals of previously unrealized gains are reported as losses in other comprehensive income and reduce accumulated other comprehensive income on the balance sheet as long as fair value is greater than original acquisition cost. In 2011, fair value falls below original acquisition cost, causing a reversal of the remainder of the accumulated unrealized gains in accumulated other comprehensive income via the recognition in other comprehensive income of €300,000 unrealized loss and recognition in net income of €100,000 unrealized loss. The land recovers its value in 2012, and the reversal of the 2011 unrealized loss reported in net income is reported in 2012 net income as an unrealized gain.

Firms must choose the class of asset to which revaluations will apply and then perform the revaluations on a regular basis. The choice is irrevocable, and as mentioned previously, the fair value of nonfinancial assets in active markets is difficult to obtain and the process takes a great deal of time and effort. As a result, few firms choose the upward revaluation option.[22]

When Will the Long-Lived Assets Be Replaced?

Forecasting future financial statements requires expectations of future tangible asset acquisitions for both replacement of existing production or service capacity and growth in capacity. Although the analyst must rely on knowledge of industry conditions and firm strategy to estimate capital expenditure growth, he or she can make two computations to gain a better understanding of when existing long-lived assets must be replaced. Because the amount of accumulated depreciation depends on the number of years for which depreciation has been taken, the *average age of depreciable assets* equals the average amount of accumulated depreciation divided by depreciation expense. Based on PepsiCo's Note 4, "Property, Plant and Equipment and Intangible Assets" (Appendix A), disclosures, $0.5 \times (\$10,889 + \$10,668)/ \$1,422$ equals 7.6 years average age. Also, the *proportion of depreciable assets consumed* equals total accumulated depreciation divided by acquisition cost. For PepsiCo, $\$10,889/\$19,911 = 54.7\%$. In the same vein, the analyst also can estimate the *remaining useful life* by dividing net depreciable PP&E by annual depreciation expense. For PepsiCo, $(\$19,911 - \$10,889)/\$1,422 = 6.3$ years average remaining life. The analyst can track average age and proportion consumed through time and compare them to competitors' numbers to ascertain whether assets are getting older on average and whether they are at a point where large capital expenditures are necessary to replace them. Also, older assets and high proportion consumed provides an indication that the firm is in a later stage of average product life cycle.

When older assets are taken out of service and scrapped, any remaining book value must be removed from the accounts and reported as a realized loss on disposal in operating income. Cash inflow from a sale of long-lived assets reduces the loss or causes a gain to be reported. These cash inflows are reported in the investing section of the statement of cash flows. Gains and losses on the sale must be adjusted out of operating income so that the total amount of cash inflow from the sale can be reported as an investing cash flow.

Assets also may be traded in for newer assets. Both U.S. GAAP and IFRS require firms to record the new asset acquired at fair value with resulting gains and losses on trade-ins reported in net income. An exception to this rule occurs if the transaction lacks commercial

---

[22] A final category of long-lived assets exists that is unique to IFRS. Biological assets are living plants and animals that will be transformed into items for sale, agricultural produce, or additional biological assets. For example, in the production of wine, the vintner has vines that produce grapes that ultimately produce wine. The vines are the biological asset. Unless fair value is clearly unreliable, biological assets are reported at fair value less estimated disposal costs at each balance sheet date, with all value changes reflected in current net income. International Accounting Standards Board, *International Accounting Standard 41*, "Agriculture" (2001).

substance, in which case the acquired asset is recorded at the book value of the assets surrendered (including the traded-in asset) and liabilities assumed with no recognition of gain or loss.[23]

Because most gains and losses on asset dispositions are reported in net income of the period, analysts must be aware of the earnings management opportunity afforded by disposal timing. Analysts must decide whether these gains and losses are persistent by looking at the past history of the firm's gain and loss reporting.

Summary

The preceding discussion suggests that an assessment of accounting quality in the area of investments in long-lived assets is determined by answering the following questions:

1. Are capitalized acquisition costs justified? Were assets created, or should the costs be expensed? Are the firm's capitalization policies clear and in line with competitors and economic reality? Were some economic assets created even though accounting rules require expense treatement?

2. Are useful lives and salvage values reasonable given the economic service and value of the assets? Are they in line with competitors? Can changes in average useful lives be explained by strategy or economic reality, or do the useful life changes appear to be opportunistic?

3. Are depreciation methods consistent with the expected economic lives of the assets? Are they similar to useful lives used by competitors with similar assets? Are methods frequently changed?

4. Are asset impairment charges consistent with the firm's economic environment? Are the charges transitory or do they occur frequently? Are asset impairment charges or IFRS upward revaluations based on reliable fair value estimates?

The analyst should understand the firm's accounting policy in the long-lived asset area. The choices that managers make can convey a wealth of information to financial statement users, but this freedom also permits managers to bias or manipulate the financial statements through manipulated accounting choices. The analyst should pay particular attention to changes in estimates used in the depreciation and amortization process and the reasons for and timing of asset impairment charges.

INVESTMENTS IN SECURITIES

Investments in a firm's own operational assets generate profits reflected in operating revenues, expenses, gains, and losses. Firms also may invest in the securities underlying the operations of other firms, such as common stock and long-term debt, thus acquiring claims to the returns from other firms' operations. In either case, the investment assets acquired increase the ROA denominator and profits from the investments increase both the denominator (assets) and numerator (net income) in computations of ROA. This section examines the accounting, reporting, and analysis issues surrounding investments in securities.

---

[23] Financial Accounting Standards Board, *Statement of Financial Accounting Standards No. 153*, "Exchanges of Nonmonetary Assets" (2004); *FASB Codification Topic 845;* International Accounting Standards Board, *International Accounting Standard 16*, "Property, Plant and Equipment" (revised 1998). A lack of commercial substance is evidenced by relatively little change in the cash flows to the firm after it replaces the asset. This provision exists to remove the past abuse of asset trading rules in which two firms trade nearly identical assets with book values below their fair values simply to record the gain on the difference between fair and book value rather than for any commercial reason.

Firms invest in the securities of governments, corporations, variable-interest entities, joint ventures, and partnerships for a variety of reasons: to earn interest or dividends; to speculate on potential price appreciation of the securities; to lock in high yields on longer-term debt securities; to exert significant influence or gain control of an important raw materials supplier, customer, technological innovator, or other valued entity; or to achieve other strategic purposes. The appropriate accounting for investments depends on the level of "controlling financial interest" by the firm making the investment, determined by the following:

1. What percentage of ownership one firm has in another entity
2. Whether the reporting firm is deemed the primary beneficiary of the investment it has made in a VIE (variable-interest entity), as defined in FASB *Interpretation No. 46R*.

The following sections discuss each criterion in turn.

Percentage of Ownership

Exhibit 7.4 identifies three types of investments based on percentage of voting stock ownership, and Exhibit 7.5 summarizes the accounting and reporting for each type of investment. The types of investments are (1) minority, passive; (2) minority, active; and (3) majority, active.

Minority, Passive Investments

Firms often acquire some stake in the debt securities or shares of capital stock of another corporation for the anticipated interest or dividends and capital gains. The percentage that a firm owns of another corporation's voting shares is not so large that the acquiring company can control or exert significant influence over the other company, and the investing firm is not deemed the VIE's primary beneficiary as defined by *Interpretation No. 46R* (discussed in a later section). Investments in debt securities, preferred stock, or common stock when the firm holds less than 20 percent of the voting stock are minority, passive investments.

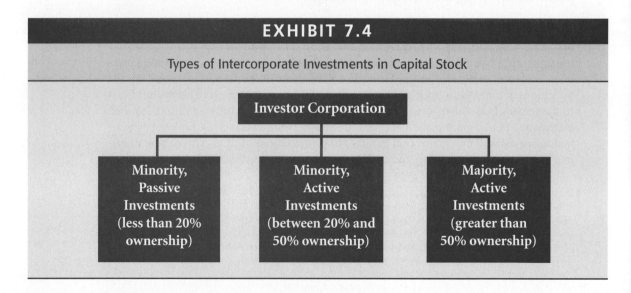

EXHIBIT 7.4

Types of Intercorporate Investments in Capital Stock

Investor Corporation

| Minority, Passive Investments (less than 20% ownership) | Minority, Active Investments (between 20% and 50% ownership) | Majority, Active Investments (greater than 50% ownership) |

EXHIBIT 7.5

Reporting Investments in Securities in the Financial Statements

Financial Statement	Minority, Passive Investments*	Minority, Active Investments*	Majority, Active Investments
Income Statement	Interest and dividend revenue	Investor's share of investee's net income	Individual revenues and expenses of investee minus the noncontrolling (that is, minority) interest's share of investee's net income included in consolidated net income
	Unrealized increases and decreases in the market value of securities classified as trading securities		
	Realized gains and losses on sales of securities		
Balance Sheet	Marketable securities and investments in securities reported at market value (except debt securities held to maturity reported at amortized acquisition cost)	Investments reported at acquisition cost plus investor's cumulative share of investee's net income minus dividends received from investee since acquisition	Investment in securities account eliminated and replaced by investee's individual assets and liabilities in preparing consolidated balance sheet
	Unrealized increases and decreases in market value of securities classified as available for sale included in Accumulated Other Comprehensive Income in the shareholders' equity section of the balance sheet		Noncontrolling interest's claim on investee's net assets shown in the shareholders' equity section of consolidated balance sheet
Statement of Cash Flows	Cash received from interest and dividends included in cash flow from operations; cash flows associated with purchases and sales included in cash flows from investing	Cash received from interest and dividends included in cash flow from operations. Cash flows associated with purchases and sales included in cash flows from investing	Individual cash flows from operating, investing, and financing activities of investee included in consolidated statement of cash flows

*The accounting for minority, passive and minority, active investments illustrated in the exhibit assumes that the investing firm is not a VIE primary beneficiary as defined by FASB Interpretation No. 46R. If the investing firm is a VIE primary beneficiary, the firm must follow the reporting for investments in securities categorized as majority, active investments.

A summary of the accounting for minority, passive investments follows: [24]

1. Firms initially record investments at acquisition cost.
2. Revenues each period equal interest and dividends received or receivable.
3. The accounting at the end of each period depends on the type of security and the firm's ability and intent to hold it. The three classifications of securities are:
   a. Debt securities for which a firm has a positive intent and ability to *hold to maturity*.
   b. Debt and equity securities held as *trading* securities.
   c. Debt and equity securities held as *available for sale*.
4. Firms must account for debt securities they expect to hold until maturity at amortized acquisition cost. That is, the firm must amortize any difference between the acquisition cost and maturity value of these debt securities as an adjustment to interest revenue over the life of the debt. This accounting is equivalent to the effective interest method demonstrated in Chapter 6. While the creditor shows bonds payable and interest expense in its financial records, the investor shows an investment in bonds and interest revenue. Firms report all other debt and equity securities at fair value at the end of each period. The reporting of any unrealized holding gain or loss depends on the purpose of holding the securities. If a firm actively buys and sells securities to take advantage of short-term differences or changes in market values, the firm will classify the securities as trading securities, a current asset on the balance sheet. Commercial banks, for example, often trade securities in different capital markets worldwide to take advantage of temporary differences in market prices. Manufacturers, retailers, and other nonfinancial firms occasionally invest funds for trading purposes, but such situations are unusual. Firms include unrealized holding gains and losses on trading securities in net income each period. Firms classify debt and equity securities that do not fit one of these first two categories (debt securities held to maturity and trading securities) as securities available for sale, including them as either current or noncurrent assets depending on the expected holding period. Unrealized holding gains or losses on securities available for sale are not included in net income each period; instead, they appear as a component of other comprehensive income, labeled Unrealized Holding Gain or Loss on Securities Available for Sale. The cumulative unrealized holding gain or loss on securities available for sale appears in the shareholders' equity section of the balance sheet as part of accumulated other comprehensive income.
5. When a firm sells a trading security, it recognizes the difference between the selling price and the book value (that is, the market value at the end of the most recent accounting period prior to sale) as a gain or loss in measuring net income. When a firm sells a security classified as available-for-sale, it recognizes the difference between the selling price and the acquisition cost of the security (or amortized cost if the available-for-sale security is a bond) as a realized gain or loss on the income

---

[24] U.S. GAAP and IFRS are consistent in the accounting and reporting of minority, passive investments. Relevant standards of investments representing passive investment (minority, passive investments) are *Statement of Financial Accounting Standards No. 115,* "Accounting for Certain Investments in Debt and Equity Securities" (1993) (referred to as *Statement No. 115); FASB Codification Topic 320;* International Accounting Standards Board, *International Accounting Standard 39,* "Financial Instruments: Recognition and Measurement" (revised 2003); International Accounting Standards Board, *International Financial Reporting Standard 7,* "Financial Instruments: Disclosure" (2005). Two key differences exist: (1) Under U.S. GAAP, unless the firm is a broker/dealer, an investment company, an insurance company, or a defined benefit plan, *unlisted* equity securities are generally carried at cost unless impaired or the fair value option is chosen, while IFRS simply requires reliably measurable fair value. (2) U.S. GAAP distinguishes between a debt securities (for example, a bond) and a loan (for example, a promissory note) and limits SFAS 115 treatment to securities, while IFRS makes no such distinction.

statement. At the time of sale, the firm must remove any amount in the shareholders' equity account, accumulated other comprehensive income, for the unrealized holding gain or loss related to that security by recognizing it in current period other comprehensive income; the realized gain or loss is then recognized in retained earnings through its net income effect.

Example 14

To understand these concepts, consider the following illustration of the accounting for investments by James Company. James had no equity investments prior to the transactions indicated below.

During 2010, James Company purchased the following common stocks:

Andrew Company	10,000 shares @ $5/sh.	$50,000	
Ball Company	5,000 shares @ $4/sh.	20,000	
Edwards Company	2,000 shares @ $6/sh.	12,000	
Watts Company	3,000 shares @ $20/sh.	60,000	$142,000
Porter Company	10,000 shares @ $3/sh.	$30,000	
Moore Company	10,000 shares @ $2/sh.	20,000	50,000
			$192,000

James intends to hold the Andrew, Ball, Edwards, and Watts shares as trading securities while holding the Porter and Moore shares as available-for-sale for an indefinite period. James does not have significant influence with any of the companies. During 2010 and 2011, James received $25,000 and $20,000, respectively, in dividends from the stock investments. James sold the investment in Watts Company in 2011 for $62,000. At the end of 2010 and 2011, market values were as follows:[25]

	2010	2011
Andrew	$ 30,000	$55,000
Ball	20,000	23,000
Edwards	10,000	10,000
Watts	63,000	0
Total	$123,000	$88,000
Porter	$ 25,000	$20,000
Moore	30,000	22,000
Total	$ 55,000	$42,000

Because James has no significant influence with the investee companies, James records these investments using the market method. In the statement of cash flows (see Exhibit 7.6), purchases and sales of investments in available-for-sale securities ($50,000 purchase in this

---

[25] Note that in this example, James holds three of the trading securities over a two-year period. By definition, a trading security is held for a short period of time (for example, 90 days). A security that is held for two years should not be classified as trading. However, the purpose of this problem is to compare and contrast the accounting for trading and available-for-sale equity security investments. Accordingly, the trading securities are artificially held over two periods so that you can compare and contrast the accounting for trading and available-for-sale equity security investments.

EXHIBIT 7.6

James Company Statement of Cash Flows (cash outflows in parentheses)

	2010	2011
OPERATING ACTIVITIES (DIRECT METHOD)		
Dividends received	$ 25,000	$20,000
Investments in trading securities	(142,000)	
Sales of trading securities		62,000
INVESTING ACTIVITIES		
Investments in available-for-sale securities	(50,000)	
Net Change in Cash	$(167,000)	$82,000

example) are listed in the investing activities section and purchases and sales of investments in trading securities ($142,000 purchase in this example) are listed in the operating activities section. Dividends received on investments accounted for under the market method are reported as revenues on the income statement, and U.S. GAAP requires that cash receipts from dividends ($25,000 and $20,000 in the two years) are reported in the operating activities section.[26]

The balance sheet (see Exhibit 7.7) shows the effects of the investments under alternative classifications. Because the available-for-sale securities are held for an indefinite period, they are classified as long-term assets. Alternatively, they could be classified as current assets if management's intent was to hold them for only a short period or to sell them whenever needed. The trading securities are classified as current. The cash balance reflects the cumulative effect of the change in cash reported in the statement of cash flows.

The investment in equity securities amounts reported in the balance sheet are determined by an analysis of the costs and fair values of the two portfolios of investments in trading and available-for-sale securities at each balance sheet date, as follows:

Trading Securities:	Costs and Fair Values in Thousands			
	December 31, 2010		December 31, 2011	
	Cost	Fair Value	New Basis	Fair Value
Andrew	$ 50	$ 30	$30	$55
Ball	20	20	20	23
Edwards	12	10	10	10
Watts	60	63	—	—
Totals	$142	$123	$60	$88
(Loss) gain reported on income statement as unrealized	$(19)		$28	

---

[26] IFRS permits reporting dividend receipts in the investing section of the statement of cash flows.

Available-for-Sale Securities:	Costs and Fair Values in Thousands			
	December 31, 2010		December 31, 2011	
	Cost	Fair Value	New Basis	Fair Value
Porter	$30	$25	$ 30	$20
Moore	20	30	20	22
Totals	$50	$55	$ 50	$42
Unrealized gain (loss) reported on balance sheet in shareholders' equity as accumulated other comprehensive income	$ 5		$ (8)	
Change from prior year reported in other comprehensive income as unrealized gain (loss)	$ 5		$(13)	

In the current assets section of the balance sheet, investments in trading equity securities are reported at their December 31, 2010, and December 31, 2011, fair values of $123,000 and $88,000, respectively. In the long-term ivestments section, the investments in available-for-sale equity securities also are reported at fair values as of December 31, 2010, and December 31, 2011, at $55,000 and $42,000, respectively.

The year-to-year fluctuations in the trading security fair values, a $19,000 unrealized loss in 2010 and a $28,000 unrealized gain in 2011, are reported in the income statement

EXHIBIT 7.7

James Company End-of-Period Balance Sheet (Effects of Investments Only)

	2010	2011
CURRENT ASSETS		
Cash	$(167,000)	$(85,000)
Investments in trading securities at fair value	123,000	88,000
LONG-TERM INVESTMENTS		
Investments in available-for-sale securities at fair value	55,000	42,000
Net effect on assets	$ 11,000	$ 45,000
SHAREHOLDERS' EQUITY		
Retained earnings (net effect in income of equity investments, ignoring income taxes)*	$ 6,000	$ 53,000
Accumulated other comprehensive income		
Cumulative unrealized gain (loss) on available-for-sale securities at fair value	5,000	(8,000)
Net Effect on Shareholders' Equity	$ 11,000	$ 45,000

*See income statement in Exhibit 7.8.

EXHIBIT 7.8

James Company Income Statement Effects

	2010	2011
Other Revenues, (Expenses), Gains, and (Losses)		
Dividend revenue	$ 25,000	$ 20,000
Unrealized gain (loss) on trading securities at fair value	(19,000)	28,000
Realized loss on sale of trading securities		(1,000)
Net Income Effect	$ 6,000	$ 47,000

James Company Statement of Comprehensive Income Effects

(Ignoring income tax effects)	2010	2011
Effect on net income (see income statement effects above)	$ 6,000	$ 47,000
Other comprehensive income		
Unrealized gain (loss) on available-for-sale securities	5,000	(13,000)
Comprehensive Income Effect	$ 11,000	$ 34,000

(Exhibit 7.8). Available-for-sale securities have a cumulative adjustment from cost to fair value reported in the accumulated other comprehensive income section of the owners' equity section (instead of in net income and retained earnings) because the current year's change is reported as other comprehensive income.

Dividend income is reported in each of the two years. A realized loss on sale of the Watts Company trading equity securities also is reported in 2011. The gain is computed by comparing the new basis (that is, the fair value at the end of 2010) to the selling price, as follows:

Sales price	$ 62,000
December 31, 2010 basis of Watts Company securities	(63,000)
Realized loss on sale	$ (1,000)

The reporting of unrealized gains and losses on available-for-sale securities in owners' equity rather than income has the advantage of deferring short-term value fluctuations on longer-term transactions. Keeping these gains and losses out of current income is a reasonable approach because the intent is not to liquidate in the short run. However, earnings management opportunities are created by the special treatment afforded available-for-sale securities: "winners" can be sold, and "losers" can be held in the portfolio. This allows realized gains to be reported as income while unrealized losses as a component of owners' equity are deferred. For example, suppose a company made two recent investments in equity securities classified as available-for-sale. Both were purchased for $10,000. Investment A has appreciated to $11,000 during the current period, and Investment B has declined in fair value to $9,500. If the company wanted to report more income during the current period, Investment A could be sold at a gain of $1,000. Otherwise, the $1,000 would be disclosed as an unrealized gain in the shareholder's equity section. Similar discretion to generate a loss exists with respect to Investment B. Comprehensive income would not be affected by the discretion indicated in this example. Available-for-sale gains and losses, realized or unrealized, are part of comprehensive income.

Exhibit 7.9 presents journal entries.

EXHIBIT 7.9: JOURNAL ENTRIES

2010 purchase of investments		
Investments in Trading Securities	142,000	
Investments in Available-for-Sale Securities	50,000	
Cash		192,000
2010 dividend receipts		
Cash	25,000	
Dividend Revenue		25,000
12/31/10 adjustments to fair value		
Unrealized Loss on Adjustment of Trading		
Securities to Fair Value	19,000	
Investments in Trading Securities		19,000
Investments in Available-for-Sale Securities	5,000	
Cumulative Unrealized Loss/Gain on		
Adjustment of Available-for-Sale		
Securities to Fair Value (OCI)		5,000
2011 dividend receipts		
Cash	20,000	
Dividend Revenue		20,000
2011 sale of Watts Company securities		
Cash	62,000	
Realized Loss on Sale of Trading Securities	1,000	
Investment in Trading Securities		63,000
12/31/11 adjustments to fair value		
Investments in Trading Securities	28,000	
Unrealized Gain on Adjustment of		
Trading Securities to Fair Value		28,000
Unrealized Loss/Gain on		
Adjustments of Available-for-Sale		
Securities to Fair Value (OCI)	13,000	
Investments in Available-for-Sale		
Securities		13,000

The different treatment given to unrealized gains and losses on available-for-sale securities in net income versus other comprehensive income creates the need to *recycle* realized gains and losses through net income when an available-for-sale security is sold. Extending Example 14, assume that the portfolio of available-for-sale securities was sold during 2012 for $42,000, the portfolio's fair value at December 31, 2011. At that date, the portfolio had a cost of $50,000 and the accumulated comprehensive loss reported in shareholders' equity was $8,000 to reflect the downward valuation of the portfolio. When the portfolio is sold, the loss of $8,000 is realized and reported in (recycled through) net income and then included in retained earnings. The accumulated other comprehensive loss of $8,000 is removed from shareholders' equity by being recognized as a gain in 2012 other comprehensive income. Therefore, the unrealized fair value gains and losses flow through accumulated other comprehensive income (described in Chapter 2 as a temporary "holding tank") until they are realized in cash, at which time they flow through net income and ultimately into retained earnings. Because the realized loss is reported in net income and the decrease in the accumulated other comprehensive loss also is reported in other comprehensive income, the two income effects cancel each other, avoiding double counting in comprehensive income. In other words, comprehensive income reflects fair value gains and losses in the available-for-sale portfolio when they occur during the first two years, not when the securities are sold.

Held-to-Maturity Investments in Debt Securities

Debt securities do not convey voting rights, so controlling influence is not an issue. Therefore, accounting for debt securities classified as trading and available-for-sale parallels the rules for investments in equity securities. Interest revenue determined using the effective interest method illustrated in Chapter 6 is reported on the income statement, and debt amortization is added back to net income in the case of a discount in the operating section of the statement of cash flows (amortization of a premium is deducted from net income in the operating section). At each reporting date, the debt securities are marked-to-market (that is, reported at fair value).

Held-to-maturity debt securities are investments for which managers have the intent and ability to hold to maturity. (Note that "maturity" does not necessarily imply a long-term holding period. If a held-to-maturity debt security is due to mature within one year, it is reported as a current asset.) While intent is quite subjective, ability is less subjective. If, for example, a company has a large liability coming due before the debt investment matures, the investment may have to be liquidated in order to extinguish the liability. Thus, the matching of maturities of assets and liabilities central to financial management is important in documenting the ability to hold to maturity. Held-to-maturity debt investments are reported at amortized cost at each balance sheet date. Standard setters have concluded that short-run fluctuations in market value are less relevant in predicting the level and riskiness of cash flows because the debt security will not be sold before it matures and, hence, will not be subject to the risk of short-run market fluctuations. Accordingly, held-to-maturity debt securities are *not* marked-to-market on the balance sheet, but fair values are *disclosed* in the notes.

Example 15

PepsiCo reports $213 million of short-term investments in the Current Assets section of its December 27, 2008 Consolidated Balance Sheet (Appendix A). In the MD&A discussion titled "Our Liquidity and Capital Resources" (Appendix B), PepsiCo discusses short-term investment activity, and PepsiCo's Statement of Cash Flows (Appendix A) confirms the discussion by reporting that net sales of short-term investments generated more than $1 billion in 2008. Note 10, "Financial Instruments" (Appendix A), provides a list of all of PepsiCo's financial assets, but it does not provide a direct explanation of the composition of the $213 million included in short-term investments. The $98 million relates to short-term investments in index funds that, due to very short maturities, approximate market value. The $41 million is classified as available-for-sale securities. The market values of these securities fell during 2008. The Comprehensive Income Statement provided as part of the Consolidated Statement of Shareholders' Equity reports a $21 million unrealized loss on these securities, net of tax.

Example 16

Qualcomm Incorporated develops, manufactures, and markets digital wireless telecommunications products and services. Qualcomm describes its accounting policy for marketable securities in the notes accompanying its 2008 Form 10-K, which follows. (Exhibit 7.10 provides a portion of the note disclosure.)

> *Marketable Securities.* The appropriate classification of marketable securities is determined at the time of purchase, and such designation is reevaluated as of each balance sheet date. Available-for-sale securities are stated at fair value as determined by the most recently traded price of each security at the balance sheet date. For securities that may not have been actively traded in a given period, fair value is determined using matrix pricing and other valuation techniques. The net unrealized gains or losses on available-for-sale securities are reported as a component of other comprehensive income (loss), net of tax. The specific identification method is used to compute the realized gains and losses on debt and equity securities.

EXHIBIT 7.10

Qualcomm Incorporated Marketable Securities Note from 2008 Form 10-K
Available-for-sale securities were comprised as follows (in millions):

	Cost	Unrealized Gains	Unrealized Losses	Fair Value
September 28, 2008				
Equity securities	$2,810	$ 90	$(283)	$2,617
Debt securities	6,966	12	(166)	6,812
	$9,776	$ 102	$(449)	$9,429
September 30, 2007				
Equity securities	$2,941	$ 492	$ (43)	$3,390
Debt securities	6,042	18	(46)	6,014
	$8,983	$ 510	$ (89)	$9,404

The following table shows the gross unrealized losses and fair values of the Company's investments in individual securities that have been in a continuous unrealized loss position deemed to be temporary for less than 12 months and for more than 12 months, aggregated by investment category, at September 28, 2008 (in millions):

	Less than 12 months		More than 12 months	
	Fair Value	Unrealized Losses	Fair Value	Unrealized Losses
Corporate bonds and notes	$1,524	$ (46)	$219	$ (9)
Mortgage- and asset-backed securities	457	(18)	8	—
Non-investment grade debt securities	864	(78)	87	(9)
Government-sponsored enterprise bonds	353	(2)	—	—
Debt mutual funds	86	(4)	—	—
Equity securities	784	(115)	6	(1)
Equity mutual funds and exchange-traded funds	1,229	(167)	—	—
	$5,297	$(430)	$320	$(19)

The unrealized losses on the Company's investments in marketable securities were caused primarily by a major disruption in U.S. and foreign credit and financial markets affecting consumers and the banking, finance and housing industries. This disruption is evidenced by a deterioration of confidence in financial markets and a severe decline in the availability of capital and demand for debt and equity securities. The result has been depressed securities values in most types of investment- and non-investment-grade bonds and debt obligations, mortgage- and asset-backed securities and equity securities. At October 31, 2008, gross unrealized gains were approximately $75 million and gross unrealized losses were approximately $1.3 billion. When assessing marketable securities for other-than-temporary declines in value, the Company considers factors including: how significant the decline in value is as a percentage of the original cost, the underlying factors contributing to a decline in the prices of securities in a single asset class, how long the market value of the investment has been less than its original cost, the performance of the investee's stock price in relation to the stock price of its competitors in the industry, expected market volatility and the market in general, analyst recommendations, the views of external investment managers, any news or financial information that has been released specific to the investee and

(Continued)

<hr>

EXHIBIT 7.10 (Continued)

the outlook for the overall industry in which the investee operates. The Company's analyses of the severity and duration of price declines, market research, industry reports, economic forecasts and the specific circumstances of issuers indicate that it is reasonable to expect marketable securities with unrealized losses to recover in fair value up to the Company's cost bases within a reasonable period of time. Further, the Company has the ability and the intent to hold such securities until they recover. Accordingly, the Company considers the unrealized losses to be temporary at September 28, 2008.

<hr>

Qualcomm has investments in both debt and equity securities classified as available-for-sale. Qualcomm uses the note disclosure to indicate the unrealized gains and losses on these securities. If these gains and losses are temporary, they will reverse. Qualcomm divides the securities into two groups based on the amount of time for which losses they consider temporary have persisted for more than 12 months. Also note that Qualcomm links the losses to the downward turn in prices in the mortgage backed securities markets of 2007 and 2008.

In assessing the quality of accounting information, analysts must decide whether to include any change in the unrealized holding gain or loss on securities classified as available-for-sale in earnings for the period. The principal argument for excluding such amounts is that the unrealized gain or loss may likely reverse or may not be realized for many years, if ever. The principal argument for including the change in earnings relates to the fact that regardless of whether it is realized, the gain or loss has economic significance and therefore has a bearing on evaluation of the firm's investment performance. The various disclosures of investment gains and losses are particularly important for financial services firms such as banks and insurers because performance and management of the investment portfolio is critically important to the profitability and risk of financial services firms and because of the sheer magnitude of the numbers. For example, Citigroup, Inc.'s 2008 annual report discloses 2008 unrealized losses on available-for-sale securities totaling $10,118 million. Although this amount appears in Citigroup's comprehensive income, it is not part of its $27,684 million net loss for 2008. Insurance giant AIG also reported a 2008 net unrealized loss on available-for-sale securities of $8,722 million.

"Other than Temporarily Impaired Securities"

As you have learned in the preceding sections, declines in fair values of available-for-sale and held-to-maturity investments are not reflected in net income until they are realized through the sale or maturity of the security. This accounting is driven by the assumption that for available-for-sale securities, the fair value declines might reverse and for held-to-maturity securities, the investor will hold the securities to maturity and collect the interest and maturity value.

If managers of the firm determine that the securities are "other than temporarily impaired," the securities must be written down to fair value, with the unrealized loss reported in net income of the period. For this reason, in each period, managers must test whether securities that have experienced unrealized losses are "other than temporarily impaired." Note that disclosures will show how long "temporarily" impaired securities have remained impaired and that discussions often will describe the reasons for management's belief that interest and maturity values of debt securities will be collected.

Minority, Active Investments

Firms often acquire shares of another corporation to exert significant influence over that company's activities. This significant influence is usually at a broad policy-making level through representation on the other corporation's board of directors. Because of wide dispersion of ownership of most publicly held corporations, and the fact that many shareholders do not vote their shares, firms can exert significant influence over another corporation with ownership of less than a majority of the voting stock. Investments of between 20 and 50 percent of the voting stock of another company are minority, active investments unless evidence indicates that the acquiring firm cannot exert significant influence or the investing firm is deemed the VIE's primary beneficiary as defined by *Interpretation No. 46R* (discussed in a later section).

U.S. GAAP and IFRS require firms to account for minority, active investments, generally those for which ownership is between 20 and 50 percent, using the *equity method.*[27] Under the equity method, the firm owning shares in another firm recognizes as income (loss) each period its share of the net income (loss) of the other firm. See, for example, the income statement of PepsiCo (Appendix A). "Bottling equity income" of $374 million in 2008 represents PepsiCo's share of the earnings from 20–50 percent-owned bottling affiliates. The investor treats dividends received from the investee as a return of investment, not as income. Therefore, PepsiCo's balance sheet reporting of "Investments in Noncontrolled Affiliates" of $3,883 million at December 27, 2008, represents its original investment plus the accumulated amount of bottling equity income it has recognized over time minus the dividends it has received from its noncontrolled affiliates.

The rationale for using the equity method when significant influence is present is best understood by considering the financial statement effects of using the (alternative) fair value method for securities classified as available-for-sale in these circumstances. Under the fair value method, the investor recognizes income or loss on the income statement only when it receives a dividend or sells all or part of the investment. Suppose, as often happens, that the investee finances its own growing operations through retention of earnings and consistently declares dividends that are significantly less than its net income. The market price of the investee's shares will probably increase to reflect the retention of assets generated by earnings. Under the fair value method, the investor's only reported income from the investment will be the modest dividends received because the investment will likely be classified as available-for-sale, and the unrealized gains from fair value changes in the investment are reported in other comprehensive income.

Because of its ownership percentage, the investor can influence the dividend policy of the investee and thereby influence the amount of income recognized under the fair value method. Under these conditions, the fair value method may not reasonably reflect the earnings of the investee generated under the investor's influence. The equity method provides a better measure of a firm's earnings and of its investment when, because of its ownership interest, it can significantly influence the operations and dividend policy of another firm.

Under the equity method, the investor reports its investment in the investee on the balance sheet at acquisition cost plus (minus) the investor's share of the investee's net income (loss) each period. In deriving cash flow from operations on the statement of cash flows,

---

[27] Relevant standards for investments representing significant influence (minority, active investments) are as follows: Accounting Principles Board, *Opinion No. 18*, "The Equity Method of Accounting for Investments in Common Stock" (1971); Financial Accounting Standards Board, *Interpretation No. 35*, "Criteria for Applying the Equity Method of Accounting for Investments in Common Stock" (1981); *FASB Codification Topic 323;* and International Accounting Standards Board, *International Accounting Standard 28*, "Investments in Associates" (1989).

the investor subtracts its share of the investee's earnings from net income and adds any cash dividends received from the investee. Many firms net these two adjustments on the statement of cash flows, in which the investor would subtract its share of the investee's *undistributed* earnings (equity income minus dividends).

Example 17

On January 1, 2010, Lake Co. bought 40 percent of Pond Co. common stock at a cost of $500,000. Pond Co.'s net assets have a book value of $1,000,000. Assume that the individual fair values of identifiable net assets are equal to the book values of Pond's assets except for a building that has a fair value that is $150,000 above book value. The building has an estimated remaining useful life of ten years. During 2010, Pond's net income is $50,000 and it pays $30,000 in dividends.

Lake Co. paid $500,000 to acquire 40 percent of Pond Co., which implies that $460,000 was paid for identifiable net assets and $40,000 for unidentifiable assets, as follows:

Price paid	$ 500,000
Fair value of identifiable net assets acquired ($1,150,000 × 40%)	(460,000)
Unidentifiable asset acquired (implied goodwill)	$ 40,000

If Lake were to use the market method, the investment in Pond Co. would be market-to-market at year-end. Further, $12,000 in dividend revenue ($30,000 × 40 percent) would be reported in the income statement. Under the equity method, however, the investee's income triggers the investor's income recognition rather than the distribution of dividends. Lake's investment income is determined as follows:

Investee earnings ($50,000 × 40%)	$20,000
Excess building depreciation ($150,000 × 40%/10 years)	(6,000)
Investment revenue	$14,000

The investee (Pond Co.) calculated its $50,000 income by basing depreciation charges on the book values of its assets. Under the equity method, the investor (Lake) records its pro rata share of investee income of $20,000 ($50,000 × 40 percent). However, from Lake's point of view, the resources committed to generating 40 percent of Pond's revenues are greater than 40 percent of Pond's costs because Lake paid $60,000 extra for the appreciated building when it purchased the 40 percent interest. Allocation of the cost of that extra investment also must be reflected in income measurement (hence, the $6,000 additional depreciation expense).

The Investment in Pond Co. account is reported in the long-term investments section of the balance sheet at the original cost plus increases in the investment from the investee's income less decreases in the investment from dividend distribution, as follows:

Investment in Pond (original cost) at January 1, 2010	$500,000
Lake's adjusted share of Pond's earnings	14,000
Lake's share of Pond's dividends ($30,000 × 40%)	(12,000)
Investment in Pond reported at December 31, 2010	$502,000

Exhibit 7.11 summarizes the financial statement effects for Lake Company of its equity method investment in Pond.

The Road Ahead

Do not follow where the path may lead.
  Go instead where there is no path, and
leave a trail.

RALPH WALDO EMERSON

In this last chapter, we'll look at the road that
lies before you. Maybe you've got a few years
of high school left, or maybe you're already
finishing up. Either way, you'll enjoy reading
these stories about independence.

You're almost at the end of this book, perhaps almost at the end of your childhood. What
lies ahead? You're leaving much behind, yet
what lies in front of you is incredibly rich in
potential and possibility. With faith in yourself
and the Lord, there isn't anything you can't do.
There is virtually no goal you can't meet, no
task you can't accomplish.

You are at a crossroads, and all roads lead
to YOU. This is your life, your future. Pray your
most fervent prayer, and set a course in the
direction of your dreams. You'll be amazed at
how swiftly the wind will carry your sail if only
you stay with God in everything you do.